13th International Conference on Natural Language Processing (ICON-2016)

Varanasi, India
17 – 20 December 2016

ISBN: 978-1-5108-3788-1

13th International Conference on Natural Language Processing

Proceedings of the Conference

17-20 December 2016
IIT (BHU), Varanasi, India

Preface

Research in Natural Language Processing (NLP) has taken a noticeable leap in the recent years. Tremendous growth of information on the web and its easy access has stimulated large interest in the field. India, with multiple languages and continuous growth of Indian language content on the web, makes a fertile ground for NLP research. Moreover, industry is keenly interested in obtaining NLP technology for mass use. The internet search companies are increasingly aware of the large market for processing languages other than English. For example, search capability is needed for content in Indian and other languages. There is also a need for searching content in multiple languages, and making the retrieved documents available in the language of the user. As a result, a strong need is being felt for machine translation to handle this large instantaneous use. Information Extraction, Question Answering Systems and Sentiment Analysis are also showing up as other opportunities.

These needs have resulted in two welcome trends. First, there is much wider student interest in getting into NLP at both postgraduate and undergraduate levels. Many students interested in computing technology are getting interested in natural language technology, and those interested in pursuing computing research are joining NLP research. Second, the research community in academic institutions and the government funding agencies in India have joined hands to launch consortia projects to develop NLP products. Each consortium project is a multi-institutional endeavour working with a common software framework, common language standards, and common technology engines for all the different languages covered in the consortium. As a result, it has already led to development of basic tools for multiple languages which are inter-operable for the tasks of machine translation, cross lingual search, hand writing recognition and OCR.

In this backdrop of increased student interest, greater funding and most importantly, common standards and interoperable tools, there has been a spurt in research in NLP on Indian languages, whose effects we have just begun to see. A great number of submissions reflecting good research is a heartening matter.

For machine learning and other purposes, linguistically annotated corpora using the common standards have become available for multiple Indian languages. They have been used for the development of basic technologies for several languages. Larger set of corpora are expected to be prepared in near future.

This volume contains papers selected for presentation in technical sessions of ICON-2016 and short communications selected for poster presentation. We are thankful to our excellent team of reviewers from all over the globe who deserve full credit for the hard work of reviewing the high quality submissions with rich technical content. From 150 submissions, 38 papers were selected, 15 for full presentation, 18 for poster presentation and 5 for poster-cum-demonstration, representing a variety of new and interesting developments, covering a wide spectrum of NLP areas and core linguistics.

We are deeply grateful to Richard Sproat, Google Inc., USA and Bruno Pouliquen, World Intellectual Property Organization, Switzerland for giving the keynote lectures at ICON-2016. We would also like to thank the members of the Advisory Committee and Programme Committee for their support and co-operation in making ICON 2016 a success.

We thank Asif Ekbal, Chair, Student Paper Competition and Amitav Das, Chair, NLP Tools Contest for taking the responsibilities of the events.

We convey our thanks to P V S Ram Babu, G Srinivas Rao, B Mahender Kumar and A Lakshmi Narayana, International Institute of Information Technology (IIIT), Hyderabad for their dedicated efforts in successfully handling the ICON Secretariat. We also thank IIIT Hyderabad team of Vineet Chaitanya, Peri Bhaskararao, Vasudeva Varma, Soma Paul, Radhika Mamidi, Manish Shrivastava, Suryakanth V Gangashetty and Anil Kumar Vuppala. We heartily express our gratitude to Sukomal Pal, Swasti Mishra and the great team of volunteers at IIT (BHU) and BHU, Varanasi for their timely help with sincere dedication and hard work to make this conference a success.

We also thank all those who came forward to help us in this task. We apologize if we have missed some names.

Finally, we thank all the researchers who responded to our call for papers and all the participants of ICON-2016, without whose overwhelming response the conference would not have been a success.

December 2016   Dipti Misra Sharma
Varanasi   Rajeev Sangal
Anil Kumar Singh

Advisory Committee:

Aravind K Joshi, University of Pennsylvania, USA (Chair)

Conference General Chair:

Rajeev Sangal, IIT (BHU), Varanasi, India

Programme Committee:

Anil Kumar Singh, IIT (BHU), India (Chair)
Dipti Misra Sharma, IIIT Hyderabad, India (Co-Chair)
Karunesh Arora, CDAC Noida, India
Sivaji Bandyopadhyay, Jadavpur University, Kolkata, India
Srinivas Bangalore, Interactions LLC, AT&T Research, USA
Peri Bhaskararao, IIIT Hyderabad, India
Rajesh Bhatt, University of Massachusetts, USA
Pushpak Bhattacharyya, IIT Patna, India
Ravindranath Chowdary C, IIT (BHU), India
Niladri Sekhar Dash, ISI Kolkata, India
Sanjukta Ghosh, BHU, Varanasi, India
Vishal Goyal, Punjabi University, Patiala, India
Harald Hammarstrom, Max Planck Institute for Psycholinguistics, Nijmegen, The Netherlands
Mohammed Hasanuzzaman, Université de Caen Normandie, Caen, France
Gerold Hintz, TU Darmstadt, Germany
Samar Husain, IIT Delhi, India
Amba Kulkarni, University of Hyderabad, India
Ramamoorthy L., CIIL, Mysore
Gurpreet Lehal, Punjabi University, Patiala, India
Roser Morante, VU University, Amsterdam, The Netherlands
Jose Moreno, Université de Caen Normandie, Caen, France
Joakim Nivre, Uppsala University, Sweden
Alexis Palmer, Heidelberg University, Germany
Martha Palmer, University of Colorado Boulder, USA
Soma Paul, IIIT Hyderabad, India
Jyoti Pawar, DCST, Goa University, India
Eugen Ruppert, TU Darmstadt, Germany
Sriparna Saha, IIT Patna, India
Shikhar Kr. Sarma, Gauhati University, India
Elizabeth Sherly, IIITM-K, Trivandrum, India
Sobha Lalitha Devi, AU-KBC, Chennai, India
Keh-Yih Su, Institute of Information Science, Academia Sinica, Taiwan

Anil Thakur, BHU, Varanasi, India
Vasudeva Varma, IIIT Hyderabad, India

Tools Contest Chairs:

POS Tagging for Code-Mixed Indian Social Media Text Rationale:

Amitav Das, IIIT, Sri City, India (Chair)

Student Paper Competition Chair:

Asif Ekbal, IIT-Patna, India

Organizing Committee:

Sukomal Pal, IIT (BHU), Varanasi, India (Chair)
Swasti Mishra, IIT (BHU), Varanasi, India

Organizers

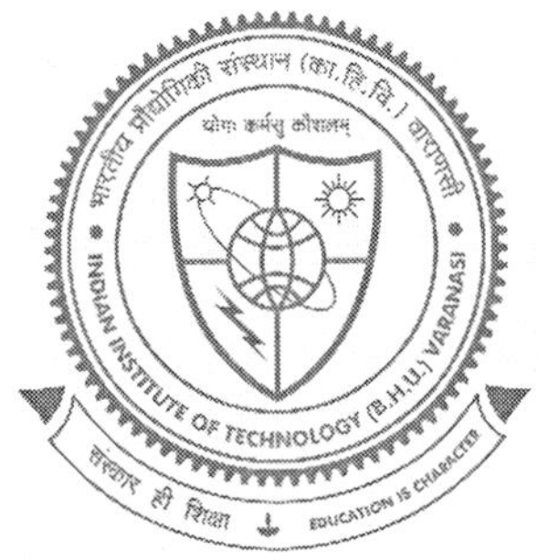

Indian Institute of Technology (BHU), Varanasi

**Natural Language Processing
Association of India**

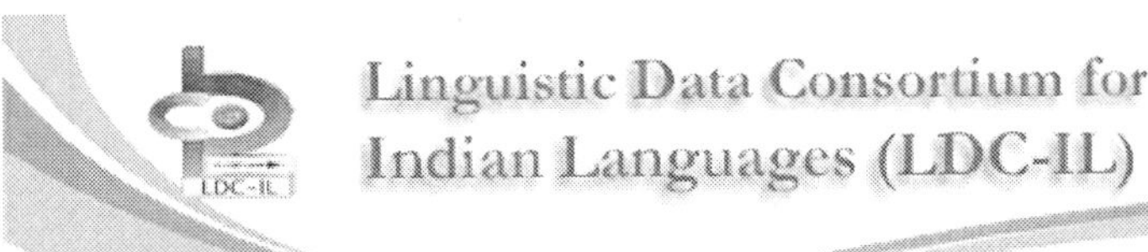

Sponsors

Referees

We gratefully acknowledge the excellent quality of refereeing we received from the reviewers. We thank them all for being precise and fair in their assessment and for reviewing the papers in time.

Abhijit Mishra
Aditya Joshi
Aishwarya N Reganti
Alexis Palmer
Alok Chakrabarty
Amba Kulkarni
Amitava Das
Amrith Krishna
Anil Kumar Singh
Anil Kumar Vuppala
Anil Thakur
Anoop Kunchukuttan
Anupam Jamatia
Aravind Ganapathiraju
Ashwini Vaidya
Asif Ekbal
Ayushi Dalmia
Ayushi Pandey
Balaji Jagan
Balamurali A R
Baskaran Sankaran
Bharat Ram Ambati
Bhuvana Narasimhan
Bibekananda Kundu
Bikash Gyawali
Bira Chandra Singh
Björn Gambäck
Brijesh Bhatt
C V Jawahar
Debasis Ganguly
Deepak Padmanabhan
Dhananjaya Gowda
Dimitris Mavroeidis
Dimple Paul
Dinesh Kumar Prabhakar
Dipankar Das
Dipasree Pal
Dipti Misra Sharma
Douwe Kiela
Dwaipayan Roy
Dwijen Rudrapal
Elizabeth Sherly
Erik Cambria
Eugen Ruppert
Ganesh Jawahar
Girish Palshikar
Gurpreet Singh Lehal
Harald Hammarström

Hema Murthy
Himanshu Sharma
Imran Rasheed
Irshad Bhat
Joakim Nivre
Joe Cheri
Jose Moreno
Jyoti Pareek
Jyoti Pawar
K V Ramakrishnamacharyulu
K V Subbarao
Kamal Garg
Karunesh Arora
Keh-Yih Su
Kishorjit Nongmeikapam
Kunal Chakma
Lars Bungum
Malhar Kulkarni
Manish Shrivastava
Marco Damonte
Martha Palmer
Mohammed Hasanuzzaman
Monojit Choudhury
Nayeemulla Khan A
Nikhil Pattisapu
Nikhilesh Bhatnagar
Niladri Sekhar Dash
Niraj Kumar
Owen Rambow
Paolo Rosso
Parth Gupta
Partha Talukdar
Pawan Goyal
Peri Bhaskararao
Pradeepika Verma
Pranaw Kumar
Prasha Shresta
Priya Radhakrishnan
Pruthwik Mishra
Pushpak Bhattacharyya
Radhika Mamidi
Raghava Krishnan
Rajendra Prasath
Rajendran S
Rajesh Bhatt
Rajiv Srivastava
Rakesh Balabantaray
Raksha Sharma

Ranjani Parthasarathi
Ratish Surendran
Ravindranath Chowdary C
Riyaz Bhat
Roser Morante
Rudramurthy V
S Arulmozi
Sachin Pawar
Sai Krishna Rallabandi
Sajini T
Samar Husain
Samudravijaya K
Sandipan Dandapat
Sandya Mannarswamy
Sanjukta Ghosh
Saptarshi Ghosh
Sara Tonelli
Satarupa Guha
Shashi Narayan
Shourya Roy
Shubhnandan Singh
Sivaji Bandyopadhyay
Sobha Lalitha Devi
Soma Paul
Srikanth Ronanki
Sriparna Saha
Sriram Chaudhury
Sruti Rallapalli
Subalalitha Navaneetha Krishnan
Sudip Kumar Naskar
Sukomal Pal
Sunayana Sitaram
Sutanu Chakraborti
Swapnil Chaudhari
T Pattabhi R K Rao
Taniya Mishra
Thamar Solorio
Thierry Declerck
Tushar Maheshwari
Umamaheswari E
Vasudeva Varma
Vasudevan N
Vijay Sunday Ram
Vinay Kumar Mittal
Vineet Chaitanya
Vishal Goyal
Vishnu G Sriram
Yuji Matsumo

Table of Contents

Conference Program

Monday, December 19, 2016

+ 9:00-9:30 Inaugural Ceremony

+ 9:30-10:00 Keynote Lecture 1 by Bruno Pouliquen

Keynote Lecture 1: Practical Use of Machine Translation in International Organizations
Bruno Pouliquen

+ 10:30-11:00 Tea Break

+ 11:00-13:00 Technical Session I: Machine Translation and WSD:

Integrating WordNet for Multiple Sense Embeddings in Vector Semantics
David Foley and Jugal Kalita

Can SMT and RBMT Improve each other's Performance?- An Experiment with English-Hindi Translation
Debajyoty Banik, Sukanta Sen, Asif Ekbal and Pushpak Bhattacharyya

Composition of Compound Nouns Using Distributional Semantics
Kyra Yee and Jugal Kalita

Towards Building a SentiWordNet for Tamil
Abishek Kannan, Gaurav Mohanty and Radhika Mamidi

+ 11:00-13:00 Technical Session II : Discourse Analysis:

Extending AIDA framework by incorporating coreference resolution on detected mentions and pruning based on popularity of an entity
Samaikya Akarapu and C Ravindranath Chowdary

Sentence Based Discourse Classification for Hindi Story Text-to-Speech (TTS) System
Kumud Tripathi, Parakrant Sarkar and K. Sreenivasa Rao

Biomolecular Event Extraction using a Stacked Generalization based Classifier
Amit Majumder, Asif Ekbal and Sudip Kumar Naskar

Syntax and Pragmatics of Conversation: A Case of Bangla
Samir Karmakar and Soumya Sankar Ghosh

+ 13:00-14:00 Lunch

+ 14:00-15:00 Technical Session III: New Trends:

Dependency grammars as Haskell programs
Tomasz Obrebski

Improving Document Ranking using Query Expansion and Classification Techniques for Mixed Script Information Retrieval
Subham Kumar, Anwesh Sinha Ray, Sabyasachi Kamila, Asif Ekbal, Sriparna Saha and Pushpak Bhattacharyya

+ 15:00-15:30 Tea Break

+ 15:30-17:30 Poster and Demo Session-1:

Feature based Sentiment Analysis using a Domain Ontology
Neha Yadav and C Ravindranath Chowdary

Cross-lingual transfer parser from Hindi to Bengali using delexicalization and chunking
Ayan Das, Agnivo Saha and Sudeshna Sarkar

Constraint Grammar-based conversion of Dependency Treebanks
Eckhard Bick

Meaning Matters: Senses of Words are More Informative than Words for Cross-domain Sentiment Analysis
Raksha Sharma, Sudha Bhingardive and Pushpak Bhattacharyya

POS Tagging Experts via Topic Modeling
Atreyee Mukherjee, Sandra Kübler and Matthias Scheutz

Graph theoretic interpretation of Bangla traditional grammar
Samir Karmakar, Sayantani Banerjee and Soumya Ghosh

A method for Automatic Text Summarization using Consensus of Multiple Similarity Measures and Ranking Techniques
Mukesh Kumar Jadon and Ayush Pareek

Monday, December 19, 2016 (continued)

Automatic Translation of English Text to Indian Sign Language Synthetic Animations
Lalit Goyal and Vishal Goyal

Towards Deep Learning in Hindi NER: An approach to tackle the Labelled Data Sparsity
Vinayak Athavale, Shreenivas Bharadwaj, Monik Pamecha, Ameya Prabhu and Manish
Shrivastava

Vaidya: A Spoken Dialog System for Health Domain
Prathyusha Danda, Brij Mohan Lal Srivastava and Manish Shrivastava

*Cosmopolitan Mumbai, Orthodox Delhi, Techcity Bangalore:Understanding City Specific
Societal Sentiment*
Aishwarya N Reganti, Tushar Maheshwari, Upendra Kumar and Amitava Das

+ 17:30-18:30 NLPAI Meeting

+ 18:30-19:30 Cultural Program

+ 19:30-20:30 Dinner

Tuesday, December 20, 2016

+ 9:30-10:30 Keynote Lecture 2:

*Keynote Lecture 2: Neural (and other Machine Learning) Approaches to Text Normaliza-
tion*
Richard Sproat

+ 10:30-11:00 Tea Break

+ 11:00-13:00 Technical Session IV: Statistical Methods:

Wisdom of Students: A Consistent Automatic Short Answer Grading Technique
Shourya Roy, Sandipan Dandapat, Ajay Nagesh and Narahari Y.

A Recurrent Neural Network Architecture for De-identifying Clinical Records
Shweta, Ankit Kumar, Asif Ekbal, Sriparna Saha and Pushpak Bhattacharyya

Twitter Named Entity Extraction and Linking Using Differential Evolution
Utpal Kumar Sikdar and Björn Gambäck

Learning Non-Linear Functions for Text Classification
Cohan Sujay Carlos and Geetanjali Rakshit

+ 13:00-14:00 Lunch

+ 14:-15:30 Poster and Demo Session-2:

A Computational Analysis of Mahabharata
Debarati Das, Bhaskarjyoti Das and Kavi Mahesh

Use of Features for Accentuation of ghañanta Words
Samir Janardan Sohoni and Malhar A. Kulkarni

Learning to Identify Subjective Sentences
Girish K. Palshikar, Manoj Apte, Deepak Pandita and Vikram Singh

Opinion Mining in a Code-Mixed Environment: A Case Study with Government Portals
Deepak Gupta, Ankit Lamba, Asif Ekbal and Pushpak Bhattacharyya

Use of Semantic Knowledge Base for Enhancement of Coherence of Code-mixed Topic-Based Aspect Clusters
Kavita Asnani and Jyoti D Pawar

Genetic Algorithm (GA) Implementation for Feature Selection in Manipuri POS Tagging
Kishorjit Nongmeikapam and Sivaji Bandyopadhyay

Effect of Syntactic Features in Bangla Sentence Comprehension
Manjira Sinha, Tirthankar Dasgupta and Anupam Basu

A New Feature Selection Technique Combined with ELM Feature Space for Text Classification
Rajendra Kumar Roul and Pranav Rai

On Why Coarse Class Classification is Bottleneck in Noun Compound Interpretation
Girishkumar Ponkiya, Pushpak Bhattacharyya and Girish K. Palshikar

Verbframator:Semi-Automatic Verb Frame Annotator Tool with Special Reference to Marathi
Hanumant Redkar, Sandhya Singh, Nandini Ghag, Jai Paranjape, Nilesh Joshi, Malhar Kulkarni and Pushpak Bhattacharyya

Towards Building A Domain Agnostic Natural Language Interface to Real-World Relational Databases
Sree Harsha Ramesh, Jayant Jain, Sarath K S and Krishna R Sundaresan

+ **15:30-16:00 Tea Break**

+ **16:00-17:30 Technical Session V: Speech Processing:**

Experimental Study of Vowels in Nagamese, Ao and Lotha: Languages of Nagaland
Joyanta Basu, Tulika Basu, Soma Khan, Madhab Pal, Rajib Roy and Tapan Kumar Basu

Perception of Phi-Phrase boundaries in Hindi.
Somnath Roy

+ **16:00-17:30 Technical Session VI : NLP Tool Contest**

+ 17:30-18:00 Valedictory Session

Keynote Lecture-1

Practical Use of Machine Translation in International Organizations

Bruno Pouliquen
World Intellectual Property Organization, Switzerland
`bruno.pouliquen@wipo.int`

We propose to present our experience in statistical machine translation, in WIPO (World Intellectual Property Organization) and in other international organizations. Special focus will be given to the recent introduction of Neural Machine Translation in production.

WIPO has developed its own MT tool, initially based on open-source Moses (phrase-based SMT - PBSMT), more recently based on open-source for Neural Machine Translation (NMT), namely Nematus and AmunMT. The PBSMT tool, trained on different documents, has been successfully installed in the UN (United Nations) and in other international organizations (ITU, IMO, FAO, WTO, ILO, WTO, TGF and FAO). The tool is fully data-driven and has been trained on various language pairs. For example, in the patent domain, it allows users to understand a patent written in a language they do not master (languages covered: English, German, Spanish, French, Portuguese, Russian, Chinese, Korean and Japanese; Arabic to be added soon). The tool is also used for dissemination, as a "translation accelerator" and used by WIPO (and other UN agencies) by translators to help them in their daily work.

It should be noted that our tool has always better automatic metrics (BLEU) for every comparison we did against general translation tool (Google) using PBSMT. The recent NMT is also clearly better (for patent texts) than GNMT (the recently published Neural machine translation engine released by Google).

The tool has now reached maturity and is successfully used in production: by translators in UN since 5 years and by users of WIPO search engine PATENTSCOPE since 6 years. NMT for Chinese has been put in production in September in WIPO. We plan to release NMT for most of the language pairs soon.

D S Sharma, R Sangal and A K Singh. Proc. of the 13th Intl. Conference on Natural Language Processing, page 1,
Varanasi, India. December 2016. ©2016 NLP Association of India (NLPAI)

Integrating WordNet for Multiple Sense Embeddings in Vector Semantics

David Foley
Kutztown University of Pennsylvania
dfole581@live.kutztown.edu

Jugal Kalita
University of Colorado, Colorado Springs
jkalita@uccs.edu

Abstract

Popular distributional approaches to semantics allow for only a single embedding
of any particular word. A single embedding per word conflates the distinct meanings of the word and their appropriate contexts, irrespective of whether those usages
are related or completely disjoint. We
compare models that use the graph structure of the knowledge base WordNet as
a post-processing step to improve vector-
space models with multiple sense embeddings for each word, and explore the application to word sense disambiguation.

Keywords: Vector Semantics, WordNet, Synonym Selection, Word Sense Disambiguation

1   INTRODUCTION

Vector semantics is a computational model of written language that encodes the usage of words in a
vector space, which facilitates performing mathematical manipulations on words as vectors (Martin and Jurafsky, 2016; Turney and Pantel, 2010).
These vectors encode the contexts of words across
a corpus, and are learned based on word distributions throughout the text. Vectors can then be
compared by various distance metrics, usually the
cosine function, to determine the similarity of the
underlying words. They also seem to possess
some modest degree of compositionality, in the
sense that the addition and subtraction of vectors
can sometimes result in equations that appear to
reflect semantically meaningful relationships between words (Mikolov et al., 2013a; Mikolov et
al., 2013b). Because it allows for the use of these
well studied techniques from linear algebra to be
brought to bear on the difficult domain of semantics, vector space models (VSMs) have been the
focus of much recent research in NLP.

While vector representations of word meaning
are capable of capturing important semantic features of words and performing tasks like meaning
comparison and analogizing, one of their shortcomings is their implicit assumption that a single written word type has exactly one meaning
(or distribution) in a language. But many words
clearly have different senses corresponding to distinct appropriate contexts. Building distributional
vector space models that account for this polysemous behavior would allow for better performance
on tasks involving context-sensitive words, most
obviously word sense disambiguation. Previous
research that attempted to resolve this issue is discussed at length in the next section. Most common
methods either use clustering or introduce knowledge from an ontology. The goal of the present
research is to develop or improve upon methods
that take advantage of the semantic groups and relations codified in WordNet, and specifically to focus on the downstream WSD task, which is often
neglected in favor of less useful similarity judgment evaluations.

The algorithm we examine in depth can in principle be implemented with any ontology, but in
the present paper we focus exclusively on Word-
Net. WordNet (WN) is a knowledge base for English language semantics (Miller, 1995). It consists of small collections of synonymous words
called synsets, interconnected with labeled links
corresponding to different forms of semantic or
lexical relations. We will be particularly interested
in the synset relation of hypernymy/hyponymy.
Hyponyms can be thought of as semantic subsets: If A is a hyponym of B, then x is A implies x is B, but the converse is not true. WordNet
is also equipped with a dictionary definition for
each synset, along with example sentences featur-
ing varying synonymous words. Often implementations that use WordNet's graph structure fail to
make use of these other features, which we will

2

D S Sharma, R Sangal and A K Singh. Proc. of the 13th Intl. Conference on Natural Language Processing, pages 2–9,
Varanasi, India. December 2016. ©2016 NLP Association of India (NLPAI)

show can improve performance on several tasks.

2 Related Work

Our work is based primarily on that of Jauhar et al's RETROFIT algorithm (Jauhar et al., 2015), which is discussed at greater length in Section 3. Below we discuss previous models for building sense embeddings.

2.1 Clustering-Based Methods

(Reisinger and Mooney, 2010) learn a fixed number of sense vectors per word by clustering context vectors corresponding to individual occurrences of a word in a large corpus, then calculating the cluster centroids. These centroids are the sense vectors. (Huang et al., 2012) build a similar model using k-means clustering, but also incorporate global textual features into initial context vectors. They compile the Stanford Contextual Word Similarity dataset (SCWS), which consists of over two thousand word pairs in their sentential context, along with a similarity score based on human judgments from zero to ten. (Neelakantan et al., 2015) introduce an unsupervised modification of the skip-gram model (Mikolov et al., 2013b) to calculate multiple sense embeddings online, by maintaining clusters of context vectors and forming new word sense vectors when a context under consideration is sufficiently far from any of the word's known clusters. The advantage of the method is that it is capable of detecting different numbers of senses for different words, unlike the previous implementations of Huang et al. and Reisinger and Mooney.

2.2 Ontology-Based Methods

(Chen et al., 2014) first learn general word embeddings from the skip-gram model, then initialize sense embeddings based on the synsets and glosses of WN. These embeddings are then used to identify relevant occurrences of each sense in a training corpus using simple-to-complex words-sense disambiguation (S2C WSD). The skip-gram model is then trained directly on the disambiguated corpus. (Rothe and Schütze, 2015) build a neural-network post-processing system called AutoExtend that takes word embeddings and learns embeddings for synsets and lexemes. Their model is an autoencoder neural net with lexeme and synset embeddings as hidden layers, based on the intuition that a word is the sum of its lexemes and a synset is the sum of its lexemes.

Our intuitions are most similar to those of (Jauhar et al., 2015) and we will be building on one of their approaches. Their RETROFIT algorithm learns embeddings for different word senses from WN by iteratively combining general embeddings according to the graph structure of WN. The approach is discussed in more detail below.

3 Improved Sense Embeddings from Word Embeddings

3.1 RETROFIT Algorithm

Because our work follows so directly from (Jauhar et al., 2015), we repeat the essential details of the RETROFIT algorithm here. Let $\Omega = (S_\Omega, E_\Omega)$ be a directed graph. We call Ω an *ontology* when the set of vertices S_Ω represent semantic objects of some kind and the set of edges E_Ω represent relationships between those objects. In the case of WN, S_Ω is the set of synsets and E_Ω are the semantic links (notably hypernyms and hyponyms). Given a set of sense-agnostic word embeddings $\hat{V}$ and an ontology Ω, RETROFIT infers a set of sense embeddings $\hat{S}$ that is maximally "consistent" with both $\hat{V}$ and Ω. By "consistency" we refer to the minimization of the objective function

$$
\begin{aligned}
D(\hat{S}) = &\sum_{ij} \alpha \left\| \hat{w}_i - \vec{s}_{ij} \right\|^2 \\
&+ \sum_{ij} \sum_{i'j' \in N_{ij}} \beta_r \left\| \vec{s}_{ij} - \vec{s}_{i'j'} \right\|^2
\end{aligned}
\tag{1}
$$

where s_{ij} is the *jth* sense of the *ith* word, N_{ij} is the set of neighbors of s_{ij} defined in E_Ω and α and β are hyperparameters controlling the importance of intial sense-agnositc embeddings and various ontological relationships, respectively. Essentially RETROFIT aims to make a sense embedding as similar to its sense-agnostic embedding as possible, while also reducing the distance between related senses as defined by Ω. It achieves this by iteratively updating sense embeddings according to

$$
\vec{s}_{ij} = \frac{\alpha \hat{w}_i + \sum\limits_{i'j' \in N_{ij}} \beta_r \vec{s}_{i'j'}}{\alpha + \sum\limits_{i'j' \in N_{ij}} \beta_r}
\tag{2}
$$

until convergence. The RETROFIT implementation discussed in (Jauhar et al., 2015) defines only synonym, hypernym and hyponym relations, with respective weights of $\beta_r = 1.0, 0.5$ and 0.5

The RETROFIT algorithm genertes embeddings for word senses only from words whose surface form matches the entry in WordNet. Below we discuss several of the limitations associated with this RETROFIT implementation and possible improvements.

3.1.1 Impoverished Synsets

Many word senses are relatively isolated in the WordNet structure. They occur in synsets with few or no synonyms or semantic relations. In the case that the word has only one meaning, this is not a problem, because the sense-agnostic embedding is in that case unambiguous. But in the case that the word has one or more other semantically rich senses (ie, senses with synonyms and hyper/hyponym relations), the impoverished sense is unduly influenced by the general embedding and its unique meaning is not distinguishable. In the extreme case both senses are identical. Thousands of such synsets exist, including the synsets for words such as *inclement* and *egalitarian*.

3.1.2 Compound Words and Multi-word Lemmas

The original RETROFIT implementation discards multi-word lemmas (and entire synsets if they consist only of multi-word lemmas.) But there exist synsets for whom most or all of the related WN synsets contain only multi-word lemmas. See, for instance, the noun form of the word *unseen*, or the more extreme case of the synset *brass.n.01*, which has eleven distinct hypernym and hyponym relations, all but two of which are compound words for types of brass. Adjusting the RETROFIT algorithm to allow for embeddings of the multi-word lemmas that appear in WN would greatly reduce the number of impoverished synsets.

3.1.3 Underrepresented Senses

The general embedding produced by word2vec[1] (Mikolov et al., 2013a; Mikolov et al., 2013b) conflates all usages of a word. If a particular sense of a word is significantly less common than others, the word2vec embedding will not be a good representation of the sense. RETROFIT indiscriminately tries to minimize the distance from any particular sense and its word2vec embedding. Consider the usage of the word *tap* given by the synset *tap.v.11*, meaning "to pierce in order to draw liquid from."

This usage occurs nowhere in the labelled SemCor corpus (Mihalcea, 1998), and is plausibly not well represented by the word2vec sense-agnostic embedding.

3.2 Modified RETROFIT Algorithm

For these reasons we make the following modifications to RETROFIT.

1) Regardless of the position of a word sense in WordNet, it will be equipped with a descriptive gloss that clarifies its usage. We incorporate all content words from each synset's gloss in the RETROFIT algorithm's objective function, where "content words" refers to any word for which we have a sense-agnostic embedding. Content words that appear more than once in the gloss are weighted according to the number of times they occur (ie, if a word is repeated in the gloss, it has a stronger influence on the sense embedding.)

2) We implement a naive model to handle a compound word by simply representing its sense-agnostic embedding as the average of the sense-agnostic embeddings of its constituent words. Although this is obviously inadequate for many compound words, we find it is already an improvement.

3) The sense-agnostic embedding of a word is assumed to be the weighted average of its sense embeddings, proportional to how common a particular word sense is. We calculate the sense-frequencies from the SemCor corpus, which consists of around 300,000 words tagged with their WordNet 3.0 synsets (Mihalcea, 1998).

3.3 Weighted RETROFIT Algorithm

Weigthed RETROFIT proceeds very similarly to RETROFIT algorithm by (Jauhar et al., 2015). We begin by intializing an embedding for each word sense as the sense-agnostic embedding (or, in the case of multi-word lemmas, the average of the sense-agnostic embeddings of the constituant words). The embeddings are then iteratively updated to make them more similar to their semantic neighbors in the WordNet ontology, and to make the weighted average of the sense embeddings of a word closer to the sense-agnostic embedding. The weighted average is learned from the SemCor counts as discussed.

More precisely, let $M = (V, \hat{V}, S, \hat{S}, P, \Omega)$ be a model consisting of a vocabulary V and sense-agnostic embeddings $\hat{V}$, a set of word senses S and sense-embeddings $\hat{S}$, a discrete probability

---

[1] https://code.google.com/archive/p/word2vec/

density function $P : V \times S \to \mathbb{R}$, and an ontology Ω. We seek the set $\hat{S}$ that minimizes the new objective function for the weighted RETROFIT algorithm (Equation 3).

$$D(M) = \sum_i \alpha \left\| \hat{w}_i - \sum_j p_{ij} \vec{s}_{ij} \right\|^2$$
$$+ \sum_{ij} \sum_{i'j' \in N_{ij}} \beta_r \left\| \vec{s}_{ij} - \vec{s}_{i'j'} \right\|^2 \qquad (3)$$
$$+ \sum_{ij} \sum_{i' \in G_{ij}} \gamma \left\| \hat{w}_{i'} - \vec{s}_{ij} \right\|^2$$

by iteratively updating embeddings according to Equation (4). where $\hat{w}_i \in \hat{V}$, $\vec{s}_{ij} \in \hat{S}$, $p_{ij} = P(s_{ij}|w_i)$, N_{ij} is the set of neighbor indices of the *jth* sense of the *ith* word defined in Ω, $G_{ij} = \{i : w_i \in \hat{V}$ is in the gloss of $s_{ij}\}$ and α, β_r and γ are the parameters controlling the weights of sense-agnostic word embeddings, relations and gloss words respectively. Note that iteratively updating the sense embeddings via Eqs. 2 or 4 is equivalent to optimizing their respective objective functions via coordinate descent.

4 Evaluation

We train three variations of the RETROFIT algorithm on the 50-dimensional global context vectors produced by (Huang et al., 2012): the unmodified RETROFIT, RETROFIT with gloss words and multi-word lemmas (which we refer to as Modified RETROFIT), and Weighted RETROFIT with weighted senses as discussed above. Training time is similar between the first two; weighted RETROFIT takes about twice as long. All converge to a solution within 0.01 within fifteen iterations.

The models are evaluated on two different tasks: Synonym Selection and Word Sense Disambiguation. We first include and discuss results from some similarity judgment tasks, but these serve more as stepping stone than an as a rigorous measure of model quality. (Faruqui et al., 2016) give a comprehensive assessment of the inadequacies of evaluating the quality of embeddings on word similarity tasks. In general, these tasks are fairly subjective and a model's performance on them does not correlate with performance on downstream NLP tasks.

4.1 Similarity Judgments

We evaluate the models on the RG-65 dataset, (Rubenstein and Goodenough, 1965) which consists of sixty-five pairs of words and an average human judgment of similarity scaled from one to four. Evaluation is a straightforward calculation of the average cosine similarity of each pair of sense embeddings, as used by (Jauhar et al., 2015) and originally proposed by (Reisinger and Mooney, 2010). As an exploration, we also consider the results of using the maximum cosine similarity, which returns the highest cosine similarity among any pair of senses from the respective words.

Our results are displayed in Table 1. Every model performs best on the task using the maximum cosine similarity metric, with our improved systems performing noticeably better. Interestingly, the commonly used average similarity metric causes our models to lose their advantage, particularly Weighted RETROFIT, whose chief credit is its ability to produce more distinct sense embeddings. Averaging these vectors together throws away the improvements gained by separating out the distinct meanings.

4.2 Synonym Selection

We test the models on two synonym selection datasets: ESL-50 (Turney, 2002) and TOEFL (Landauer and Dumais, 1997). ESL-50 is a set of fifty English sentences with a target word for which a synonym must be selected from four candidate words. TOEFL consists of eighty context-independent words and four potential candidates for each. For both datasets, we use the same maxSim selection criteria as (Jauhar et al., 2015). We select the sense vector $\vec{s}_{ij}$ that corresponds to:

$$maxSim(w_i, w_{i'}) = \max_{j,j'} cos(\vec{s}_{ij}, \vec{s}_{i'j'})$$

Our results are presented in Table 2. The results on this task are less straightforward. Although the ESL-50 and TOEFL datasets are remarkably similar in form, the models do not perform consistently across them. Our modified RETROFIT method produces an enormous improvement on TOEFL, while ESL-50 gives our models some difficulties. Whether this is an effect of the relatively small number of words in the task or whether there are specific features about how the datasets were assembled is unclear.

$$\bar{s}_{ij} = \frac{\alpha p_{ij}\hat{w}_i - \alpha p_{ij}\sum_{k\neq j} p_{ik}\vec{s}_{ik} + \sum_{i'j'\in N_{ij}} \beta_r \vec{s}_{i'j'} + \gamma \sum_{i'\in G_{ij}} \hat{w}_{i'}}{\alpha p_{ij}^2 + \sum_{i'j'\in N_{ij}} \beta_r + \sum_{i'\in G_{ij}} \gamma} \qquad (4)$$

Similarity Judgments		
	RG-65	
	AVG	MAX
RETROFIT	**0.73**	0.79
Modified RETROFIT	0.72	**0.85**
Weighted RETROFIT	0.69	0.84

Table 1: Performance on RG-65 word similarity dataset. Scores are Spearman's rank correlation.

Synonym Selection		
	ESL-50	TOEFL
RETROFIT	**64.0**	68.75
Modified RETROFIT	62.0	**81.25**
Weighted RETROFIT	60.0	75.0

Table 2: Percent accuracy on ESL-50 and TOEFL synonym selection using maxSim comparison

4.3 Word Sense Disambiguation

We use Semeval 2015 task 13 (Moro and Navigli, 2015) as our English WSD test. The corpus for the task consists of four documents taken from the biomedical, mathematical and social issues domains, annotated with part of speech information. The task also includes named entity disambiguation, which we do not handle, except in the incidental case where there is a WN synset for a named entity. We explore two different methods for WSD. The first chooses a word sense by identifying a word that co-occurs in the sentence and has a sense that is closest to a sense of our target word. The intuition of the model is that although particular words may be totally unrelated to the sense of the target word, there should exist somewhere in the sentence a word pertaining to the subject described by the ambiguous word. Formally, this method is described as the *contextMax* function:

$$contextMax(w,c) =$$
$$\arg\max_{s\in S_i}(\max_{c\in\bigcup_{k\neq i} S_k} cos(\vec{s},\vec{c})\cdot p(s|w)) \qquad (5)$$

where S_i is the set of senses of the *ith* word of the context sentence.

The second WSD method incorporates both local and global context in equal parts. The intuition is that nearby words in a particular sentence will capture information about the particular usage of a word, while words that appear over the course of a passage will characterize the subject matter being discussed. Both of these component are essential to human understanding and should aid WSD algorithms, as discussed in (Weissenborn et al., 2015). Formally, we define the localGlobal WSD function as

$$localGlobal(w,c) = \arg\max_{s\in W_{ij}}(cos(\vec{s},\vec{c}_{ij})\cdot p(s|w)) \qquad (6)$$

where the context vector $\vec{c}_{ij}$ for the *jth* word of the *ith* sentence is given by

$$\vec{c}_{ij} = \frac{\vec{l}_{ij}}{|\vec{l}_{ij}|} + \frac{\vec{g}_i}{|\vec{g}_i|}$$

and the local context vector $\vec{l}_{ij}$ of the *jth* word of the *ith* sentence and global context vector $\vec{g}_i$ of the *ith* sentence are given by

$$\vec{l}_{ij} = \sum_{k\neq j} \frac{1}{|j-k|}\hat{w}_{ik}$$

$$\vec{g}_i = \sum_{n=i-2}^{i+2} \sum_k \hat{w}_{nk}$$

As a baseline we compare against the most-frequent sense tagger (MFS) trained on the Semcor corpus (Moro and Navigli, 2015), defined simply as

$$mfs(w) = \arg\max_{s\in S_w}(p(s|w)) \qquad (7)$$

6

Word Sense Disambiguation					
	Nouns	Verbs	Adjectives	Adverbs	All
MFS	45.8	49.9	67.5	70.6	53.5
RETROFIT	49.1	52.0	67.3	75.3	56.2
Modified RETROFIT	**50.6**	50.0	**69.2**	**76.5**	**57.0**
Weighted RETROFIT	50.0	**52.8**	65.4	**76.5**	56.8

Table 3: Semeval 2015 task 13 F1 scores of the models using the contextMax disambiguation function.

	Nouns	Verbs	Adjectives	Adverbs	All
RETROFIT	52.5	57.2	**77.3**	77.8	61.1
Modified RETROFIT	53.6	56.4	76.0	**79.0**	61.6
Weighted RETROFIT	**53.9**	**59.2**	75.4	77.8	**62.1**

Table 4: Semeval 2015 task 13 F1 scores of the models using the contextMax disambiguation function, restricted to correct POS

Tables 3 and 4 display results for our models using contextMax disambiguation with and without restriction by POS information, along with the MFS tagging baseline. In both cases, RETROFIT and MFS are outperformed overall by our improvements. Tables 5 and 6 show the WSD results using localGlobal disambiguation, which for the most part appears to be a strictly better metric. Results are ranked by F1 score, the harmonic mean of precision and recall (uniformly weighted). Although it underperforms on the compartively easier task of disambiguating adjectivs and adverbs, Weighted RETROFIT is the best model of verbs by every single metric.

By all measures, the various RETROFIT implementations outperform the MFS baseline. Weighted RETROFIT and Modified RETROFIT both improve the initial model. The best performing systems on the Semeval 2015 task 13 English corpus are LIMSI and SUDOKU (Moro and Navigli, 2015), which achieve F1 scores of 65.8 and 61.6 respectively. This would position both Weighted RETROFIT and RETROFIT with compound words and gloss words as second only to the top system, even with the use of relatively low dimensional embeddings.

5 Discussion

Results on similarity judgment are mixed, although it should be noted that despite the fact that in principle average similarity appears to be a good measure of word relatedness, in our trials the maximum similarity between two words is a better predictor of human judgments on RG-65 with all algorithms. It's possible that in the absence of disambiguating context human judges are not actually good at combining the relatedness of different senses of words and instead specifically search for related meanings when evaluating similarity. It's worth noting that the metric by which our modifications provide the largest improvements is the metric which RETROFIT itself also performs best by. But, as discussed above and in [4], even human judges often do not score particularly well similarity tasks, and in fact there may be no real "gold standard" on such a task.

The results of the synonym selection task are also mixed. On the ESL-50 dataset our modifications slightly underperform, while on the TOEFL dataset they provide an enormous improvement. We have not investigated the particulars of the datasets enough to see if there are anomolous features (over or under-representation of certain parts of speech, rare word senses, etc), or if these performance gaps are due more to the small sample size of the test data. Testing on a wider array of larger synonym selection datasets could yield insight into the models' shortcomings.

Our models are a noticeable improvement on WSD. Interestingly, the Weighted RETROFIT algorithm achieves the best scores on verbs across

	Nouns	Verbs	Adjectives	Adverbs	All
RETROFIT	49.5	49.2	64.2	**79.0**	55.7
Modified RETROFIT	**54.8**	50.0	**67.9**	77.8	**59.5**
Weighted RETROFIT	53.0	**52.4**	62.3	74.1	57.9

Table 5: Semeval 2015 task 13 F1 scores of the models using the localGlobal disambiguation function

	Nouns	Verbs	Adjectives	Adverbs	All
RETROFIT	52.2	55.6	73.5	**80.2**	60.2
Modified RETROFIT	**56.6**	57.6	**74.1**	**80.2**	**63.4**
Weighted RETROFIT	55.6	**59.2**	72.9	76.5	62.1

Table 6: Semeval 2015 task 13 F1 scores of the models using the localGlobal disambiguation function, restricted to correct POS

all metrics. Again, whether this is a quirk of the specific corpus is unclear. If not, it may indicate that homophonous verbs in English tend to be more distinct from each other than other parts of speech, perhaps because of more common metaphorical language use. We at least can say confidently that utilizing more features from WN is an across the board improvement.

Future Work

As mentioned above, the limited size and scope of the test sets leaves room for doubt about the models' performance on new datasets, especially when two datasets for the same task yield strikingly different results, like synonym selection. A useful exploration may be looking at domain-specific datasets for this task, as the results might suggest that the performance discrepancies are present between domains. It is possible, for example, that WordNet underrepresents certain domains. (Consider the case of the word *nugget*, which in Word-Net has no synsets related to food, but in American English is most often used in the compound *chicken nugget*.) It will also be important to try the same task with significantly larger datasets.

We also use only a crude model of compound word vectors. An investigation of better compositional semantic models could greatly benefit the algorithm, as a large percentage of WN synsets contain compound words.

The RETROFIT algorithm may also be discarding valuable information by constructing the sense vectors only from the sense-agnostic embeddings for words whose exact surface form matches entries in WordNet. But word2vec and most other VSM algorithms learn embeddings for many different conjugations of words, and in fact those conjugations may themselves contain information (such as part-of-speech) that can help further differentiate senses.

Our models are all trained on the relatively low dimensional global feature vectors produced by (Huang et al., 2012), but significantly richer embeddings exist, such as the GoogleNews vectors, which are 300 dimensional and were trained on a 100 billion word corpus using CBOW (Mikolov et al., 2013a; Mikolov et al., 2013b). We expect that the quality of the embeddings produced by the RETROFIT algorithms will scale with the quality of the underlying embeddings, and can hope for continual improvement as larger and better datasets become available.

6   Acknowledgement

This work was funded under NSF grant 1359275. The authors would also like to thank Feras Al Tarouti for his valuable input.

References

Xinxiong Chen, Zhiyuan Liu, and Maosong Sun. 2014. A unified model for word sense representation and disambiguation. In *EMNLP*, pages 1025–1035.

Manaal Faruqui, Yulia Tsvetkov, Pushpendre Rastogi, and Chris Dyer. 2016. Problems with evaluation of word embeddings using word similarity tasks. *arXiv preprint arXiv:1605.02276*.

Eric H Huang, Richard Socher, Christopher D Manning, and Andrew Y Ng. 2012. Improving word representations via global context and multiple word prototypes. In *Proceedings of the 50th Annual Meeting of the Association for Computational Linguistics: Long Papers-Volume 1*, pages 873–882.

Sujay Kumar Jauhar, Chris Dyer, and Eduard Hovy. 2015. Ontologically grounded multi-sense representation learning for semantic vector space models. In *Proceedings of National Association for Computational Linguistics (NAACL)*.

Thomas K Landauer and Susan T Dumais. 1997. A solution to plato's problem: The latent semantic analysis theory of acquisition, induction, and representation of knowledge. *Psychological review*, 104(2):211.

James H Martin and Daniel Jurafsky. 2016. Semantics with dense vectors, in speech and language processing. *Third Edition, Draft*.

Rada Mihalcea. 1998. SemCor semantically tagged corpus. *Unpublished manuscript*.

Tomas Mikolov, Kai Chen, Greg Corrado, and Jeffrey Dean. 2013a. Efficient estimation of word representations in vector space. *arXiv preprint arXiv:1301.3781*.

Tomas Mikolov, Ilya Sutskever, Kai Chen, Greg Corrado, and Jeffrey Dean. 2013b. Distributed representations of words and phrases and their compositionality. *Advances in Neural Information Processing Systems*, pages 3111–3119.

George A Miller. 1995. Wordnet: A lexical database for english. *Communications of the ACM*, 38(11):39–41.

Andrea Moro and Roberto Navigli. 2015. Semeval-2015 task 13: Multilingual all-words sense disambiguation and entity linking. *Proceedings of SemEval-2015*.

Arvind Neelakantan, Jeevan Shankar, Alexandre Passos, and Andrew McCallum. 2015. Efficient non-parametric estimation of multiple embeddings per word in vector space. *arXiv preprint arXiv:1504.06654*.

Joseph Reisinger and Raymond J Mooney. 2010. Multi-prototype vector-space models of word meaning. In *Human Language Technologies: The 2010 Annual Conference of the North American Chapter of the Association for Computational Linguistics*, pages 109–117.

Sascha Rothe and Hinrich Schütze. 2015. Autoextend: Extending word embeddings to embeddings for synsets and lexemes. *arXiv preprint arXiv:1507.01127*.

Herbert Rubenstein and John B Goodenough. 1965. Contextual correlates of synonymy. *Communications of the ACM*, 8(10):627–633.

Peter D Turney and Patrick Pantel. 2010. From frequency to meaning: Vector space models of semantics. *Journal of artificial intelligence research*, 37(1):141–188.

Peter D Turney. 2002. Mining the web for synonyms: Pmi-ir versus lsa on toefl. *arXiv preprint cs/0212033*.

Dirk Weissenborn, Leonhard Hennig, Feiyu Xu, and Hans Uszkoreit. 2015. Multi-objective optimization for the joint disambiguation of nouns and named entities. In *Proceedings of the 53rd Annual Meeting of the Association for Computational Linguistics and the 7th International Joint Conference on Natural Language Processing of the Asian Federation of Natural Language Processing*, pages 596–605.

Can SMT and RBMT Improve each other's Performance?- An Experiment with English-Hindi Translation

Debajyoty Banik, Sukanta Sen, Asif Ekbal, Pushpak Bhattacharyya
Department of Computer Science and Engineering
Indian Institute of Technology Patna
{debajyoty.pcs13,sukanta.pcs15,asif,pb}@iitp.ac.in

Abstract

Rule-based machine translation (RBMT) and Statistical machine translation (SMT) are two well-known approaches for translation which have their own benefits. System architecture of SMT often complements RBMT, and the vice-versa. In this paper, we propose an effective method of serial coupling where we attempt to build a hybrid model that exploits the benefits of both the architectures. The first part of coupling is used to obtain good lexical selection and robustness, second part is used to improve syntax and the final one is designed to combine other modules along with the best phrase reordering. Our experiments on a English-Hindi product domain dataset show the effectiveness of the proposed approach with improvement in BLEU score.

1 Introduction

Machine translation is a well-established paradigm in Artificial Intelligence and Natural Language Processing (NLP) which is getting more and more attention to improve the quality (Callison-Burch and Koehn, 2005; Koehn and Monz, 2006). Statistical machine translation (SMT) and rule-based machine translation (RBMT) are two well-known methods for translating sentences from one to the other language. But, each of these paradigms has its own strengths and weaknesses. While SMT is good for translation disambiguation, RBMT is robust for morphology handling. There is no systematic study involving less-resourced languages, where the coupling of SMT and RBMT has been shown to achieve better performance. In our current research we attempt to provide a systematic and principled way to combine both SMT and RBMT for translating product related catalogs from English to Hindi. We consider English-Hindi scenario as an ideal platform as Hindi is a morphologically very rich language compared to English. The key contributions of our research are summarized as follows:

(i). Proposal of an effective hybrid system that exploits the advantages of both SMT and RBMT.

(ii). Developing a system for translating product catalogues from English to Hindi, which is itself a difficult and challenging task due to the nature of the domain. The data is often mixed, comprising of very short sentences (even the phrases) and the long sentences. To the best of our knowledge, for such a domain, there is no work involving Indian languages.Below we describe SMT and RBMT very briefly.

1.1 Statistical Machine Translation (SMT)

Statistical machine translation (SMT) systems are considered to be good at capturing knowledge of the domain from a large amount of parallel data. This has robustness in resolving ambiguities and other related issues. SMT provides good translation output based on statistics and maximum likelihood expectation (Koehn et al., 2003a):

$$e_{best} = argmax_e P(e|f)$$

$$= argmax_e [P(f|e)P_{LM}(e)]$$

where f and e are the source and target languages, respectively. $P_{LM}(e)$ and $P(f|e)$ are the language and translation model, respectively. The best output translation is denoted

D S Sharma, R Sangal and A K Singh. Proc. of the 13th Intl. Conference on Natural Language Processing, pages 10–19,
Varanasi, India. December 2016. ©2016 NLP Association of India (NLPAI)

by e_{best}. Language model corresponds to the n-gram probability. The translation probability $P(f|e)$ is modeled as,

$$P(f_1^{-I}|e_1^{-I}) = \prod_{i=1}^{I} \phi(\bar{f_i}|\bar{e_i})d(start_i - end_{i-1} - 1)$$

ϕ is phrase translation probability and d(.) is distortion probability.

$start_i - end_{i-1} - 1$, which is the argument of d(.) is a function of i, whereas $start_i$ and end_{i-1} are the starting positions of the translation of ith phrase and end position of the $(i-1)^{th}$ phrase of e in f. In the above equation, it is well defined that most probable phrases present in training corpora will be chosen as the translated output. This could be useful in handling ambiguity at the translation level. The work reported in (Dakwale and Monz, 2016) focuses on improving the performance of a SMT system. Along with the translation model authors allow the re-estimation of reordering models to improve accuracy of translated sentences. The authors in their work reported in (Carpuat and Wu, 2007) show how word sense disambiguation helps to improve the performance of a SMT system. Literature shows that there are few systems available for English-Indian language machine translation (Ramanathan et al., 2008; Rama and Gali, 2009; Pal et al., 2010; Ramanathan et al., 2009).

1.2 Rule-based Machine Translation (RBMT)

Rule-based system generates target sentence with the help of linguistic knowledge. Hence, there is a high chance that translated sentence is grammatically well-formed.There are several steps required to build linguistic rules for translation. Robustness of a rule-based system greatly depends on the quality of rules devised. A set of sound rules ensures to build a good accurate system. Generally, the steps can be divided into three sub parts:

1. Analysis
2. Transfer
3. Generation

Analysis step consists of pre-processing, morphological analysis, chunking, and pruning. Transfer step consists of lexical transfer, transliteration, and WSD. Finally, generation step consists of genderization, vibhakti computation, TAM computation, agreement computing, word generator and sentence generator. The agreement computing can be accomplished with three sub steps: intra-chunk, inter-chunk and default agreement computing. In (Dave et al., 2001) authors have proposed an inter-lingua based English–Hindi machine translation system. In (Poornima et al., 2011), authors have described how to simplify English to Hindi translation using a rule-based approach. AnglaHindi is one of the very popular English-Hindi rule-based translation tools proposed in (Sinha and Jain, 2003). Multilingual machine aided translation for English to Indian languages has been developed in (Sinha et al., 1995). Apertium is an open source rule-based machine translation tool proposed in (Forcada et al., 2011). Rule-based approach for machine translation has been proposed with respect to Indian language (Dwivedi and Sukhadeve, 2010).

1.3 Hybrid Machine Translation

A hybrid model of machine translation can be developed using the strengths of both SMT and RBMT. In this paper, we develop a hybrid model to exploit the benefits of disambiguation, linguistic rules, and structural issues. Knowledge of coupling is very useful to build hybrid model of machine translation. There are different types of coupling, *viz.* serial coupling and Parallel coupling. In serial coupling, SMT and RBMT are processed one after another in sequence. In parallel coupling, models are processed in parallel to build a hybrid model. In Indian languages, few hybrid models have been proposed as in(Dwivedi and Sukhadeve, 2010; Aswani and Gaizauskas, 2005).

The rest of the paper is structured as follows. We present a brief review of the existing works in Section 2. Motivations and various characteristic features have been discussed in Section 3. We describe our proposed method in Section 4. Experiential setup and results are discussed in Section 5. Finally, we conclude in Section 6.

2 Related work

In rule-based MT, various linguistic rules are defined and combined in (Arnold, 1994). Statistical machine translation models have resulted from the word-based models (Brown et al., 1990). This has become so popular because of its robustness in translation only with the parallel corpora. As both of this approaches have their own advantages and disadvantages, there is a trend nowadays to build a hybrid model by combining both SMT and RBMT (Costa-Jussa and Fonollosa, 2015). Various architectures of hybrid model have been compared in (Thurmair, 2009). Among the various existing architectures, serial coupling and parallel coupling are the most popular (Ahsan et al., 2010).Rule-based approach along with post-processed SMT outputs are described in (Simard et al., 2007). A review for hybrid MT is available in (Xuan et al., 2012). In (Eisele et al., 2008), authors proposed an architecture to build a hybrid machine translation engine by following a parallel coupling method. They merged phrase tables of general training data of SMT and the output of RBMT. However, they did not consider the source and target language ordering characteristics. In this paper, we combine both SMT and RBMT in order to exploit advantages of both the translation strategies.

3 Necessity for Combining SMT and RBMT

In this work we propose a hybrid architecture for translating English documents into Hindi. Both of these languages are very popular. English is an international language, whereas Hindi is one of the very popular languages. Hindi is the official language in India and in terms number of native speakers it ranks fourth in the world.Linguistic characteristics of English and Hindi are not similar and their differences are listed below:

- Hindi is a relatively morphologically richer language compared to English.

- Word orders are not same for English and Hindi. Subject-Object-Verb (SOV) is the standard way to represent Hindi whereas SVO ordering is followed for English.

- Hindi uses postposition whereas English uses preposition.

- Hindi uses pre-modifiers, whereas English uses post-modifiers.

SMT and RBMT can not solve the problems as mentioned above independently.So, main focus of our current work is to develop a hybrid system combining both SMT and RBMT which can efficiently solve the problems.In addition to combining these two methods we also introduce reordering to improve the translation quality. Our main motivation was to make use of the strength of SMT (better in handling translation ambiguities) and RBMT (better for dealing with rich morphology)

3.1 Morphology

As already mentioned Hindi is a morphologically richer language compared to English. Morphology plays an important role in the translation quality of English-Hindi. Let us consider the examples: case: ए (e – plural direct) or ओं (on – plural oblique) is used as plural-marker for "boy". But in the case of "girl" याँ (on) is used for plural direct, and ओं (on) is used for plural oblique.

Singular direct:
E: The boy is going.
H: लड़का जा रहा है।
HT: Ladka ja raha hai.
E: The girl is going.
H: लड़की जा रही है।
HT: Ladki ja rahi hai.

Plural direct:
E: The boys are going.
H: लड़के जा रहे हैं।
HT: Ladke ja rahe hain.
E: The girls are going.
H: लड़कियाँ जा रही हैं।
HT: Ladkiya ja rahi hae.

Singular oblique:
E: I have seen a boy.
H: मैं ने एक लड़के को देखा।
HT: Main ne ek ladke ko dekha.
E: I have seen a girl.
H: मैं ने एक लड़की को देखा।
HT: Main ne ek ladki ko dekha.

plural oblique:

E: I have seen five boys.

H: मैं ने पाँच लड़कों को देखा।

HT: Main ne paanch ladkon ko dekha.

E: I have seen five girls.

H: मैं ने पाँच लड़कियों को देखा।

HT: Main ne paanch ladkiyon ko dekha.

Tense: Tenses are directed by the verbs. For example, एगा (aega) and एगी (aegi) denote future connotation in singular form for masculine gender and feminine gender, respectively. आएगा (ayega), आएगी (ayegee). एंगे (aenge) and एंगी (aengi) denote future tense in plural form for masculine and feminine geneder, respectively. Here we show the few usages:

Singular form in future tense:-

E: The boy will come.

H: लड़का आएगा ।

HT: ladka ayenga

E: The girl will come.

H: लड़की आएगी ।

HT: ladki ayegi

Plural form in future tense:-

E: Boys will come.

H: लड़के आएंगे ।

HT: ladke ayenge.

E: Girls will come.

H: लड़कियाँ आएंगी ।

HT: ladkiyan ayengi.

The above examples describe how morphology influences the structure and meaning of the language. A root word can appear in different forms in different sentences depending upon tense, number or gender. Such kinds of diversities can not be handled properly by a SMT system because of lack of data or enough grammatical evidences. This can, however, be handled efficiently in a RBMT system due to the richness of linguistic rules that it embeds. It is very important to have all the morphological forms and case structures along with their equivalent representations in the target language. Under this scenario, hybridization of SMT and RBMT is a more preferred approach.

3.2 Data Sparsity

While translating from English to Hindi we encounter with the problems of data sparsity due to the variations in morphology and case marking in source and target language pairs.

From the examples shown in the previous subsection, it is seen that same word may appear in different positions of a sentence, often followed or preceded by different words, due to varying morphological properties such as case, gender and number information. For example, the English word 'girl' can be translated to लड़की (ladki), लड़कियाँ (ladkiyan), लड़कियों (ladkiyon) etc. in Hindi based on case and number information. Even though both लड़कियाँ (ladkiyan) and लड़कियों (ladkiyon) are in plural forms, they convey differnt meanings based on the context. The word लड़कियों (ladkiyon) is placed with case markers, but लड़कियाँ (ladkiyan) is used without it. The word 'Child' can be बच्चा (bachcha) and बच्चे ने (bachche ne) in singular form in direct and oblique cases, respectively. Here, ने is followed by बच्चों (bachchon), but if बच्यों ने (bachchon) ne) does not occur in corpora then it can not be translated.

Such problems can be resolved using proper linguistic knowledge, which is the strength of a rule-based system. In statistical approach, system is modeled using a probabilistic method that retrieves the target phrase based on maximum likelihood estimates. Hence, this may not be possible to resolve the issues using a SMT system. In contrast, RBMT has the power to deal with such situation that incorporates proper grammatical knowledge.

3.3 Ambiguity

Ambiguity is a very common problem in machine translation. Ambiguities can appear in many different forms. For example, the following sentence has ambiguities at the various levels:

E: I went with my friend Washington to the bank to withdraw some money, but was disappointed to find it closed.

Bank may be verb or noun-Part of speech ambiguity.

Washington may be a person name or place-Named entity ambiguity.

Bank may be placed for the borders of a water body or financial transaction- Sense ambiguity.

The word `it' has to be disambiguated to

understand its proper reference-Discourse/co-reference ambiguity.

It is not understood who was disappointed for the closure of bank (Pro-drop ambiguity).

3.3.1 Semantic Role Ambiguity

Let us consider the following example sentence:

H: मुझे आपको मिठाई खिलानी पड़ेगी

HT: Mujhe aapko mithae khilani padegee.

In this sentence, it is not properly disclosed who will feed the sweets (to/by me or to/by you). Thus, English sentence for the above Hindi sentence may take any of the following forms:

E1: I have to feed you sweets.

E2: You have to feed me sweets.

3.3.2 Lexical Ambiguity

We discuss the problem of lexical ambiguity with respect to the following example sentence. E: I will go to the bank for walking today.

Here, bank may be a financial institution or the shore of a river or sea. It is difficult to interpret exact meaning of bank. Context plays an important role in interpreting the current sense. Here, bank is used in the context of walk. Hence, there is a greater chance that it denotes the `bank of river`' instead of `financial institution`.   Use of proverbs complicates translation further.

E: An empty vessel sounds much.

H: थोथा चना बाजे घना. / अधजल गगरी छलकत जाय.

HT: Thotha chana baaje ghana./ adhajal gagaree chhalkat jai.
Its actual meaning should be जिसको कम ज्ञान होता है वो दिखावा करने के लिए अधिक बोलता है. (jisko kam gyan hota hai wo dikhava karne ke liye adhik bolta hai.)

All of the above mentioned issues can not be efficiently handled by statistical or rule-based approach independently. Some of the issues are better handled by a RBMT approach whereas some are better handled by a SMT system. In this paper we develop a hybrid model by combining the benefits of both rules and statistics.

3.4 Ordering

We further study the effect of ordering in our proposed model. Ordering can be considered as a basic structure of any language. Different languages have different structure patterns at sentence which can be achieve after merging PoS. For example, English uses subject-verb-object (SVO) whereas Hindi uses subject-object-verb (SOV). These structural differences of language pair can be the vital cause of affecting the accuracy. So, we shall incorporate the concept of ordering along with SMT and RBMT to build the hybrid model.

4 Proposed MT Model: A Multi-Engine Translation System

We propose a novel architecture that improves translation quality by combining the benefits of both SMT and RBMT. We also devise a mechanism to further improve the performance by integrating the concept of reordering at the source side. This architecture is trying to combine the best parts from multiple hypothesis to achieve maximum advantages of different MT engines and remove the pitfall of the translated texts so that the quality of the translated text could be improved. Translation models are combined in such a way that the overall performance is improved over the individual models. In literature it was also shown that an effective combination of different complimentary models could be more useful (Rayner and Carter, 1997; Eisele et al., 2008).

Combining multiple models of machine translations is not an easy task because of the following facts: RBMT is linguistically richer than SMT; RBMT can produce different word orders in the target sentence compared to SMT; and there may have different word orders for the SMT and RBMT outputs. After using linguistic rules at the source side of the test set, we combine the outputs obtained to the training set, and generate new hypothesis to build a better phrase table. Finally, we use argmax computation of SMT decoder to find the best possible sequence.   A combined model can not produce expected output if the individual component models are not strong enough. Word ordering plays an important role to improve the quality of translation, es-

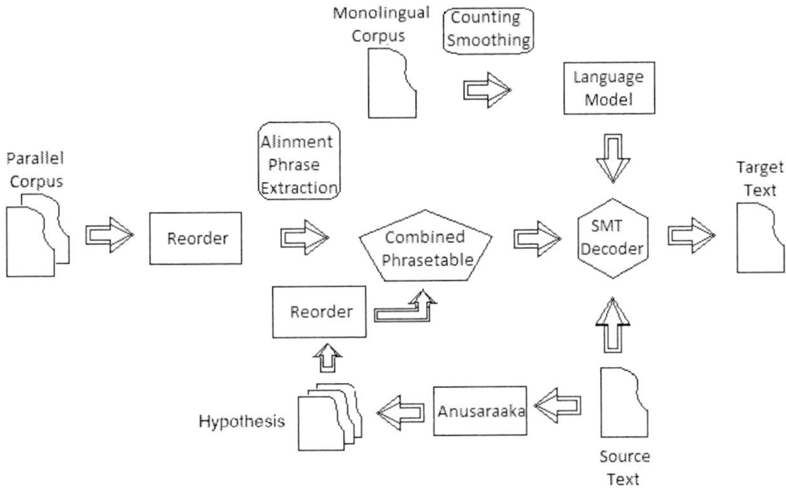

Figure 1: Architecture for multi-engine MT driven by a SMT decoder

pecially for the pair of languages where source language is relatively less-rich compared to the target. Our source language, which is English, follows a Subject-Verb-Object (SVO) fashion whereas Hindi follows a Subject-Object-Verb (SOV) ordering scheme. At first we extract syntactic information of the source language. The syntactic order of source sentence is converted to the syntactic order of target language. The source language sentences are pre-processed following the set of transformation rules as detailed in (Rao et al., 2000).

$$SS_m VV_m OO_m C_m \rightarrow C'_m S'_m S' O'_m O' V'_m V'$$

where,

S: Subject

V : Verb

O: Object

X': Hindi corresponding constituent, where X is S, V, or O X_m: modifier of X

C_m: Clause modifier

Pre-ordering alters the English SVO order to Hindi SOV order, and post-modifiers generate the pre-modifiers. Our prepossessing module performs this by parsing English sentence and applying the reordering rules on the parse tree to generate the representations in the target side. After pre-ordering of source sentences, we combine the RBMT and SMT based models.After pre-ordering of training and tuning corpora we also do the same for the test set. Alignment was done using the hypothesis of

RBMT.Beam search algorithm of SMT decoder is used to obtain the best target sentence. Detailed architecture of the proposed technique is shown in Figure 1. In this figure, lower portion represents different modules and resources used in the RBMT model, whereas the upper portion represents the SMT model. Because of this effective combination we obtain a model that produces target sentences of better qualities compared to either RBMT or SMT with respect to morphology and disambiguation (at the level of lexical and structural).

Sets	Number of sentences
Training Set	111,586
Tune Set	602
Test Set	5,640

Table 1: Datasets statistics

5 Data Set, Experiential setup, Result and analysis

5.1 Data Set

In this paper we develop a hybridized translation model for translating product catalogs from English to Hindi.The training corpus consists of 111,586 English-Hindi parallel sentences. Tune and test sets comprise of 602 and 5,640 sentences, respectively. Brief statistics of training, tune and test sets are shown in Table 4. The domain is, itself, very challenging due to the mixing of various types of sentences. There

Approach	BLEU Score
~~Baseline (Phrase-based SMT)~~	~~45.66~~
RBMT	5.34
SMT & RBMT	46.66
Our Approach	50.71
Improvement from Baseline	11.06%
Improvement from SMT & RBMT	8.67%

Table 2: Results of different models

are sentences of varying lengths consisting of minimum of 3 tokens to the maximum of 80 tokens. Average length of the sentences is approximately 10. In one of our experiments we distributed the sentences into short and long sets, containing less than 5 and more than equal to 5 sentences, respectively. Training, tuning and evaluation were then carried out, which reveals that performance deteriorates due to the reduction in size. Hence, we mix all kinds of sentences for training, and then tune and test.

5.2 Experiential Setup

We use the pre-order tool developed at CFILT lab. (Dwivedi and Sukhadeve, 2010) We use Moses [1] setup for SMT related experiments. The model is tuned using a tuning set. We use ANUSAARAKA (Ramanathan et al., 2008) rule-based system for translation. Phrase tables are generated by training SMT model on the parallel corpora of English-Hindi. The RBMT system is evaluated on the test data. The outputs produced by this model are used as the silver standard data. The SMT model is trained on this silver standard data to produce a phrase table. The phrase table, thus obtained, is added to the phrase table generated using the original training data. Secondly, the silver standard parallel corpora is added to the original training corpora and a new parallel corpora is generated. The SMT model is again built on this new data-set. This generated model is used to evaluate the test set thereafter.

5.3 Results and Analysis

We report the experimental results in Table 4. Accuracy is calculated using the standard evaluation metric called BLEU (Papineni et al., 2002). A baseline model (Phrase-based SMT model) is developed by training Moses with default parameter settings (Koehn et al., 2003b). We achieve a BLEU score of 45.66. Our proposed hybrid model attains a BLEU score of 46.66, which is 2.19% higher compared to the baseline model. When re-ordering is performed at the source side, we obtain the BLEU score of 50.71, which is nearly 8.68% higher compared to the hybrid model (without re-ordering) . This is 11.06% higher compared to the baseline phrase-based model. Generated outputs of the proposed model are better in various respects like structure, morphology etc. With the following examples, we describe how the proposed model can be used to improve the performance over SMT or RBMT model. Here ST, SMT, AMT, HMT, and PMT denote source sentence, SMT output, RBMT output, output of the hybrid model and output of the proposed system, respectively.

a.　SMT output is incomplete while PMT output is complete and better than SMT output.

ST: All applicable shipping fees and custom duties up to customers address are included in the price

SMT: डिलीवरी तक लागू सभी कस्टम और शुल्क जोड़े जा चुके हैं इस दाम में

HT: Delivary tak lagu sabhi custom aur shulk joden ja chuke hain is daam mein

PMT: डिलीवरी तक लागू सभी कस्टम और शुल्क ग्राहक के घर तक शिपिंग के मूल्य में शामिल हैं

HT: Delivery tak lagu sabhi custom aur shulk grahak ke ghar tak shipping ke mullya mein samil hain

AMT: सब ग्राहकों जहाँ तक कि शुल्क और रिवाज कार्य जहाज से भेजता हुआ लागू होना पते मूल्य में सम्मिलित हुए गये हैं

HT: Sab grahakon jahan tak ki shulk aur rivaz karya jahaz se bhejta hua lagu hona pate mulya mein sammilithue gaye hain

---

[1] http://www.statmt.org/moses/

b. PMT output is a reordered version of SMT which is an exact translation. Hence, this is better compared to the others. Also PMT retrieves proper phrase to generate better quality. ST: Add loads of flirty colours to your wardrobe!

SMT: में शोख रंगों को शामिल करें अपनी अलमारी

HT: mein shokh rangon ko shamiln karen apni almaree

PMT: अपनी अलमारी में शोख रंगों को शामिल करें

HT:apni almaree mein shokh rangon ko shamil karen

AMT: आपकी अलमारी को इश्कबाज रङ्गों के बहुत जोडिए!

HT:aapki almaree ko ishqbaaz radgon ko bahut jodiye

c. PMT is capable to select better sentence of generated translated output by both of the systems. AMT is better than SMT. PMT produces quite simliar output as AMT. Hence, the overall quality will improve.

ST: A classy way to hang your clothes
SMT: एक उत्तम दर्जे के तरीका अपने कपड़े सिर्फ लटका कर

HT Ek utam darje ke tareeka apne kapde sirf latka kar

PMT: एक विशेष एवं उच्चतम मार्ग आपके वस्त्र लटकाने का

HT: Ek vishesh evam uchchtam marg apke vastra latkane ka.

AMT: एक विशेष एवं उच्चतम मार्ग आपके वस्त्र लटकाने का

HT: Ek vishesh evam uchchtam marg apke vastra latkane ka.

d. PMT output is better because it is in correct syntax order (ends in verb).

ST: 11 Diamonds provides lifetime manufacturing & exchange warranty

SMT: प्रदान करता है 11 हीरे और एक्सचेंज वारंटी जीवन भर निर्माण

HT: Pradan karta hai 11 hire or exchange warranty jeevan bhar nirman

PMT: 11 डायमंड आजीवन निर्माता और एक्सचेंज वांरटी देता है

HT: 11 diamond aajeevan nirmata aur exchange warranty deta hai

AMT: 11 डाइमन्ड्ज जीवन-काल उत्पादन और अदला बदला अधिकार देता है

HT: Diamond jeevan-kaal utpadan aur adla badla adhikar deta hai

It is out-of-scope to compare the existing English-Hindi MT systems (as mentioned in the related section) as none of the techniques was evaluated on the product catalogue domain. Since the domain as well as the training and test data are different, we can not directly compare our proposed system with the others. It is also to be noted that none of the existing systems makes use of an infrastructure like ours. The multi-engine MT model proposed in (Eisele et al., 2008) can not be compared as this was not evaluated for the language pair and domain that we attempted.

6   Conclusion

In this paper we have proposed a hybrid model to study whether RBMT and SMT can improve each other's efficiency. We use an effective method of serial coupling where we have combined both SMT and RBMT. The first part of coupling has been used to obtain good lexical selection and robustness, second part has been used to improve syntax and the final one has been designed to combine other modules along with source-side phrase reordering. Our experiments on a English-Hindi product domain dataset show the effectiveness of the proposed approach with improvement in BLEU score. In future we would like to evaluate the proposed model on other domains, and study hierarchical SMT model for the product catalogues domain.

References

Arafat Ahsan, Prasanth Kolachina, Sudheer Kolachina, Dipti Misra Sharma, and Rajeev Sangal. 2010. Coupling statistical machine translation with rule-based transfer and generation. In Proceedings of the 9th Conference of the Association for Machine Translation in the Americas.

Doug Arnold. 1994. Machine translation: an introductory guide. Blackwell Publisher.

Niraj Aswani and Robert Gaizauskas. 2005. A hybrid approach to align sentences and words in english-hindi parallel corpora. In Proceedings of the ACL Workshop on Building and Using Parallel Texts, pages 57--64. Association for Computational Linguistics.

Peter F Brown, John Cocke, Stephen A Della Pietra, Vincent J Della Pietra, Fredrick Jelinek, John D Lafferty, Robert L Mercer, and Paul S Roossin. 1990. A statistical approach to machine translation. Computational linguistics, 16(2):79--85.

Chris Callison-Burch and Philipp Koehn. 2005. Introduction to statistical machine translation. Language, 1:1.

Marine Carpuat and Dekai Wu. 2007. Improving statistical machine translation using word sense disambiguation. In EMNLP-CoNLL, volume 7, pages 61--72.

Marta R Costa-Jussa and José AR Fonollosa. 2015. Latest trends in hybrid machine translation and its applications. Computer Speech & Language, 32(1):3--10.

Praveen Dakwale and Christof Monz. 2016. Improving statistical machine translation performance by oracle-bleu model re-estimation. In The 54th Annual Meeting of the Association for Computational Linguistics, page 38.

Shachi Dave, Jignashu Parikh, and Pushpak Bhattacharyya. 2001. Interlingua-based english--hindi machine translation and language divergence. Machine Translation, 16(4):251--304.

Sanjay K Dwivedi and Pramod P Sukhadeve. 2010. Machine translation system in indian perspectives. Journal of computer science, 6(10):1111.

Andreas Eisele, Christian Federmann, Hans Uszkoreit, Hervé Saint-Amand, Martin Kay, Michael Jellinghaus, Sabine Hunsicker, Teresa Herrmann, and Yu Chen. 2008. Hybrid architectures for multi-engine machine translation. Proceedings of Translating and the Computer, 30.

Mikel L Forcada, Mireia Ginestí-Rosell, Jacob Nordfalk, Jim O'Regan, Sergio Ortiz-Rojas, Juan Antonio Pérez-Ortiz, Felipe Sánchez-Martínez, Gema Ramírez-Sánchez, and Francis M Tyers. 2011. Apertium: a free/open-source platform for rule-based machine translation. Machine translation, 25(2):127--144.

Philipp Koehn and Christof Monz. 2006. Shared task: Exploiting parallel texts for statistical machine translation. In Proceedings of the NAACL 2006 workshop on statistical machine translation, New York City (June 2006).

Philipp Koehn, Franz Josef Och, and Daniel Marcu. 2003a. Statistical phrase-based translation. In Proceedings of the 2003 Conference of the North American Chapter of the Association for Computational Linguistics on Human Language Technology-Volume 1, pages 48--54. Association for Computational Linguistics.

Philipp Koehn, Franz Josef Och, and Daniel Marcu. 2003b. Statistical phrase-based translation. In Proceedings of the 2003 Conference of the North American Chapter of the Association for Computational Linguistics on Human Language Technology-Volume 1, pages 48--54. Association for Computational Linguistics.

Santanu Pal, Sudip Kumar Naskar, Pavel Pecina, Sivaji Bandyopadhyay, and Andy Way. 2010. Handling named entities and compound verbs in phrase-based statistical machine translation. Association for Computational Linguistics.

Kishore Papineni, Salim Roukos, Todd Ward, and Wei-Jing Zhu. 2002. Bleu: a method for automatic evaluation of machine translation. In Proceedings of the 40th annual meeting on association for computational linguistics, pages 311--318. Association for Computational Linguistics.

C Poornima, V Dhanalakshmi, KM Anand, and KP Soman. 2011. Rule based sentence simplification for english to tamil machine translation system. International Journal of Computer Applications, 25(8):38--42.

Taraka Rama and Karthik Gali. 2009. Modeling machine transliteration as a phrase based statistical machine translation problem. In Proceedings of the 2009 Named Entities Workshop: Shared Task on Transliteration, pages 124--127. Association for Computational Linguistics.

Ananthakrishnan Ramanathan, Jayprasad Hegde, Ritesh M Shah, Pushpak Bhattacharyya, and M Sasikumar. 2008. Simple syntactic and morphological processing can help english-hindi statistical machine translation. In IJCNLP, pages 513--520.

Ananthakrishnan Ramanathan, Hansraj Choudhary, Avishek Ghosh, and Pushpak Bhattacharyya. 2009. Case markers and morphology: addressing the crux of the fluency problem in english-hindi smt. In Proceedings of the Joint Conference of the 47th Annual Meeting of the ACL and the 4th International Joint Conference on Natural Language Processing of the AFNLP: Volume 2-Volume 2, pages 800--808. Association for Computational Linguistics.

Durgesh Rao, Kavitha Mohanraj, Jayprasad Hegde, Vivek Mehta, and Parag Mahadane. 2000. A practiced framework for syntactic transfer of compound-complex sentences for english-hindi machine translation. In Knowledge Based Computer Systems: Proceedings of the International Conference: KBCS--2000, page 343. Allied Publishers.

Manny Rayner and David Carter. 1997. Hybrid language processing in the spoken language translator. In Acoustics, Speech, and Signal Processing, 1997. ICASSP-97., 1997 IEEE International Conference on, volume 1, pages 107--110. IEEE.

Michel Simard, Nicola Ueffing, Pierre Isabelle, and Roland Kuhn. 2007. Rule-based translation with statistical phrase-based post-editing. In Proceedings of the Second Workshop on Statistical Machine Translation, pages 203--206. Association for Computational Linguistics.

RMK Sinha and A Jain. 2003. Anglahindi: an english to hindi machine-aided translation system. MT Summit IX, New Orleans, USA, pages 494--497.

RMK Sinha, K Sivaraman, A Agrawal, R Jain, R Srivastava, and A Jain. 1995. Anglabharti: a multilingual machine aided translation project on translation from english to indian languages. In Systems, Man and Cybernetics, 1995. Intelligent Systems for the 21st Century., IEEE International Conference on, volume 2, pages 1609--1614. IEEE.

Gregor Thurmair. 2009. Comparing different architectures of hybrid machine translation systems. In Proceedings of MT Summit XII, Ottawa (2009).

HW Xuan, W Li, and GY Tang. 2012. An advanced review of hybrid machine translation (hmt). Procedia Engineering, 29:3017--3022.

Composition of Compound Nouns Using Distributional Semantics

Kyra Yee
Pomona College
333 N College Way
Claremont, CA 91711, USA
`kny02014@mymail.pomona.edu`

Jugal Kalita
University of Colorado, Colorado Springs
1420 Austin Bluffs Pkwy
Colorado Springs, CO 80918, USA
`jkalita@uccs.edu`

Abstract

The use of distributional semantics to represent the meaning of a single word has proven to be very effective, but there still is difficulty representing the meaning of larger constituents, such as a noun phrase. In general, it is unclear how to find a representation of phrases that preserves syntactic distinctions and the relationship between a compound's constituents. This paper is an attempt to find the best representation of nominal compounds in Spanish and English, and evaluates the performance of different compositional models by using correlations with human similarity judgments and by using compositional representations as input into an SVM classifying the semantic relation between nouns within a compound. This paper also evaluates the utility of different function's compositional representations, which give our model a slight advantage in accuracy over other state-of-the-art semantic relation classifiers.

Keywords compositional distributional semantics, nominal compounds, nominal compounds in Spanish

1 Introduction

The use of distributional semantics has become increasingly popular due to its effectiveness in a range of NLP tasks. The vector-based representation is computed by looking at the context of every instance of a specific word within a large corpus, which is based on the idea that the meaning of a word is determined by its associations with other words (Erk, 2012). Despite the success of vector-based representation in a wide variety on contexts, this method still has difficulty handling larger phrase structures and function words, as opposed to just isolated content words (Mitchell and Lapata, 2008). Vectors for larger phrases cannot be reliably used due to the sparseness of data (Erk, 2012).

Ways of representing compositional models for constituents larger than a single word that preserve the lexical and syntactic function of a word in a phrase and best represent the relation between the constituents of a phrase is desired in creating a more general and powerful framework for natural language semantics. (Mitchell and Lapata, 2008; Mitchell and Lapata, 2010), and (Guevara, 2010) have compared and empirically tested the effectiveness of different mathematical compositions in representing adjective-noun, verb-object, and noun-noun compounds, but there has been little research into representing nominal compounds that are longer than two words, and the vast majority of research has been in English, without cross-linguistic inquiries (Mitchell and Lapata, 2010). This paper will investigate the effectiveness of a variety of different compositional functions using two metrics: correlation of the model's cosine similarity predictions with human similarity judgments for two, three and four word Spanish and English noun compounds, and by using the composition of two vectors as input into an SVM used to classify the relations between constituent nouns for two-word English noun compounds. For the human correlation task, this paper builds on (Mitchell and Lapata, 2010) by analyzing compounds longer than two words, which is a previously unexplored topic, and by analyzing the composition of Spanish compound nouns. As far as we know, compositional models have never been applied to Spanish word vectors be-

D S Sharma, R Sangal and A K Singh. Proc. of the 13th Intl. Conference on Natural Language Processing, pages 20–29,
Varanasi, India. December 2016. ©2016 NLP Association of India (NLPAI)

fore. Previous work have utilized word embeddings as input for relation classification, but we use the composed vectors as input as well, which also has never before been tested. This paper is also the first to use noun-relation classification accuracy as a metric for the utility of compositional functions, which gives a new level of insight into the

2   Compounding in English and Spanish

What constitutes a nominal compound is contested among linguists and computational linguists(Moyna, 2011; Finin, 1980). For our purposes, we will use the definition given by Finin (Finin, 1980):

> *A nominal compound is the concatenation of two or more nominal concepts which functions as a third nominal concept.*

The structure N N in English is productive, recursive, and compositional (Bauke, 2014). In Spanish, N N compounds are rarely productive, rarely contain more than two elements and are highly stylistic (Bauke, 2014; Moyna, 2011). The process is that of lexical word-formation, as opposed to English,which has syntactic word-formation for N N compounds (Bauke, 2014). In Spanish, the creation of N N compounds more closely resembles the invention of a new morpheme, which is reflected by the fact that only 2% of N N constructions are written as two words or a hyphenated word without one-word alternates (Moyna, 2011). Because of the limitations of N N constructions in Spanish, many consider the Spanish equivalent to the English N N structure to be the N P N structure, with a semantically empty preposition. This structure, similar to the English N N structure, is productive, recursive, and compositional (Bauke, 2014). We do not consider the more theoretical qualifications for compounds nouns proposed by (Moyna, 2011) for a more linguistically rigorous definition for Spanish compound nouns.

Restricting our attention to compounds only consisting of two nouns in English, analyzing the meaning of nominal compounds computationally has proven to be a difficult task because the listener must discern the relationship between the two words, which must be inferred contextually without any syntactic clues (Finin, 1980). Consider the cases of "meeting room", "salt water" and "aircraft engine". "Room" defines the location for "meeting", "engine" is a part of the "aircraft", and "salt" is dissolved in "water" (Finin, 1980). This problem of determining relations between the constituent nouns becomes even more difficult for longer phrases, because we now must determine the parse of the compound using contextual clues. In the phrase "computer science department", "computer science" modifies "department", instead of having "computer" modify "science department". These factors pose challenges to vector-based representations of longer compound noun phrases.

In Spanish N P N constructions, despite the presence of a preposition or potentially determiners, is it still difficult to discern the relation between the constituent nouns. Spanish definite determiners are used in a much wider context than their English counterparts, so they do not provide much useful insight into the relation between the two nouns. In the majority of cases, the preposition is "de", which is semantically empty in this construction (Bauke, 2014), and is used to represent a multitude of relations, as seen from Table I (taken from (Valle, 2008)).

English	Spanish	Meaning Implied
leather shoes	zapatos de piel	shoes made of leather
sports shoes	zapatos de deporte	shoes used to play sports with
winter shoes	zapatos de invierno	shoes to be worn in winter time
high-heel shoes	zapatos de tacón	shoes with high heels
display shoes	zapatos de muestra	shoes on display
Gucci shoes	zapatos de Gucci	shoes designed by Gucci

Table 1: Spanish Semantic Relations.

Thus the Spanish N P N construction poses similar challenges to the English N N construction. Our goal is to analyze compound nouns in English (which take on the form of N N) and semantically equivalent structures in Spanish, which take on the form N P N (Girju, 2009).

3 Previous Work

3.1 Word Embeddings

A variety of methods for generating word embeddings have been proposed, most famously the GloVe, word2vec, CW, and HPCA embeddings. The word2vec model, proposed by (Mikolov and Dean, 2013), is a continuous skip-gram model, built using neural neworks, which is able to capture precise syntactic and semantic word relationships to generate a vector representation of a word. The GloVe model (Pennington et al., 2014) is a global bilinear regression model which combines the advantages of global matrix factorization and local context window methods. It utilizes statistical information by training on "non-zero elements in a word-word cooccurrence matrix, rather than on the entire sparse matrix or on individual context windows in a large corpus". The CW model, proposed by (Collobert et al., 2011), implements a multilayer neural network, where the first layer extracts features for each word and the second layer extracts features from a window of words. The model is refined using a supervised training step utilizing data from part-of-speech tagging, chunking, named entity recognition and semantic role labeling (Collobert et al., 2011; Dima and Hinrichs, 2015). The HPCA model (Lebret and Collobert, 2013) is generated by applying Hellinger PCA to a word co-occurance matrix, which has the advantage of being much faster than training a neural net.

3.2 Compositional Models

Very little work has been done in distributional semantics for Spanish. Some studies have been done on the effectiveness of vector-based representations on Spanish (Etcheverry and Wonsever, 2016; Al-Rfou et al., 2013), but none have considered compositional models. Many studies have been done in English studying compositional models, (Mitchell and Lapata, 2010; Mitchell and Lapata, 2008; Reddy et al., 2011; Im Walde et al., 2013; Baroni and Zamparelli, 2010; Guevara, 2010; Socher et al., 2012; Polajnar and Clark, 2014) but none have considered three or four word compound nouns.

There have been many functions suggested for how to compose two vectors. The general class of models representing the vector composition is defined by:

$$\mathbf{p} = f(\mathbf{u}, \mathbf{v}, R, K) \qquad (1)$$

where $\mathbf{u}$ and $\mathbf{v}$ are the constituent vectors, R represents their syntactic relation, and K represents any additional information required to interpret the semantics of $\mathbf{p}$ (Mitchell and Lapata, 2010). Since we are only considering the composition of compound nominals, we can hold R fixed. We can also ignore K for simplicity, attempting to glean as accurate of a meaning as possible without further pragmatic context (Mitchell and Lapata, 2010). From these assumptions, we arrive at several more common potential functions: additive, multiplicative, and tensor product, respectively (Mitchell and Lapata, 2010).

$$p_i = u_i + v_i \qquad (2)$$

$$p_i = u_i \cdot v_i \qquad (3)$$

$$p_{ij} = u_i \otimes v_j \qquad (4)$$

The tensor product has interested some researchers since it does a better job of encoding syntactic information (the tensor product is not commutative, so it is seen as a representation that can distinguish "blood donor" from "donor blood"). However, the tensor product becomes very computationally expensive, as the number of dimensions grows exponentially as more constituents are composed (Mitchell and Lapata, 2010; Polajnar and Clark, 2014). The effectiveness of each of these equations, especially between the additive and multiplicative model, is still contested (Baroni and Zamparelli, 2010). Another well-known function is the weighted additive function, which is regarded as being better at representing the syntactic relation between its constituents:

$$p_i = \alpha u_i + \beta v_i. \qquad (5)$$

With regard to nominal compounds, one study showed that the influence of the modifier noun has a much greater influence on the overall meaning of the compound than the head noun in German, with respect to both human ratings and vector-space models (Im Walde et al., 2013). In contrast, another study determined that the semantic contribution of the modifier and head to a compound noun are approximately equal in English (Kim and Baldwin, 2005).That being said, it could be the case that the average contribution of the modifier and head varies between languages, so determining a weighting for Spanish and English could yield different results to obtain the optimal weighted additive model. An extreme form of this formula would be to only use the vector from either the head or modifying noun:

$$p_i = u_i \tag{6}$$

$$p_i = v_i. \tag{7}$$

It is also possible to combine the weighted additive and multiplicative model:

$$p_i = \alpha u_i + \beta v_i + \gamma u_i v_i. \tag{8}$$

One major disadvantage to the multiplicative model is that the presence of a zero in either two component vectors will lead to a zero in the resulting vector, essentially meaning information from the noun-zero entries multiplied by zero was thrown away; combining these two models could help alleviate that effect (Mitchell and Lapata, 2010).

Other models for composition include utilizing a partial least squares regression (Guevara, 2010) or using a recursive neural tensor network (Socher et al., 2012). This paper will compare different models for the composition of two, three, and four word compounds in Spanish and English.

3.3 Automatic Compound Noun Interpretation

A variety of taxonomies have been proposed for the classification of compound noun relations, some of which consist of a relatively small number of semantic relations, while others propose an unbounded number (Tratz and Hovy, 2010). The taxonomy created by (Tratz and Hovy, 2010) has been widely used because of its comparatively high level of inter-annotator agreement for its relations and the large size of the data set. (Kim and Baldwin, 2005) use wordnet similarity to classify a set of 2169 compounds into 20 semantic categories, achieving 53% accuracy. (Girju, 2007) uses cross-linguistic data and an SVM model to achieve an accuracy of 77.9% on an unseen test set. (Tratz and Hovy, 2010) use a dataset of 17509 compounds and a maximum entropy classifier to achieve 79.3% for cross-validation and 51% accuracy on an unseen test set using a set of 43 semantic relations, using wordnet, surface level, thesaurus based, and N-gram features. (Verhoeven et al., 2012) uses word embeddings to classify Dutch and Afrikaans compound nouns, achieving 47.8 % and 51.1%, respectively. (Dima and Hinrichs, 2015) use a neural net on the concatenation of CW-50, FloVe-300, HPCA-200, and word2vec embeddings on the tratz dataset to achieve 77.7% accuracy on a ten-fold cross-validation and 77.12% accuracy on an unseen test set. Although (Dima and Hinrichs, 2015) and (Verhoeven et al., 2012) use word embeddings, none of the previously proposed models used the composition of word embeddings as input for their model.

4 Experimental Setup

4.1 Overview of the Procedure

For the human similarity judgment correlation task, we first created our own dataset for two, three, and four word compounds in Spanish and English, since longer compounds and Spanish compounds have been previously unexplored. We then generated embeddings for the constituent nouns from the noun compounds using word2vec and the BNC and the Spanish Wikipedia corpus. Next, we applied the compositional functions to the constituent nouns to create a representation for the compound. To apply functions with parameters in them, we used grid search to optimize the parameters, taking the best parameters as the ones with highest correlations to the human judgments. We then took the cosine similarity of noun compound pairs and correlated this with human judgments to determine how accurately each function represents the compound noun.

For the noun classification task, we experimented with a variety of embedding types to see which had the best results. We used the Tratz dataset and used the concatenation of the constituent embeddings and the composition embedding as input for the classifier to train an SVM. We took the performance of the difference classifier using different composition functions as evidence for the accuracy of a composition function to represent noun compounds.

4.2 Materials and Tools

We will evaluate the performance of each composition function in two ways: by analyzing its correlation with human similarity judgments, and also by seeing which composition function yields the best result for classifying compound noun relations using an SVM for English two-word compounds. For evaluating human judgments, we used the British National Corpus (`http://www.natcorp.ox.ac.uk/`) for English and the most recent wikidump from July 3, 2016 (https://dumps.wikimedia.org/eswiki/latest/) for Spanish to train word2vec embeddings. The WikiExtractor was used to extract and clean the wikidump (https://github.com/attardi/wikiextractor). The gensim package was used to extract 500 dimensional word2vec vectors, using the CBOW algorithm. For both corpora, stop-words were removed, and words that occurred less than 100 times for English and 50 times for Spanish were excluded from the model's vocabulary. We resorted to creating our own datasets due to the unavailability of preexisting ones for three and four word compounds and Spanish compounds. The Stanford POS tagger version 3.5.2 was used to extract Spanish nominal compounds (Toutanova et al., 2003), and the BNC's tagset was used to extract English compounds. Spanish and English compounds for the test set were randomly chosen from looking at the list of compounds that included one of the top 400 words that occurred in the most compounds. This was to ensure that for each compound in the test set, there would be a sufficient number of compounds that share one constituent word for comparison. There were six test sets: two, three and four word compounds for Spanish and English. For Spanish, this is with respect to nouns only, not counting the preposition or determiners when determining the length of the compound. 25 compounds were chosen for each test set, totaling up to 150 test compounds. For each word in the test compound, another two-word compound sharing that word was chosen for comparison. So for the four word-test sets, there were 100 pairs for comparison, for the three-word compound sets, there were 75 pairs for comparison, and for the two-word compound sets, there were 50 pairs for comparison.

For example, "periodo de expansión del imperio" was paired with "expansión del universo", "embajador del imperio", and "periodo de ausencia". "Bomb squad chief" was paired with "bomb damage", "drug squad", and "police chief".

The goal of analyzing compound noun relation classification is twofold; it will serve as another metric for comparing composition functions, a previously unused metric, and we will be able to determine if using the composition vectors as input to a classifier can improve overall performance of the classifier, a previously untried strategy. We only perform this experiment in English for two-word compounds due to the availability of large preexisting annotated data sets. (Verhoeven et al., 2012) and (Dima and Hinrichs, 2015) use word embeddings for semantic classification; however, they simply concatenate the embeddings for the constituent vectors as input. For classifying semantic relations in English, we experimented with our BNC model, Google News Vectors (available at https://code.google.com/archive/p/word2vec/), GloVe vectors (Pennington et al., 2014), CW vectors (Collobert et al., 2011) and HPCA vectors (Lebret and Collobert, 2013). For the utilization of word2vec vectors, we found better results with the Google News Vectors, probably due to the amount of data used to train them, so we report only classification results utilizing those here. For each embedding type, we chose the largest possible dimensions, since that has yielded the best results in (Dima and Hinrichs, 2015). Table II gives an overview of the information used to train each set. We used the dataset described

Method	Embedding Size	Dictionary Size	Training Data Size	Support Corpora
word2vec	300	3,000,000	100.00 bn	Google News
GloVe	300	400,000	42.00 bn	Common Crawl
HPCA	200	178,080	1.65 bn	enWiki+Reuters +WSJ
CW	50	130,000	0.85 bn	enWiki+Reuters RCV1
word2vec	500	30,025	100 mn	BNC
word2vec	500	19,679	120 mn	esWiki

Table 2: Overview of different embeddings

in (Tratz, 2011) (available at `http://www.isi.edu/publications/licensed-sw/fanseparser/index.html`), which consists of 37 relations and 19,158 annotated compound nouns. Compounds with words that were not included in all of the different model embeddings' vocabularies were not included in the analysis, leaving a total of 18669 compounds. The set was partitioned into a training module that was 80% of the original set and a test set that was 20%. After experimenting with a variety of different classifiers and architectures, we used the Weka machine learning software (https://weka.wikispaces.com/) to implement an SVM with a polykernel, with feature selection using a gain ratio attribute evaluator and a ranker search. To create the input features, we concatenated the vectors for the constituent nouns and the composition function vector. We experimented with using the different word embeddings individually and in conjunction, and found the best results by concatenating the constituent and composition embeddings from the Google News word2vec, GloVe, HPCA, and CW sets, similar to the work done by (Dima and Hinrichs, 2015).

4.3 Collecting Similarity Judgments

Responses were collected using Survey Gizmo (`https://www.surveygizmo.com/`), using unpaid volunteers. Subjects were asked to rate how similar or dissimilar compound noun pairs were on a Likert scale. Each pair was presented twice, once as "compound 1, compound 2" and again as "compound 2, compound 1" to account for a asymmetry of human judgments. Pairs were presented in random order. Surveys were self paced and took approximately fifteen minutes. For the English survey, there were 7 participants. For the Spanish survey, there were 4 participants. Participants ranged in age from 15-55, and were self-reportedly fluent in the language of the survey. For each pair, the average similarity was calculated on a scale of 1 to 5, 5 being most similar and 1 being the most dissimilar. Ratings from each participant were averaged to use to correlate with the model's cosine similarity predictions.

4.4 Composition Methods

For the human judgment correlation task, for each compound in the test and comparison set, representations were generated by taking the vector representations from the word2vec model using the CBOW

	Combined Model			OWA		NWA	
	α	β	γ	α	β	α	β
two-word Spanish	0.099	0.101	0.000	0.098	0.098	0.5	0.5
two-word English	0.267	0.264	9.697	0.874	0.898	0.5	0.5
three-word Spanish	1.452	1.943	-0.006	1.333	1.749	0.2	0.8
three-word English	0.842	0.724	0.000	0.821	0.719	0.9	0.1
four-word Spanish	0.949	1.387	4.422	1.065	1.639	0.1	0.9
four-word English	0.939	0.869	2.580	0.927	0.869	0.1	0.9

Table 3: Parameters for the combined, optimized weighted additive, and normalized weighted addtive models

algorithm trained from the BNC and esWiki corpora. For entries in the Spanish test set, only the nouns were considered for composing the phrase. Since the preposition is largely semantically empty and only serves to illustrate the syntactic connection between the nouns, it is ignored. As we have previously seen, the preposition "de" encodes a wide variety of semantic relations; however, there is a minority of nominal compounds that use different prepositions like "por","para", "entre", etc. We will naively assume here that the preposition does not encode semantic information and focus only on compounds using the most common preposition "de", which is a bit of a generalization. Articles were also ignored, since they also do not provide much semantic meaning, especially considering their more generalized usage in Spanish compared to English. The composition of the constituent words for each compound was then calculated using the following functions: simple additive (equation (2)), multiplicative (equation (3)), tensor product (equation (4)), head only (equation (7) for English, (6) for Spanish), modifier only(equation (6) for English, (7) for Spanish), weighted additive(equation (5)), and combined weighted additive and multiplicative(equation (8)). For three word compounds, data was parsed by hand into (n1 n2) n3 or n1 (n2 n3) so that syntactically sensitive functions could be properly applied recursively. The same method was applied to four-word compounds. For compounds longer than two words, the head only and modifier only models were not calculated, since there are multiple modifiers and heads.

4.5 Determining the Parameters of the Weighted Additive and Combined Models

The parameters of the weighted additive model were determined in two different ways. First, we considered nine models, with weights varying from 0.1 to 0.9 in a step size of 0.1, where the sum of α and β adds to one, where the model with the highest correlation to the human judgments was taken as optimal. For the purposes of this experiment, the magnitude of the vector does not matter, because the cosine similarity is taken for the final metric, which does not take magnitude into account. We used grid search to find the optimal values for α and β, but without the constraint that they had to add to one, again maximizing the correlation to human judgments. Likewise, for the combined model, we used a similar grid search, without the traditional constraint. The model parameters are described in Table III, where NWA stands for normalized weighted additive and OWA stands for optimized weighted additive.

In Spanish, the head is the first noun, and would be weighted with α, whereas the head is the second noun in English, and would be weighted with β. So we see that heavily weighting the modifier is a consistent trend across the combined, normalized additive, and optimized additive models in English and Spanish for compounds longer than two words, with the exception of the four-word normalized additive English set. This inconsistency could be due to idiosyncrasies in the relatively small data set. For two-word compounds in English and Spanish, an even weight distribution yielded the best results. This could imply that as the length of the compound noun grows, the semantic importance of the modifier increases.

5 Evaluation

For the human similarity judgments, we calculated intersubject agreement using Spearman's ρ, using leave-out one resampling as employed by (Mitchell and Lapata, 2008), with the results given in Table 4.

2W Spanish	2W English	3W Spanish	3W English	4W Spanish	4W English
0.341	0.441	0.357	0.347	0.170	0.321

Table 4: Intersubject Agreement for Human Similarity Judgments

For the two-word English set, we see that the similarity judgment is consistent with previous work, where (Mitchell and Lapata, 2010) achieved a Spearman's correlation coefficient of 0.49. As a general trend, inter-subject agreement declines as the compounds get longer.

	2W Span	2W Eng	3W Span	3W Eng	4W Span	4W Eng
simple additive	0.365	0.617	0.585	0.331	0.230	0.650
multiplicative	0.258	0.624	0.227	-0.057	0.105	0.372
tensor	0.357	0.621	0.040	-0.041	0.266	0.321
head	0.280	0.443				
modifier	0.191	0.060				
normalized weighted additive	0.365	0.617	0.521	0.312	0.289	0.336
optimized weighted additive	0.371	0.633	0.690	0.330	0.435	0.654
optimized combined	0.342	0.670	0.652	0.338	0.434	0.658

Table 5: Spearman's correlation between human similarity judgments and cosine similarity predictions

We evaluated the similarity of two compounds by taking the cosine of their vectors, a commonly used metric (Mitchell and Lapata, 2010). To test if a composition model's results were consistent with human judgments, we used Spearman's correlation, where we compared the cosine with the average human similarity judgment. Similar to (Mitchell and Lapata, 2010), the results indicate that the similarity judgment task was relatively difficult, but there still was a decent amount of consistency between participants. Our study finds that this task becomes more difficult as the compounds get longer.

For noun relation classification, we used two metrics. We performed a ten-fold cross-validation on the training set, and also tested each model on the unseen test set. For the parameterized functions, we used the optimized parameter values from the corresponding human judgment correlation test. Since the optimal normalized parameters from the 2-word English set was 0.5 and 0.5, we did not perform a test for the normalized weighted additive set, since the proportions are the same as the simplified additive model. We also did not test the tensor product model, due to constraints in dimensionality.

6 Results

6.1 Correlation with Human Similarity Judgments

Table 5 shows the model's predictions correlated with the human judgment using Spearman's ρ.

Consistent with the work of (Mitchell and Lapata, 2010), all compositional models outperform the head-only and modifier-only models, indicating the utility of the composition functions. The simple additive model and the multiplicative model yield comparable results for two-word compounds, but the effectiveness of the multiplicative model declines for longer compounds. This could be due to the previously discussed fact that zero or low-valued entries in the vector can essentially "throw away" data in the component vector, leading to poor results as more vectors are composed. As more and more vectors are composed, this problem is exacerbated and begins to affect performance. Likewise, the tensor product performs well on two-word compounds in comparison with the additive model, but less so on longer compounds, especially three-word compounds. This may imply that in addition to dimensionality challenges, the tensor product may face similar limitations to the multiplicative model for composing larger phrases. For the optimized weighted additive and combined models, the results are very comparable, with the optimized additive model slightly outperforming the normalized additive model. The combined and weighted additive models yield the most promising results, especially since their accuracy is relatively consistent for handling longer phrases. The increasing inaccuracy of the multiplicative and tensor models and the consistency of the combined and weighted additive models for longer compounds are new insights for the effectiveness of these models, which has serious consequences for attempting to build models that can handle longer phrase structures in general. This work suggests that the utility of each function can vary with the length of the sentence, which suggests the importance of performing more work on structures longer than two-words, which has been the standard for work in compound nouns until now. This paper presents strong evidence that the multiplicative model, although promising in previous work handling two-word phrases, has serious shortcomings for handling more complex phrases.

6.2 Compound Noun Relation Classification

Table 6 gives the results for each tested function on the different word embeddings, including the concatenation of all the different embeddings. The CV column represents the 10-fold cross-validation accuracy, and the test set is comprised of unseen noun compounds. Input with only the constituent vector embeddings without the composition function was also tested to give a baseline. Adding the composition function improves the performances for every type of embedding, with the most dramatic improvement in the concatenated word2vec+HPCA+CW+GloVe model.

We achieved the best results using the concatenation of the word2vec, HPCA, CW, and GloVe embeddings. Adding the composition function improves this models performance by as much as 2.02% using the multiplicative function, demonstrating the utility of using a compositional function during classification. The simple additive and weighted additive models actually perform worse in cross-validation than using no composition function at all. The combined models γ parameter was 9.697, so the multiplicative component of the combined model mostly overpowers the additive components, which explains why its performance is similar to that of the multiplicative model.

Our model slightly outperforms (Dima and Hinrichs, 2015), with its high cross-validation score being 77.7%, and is comparable to the state of the art model of (Tratz and Hovy, 2010), achieving 79.3%.

	word2vec+HPCA+CW+GloVe		word2vec		GloVe		HPCA		CW	
	CV	test set	CV	test set	CV	test set	CV	test set	CV	test set
no composition function	76.76	77.3	75.41	76.67	73.35	73.21	71.60	72.39	61.96	62.26
simple additive	76.52	76.95	75.85	76.01	72.63	73.59	71.36	71.59	61.98	62.23
weighted additive	76.47	77.70	74.80	76.76	72.70	73.62	71.37	71.48	62.02	62.31
multiplicative	**78.78**	**78.23**	75.82	76.04	73.42	73.30	71.95	72.50	62.52	62.58
combined	78.69	78.09	75.99	76.09	73.38	73.30	71.36	71.59	62.27	62.18

Table 6: Cross-validation accuracy and accuracy on an unseen test set for semantic relation classification

However, the model of (Tratz and Hovy, 2010) only achieves 51% accuracy on an unseen test set, whereas our model is much more consistent, with 78.23% accuracy. Again, we narrowly outperform (Dima and Hinrichs, 2015), with its accuracy on an unseen test set, which was 77.12% (Dima and Hinrichs, 2015). (Tratz and Hovy, 2010) use a slightly different set of relations and data set, but similar to the work of (Dima and Hinrichs, 2015), the consistency when testing unseen compounds points to the robustness of our model in comparison to (Tratz and Hovy, 2010). It is also clear that the small performance increase spurred by the addition of the composition function gives our model its slight increase in accuracy over the model of (Dima and Hinrichs, 2015), with a 4.84% decrease in relative error for cross-validation and 4.85% decrease in relative error for an unseen test set.

7 Discussion

With regards to the effectiveness of the additive and multiplicative classes of models, this paper presents strong evidence that multiplicative class models do not perform well for longer compound nouns, which have been previously untested. This idea is further supported by the low γ parameters in the optimized combined model for three and four word compounds. However, within the context of semantic relation classification, the multiplicative model is the strongest, whereas the additive model does not improve performance significantly, and sometimes even worsens performance. One interesting direction of future study would be to see which function performs best for classifying longer compounds, since the multiplicative model did not perform well for the human similarity correlation task

for longer compounds. This paper also suggests that the semantic importance of the head noun diminishes as the compound gets longer, and that the semantic importance of the modifier becomes greater, as illustrated by the optimized parameters of the weighted additive models. One future direction of study would be to implement more complex composition functions, or to incorporate information from the prepositions in Spanish compound nouns into the composition vector. Another direction of study would be to expand the noun relation classification task to a Spanish data set, and compare results, or to expand the classification task to three or four word compounds in English. This study points to the robustness of the combined model, since it is able to capture information from both the additive and multiplicative models. It performs well for three and four word compound human judgment similarity correlation, and it performs well in the relation classification task. The flexibility of its parameters, which can vary between languages and for compound nouns differing in length, makes it very promising.

8 Conclusion

The goal of this research is to find the optimal way to represent compound nouns of length two or greater using a vector-based representation. We have illustrated the utility of the multiplicative model in relation classification, but it has shortcomings in representing larger phrases in comparison to the additive class of models. Our new classification system, which incorporates composition vectors into SVMs, is comparable to other state-of-the-art models using cross-validation, or slightly outperforms them using an unseen test set.

References

[Al-Rfou et al. 2013] Rami Al-Rfou, Bryan Perozzi, and Steven Skiena. 2013. Polyglot: Distributed word representations for multilingual NLP. *CoNLL-2013 (2013): 183.*.

[Baroni and Zamparelli 2010] Marco Baroni and Roberto Zamparelli. 2010. Nouns are vectors, adjectives are matrices: Representing adjective-noun constructions in semantic space. In *2010 Conference on Empirical Methods in NLP*, 1183-1193.

[Bauke 2014] Leah S Bauke. 2014. *Symmetry breaking in syntax and the lexicon*, volume 216. John Benjamins Publishing Company.

[Collobert et al. 2011] Ronan Collobert, Jason Weston, Léon Bottou, Michael Karlen, Koray Kavukcuoglu, and Pavel Kuksa. 2011. Natural language processing (almost) from scratch. *Journal of Machine Learning Research*, 12 (Aug):2493-2537.

[Dima and Hinrichs 2015] Corina Dima and Erhard Hinrichs. 2015. Automatic noun compound interpretation using deep neural networks and word embeddings. *IWCS 2015*,173.

[Erk 2012] Katrin Erk. 2012. Vector space models of word meaning and phrase meaning: A survey. *Language and Linguistics Compass*, 6(10):635–653.

[Etcheverry and Wonsever 2016] Mathias Etcheverry and Dina Wonsever. 2016. Spanish word vectors from wikipedia. In *LREC 2016*, May.

[Finin 1980] Timothy Wilking Finin. 1980. The semantic interpretation of compound nominals.

[Girju 2007] Roxana Girju. 2007. Improving the interpretation of noun phrases with cross-linguistic information. In *annual meeting for computation linguistics*, volume 45, page 568.

[Girju 2009] Roxana Girju. 2009. The syntax and semantics of prepositions in the task of automatic interpretation of nominal phrases and compounds: A cross-linguistic study. *Computational Linguistics*, 35(2):185–228.

[Guevara 2010] Emiliano Guevara. 2010. A regression model of adjective-noun compositionality in distributional semantics. In *2010 Workshop on Geometric Models of NL Semantics*, pages 33-37. ACL.

[Im Walde et al. 2013] Sabine Schulte Im Walde, Stefan Müller, and Stephen Roller. 2013. Exploring vector space models to predict the compositionality of german noun-noun compounds. In 2nd Joint Conference on Lexical and Computational Semantics, 255-265.

[Kim and Baldwin 2005] Su Nam Kim and Timothy Baldwin. 2005. Automatic interpretation of noun compounds using wordnet similarity. In *ICON*,945-956.

[Lebret and Collobert 2013] Rémi Lebret and Ronan Collobert. 2013. Word embeddings through Hellinger PCA. *EACL 2014 (2014): 482.*.

[Mikolov and Dean 2013] T Mikolov and J Dean. 2013. Distributed representations of words and phrases and their compositionality. *Advances in neural information processing systems*.

[Mitchell and Lapata 2008] Jeff Mitchell and Mirella Lapata. 2008. Vector-based models of semantic composition. In *ACL*, pages 236–244.

[Mitchell and Lapata 2010] Jeff Mitchell and Mirella Lapata. 2010. Composition in distributional models of semantics. *Cognitive science*, 34(8):1388-1429.

[Moyna 2011] María Irene Moyna. 2011. *Compound words in Spanish: theory and history*, volume 316. John Benjamins Publishing.

[Pennington et al. 2014] Jeffrey Pennington, Richard Socher, and Christopher D Manning. 2014. Glove: Global vectors for word representation. In *EMNLP*, volume 14, 1532-43.

[Polajnar and Clark 2014] Tamara Polajnar and Stephen Clark. 2014. Reducing dimensions of tensors in type-driven distributional semantics.

[Reddy et al. 2011] Siva Reddy, Ioannis P Klapaftis, Diana McCarthy, and Suresh Manandhar. 2011. Dynamic and static prototype vectors for semantic composition. In *IJCNLP*, 705-713.

[Socher et al. 2012] Richard Socher, Brody Huval, Christopher D Manning, and Andrew Y Ng. 2012. Semantic compositionality through recursive matrix-vector spaces. In *2012 Conference on Empirical Methods in NLP and Comp. Natural Language Learning*, pages 1201-1211.

[Toutanova et al. 2003] Kristina Toutanova, Dan Klein, Christopher D Manning, and Yoram Singer. 2003. Feature-rich part-of-speech tagging with a cyclic dependency network. In *2003 Conference of the North Amer. Chapter of the ACL on Human Language Technology-Volume 1*, pages 173-180.

[Tratz and Hovy 2010] Stephen Tratz and Eduard Hovy. 2010. A taxonomy, dataset, and classifier for automatic noun compound interpretation. In *48th Annual Meeting of the ACL*, pages 678-687.

[Tratz 2011] Stephen Tratz. 2011. *Semantically-enriched parsing for natural language understanding*. USC.

[Valle 2008] Ana Bocanegra Valle. 2008. On the teachability of nominal compounds to spanish learners of english for specific purposes. *English for Specific Purposes: Studies for Classroom Development and Implementation*, page 249.

[Verhoeven et al. 2012] Ben Verhoeven, Walter Daelemans, and Gerhard B Van Huyssteen. 2012. Classification of noun-noun compound semantics in dutch and afrikaans. In *PRASA 2012*, 121-125.

29

Towards Building a SentiWordNet for Tamil

Abishek Kannan
LTRC
IIIT Hyderabad
abishek.kannan
@research.iiit.ac.in

Gaurav Mohanty
LTRC
IIIT Hyderabad
gaurav.mohanty
@research.iiit.ac.in

Radhika Mamidi
LTRC
IIIT Hyderabad
radhika.mamidi
@iiit.ac.in

Abstract

Sentiment analysis is a discipline of Natural Language Processing which deals with analysing the subjectivity of the data. It is an important task with both commercial and academic functionality. Languages like English have several resources which assist in the task of sentiment analysis. SentiWordNet for English is one such important lexical resource that contains subjective polarity for each lexical item. With growing data in native vernacular, there is a need for language-specific SentiWordNet(s). In this paper, we discuss a generic approach followed for the development of a Tamil SentiWordNet using currently available resources in English. For Tamil SentiWordNet, a substantial agreement Fleiss Kappa score of 0.663 was obtained after verification from Tamil annotators. Such a resource would serve as a baseline for future improvements in the task of sentiment analysis specific to Tamil data.

1 Introduction

Tamil has over 70 million native speakers spread across the world and digitized data for Tamil is ever increasing on the web. From news data to movie review sites, usage of Tamil on the web is more than it ever was. In an era driven by social media, the focus shifts from an objective application (News) to a subjective environment (Surveys, Online Review Systems). Applications of sentiment analysis are endless and it is in demand because it has proved to be efficient. Thousands of text documents can be processed for sentiment in seconds compared to the hours it would take for a team to manually complete the task. Commer-

cial Organisations are therefore incorporating sentiment analysis systems[1] for customer feedback and product review. For good governance, feedback from the public through social media and other surveys is monitored at a large scale. The public prefers to give feedback in its own vernacular. Analysing the sentiment in their feedback in various Indian languages hence demands language specific subjective lexicons. This served as the motivation for the creation of SentiWordNet for Tamil.

A translation based approach has been adopted to build this resource using various lexicons in English. Each of these lexicons comprises of English words with certain polarity. After several levels of preprocessing, a final set of English words was obtained. These words were then translated into Tamil using Google Translate[2]. The final set of words were annotated with either positive or negative polarity based on its prior polarity in English. The final lexicon was checked by Tamil annotators to remove any ambiguous entries and also for accuracy of translation.

The various tools used for the construction of SentiWordNet for Tamil include English SentiWordNet (Esuli and Sebastiani, 2006), AFINN-111 lexicon (Nielsen, 2011), Subjectivity Lexicon (Wilson et al., 2005), Opinion Lexicon (Liu et al., 2005) and Google Translate.

The rest of the paper is organized into various sections. Section 2 deals with related work and progress towards building SentiWordNets for Indian languages followed by Section 3 describing the resources and tools used. Section 4 contains a detailed explanation of the approach followed to build the Tamil SentiWordNet. Section 5 defines the evaluation scheme for verification of resource

---

[1] http://www.sas.com/en$_u$s/home.html
[2] https://translate.google.co.in/

D S Sharma, R Sangal and A K Singh. Proc. of the 13th Intl. Conference on Natural Language Processing, pages 30–35,
Varanasi, India. December 2016. ©2016 NLP Association of India (NLPAI)

created. An insight on future work and extensibility of the SentiWordNet is provided in Section 6.

2 Related Work

Sentiment analysis has been an age-old task and has been improving steadily over the past few decades. "It is one of the most active research areas in natural language processing and is also widely studied in data mining, web mining, and text mining" (Liu, 2012). Initially the analysis was only restricted to adjectives and adverbs but now many lexical resources contain nouns and verbs also. Various approaches have been proposed for building a SentiWordNet in the past.

Turney worked on sentiment analysis for customer reviews dataset, using an unsupervised learning algorithm (Turney, 2002). Wiebe proposed methods to generate a resource, with subjective information, for a given target language from resources present in English (Wiebe and Riloff, 2005). Translation methods included using a bilingual dictionary and a parallel corpora based approach.

For English, SentiWordNet was developed by Esuli (Esuli and Sebastiani, 2006) with improvements over the years (Baccianella et al., 2010). English SentiWordNet 3.0 is based off the Princeton English WordNet (Miller, 1995). Expansion strategies were suggested to increase the coverage of English SentiWordNet by assigning scores to antonym and synonym synsets.

Less resourced languages depend on resources present in English to build such lexical tools. Whalley and Medagoda propose a method to build a sentiment lexicon for Sinhala using Sentiwordnet 3.0 (Whalley and Medagoda, 2015). The Sentiwordnet is mapped to an online Sinhala dictionary. Scores for each lexicon and its synonyms is assigned based on English Sentiwordnet scores. Similar work is prevalent in literature for many Indian languages as well. Joshi built a SentiWordNet for Hindi using English SentiWordNet and linking English and Hindi WordNets (Joshi et al., 2010). Polarity scores were copied from the words in English SentiWordNet to the corresponding translated words in Hindi SentiWordNet.

Another approach was proposed by Amitava Das (Das and Bandyopadhyay, 2010) (Das and Bandyopadhyay, 2011) (Das and Gambäck, 2012) in order to build SentiWordNet for three Indian languages (Bengali, Hindi and Telugu). This approach used two resources available in English which provided subjectivity information: SentiWordNet 3.0 and Subjectivity Lexicon. A bilingual dictionary based translation was carried out in order to obtain the target lexicon. A Wordnet based approach, to assign scores to synsets, and an automatic corpus based approach were also suggested.

3 Resources Used

For the creation of Tamil SentiWordnet, English SentiWordNet 3.0 and Subjectivity Lexicon were the two most reliable resources. On reviewing English SentiWordNet and comparing it with the Subjectivity Lexicon, it was found that many words had contradicting sentiments in both the lists. Therefore, for a better estimate of sentiment for each word and reduction of ambiguities, two more resources, AFINN-111 and Opinion Lexicon, were also used. The resources used are described below:

List Name	Number of Tokens
SentiWordNet	2000K
Subjectivity Lexicon	8222
AFINN-111	2477
Opinion Lexicon	6789

Table 1: Resource Table.

- **English SentiWordNet** is a lexical resource for opinion mining which has a rich dataset of about 2 million lexical entries. SentiWordNet assigns, to each synset of WordNet, sentiment scores: positive and negative. Each synset is uniquely identified by a synset ID corresponding to the synset ID in Princeton WordNet. Other information includes Part-Of-Speech Tag (Adjective, Adverb, Noun, Verb). Positive and negative scores are a decimal ranging from zero to one. Objectivity score defines how factual a given word is and is obtained by 1 - (Positive Score + Negative Score).

- **Subjectivity Lexicon** is also a highly reliable lexicon for sentiment information and is robust in terms of performance. It is used as a part of OpinionFinder[3] (Wilson et al., 2005).

---

[3]http://mpqa.cs.pitt.edu/opinionfinder/

The list contains for a given word, Part-of-Speech tag, its polarity and subjectivity parameter. Subjectivity parameter classifies the word as either strongly or weakly subjective.

- **AFINN-111** is a list of English words rated for valence with an integer between minus five (negative) and plus five (positive). Words have been manually labeled by Finn rup Nielsen (Nielsen, 2011).

- **Opinion Lexicon** comprises of a relatively large dataset of positive and negative words without any specific scores. This dataset is based off annotated twitter corpora (Hu and Liu, 2004).

- **Translation-Dictionary** . In order to translate the final collection of words from English to Tamil, we used Google Translate[4] by running every single word on the Google Translate web application. The final list of translated words was cross checked by Tamil annotators in order to remove multi-word entries, incorrect translations and other ambiguous words.

4   Approach

Figure 1 shows a step by step procedure followed to build the Tamil SentiWordNet. The methodology is generic and can be used to build a SentiWordNet in any language. The entire procedure is divided into three parts :

- **Collecting Source Lexicon** - In order to build a SentiWordNet for any Indian language, one can use available resource(s), with sentiment information, from English.

- **Translation to Target Lexicon** - Once source lexicon is acquired, it needs to be translated to target lexicon using a translation method such as usage of a bilingual dictionary, an online translation resource, or a parallel corpus.

- **Evaluation of Target Lexicon** - The created target lexicon needs to be evaluated for errors. This paper adopts manual evaluation by language specific annotators and reports annotator agreement score.

---

[4]https://translate.google.co.in/

4.1   Source Lexicon

In order to obtain the source lexicon, multiple filtering techniques were applied to the existing resources in English. Source Lexicon acquisition starts with Subjectivity Lexicon and SentiWordNet, which are the primary resources for sentiment analysis in English. SentiWordNet polarity scores are obtained from learning through large English corpora. A threshold of 0.4 was considered (Das and Bandyopadhyay, 2010), as those words which have a score lower than the threshold may lose subjectivity upon translation to the target language. Words which have scores above 0.4 are assumed to be strongly subjective. Upon filtering words from English SentiWordNet based on the above criteria, a total of 16,791 tokens were obtained.

The Subjectivity Lexicon contains 8,222 words in total. From this set, all words which were annotated as weakly subjective were removed (Riloff et al., 2006). A total of 2,652 weakly subjective words were discarded resulting in a new set of only strongly subjective words. As mentioned before, this list also contains Part-of-Speech tags. Those words which were tagged 'anypos' were also removed to prevent context related ambiguities. Since the main aim was only to capture positive or negative sentiment, words tagged as neutral were also removed. The final list of words from Subjectivity Lexicon comprised of 4,526 tokens.

On merging the two filtered lists it was found that 2,199 tokens were common between the both. Among these duplicates only words which had the same Part-of-Speech tag in both the lists were sent forward and the others were discarded. Some of the duplicates included words which had conflicting tags in the SentiWordNet and the Subjectivity Lexicon. For example, the word 'pride' was tagged as positive in the Subjectivity Lexicon and the same word was given a higher negative score in SentiWordNet. Subjectivity of such words depend upon context and hence were also removed.

The final list now contained words which were strongly subjective and would more likely hold their subjectivity after translation. To ensure this, the list was manually checked. The final list now contained 15,823 tokens.

Since many entries in the SentiWordNet had opposing scores to that in the Subjectivity Lexicon, it was decided to add two more lists to increase the reliability of the source lexicon. AFINN-

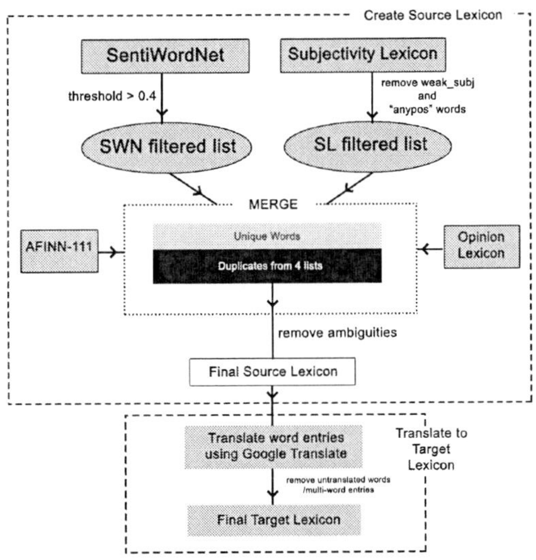

Figure 1: Flow of Design for Tamil SentiWordNet

111 (Nielsen, 2011) and Opinion Lexicon (Liu et al., 2005) were the two lists that were added and they were used to filter out more words which had ambiguous sense. For example, the word 'rid' had a positive score in SentiWordNet and it was tagged as negative in the Subjectivity Lexicon. Such words had to be avoided because they could be either positive or negative, depending on the context. A total of 4,954 words were present in more than one list. If a given word was present in a majority of the lists it appeared in, the majority opinion (positive or negative) was considered. The final list only contained strongly subjective words which served as the source lexicon before translation.

4.2 Target Lexicon

Each of the words from the final list was then translated using Google translate. Bilingual dictionaries may not account for all the words because of language variations (Bakliwal et al., 2012). This method of translation is also labour intensive. Context dependent word mapping between two languages is a tough task in general. Though Google Translate has its own challenges, this method was used for faster translation of words and better translation performance.

Some words were not translated into Tamil because the target language lacks such words. Multi-word entries in the source lexicon were challenging to translate as sometimes the first word would get translated but not the rest. In a few cases a multi-word entry would get translated to an accurate single word and in some cases a single word entry would get translated to a multi-word entry in the target language. Such cases had to be individually checked during pre-processing before evaluation.

The final list of words which were properly translated contained 10,225 single word entries tagged as positive or negative. One must note that this method does not copy English SentiWordNet scores for positivity or negativity. Copying scores was suggested previously in literature (Das and Bandyopadhyay, 2010). This was not followed because English SentiWordNet scores are based on English corpus. Same scores may not necessarily work for Tamil. Subjectivity of a word may transcend across languages but not in the same magnitude. Hence, a given word is only marked as carrying either positive or negative sentiment.

5 Evaluation Methodology

After translation to target lexicon, the list comprised of a set of English words along with their corresponding Tamil translations. Each of these words is either marked with positive or negative polarity based on its polarity in source lexicon(s).

This list was sent to 5 Tamil annotators to verify the correctness of the translation. Words which did not retain subjectivity after translation were removed. In case of conflict over any word, the majority of opinion was taken into account. When we say majority, we assume that at-least 4 out of 5 annotators agree on a given sentiment. If not, the word is removed from the list for future inspection. Words which did not transfer contextual meaning were also removed. For example, the word *inclination* was translated wrongly in the target language. The translation only captured the words meaning as a slope or an incline and not a person's tendency to act or feel in a certain way. Words which were wrongly translated were also removed.

The evaluation resulted in 190 words being marked as ambiguous and 540 words being marked as wrongly translated. These words were eliminated and the final lexicon contained a total of 9495 words with strong subjectivity. 3336 words were tagged as positive and 6159 words were tagged as negative. In order to capture inter-annotator agreement Fleiss Kappa[5] score for the final set was also calculated. Fleiss Kappa is calculated using the following formula:

$$\kappa = \frac{\bar{P} - \bar{P_e}}{1 - \bar{P_e}} \qquad (1)$$

$\bar{P}$ is the sum of observed agreement. $\bar{P_e}$ is the sum of agreement by chance. Fleiss kappa score is calculated using five raters.There are two categories (positive/negative). A substantial agreement score of $\kappa = \mathbf{0.663}$ is reported for Tamil SentiWordNet.

Initial Token Count	10225
Wrongly Translated	540
Ambiguous Entries	190
Final Token Count	9495
Inter-Annotator Agreement (**Fleiss Kappa**)	
0.663	

Table 2: Evaluation Details

6   Conclusion and Future Work

The Tamil SentiWordNet lexicon serves as a baseline for future improvements. The approach followed can be used to build SentiWordNet for any Indian Language. Other methods of translation to target language include usage of a bilingual dictionary or a parallel corpora for English and Target language pair. Various techniques can be applied to improve the accuracy and expand the lexicon

content. Tamil WordNet (Rajendran et al., 2002) is available publicly[6] and contains 1916 synset entries. Lexicon can be expanded by using, for a given word in the Tamil SentiWordNet, its corresponding synsets in the Tamil WordNet. Synonyms and antonyms can be classified with similar and opposite subjectivity respectively.

The SentiWordNet can also be expanded using a corpus based approach to capture language-specific words. SentiWordNet lexicon can be used as a seed list and the corpus can be tagged based on this seed list. Machine learning techniques can then be applied on this corpus to find new words to be added to the lexicon.

Currently, the lexicon has only been divided into two classes (positive and negative) This classification can be replaced by a five point scale in the future (Nakov et al., 2016). Furthermore, for getting subjectivity scores of individual words in the SentiWordNet one can use sentiment annotated Tamil corpora. The accuracy of any lexical resource is best calculated when it is actually usable in practical applications. With Tamil social media data being more readily available, manually annotating this data for positive and negative sentiment and using Tamil SentiWordNet to annotate the same data to check for accuracy is one possible method. One of the challenges which needs to be addressed in the future is capturing the sentiment of multi-word entries.

References

Stefano Baccianella, Andrea Esuli, and Fabrizio Sebastiani. 2010. Sentiwordnet 3.0: An enhanced lexical resource for sentiment analysis and opinion mining. In *LREC*, volume 10, pages 2200–2204.

Akshat Bakliwal, Piyush Arora, and Vasudeva Varma. 2012. Hindi subjective lexicon: A lexical resource for hindi polarity classification. In *Proceedings of the Eight International Conference on Language Resources and Evaluation (LREC)*.

Amitava Das and Sivaji Bandyopadhyay. 2010. Sentiwordnet for indian languages. *Asian Federation for Natural Language Processing, China*, pages 56–63.

Amitava Das and Sivaji Bandyopadhyay. 2011. Dr sentiment knows everything! In *Proceedings of the 49th annual meeting of the association for computational linguistics: human language technologies: systems demonstrations*, pages 50–55. Association for Computational Linguistics.

---

[5]https://en.wikipedia.org/wiki/Fleiss'`kappa

[6]https://www.amrita.edu/center/computational-engineering-and-networking/research/computational

Amitava Das and Björn Gambäck. 2012. Sentimantics: conceptual spaces for lexical sentiment polarity representation with contextuality. In *Proceedings of the 3rd Workshop in Computational Approaches to Subjectivity and Sentiment Analysis*, pages 38–46. Association for Computational Linguistics.

Andrea Esuli and Fabrizio Sebastiani. 2006. Sentiwordnet: A publicly available lexical resource for opinion mining. In *Proceedings of LREC*, volume 6, pages 417–422. Citeseer.

Minqing Hu and Bing Liu. 2004. Mining and summarizing customer reviews. In *Proceedings of the tenth ACM SIGKDD international conference on Knowledge discovery and data mining*, pages 168–177. ACM.

Aditya Joshi, AR Balamurali, and Pushpak Bhattacharyya. 2010. A fall-back strategy for sentiment analysis in hindi: a case study. *Proceedings of the 8th ICON*.

Bing Liu, Minqing Hu, and Junsheng Cheng. 2005. Opinion observer: analyzing and comparing opinions on the web. In *Proceedings of the 14th international conference on World Wide Web*, pages 342–351. ACM.

Bing Liu. 2012. Sentiment analysis and opinion mining. *Synthesis lectures on human language technologies*, 5(1):1–167.

George A Miller. 1995. Wordnet: a lexical database for english. *Communications of the ACM*, 38(11):39–41.

Preslav Nakov, Alan Ritter, Sara Rosenthal, Fabrizio Sebastiani, and Veselin Stoyanov. 2016. Semeval-2016 task 4: Sentiment analysis in twitter. In *Proceedings of the 10th international workshop on semantic evaluation (SemEval 2016), San Diego, US*.

Finn Årup Nielsen. 2011. A new anew: Evaluation of a word list for sentiment analysis in microblogs. *arXiv preprint arXiv:1103.2903*.

S Rajendran, S Arulmozi, B Kumara Shanmugam, S Baskaran, and S Thiagarajan. 2002. Tamil wordnet. In *Proceedings of the First International Global WordNet Conference. Mysore*, volume 152, pages 271–274.

Ellen Riloff, Siddharth Patwardhan, and Janyce Wiebe. 2006. Feature subsumption for opinion analysis. In *Proceedings of the 2006 Conference on Empirical Methods in Natural Language Processing*, pages 440–448. Association for Computational Linguistics.

Peter D Turney. 2002. Thumbs up or thumbs down?: semantic orientation applied to unsupervised classification of reviews. In *Proceedings of the 40th annual meeting on association for computational linguistics*, pages 417–424. Association for Computational Linguistics.

J Whalley and N Medagoda. 2015. Sentiment lexicon construction using sentiwordnet 3.0. *ICNC'15 - FSKD'15, School of Information Science and Engineering, Hunan University, China*.

Janyce Wiebe and Ellen Riloff. 2005. Creating subjective and objective sentence classifiers from unannotated texts. In *International Conference on Intelligent Text Processing and Computational Linguistics*, pages 486–497. Springer.

Theresa Wilson, Paul Hoffmann, Swapna Somasundaran, Jason Kessler, Janyce Wiebe, Yejin Choi, Claire Cardie, Ellen Riloff, and Siddharth Patwardhan. 2005. Opinionfinder: A system for subjectivity analysis. In *Proceedings of hlt/emnlp on interactive demonstrations*, pages 34–35. Association for Computational Linguistics.

Extending AIDA framework by incorporating coreference resolution on detected mentions and pruning based on popularity of an entity

Samaikya Akarapu
Department of Computer Science
and Engineering
Indian Institute of Technology (BHU)
Varanasi, India 221005
samaikyaakarapu@gmail.com

C Ravindranath Chowdary
Department of Computer Science
and Engineering
Indian Institute of Technology (BHU)
Varanasi, India 221005
rchowdary.cse@iitbhu.ac.in

Abstract

Named Entity Disambiguation (NED) is gaining popularity due to its applications in the field of information extraction. Entity linking or Named Entity Disambiguation is the task of discovering entities such as persons, locations, organizations, etc. and is challenging due to the high ambiguity of entity names in natural language text. In this paper, we propose a modification to the existing state of the art for NED, Accurate Online Disambiguation of Entities (AIDA) framework. As a mention's name in a text can appear many times in shorter forms, we propose to use coreference resolution on the detected mentions. Entity mentions within the document are clustered to their longer form. We use the popularity of candidate entities to prune them and based on the similarity measure of AIDA the entity for a mention is chosen. The mentions are broadly classified into four categories person, location, organization and miscellaneous and the effect of coreference and pruning were analyzed on each category.

1 Introduction

One of the unsolved problems in computer science is understanding and producing natural language by machines. The goal of fully understanding is out of reach but there have been significant advances recently. Systems are able to understand words or phrases of text by explicitly representing their meaning. Once the meanings of individual words are known, next is to find the relation among them.

1.1 Named Entity Disambiguation

A real word object that is designated by a proper name that identifies itself from other objects having similar attributes is called as named entity. Names can be rigid or non-rigid. Rigid names refer to one and only one thing like "*Narendra Modi*". Non-rigid names refer to different objects like "*Home Minister*" (Home Minister of India or Srilanka). In general, we can say proper names are rigid and common names are non-rigid. Articles on the web consist of names of persons, locations, organizations, events etc. The same name can have a different meaning. For example, consider the following sentence:

Example 1.1 " *Michael is the father of two relational database systems, Ingres and Postgres developed at Berkeley. Page and Brin did research at Stanford.*"

Here "*Michael*" refers to the person *Michael Stonebraker* who is a computer scientist and not the singer *Michael Jackson*, "*Berkeley*" and "*Standford*" refer to the universities- *University of California, Berkeley* and *Standford University* and not to the places *Berkeley* and *Standford*, "*Page*" refers to *Larry Page* the founder of Google and not *Jimmy Page* who is a guitarist. Looking at the sentence, humans barely notice the ambiguity as they subconsciously resolve it. The ability to understand single words was made possible by associating phrases and words with their senses. The WordNet (Fellbaum, 1998) contains a collection of senses for nouns, adjectives and verbs and word sense disambiguation (Navigli, 2009) has benefited from it. Mapping these mention names to the actual entities is referred to as Entity Linking or Named Entity Disambiguation.

1.2 Named Entity Recognition

Before applying NED, the first step would be to recognize a word or multiple word phrases that could possibly represent a real word entity. For the last two decades, entity recognition has received a lot of attention. The task of finding and categorizing elements of text into different classes

D S Sharma, R Sangal and A K Singh. Proc. of the 13th Intl. Conference on Natural Language Processing, pages 36–45,
Varanasi, India. December 2016. ©2016 NLP Association of India (NLPAI)

such as names of persons, locations, organizations, quantities, expressions of times, percentages, monetary values, etc. is termed as Named Entity Recognition or entity identification, in short as NER. Most NER methods use machine learning to label the input texts. The data for the training is mostly obtained from MUC (Message Understanding Conference) (Grishman and Sundheim, 1996), where NER was first introduced, and CoNLL (Computational Natural Language Learning) (Tjong Kim Sang and De Meulder, 2003). The most widely used system for NER is the Standford NER (Finkel et al., 2005) that uses the conditional random fields.

1.3 Representation

The NED maps ambiguous names to its canonical entities. It assumes that the names or phrases that could potentially represent a real world entity are discovered by using a NER. These names are called as mentions. M are the set of mentions which are given as input. KB is the knowledge base that is used as the reference list of entities. E is the set of entities. If Wikipedia is taken as a knowledge base, each page of the Wikipedia is an entity. $m \in M$, $D \subset (N \times E)$ is the dictionary that contains the pairs of (n, e) where n is a name $\in N$ and $e \in E$. N is the set of all names of each e. Suppose if the entity *Michael Jackson* is considered *MJ, Michael Joseph Jackson, King of Pop* etc. would be the set of names for this entity. $CE(m)$ are the candidate entities for a mention m. To find $CE(m)$, m is matched against names in N. The goal of NED is to map m to an entity in $CE(m)$. If the entity is not in the knowledge base it is mapped to *NULL*, i.e. it is not registered. If $CE(m)$ is empty by default m is mapped to *NULL*.

2 Related Work

NED requires a knowledge base to map the mention names to the corresponding entities registered in a specific knowledge base. One of the popular choices of a knowledge base is Wikipedia, where each page is considered as an entity. Bunescu and Pasca (2006) were the first to use Wikipedia to link entities. The basis of disambiguation is to compare context of mention and candidate entities. Milne and Witten (2008), Kulkarni et al. (2009) also considered the semantic relations between the candidate entities for disambiguation.

Pershina et al. (2015) represented NED as a graph model and disambiguated based on PersonalizedPageRank(PPR). The local similarity score includes the similarity between Wikipedia title, mention and category type. The global similarity is measured based on the link counts of Freebase and Wikipedia. Either of these measures is assumed as the initial similarity score. The coherence of entity is obtained as a pairwise relation of PPR scores with entities of other mentions. The final score of entity is a combination of coherence and initial similarity score weighted with PPR average. The entity with the highest score is selected and evaluation was done on CoNLL 2003 dataset used by Hoffart et al. (2011).

Luo et al. (2015) jointly recognize and disambiguate entities by identifying the dependency between the tasks (JERL). It defines three feature sets on a segment assignment of a word sequence: NER features (various unigram and bigram features, dictionaries, WordNet clusters, etc.), linking features (entity priors, context scores), mutual dependency (type-category correlation) and is modeled as Semi-CRF. Evaluation was done on CoNLL 2003 dataset used by Hoffart et al. (2011).

Usbeck et al. (2014) (AGDISTIS) finds an assignment that maximizes similarity with the named entities and coherence with the knowledge base. The candidate entities are found using trigram similarity and belong to categories of person, place, and organization. With candidate entities as initial vertices in a graph, it is expanded by DFS with a certain depth. The edge between vertices is present if they form an RDF triplet. They use HITS algorithm (Kleinberg, 1999) to find the authoritative candidates, sort them and assign them. They evaluated on eight different datasets: Reuters-21578 (Röder et al., 2014), news.de (Röder et al., 2014), RSS 500 (Röder et al., 2014), AIDA-YAGO2 (Hoffart et al., 2011), AIDA/CoNLL-TestB (Hoffart et al., 2011), AQUAINT (Hoffart et al., 2011), IITB (Kulkarni et al., 2009), and MSNBC (Cucerzan, 2007).

Moro et al. (2014) address Entity Linking and Word Sense Disambiguation. They consider the semantic network Babelnet (Navigli and Ponzetto, 2012), where each concept and named entity is a vertex and relations between them are edges. They perform Random Walk with Restart (Tong et al., 2006) to reweigh the edges and to obtain a semantic signature. In the input document, text fragments which contain noun and substrings of entities in Babelnet are considered as candidate entities. Edges are added between candidate entities based on the previously computed semantic signature. A dense subgraph is found and the candidates are selected based on the score obtained from incident edges. They evaluated on two datasets for NED: KORE50 (Hoffart et al., 2012) and CoNLL 2003 dataset used by Hoffart et al. (2011).

Almost all the methods use the similar features to find similarity between the context of mentions and their candidate entities but differ in disambiguation method. The methods can be broadly divided into two types: local method and global method. While disambiguating, the local method only considers mention and its candidate entities but the global method also consider relations among the entities. Thus, the complexity of the global method is high. The systems assume the annotations are correct if they strictly match the ground truth. The difficult part for the systems would be disambiguating entities that don't belong to Wikipedia as the features of these entities are absent. All the above methods use different data sets for evaluation. Pershina et al. (2015), Luo et al. (2015) did not consider the assignment of null entities. Usbeck et al. (2014) used DBpedia as knowledgebase but with Yago2, AIDA performed well.

3 AIDA

AIDA (Hoffart et al., 2011) is a framework developed by the *Databases and Information Systems Group at the Max Planck Institute for Informatics* for named entity recognition and disambiguation. The framework presents both local and global disambiguation methods for NED. In the local disambiguation technique, the disambiguation is done based on prior probability and context similarity with a prior test. The prior test decides whether prior probability has to be considered or not. In the global disambiguation technique, the NED is presented as a graph problem with mentions and entities as nodes and weighted edges between them. An edge is present between mention and its candidate entities. An edge between e_1 and e_2 is present if they are candidate entities of different mentions and have a link to their pages. The edge weight between a mention and an entity is the similarity between the context of mention and context of the entity. The edge weight between entities is

proportional to their coherence. Not all mentions are disambiguated by the global method. A coherence test decides whether the disambiguation should be done locally or globally. The goal is to find a subgraph with each mention having only one edge with an entity thus disambiguating collectively. Collective disambiguation was proposed by Kulkarni at el. (2009). The AIDA was evaluated on 1393 articles of CoNLL 2003 dataset and mentions were recognized using Standford NER (Finkel et al., 2005) tagger. The following features of AIDA are used later in the experiments:

Prior Probability: Popularity, in general, gives an estimate of what a mention could be referring to. The measure is obtained based on Wikipedia link anchors. The probability distribution of candidate entities is estimated as the number of times the entity referred with that mention as the anchor text in Wikipedia.

KeyPhrase-based Similarity: The important measure for mapping is the similarity between the context of mention and entity. All the tokens in the document are considered as the context of the mention. The keyphrases extracted from Wikipedia link anchor texts, category names, citation titles, external references of the entity and the entities linking to it are considered as the context of the entity. These are the set of keyphrases of entity $KP(e)$. The Mutual Information **MI** between an entity e and a word w occurring in a keyphrase is calculated as (Hoffart et al., 2011):

$$MI(e,w) = \frac{\begin{array}{c}\#elements\ in\ KP(e)\\ in\ which\ w\ occurs\end{array}}{N} \quad (1)$$

where N is the total number of entities.

Each keyphrase q in $KP(e)$ is associated with a score by obtaining a *cover(q)*- the smallest window in the text such that maximum number of words in q occur in the window. The score of a phrase q is given by (Taneva et al., 2011):

$$score(e,q) = z_q \left(\frac{\sum_{w \in \{cover(q) \cap q\}} MI(e,w)}{\sum_{x \in q} MI(e,x)} \right)^2 \quad (2)$$

where $z_q = \frac{\#\ matching\ words\ in\ cover(q)\ and\ q}{length\ of\ cover(q)}$.

The similarity between mention and a candidate entity is given as the sum of scores of all keyphrases of entity (Hoffart et al., 2011):

$$sim(e) = \sum_{q \in KP(e)} score(e,q) \quad (3)$$

4   Coreference and Pruning

Coreference resolution is defined as finding all expressions that refer to the same entity in a text. In a text, it can happen that one of the names of an entity is long and later the same names of the entity are referred with short forms. Our concern is coreference resolution on the mentions detected in the text. For example,

> *"Sir Jagadish Chandra Bose is one of the fathers of radio science. Bose was the first to use semiconductor junctions to detect radio signals."*

The idea is to map the shorter forms to the longer forms. Longer forms are more explicit and can have few candidate entities or just one as compared to the shorter forms.

We use the Standford NER tagger to obtain the tokens and their labeling. A mention is a span of token/tokens. AIDA also uses Standford NER for detecting the mentions. A mention phrase is found if the span of token/tokens has the same label. Thus a mention is labeled accordingly into one of the four categories person, location, organization and miscellaneous. While coreferencing, the labeling information is used. The shorter forms are mapped to the longer form of a mention if the label of both the forms are same and the shorter form occurs in the longer form. Consider the following example:

> *"Ram Prasad, designer of .... Shiva Prasad works as a doctor at AIMS.... Dr. Prasad ...."*

here *"Dr. Prasad"* refers to *"Shiva Prasad"*. The way we match would map *"Prasad"* to *"Ram Prasad"*, since the mapping is based on text matching. To map *"Prasad"* to *"Shiva Prasad"* the context *"Dr."* should be considered. But usually in a text, if people with same family name appear they would be referred using their first name, so the matching is kept to a simple string matching. The condition that the labeling should be same is imposed to ensure that the short name occurring in the long name but belonging to different entities are not clustered. For example,

> *"Universtiy of Delhi is a central collegiate university, located in Delhi."*

"University of Delhi" is an organization and *"Delhi"* is a place. *"Delhi"* occurs in *"University of Delhi"*. If the condition is not imposed

both names of different entities would be clustered which is incorrect. The experiments were done both imposing and not imposing the condition.

At the next stage, the mentions are queried for the candidate entities. For all the candidate entities of a mention, prior probability $prior(e)$ and keyphrase-based similarity (not the mention-entity similarity which may include prior probability) $sim(e)$ is obtained using AIDA. The mentions which have only one candidate entity are mapped to it directly and which have no candidate entities are mapped to null. We calculate the global average of the prior probability of the candidate entities of all mentions, local average of the prior probability of the candidate entities of each mention.

$$global\_avg_M = \frac{\sum_{m \in M} \sum_{e \in CE(m)} prior(e)}{\sum_{m \in M} size(CE(m))} \quad (4)$$

$$local\_avg_m = \frac{\sum_{e \in CE(m)} prior(e)}{size(CE(m))} \quad (5)$$

where m is a mention, M is the mention set, e is an entity, $CE(m)$ is the set of candidate entities of m, $size(CE(m))$ is the number of candidate entities of m, $prior(e)$ is the popularity or prior probability of e.

The candidate entities whose prior probability is lower than either $global\_avg_M$ or $local\_avg_m$ are pruned. Among the candidate entities left, the one with the highest keyphrase-based similarity $sim(e)$ is associated to the mention. Pruning is done to remove those entities whose popularity is very low as compared to those entities whose popularity and similarity are reasonably high. Popularity captures a notion of commonness. The frequency of occurrence of entities varies for different categories. On an average, places tend to occur more frequently or more popular than persons. Experiments were done with and without pruning and its trend in each category is examined and decided whether it should be applied or not. Later coreference and pruning are combined.

4.1   Finding and labeling the mentions:

Standford NER takes text as input and gives tokens $t_1, t_2, ... t_n$ and their labels $t_1.label, t_2.label .. t_n.label$ as output. A mention is a span of tokens whose labels are same and the mention type is the label type, i.e. $m = \{t_k ... t_{k+l} \mid t_k.label = ... = t_{k+l}.label\}$ and $m.label = t_k.label$.

4.2 Mapping short forms on to longer forms:

A mention is a span of tokens. A mention $m_1 = t_i...t_{i+p}$ is mapped to a mention $m_2 = t_j....t_{j+q}$ if m_1 occurs in m_2, i.e. $t_i = t_k \wedge...\wedge t_{i+p} = t_{k+p} \wedge j <= k <= j + q - p \wedge m_1.label = m_2.label$.

Algorithm 1 NED

1: **Input:**Text
2: **Output:** Mention Mappings
3: Find mentions and label them as discussed in Section 4.1;
4: Map short forms on to longer forms as discussed in Section 4.2;
5: **for** m **do**
6:     **if** $CE(m) == null$ **then**
7:         $result\_entity(m) \leftarrow null$;
8:     **end if**
9:     **if** $size(CE(m)) == 1$ **then**
10:         $result\_entity(m) \leftarrow e$;
11:     **end if**
12:     **if** $size(CE(m)) > 1$ **then**
13:         **for** $e \in CE(m)$ **do**
14:             **if** $prior(e) < min(local\_avg_m,$
15:             $global\_avg_M)$ **then**
16:                 $CE(m) \leftarrow CE(m) - \{e\}$;
17:             **end if**
18:         **end for**
19:         $result\_entity(m) \leftarrow \{e_i \mid$
20:             $\underset{i}{argmax}\ sim(e_i)\}$;
21:     **end if**
22: **end for**

4.3 Datasets

The experiments were carried on two data sets. First one is the TIPSTER[1] data set from which 45 documents were randomly chosen. These documents were related to news. The second dataset is the IITB dataset by Kulkarni et al.(2009), out of which 50 documents were taken. The IITB documents were collected from online news sources and are not well formatted and sometimes had comments of online users. The CoNLL 2003 dataset used by the AIDA is copyright protected but the annotations are available. We have manually annotated all the documents, i.e. both 45 documents of Tipster dataset and 50 documents of IITB dataset. The properties of the dataset are given in Table 1.

---

[1] http://www.nist.gov/tac/data/data_desc.html#TIPSTER

	Tipster	IITB
Documents	45	50
Mentions retrieved	1681	1666
Relevant mentions	1661	1595
Average mentions per document	37	32
Mentions marked as null in ground truth	383	457
Mentions not null	1278	1138
Mentions whose query resulted null	207	319

Table 1: Dataset Properties

	null	not null	total	%
p	240	337	577	34.74
l	48	621	669	40.28
o	58	206	264	15.89
m	37	114	151	9.09
total	383	1278	1661	
%	23.06	76.94		

Table 2: Mentions whose entity mappings marked as NULL and not NULL for Tipster dataset

Only the relevant mentions retrieved by AIDA are considered. For example, "…. *Bermuda-based company* …." where AIDA retrieves "*Bermuda-based*" as mention which is considered irrelevant. Similarly, "….*Cuban-Soviet friendship*…" is retrieved as "*Cuban-Soviet*" which is irrelevant.

The mention mappings can be of four types: A mention whose entity is not registered in the database and mapping gives NULL, a mention whose entity is not registered in the database and maps to some entity, a mention whose entity is registered in the database and maps to an incorrect entity and mention whose entity is registered in the database and maps to the correct entity. Precision is the fraction of mention entity mappings that match the ground truth assignments. Macro average precision is the average of precision of each document. Micro average precision is the fraction of mention entity mappings in all documents that match the ground truth assignments. Table 2 and Table 3 give the details of NULL entities in ground truth. The recall remains the same for the AIDA and for the experiments done as both use the same retrieval methods. The mentions were retrieved using the Stanford NER which classifies the men-

	null	not null	total	%
p	239	149	388	24.33
l	35	580	615	38.56
o	145	330	475	29.78
m	38	79	117	7.36
total	457	1138	1595	
%	28.65	71.35		

Table 3: Mentions whose entity mappings marked as NULL and not NULL for IITB dataset

	p	l	o	m	total
p	563	7	5	2	577
l	3	522	21	123	669
o	3	12	231	18	264
m	4	2	26	119	151

Table 4: Confusion Matrix for Tipster dataset

tions into four categories namely person (p), location (l), organization (o) and miscellaneous (m). The mentions were also annotated for their labels manually. Table 4, Table 5 gives the Confusion Matrix for both the datasets. The column is the actual label and the row is the labels predicted by NER.

4.4 Experiments

AIDA was run with four settings:

- *LocalDisambigautionSetting()-* uses prior and similarity with a prior test, described in Section 3;

- *LocalDisambiguationWithNullSettings()-* uses the above method but uses a threshold to find NULL entities;

- *CocktailDisambiguationSettings()-* uses the graph method, described in Section 3;

- *CocktailDisambiguationWithNullSettings()-* uses the above method but uses a threshold to find NULL entities;

	p	l	o	m	total
p	374	8	3	3	388
l	27	494	32	62	615
o	27	60	360	28	475
m	6	2	22	87	117

Table 5: Confusion Matrix for IITB dataset

The experiments were carried out with the following 8 methods:

- **Method 1 (AG):** AIDA graph Disambiguation.

- **Method 2 (AGN):** AIDA graph Disambiguation with NULL settings.

- **Method 3 (AL):** AIDA local Disambiguation.

- **Method 4 (ALN):** AIDA local Disambiguation with NULL settings.

- **Method 5 (NP):** No Pruning- The method is run based on Algorithm 1 except the lines 4, 13 to 18 are not performed.

- **Method 6 (WP):** With Pruning- The method is run based on Algorithm 1 except the line 4 is not performed.

- **Method 7 (CNCP):** Coreference without labeling condition and pruning- The method is run based on Algorithm 1 but in line 4 short forms are mapped to longer forms of mention without the condition that both the forms should have the same label and pruning is done for all mentions labeled as location, organization, misc and not done for mentions labeled as persons.

- **Method 8 (CCP):** Coreference with labeling condition and pruning- The method is run based on Algorithm 1 but in line 4 short forms are mapped to longer forms of mention with the condition that both the forms should have the same label and pruning is done for all mentions labeled as location, organization, misc and not done for mentions labeled as persons.

Table 6 and Table 7 show the number of correct mappings for each category by various methods on the two datasets used. Among the AIDA methods, on the Tipster dataset, the graph disambiguation performs well. When considered for individual categories, it performs well on person and organization, while local disambiguation performs well on location and misc. On the IITB dataset, the local disambiguation performs well. When considered for individual categories, graph disambiguation performs well on person and organization, local disambiguation performs well on location and

	AL	ALN	AG	AGN	NP	WP	CNCP	CCP
person null	44.58	52.92	44.58	61.25	44.58	44.58	**83.75**	82.92
location null	**70.83**	**70.83**	**70.83**	**70.83**	**70.83**	**70.83**	**70.83**	**70.83**
organization null	82.76	82.76	82.76	84.48	82.76	82.76	**86.21**	84.48
misc. null	37.84	37.84	37.84	**40.54**	37.84	37.84	**40.54**	**40.54**
person not null	84.57	82.20	**95.55**	92.58	85.46	81.01	93.77	94.66
location not null	88.89	88.89	84.70	84.70	82.14	**91.79**	87.28	90.34
organization not null	86.89	86.89	**88.83**	**88.83**	83.50	85.44	84.47	84.47
misc. not null	65.79	65.79	64.04	64.04	57.89	**69.30**	68.42	68.42

Table 6: Percentage of correct mappings for each category by various methods on Tipster dataset

	AL	ALN	AG	AGN	NP	WP	CNCP	CCP
person null	53.56	61.51	53.56	66.95	53.56	53.56	**73.64**	**73.64**
location null	54.29	54.29	54.29	54.29	54.29	54.29	**71.43**	**71.43**
organization null	70.34	70.34	70.34	70.34	70.34	70.34	**72.41**	71.72
misc. null	**71.05**	**71.05**	**71.05**	**71.05**	**71.05**	**71.05**	**71.05**	**71.05**
person not null	85.91	85.91	**94.63**	93.29	86.58	79.87	93.96	93.96
location not null	85.86	85.86	82.59	82.07	81.90	**87.59**	87.07	87.41
organization not null	79.70	79.70	**81.56**	75.168	78.48	74.24	73.03	73.03
misc. not null	**72.15**	**72.15**	56.96	56.96	62.03	68.35	68.35	68.35

Table 7: Percentage of correct mappings for each category by various methods on IITB dataset

misc. Thus, AIDA graph disambiguation performs well for person and organization while local disambiguation performs well for location and misc.

The method 5 (NP) maps the mentions with the highest similarity, without considering the prior probability. When the method 6- with pruning is compared with method 5- no pruning, for Tipster dataset there is an increase in accuracy for location, organization and misc and decrease for person. For IITB dataset there is an increase in accuracy for location and misc and decrease for person and organization. So for method 7 (CNCP) and method 8 (CCP) pruning was done for location, organization, misc. Table 8 and Table 9 shows the results for various methods for both the datasets. Comparing the results, Coreference helps increase the accuracy of mapping especially for person, pruning for location while AIDA performs well on organization, for misc pruning increased accuracy on Tipster dataset. Pruning decreases the accuracy for organization showing that some potential entity that could be mapped is removed. Coreferenece decreases accuracy for location on Tipster dataset while not much effective on IITB dataset because the shorter forms accuracy depends on the longer form it is mapped to. For misc every method is equally competitive. After the modifica-

tion, the mentions whose longer forms are mapped as NULL are ensured that the shorter forms too are mapped as NULL but in the case of AIDA, the shorter forms were mapped to some other entity in Yago2. For mentions whose longer forms are mapped to the right entity, the shorter forms are mapped to the right entities by both the methods AIDA and CCP. In one of the documents,

"Naomi Foner, who wrote.... Her own experiences made Foner....."

AIDA just gives only *Naomi Foner Gyllenhaal* as candidate entity of mention *"Naomi Foner"*, but the mention *"Foner"* doesn't contain *Naomi Foner Gyllenhaal* as one of its candidate entity. This might be because of some error in retrieval by AIDA. Coreferencing them ensured that mention *"Foner"* is mapped to the right entity. If the longer surface form is mapped to a wrong entity, then all the shorter forms too are mapped to the wrong entity. Thus, the accuracy depends on the mapping of longer forms.

"Nicholas Calas a poet and..... Calas..."

The longer form *"Nicholas Calas"* has no candidate entities and shorter form *"Calas"* has been mapped to the right entity *Nicolas Calas*. Here

Method	person	location	organization	misc	true	Macro (%)	Micro (%)
AG	429	560	231	87	1307	77.22	78.69
AGN	459	560	**232**	88	1339	79.45	80.61
AL	392	586	227	89	1294	76.41	77.90
ALN	404	586	227	89	1306	77.19	78.63
NP	395	544	220	80	1239	73.84	74.59
WP	380	**604**	224	**93**	1301	77.27	78.33
CNCP	517	576	224	**93**	1410	85.41	84.89
CCP	**518**	595	223	**93**	**1429**	**86.23**	**86.03**

Table 8: Results of various methods on Tipster dataset

Method	person	location	organization	misc	true	Macro (%)	Micro (%)
AG	269	498	**371**	72	1210	79.72	75.86
AGN	299	495	350	72	1216	80.07	76.24
AL	256	508	365	**84**	1213	79.53	76.05
ALN	275	508	365	**84**	1232	80.69	77.34
NP	275	508	365	84	1232	80.69	77.34
WP	247	527	347	81	1202	79.21	75.36
CNCP	**316**	530	346	81	1273	82.52	79.81
CCP	**316**	**532**	345	81	**1274**	**83.03**	**79.87**

Table 9: Results of various methods on IITB dataset

coreferencing shorter form *"Calas"* to longer form maps it to NULL. Instead of *"Nicholas"* if it had been *"Nicolas"* it would had mapped to right entity. The mention was just misspelled.

The coherence graph algorithm of AIDA makes sense.

> *"....Maj. Gadi, commander of a battalion...."*

When only similarity is considered it maps to *"Gadi Brumer (Israeli footballer)"* but with coherence, it maps to *"Gadi Eizenkot (Chief of general staff of Israel Defence Forces)"*. Coherence too causes errors. All mentions with the same syntax are mapped to the same entity.

> *"...all Chinese in Tibet stop carrying... The demonstrators were carrying banners in Tibetian and Chinese..."*

Here the former *"Chinese"* means *Chinese people* and later means the *Chinese language*.

> *"...Jewish dietary laws....intones the Hebrew words.."*

both *"Jewish"* and *"Hebrew"* are mapped to *Hebrew language*.

> *"...The runners-up for the charisma title were San Francisco and Washington ..."*, here, *"San Francisco"* should be mapped to the teams *San Francisco 49ers* and *"Washington"* to *Washington Redskins* but are mapped to places. These entities occur at the top when sorted with respective to the similarity measure. If it is known that these mentions represent a team (organization), other candidate entities which are not team (organization) could be pruned by finding the yago types.

5 Conclusions

The proposed modifications to the AIDA improved the overall accuracy of entity mappings. The first modification is mapping short forms on to their long form. As long forms are more explicit, they are less ambiguous. It especially helps in identifying null entities, about an increase in 17.58% for Tipster dataset and 5.25% for IITB dataset. The second modification is pruning based on popularity. Experiment results show that applying pruning selectively on categories help in increase of accuracy of the system.

6 Acknowledgement

This project was supported by DST-SERB No. YSS/2015/000906.

References

Razvan Bunescu and Marius Pasca. 2006. Using encyclopedic knowledge for named entity disambiguation. In *Proceesings of the 11th Conference of the European Chapter of the Association for Computational Linguistics (EACL-06)*, pages 9–16, Trento, Italy. Association for Computational Linguistics.

Silviu Cucerzan. 2007. Large-scale named entity disambiguation based on Wikipedia data. In *Proceedings of the 2007 Joint Conference on Empirical Methods in Natural Language Processing and Computational Natural Language Learning (EMNLP-CoNLL)*, pages 708–716, Prague, Czech Republic, June. Association for Computational Linguistics.

Christiane Fellbaum. 1998. Wordnet: An electronic lexical database.

Jenny Rose Finkel, Trond Grenager, and Christopher Manning. 2005. Incorporating non-local information into information extraction systems by gibbs sampling. In *Proceedings of the 43rd Annual Meeting on Association for Computational Linguistics*, ACL '05, pages 363–370, Ann Arbor, Michigan. Association for Computational Linguistics.

Ralph Grishman and Beth Sundheim. 1996. Message understanding conference-6: A brief history. In *Proceedings of the 16th Conference on Computational Linguistics - Volume 1*, COLING '96, pages 466–471, Copenhagen, Denmark. Association for Computational Linguistics.

Johannes Hoffart, Mohamed Amir Yosef, Ilaria Bordino, Hagen Fürstenau, Manfred Pinkal, Marc Spaniol, Bilyana Taneva, Stefan Thater, and Gerhard Weikum. 2011. Robust disambiguation of named entities in text. In *Proceedings of the Conference on Empirical Methods in Natural Language Processing*, EMNLP '11, pages 782–792, Edinburgh, United Kingdom. Association for Computational Linguistics.

Johannes Hoffart, Stephan Seufert, Dat Ba Nguyen, Martin Theobald, and Gerhard Weikum. 2012. Kore: Keyphrase overlap relatedness for entity disambiguation. In *Proceedings of the 21st ACM International Conference on Information and Knowledge Management*, CIKM '12, pages 545–554, Maui, Hawaii, USA. ACM.

Jon M Kleinberg. 1999. Authoritative sources in a hyperlinked environment. *Journal of the ACM (JACM)*, 46(5):604–632.

Sayali Kulkarni, Amit Singh, Ganesh Ramakrishnan, and Soumen Chakrabarti. 2009. Collective annotation of wikipedia entities in web text. In *Proceedings of the 15th ACM SIGKDD International Conference on Knowledge Discovery and Data Mining*, KDD '09, pages 457–466, Paris, France. ACM.

Gang Luo, Xiaojiang Huang, Chin-Yew Lin, and Zaiqing Nie. 2015. Joint entity recognition and disambiguation. In *Proceedings of the 2015 Conference on Empirical Methods in Natural Language Processing*, pages 879–888, Lisbon, Portugal, September. Association for Computational Linguistics.

David Milne and Ian H. Witten. 2008. Learning to link with wikipedia. In *Proceedings of the 17th ACM Conference on Information and Knowledge Management*, CIKM '08, pages 509–518, Napa Valley, California, USA. ACM.

Andrea Moro, Alessandro Raganato, and Roberto Navigli. 2014. Entity linking meets word sense disambiguation: a unified approach. *Transactions of the Association for Computational Linguistics*, 2:231–244.

Roberto Navigli and Simone Paolo Ponzetto. 2012. Babelnet: The automatic construction, evaluation and application of a wide-coverage multilingual semantic network. *Artificial Intelligence*, 193:217–250.

Roberto Navigli. 2009. Word sense disambiguation: A survey. *ACM Comput. Surv.*, 41(2):10:1–10:69, February.

Maria Pershina, Yifan He, and Ralph Grishman. 2015. Personalized page rank for named entity disambiguation. In *Proceedings of the 2015 Conference of the North American Chapter of the Association for Computational Linguistics: Human Language Technologies*, pages 238–243, Denver, Colorado, May–June. Association for Computational Linguistics.

Michael Röder, Ricardo Usbeck, Sebastian Hellmann, Daniel Gerber, and Andreas Both. 2014. N3-a collection of datasets for named entity recognition and disambiguation in the nlp interchange format. *9th LREC*.

Bilyana Taneva, M Kacimi El Hassani, and Gerhard Weikum. 2011. Finding images of rare and ambiguous entities. *Technical Report*.

Erik F. Tjong Kim Sang and Fien De Meulder. 2003. Introduction to the conll-2003 shared task: Language-independent named entity recognition. In *Proceedings of the Seventh Conference on Natural Language Learning at HLT-NAACL 2003 - Volume 4*, CONLL '03, pages 142–147, Edmonton, Canada. Association for Computational Linguistics.

Hanghang Tong, Christos Faloutsos, and Jia-Yu Pan. 2006. Fast random walk with restart and its applications. In *Proceedings of the Sixth International Conference on Data Mining*, ICDM '06, pages 613–622, Washington, DC, USA. IEEE Computer Society.

Ricardo Usbeck, Axel-Cyrille Ngonga Ngomo, Michael Röder, Daniel Gerber, Sandro Athaide Coelho, Sören Auer, and Andreas Both. 2014. Agdistis - graph-based disambiguation of named entities using linked data. In *Proceedings of the*

*13th International Semantic Web Conference - Part
I*, ISWC '14, pages 457–471, New York, NY, USA.
Springer-Verlag New York, Inc.

Sentence Based Discourse Classification for Hindi Story Text-to-Speech (TTS) System

Kumud Tripathi, Parakrant Sarkar and **K. Sreenivasa Rao**
Department of Computer Science and Engineering
Indian Institute Technology Kharagpur, India
{kumudtripathi.cs, parakarantsarkar}@gmail.com, ksrao@iitkgp.ac.in

Abstract

In this work, we have proposed an automatic discourse prediction model. It predicts the discourse information for a sentence. In this study, three discourse modes considered are descriptive, narrative and dialogue. The proposed model is developed using story corpus. The story corpus comprises of audio and its corresponding text transcription of short children stories. The development of this model entails two phases: feature extraction and classification of the discourse. The feature extraction is carried out using 'Word2Vec' model. The classification of discourse at sentence-level is explored by using Support Vector Machines (SVM), Convolutional Neural Network (CNN) and a combination of CNN-SVM. The main focus of this study is on the usage of CNN for developing the model because it has not been explored much for the problems related to text classification. Experiments are carried out to find the best model parameters (such as the number of the filter, filter-height, cross-validation number, dropout rate, and batch-size) for the CNN. The proposed model achieves its best accuracy 72.6% when support vector machine (SVM) is used for classification and features are extracted from CNN (which is trained using the word2vec feature). This model can leverage the utilization of the discourse as a suprasegmental feature from the perspective of speech.

1 Introduction

In recent years, there has been a lot of works on analysis of storytelling style speech. In (Montao et al., 2013), TTS system was developed for synthesizing story style speech in Spanish. The main focus was on the analysis of prosodic patterns (such as pitch, intensity, and tempo) based on discourse modes. The three discourse modes considered for the study are narrative, descriptive and dialogue. Further, the authors introduced narrative situations such as neutral narrative, post-character, suspense and affective situations within the narrative mode. The discourse information was manually assigned to each sentence of the story by text experts. Based on the discourse modes, the sentence was grouped, and prosodic rules are derived. These prosodic rules implemented using Harmonic plus Noise Model (HNM) for synthesizing storytelling style speech. In (Delmonte and Tripodi, 2015), an analysis based on discourse mode was carried out to make TTS system more expressive for English. The analysis of text was carried out at phonetic, phonological, syntactic and semantic level. The prosodic manager is proposed which takes discourse structures as input and uses the information to modify the parameters of the TTS. The authors further carried out studies by proposing various discourse relations (Delmonte, 2008; Delmonte et al., 2007).

In storytelling style speech (Theune et al., 2006), a storyteller uses his/her skill by putting variation in the speech for the better understanding of the listeners (especially children). The variation in speech is produced by mimicking various character's voices present in the story, making various sound effects, and using prosody to convey emotions. It creates a pleasant listening experience for the listeners. In Indian Languages, development of TTS systems for Hindi, Bengali and Telugu are carried out in (Verma et al., 2015; Sarkar et al., 2014). In most of the earlier works, discourse information of sentence is obtained by manual annotation. This information is annotated by the text experts of the particular language. In this work, we are developing a method to auto-

D S Sharma, R Sangal and A K Singh. Proc. of the 13th Intl. Conference on Natural Language Processing, pages 46–54,
Varanasi, India. December 2016. ©2016 NLP Association of India (NLPAI)

matically classify the sentence based on discourse modes. This information will be processed further to improve the prediction performance of the prosody models that are developed for Story TTS systems. In Hindi Story TTS system, discourse information plays a vital role in capturing the story semantic information. The prosody modeling for duration, intonation, intensity and pause using discourse information are carried out in (Sarkar and Rao, 2015). In view of this, we have explored various machine learning techniques to automatically predict the discourse of the sentence in a story.

In NLP, sentence classification has been carried out using machine learning techniques such as SVM, KNN and K-fold cross-validation. There have various types of deep learning architectures like recurrent neural network (RNN), deep neural network (DNN) etc. In this work we have used a convolutional neural network (CNN) which is motivated from (Yoon, 2006). For the first time (Yoon, 2006) proposed a framework for using convolutional neural network (CNN) for text classification (i.e. emotion and question classification) at sentence level. The fundamental property of CNN (shared weight and local connectivity) make it different and suitable for sentence classification. Rather than learning single global weight matrix between layers, they expect to find an arrangement of locally connected neurons. Similarly, In the case of sentence classification, we need to find out the relationship between words in a sentence. Experiments were carried out using CNN and DNN, among these CNN gave better performance.

In this work, our aim is to create a model which can recognize the discourse of sentences. We have implemented Convolutional neural network (CNN) for automated sentence (from Hindi story corpus) level discourse classification that has not been addressed yet. We have considered three discourse modes- a Descriptive mode which enables the audience to develop a mental picture of what is being discussed, Narrative mode, it relies on stories and Dialogue mode, which includes the exchange of conversation in a group or between two persons directed towards a particular subject. The performance of these models is evaluated by using confusion matrix.

The work flow of this paper is as follows; the story-speech corpus is discussed in section II. Section III describes the proposed architecture for discourse classification. This section also explains about the vector representation of words, convolutional neural network (CNN), multiclass SVM and combined CNN-SVM model. The Section IV, discuss the experiments and results of the systems. The conclusion and future work of this paper have been included in section V.

2 Story Speech Corpus

The story speech corpus in Hindi consists of both story text and its corresponding story wave files. The children story texts are collected from story books like *Panchatantra*[1] and *Akbar Birbal*[2]. The speech corpus comprises of 105 stories with a total of 1960 sentences and 25340 words. These stories were recorded by a professional female storyteller in a noise free studio environment. For maintaining the high recording quality of the stories, continuous feedback is given to the narrator for improving the quality of the recordings. The speech signal was sampled at 16 kHz and represented as 16-bit numbers. The total duration of the story corpus is about 3 hours.

In this study, we considered only three different kinds of discourse modes (i.e. narrative, descriptive and dialogue). In literature, there are discourse modes such as narrative, descriptive, argumentative, explanatory and dialogue (Adell et al., 2005). It is been observed in the children stories that the different parts of story are narrated in different styles based on the semantics present at that part of story. In general, most of the children stories in Hindi, begins with introducing the characters present in story, followed by various events related to the story and finally story will conclude with a moral. In the narration of the story, as it progresses one event after another, narrative mode is used to depict the listener/reader about the actions taking place in story. The descriptive mode shows the various activities that the main character is experiencing. Dialogue mode is used for any type of conversation taking place between any two characters. Generally, a greater amount of the text comprises of narrative mode. A storyteller uses his/her skills to add various expressive registers at sentence-level while narrating a story.

For Hindi children stories text classifications are shown in (Harikrishna and Rao, 2015) and (Harikrishna et al., 2015). Similar approached is followed for manually annotating the story-corpus

---

[1]https://en.wikipedia.org/wiki/Panchatantra
[2]https://en.wikipedia.org/wiki/Akbar_Birbal

Data	C	N	V	L	Test
Hindi Storyteller Speech	3	1960	3512	44	CV

Table 1: Dataset information. *C*: Number of Output classes. *N*: Number of sentences in storyteller speech corpus. $|V|$: Size of vocabulary. *L*: Maximum length of a sentence. *Test*: Size of test data (CV: train/test data partition is done by using 6-fold crossvalidation (CV)).

based on the three discourse modes. At sentence-level, text of the story was entrusted by four native Hindi speakers on text classification. They have been trained separately and work independently in order to avoid any labeling bias. In order to make the task of the annotation more focused, various discourse modes are annotated from the point of view of the text. Each annotator's task is to label the sentence with one of the modes of discourse (i.e. descriptive, dialogue and narrative). In the story corpus, there are 1960 sentences in which narrative, descriptive, and dialogue mode have 1127, 549, and 294 sentences, respectively. The inter-annotator agreement is given by Fleiss Kappa (κ). The κ values above 0.65 or so can be considered to be substantial. The κ value is 0.73 for the annotating the discourse mode to each sentence. Following are the example sentences of given discourse mode:

Descriptive mode

- ek taalaab men do machchha rahate the

- yah kah kar mendhak vahaan se chala gaya

- tabhi dono ne hi samajha ki ab to jaan bachi

Narrative mode

- tab tak birbal bhi darbar men aa pahunche

- baadshah ne vahi prashna unse bhi puchha

- rakhvala sevak ghabra gaya

Dialogue mode

- aisa mat karo isase to ham donon hi maare jaenge

- soch lo na dikha sakhe to saja milegi

- tumne yah chamatkar kaise kiya

3 Proposed Model

In the work, we have used three model for discourse classification. In the first and second model, word2vec is used for feature extraction, and CNN and SVM (Joachims, 1998) respectively are used for classification. The third model is the combination of CNN and SVM (Cao et al., 2015), where CNN is used for feature extraction and SVM is used for classification. All these models are described in details, further.

3.1 Word to Vector

In text processing problems, words act as an important (Turian et al., 2010) feature. The words are considered as a distinct atomic (Collobert et al., 2011) attribute, for example, a word 'car' might be expressed as '*id123*'. This representation of a word is not sufficient enough to highlight the relation that may exist between the words in a story. In order to train the models successfully, there is a need for better representation of words. The vector representation of the word allows capturing the relevant information of the word for a task at hand. The values for the vector of words either could be generated randomly or by using some learning model like word2vec. Traditionally TTS system used uniform distribution for vector representation of words. Uniform distribution provides random values to word vector. Training using these vectors require large training data. For less training data, word vector cannot be learned properly, and they may be overfitted.

Therefore, instead of randomly initialization of word, we used word2vec model for vector representation of words. In general, word2vec model uses two types of algorithms (i)Continuous Bag-of-word (CBOW) model and (ii) Skip-Gram model (Mikolov and Dean, 2013). In this work, CBOW model is used for obtaining the vector representation of the word.

The architecture of the CBOW model can be seen as a fully connected neural network with a single hidden layer. The bag-of-word represents the relationship between a word and its surrounding word. In this work, two successor and two predecessor words are taken as input to recognize the current word. We have evaluated the accuracy of the CBOW by varying the dimension of the word vector such as 10, 15, 20, 25, 30, 40, 50 and 100. The 20-dimensional feature vector gave the optimal performance for the training data. Table 2 shows that similar words (Mikolov et al., 2013) in the vocabulary is extracted by measuring the cosine distance between the word vectors.

Query Word	Similar Word
birbal	manoranjak
	akabar
	baadshaah
	taariph
	samjhaya
pyaara	sajidhaji
	aanandit
	chaahti
	bhaabhi
	ijjat

Table 2: Top five similar words (calculated using cosine distance measure technique) from the vocabulary size of 3512 words.

3.2 Convolution Neural Network (CNN)

In this work, CNN has been explored for sentence based discourse classification problem. The reason for using CNN is to have a model that can easily manage the word sequence in a sentence and finds the relationship between the surrounding words. The key concept in CNN is the convolution operation. The convolution is between the input and filter matrices to find the relation in a sequence. In this work, input matrix of the CNN corresponds to a sentence. Figure 1 represents the complete process of training and testing the CNN model with an example of training and testing sentence. A sentence in the CNN model is represented by $S_1 \in \Re^{n \times v}$, where S denotes an input matrix to the CNN, n is the number of words in a sentence and v is the word vector dimension which is extracted from word2vec model[3]. Zero-padding is done for the varying sentence length. Let $F \in \Re^{h \times v}$ corresponds to a filter for performing mathematical convolution operation which convolve with each possible pair of h words in a sentence $[S_{1:h}, S_{2:h+1}, ..., S_{n-h+1:n}]$ to generate a feature map

$$m = [m_1, m_2, ..., m_{n-h+1}]$$

The next task is to perform max-pooling operation on the feature maps generated using a convolution filter and calculates the maximum value

---

3https://code.google.com/p/word2vec/

$M = max\{m\}$. In this way CNN extract dominant features for each feature map. CNN learns

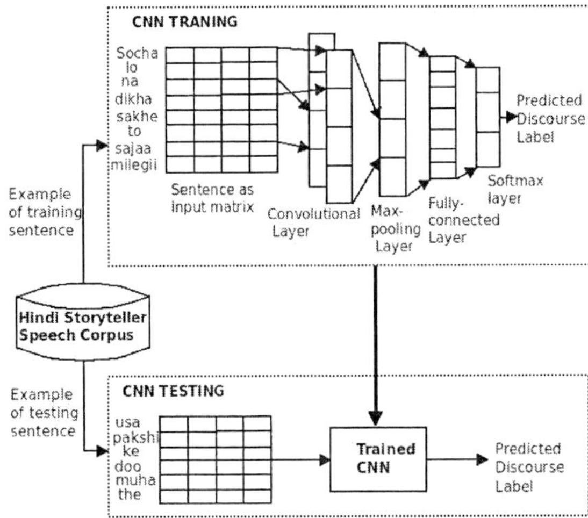

Figure 1: CNN Achitecture for discourse classification.

to convert a given sentence into a discourse label by calculating discriminant features (Dosovitskiy et al., 2014).

Model Hyperparameters Finding a set of hyperparameters (Hoos et al., 2014) is a neccessary task for optimising convolutional networks. There are various hyperparameters to tune in CNN such as the number and the height of filters, learning rate, dropout rate (Krizhevsky et al., 2012), L2 constraint, etc. Value of these hyperparameters depends (Zhang and Wallace, 2015) on the task at hand.

We observed that model performance is varying by using various hyperparameters. In the case of discourse classification, the proposed model achieves the best performance at the following values of the hyperparameters. It includes three filters for convolution operation, and their corresponding sizes are $(3 \times 100, 4 \times 100$ and $5 \times 100)$ where 3,4,5 is the height of the filter with 100 feature map. AdaGrad (Duchi et al., 2011) technique is used for training the model where the parameter for learning rate is 0.05. The value for L2-constraint is 3 which is used for regularizing the model parameters. The penultimate layer of the model is regularized using dropout rate of 0.7. We observe that model performance is varying as per the various dropout rate. In the case of discourse classification model performance is reduced if dropout rate is more or less than 0.7.

Model Regularization CNN is more prone to overfitting because of a large number of hyper-parameter tuning while training. Overfitting is a situation when the model is overtrained for training data, and it will be unable to predict the new data correctly. This problem is resolved by using regularization. For Regularization, dropout technique is implemented at the second last layer of CNN. Dropout is a method to deactivate (Miao and Metze, 2013) randomly selected hidden nodes. The dropped out nodes does not contribute to the training of the model. With the help of the dropout, technique model will learn more generalize feature. Also, the performance of the model increases because the active nodes are now insensitive to dropped-out nodes. In this work, we have seen dropout rate of 0.7 gives good result compare to values greater and less than this.

3.3 Multiclass Support Vector Machine

In this section, we discuss SVM (Rennie and Rifkin, 2001) for the multiclass problem by utilizing one-vs-rest method. The process involves L binary SVM for L classes and data from that class is taken as positive and remaining data is taken as negative. In the Hindi story corpus, at sentence level features are extracted to train the SVM. The words $w \in \Re^v$ in the sentence is represented by v dimensional vector extracted using word2vec model. The input sentence is represented as:

$$S_2 = [w_1 + w_2 + ... + w_n]$$

Here, the plus + symbol denotes the concatenation of the word vector. The Figure 2 shows the framework of the procedure followed for training and testing of SVM model.

3.4 CNN-SVM Model

In this section, we explored the combination of CNN-SVM model for developing the automatic discourse predictor. The CNN generates discriminant features, and SVM gives better generalization on the new data. During learning SVM tries to find out global hyperplane and CNN tries to minimize cross-entropy value. SVM provides better classification results than the softmax function at the fully-connected layer of the CNN. Here, the architecture of the CNN model is same as we have used before in this work 3.2. In this model, CNN is used for extraction of the feature for the sentence and then these features are used for training the SVM. The softmax function used to generate the

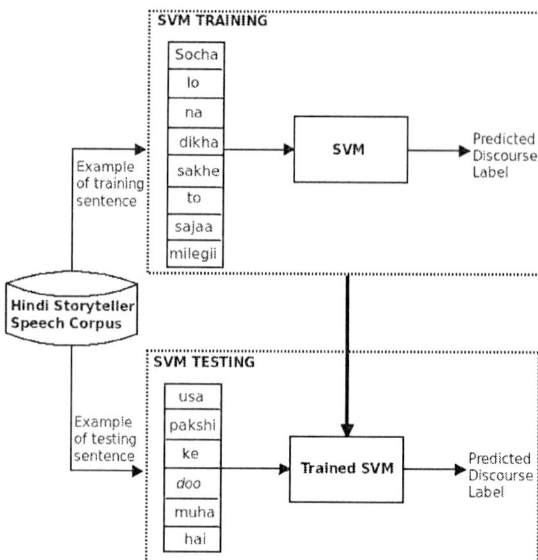

Figure 2: SVM Achitecture for discourse classification.

probabilistic value for the input data. This value is treated as a feature produced by CNN.

The Figure 3 shows that CNN takes a sentence as an input matrix S_1 which is generated using word2vec model. For feature extraction task CNN uses its original model in which softmax function is used at the output layer. After training of CNN, the features are obtained. These features are used for training the SVM model. The testing is carried out by extracting the features from CNN and using SVM classification.

4 Experimental Results

In this section, we discuss the experiments carried out on Hindi story corpus to analyze the accuracy of the discourse prediction model. The evaluation is performed using a various parameter of CNN (number of the filter (N), filter-height (H), cross-validation (CV) number, dropout rate (D), and batch-size (B)). Effect of each value of the parameters significantly alters the performance of the model. During experiment value of CV varies from 8 to 10, the value of N in between 1 to 3, the value of H ranges in between 3 to 5, the value of B varies from 50, 100 and 150 and D lies in the range of 0.2 to 0.8. After several experiments, we got optimal results at the number of filter 3, filter-height [3,4,5], Cross-validation (CV) 8, batch-size 50 and dropout rate 0.7.

At the time of training and testing, input to the

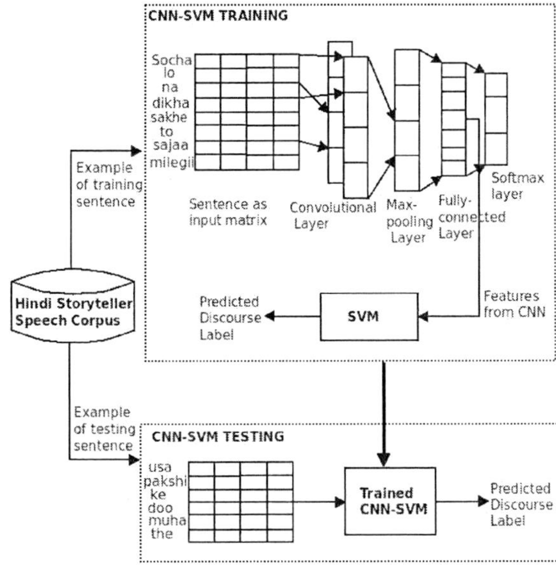

Figure 3: CNN-SVM Achitecture for discourse classification.

	DS (in %)	NR (in %)	DL (in %)
DS	**70 .1**	22.4	7.5
NR	19.4	**78.3**	2.3
DL	10.6	20	**69.4**

Table 3: Discourse classification results for the Hindi story corpus using CNN-SVM.

model is a sentence. In training, each story is divided into a set of sentences. Each of the sentences are labeled with one of the discourse mode (descriptive (*DS*), dialogue (*DL*), narrative (*NR*)). 1613 sentences are used in training and remaining, 347 sentences are used for testing the performance of the model.

The performance of the proposed methods is evaluated using confusion matrix, ROC curve, and F-Score. A graphical plot of the performance is shown by ROC curve. This curve considers only true positive rate and false positive rate of the testing data. F-Score tells about the sensitivity, specificity, precision, recall, f-measure, and g-mean. Here sensitivity and recall show the true positive rate, specificity shows the true negative rate, precision gives the positive predicted value, f-measure (Espíndola and Ebecken, 2005) is the harmonic mean of precision and recall and g-mean is the geometric mean of precision and recall (Powers, 2014).

Table 3 represents that each discourse is classified (using SVM which is trained on features extracted from CNN) correctly by almost 72.6%. Narrative mode classification is 76.3% because of more training data for this mode, and dialogue mode classification is 65.5%, and descriptive mode classification is 65% because for this class we have fewer data to train our model.

Figure 4 represents the receiver operating char-acteristic (ROC) for CNN-SVM model where class 1, class 2 and class 3 accounts for the descriptive, narrative, and dialogue mode respectively. Class 2 (narrative mode) has larger true positive rate than other two classes.

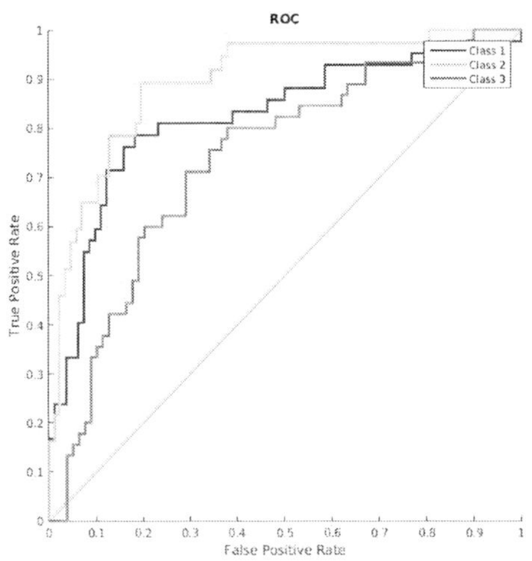

Figure 4: ROC curve for CNN-SVM model.

Table 4 shows that each discourse is classified (using CNN with softmax function which is trained on features extracted from word2vec model) correctly by almost 62.66%. Dialogue mode classification is 39.58% which is lesser than descriptive and narrative mode classification because for dialogue mode we have fewer data to train our model. CNN learns better feature if a particular mode has sufficiently large amount of training data.

Figure 5 represents the ROC curve for CNN model. Class 1 (Descriptive mode) has larger true positive rate than other two classes.

Table 5 shows that each discourse is classified (using SVM which is trained on features extracted from word2vec model) correctly by almost 54.3%. Dialogue mode classification is 18.75% which is

	DS (in %)	NR (in %)	DL (in %)
DS	**77.08**	8.33	14.58
NR	10.86	**71.73**	17.39
DL	25	35.41	**39.58**

Table 4: Discourse classification results for the Hindi story corpus using CNN.

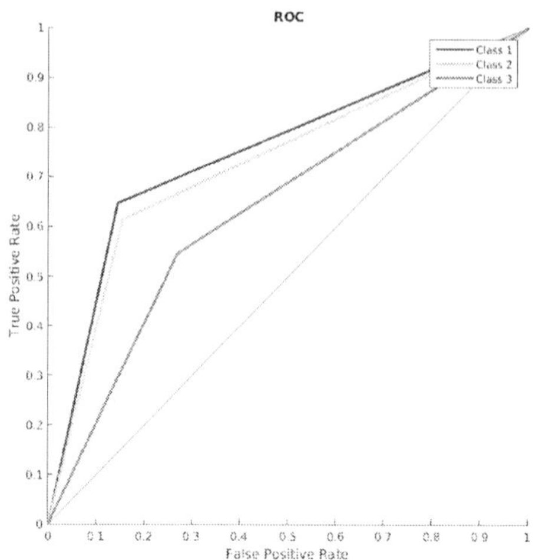

Figure 5: ROC curve for CNN model.

lesser than descriptive and narrative mode classification because for dialogue mode we have fewer data to train our model. SVM give worse results if a class does not have sufficient amount of training data.

	DS (in %)	NR (in %)	DL (in %)
DS	**67.39**	17.39	15.29
NR	10.41	**77.08**	12.5
DL	37.5	43.75	**18.75**

Table 5: Discourse classification results for the Hindi story corpus using SVM.

Figure 6 represents the ROC curve for SVM model. Class 2 (Narrative mode) has larger true positive rate than other two classes. In class 3 (Dialogue mode) false positive rate is greater than true positive rate.

Table 6 represents f-score for all the proposed model. F-score gives almost complete knowledge about the methods. It can be observed that the best performance for discourse classification is 72.6%

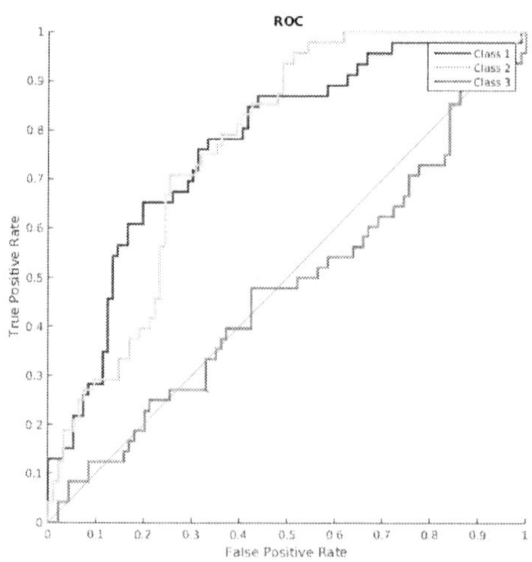

Figure 6: ROC curve for SVM model.

using CNN-SVM model. SVM model gives worst performance against all given model.

F-Score	CNN (in %)	SVM (in %)	CNN-SVM (in %)
Accuracy	62.66	54.3	**72.6**
Sensitivity	77.08	77.08	58.86
Specificity	55.32	42.55	71.97
Precision	46.84	40.66	52.06
Recall	77.08	77.08	58.86
F-measure	58.27	53.24	59.55
G-mean	65.30	57.27	70.88

Table 6: F-Score for discourse classification models.

5 Summary and Conclusion

In this work, we have developed automatic discourse classification model which determine the discourse information of the sentence. We explored SVM and CNN for developing the automatic discourse classification model. In view of this, we collected short children stories to develop story corpus. This corpus is used for developing the automatic discourse predictor. Three modes of discourse are considered, narrative, descriptive and dialogue. The features are used for training the SVM and CNN model are obtained using word2vec method. Our current model achieves its best accuracy (72.6%) when the feature is obtained using CNN (which is trained on word2vec feature) and classification is done by using SVM.

Future scope of this work is to increase the corpus size to improve the accuracy of the model. Apart from word2vec, we can explore Latent Semantic Analysis (LSA) for obtaining the features. We can also compare the current work by using recurrent neural network (RNN).

Acknowledgments

The authors would like to thank the Department of Information Technology, Government of India, for funding the project, *Development of Text-to-Speech synthesis for Indian Languages Phase II*, Ref. no. 11(7)/2011HCC(TDIL).

References

Jordi Adell, Antonio Bonafonte, and David Escudero. 2005. Analysis of prosodic features towards modelling of emotional and pragmatic attributes of speech. *Procesamiento de Lenguaje Natural*, 35:277–284.

Yuhui Cao, Ruifeng Xu, and Tao Chen. 2015. Combining convolutional neural network and support vector machine for sentiment classification. In *Chinese National Conference on Social Media Processing*, pages 144–155. Springer.

Ronan Collobert, Jason Weston, Léon Bottou, Michael Karlen, Koray Kavukcuoglu, and Pavel Kuksa. 2011. Natural language processing (almost) from scratch. *Journal of Machine Learning Research*, 12(Aug):2493–2537.

Rodolfo Delmonte and Rocco Tripodi. 2015. Semantics and discourse processing for expressive tts. In *Workshop on Linking Models of Lexical, Sentential and Discourse-level Semantics (LSDSem)*, page 32.

Rodolfo Delmonte, Gabriel Nicolae, Sanda Harabagiu, Cristina Nicolae, Stefan Trausan-Matu, Cristina Grigore, and Liviu Dragomirescu. 2007. A linguistically-based approach to discourse relations recognition. *Natural Language Processing and Cognitive Science: Proc. of 4th NLPCS (Funchal, Portugal)*, pages 81–91.

Rodolfo Delmonte. 2008. A computational approach to implicit entities and events in text and discourse. *International Journal of Speech Technology*, 11(3-4):195–208.

Alexey Dosovitskiy, Jost Tobias Springenberg, Martin Riedmiller, and Thomas Brox. 2014. Discriminative unsupervised feature learning with convolutional neural networks. In *Advances in Neural Information Processing Systems*, pages 766–774.

John Duchi, Elad Hazan, and Yoram Singer. 2011. Adaptive subgradient methods for online learning and stochastic optimization. *Journal of Machine Learning Research*, 12(Jul):2121–2159.

RP Espíndola and NFF Ebecken. 2005. On extending f-measure and g-mean metrics to multi-class problems. *WIT Transactions on Information and Communication Technologies*, 35.

DM Harikrishna and K Sreenivasa Rao. 2015. Children story classification based on structure of the story. In *Advances in Computing, Communications and Informatics (ICACCI), 2015 International Conference on*, pages 1485–1490. IEEE.

DM Harikrishna, Gurunath Reddy, and K Sreenivasa Rao. 2015. Multi-stage children story speech synthesis for hindi. In *Contemporary Computing (IC3), 2015 Eighth International Conference on*, pages 220–224. IEEE.

Holger Hoos, UBC CA, and Kevin Leyton-Brown. 2014. An efficient approach for assessing hyperparameter importance.

Thorsten Joachims. 1998. Text categorization with support vector machines: Learning with many relevant features. In *European conference on machine learning*, pages 137–142. Springer.

Alex Krizhevsky, Ilya Sutskever, and Geoffrey E Hinton. 2012. Imagenet classification with deep convolutional neural networks. In *Advances in neural information processing systems*, pages 1097–1105.

Yajie Miao and Florian Metze. 2013. Improving low-resource cd-dnn-hmm using dropout and multilingual dnn training. In *INTERSPEECH*, pages 2237–2241. ISCA.

T Mikolov and J Dean. 2013. Distributed representations of words and phrases and their compositionality. *Advances in neural information processing systems*.

Tomas Mikolov, Wen-tau Yih, and Geoffrey Zweig. 2013. Linguistic regularities in continuous space word representations. In *HLT-NAACL*, volume 13, pages 746–751.

Ral Montao, Francesc Alas, and Josep Ferrer. 2013. Prosodic analysis of storytelling discourse modes and narrative situations oriented to text-to-speech synthesis. In *8th ISCA Workshop on Speech Synthesis*, pages 191–196, Barcelona, Spain, August.

David MW Powers. 2014. What the f–measure doesnt measure.

Jason DM Rennie and Ryan Rifkin. 2001. Improving multiclass text classification with the support vector machine.

Parakrant Sarkar and K Sreenivasa Rao. 2015. Analysis and modeling pauses for synthesis of storytelling speech based on discourse modes. In *Contemporary Computing (IC3), 2015 Eighth International Conference on*, pages 225–230. IEEE.

Parakrant Sarkar, Arijul Haque, Arup Kumar Dutta, Gurunath Reddy, DM Harikrishna, Prasenjit Dhara, Rashmi Verma, NP Narendra, Sunil Kr SB, Jainath Yadav, et al. 2014. Designing prosody rule-set for converting neutral tts speech to storytelling style speech for indian languages: Bengali, hindi and telugu. In *Contemporary Computing (IC3), 2014 Seventh International Conference on*, pages 473–477. IEEE.

Mariët Theune, Koen Meijs, Dirk Heylen, and Roeland Ordelman. 2006. Generating expressive speech for storytelling applications. *IEEE Transactions on Audio, Speech, and Language Processing*, 14(4):1137–1144.

Joseph Turian, Lev Ratinov, and Yoshua Bengio. 2010. Word representations: a simple and general method for semi-supervised learning. In *Proceedings of the 48th annual meeting of the association for computational linguistics*, pages 384–394. Association for Computational Linguistics.

Rashmi Verma, Parakrant Sarkar, and K Sreenivasa Rao. 2015. Conversion of neutral speech to storytelling style speech. In *Advances in Pattern Recognition (ICAPR), 2015 Eighth International Conference on*, pages 1–6. IEEE.

Ye Zhang and Byron C. Wallace. 2015. A sensitivity analysis of (and practitioners' guide to) convolutional neural networks for sentence classification. *CoRR*, abs/1510.03820.

Biomolecular Event Extraction using a Stacked Generalization based Classifier

Amit Majumder
Dept. of MCA
Academy Of Technology
West Bengal, India
cseamit48@yahoo.co.in

Asif Ekbal
Dept. of CSE
IIT Patna, Patna
India
asif@iitp.ac.in

Sudip Kumar Naskar
Dept. of CSE
Jadavpur University
West Bengal, India
sudip.naskar@gmail.com

Abstract

In this paper we propose a stacked generalization (or stacking) model for event extraction in bio-medical text. Event extraction deals with the process of extracting detailed biological phenomenon, which is more challenging compared to the traditional binary relation extraction such as protein-protein interaction. The overall process consists of mainly three steps: event trigger detection, argument extraction by edge detection and finding correct combination of arguments. In stacking, we use Linear Support Vector Classification (Linear SVC), Logistic Regression (LR) and Stochastic Gradient Descent (SGD) as base-level learning algorithms. As meta-level learner we use Linear SVC. In edge detection step, we find out the arguments of triggers detected in trigger detection step using a SVM classifier. To find correct combination of arguments, we use rules generated by studying the properties of bio-molecular event expressions, and form an event expression consisting of event trigger, its class and arguments. The output of trigger detection is fed to edge detection for argument extraction. Experiments on benchmark datasets of BioNLP-2011 show the recall, precision and F-score of 48.96%, 66.46% and 56.38%, respectively. Comparisons with the existing systems show that our proposed model attains state-of-the-art performance.

1 Introduction

Huge amount of electronic bio-medical documents, such as molecular biology reports, genomic papers or patient records are generated daily. These contents need to be organized in a more principled way so as to enable advanced search and efficient information retrieval and information extraction methods. This can be beneficial to the practitioners and researchers in biology, medicine and the other allied disciplines. Success of text mining (TM) is evident from the organization of different shared-task evaluation campaigns. The bulk of research in the field of biomedical natural language processing (BioNLP) have mainly focused on the extraction of simple binary relations. Some of the very popular bio-text mining evaluation challenges include TREC Genomics track (Voorhees, 2007), JNLPBA[1], LLL (Nedellec, 2005) and BioCreative (Lynette Hirschman, 2007). While the first two evaluation challenges were concerned with the issues of information retrieval and named-entity recognition (NER), the last two addressed the issues of information extraction and seeking relations between bio-molecules. Relations among biomedical entities (i.e. proteins and genes) must be extracted automatically from a large collection of biomedical datasets since they are very important in understanding biomedical phenomena. Simple binary relations are not itself sufficient for capturing the detailed phenomenon, and there is a growing demand for capturing more detailed and complex relations. Two large corpora, BioInfer (Pyysalo S, 2007) and GENIA (Tomoko Ohta and Tsujii, 2009), have been proposed for this purpose.

In recent times there has been a trend for fine-grained information extraction from text (Kim J-D, 2009). This was addressed in three consecutive text mining challenges, BioNLP-2009 (Hyoung-Gyu Lee, 2009), BioNLP-2011 (Jin-Dong Kim, 2011) and BioNLP-2013 (Lishuang Li, 2013). In this paper we propose an effective technique for

---

[1] http://www.geniaproject.org/
shared-tasks/bionlp-jnlpba-shared-task-2004

D S Sharma, R Sangal and A K Singh. Proc. of the 13th Intl. Conference on Natural Language Processing, pages 55–64,
Varanasi, India. December 2016. ©2016 NLP Association of India (NLPAI)

information extraction (more specifically, event extraction) at more finer level. This is known as event extraction where the focus is to extract events and their different properties that denote detailed biological phenomenon. This can be thought of as a three-steps process, *viz.* event trigger detection, classification of triggers into pre-defined categories and argument extraction. The events are classified into 9 potential events, out of which 5 are simple which corresponds to *gene expression, transcription, protein catabolism, phosphorylation* and *localization*. Among the rest four events, one *binding* event and three regulatory or complex events namely *regulation, positive regulation* and *negative regulation*. For simple events we have a single primary theme, which is usually a protein. But a complex event can include a theme as well as a cause argument. These themes and causes can be either proteins or events. Moreover, number of themes could also vary. In order to explain this, we consider the following sentence as an example, where TRAF2 and CD40 denote proteins.

Sentence: *In this study we hypothesized that the phosphorylation of TRAF2 inhibits binding to the CD40 cytoplasmic domain.*

This sentence contains simple, binding and complex events. Each bio-molecular event expression contains a trigger word and one or more arguments. The identified events from the sentence are:

Simple event: The word *phosphorylation* is a trigger of type *Phosphorylation*. Argument of this trigger is *TRAF2* as theme.

Binding event: The word *binding* is a trigger word of *Binding* type. Arguments of this trigger are *TRAF2* and *CD40*.

Complex event: The word *inhibits* is a trigger word of *Negative_regulation* type. The previously mentioned two events(i.e. *Phosphorylation* and *Binding*) are *theme* type arguments of this trigger word.

Here, we propose a stack model for event extraction. In stacking, Linear Support Vector Classification (Linear SVC)[2], Logistic Regression (LR)[3] and Stochastic Gradient Descent (SGD)[4]

from Scikit-learn (sklearn)[5] have been used as base-level learning algorithms. Linear SVC is an implementation of Support Vector Machine using liblinear library[6]. For meta learning we use Linear Support Vector Classification. The system is evaluated based on the framework of BioNLP 2011 shared task[7].

Event extraction systems find both triggers and their associated arguments. These could pose a number of challenges. Exact interpretation of triggers depend upon the context, e.g. expression of [gene] is an event of type Gene Expression, but expression of [mRNA] is of type Transcription. So there is ambiguity in sense of trigger words. It is a challenge to fix these ambiguities. Event arguments can be difficult to detect in case of binding and regulatory type of arguments, because in these cases, number of arguments is not fixed. Number of arguments in binding events can be one or more. Finding correct combination of arguments is very challenging. More precisely, we use the annotated data collected for these tasks and report the results returned by the evaluation servers on the test sets of the 2011 GE task. From the experiment it has been seen that evaluation on test data shows 2-3% less in performance than the performance on development data. So it is challenge to increase the performance on test data. Coreference resolution is required for the correct interpretation of certain event arguments. For example, in the sentence M-CSF treatment was also associated with a rapid induction of the jun-B gene, although expression of this gene was prolonged compared to that of c-jun. In this example, the word this gene refers jun-B and the word that refers expression. There are two gene expression events in the sentence. Arguments of these events can be identified correctly if coreference resolution method is applied on the dataset and it is a challenging issue.

2 Few Existing Methods for Combining Classifiers

In our day to day life, when crucial decisions are made in a meeting, a voting among the members present in the meeting is conducted when the opinions of the members conflict with each other.

---

[2]http://scikit-learn.org/stable/modules/generated/sklearn.svm.LinearSVC.html

[3]http://scikit-learn.org/stable/modules/generated/sklearn.linear_model.LogisticRegression.html

[4]http://scikit-learn.org/stable/

[5]http://scikit-learn.org/stable/modules/generated/sklearn.linear_model.SGDClassifier.html

[6]https://www.csie.ntu.edu.tw/~cjlin/liblinear/

[7]http://2011.bionlp-st.org/

This principle of "voting is very popular in data mining and machine learning. In voting, when classifiers are combined, the class assigned to a test instance will be the one suggested by most of the base level classifiers involved in the ensemble process. Bagging (Breiman, 1996) and boosting (SCHAPIRE, 1990) are the widely used variants of voting schemes. Bagging is a voting scheme in which n models, usually of same type, are constructed. For an unknown instance, each models predictions are recorded. Finally, that particular class is assigned which has the maximum votes among the predictions from models. Boosting is very similar to bagging in which only the model construction phase differs. Here the instances which are often misclassified are allowed to participate in training more number of times. There will be n classifiers which themselves will have individual weights for their accuracies. Finally, the class is assigned which is having the maximum weight.

The classifiers can be combined using two popular approaches, viz. majority voting and weighted voting. In majority voting, we select the class that receives maximum votes. In weighted voting, classifiers are combined based on the strengths and weaknesses of classifiers.

Stacked generalization or stacking is a method for combining multiple classifiers. The idea of stacked generalization (Wolpert, 1992; Georgios Sigletos, 2005) is to learn a meta-level (or level-1) classifier based on the output of base-level (or level-0) classifiers, estimated as follows:
Define D as a training data set consisting of feature vectors, also referred to as level-0 data, and $L^1...L^N$ as a set of N different learning algorithms. During the K-fold cross-validation process, D is randomly split into K disjoint parts $D^1...D^K$ of almost equal sizes. At each j-th fold, j =1..K , the $L^1...L^N$ learning algorithms are applied to the training part D-D^j (i.e. part of training data excluding D^j, where D is the whole training data and D^j is the current test part for cross-validation) and the induced classifiers C^1(j)...C^N(j) are applied to the test part D^j. The concatenated predictions of the induced classifiers on each feature vector x_i in D^j, together with the original class value $y_i(x_i)$, form a new set MD^j of meta-level vectors.

At the end of the entire cross-validation process,
$$MD= \bigcup_{j=1}^{K} MD^j$$ constitutes the full meta-level data set, also referred to as level-1 data, which is used for applying a learning algorithm L^M and inducing the meta-level classifier C^M . The learning algorithm L^M that is employed at meta-level could be one of the $L^1...L^N$ or a different one. Finally, the $L^1...L^N$ learning algorithms are applied to the entire data set D inducing the final base-level classifiers $C^1...C^N$ to be used at runtime. In order to classify a new instance, the concatenated predictions of all base-level classifiers $C^1...C^N$ form a meta-level vector that is assigned a class value by the meta-level classifier C^M.

3   Proposed Approach

In this section we describe our proposed approach for event extraction. The steps to extract event expression are sentence splitting, tokenization, trigger detection, argument extraction by edge detection and finding correct combination of arguments as shown in figure 1. In sentence splitting and tokenization steps we use sentence split and tokenised data which was made available as the supportive resources in BioNLP-2011 shared task[8]. We use SVM to extract arguments and its correct combinations.

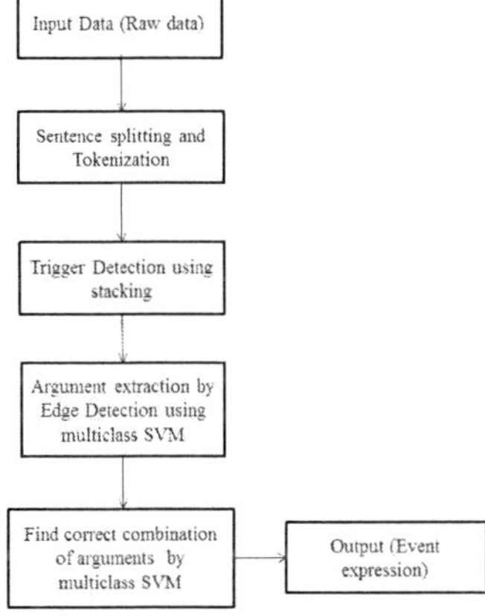

Figure 1: Steps to extract event expression

Our method is based on the principle of stacking. We generate 10 classifiers for each of the algorithms (i.e. Linear SVC, SGD and LR) mentioned above. We describe the algorithms in the subsequent sections.

<hr>

[8]`http://weaver.nlplab.org/~bionlp-st/ BioNLP-ST/downloads/support-downloads. html#parse-formats`

3.1 Linear Support Vector Classification (Linear SVC)

Linear SVC is learning algorithm for classification. Using Linear SVC algorithm, we generate 10 classifiers by varying C parameter of the algorithm. The C parameter is a parameter for optimization that specifies the learning algorithm how much it wantS to avoid misclassifying each training example. Starting C value (here, 0.001) is chosen by running the algorithm using C values as 1000, 100, 1, 0.1, 0.001, 0.00001, and choose final value based on the highest accuracy obtained.

$$C_i^{SVC} = 0.001 + i \times 0.05 \tag{1}$$

where C_i^{SVC} represents C parameter for SVC_i classifier.

3.2 Stochastic Gradient Descent (SGD)

We generate 10 classifiers by varying the *alpha* parameters of SGD algorithm. The parameter *alpha* is Constant that multiplies the regularization term used in the implementation of the algorithm. These 10 classifiers are SGD_i, for i=0 to 9. The value of *alpha* is set to 0.000029 based on the different experiments executed.

$$alpha_i^{SGD} = 0.000029 + i \times 0.000015 \tag{2}$$

where $alpha_i^{SGD}$ represents *alpha* parameter for SGD_i classifier.

3.3 Logistic Regression (LR)

We generate 10 classifiers by varying the C parameter of LR algorithm. These classifiers are LR_i, for i=0 to 9. The value of C is set to 7.2101 which is chosen by running the algorithm with different C values.

$$C_i^{LR} = 7.2101 + i \times 0.05 \tag{3}$$

where C_i^{LR} represents C parameter for LR_i classifier.

The architecture of our proposed stacked method is shown in Fig 2 where SVC, SGD and LR have been used as base level classifiers. Here, SVC is used as meta-level classifier.

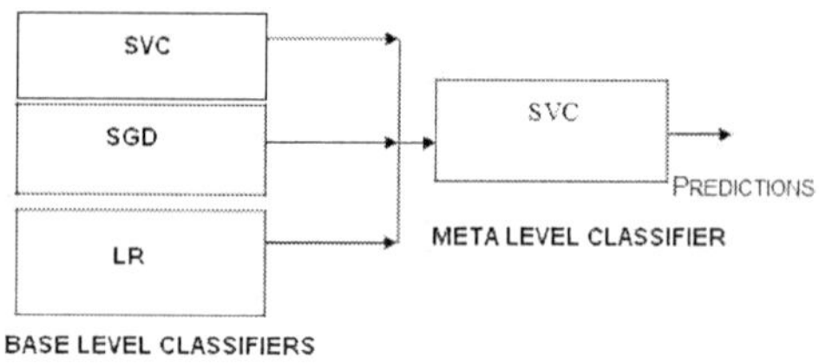

Figure 2: Model ensemble using stacking

4 Features

In this section we describe the features that we use for developing the models. To explain the features, let us consider the following example sentence: *"BMP-6 inhibits growth of mature human B cells; induction of Smad phosphorylation and upregulation of Id1"*. The sentence is tokenised and features are extracted for every token. We use token *"upregulation"* in the above example to explain the features.

4.1 Features for trigger detection and classification

Here, we describe the set of features that we use for event trigger detection and classification.

1. **Surface Word, Stem, PoS, Chunk and Named Entity:** We use surface forms, lemma, Part-of-Speech (PoS), chunk and named entity (NE) as features for trigger detection and classification. These information were extracted from the GENIA tagger[9]. For the token *"upregulation"*, the feature values extracted are *upregulation, upregulate, NN, I-NP and O* for the surface form, lemma, PoS, Chunk and NE features, respectively. All these information are very critical to identify the trigger and its class.

2. **Bag-of-Words:** The bag-of-word (BoW) feature plays a crucial role in many text mining tasks. This particular feature is defined in different ways. At first we extract BoWs within the context of sizes 3 and 5 (i.e., ± 1 and ± 2). We also extract NEs from this context, and use their counts as features. Entire sentence is then considered as a context and BoWs and NE features are extracted. For

---

[9]http://www.nactem.ac.uk/GENIA/tagger/

example, BoW feature for the token *"up-regulation"* are *"and upregulation of"* and *"phosphorylation and upregulation of Id1"* for window sizes 3 and 5, respectively.

3. **Linear Features:** Linear features are generated by marking token with a tag that denotes their relative positions in the linear order. This feature is defined with respect to a context window. If i is a position (i.e. index) of the token under consideration, then the linear features are calculated from the words with indices $i-3$ to $i+3$. In our experiment we use the word along with its PoS tag to generate linear features.

4. **upper_case_start, upper_case_middle, has_digits, has_hyphen:** These features are defined based on the orthographic constructions: whether the token starts with an uppercase character, or it has any uppercase character in the middle, or has any digit(s) or hyphen inside it.. These features are important from the observations that there are some trigger words in the dataset which start with uppercase character or hyphen inside it. For example, in the sentence *TGF-beta mediates RUNX induction and FOXP3 is efficiently up-regulated by RUNX1 and RUNX3 in human CD4+ T cells.*, the word *up-regulated* is *Positive_regulation* type rvent trigger which has hyphen inside it.

5. **Bi-gram and Tri-gram Features:** We use the character bi-gram and tri-gram sequences extracted from a token as features. For example, for the token *"upregulation"*, the bi-gram features will be *up pr re eg gu ul la at ti io on* and tri-gram features will be *upr pre reg egu gul ula lat ati tio ion* .

6. **Dependency Path Features:** There are are some trigger words which ca not be detected using context features or b-gram or tri-gram features. So we depend on dependency relations inside sentence. Dependency features are extracted from dependency graph generated by dependency parser(David McClosky and Manning, 2011; David McClosky and Johnson, 2006) . Figure 3 shows the dependency graph for the sentence *"BMP-6 inhibits growth of mature human B cells; induction of Smad phosphorylation and upreg-duction of Smad phosphorylation and upreg-*

ulation of Id1", generated by the Charniak-McCloskey parser (David McClosky and Johnson, 2006). In the graph, an edge label represents the dependency relation between two nodes. Each node in the graph is labelled by a number which represents a word appearing in that position (0-based index) of the sentence. For example, node labelled with number 0 indicates the word *BMP-6* and node labelled with number 1 indicates the word *inhibits*.

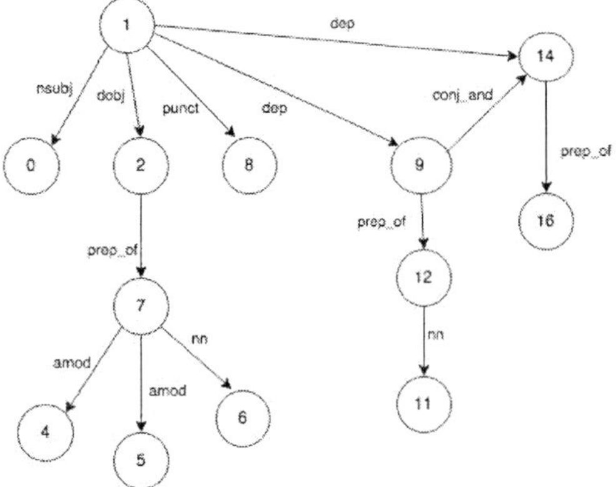

Figure 3: Dependency graph for the example sentence *"BMP-6 inhibits growth of mature human B cells; induction of Smad phosphorylation and upregulation of Id1"*

In the graph, node 0 and 16 represent proteins (i.e. NE) as specified in the training dataset. In the feature value NE is denoted by _NAMED_ENT.

Edges in a dependency graph are directed arcs. Each edge connects two nodes. Nodes represent words along with other information like PoS tags of the words. A node can be connected to two types of edges: one is in-type (or incoming) edges which are incident on the node and the other type is out-type (or outgoing) edges which emanate from the node.

Features for in-type edges:
For the in-type edges we consider the features as defined below. For illustration purpose, we consider node numbered 14 (*upregulation*) as the target node and we present below the feature values generated for the in-type edge emanating from node 1 (*inhibits*) and incident on

node numbered 14.

   (a) Edge type (i.e. dependency relation) – *dep*

   (b) PoS of source node – *VBZ*

   (c) Edge type combined with PoS – *dep_VBZ*

   (d) Text of the source node – *inhibits*

   (e) Edge type merged with PoS and token of source node – *dep_VBZ_inhibits*

   (f) Stem of the source node – *inhibit*

   (g) Edge type combined with stem of the source node – *dep_inhibit*

   (h) Stem of the current word combined with edge-type and stem of the source node – *upregul_dep_inhibit*

Features for out-type edges:

For out-type edges emanating from the target word, in addition to the target word feature we also take into consideration the features belonging to the edge (i.e. the dependency relation) and the destination node on which the edge is incident.

The list of features considered for out-type edges are listed below. For illustration, we consider node 14 (*upregulation*) as the target node and the corresponding feature values are shown next to the out-type edge features for the out-type edge emanating from node 14 (*upregulation*) and incident on node 16 (*Id1*).

   (a) Edge type – prep_of

   (b) PoS of destination node – NN

   (c) Edge-type combined with PoS of destination node – prep_of_NN

   (d) Text of the destination node – NAMED_ENT

   (e) Edge-type combined with the token text of the destination node – prep_of_NAMED_ENT

   (f) Stem of the current word combined with the edge-type and stem of the destination node – upregul_prep_of_NAMED_ENT

7. **Dependency chain:** These features are syntactic dependencies up to a certain depth limit, starting from a token of interest. In our case we consider the depth of limit three. They are used to define the immediate context of these words.

4.2 Features for argument extraction by edge detection

To find out features for argument extraction, for every sentence, we form a dependency graph consisting of the triggers detected in trigger detection step and proteins mentioned in the data set for that sentence. Following features are extracted for argument extraction.

1. **Token features:** These are features of two tokens connected by an edge. A token can potentially be a protein (i.e NE) or a trigger word detected during the trigger detection phase. The token features are surface word, stem, PoS, chunk and NE, BoW, prefix and suffix, linear features, bi-gram and tri-gram features. These have been discussed in details in Section 4.1.

2. **Dependency Features:** Dependency features play important role to extract arguments of triggers. The following dependency features are extracted from dependency graph.

   Single element feature: A path in dependency graph has a starting token, ending token and some intermediate tokens. Token can be considered as a node in the graph. A path consists of a sequence of edges starting from the initial node, followed by a set of intermediate nodes, and ending in a terminal node.

   (a) For each pair of adjacent tokens, all the dependency relations are considered.

   (b) Lexical features of all the internal tokens in the path are also considered. These are surface word, stems, PoS, chunk, NE, BoW, prefix, suffix, linear features, bi-gram and tri-gram features.

   (c) Dependency features that we use are mentioned in Section 4.1.

   N-gram feature: We compute the shortest path from starting to the end token in the dependency graph in figure-3. From this walk we compute bi-grams from all the combinations of two consecutive edges. In the same way, we compute n-grams (n=3,4) by considering three and four consecutive edges, respectively.

   Path edge feature: For each edge in the path, we use the edge features. Edge feature is defined as consisting of all the lexical-level features of the nodes connected by an edge.

5   Experimental Results and Analysis

We perform experiments on BioNLP-11 Genia event dataset[10]. Statistics of BioNLP-11 dataset for genia event extraction has been mentioned in table 1.

Attributes	Training	Development	Test
Abstracts+Full articles	908 (5)	259 (5)	347 (5)
Sentences	8,759	2,954	3,437
Proteins	11,625	4,690	5,301
Total events	10,287	3,243	4,457

Table 1: Statistics of BioNLP-ST 2011 Genia Event dataset (training, development and test). Value inside parentheses indicates the number of full articles

The overall algorithm comprises of three basic steps: trigger detection, edge detection and argument extraction. Trigger detection is performed using the stacked generalization method. Experimental results are shown in Table 2. From the ex-

Base/Meta classifier	Classifiers	Recall	Precision	F-score
	SVC0	48.22	84.81	61.48
	SVC1	74.42	67.58	70.84
	SVC2	65.82	76.61	70.81
	SVC3	71.46	70.42	70.94
	SVC4	66.07	75.49	70.46
	SVC5	70.25	71.20	70.72
	SVC6	66.13	74.92	70.25
	SVC7	69.57	71.81	70.67
	SVC8	66.04	74.54	70.03
	SVC9	68.89	72.08	70.45
	LR0	64.69	76.08	69.92
	LR1	64.95	76.28	70.16
	LR2	65.22	76.37	70.36
	LR3	65.91	76.46	70.80
Base level classifiers	LR4	65.72	77.33	71.05
	LR5	65.91	77.43	71.21
	LR6	65.16	78.67	71.28
	LR7	66.13	78.10	71.62
	LR8	65.47	78.57	71.43
	LR9	64.97	79.66	71.57
	SGD0	71.43	71.35	71.39
	SGD1	71.38	71.34	71.36
	SGD2	71.43	71.33	71.38
	SGD3	71.34	71.36	71.35
	SGD4	71.39	71.38	71.38
	SGD5	71.42	71.39	71.41
	SGD6	71.38	71.38	71.38
	SGD7	71.41	71.36	71.38
	SGD8	71.38	71.42	71.40
	SGD9	71.38	71.37	71.37
Meta level classifier	SVC	69.13	74.96	71.93

Table 2: Stacked generalization result in trigger detection

perimental results of stacking mentioned in table 2, it is evident that performances of LR and SGD

algorithms are better than Linear SVC. SGD classifier is an implementation of SVM with stochastic gradient descent (SGD) learning, whereas Linear SVC is an implementation of SVM using liblinear library. Linear SVC shows low performance, but it is very fast. We recorded the results for each class label (though, not shown in table) and we see that linear SVC generates best result for *Transcription* and *Regulation* type triggers. LR classifier shows best result, but it takes more time than the other two algorithms. This happens due to the fact that each of these classifiers have their own default parameter settings in sklearn tool. We have tuned *C* parameter in SGD and Linear SVC. In SGD classifier, we tune *alpha* parameter. Among all the base-level classifiers, classifier LR7 using Logistic Regression algorithm provides best result (F-score=71.62). Results show that stacked model achieves better performance compared to the best base-level classifier. Output of trigger detection is fed to the input of edge detection step. In this step we use multi-class SVM[11] as a classification algorithm to find out *theme* and/or *cause* relationships between triggers and proteins. After finding the relationships we generate the event expression. In Table 3 and Table 4, we show the results of experiments on BioNLP-11 shared task dataset on development and test set, respectively. We achieve satisfactory F-score of 80.04% on development dataset and 78.15% on test dataset for *Gene_expression* type event. System also performs well for *protein_catebolism* event with an F-score of 91.30% on the development set. Results of *phosphorylation* event is also satisfactory for the test and development datasets (around 84% F-score). The system suffers most for the relatively complex regulatory events where it shows around 42% to 51% F-score.

Event Class	gold (match)	answer (match)	recall	precision	fscore
Gene_expression	749 (582)	704 (581)	77.70	82.53	80.04
Transcription	158 (79)	93 (79)	50.00	84.95	62.95
Protein_catabolism	23 (21)	23 (21)	91.30	91.30	91.30
Phosphorylation	111 (94)	111 (94)	84.68	84.68	84.68
Localization	67 (49)	58 (49)	73.13	84.48	78.40
=[SVT-TOTAL]=	1108 (825)	989 (824)	74.46	83.32	78.64
Binding	373 (171)	311 (171)	45.84	54.98	50.00
==[EVT-TOTAL]==	1481 (996)	1300 (995)	67.25	76.54	71.60
Regulation	292 (104)	182 (104)	35.62	57.14	43.88
Positive_regulation	999 (376)	667 (376)	37.64	56.37	45.14
Negative_regulation	471 (168)	264 (168)	35.67	63.64	45.71
==[REG-TOTAL]==	1762 (648)	1113 (648)	36.78	58.22	45.08
==[ALL-TOTAL]==	3243 (1644)	2413 (1643)	50.69	68.09	58.12

Table 3: Result on development data [Approximate Span/Approximate Recursive]

---

[10] http://2011.bionlp-st.org/

[11] https://www.cs.cornell.edu/people/tj/svm_light/svm_multiclass.html

Event Class	gold (match)	answer (match)	recall	precision	fscore
Gene_expression	1002 (728)	861 (728)	72.65	84.55	78.15
Transcription	174 (87)	123 (87)	50.00	70.73	58.59
Protein_catabolism	15 (7)	9 (7)	46.67	77.78	58.33
Phosphorylation	185 (154)	184 (154)	83.24	83.70	83.47
Localization	191 (99)	116 (99)	51.83	85.34	64.50
=[SVT-TOTAL]=	1567 (1075)	1293 (1075)	68.60	83.14	75.17
Binding	491 (234)	408 (234)	47.66	57.35	52.06
==[EVT-TOTAL]==	2058 (1309)	1701 (1309)	63.61	76.95	69.65
Regulation	385 (120)	221 (120)	31.17	54.30	39.60
Positive_regulation	1443 (549)	980 (549)	38.05	56.02	45.32
Negative_regulation	571 (204)	381 (204)	35.73	53.54	42.86
==[REG-TOTAL]==	2399 (873)	1582 (873)	36.39	55.18	43.86
==[ALL-TOTAL]==	4457 (2182)	3283 (2182)	48.96	66.46	56.38

Table 4: Results on test data [Approximate Span/Approximate Recursive]

5.1 Effectiveness of features

Finding importance of individual feature (e.g. root words, n-gram features, linear features etc.) used in our experiment is not an easy task. Transformation of textual features into numeric features generates a lot of features. For example, in trigger detection step we use 38 features, but when these are converted to numerical data for machine learning purpose, number of features increases to 5 lakhs. Finding the most relevant set of features from this collection is a complex problem. We keep a record of how the original 38 features (represented in text format) are mapped in higher dimensional space containing more than 5 lakh of features. For example, if we use 0-based index for feature, then in trigger detection 0-th feature (from the 38 original features) is mapped to feature indices in the range of 0 to 11,036 and 1-st feature (from 38 original features) is mapped to feature indices in the range of 11,037 to 20,080 in higher dimensional space and so on. Using Linear SVC classifier we select some of the top features which are mapped to the original features. We observe that the features for outgoing edges from the dependency graph are most important for *Gene_expression, Transcription, Localization, Phosphorylation and Binding* type event triggers. For *Positive_regulation,Negative_regulation and Regulation* type event triggers, the most important feature is the dependency chain features.

5.2 Comparison with existing systems

For bio-molecular event extraction, the state-of-the-art system is TEES (Björne, 2014), which ranked first place in BioNLP-ST-2009[12]. Along with this we also compare our proposed system with the other existing systems, which participated

[12]http://www.nactem.ac.uk/tsujii/GENIA/SharedTask/

in BioNLP-2011 shared task (Jin-Dong Kim, 2011) . Our experimental results show recall, precision and F-score values of 50.69%, 68.09% and 58.12%, respectively on development dataset, whereas official result attained by TEES (Björne, 2014) is 52.45%, 60.05% and 55.99% respectively. As compared to the official scores of TEES on the test set (recall: 49.56%, precision: 57.65% and F-score: 53.30%), our system achieves recall, precision and F-score values of 48.96%, 66.46% and 56.38%, respectively. Hence, our system performs better with more than 3 points. While we compare our proposed model with the systems presented in BioNLP-2011 (Jin-Dong Kim, 2011), it shows that we achieve performance very close to the best performing system, FAUST (Sebastian Riedela and Manning, 2011)(recall:49.41%, precision: 64.75% and F-score:56.04%) and better than the second ranked system, UMass, (McCallum, 2011) (recall:48.49%, precision:64.08% and F-score:55.20%). A recently developed system named as EventMine (Makoto Miwa and Ananiadou, 2013), which made use of coreference resolution obtains significant improvement with recall, precision and F-score of 51.25%, 64.92% and 57.28%, respectively. The performance in our model is very close to system, EventMine (Makoto Miwa and Ananiadou, 2013).

5.3 Error Analysis

In order to gain more insights we analyse the outputs to find the errors and their possible causes. We perform quantitative analysis in terms of confusion matrix, and qualitative analysis by looking at the outputs produced by the systems. For trigger detection and classification we observe that the system performs satisfactorily well for gene_expression and phosphorylation types. However, the classifier does not show convincing results for regulation type events which are, in general, difficult to identify and classify. One of the reasons may be the less number of training instances of regulatory events. Classifier finds it difficult to disambiguate the cases when any particular instance belongs to more than one type. For example, token *transfection* originally belongs to both the types, Gene_expression and Positive_regulation, but our system is unable to detect it even as a trigger word. On the other hand, the word *Overexpression* is originally a non-trigger word, but our system detects *Overexpression* as trigger word of types Gene_expression and Positive_regulation both.

In argument extraction step, arguments of the triggers detected in trigger detection and classification step are identified. Relation between a trigger word and its argument is also found out in this step. Possible arguments are proteins and/or event trigger words. Possible relations are *theme* and *cause*. From a closer analysis we see that our system performs satisfactorily in detecting *theme* argument, but for detecting *cause* argument classifier is not very robust. This may be due to the fact that a cause expression could be both a protein (or, NE) or an event trigger expression. The system suffers most for the regulatory events as the errors might have propagated from the earlier step, i.e. trigger detection and classification step. For example trigger word *phosphorylation* in one example sentence is originally a *theme* argument of a regulatory event, but our system is unable to detect the trigger word *phosphorylation* as an argument of that regulatory event.

6   Conclusion and Future Works

In this paper we propose a stacking approach for event extraction. The idea of stacking is to perform cross-validation on the training data set using some learning algorithms in order to create a meta-level data set. Meta-level dataset is formed using predictions generated by the learning algorithms along with the actual output class. In edge detection step, we find out arguments of the triggers detected in trigger detection step using SVM algorithm. To find correct combination of arguments we use rules of bio-molecular events and form an event expression consisting of event trigger, its class and arguments. Experiments on BioNLP-2011 datasets show the efficacy of our proposed model with significant performance improvement over the state-of-the-art systems. This improvement is due to application of stacking aproach along with efficient features. In future we would like to study whether coreference resolution could improve the performance of the system.

References

Jari Björne. 2014. *Biomedical Event Extraction with Machine Learning*. Ph.D. thesis, University of Turku.

L Breiman. 1996. Bagging predictors. In *Machine Learning*, pages 123–140.

Eugene Charniak David McClosky and Mark Johnson. 2006. Effective self-training for parsing. In *Proceedings of the Human Language Technology Conference of the North American Chapter of the ACL*, pages 152–159. New York.

Mihai Surdeanu David McClosky and Christopher D. Manning. 2011. Event extraction as dependency parsing for bionlp 2011. In *Proceedings of BioNLP Shared Task 2011 Workshop*, pages 41–45. June.

Constantine D. Spyropoulos Georgios Sigletos. 2005. Combining information extraction systems using voting and stacked generalization. In *Journal of Machine Learning Research*, volume 6, pages 1751–1782.

Min-Jeong Kim Joo-Young Lee Gumwon Hong Hae-Chang Rim Hyoung-Gyu Lee, Han-Cheol Cho. 2009. A multi-phase approach to biomedical event extraction. in bionlp 09. In *Proceedings of the Workshop on BioNLP*, pages 107–110.

Tomoko Ohta-Robert Bossy Ngan Nguyen Junichi Tsujii Jin-Dong Kim, Sampo Pyysalo. 2011. Overview of bionlp shared task 2011. In *Proceedings of BioNLP Shared Task 2011 Workshop*, pages 1–6. June.

Pyysalo S-Kano Y Tsujii J Kim J-D, Ohta T. 2009. Overview of bionlp09 shared task on event extraction. In *BioNLP 09: Proceedings of the Workshop on BioNLP*, pages 1–9.

Degen Huang Lishuang Li, Yiwen Wang. 2013. Improving feature-based biomedical event extraction system by integrating argument information. In *Proceedings of the BioNLP Shared Task 2013 Workshop*, pages 109–115. August.

Alfonso Valencia Lynette Hirschman, Martin Krallinger. 2007. Proceedings of the second biocreative challenge evaluation workshop. In *CNIO Centro Nacional de Investigaciones Oncologicas*.

Tomoko Ohta Makoto Miwa, Sampo Pyysalo and Sophia Ananiadou. 2013. Wide coverage biomedical event extraction using multiple partially overlapping corpora. In *BMC Bioinformatics*.

Sebastian Riedel Andrew McCallum. 2011. Robust biomedical event extraction with dual decomposition and minimal domain adaptation. In *Proceedings of BioNLP Shared Task 2011 Workshop*, pages 46–50.

Claire Nedellec. 2005. Learning language in logic - genic interaction extraction challenge. In *Proceedings of the 4th Learning Language in Logic Workshop (LLL05)*, pages 31–37.

Heimonen J Bjorne J Boberg J Jarvinen J Salakoski T Pyysalo S, Ginter F. 2007. A corpus for information extraction in the biomedical domain. In *BMC Bioinformatics*, pages 8–50.

ROBERT E. SCHAPIRE. 1990. The strength of weak learnability. In *Machine Learning*, pages 197–227.

Mihai Surdeanub Andrew McCalluma Sebastian Riedela, David McCloskyb and Christopher D. Manning. 2011. Model combination for event extraction in bionlp 2011. In *Proceedings of BioNLP Shared Task 2011 Workshop*, pages 51–55.

Sampo Pyysalo Tomoko Ohta, Jin-Dong Kim and Junichi Tsujii. 2009. Incorporating genetag-style annotation to genia corpus. In *Proceedings of Natural Language Processing in Biomedicine (BioNLP)*, pages 1–9.

Ellen Voorhees. 2007. Overview of trec 2007. In *Sixteenth Text REtrieval Conference (TREC 2007) Proceedings*, pages 1–16. Gaithersburg,Maryland,USA.

D. Wolpert. 1992. Stacked generalization. In *Neural Networks*, pages 241–260.

Syntax and Pragmatics of Conversation: A Case of *Bangla*

Samir Karmakar
School Of Languages and Linguistics
Jadavpur University
India
samirkrmkr@yahoo.co.in

Soumya Sankar Ghosh
School Of Languages and Linguistics
Jadavpur University
India
ghosh.soumya73@yahoo.com

Abstract

Conversation is often considered as the most problematic area in the field of formal linguistics, primarily because of its dynamic emerging nature. The degree of complexity is also high in comparison to traditional sentential analysis. The challenge for developing a formal account for conversational analysis is bipartite: Since the smallest structural unit at the level of conversational analysis is utterance, existing theoretical framework has to be developed in such a manner so that it can take an account of the utterance. In addition to this, a system should be developed to explain the interconnections of the utterances in a conversation. This paper tries to address these two tasks within the transformational and generative framework of Minimalism, proposed by Chomsky, with an emphasis on the Bengali particle *to* – traditionally classified as indeclinable.

1   Introduction

Formal modeling of conversation is still considered as daunting task in the fields of both computational and cognitive linguistics. In spite of the emphasis by Chomsky (1986) on the questions of (a) what constitutes the knowledge of language, (b) how is knowledge of language acquired, and (c) how is knowledge of language put to use, a few approaches has really dealt with the last questions of the above mentioned series. Though formal theories are proposed to deal with the very nature of knowledge of language in linguistics, very less has been done to understand how this knowledge is put to use within the general framework of Transformational and Generative Grammar (henceforth, T-G Grammar). Under this situation, the paper seeks to investigate how knowledge of language is put to use. More specifically, the paper intends to explore how efficiently the semantics and pragmatics of conversation can be explained within the existing theoretical framework of T-G Grammar. Consider the following example:

1.	Speaker_1	*suśīl-ϕ*	*ās-ϕ-b-e*	*to*
		Sushil-Nom	come-ϕ-fut-3.fut	prt
		Will Sushil come?		
	Speaker_2	*hyā suśīl-ϕ*	*ās-ϕ-b-e*	
		yes Sushil-Nom	come-ϕ-fut-3.fut	
		Yes, Sushil will come.		

In this piece of communication, Speaker_1 asks a question about the arrival of Sushil. In response to Speaker_1's query Speaker_2 confirms Sushil's arrival. The current status of linguistic enquiry in the field of syntax and semantics does not deal with this type of connected speech which we encounter often in our daily life. In most of the cases, idealized sentential representation is discussed to unveil the grammatical intricacies. Interestingly, what falls outside of the scope of these sorts of investigation is a systematic exploration into what we would call the grammar of conversation. The importance of studying the grammar of conversation also lies with the fact that conversation embodies many principles of complex dynamic system. Under this situation, this paper attempts to address those problems involved in the formal modeling of the conversational discourse with in framework of Minimalist Program (Chomsky, 1995) with a specific emphasis on the behavior to Bengali particle *to* – traditionally classified as indeclinable.

D S Sharma, R Sangal and A K Singh. Proc. of the 13th Intl. Conference on Natural Language Processing, pages 65–70,
Varanasi, India. December 2016. ©2016 NLP Association of India (NLPAI)

Unlike the major lexical expressions, *to* as a discourse particle hardly contributes in the content of the sentence; rather, it is used to induce some effect of emotional coloring on the content itself. By emotional coloring we do mean various states of minds involved in the act of *questioning, doubting, confirming, requesting* etc. From the perspective of conversation analysis, the expressions like *to* are extremely crucial primarily because of their role in ongoing epistemic negotiations happening between the interlocutors, i.e. the negotiation holding between Speaker_1 and Speaker_2. In virtue of contributing in the epistemic negotiation in terms of various emotional colors as is mentioned above, it expects other sentential discourses. As a consequence, it becomes quite essential to investigate how this capacity of meaning making can be talked about in terms of the pragmatic, semantic and syntactic behaviors of *to*.

To attain the above stated goal, the paper will explore the sentential level semantics and pragmatics of *to* in Bengali in Section 2. In Section 3, this discussion will be further augmented with a discussion of some pragmatic observations regarding the linguistic behavior of *to* to elucidate how current understanding of Pragmatics can provide some important clues about the formalization of the problem stated above. Finally in Section 4, we have proposed a theoretical framework which is crucial in providing a systemic formal account of conversation.

2 Indeclinable *to* in Bengali

Traditionally, *to* is classified as indeclinable for the reason of not being affected by the inflections. It is not being expected by the major lexical categories of a sentence. Its significance lies with its capacity to change the overall sense of a sentence. In addition to this it is also noticed that the incorporation of *to* has its direct bearing on the pitch contour of the sentence itself. Compare the sentences cited in (2) and (3):

2.   *suśīl-ϕ*   *kāl-ϕ*   *bājār-e*
    Sushil-Nom   yesterday-Loc$_{temp}$ market-Loc$_{spatial}$
    giy-ech-il-o
    go-perf-past-3.past
    Sushil had gone to the market yesterday
3.   *suśīl-ϕ*   *to*   *kāl-ϕ*   *bājār-e*
    Sushil-Nom   prt   yesterday-Loc$_{temp}$ market-Loc$_{spatial}$
    giy-ech-il-o
    go-perf-past-3.past
    Sushil had gone to the market yesterday

As per the traditional practice, articulations of declarative sentences seem to be the objective rendition of the *real* world phenomena. For the interpretation of a declarative sentence like (2), one has no need to invoke the knowledge of preceding and following sentences, as if (2) is self-sufficient. In contrast, the sentences like the one cited in (3) is considered as unreal in virtue of being stated in a mood other than declarative. What distinguishes (3) as *unreal* is the presence of *to* in it. Incorporation of *to* in (2) results into an articulation stated in *irrealis* mood. *Irrealis* mood covers a wide range of emotional involvements like questioning, affirming etc. In other words, (3) is not an objective rendition about any worldly phenomena but involves a wide range of subjective necessities to satiate its meaning construing capacity. At least in case of *to*, it is also possible to show that change of its position in (3) confirms different types of requirements raised by the context of communication within which the sentence is embedded in. Consider the following sentences:

4.   *suśīl-ϕ*   *kāl-ϕ*   *to*
    Sushil-Nom   yesterday-Loc$_{temp}$ prt
    bājār-e   *giy-ech-il-o*
    market-Loc$_{spatial}$ go-perf-past-3.past
    Sushil had gone to the market **yesterday**
5.   *suśīl-ϕ*   *kāl-ϕ*   *bājār-e*
    Sushil-Nom   yesterday-Loc$_{temp}$ market-Loc$_{spatial}$
    to   *giy-ech-il-o*
    prt   go-perf-past-3.past
    Sushil had gone **to the market** yesterday
6.   *suśīl-ϕ*   *kāl-ϕ*   *bājār-e*
    Sushil-Nom   yesterday-Loc$_{temp}$ market-Loc$_{spatial}$
    giy-ech-il-o   *to*
    go-perf-past-3.past   prt
    Sushil **had gone** to the market yesterday

The other point which needs to be brought into the notice is the capacity of *to* of putting emphasis on the different constituents of a sentence. To represent emphasis, bold letters are used. Change in position changes the pattern of emphasizing while keeping the emotional content intact. Change in emotional content can only be initiated by ensuring the change in the pitch contour: From Fig. 1, it is visible that in case of *affirming* the stress is put on the syllables quite differently than it is put in case of *questioning*. Moreover the point we want to make here is that emotional conditioning has the power to supersede the lexical conditioning while emphasizing the communicative intention.

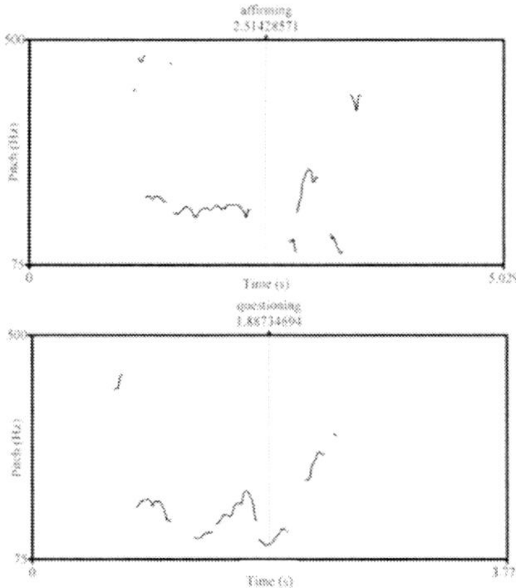

Fig. 1. *suśil kāl bājāre giyechilo to*

It is not hard to show that the ambiguity in the emotional content is always relative to pitch contour carried by an utterance. For example the ambiguity between affirming and questioning/doubting in case of (7) can be solved by taking an account of the associated pitch contour.

7. *suśil-ϕ   ās-ϕ-b-e   to*
    Sushil-Nom   come-ϕ-fut-3.fut   prt
    Will Sushil come?

However, when the sense of request is prevailing, no such ambiguity in terms of emotional content is noticed:

8. *ekhār   es-ϕ-ϕ-o   to*
    once   come-ϕ-pres-2.pres   prt
    Come once.

Beside this, *to* can also appear with *tāi* and *hay*. The resultant forms *tāito* and *hay-to*, can mean several things depending on the context:

9.   *tāi   to   bal-ch-ϕ-i*
     because   prt   tell-cont-pres-1pres
     That is why, I am telling (this).
10   *ha-ϕ-ϕ-y   to   tā-i   bal-ech-ϕ-i*
     be-ϕ-ϕ-3pres.Imp   prt   that-emph   tell-perf-pres-1pres
     Probably, I have said so.

Though *tāito* and *hayto* are composed of two different morphemes, they are often treated as single forms. Because of the anaphoric nature of *tāi*, *tāito* establishes a relation between the current articulation and the previous articulations.

In a conditional construction like (11), inclusion of *to* as in (12) brings different shades of interpretation which is equivalent to *ādau jadi balte dāo* "if at all you allow me to speak".

11. *bal-te   di-le   bal-ϕ-ϕ-i*
     tell-prt   give-prt   tell-ϕ-pres-1.pres
     If you allow then only I speak.
12. *bal-te   di-le   to   bal-ϕ-ϕ-i*
     tell-prt   give-prt   prt   tell-ϕ-pres-1.pres
     If you at all allow me to speak.

to can also be used in a negative sense:

13   *bal-te   di-le   to*
     tell-prt   give-prt   prt
     We are not allowed to speak

When *to* is used in conjunction with the future tense, it results into the sense of doubt and/or questioning. Consider (14):

14. *bal-te   de- ϕ-b-e   to*
     tell-prt   give-ϕ-fut-3.fut   prt
     Will they allow us to speak?

On the basis of this discussion, what we can argue that *to* is primarily an expression not containing anything which is propositional in nature. As a consequence, the meaning construing capacity of it cannot be discussed in terms of the truth conditions. Under this situation what will be of interest is the way we understand the meaning construing capacity of *to*: *to* as an emphatic indeclinable has the power to change the meaning of the propositional content of the sentence within which it is embedded. The appearance of *to* in a sentence has distinct phonological bearing which is directly connected with the emotional coloring effect. Therefore, a theoretical account of the meaning construing capacity of *to* should have some component to deal with the phonological aspect involved with it.

3   Bengali particle to in the light of Pragmatics

On the basis of discussion of Section 2, at least two different aspects of *to* can be talked about: *Firstly*, during conversation, the indeclinable *to* plays a crucial role in imposing the illocutionary force on the propositional content of the articulation. As a consequence the syntax and semantics of *to* is not interpreted within the scope of IP (= Inflectional Phrase); rather we do feel IP is dominated by the dis-course particles like *to*. A similar observation is also made by Searle (1969) while explaining the interrelation holding between illocutionary force (= F) and the propositional content (= p). To represent the interaction, Searle proposes the following scheme: F(p).

Vanderveken (1990) has also supported this proposal.

Secondly, a point to be noted here regarding the linguistic behavior of discourse particles like *to*: The meaning construing behavior of discourse particle *to* is not restricted within the scope of the utterance where it is embedded. Its meaning construing behavior often invokes the context for other utterances. This has already been noticed in the discussions of Section 1 and 2. Therefore, to exhaust its meaning construing capacity, an analytical framework should have some provisions.

Under this situation, then, what we want to look for in this paper is an unified theoretical account which can take care of aforementioned bilayered meaning construction: In one layer, *to* as an emphatic particle will determine the illocutionary aspect of the utterance; and, in other layer it will motivate a move to satisfy the requirements possed by the perlocutionary act of the following utterance. Note the concepts of locution, illocution and perlocution are first proposed by Austin (1975).

4 Discussion

While dealing with the problem of *to*, Bayer *et al.* (2014) considers Rizzi's model, proposed in the year of 1997, where the syntactic representation of force is proposed as the highest functional projection: Rizzi argues CP (= Complimentizer Phrase) is composed of ForceP (= Force Phrase), FocP (= Focus Phrase) and TopP (= Topic Phrase) just like the way IP contains information about TP (= Tense Phrase) and AgrP (= Agreement Phrase). Rizzi's proposal in this regard can be summarized in the following figure:

Rizzi's proposal provides some solution to the incorporation of pragmatic content in the existing framework of syntax. In other words, syntax is now capable enough in taking an account of the utterance.

4.1 Incorporating Illocution

To incorporate the illocutionary aspect of an utterance, the existing theoretical framework has to undergo certain types of modifications. These modifications will be elaborated now in this section. Consider the following examples:

15.   *suśīl-ɸ*   *to*   *ās-ɸ-b-e*
    Sushil-Nom   prt   come-ɸ-fut-3 fut
    Sushil will come.
    [Confirming: *keu nā eleo, suśīl to āsbe*
    "even if nobody comes, (I do believe),
    Sushil will come"]
16.   *suśīl-ɸ*   *ās-ɸ-b-e*   *to*
    Sushil-Nom   come-ɸ-fut-3 fut   prt
    Will Sushil come?

Following Rizzi's proposal, for (15) we get the syntactic representation of Figure 3. As per this representation, *to* originates at the Head-FocP position. As an emphatic particle *to* contains [+emph] feature which belongs to the [+F] class. The DP moves from Spec-AgrSP (= Specifier position of Subject-Agreement-Phrase) to Spec-FocP (= Specifier position of Focus Phrase) in order to get the focus feature checked:

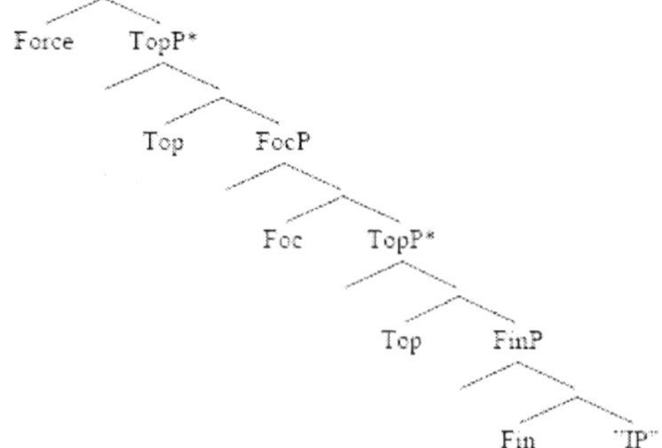

Fig. 2. Rizz's proposal: Pragmatization of Syntax

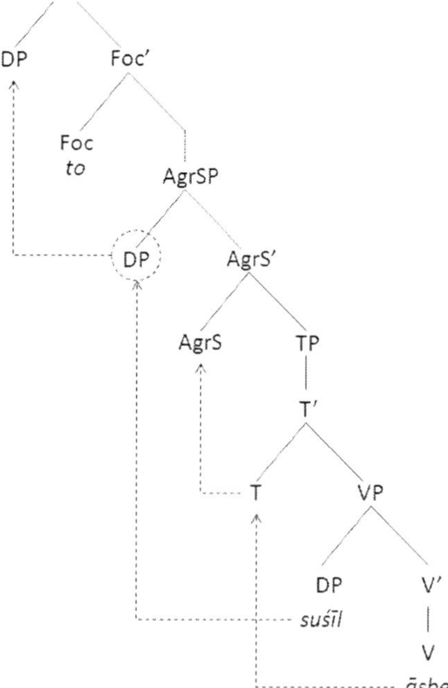

Fig. 3. Syntactic representation of 15

In other words, [+emph] feature belonging to [+F] class feature is attributed to phrase migrated from Spec-AgrSP position to Spec-FocP. The syntactic representation for (16) is can also be provided following the same line of reasoning:

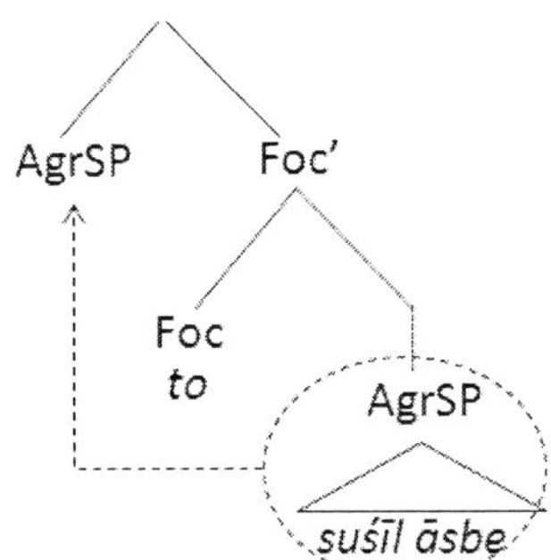

Fig. 4. Syntactic representation of 16

As per these representations, *to* originates in the Head-FocP (= Head position of the Focus Phrase) position with head feature +F. Solution to this specific problem can be generalized over a class of linguistic constructions involving the phenomenon of focusing. The generalization, then, would provide an interpretation (Fig. 5) that Head-FocP attracts the emphasized XP towards itself in order to get the +F feature checked; and this in turn remains the sole motivation for the movement of emphasized XP to the Spec-FocP position.

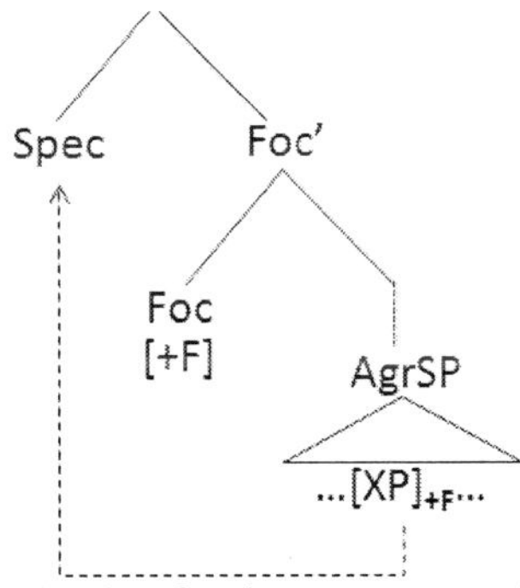

Fig. 5. Motivation for the movement of the emphasized phrase in the Spec-FocP position

In other words, the proposal creates a motivation for the phrase marked with +F to move out from its original position to a higher node to satisfy the need of interpretation: What remains uninterpreted in its original position becomes completely interpretable due to its movement to the Spec-ForceP position. Till now, the first layer of the bilayered representation discussed in Section 3 is outlined. Rest of this article will now deal with the second layer of the bilayered representation.

To address the problem of capturing illocutionary aspect of an utterance, we will adopt a way similar to the one we have discussed above following the proposal developed in Karmakar *et al.* (2016). As per this proposal the FocP moved to Spec-ForceP position to check the head feature of the ForceP. Note that in (15) the head feature is [+R]; and, in (16) it is [+Dr].

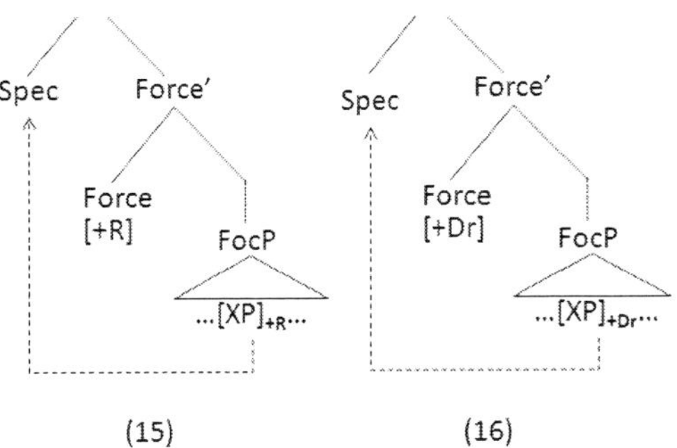

Fig. 6. Capturing illocution

To propose an effective way to capture illocution we would like to accommodate the taxonomy of speech acts as is proposed by Searle (1976): As per this proposal, speech acts can be reduced into five main types namely (a) representatives (= [+R] = asserting, concluding etc.), (b) directives (= [+Dr] = requesting, questioning etc.), (c) commissives (= [+C] = promising, threatening, offering etc.), (d) expressive (= [+E] = thanking, apologizing, welcoming, congratulating etc.), and (e) declarations (= [+Dl] = excommunicating, declaring, christening etc.)

4.2 Conversation in terms of illocution and perlocution

Conversation differs from the isolated utterances in several respects: In conversation, utterances often stand in some relation to the other utterances in order to satisfy different degrees of expectancies. Conversation is not something static rather it is a dynamic network of different intentions. Following Austin, these intentions can be best talked about in terms of different acts – namely locutionary act, illocutionary act and perlocutionary act. Locutionary act is primarily concerned about those facts which are central in making sense in language; Illocutionary act is performed by the speaker to express that intention which is not directly associated with the discrete lexicalized content of the articulation; And, perlocutionary act is all about what follows an utterance in a conversation.

Following *Karmakar et al.* (2016), we propose a further split of ForceP into perlocutionary phrase (= PerlocP) and illocutionary phrase (= IllocP) to capture the way different types of speech acts interacts with each other during conversation. In our earlier discussion, we have shown how illocutionary act can be handled within the syntactic framework of minimalist program; and, now we are proposing the following scheme of representation for (1) as an exemplar to show how syntax of conversation can be modeled to take an account of the emerging network of intentions during different turns:

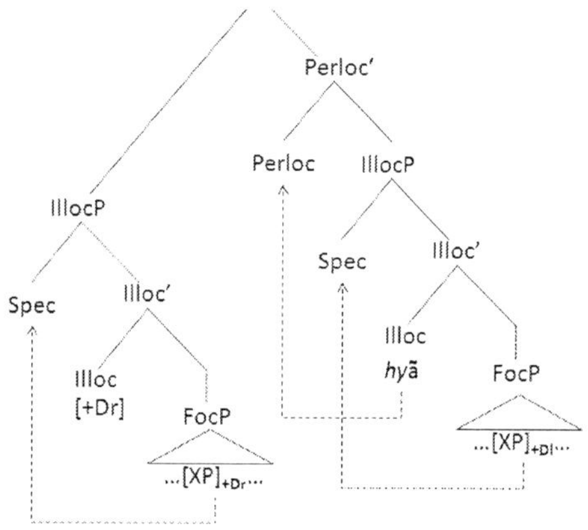

Fig. 7. A Minimalist representation of (1) in terms of perlocution and illocution

As per this representation IllocP dominating …[XP]$_{+Dr}$… connected with the IllocP dominating …[XP]$_{+Dl}$… not under any influence of the illocutionary acts (marked with subscripts +Dr and +Dl respectively) but definitely due to the act of perlocution expected by the utterance of Speaker_1. Also note that, *hyã* appears in the Head-IllocP position and moves to the Head-PerlocP position to satisfy the expectancy of the speech act performed by Speaker_1. This position is a bit different from what Karmakar *et al.* (2016) has claimed in their paper.

5   Conclusion

Since conversation is the most prevalent form of human communication, a formal study of conversation as an embodiment of complex adaptive system may reveal various intricacies involved in the process of conversing. We have attempted one such intricacy to explore which *principles* and *parameters* are in work to make a communication meaningful. A little attention will reveal the fact that the approach we have argued for encompasses the questions of both "what constitutes the knowledge of language" as well as "how this knowledge is put to use". Future research along this line demands a more rigorous characterization of various concepts which remain crucial in defining their role in construing the structure of conversation in general.

Reference

Austin, J. (1975). *How to Do Things with Words* (2nd ed.). Oxford: Clarendon Press.

Bayer, J., Dasgupta, P., Mukhopadhyay, S., & Ghosh, R. (2014, February 06-08). *Functional Structure and the Bangla Discourse Particle to*. Retrieved July 19, 2015, from http://ling.uni-kon-stanz.de/pages/StructureUtterance/web/Publications_&_Talks_files/Bayer_Dasgupta_MukhopadhyayGhosh_SALA.pdf

Chomsky, N. (1986). *Knowledge of Language*. New York: Praeger.

Chomsky, N. (1995). *The Minimalist Program* (3rd ed.). Massachusets: The MIT Press.

Karmakar, S., Ghosh, S., & Banerjee, A. (2016). *A Syntactic Framework of Conversational Pragmatics of Bengali*. Unpublished manuscript.

Rizzi, L. (1997). The fine structure of the left periphery. In L. Haegeman, *Elements of Grammar* (pp. 281-337). Dordrecht: Kluwer.

Searle, J. (1969). *Speech Acts*. Cambridge: Cambridge University Press.

Searle, J. (1976). The classification of illocutionary acts. *Language in Society*, 5, 1-23.

Vanderveken, D. (1990). *Meaning and Speech Acts* (Vol. I). Cambridge: Cambridge University Press.

Dependency grammars as Haskell programs

Tomasz Obrębski
Adam Mickiewicz University
Poznań, Poland
obrebski@amu.edu.pl

Abstract

In the paper we try to show that a lazy functional language such as Haskell is a convenient framework not only for implementing dependency parsers but also for expressing dependency grammars directly in the programming language in a compact, readable and mathematically clean way. The parser core, supplying necessary types and functions, is presented together with two examples of grammars: one trivial and one more elaborate, allowing to express a range of complex grammatical constraints such as long distance agreement. The complete Haskell code of the parser core as well the grammar examples is included.

1 Introduction

Functional programming is nowadays probably the most rapidly developing subfield in the domain of theory and implementation of programming languages. Functional languages, with Haskell as their flagship, are continuously evolving, mostly by absorbing more and more mathematics (abstract algebra, category theory). This translates into their increasing expressiveness, which is directly usable by programmers.

The combination of keywords *functional programming* and *parsing* usually brings to mind the monadic parsing technique (Hutton and Meijer, 1998) developed as an attractive functional offer for parser builders. This technology is dedicated mostly to artificial languages. Much less work has been done in functional programming paradigm regarding natural language parsing technologies. The outstanding exception is the *Grammatical Framework* environment (Ranta, 2011). Written in Haskell with extensive use of higher-order abstraction and laziness property, it offers impressive capabilities of making generalizations in all conceivable dimensions in a large and highly multilingual language model including morphological, syntactic and semantic layers. Some other works, which may be mentioned here, are due to Ljunglöf (2004), de Kok and Brouwer (2009), Eijck (2005).

As far as dependency-based parsing and language description is concerned (Kubler et al., 2009), the author is not aware of any attempts to apply functional programming techniques.

Below we try to show that a lazy functional language such as Haskell is a convenient framework not only for implementing dependency parsers but also for expressing dependency grammars directly as Haskell code in a compact, readable, and mathematically clean way.

A question may arise: why the ability to write a grammar directly in a programming language should be considered desirable. There are already plenty of grammatical formalisms to choose from. And what makes Haskell more interesting target language then others, e.g. Python. The answer to the first questions is: (1) the grammar writer is free in choosing the way the lexical and grammatical description is formulated; (2) full strength of the language may be used according to the needs. DCG grammars (Pereira and Warren, 1980) are a good example here. The answer to the second one is: (1) the grammar may be expressed in declarative way in the language very close to that of mathematics, in terms of basic mathematical notions such as sets, functions, and relations; (2) functional character of Haskell allows for making generalizations wherever the grammar writer finds it advantageous; (3) Haskell syntax allows for formulating grammatical statements in a compact, clean, mathematical manner; (4) Haskell libraries supply support for mathematical objects frequently used in language description, e.g. lattices (cf. Koster, 1992; Levy and Pollard, 2001),

D S Sharma, R Sangal and A K Singh. Proc. of the 13th Intl. Conference on Natural Language Processing, pages 71–80,
Varanasi, India. December 2016. ©2016 NLP Association of India (NLPAI)

semirings (cf. Goodman, 1999), to mention just two.

2 The Haskell toolbox

Haskell is a purely functional programming language, applying lazy evaluation strategy, see (Jones, 2002) for language specification, (Lipovaca, 2011) for introductory course, and (Yorgey, 2009) for information on advanced Haskell algebraic type classes. We will take a closer look at two Haskell types on which the parser and grammar implementation is based:

[a]   – list of elements of type a

a →[a] – a function taking an argument of type a and returning a list of elements of type a.

Below, we are going inspect the properties of those types as well as functional tools which will allow us to operate on them conveniently.

Lists are used to store collections of values. Their interpretation depends on the context. We use lists for representing sequences, sets, alternatives of values as well as possible lack of a value (singleton list - value exists, empty list - no value). The other important type is the type of functions that take an argument of some type a and return a list of values of type a, i.e. the type a →[a]. These are functions which return sequences, sets, alternatives, or a possibly lacking value, all represented by lists. Here are some examples:

- the function which extends the parse with a new node produces several alternative results for the word "fly" (type Parse →[Parse]);

- the function returning the preceding node has no value for the first node (type Node →[Node]);

- the function computing transitive heads of a node returns a set of nodes (type Node →[Node]).

A list type [a] is obtained by applying the list functor [] to some type a, with no constraints on what a is. Two properties are particularly useful: (1) the list functor [] is an instance of Monad; (2) a list of elements of any type is an instance of Monoid.

Functions and operators from both classes (Monoid and Monad) may be intermixed for lists

because they share the value-combining operation: both the *join*[1] operation in the list monad and the operation in the monoid [a] is concatenation. An important consequence of the fact that [a] is an instance of Monoid is that all functions which return [a] are also instances of Monoid. Below we summarize the list of operators on values of type [a] and a -> [a], supplied by classes Monad and Monoid, which we will make use of.

- $\oplus :: [a] \to [a] \to [a]$
  (instance Monoid [a])

  xs $\oplus$ ys combines values contained in xs with those in ys producing one list with both xs and ys;

- $\oplus :: (a \to [a]) \to (a \to [a]) \to (a \to [a])$
  (instance Monoid (a -> [a]))

  f $\oplus$ g combines functions f and g, which both return a list of values of type a, into a single function returning one list that contains the return values of both f and g;

- >=> :: $(a \to [a]) \to (a \to [a]) \to (a \to [a])$
  (instance Monad [])

  f >=> g composes functions f and g in one function (of the same type). The resulting function applies g to each value from the list returned by f and returns the results combined in one list;

- >>= :: $[a] \to (a \to [a]) \to [a]$
  (instance Monad [])

  [a] >>= f applies f to all values from [a] and combines the results.

In addition to the operators listed above, we will use the function:

- pure :: $a \to [a]$
  (instance Applicative [])

  which returns a singleton list containing its argument. It is equivalent to the monadic return function, but it reads much better in our contexts.

Having a function of type $a \to [a]$, we will be frequently also interested in its transitive closure or reflexive transitive closure (strictly speaking - the term *transitive closure* refers to the underlying

---

[1]The operation which transforms a list of lists into a flat list.

relation). We will introduce the family of closure functions. They are used for example to obtain the function which computes transitive heads from the function that returns the head.

```
clo,mclo,rclo,mrclo :: (a → [a]) → a → [a]
clo f    = f >=> ( pure ⊕ clo f )
rclo f   = pure ⊕ clo f
mclo f   = f >=> mrclo f
mrclo f x = let fx = f x in if null fx
                            then pure x
                            else fx >>= mrclo f
```

The function `clo` computes the closure of its argument function `f`. The function `f` is (Kleisli) composed with the function which combines ($\oplus$) its arguments (pure values of `f`) with the values of recursive application of `clo f` on each of those arguments. The function `rclo` computes the reflexive transitive closure of its argument function `f`. The argument itself (`pure`) is combined ($\oplus$) with the values returned by `clo f` applied to this argument. The `m*` versions of `clo` and `rclo` return only maximal elements of closures, i.e. those for which the argument function `f` returns no value.

The operators and functions presented above will be expecially useful for working with relations. This is undoubtedly the most frequently used mathematical notion when talking about dependency structures. We use relations to express relative position of a word (node) with respect to another word (predecessor, neighbor, dependent, head). We also frequently make use of such operations on relations as transitive closure transitive head, reflexive transitive dependent) or composition (transitive head <u>of</u> left neighbour).

Haskell is a functional language. We will thus have to capture operations on relations by means of functions. The nearest functional relatives of a relation are image functions.

Given a relation $\mathbf{R} \subset A \times B$, the image functions $\mathbf{R}[\cdot]$ are defined as follows (1 – image of an element, 2 – image of a set):

$$
\begin{aligned}
(1) \quad & \mathbf{R}[x] & = & \quad \{y \mid xRy\} & \text{where } x \in A \\
(2) \quad & \mathbf{R}[X] & = & \quad \{y \mid x \in X \land xRy\} & \text{where } X \subset A
\end{aligned}
$$

Haskell expressions corresponding to image functions and their use are summarized below (x has type `a`, xs has type `[a]`, r and s have type `a → [a]`):

$$
\begin{aligned}
&\mathbf{R}[x] & &\text{r x} & &\text{(or pure x >>= r)} \\
&\mathbf{R}[X] & &\text{xs >>= r} \\
&(\mathbf{R} \circ \mathbf{S})[\cdot] & &\text{s >=> r} \\
&(\mathbf{R} \cup \mathbf{S})[\cdot] & &\text{r} \oplus \text{s} \\
&\mathbf{R}^{+}[\cdot] & &\text{clo r} \\
&\mathbf{R}^{*}[\cdot] & &\text{rclo r}
\end{aligned}
$$

3 Data structures

The overall design of the parser is traditional. Words are read from left to right and a set of alternative parses is built incrementally. We start with describing data types on which the parser core is based. They are designed to fit well into the functional environment[2].

3.1 The Parse type

A (partial) parse is represented as a sequence of parse steps. Each step consumes one word and introduces a new node to the parse. It also adds all the arcs between the new node and the nodes already present in the parse. All the data added in a parse step – the index of the new node, its category and the information on its connections with the former nodes – will be encapsulated in a value of type `Step`:

```
type Parse = [Step]
data Step  = Step Ind Cat [Arc] [Arc]
             deriving (Eq,Ord)
```

A value of type `Step` is built of the type constructor of the same name and four arguments:

(1) the word's index of type `Ind`. It reflects the position of the word in the sentence. It is also used as the node identifier within a parse;

(2) the syntactic category of the node represented by a value of type `Cat`;

(3) the arc linking the node to its left head. This value will be present only if the node is preceded by its head in the surface ordering. List is used to represent a possibly missing value.

(4) the list of arcs which connect the node with its left dependents.

We also make `Step` an instance of the classes `Eq` and `Ord`. This will allow us to use comparison operators (based on node index order) with values of type `Node` introduced below.

The value of type `Arc` is a pair:

---

[2]The functional programming friendly representation of a parse was inspired by (Erwig, 2001).

```
type Arc = (Role,Ind)
```

where `Ind` is the integer type.

```
type Ind = Int
```

For the sentence *John saw Mary.* we obtain the following sequence of the parse steps:

```
[ Step 3 N [(Cmpl,2)] [],
  Step 2 V [] [(Subj,1)],
  Step 1 N [] []          ]
```

We introduce three operators for constructing a parse:

```
infixl 4 <<, +->, +<-
(<<) :: Parse -> (Ind,Cat) -> Parse
p << (i,c) = Step i c [] [] : p

(+->),(+<-) :: Parse -> (Role,Ind) -> Parse
(Step i c [] d : p) +-> (r,j) = Step i c [(r,j)] d  : p
(Step i c h  d : p) +<- (r,j) = Step i c h ((r,j):d) : p
```

The operator `<<` adds an unconnected node with index `i` and category `c` to the parse `p`. The operator `+->` links the node `i` as the head of the current (last) node with depencency of type `r`. The operator `+<-` links the node `i` as the dependent of the current node with depencency of type `r`. All the operators are left associative and can therefore be sequenced without parentheses. The expression constructing the parse for the sentence *John saw Mary.* is presented in Figure 1.

3.2 The `Node` type

In i-th step, the parser adds the node i to the parse and tries to establish its connections with nodes $i-1$, $i-2$, ..., 1. In order to make a decision whether the dependency of type r between nodes i and j, $j < i$, is allowed, various properties of the node j has to be examined. They depend on the characteristics of the grammar. Some of them are easily accessible, such as the node's category. Other ones are not accessible directly, such as e.g. the set of roles on outgoing arcs, categories of dependent nodes.

When the parser has already performed n steps, full information on each node $i, i < n$, including its connections with all nodes $j, j < n$, is available. In order to make this information accessible for the node i, we use the structure of the following type for representing a node:

```
data Node = Node [Step] [Step] deriving (Eq,Ord)
```

The first list of steps is the parse history up to the step i. The second list contains the steps which follow i, arranged from the one directly succeeding i up to the last one in the partial parse.

The node representation contains the whole parse, as seen from the node's perspective. The redundancy in the node representation, resulting from the fact that the whole parse is stored in all nodes during a computation, is apparent only. Lazy evaluation guarantees that those parts of the structure, which will not be used during the computation, will never be built. Thus, we can see a value of type `Node`, as representing a node equipped with the potential capability to inspect its context. In the last node of a parse, the *history* list will contain the whole parse and the *future* list will be empty.

```
lastNode :: Parse → Node
lastNode p = Node p []
```

The following functions will simplify extracting information from a `Node` value.

```
ind :: Node → Ind
ind (Node (Step i _ _ _ : _) _) = i
cat :: Node → Cat
cat (Node (Step _ c _ _ : _) _) = c

hArc, dArcs :: Node → [Arc]
hArc (Node (Step _ _ h _ : _) _) = h
dArcs (Node (Step _ _ _ d : _) _) = d
```

The most essential property of a `Node` value is probably that all the other nodes from the partial parse it belongs to may be accessed from it.

```
lng, rng :: Node → [Node]
lng (Node (s:s':p) q) = [Node (s':p) (s:q)]
lng _                 = []
rng (Node p (s:q))    = [Node (s:p) q]
rng _                 = []

preds, succs :: Node → [Node]
preds = clo lng
succs = clo rng
```

The function `lng` (left neighbour) returns the preceding node. The last step in the *history* list is moved to the beginning of the *future* list, provided that the *history* list contains at least two nodes. The function `rng` (right neighbour) does the opposite and returns the node's successor. The `clo` function was used to compute the list of predecessors and successors of a node.

The next group of functions allows for accessing the head and dependents of a node. List comprehensions allow for their compact implementation:

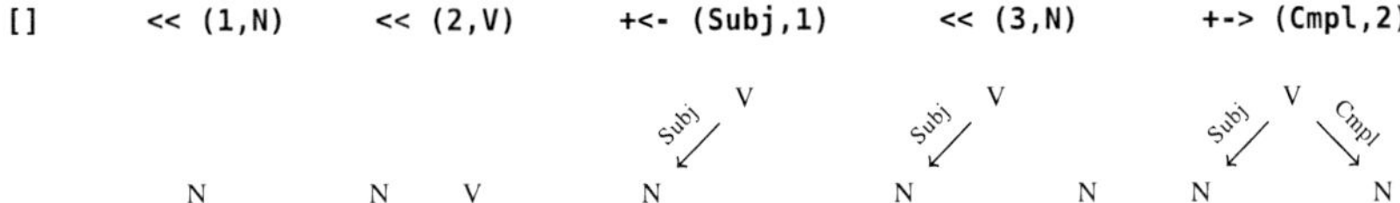

Figure 1: The expression for the parse: [Step 3 N [(Cmpl,2)] [], Step 2 V [] [(Subj,1)], Step 1 N [] []]

```
ldp',rdp',dp',lhd',rhd',hd' :: Node → [(Role, Node)]
ldp' v = [(r,v')|v'←preds v,(r,i)←dArcs v,ind v'≡i]
rdp' v = [(r,v')|v'←succs v,(r,i)←hArc v',ind v≡i]
dp'    = ldp' ⊕ rdp'

lhd' v = [(r,v')|v'←preds v,(r,i)←hArc v,ind v'≡i]
rhd' v = [(r,v')|v'←succs v,(r,i)←dArcs v',ind v≡i]
hd'    = lhd' ⊕ rhd'
```

The function `ldp'` (left dependent) returns the list of left dependents of the node v together with corresponding roles: these are such elements v' from the list of predecessors of v, for which there exists an arc in dArcs v with index equal to the index of v'. To get the list of right dependents (rdp') of v, we select those nodes from the list succs v, whose left head's index is equal to that of v. The functions rhd' (right head) and lhd' (left head) are implemented analogously. The function dp' which computes all dependents is defined by combining the functions ldp' and rdp' with the operator ⊕ (similarly hd').

These primed functions are not intended to be used directly by grammar writers (hence their primed names)[3]. They will serve as the basis for defining the basic parser interface functions: group of functions for computing related nodes (ldp, rdp, ...), group of functions for computing roles on in- and outgoing arcs (ldpr, rdpr, ...), and finally the group of function for accessing nodes linked with dependency of a specific type (ldpBy, rdpBy, ...).

```
ldp, rdp, dp, lhd, rhd, hd :: Node → [Node]
ldp = fmap snd . ldp'
( similarly rdp, dp, lhd, rhd, hd)

ldpBy, rdpBy, dpBy :: Role → Node → [Node]
ldpBy r v = [ v' | (r,v') ← ldp' v ]
rdpBy r v = [ v' | (r,v') ← rdp' v ]
dpBy r    = ldpBy r ⊕ rdpBy r

ldpr, rdpr, dpr, lhdr, rhdr, hdr :: Node → [Role]
ldpr = fmap fst . ldp'
( similarly rdpr, dpr, lhdr, rhdr, hdr)

lhdBy,rhdBy,hdBy :: Role → Node → [Node]
```

```
lhdBy r v = [ v' | (r,v') ← lhd' v ]
rhdBy r v = [ v' | (r,v') ← rhd' v ]
hdBy r    = lhdBy r ⊕ rhdBy r
```

The functions for navigating among nodes[4] are summarized in Figure 2.

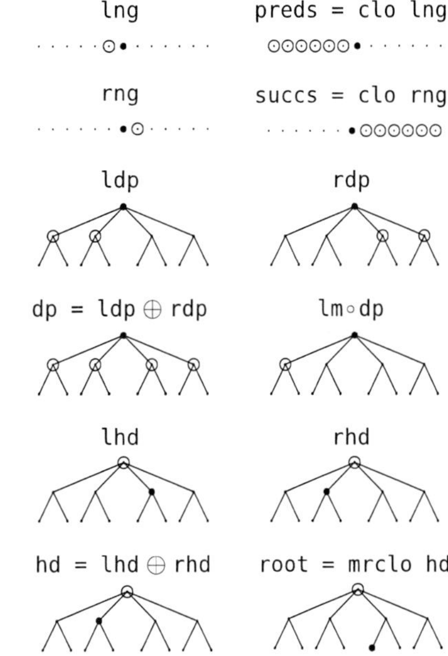

Figure 2: Node functions (black dot - the argument, circles - values)

We will end with defining three more useful functions: lm and rm for choosing the leftmost/rightmost node from a list of nodes, and hdless for checking whether the argument node has no head.

```
lm, rm :: [Node] -> [Node]
lm [] = []
lm xs = [minimum xs]
rm [] = []
rm xs = [maximum xs]

hdless :: Node → Bool
hdless = null ∘ hd
```

---

[3]They are not of type a →[a] and are far less usefull then e.g. functions of type Node →[Node] defined below (ldp, rdp, ...).

[4]Many other useful functions for navigating among parse nodes may be defined using the ones introduced above, for example: subtree = rclo dp, root = mrclo hd, tree = root >=> subtree, siblings = hd >=> dp, etc.

4   The parser core

We will begin by defining the `step` function. Given a parse and a word, it computes the next `Step`. This computation may be decomposed into two independent operations: `shift` – add a new `Step` with only word's category and the index, with no connections; and `connect` – create dependency connections for the last node in the parse. The operations `shift` and `connect` will resort to two different information sources external to the parser: the lexicon and the grammar, respectively. In the impelementation of `shift` we assume the existence of an external lexicon (see Section 5), which provides a function `dic` of type `Word -> [Cat]`. This function, given a word `w` as argument, returns a list of its syntactic categories.

```
type Word = String

shift :: Word → Parse → [Parse]
shift w p = [ p << (nextId p, c) | c←dic w]
          where nextId [] = 1
                nextId (Step i _ _ _ : _) = i + 1
```

The `shift` function adds to the parse `p` a new unconnected node with `w`'s syntactic category and the appropriately set index. As the word `w` may be assigned many alternative syntactic categories due to its lexical ambiguity, a list of parses is produced – one parse for each alternative reading of `w`.

In the impelementation of `connect` we assume the existence of an external grammar (see Section 5), which is required to offer the functions `heads`, `deps` of type `Node -> [(Role,Node)]` and `pass` of type `Node -> Bool`. The functions `heads` and `deps` take a node as argument and return the list of all candidate connections to heads or dependents, respectively. The `pass` function allows the grammar to perform the final verification of the complete parse (the last node is passed as the argument).

We first define two functions `addHead` and `addDep`. They add connections proposed by the grammar for the last node in the parse. The functions also check whether the candidate for the dependent node has no head attached so far.

```
addHead, addDep :: Parse → [Parse]
addHead p = [ p +-> (r,ind v') | let v = lastNode p,
                                 hdless v,
                                 (r,v') ← heads v ]
addDep p  = [ p +<- (r,ind v') | let v = lastNode p,
                                 (r,v') ← deps v,
                                 hdless v' ]
```

With these functions we can define `connect` as follows:

```
connect :: Parse → [Parse]
connect = (addDep >=> connect) ⊕ addHead ⊕ pure
```

Parses returned by `addDep`, `addHead`, are combined together with the unchanged parse (`pure`). Parses returned by `addDep` are recursively passed to `connect`, because there are may be more than one dependent to connect. The `connect` function produces parses with all possible combinations of valid connections.

Now, the step computation may be implemented by combining `shift w` and `connect`.

```
step :: Word → Parse → [Parse]
step w = shift w >=> connect
```

The whole parse will be computed (function `steps`) by applying left fold on a word list using the `step` function inside the list monad – we just have to flip the first two arguments of `step` to get the type needed by `foldM`.

```
steps :: [Word] → [Parse]
steps = foldM (flip step) []
```

Finally, the `parser` function selects complete parses (containing one tree, thus satisfying $(\equiv 1) \circ size$) and asks the grammar for final verification (`pass ∘ lastNode`).

```
parser :: [Word] → [Parse]
parser = filter ((≡1)∘size ∧ pass∘lastNode) ∘ steps
```

5   Lexicons and grammars

In order to turn the bare parser engine defined above into a working syntactic analysis tool we has to provide it with a lexicon and a grammar. We are short of exactly six elements: the types `Cat` and `Role`, and the functions `dic`, `heads`, `deps`, and `pass`.

Definition of a lexicon and a grammar accounts to defining these six elements making use of the set of 30 interface functions, namely: `cat`, `lng`, `rng`, `preds`, `succs`, `ldp`, `rdp`, `dp`, `lhd`, `rhd`, `hd`, `ldpr`, `rdpr`, `dpr`, `lhdr`, `rhdr`, `hdr`, `ldpBy`, `rdpBy`, `dpBy`, `lhdBy`, `rhdBy`, `hdBy`, `lm`, `rm`, `hdless`, `clo`, `rclo`, `mclo`, `mrclo` supplemented with ... the whole Haskell environment. Two examples are given below. It should be stressed that the examples are by no means meant to be understood as proposals of grammatical systems or descriptive solutions, they unique role is the illustration of using Haskell language for the purpose of formulating grammatical description.

5.1 Example 1

The first example is minimalistic. We will implement a free word order grammar which is able to analyze Latin sentences composed of words *Joannes, Mariam, amat.* The six elements required by the parser are presented below. The part of speech affixes 'n' and 'a' stand for 'nominative' and 'accusative'.

```
data Cat  = Nn | Na | V deriving (Eq,Ord)
data Role = Subj | Cmpl deriving (Eq,Ord)

dic "Joannes"   = [Nn]
dic "Mariam"    = [Na]
dic "amat"      = [V]

heads d = [ (r,h) | h ← preds d,
                    r ← link (cat h) (cat d) ]

deps  h = [ (r,d) | d ← preds h,
                    r ← link (cat h) (cat d) ]

pass    = const True

link V Nn       = [Subj]
link V Na       = [Cmpl]
link _ _        = []
```

There is one little problem with the above grammar: duplicate parses are created as a result of attaching the same dependents in different order. we can solve this problem by slightly complicating the definition of deps function and substituting the expression $lm \circ (ldp \oplus pure) >=> preds$ in the place of preds. This expression defines a function which returns predecessors (preds) of the leftmost (lm) left dependent (ldp) of the argument node or of the node itself (pure) if no dependents are present yet.

Examples of the parser's output:

```
> parse "Joannes amat Mariam"

[ [ Step 3 Nacc [(Cmpl,2)] [],
    Step 2 V [] [(Subj,1)],
    Step 1 Nnom [] [] ] ]

> parse "Joannes Mariam amat"

[ [ Step 3 V [] [(Subj,1),(Cmpl,2)],
    Step 2 Nacc [] [],
    Step 1 Nnom [] [] ] ]
```

The parsing algorithm which results from combining the parser from Section 4 with the above grammar is basically equivalent to the ESDU variant from (Covington, 2001).

5.2 Example 2

The second example shows a more expressive grammar architecture which allows for handling some complex linguistic phenomena such as: constraints on cardinality of roles in dependent connections; local[5] agreement; non-local agreement between coordinated nouns; non-local requirement of a relative pronoun to be present inside a verb phrase in order to consider it as a relative clause; long distance agreement between a noun and a relative pronoun nested arbitrarily deep in the relative clause.

These phenomena are present for example in Slavonic languages such as Polish. In this example the projectivity requirement will be additionally imposed on the tree structures.

In the set of categories, the case and gender markers are taken into account: n=nominative, a=accusative, m=masculine, f=feminine; REL=relative pronoun. The lexicon is implemented as before[6]:

```
data Cat  = Nmn | Nfn | Nma | Nfa | Vm | Vf
            | ADJmn | ADJfn | ADJma | ADJfa
            | RELmn | RELfn | RELma | RELfa | CONJ
          deriving (Eq,Ord)

data Role = Subj | Cmpl | Coord | CCmpl | Rel | Mod
          deriving (Eq,Ord)

dic "Jan"      = [Nmn]    dic "widział" = [Vm]
dic "Jana"     = [Nma]    dic "widziała"= [Vf]
dic "Maria"    = [Nfn]    dic "czyta"   = [Vm,Vf]
dic "Marię"    = [Nfa]    dic "czytał"  = [Vm]
dic "książka"  = [Nfn]    dic "czytała" = [Vf]
dic "książkę"  = [Nfa]    dic "który"   = [RELmn]
dic "dobra"    = [ADJfn]  dic "którego" = [RELma]
dic "dobrą"    = [ADJfa]  dic "która"   = [RELfn]
                          dic "którą"   = [RELfa]
                          dic "i"       = [CONJ]
```

We introduce word classes, which are technically predicates on nodes. Functions of type a →Bool are instances of Lattice class and may be combined with operators ∨ (join) and ∧ (meet), e.g. nominal class:

```
v,n,adj,rel,conj :: Node → Bool
v    = (∈ [Vm,Vf]) ∘ cat
n    = (∈ [Nmn,Nma,Nfn,Nfa]) ∘ cat
adj  = (∈ [ADJmn,ADJma,ADJfn,ADJfa]) ∘ cat
rel  = (∈ [RELmn,RELma,RELfn,RELfa]) ∘ cat
conj = (≡ CONJ) ∘ cat

nominal :: Node → Bool
nominal = n ∨ rel

nom,acc,masc,fem :: Node → Bool
```

---

[5]By the term *local* we mean: limited to the context of a single dependency connection.

[6]*Jan(a)* = John, *Mari(a/ę)* = Mary, *książk(a/ę)* = book, *dobr(a/ą)* = good, *widział(a)* = to see$_{PAST}$, *czyta*=to read$_{PRES}$, *czytał(a)* = to read$_{PAST}$, *któr(y/ego/a/ą)* = which/who/that, *i* = and

```
nom  = (∈ [Nmn,Nfn,ADJmn,ADJfn,RELmn,RELfn]) ∘ cat
acc  = (∈ [Nma,Nfa,ADJma,ADJfa,RELma,RELfa]) ∘ cat
masc = (∈ [Vm,Nmn,Nma,ADJmn,ADJma,RELmn,RELma]) ∘ cat
fem  = (∈ [Vf,Nfn,Nfa,ADJfn,ADJfa,RELfn,RELfa]) ∘ cat
```

The grammar has the form of a list of rules. The type Rule is defined as follows:

```
data Rule = Rule Role (Node→Bool) (Node→Bool) [Constr]
```

A value of type Rule is built of the type constructor of the same name and four arguments: the first is the dependency type (role), the next two specify categories allowed for the head and the dependent, given in the form of predicates on nodes. The fourth argument of is the list of constraints imposing additional conditions. The type of a constraint in a function from a pair of nodes (head, dependent) to Bool.

```
type Constr = (Node,Node) → Bool
```

The functions heads, deps, and pass take the following form:

```
heads d = [ (r,h) | h ← visible d, r ← roles h d ]
deps  h = [ (r,d) | d ← visible h, r ← roles h d ]
pass    = const True

visible = mrclo (lm ∘ dp) >=> lng >=> rclo lhd

roles h d = [ r | Rule r p q cs ← rules,
                  p h,  q d,
                  all ($ (h,d)) cs ]
```

The function visible (see Figure 3) returns the list of nodes connectable without violating the projectivity requirement. These are reflexive transitive left heads (rclo lhd) of the left neighbour (lng) of the maximal transitive leftmost dependent (mrclo (lm∘dp)). The function roles, given two nodes as arguments, selects roles which may label dependency connection between them. For each rule Rule r p q cs in the list of rules, it checks whether the head and dependent nodes satisfy the predicates imposed on their categories (p and q, respectively), then verifies whether all constrains cs apply to the head-dependent pair (($ (h,d)).

```
visible = mrclo (lm∘dp) >=> lng >=> rclo lhd
```

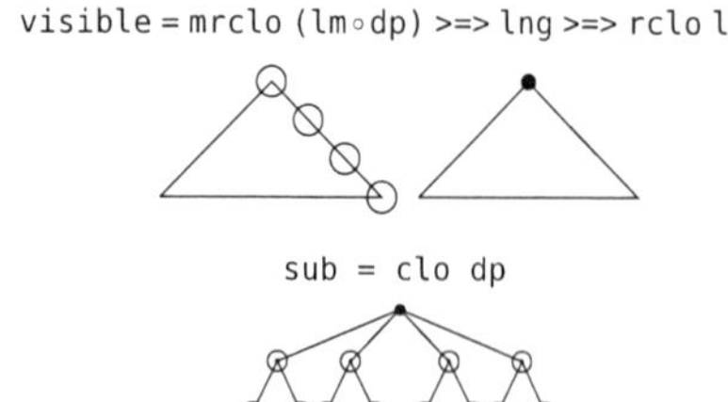

```
sub = clo dp
```

Figure 3: Node functions visible and sub

The set of constraints for our example include order constraints (left, right), agreement in gender (agrG), case (agrC), both case and gender (agrCG), agreement between coordinated nouns (agrCoord), and the constraint related to relative close attachment (agrRel, see below).

```
right      (h,d) = h < d
left       (h,d) = d < h
agrG       (h,d) = (all masc ∨ all fem) [h,d]
agrC       (h,d) = (all nom ∨ all acc) [h,d]
agrCG            = agrC ∧ agrG
agrCoord (h,d) = or [ agrC  (h',d) | h'← hdBy Coord h ]
agrRel     (h,d) = or [ agrCG (h,d') | d'← sub d, rel d']
    where sub = clo dp
```

The constraint agrCoord[7] checks whether the node h has the head h' linked by dependency of type Coord and the agrC constraint for h' and d evaluates to True; agrRel checks whether the node d has a transitive dependent d' (i.e. subordinate node, function sub – see Figure 3) belonging to the category rel which agrees with the node h in case and gender. Finally, the list of grammar rules may be stated as:

```
rules = [ Rule Subj  v     (nominal ∧ nom)  [agrG],
          Rule Cmpl  v     (nominal ∧ acc)  [],
          Rule Coord n     conj             [right],
          Rule CCmpl conj n                 [right,agrCoord],
          Rule Rel   n     v                [agrRel],
          Rule Mod   n     adj              [agrCG]          ]
```

Now, we will extend our grammar with constraints on the cardinality of roles. Let's introduce two more components to the grammar: the set of roles, which may appear at most once for each head (sgl) and the statements indicating roles which are obligatory for word categories (obl).

```
sgl :: [ Role ]
sgl = [ Subj, Cmpl, CCmpl, Rel ]

obl :: [ ((Node → Bool), [Role]) ]
obl = [ (conj,[CCmpl]) ]
```

Singleness constraint will be defined as an instance of a more general mechanism: universal constraints – similar to constraints in rules but with global scope.

```
type UConstr = (Role,Node,Node) → Bool

singleness :: UConstr
singleness (r,h,d) = ¬ (r ∈ sgl ∧ r ∈ dpr h)

uc :: [UConstr]
uc = [singleness]
```

---

[7]We used the standard Haskell function or here, despite its name is not intuitively fitting the context, because it does exactly what we need: it checks both whether the constraint agrC returns True and whether there esists h' for which the agrC is evaluated.

Universal constraints will be checked before each dependency is added and will block the addition in case any of them is violated. In order to incorporate them into our grammar we have to replace the function `roles` used in the definition of `heads` and `deps` functions with `roles'` defined as follows:

```
roles' h d = [ r | r ← roles h d, all ($ (r,h,d)) uc ]
```

The function `roles'` extends `roles` by additionally checking if all universal constraints (the list uc) apply to the connection being under consideration.

The obligatoriness constraint will be checked after completing the parse, in the `pass` function. The `sat` function looks for all roles which are obligatory for the argument node, as defined in the statements in the `obl` list, and verifies if all of them are present.

```
sat n = all (∈ dpr n) [ r | (p,rs) ← obl, p n, r ← rs ]

pass = all sat ∘ (pure ⊕ preds)    (redefinition)
```

Here are some examples of the parser's output:

```
> parse "widział Marię i Jana"⁸

[ [ Step 4 Nma   [(CCmpl,3)] [],
    Step 3 CONJ  [(Conj,2)]  [],
    Step 2 Nfa   [(Cmpl,1)]  [],
    Step 1 Vm    []          []  ]
]


> parse "widział Marię i Jan"⁹

[ ]


> parse "Jan widział książkę którą czyta Maria"¹⁰

[ [ Step 6 Nfn    [(Subj,5)] [],
    Step 5 Vf     [(Rel,3)]  [(Cmpl,4)],
    Step 4 RELfa  []         [],
    Step 3 Nfa    [(Cmpl,2)] [],
    Step 2 Vm     []         [(Subj,1)],
    Step 1 Nmn    []         []          ]
]


> parse "Jan widział książkę którego czyta Maria"¹¹

[ ]
```

---

[8] *he-saw Mary+acc and John+acc*

[9] *he-saw Mary+acc and John+nom* (`agrCoord` constraint violated)

[10] *John saw the-book+fem+acc which+fem+acc Mary is-reading*

[11] *John saw the-book+fem+acc which+masc+acc Mary is-reading* (`agrRel` constraint violated)

6 Efficiency issues

As far as the efficiency issues are concerned, the most important problem appears to be the the number of alternative partial parses built, because partial parses with all possible combinations of legal connections (as well subsets thereof) are produced during the analysis. This may result in unacceptable analysis times for longer and highly ambiguous sentences.

This problem may be overcome by rejecting unpromising partial parses as soon as possible. One of the most obvious selection criteria is the forest size (number of trees in a parse). The relevant parser modification accounts to introducing the selection function (for simplicity we use the fixed value of 4 for the forest size to avoid introducing extra parameters) and redefining the `step` function appropriately:

```
select :: Parse → [Parse]
select p = if size p ≤ 4 then [p] else []

step w = shift w >=> connect >=> select
```

The function `size` which used to compute the number of trees in a parse may be defined as follows:

```
size :: Parse -> Int
size = foldr acc 0
  where acc (Step _ _ h ds) n = n + 1 - length (h ++ ds)
```

7 All/first/best parse variants

The parser is designed to compute all possible parses. If, however, only the first n parses are requested, then only these ones will be computed. Moreover, thanks to the lazy evaluation strategy, only those computations which are necessary to produce the first n parses will be performed. Thus, no modifications are needed to turn the parser into a variant that searches only for the first or first n parses. It is enough to request only the first n parses in the parser invocation. For example, the `parse1` function defined below will compute only the first parse.

```
parse1 = take 1 ∘ parse
```

In order to modify the algorithm to always select the best alternatives according to `someScoringFunction`, instead of the first ones, the parser may by further modified as follows:

```
someScoringFunction :: (Ord a) ⇒ Parse → a
someScoringFunction = ...
```

```
sort :: [Parse] → [Parse]
sort = sortWith someScoringFunction

step w = shift w >=> connect >=> (sort ∘ select)
```

8 Conclusion

In the paper we have tried to show that a lazy functional language such as Haskell is a convenient framework not only for implementing dependency parsers but also for expressing dependency grammars directly as Haskell code. Even without introducing any special notation, language constructs, or additional operators, Haskell itself allows to express the grammar in compact, readable and mathematically clean manner.

The borderline between the parser and the grammar is shifted compared to the traditional view, e.g. CFG/Earley. In the part, which we called the parser core, minimal assumptions are made about structural properties of the syntactic trees allowed (e.g. projective, nonprojective) and the nature of grammatical constraints which are formulated. In fact the only hard-coded requirements are that the syntactic structure is represented in the form of a dependency tree and that the parse is built incrementally.

In order to turn the ideas presented above into a useful NLP tool for building grammars it would be obviously necessary to rewrite the code in more general, parametrizable form, abstracting over word category type (e.g. to allow structural tags), role type, parse filtering and ranking functions, the monad used to represent alternatives, allowing for representing some kinds of weights or ranks etc.

In fact, the work in exactly this direction is already in advanced stage of development. In this paper it was reduced to the essential part (without parameterized data types, multi-parameter classes, monad transformers, and so on), which size allows to present it in full detail and with the complete source code in a conference paper.

References

Covington, M. A. (2001). A fundamental algorithm for dependency parsing. In *In Proceedings of the 39th Annual ACM Southeast Conference*, pages 95–102.

de Kok, D. and Brouwer, H. (2009). Natural language processing for the working programmer. http://freecomputerbooks.com/books/nlpwp.pdf. Accessed: 2016-11-22.

Eijck, J. V. (2005). Deductive parsing with sequentially indexed grammars. http://homepages.cwi.nl/~jve/papers/05/sig/DPS.pdf. Accessed: 2016-11-22.

Erwig, M. (2001). Inductive graphs and functional graph algorithms. *J. Functional Programming*, 11(5):467–492.

Goodman, J. (1999). Semiring parsing. *Computational Linguistics*, 25(4):573–605.

Hutton, G. and Meijer, E. (1998). Monadic parsing in haskell. *J. Funct. Program.*, 8(4):437–444.

Jones, S. P., editor (2002). *Haskell 98 Language and Libraries: The Revised Report.* http://haskell.org/.

Koster, C. H. (1992). Affix grammars for natural languages. In Alblas, H. and Melichar, B., editors, *Attribute Grammars, Applications and Systems*, volume 545 of *LNCS*, pages 469–484. Springer-Verlag.

Kubler, S., McDonald, R., Nivre, J., and Hirst, G. (2009). *Dependency Parsing.* Morgan and Claypool Publishers.

Levy, R. and Pollard, C. (2001). Coordination and neutralization in hpsg. In Eynde, F. V., Hellan, L., and Beermann, D., editors, *Proceedings of the 8th International Conference on Head-Driven Phrase Structure Grammar*, pages 221–234. CSLI Publications.

Lipovaca, M. (2011). *Learn You a Haskell for Great Good!: A Beginner's Guide.* No Starch Press, San Francisco, CA, USA, 1st edition.

Ljunglöf, P. (2004). Functional chart parsing of context-free grammars. *Journal of Functional Programming*, 14(6):669–680.

Pereira, F. C. N. and Warren, D. H. D. (1980). Definite Clause Grammars for Language Analysis - A Survey of the Formalism and a Comparison with Augmented Transition Network. *Artificial Intelligence*, pages 231–278.

Ranta, A. (2011). *Grammatical Framework: Programming with Multilingual Grammars.* CSLI Publications, Stanford. ISBN-10: 1-57586-626-9 (Paper), 1-57586-627-7 (Cloth).

Yorgey, B. (2009). The typeclassopedia. *The Monad. Reader Issue 13*, pages 17–66.

Improving Document Ranking using Query Expansion and Classification Techniques for Mixed Script Information Retrieval

Subham Kumar, Anwesh Sinha Ray, Sabyasachi Kamila, Asif Ekbal, Sriparna Saha, Pushpak Bhattacharyya

Department of Computer Science and Engineering

Indian Institute of Technology Patna

Bihta, Patna-801103 (Bihar)

`{shubham.ee12,anwesh.cs12,sabyasachi.pcs16,asif,sriparna,pb}@iitp.ac.in`

Abstract

A large amount of user-generated translit-erated contents in Roman scripts are avail-able in the Web for the languages that use non-Roman based indigenous scripts. This creates a mixed script space which is mono-lingual or multilingual having more than one script. Information retrieval (IR) in the mixed-script space is challenging as both query and documents can be writ-ten in either native or Roman script, or may be in both the scripts. Moreover, due to lack of any standard ways of spelling a word in a non-native script, translit-erated contents can be written with dif-ferent spelling variations. In this paper, we propose the effective techniques for query expansion and query classification for mixed-script IR. The proposed tech-niques are based on deep learning, word embedding and traditional TF-IDF. We generate our own resources for creating the test-bed for our experiments. Exten-sive empirical analyses show that our pro-posed methods achieve significantly better performance (20.44% increase in MRR, 22.43% increase in NDCG@1 & 15.61% increase in MAP) over a state-of-the-art baseline model.

1 Introduction

Information Retrieval (Manning et al., 2008) refers to finding material (usually, in the form of documents) of a semi-structured nature (usually, in text) that satisfies an information need within a large document collections. Nowadays, due to var-ious socio-cultural and technological reasons, of-ten the websites and the user-generated contents in languages such as Arabic, Russian, Indic etc., are

written using Roman scripts. Such contents create a mono-lingual or multi-lingual space with more than one script which we refer to as the Mixed-Script space. Information retrieval in the mixed-script space, known as Mixed-Script IR (MSIR), is more challenging because queries can be writ-ten in both the native as well as Roman scripts, and these should also be matched to the documents written in both the scripts.

Transliteration (Lopez, 2008) is the process of phonetically describing the words of a given lan-guage using a non-native script. For both the web documents and intended search queries to retrieve those documents, transliteration, especially into Roman script, is generally used. Since no stan-dard ways of spelling any word into a non-native script exist, transliterated contents offer extensive spelling variations; typically, we can transliterate a native term into Roman script in many ways (Gupta et al., 2012). For example, the word *khus-boo* ("fragrance") can be written in Roman script using different variations such as *kushboo, khusbu, khushbu* and so on. This type of problem is termed as a non-trivial term matching problem for search engines with the aim to match the native-script or Roman-transliterated query with the documents in multiple scripts after considering the spelling variations. Many single (native) script queries and documents with spelling variations have been studied (French et al., 1997; Zobel and Dart, 1996) as well as transliteration of named entities (NE) in IR (Collier et al., 1998; Wang et al., 2009).

It is important for every IR engine to present users with information that are most relevant to the users' needs. While searching, user has an idea of what s/he wants, but in many instances, due to the variations in query formulations, re-trieved results could greatly vary. As a result, un-derstanding the nature of information need behind the queries issued by Web users has become an im-

81

D S Sharma, R Sangal and A K Singh. Proc. of the 13th Intl. Conference on Natural Language Processing, pages 81–89,
Varanasi, India. December 2016. ©2016 NLP Association of India (NLPAI)

portant research problem. Classifying queries into predefined target categories, also known as query classification, is important to improve search relevance. Successfully classifying incoming general user queries to topical categories can bring improvements in both the efficiency and the effectiveness of general web search. Query classification encounters two important challenges: (i) many queries are very short and contain noise. (ii) a query can often have multiple meanings. In our work we propose a query classification technique for improving document ranking in mixed-script IR scenario. The query can be in multiple scripts, and the dataset is of mixed-domain [1]. At first we develop a baseline model for query expansion in line with (Gupta et al., 2014) using a deep learning architecture. We develop the query classification technique based on distributed word representation and traditional TF-IDF weighting scheme. The proposed method is proven to be effective in improving the ranking of relevant documents.We present an extensive empirical analysis of the proposed technique that achieves significantly better performance (20.44% increase in MRR, 22.43% increase in NDCG@1 & 15.61% increase in MAP) over the baseline model. We summarize the contributions of our current work as follows:

(i) proposal of an effective query classification (traditional tf-idf along with word-embedding) technique that improves the performance in a mixed-script IR scenario.

(ii) development of a model of query expansion based on deep learning architecture.

(iii) creation of resources for mixed-script IR.

The remaining of the paper is organized as follows. In Section 2, we introduce the concept of MSIR in correspondence to our task and show the possible application scenarios and challenges. Section 3 presents different approaches that we developed to improve the document ranking in an ad-hoc retrieval setting of mixed-script IR over the baseline. In Section 4, we present the details of resources that we created for our experiments. Section 5 reports the experimental setup and the results of evaluation with some empirical analysis. Finally, we conclude in Section 6.

---

[1]Refers to the dataset that contains texts written in more than one domain

2 MSIR: Definition and Challenges

In this section, we present the definition of mixed-script information retrieval (MSIR) with respect to our work.

2.1 Mixed Script IR

The task of IR engine is to rank the documents retrieved from a document pool D, such that documents which are relevant to query q appear at the top of the ranked list. For a *Mixed Script IR* setup, the queries and the documents are all in the same language, i.e., Hindi in our case, but those are written in more than one different scripts, i.e., Roman and Devanagari scripts in our case. The task of IR engine is to search across the scripts.

More specifically, we define our problem statement as: Given a query in Roman or Devanagari script, the system has to retrieve the top-k documents from a corpus that contain mixed scripts (i.e., either Roman or Devanagari or both).

Input: a query written in Roman (transliterated) or Devanagari script

Output: a ranked list of ten (k=10 here) documents both in Devanagari and Roman scripts generated from some given document collections.

As part of our contribution to FIRE 2015 shared task (Sequiera et al., 2015), we had access to the queries which cover three different genres, i.e., Hindi songs lyrics, movie reviews, and astrology. In line with this we prepare 25 queries as a test collection for various information needs. Queries related to lyrical documents express the need to retrieve relevant song lyrics while queries related to movie reviews and astrology are informational in nature (Sequiera et al., 2015).

2.2 Challenges in MSIR

There are mainly two challenges exist in mixed-script information retrieval (MSIR) which are: (a) problems in handling extensive spelling variations in transliterated queries and documents during term matching phase? and (b) problems in identifying, representing and processing a mixed type query, mixed and transliterated documents? The solution for the first problem could be the following: the given text can be transliterated and converted into a common space and finally some standard matching techniques in single-script space can be applied. Otherwise as shown in (Gupta et al., 2014) an abstract orthographic space can be created to represent the words of different scripts.

Here the words can be matched to obtain variants of a query word across scripts.

In mixed query processing, language identification of query words adds another interesting challenge. Query words should be assigned appropriate semantic classes, which denote either native or transliterated scripts. This is challenging as depending upon the context of the query a same word may have different meanings. For example a word *man* can be a representative of the English word *man*, or the transliterated Hindi word of *man* having meaning *mind*, or another transliterated Hindi word *maan* meaning *reputation*. Hence, language identification seems to be an extremely important problem in MSIR setting, especially when multiple languages are involved. Our algorithm for language identification is based on supervised machine learning, which is in line with the system as described in (Gupta et al., 2015).

There are some other problems apart from these basic challenges like how to present information etc. This requires some additional information to be known in advance like whether the user can read all the scripts, or prefer some scripts over the other.

3 Methodology

Having defined the basic MSIR setting, and establishing its prevalence in Web search through availability of several mixed-script contents in the web, i.e., Indian Astrology, Bollywood movie reviews, Hindi song lyrics etc., we now present the approaches that we develop along with the baseline system. An overall architecture of the system showing the basic components is depicted in Figure 1.

3.1 Baseline System

We develop a baseline model based on deep-learning architecture in line with the prior work as proposed in (Gupta et al., 2014). This is based on *restricted Boltzmann machine*(RBMs) (Hinton, 2010) model. Our baseline, though uses the concept proposed in (Gupta et al., 2014), is developed to handle a bigger dataset comprising of multiple domains instead of only Hindi song lyrics dataset of FIRE 2014, thus extending the research challenges in a MSIR setup. The baseline proposes a principled solution to handle the mixed-script term matching and spelling variation. The mixed-script features are modeled jointly in

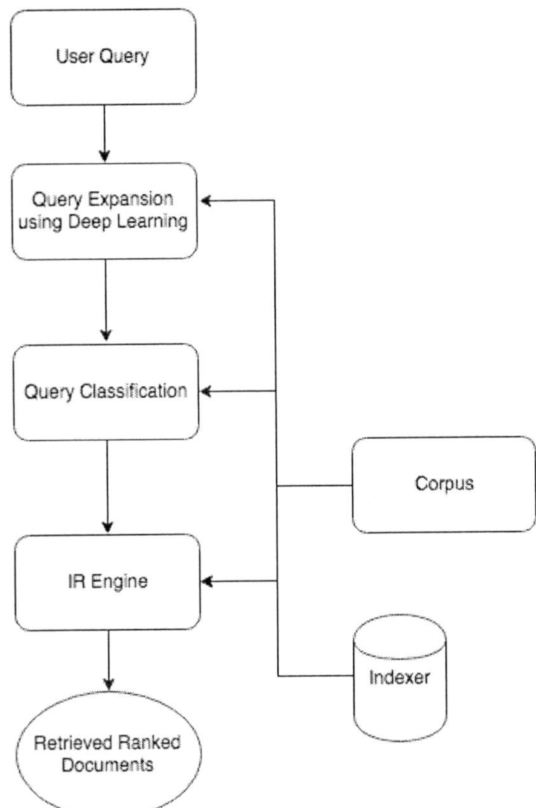

Figure 1: Block Diagram of the system

a deep-learning architecture in such a way that these can be compared in a low-dimensional abstract space where term equivalents are close to each other. The principle behind the formation of common abstract space for mixed-script modeling is that original words and the corresponding transliterated words into a non-native script share the same sound/pronunciation. This process can help in determining possible equivalents of the query term across the script. Finally the expansion of the original query can be done using the thus found equivalents.

3.1.1 Formulation

The phonemes are considered as character-level *topics* in the terms. Terms are the representatives of mixtures of *topics*, with each topic representing a probability distribution over character n-grams. Let us assume that the feature set $F = \{f_1, ..., f_K\}$ contain character grams of scripts s_i for all i $\in \{1, ., r\}$ and $|F| = K$.

$$t_1 = \bigcup_{i=1....r} w_{1,i}$$

83

represents a data-point from training data T of language l_1 where $w_{1,i}$ denotes word w written in language l_1 and script s_i. Here r counts the number of jointly modeled scripts. Each data-point is assumed to be a K-dimensional feature vector x where x_k is a measurement of kth feature $f_k \in F$ in data-point t_1. The count for character grams within terms can be measured using Dirichlet multi-nomial distribution[2]. We have considered total N independent draws from a categorical distribution with K different output classes. In the current context, the value of N can be computed as follows:

N = $\sum_{i=1}^{k} x_i$ and $\{f_1, \ldots, f_K\}$ denote K categories. Here x_k indicates the number of times a particular feature f_k appears in the data-point t_1. Here x = $\{x_1, \ldots, x_K\}$ satisfies a multinomial distribution with two parameters N and p. Here p = $(p_1, \ldots, p_K)$ and p_k denotes the probability that k^{th} feature obtains the value of x_k. The parameter p can not be directly computed in our case rather it is computed using a conjugate prior distribution.

In the current paper we have proposed a model based on non-linear dimensionality reduction procedures like deep auto-encoder. A deep learning based architecture is proposed after stacking several RBMs together. The bottom-most RBM in our framework is used for modeling the input terms. This can be viewed as a character-level variant of the replicated softmax (RSM) model presented in for documents. In general character n-grams follow Dirichlet multi-nomial distribution. But in the current work RSM has been used to model these as at the time of applying the inference, methods like Gibbs sampling, Dirichlet prior distributions are often marginalized out. We assume that $v \in \{0, 1, , N\}^k$ denotes the visible multinomial units and $h \in \{0, 1\}^m$ denotes a stochastic binary hidden latent unit. Also assume that v is a K-dimensional input vector such as feature vector x for data-point t_1. h denotes the m-dimensional latent feature vector and N = $\sum_{i=1}^{k} x_i$. The energy of the state $\{v, h\}$ is calculated as follows:

$$E(v, h) = -\sum_i a_i v_i - \sum_j b_j h_j - \sum_i \sum_j v_i w_{i,j} h_j$$

Here the following terms are used: v_i denotes the measurement of x_i, $w_{i,j}$ is the weight matrix entry between i^{th} visible node and j^{th} hidden node, while a_i and b_j are bias terms of visible and hidden layers, respectively. A large number of layers are inserted to develop a deep auto-encoder. A cascaded structure of binary RBMs is created in such a way that output of a lower RBM is passed as an input to the immediate next RBM.

3.1.2 Training

In our proposed model, the visible layer of the bottom-most RBM is the character-level replicated soft-max layer. The feature space F is a combination of character uni- and bi-grams of training data (r = 2). The terms are represented as low dimensional embedding in the abstract space. The hidden layer of the top-most RBM is kept linear for this purpose. A two-phased training procedure is carried out for the developed auto-encoder i) pre-training the layers in a greedy manner and; ii) updation of the weights using backpropagation process.

3.1.3 Finding Equivalents

After the training of the model is finished, the process of equivalent- discovery has started. This is composed of two steps: i) the index of mining lexicon in abstract space is produced and; ii) the equivalents for the query term are generated. The mining-lexicon is a lexicon of reference collection (ideally, mixed-script) . This is later on utilized to extract term equivalents. This is executed after projecting each term in the mining lexicon into an abstract space. For each term, one index entry is stored which contains the corresponding projected term. Finally the query term x_q is also projected into the abstract space h_q and the corresponding cosine similarity with respect to all terms in the index is calculated. For a given query word, x_q, the terms with cosine similarity $> \theta$ are considered as equivalents. Here θ is used as the similarity threshold.

For developing the baseline system, similarity thresholds of 0.95 and 0.98 are considered.

3.2 Query Classification

Query classification helps identifying intents behind each query, which, in turn, provides better retrieval search results.We divide our dataset into 3 broad domains, namely *Music Lyrics*, *Movie Reviews* and *Astrology*.

---

[2] http://en.wikipedia.org/wiki/Dirichlet-multinomial_distribution

3.2.1 TF-IDF based Technique

Term frequency (TF)-inverse document frequency (IDF) is a technique to show the importance of a word in a document given a large collection of documents or corpus. TF-IDF technique is widely used in information retrieval or text mining as a weighting factor. In general if a word appears multiple times in a document then TF value would be more. But this is offset by the frequency of the word appearing in the other documents of the corpus. This way the TF-IDF scores of words which appear frequently in general can be reduced.

We create the minion lexicon for each domain through indexing along with the normalized TF-IDF scores of each term in that respective domain.

For each domain d, we obtain normalized term frequency of the term t as follows:

$$TF(t, d) = \frac{tf(t, d)}{\max_t tf(t, d)}$$

Here, $tf(t, d)$: term frequency of the tth term in document d; $max_t tf(t, d)$: frequency of the most frequent term.

For each domain d, we obtain normalized inverse document frequency of the term t

$$IDF(t, d) = \frac{idf(t, d)}{\max_t idf(t, d)}$$

Here, $idf(t, d)$: inverse document frequency of term t in document d; $max_t idf(t, d)$: maximum inverse document frequency obtained throughout the corpus.

The corresponding normalized TF-IDF score of a term t is obtained by

$$TF - IDF(t, d) = TF(t, d).IDF(t, d)$$

After obtaining the above TF-IDF score for each minion lexicon of each domain, the TF-IDF score of a query for a domain is obtained by summing up the TF-IDF score of every expanded query term obtained from that domain. If a expanded query term is not found in that domain, its TF-IDF score is set to 0. Once the score for a query is obtained for each domain, the query is classified to the domain for which it has the highest score.

3.2.2 Word Embedding based Technique

We use word2vec tool (Mikolov et al., 2013) which efficiently captures the semantic properties of words in the corpus. Word2vec is a group of related models (i.e., CBOW: continuous bag-of-words model and Skip-grams) which can be utilized to generate different word embeddings. The linguistic contexts of words can be generated using some models based on shallow-ed, two-layered neural networks. A word is given as an input to the network and the task is to predict the words which can appear in adjacent positions given an input text. Order of the remaining words is not important.

For each domain d, we merge the contents of all the documents belonging to that domain to obtain its respective document collection. We train Word2Vec using CBOW model for each domain dataset by setting window size to 5, and dimension of the final vectors to 100. For each domain, we create a normalized vector *norm_vec(d)* by summing up all the vectors of all the tokens t of that domain, and dividing resultant vector by the total number of documents *N(d)* in that domain. For the expanded query vectorization, we obtain the vectors *vec(t,d)* of each query term t from the trained model of the domains in which that term is present, sum up the vectors, and divide the final vector by the number of domains in which it has occurred (denoted by *N(t,d)*: number of domains d in which the term appears). The final vector of a query Q is obtained by summing up the individual word vectors of each query term. The processes are described mathematically as follows: $N(t, d)$ = No. of domains where the term t has occurred; $N(d)$ = No. of documents in the domain d; $vec(t, d)$ = Vector of term t in domain d; $norm\_vec(d)$ = Normalized vector for domain d; $norm\_vec(Q)$ = Query vector of a query Q;

$$norm\_vec(d) = \frac{\sum_{t \in d} vec(t, d)}{N(d)}$$

$$norm\_vec(Q) = \sum_{t \in Q} \frac{\sum_d vec(t, d)}{N(t, d)}$$

For classifying the queries into one of the 3 domains, we use two similarity measures (i.e., cosine similarity and Euclidean distance) between the query vector *norm_vec(Q)* and the domain vector *norm_vec(d)*.

4 Dataset

4.1 Resource Creation

We create our own resources for experiments. We develop a web crawler using Python modules - *BeautifulSoup, mechanize* to crawl the documents from different web sources. For data creation we had to deal with the following issues: (i) very few web-sites having good amount of transliterated contents of Devanagari documents; (ii) no standard html tag containing actual contents of documents, and so manual intervention was necessary. We crawl total 1,503 documents covering all the 3 domains- *Astrology, Bollywood Movie Reviews* and *Bollywood Movie Dialogues*. Following sources were used: Bollywood movie reviews: http://www.jagran.com/, Astrology: http://astrology.raftaar.in/ and Bollywood movie dialogues: http://filmyquotes.com/. We contributed to the FIRE-2015 Shared Task on MSIR in Subtask 2 problem[3], which is related to the mixed-script Ad-hoc retrieval. In Table 1, we present some statistics for the datasets.

Domain	No. of documents	Script
Astrology	343	Devanagari
Movie Reviews	97	Devanagari
Movie Dialogues	1,063	Mixed

Table 1: Statistics of Crawled Datasets

4.2 Pre-processing

The dataset has to be pre-processed for removing inconsistencies and other typical errors. Some of the examples are shown in Table 2. The errors were manually corrected. Some typical examples are shown in Table 2.

Errors	Example	Correct Word
Unicode Characters		-
Punctuation Marks	hai.n, maine;	hain, maine
XML Tags	⟨text⟩	-
Hash Tags	###	-
Underscore	ko_ii	koii
Website Name	MusicMaza.Com	-
Backslash	be\-sadaa	be sadaa

Table 2: Typical Examples of the Dataset

4.3 Dataset Statistics

We use the FIRE 2013 shared task collection on Transliterated Search (Roy et al., 2007) for training the deep auto-encoder (stacked RBMs). The dataset comprises of document collection (D), queryset (Q) and relevance judgments. The collection contains 63,334 documents containing song titles and lyrics in Roman, Devanagari and mixed scripts; Hindu astrology and Bollywood movie reviews in Devanagari. Statistics are shown in Table 3. The query set (Q) contains 25 lyrics search queries covering Bollywood songs; Movie reviews and Hindu astrology in Roman and Devanagari scripts with mean query length of 4.04 words. Queries related to lyrics documents express the need to retrieve relevant song lyrics, while queries related to movie reviews and astrology are informational in nature. The queries are of different difficulty levels: word level joining and splitting, ambiguous short queries, different script queries and mixing of different language keywords. On an average, there are 47.52 qrels per query with average relevant documents per query is set to 5.00. Some example queries are shown in Table 4.

No. of documents	63,334
No. of tokens	1,40,39,002
No. of vocabulary words	1,45,478

Table 3: Corpus Statistics

Sample Queries
tujho nahi lyrics
vicky donor movie reviews
ill effects of rahu kaal

Table 4: Example of Queries

5 Experiments and Results

In this section we describe the experimental results along with necessary analysis for evaluating the effectiveness of the proposed method for retrieval in *mixed-script space*.

5.1 Baseline System

The experimental setup for baseline model is based on a standard ad-hoc retrieval setting. The document collection of three domains is first indexed to create an inverted index. We set the following experimental setups for each domain:

---

[3]http://fire.irsi.res.in/fire/2015/home

(i) for lyrical retrieval, the sequential information among the terms is crucial for effectiveness evaluation (Gupta et al., 2014), e.g., *love me baby* and *baby love me* are completely different songs. In order to capture the word-ordering we consider word bi-grams as a unit for indexing and retrieval; and (ii) for bollywood movie reviews and astrology, we consider word uni-gram as a unit for indexing and retrieval[4] Every query is enriched with equivalents of the query terms using the deep-learning based query expansion technique (c.f. Section 3.1.3).Suppose a query has n terms in it, and has m equivalents, then the query gets expanded into m^n queries. After the queries are expanded, they are first pre-processed, i.e., converted to word bi-grams for song lyrics and word uni-grams for astrology and movie reviews, and then fed to the retrieval engine to get the top 10 relevant documents.

5.2 Results using Query Classification

Here we present the results using different query classification techniques.

- **Query Classification using TF-IDF**: After expanding the queries with term equivalents (0.98 as the similarity threshold), the document collection is divided into 3 pre-defined domains, and are indexed separately. We consider the same indexing schemes as that of the baseline model (i.e., word bi-gram for song lyrics and word uni-gram for astrology and movie reviews).Every query is classified into one of the 3 domains in which the corresponding TF-IDF score is the highest, and the documents are retrieved from their respective classified domain.

- **Rule-based Query Classification using TF-IDF and Word Embedding**: We compute word embeddings using the process as described in Section 3.2.2. Once the similarity scores of each query for all the three domains are obtained using the word embedding technique as described in Section 3, we propose a rule-based system to classify the queries. We first classify using the traditional TF-IDF based approach. If the score is below a certain threshold level (in this case, it is 0.85), we use the word embedding based approach for query classification. Vector representation of each word in the query is obtained by

following the process as mentioned in Section 3.2.2. For Euclidean distance based classification, we classify the queries to the domain for which the distance is minimum and for cosine similarity based classification, we classify the queries to the domain for which the score is the highest.

5.3 Results and Analysis

We evaluate the effectiveness of the proposed methods, referred to as **Deep-TF-IDF** and **Deep-Rule-based** and compare with the baseline system which we refer to as **Deep-baseline**. For a fair comparison between the baseline and our proposed methods, we develop the *baseline from scratch*, and evaluate using the cleaned dataset keeping the parameter θ to be 0.98. The retrieval performance of the proposed systems are computed using three evaluation measures, mean average precision (MAP), mean reciprocal rank (MRR) and normalized discounted cumulative gain (NDCG@1). The optimal value θ is set by conducting experiments for a range of θ values starting from 0.90 to 0.99 with a step size of 0.01 and finding the value of θ which yields the highest MAP, MRR and NDCG@1 values. For a particular query, the ranked-list which is a collection of top 10 documents is first created. The ranking model used in the current work is a parameter free divergence from randomness (unsupervised DFR) as described in (Amati, 2006). This model is suitable for short-queries. The obtained average results over Q measured in terms of MAP, MRR and NDCG@1 are illustrated in Table 5. We choose θ for **Deep-baseline** following the process as described in (Gupta et al., 2014). The proposed Deep-Rule-based technique attains the high MRR score. This shows its utility in fetching the first relevant document at very high ranks which is required in case of web search. Moreover Deep-Rule-based technique also attains the highest value of MAP compared to all other techniques. High NDCG@1 describes its ability to fetch useful and the most relevant documents at the first position.

Results of query classification using TF-IDF technique are presented in Table 6. This shows the TF-IDF scores of each query for each domain.

The actual music queries are from 51 to 60, actual movie queries are from 61 to 67 and astrology queries are from 68 to 75. From the above experiments, we come to the conclusion that out of

---

[4]Since the queries are informational in nature.

Method	NDCG@1	MRR	MAP	θ
Deep	0.6633	0.5613	0.3338	0.95
Deep	0.7133	0.6144	0.3587	0.98
Deep-TF-IDF	**0.7633**	**0.6600**	**0.3347**	0.98
Deep-Rule-Based	**0.8733**	**0.7400**	**0.4147**	0.98

Table 5: Results of Retrieval Performance Measured by MAP, MRR & NDCG@1

Query No.	Music	Movie	Astrology
51	158.93	0.0	4.21
52	461.02	3.97	0.0
53	33.53	0.0	0.0
54	473.83	0.0	846.14
55	389.19	0.0	175.04
56	306.56	31.14	21.60
57	101.15	61.44	74.01
58	525.55	81.94	273.98
59	981.11	84.30	138.07
60	188.33	3.97	4.21
61	1.58	33.73	0.0
62	13.52	7.95	21.33
63	2.88	0.0	4.21
64	0.30	3.97	0.0
65	1.37	29.75	0.0
66	1.29	25.77	0.0
67	12.71	23.85	14.85
68	34.53	3.97	366.12
69	146.84	25.06	1054.97
70	33.07	12.79	125.16
71	6.11	0.0	140.84
72	208.50	15.02	209.04
73	4.41	13.45	645.70
74	4.11	6.72	149.76
75	249.27	10.09	343.47

Table 6: TF-IDF Score of Queries($\times 10^{-4}$)

Query No.	Music	Movie	Astrology
51	267.89	1393.75	540.52
52	414.86	1412.81	593.60
53	272.40	1398.45	542.50
54	597.42	1390.06	702.43
55	398.54	1410.33	665.43
56	260.86	1397.78	542.05
57	279.56	1394.62	559.91
58	2491.55	2771.60	2556.23
59	4112.95	4249.52	4245.69
60	331.28	1399.07	613.57

Table 7: Euclidean Distance Measures between Queries and Domains: Music, Movie and Astrology

Query No.	Music	Movie	Astrology
61	0.22	0.30	0.27
62	0.07	0.19	0.12
63	0.11	0.135	0.132
64	0.10	-0.17	-0.18
65	0.27	0.13	0.03
66	0.18	0.25	0.09
67	0.14	0.34	0.21
68	0.08	0.23	0.44
69	0.35	0.24	0.36
70	0.171	0.178	0.24
71	0.09	0.11	0.06
72	0.15	0.28	0.31
73	0.15	0.17	0.33
74	0.07	0.30	0.29
75	0.16	0.44	0.50

Table 8: Cosine Similarity between Queries Domains: Music, Movie and Astrology

25 queries, there are three queries (i.e., 54,62,63) that are incorrectly classified into astrology domain.Results of query classification using word embedding technique are presented in Table 7 and Table 8 for music queries, and movie and astrology queries, respectively. We use Euclidean distance to classify music queries as this metric gives weight-age to long documents. In our case, out of total 63,334 documents, Hindi song lyrics domain has 62,894 documents. For movie and astrology queries, we use cosine similarity which penalizes long documents by normalizing the vector length.

From the above results, it is evident that the queries which are incorrectly classified by simple TF-IDF based technique (i.e., 54,62,63) are now correctly classified using word embedding based technique.

6 Conclusion

Although Mixed-Script IR (MSIR) is a very important and prevalent problem, it has attained very little attention. In this work we have shown how query classification aids in document retrieval. Our baseline is developed using a deep learning architecture. We develop query classification using TF-IDF and word embedding based models that improve the document ranking of the baseline. We have presented extensive empirical analyses of the proposed techniques for ad-hoc retrieval settings of Hindi songs lyrics, Astrology and Bollywood Movie reviews, where the proposed methods achieve significantly better results (20.44% increase in MRR, 22.43% increase in NDCG@1 & 15.61% increase in MAP) over the baseline.

In future we would like to investigate a more general setup of MSIR such as Mixed-Script Multilingual IR (MS-MLIR).

References

Giambattista Amati. 2006. Frequentist and bayesian approach to information retrieval. In *Proceedings of the 28th European Conference on Advances in Information Retrieval*, ECIR'06, pages 13–24, Berlin, Heidelberg. Springer-Verlag.

Nigel Collier, Hideki Hirakawa, and Akira Kumano. 1998. Machine translation vs. dictionary term translation: A comparison for english-japanese news article alignment. In *Proceedings of the 36th Annual Meeting of the Association for Computational Linguistics and 17th International Conference on Computational Linguistics - Volume 1*, ACL '98, pages 263–267, Stroudsburg, PA, USA. Association for Computational Linguistics.

James C. French, Allison L. Powell, and Eric Schulman. 1997. Applications of approximate word matching in information retrieval. In *Proceedings of the Sixth International Conference on Information and Knowledge Management*, CIKM '97, pages 9–15, New York, NY, USA. ACM.

Kanika Gupta, Monojit Choudhury, and Kalika Bali. 2012. Mining hindi-english transliteration pairs from online hindi lyrics. In *Proceedings of the Eighth International Conference on Language Resources and Evaluation (LREC-2012), Istanbul, Turkey, May 23-25, 2012*, pages 2459–2465.

Parth Gupta, Kalika Bali, Rafael E. Banchs, Monojit Choudhury, and Paolo Rosso. 2014. Query expansion for mixed-script information retrieval. In *The 37th International ACM SIGIR Conference on Research and Development in Information Retrieval, SIGIR '14, Gold Coast , QLD, Australia - July 06 - 11, 2014*, pages 677–686.

Deepak Kumar Gupta, Shubham Kumar, and Asif Ekbal. 2015. Machine learning approach for language identification & transliteration. In *Proceedings of the Forum for Information Retrieval Evaluation*, FIRE '14, pages 60–64, New York, NY, USA. ACM.

Geoffrey Hinton. 2010. A practical guide to training restricted boltzmann machines. *Momentum*, 9(1):926.

Adam Lopez. 2008. Statistical machine translation. *ACM Comput. Surv.*, 40(3):8:1–8:49, August.

Christopher D. Manning, Prabhakar Raghavan, and Hinrich Schütze. 2008. *Introduction to Information Retrieval*. Cambridge University Press, New York, NY, USA.

Tomas Mikolov, Kai Chen, Greg Corrado, and Jeffrey Dean. 2013. Efficient Estimation of Word Representations in Vector Space. *arXiv preprint arXiv:1301.3781*.

Rishiraj Saha Roy, Monojit Choudhury, Prasenjit Majumder, and Komal Agarwal. 2007. Overview of the fire 2013 track on transliterated search. In *Post-Proceedings of the 4th and 5th Workshops of the Forum for Information Retrieval Evaluation*, FIRE '12 & '13, pages 4:1–4:7, New York, NY, USA. ACM.

Royal Sequiera, Monojit Choudhury, Parth Gupta, Paolo Rosso, Shubham Kumar, Somnath Banerjee, Sudip Kumar Naskar, Sivaji Bandyopadhyay, Gokul Chittaranjan, Amitava Das, and Kunal Chakma. 2015. Overview of FIRE-2015 shared task on mixed script information retrieval. In *FIRE Workshops*, volume 1587 of *CEUR Workshop Proceedings*, pages 19–25. CEUR-WS.org.

Xuerui Wang, Andrei Z. Broder, Evgeniy Gabrilovich, Vanja Josifovski, and Bo Pang. 2009. Cross-language query classification using web search for exogenous knowledge. In *Proceedings of the Second International Conference on Web Search and Web Data Mining, WSDM 2009, Barcelona, Spain, February 9-11, 2009*, pages 74–83.

Justin Zobel and Philip Dart. 1996. Phonetic string matching: Lessons from information retrieval. In *Proceedings of the 19th Annual International ACM SIGIR Conference on Research and Development in Information Retrieval*, SIGIR '96, pages 166–172, New York, NY, USA. ACM.

Feature based Sentiment Analysis using a Domain Ontology

Neha Yadav
Department of Computer Science
and Engineering
Indian Institute of Technology (BHU)
Varanasi, India 221005
neharao.rao8@gmail.com

C Ravindranath Chowdary
Department of Computer Science
and Engineering
Indian Institute of Technology (BHU)
Varanasi, India 221005
rchowdary.cse@iitbhu.ac.in

Abstract

With the increase of unstructured social media data, sentiment analysis can be applied to infer useful information to assist organizations and their customers. We propose a model for feature-based sentiment analysis using ontology to address queries like:*"which car is more comfortable?, which car has better performance and interior?"*. Feature based sentiment analysis is done using SentiWordNet with word sense disambiguation and an ontology that is developed by us. Data Tables are prepared from the RDF triples of parsed ontology and the sentiment ranks of car attributes. To relate the RDBM data to the built ontology of car, mapping axioms are proposed to connect them using OBDA model. Using SPARQL query, the results of the proposed model are compared with a dictionary-based method with respect to different car attributes. The performance of our model is better than dictionary based method.

1 Introduction

With the development of Web 2.0, the measure of individual feeling (reviews, ratings, recommendations, feedbacks, comments) in online social networking has been seriously studied by many groups. The challenge is to decipher enormous amount of data for analyzing sentiments, feelings or emotions from the web. There are two types of approaches for sentiment analysis (SA): corpus-based and dictionary-based. The classification of customers' reviews at either sentence or complete document level is not adequate for many applications as these do not recognize right conclusion or sentiment targets. In this work, we emphasize on word-phrase and word-level-based sentiment clas-

sification also called feature-based opinion mining which covers both entities and aspects. In our approach, there are two major tasks: feature extraction and feature sentiment classification to determine sentiments on targets, for example, *"The speed of bmw 3.0 is great but the navigation is not good."*. Here there are two attributes of car (*bmw3.0*); *speed* and *navigation*.

According to Liu (2012), there are four principle approaches to recognize every assessment expression and its objective from the opinion: *"extraction based on frequent nouns and noun phrases, extraction by exploiting opinion and target relations, extraction using supervised learning and topic modeling"*. We used the second approach using nltk[1] lexical resources. Feature-based sentiment analysis (FBSA) is done on car customers' reviews in which features are extracted using our ontology on car domain. According to Gruber (1993), an ontology is an *"explicit and formal specification of a conceptualization"*. We proposed FBSA on car reviews using SentiWordNet with word sense disambiguation (WSD) and an ontology associated with mappings.

2 Related Work

Guzman and Maalej, (2014) suggested an automated technique in three phases to analyze relevant features: 1) collocation finding algorithm to extract fine-grained (two keywords) features, 2) SentiStrength for SA on sentence level 3) Latent Dirichlet Allocation (LDA) topic modeling technique to group into high-level or coarse-grained features and used weighted average sentiment score to each topic. The coherence of ten most popular features in app reviews are measured on a five-point scale, which represents a logical and consistent level of shared theme. The authors compared the results with the manually created

---

[1] http://www.nltk.org/

D S Sharma, R Sangal and A K Singh. Proc. of the 13th Intl. Conference on Natural Language Processing, pages 90–98,
Varanasi, India. December 2016. ©2016 NLP Association of India (NLPAI)

truth sets by content analysis and reported 91% precision and 73% recall.

Virmani et al., (2014) proposed an algorithm for aspect-level sentiment analysis on reviews used in Letter of recommendation (LOR) system. The authors made an aspect-tree of different aspect levels and sentiment weightage is assigned to each branch. Their idea is based on Sentiment Ontology Tree (SOT) and hierarchical classification algorithm (Wei and Gulla, 2010). After extracting aspects, each aspect value is computed by multiplying score of branches from the aspect location to root while traversing the aspect tree. The sentiment values of aspects are calculated using a dictionary-based method.

Thakor and Sasi, (2015) proposed partially automated ontology-based SA method (OSAPS) on social media data. Their aim is to identify the problem area on the customers' feedback on delivery issues of postal services and to generate automated online reply for those issues. They build ontology model from extracted data and use it to determine issues from the negative sentiments with SentiStrength. Their process includes data cleaning, extract only combination of nouns and verbs tags for query building and retrieves information from SPARQL Query from ontology model. Their ontology model with SPARQL query extract combinations of various nouns and verbs from negative tweets.

Tran and Phan, (2015) suggested a model for construction of sentiment ontology based Vietnamese reviews. This model comprised three phases: conceptual relation identification to determine the relationship among newly extracted features, feature extraction using word relationship in dependency tree and sentiment polarity assignment using corpus. Extraction of new features and sentiments is done by double propagation algorithm which proposed rules of syntactic relationship of sentiment words with feature, feature with feature and among sentiment words. They proposed six conceptual rules based on Vietnamese grammar to identify the semantic relationship of sentiment words with features present in opinion and reported an accuracy of 58.15% in terms of F-measure.

Ankit Ramteke et al., (2013) proposed rule based and machine learning (ML) approach for detection of thwarting and sarcasm using ontology in camera domain. They find document polarity by determining weights for the nodes of camera domain ontology from sentiment lexicons and used polarity reversal in opinion on different parts of product. Their ML based approach (SVM) outperforms rule based approach.

The topic modeling technique used in Guzman and Maalej, (2014) does not involve detection of infrequent features, lexical SA on sarcasm level, negation and conditionals. By measuring coherency of extracted features or using aspect tree, more significant features in the opinion can be obtained. Building unsupervised sentiment lexicon with SentiWordNet resulted in better accuracy. The ontology provides hierarchical semantic data to identify and extract features in an efficient way. Ramanathan and Ramnath, (2010) got the best accuracy at 80% for software dataset using ontology-domain mapping sentences on the objects contained in the ontology. Recupero et al.,(2014) suggested SA scoring algorithm to build a framework called Sentilo for extraction of sentiment relations in a sentence. Their framework identified topics in different context and target holders which are stored in RDF (Resource Description Framework) representation using Linked data and an opinion ontology. Thakor and Sasi, (2015) approach to identify negative sentiments for query data isn't efficient and needs updating and extraction of more logical data to optimize SPARQL query. Tran and Phan, (2015) work did not identify features in phrases.

3 FBSA using Dictionaries

Customer car reviews are extracted from *edmund*[2] site.

3.1 Dictionary-based sentiment analysis

According to Liu (2012), a sentiment is defined as 5-tuple (quintuple) in a given document d as follows:

$$S = (e_i, a_{ij}, s_{ijkl}, h_k, t_l) \qquad (1)$$

where e_i is the ith target under consideration, a_{ij} is a jth feature of the target i, h_k is the user who expresses the opinion, t_l is the time at which the review is conveyed, s_{ijkl} is the sentiment of jth feature a_{ij} of ith target e_i by h_k at time t_l.

For example, *"Last Sunday, David found out that the bmw 3.0 navigation is very poor"*. In this sentence, $e_i = $ *bmw 3.0*, $a_{ij} = $ *navigation*, $h_k = $

---

[2]http://www.edmunds.com/car-reviews/

David, $t_l = last\ Sunday$, $s_{ijkl} = poor$, which should be negative on sentiment analysis.

For dictionary-based SA, two dictionaries of text files containing positive and negative sentiment word list is taken from the Opinion Lexicon [3] (English) (Hu and Liu, 2004) for sentiment analysis.

3.2 Algorithm for FBSA using dictionaries

This is a naïve method for SA. $stSum$ is the overall sentiment score for the review and sc is the sentiment score of a feature. Table 1 and 2 give labels to the ranges of $stSum$, sc (second and third column respectively) of the four functions $rR1(stSum)$, $rR2(stSum)$, $rF1(sc)$, $rF2(sc)$. These ranges are decided on the basis of selection of better distribution of scores of reviews. The $rR1(stSum)$, $rR2(stSum)$ functions give labels to sentiment polarity ($stSum$) for each review and $rF1(sc)$, $rF2(sc)$ functions add labels to sentiment polarity (sc) for each key in $carD$.

labels	$rR1(stSum)$	$rF1(sc)$
VERY_BAD	≤ -5	≤ -2
BAD	(-5,-2]	(-2,-1]
NOT_GOOD	(-2,0)	(-1,0)
NEUTRAL	{0}	{0}
GOOD	(0,8]	(0,5]
VERY_GOOD	(8,14]	(5,7]
EXCELLENT	> 14	> 7

Table 1: sentiment labels of reviews and features for Algorithm 1

In Algorithm 1 and 3, $carD$ is a dictionary having car attributes or features as keys and their values are relevant sentiment words in the user review, sentiment score and labels (ranks) of the features. The words (attributes) in $carJ$ is a jargon or list of features extracted from the RDF triples obtained from built ontology of car ($Car\_Ontology$) as described in Section 5.

Generating $stList$ of sentence s_i : $stList$ is a list of tuples of form (word, part-of-speech tag, polarity, position) denoted as (w, pos, pol, p). First, sentence s_i is tokenized into words. Each word is represented as a tuple (w, pos, pol, p), where p is position of w in sentence s_i, pos are pos-tag using $nltk.pos\_tag$ and pol (default value is 0) is computed by checking, if w is in positive dictionary,

[3] https://www.cs.uic.edu/~liub/FBS/sentiment-analysis.html

pol is 1 and if w is in negative dictionary, pol is -1.

Breaking into segments: The sentence segments are formed by finding positions of the conjunction words ('but', 'and','or', ',' and 'because'). For e.g, sentence s_i: *"The mileage is not good but engine is smooth, sound system is good"*. The segments of this example are: *"The mileage is not good","engine is smooth", "sound system is good"* which are formed by breaking sentence at positions of conjunction words. Within each segment S_{s_i}, each word in $carD$ (having car attributes as keys) is tagged with tuples of $stList$ of words of S_{s_i} except the tuples having words as keys.

Algorithm 1 FBSA using dictionaries

1: **Input:** reviews, $carJ$, sentiment dictionaries
2: **Output :** files of FB sentiment ranks of cars.
3: **for** each review R in review-list of f **do:**
4:     Break R into sentences;
5:     $stSum \leftarrow 0$;   ▷ total review polarity
6:     $stList \leftarrow []$;
7:     $carD \leftarrow \{\}$;
8:     make car attributes of $carJ$ as $carD$ keys;
9:     **for** each sentence s_i in R **do:**
10:         generate $stList$ of s_i as explained in Section 3.2;
11:         $stSum \leftarrow stSum + \sum pol$ of each w in $stList$;
12:         make segments of s_i as explained in Section 3.2;
13:         **for** each segment $S_{s_i} \in s_i$ **do:**
14:             add tuples of S_{s_i} to $carD$ keys as explained in Section 3.2;
15:         ▷ add ranks and score of each $carD$ key;
16:     **for** each key $k_j \in carD$ **do:**
17:         $sc = \sum pol$ of tuples of $carD[k_j]$;
18:         $carD[k_j].append(rF1(sc))$;
19:         ▷ ranks to sentiment of each review;
20:     $rR1\{stSum\}$;
21:         ▷ overall polarity of each review;
22:     $stType \leftarrow "NEUTRAL"$;
23:     **if** $stSum > 0$ **then:**
24:         $stType \leftarrow "POSITIVE"$;
25:     **if** $stSum < 0$ **then:**
26:         $stType \leftarrow "NEGATIVE"$;

---

4 FBSA using lexical resources

4.1 SentiWordNet

SentiWordNet 3.0[4] is an explicit lexical resource document for assignment of sentiment weightage for opinion mining. It contains English words, derived from WordNet[5] which carry semantic word relations, attached with a score. The POS in SentiWordNet contains sentiment subjectivity of adverb (r), noun (n), verb (v), adjective (a) synsets i.e. according to the meaning of each word used in a sentence. Its output contains five elements: pos tag, offset-id (identify synset), positive score, negative score and list of synsets. The sentiment score of each synset in SentiWordNet varies from 0 to 1.

4.2 Word Sense Disambiguation

Word Sense Disambiguation (WSD) (Navigli, 2009) recognizes which feeling of a word (which means) is utilized as a part of a sentence, when there are polysemy words or phrases. WSD needs dictionary for word reference to determine the possible meanings or glossary and a corpus database for disambiguated words identification. The WSD based on corpus method is not much practical because for word target labeling, a user has to refer to the word-phrase glossary repeatedly for the same word. The proposed method used fine-grained computational lexicon of WordNet (Fellbaum and Christiane, 1998) dictionary for WSD by finding semantic word relations to find the sentiment polarity furthermore.

4.3 Feature based Sentiment Analysis

4.3.1 Building Lexicon:

Following types of sentiment lexicons are created manually (Palanisamy et al., 2013) for FBSA:

1. *Regular Lexicons:*
   This sort of lexicon comprises of sentiment information having consistent semantics or connotation crosswise over various classes and the opinion words.

   (a) *Default Sentiment Words:* Common list of words (adjective, adverbs) having consistent sentiment semantic value (positive or negative weightage) across different fields.

   (b) *TNgList words:* These reverse the sentiment subjectivity ($\pm$) sign. For e.g.,

"The mileage is not good" has sentiment word *"good"* but it is negative subject.

   (c) *HdNg Words:* the words (*'absence'*, *'deals'*, *'needs'*, *'presence' etc.*), which remain undetected by common sentiment words, have hidden sentiment in statement. In the sentence, *"The car needs a better wheel"*, word *"needs"* have a negative sense.

   (d) *Conjunctive Words:* the words which connect sub-statements like commas, conjunctions like *'and'* etc. The sentence is segmented for feature extraction. For e.g., *"Speed is good but the mileage is bad"* contains two fragments *"Speed is good"* and *"mileage is bad"*.

2. *Feature-based Lexicon:*
   For an entity: cars, the entity names are car brands e.g. *bmw3.0* and aspects/attributes like *performance, mileage* etc. This lexicon type includes: entity or product list which identifies users' target entities, a list of car properties for features, entity-based word-list of sentiments related to subjectivity.

4.3.2 Sentiment Calculation:

We apply sentiment analysis based on sentence-level and entity-level. FBSA is done by feature extraction using ontology. The sentiment labels are also assigned based on the overall review and feature-based sentiment polarity value mentioned in *rR2()*, *rF2()* respectively. After pre-processing, the sentiment is calculated as given in Algorithm 3:

1. WSD on the tokenized word list is performed to identify correct word sense in a review.

2. Compute sentiment list ($stList$) having (w, pos, pol, p) tuples. $stList$ contains nouns, verbs, adjectives and adverbs.

3. To calculate polarity, we check (Algorithm 2) if the word is not present in SentiWordNet but present in *NgList* or *HdNg* list, then the word tuple is added to the $stList$ along with the corresponding sentiment polarity. For e.g., in review, *"The car needs a better wheel"*, word *"needs"* has negative aspect for *"speed"* feature.

---

[4]http://sentiwordnet.isti.cnr.it/
[5]http://wordnet.princeton.edu

labels	$rR2(stSum)$	$rF2(sc)$
VERY_BAD	≤ -2	≤ -1
BAD	(-2,-1]	(-1,-0.5]
NOT_GOOD	(-1,0)	(-0.5,0)
NEUTRAL	$\{0\}$	$\{0\}$
GOOD	(0,1]	(0,1]
VERY_GOOD	(1,2]	(1,1.5]
EXCELLENT	> 2	> 1.5

Table 2: sentiment labels of reviews and features for Algorithm 3

4. In Algorithm 2, if the word is in $TNgList$, then the polarity of all the words present within word length of 2 in both the directions (4 units proximity by checking distance) will be reversed.

5. The sentiment of an entity is given by sc which is computed by summing the sentiment scores i.e. pol's of the entity in the review. The overall sentiment of the review is given by $stSum$.

4.3.3 Feature Extraction:

1. Only those features that are present in both the reviews and $CarJ$ are the candidate for features in this phase.

2. These candidate features and their sentiment word list is appended to $CarD$ dictionary.

4.4 Algorithm for FBSA Using Lexical Resources

In Algorithm 2, $HdNgList$ is the list of sentiment words (not present in SentiWordNet): 'needs', 'absence', 'deficient', 'lack', 'incomplete', 'partial', 'fragmental'. $TNgList$ is the list of words to reverse polarity.

Data preprocessing of sentence s_i:
This aims at normalizing the text into an appropriate form for sentiments extraction. Data preprocessing includes:

- *Tokenizing*: We break each review R into sentences and each sentence s_i is tokenized into words with part-of-speech tagging (identifying n, v, a, r) by *nltk pos_tokenizer*.

- *Reduction to root words*: We reduce words to derived form or stem, which helps in building lexicons. For e.g., words: 'hates', 'hating' reduced to 'hate'. It is done by *nltk stemmer*.

- *Expansion of abbreviated words*: After removing stopwords, we expand abbreviated words in s_i manually. We identify words, having some repetition of letters, and convert them to proper form like "wooowwww" to "wow".

- *Slang words or spelling correction*: We correct spellings and convert slang words to standard English by replacing the words with their expansion or correct form.

- *Appending sentiments of emoticons*: We add sentiments of the emoticons by replacing the smileys with appropriate words : happy, very happy, winky, sad, crying, angry.

- *Word Sense Disambiguation*: We generate $wsdList$ which is a list of word-synsets (having correct word sense, i.e. *pos* tag, in the sentence) after applying WSD. In this step, we apply WSD using maximum path similarity method, which is based on the idea that path length of more similar word sense of the word w is lesser than other less similar words, i.e. computes the shortest word sense edge from all edges of w.

Generating $stList$ of sentence s_i:

- $stList$ is a list of tuples of form (w, pos, pol, p) as mentioned in Section 3.2. But pol value is computed using SentiWordNet method which is the difference of positive and negative SentiWordNet score considering WSD

- *capitalization weightage*: Add extra $\pm\alpha$ sentiment weightage for capital emotion words

- *exclamation mark weightage:* Add extra sentiment score $\pm\beta/(\#('!'))$ to the words with attached exclamation mark

- *start sentence weightage:* if s_i is start sentence and has more positive or negative score, then add $\pm\gamma$ to $stSum$

- *last sentence weightage:* if s_i is last sentence and has more positive or negative score, then add $\pm\delta$ to $stSum$

The values of α, β, γ and δ are fixed empirically.

Algorithm 2 reverse polarity of negation words

1: **function** RVP($stList$, $stNgList$)
2:     **if** $stList \neq \emptyset$ and $stNgList \neq \emptyset$ **then:**
3:         **for** each word $w_1 \in stList$ **do:**
4:             **for** each word $w_2 \in stNgList$ **do:**
5:                 **if** proximity distance $|w_1 - w_2|$ ≤ 2 **then:**   ▷ both side
6:                     Reverse polarity of w_1;
7:     **else**
8:         **if** $stNgList \neq \emptyset$ **then:**
9:             **for** each word $w_i \in stNgList$ **do:**
10:                 **if** $w_i \notin stList$ **then:**
11:                     $stList.append((w_i, pos_i, pol_i, p_i))$;
12:     $HdNg \leftarrow$ tuples of $stList$ having words from $HdNgList$;
13:     **for** each word $w_i \in HdNg$ **do:**
14:         **if** $w_i \notin$ SentiWordNet **then:**
15:             $stList.append((w_i, pos_i, pol_i, p_i))$;
16:     **return** $stList$;

5 Building ontology in car domain

The car ontology ($Car\_Ontology$) about car properties shown in Figure 1 is built using Protégé[6] (protege-5.0.0-beta-15).

Figure 1: $Car\_Ontology$: classes, subclasses, data properties of Car attributes.

6 Data Parsing

The list of features of car is collected from parsing RDF syntax of built $Car\_Ontology$. RDF triples

---

Algorithm 3 FBSA using Lexical Resources

1: **Input:** $HdNgList$, $TNgList$, reviews, $carJ$;
2: **Output:** files of FB sentiment ranks of cars
3: **for** each review R in review-list of f **do:**
4:     Break R into sentences;
5:     $stSum \leftarrow 0$;   ▷ total review polarity;
6:     $stList \leftarrow []$;
7:     $carD \leftarrow \{\}$;
8:     make car attributes of $carJ$ as $carD$ keys;
9:     **for** each sentence s_i in R **do:**
10:         $wsdList \leftarrow []$;
11:         data preprocessing of s_i and make $wsdList$ as explained in Section 4.4;
12:         generate $stList$ of s_i as explained in Section 4.4;
13:         ▷ reverse pol of $TNgList$ words;
14:         $stNgList \leftarrow$ list of tuples of $stList$ having words present in $TNgList$;
15:         $stList \leftarrow$ RVP($stList$, $stNgList$);
16:         $stSum \leftarrow stSum + \sum pol$ of each w in $stList$;
17:         make segments of s_i as explained in Section 3.2;
18:         **for** each segment $S_{s_i} \in s_i$ **do:**
19:             add tuples of S_{s_i} to $carD$ keys as explained in Section 3.2;
20:     ▷ add ranks and score of each $carD$ key;
21:     **for** each key $k_j \in carD$ **do:**
22:         $sc = \sum pol$ of tuples of $carD[k_j]$;
23:         $carD[k_j].append(rF1(sc))$;
24:     ▷ ranks to sentiment of each review;
25:   $rR2\{stSum\}$;
26:     ▷ overall polarity of each review;
27:   $stType \leftarrow$ "$NEUTRAL$";
28:   **if** $stSum > 0$ **then:**
29:     $stType \leftarrow$ "$POSITIVE$";
30:   **if** $stSum < 0$ **then:**
31:     $stType \leftarrow$ "$NEGATIVE$";

(subject-predicate-object) between tags are stored by a graph (tree form) method which is used by previous Algorithms 1 and 3 for FBSA in collecting sentiment words related to defined category. We made a car database with thirteen data tables using the parsed and extracted data from Algorithm 1 and 3 which represents the customers' opinion about different car attributes.

---

[6]http://protege.stanford.edu/

7 Modeling in OBDA

7.1 Experimentation using ontop

An OBDA model (obdaModel, 2009) includes only single data source which is the database that constitutes information about the system and from which the queries would be executed in the framework. This model contains a set of mapping axioms in the ontology.

7.1.1 Mapping axioms

A mapping axiom in this model consists of the following three elements: mappingId (name: any string which recognizes the axiom), source (randomly selected SQL query processed over the car database) and target (RDF triple template that contains placeholders to refer the column names described in source query). For e.g., a valid ontop mapping in *Car_Ontology* is given below:

mappingId: Car_Attrbiutes
source : SELECT userid, appearance FROM carAppearanceTable
target : *<http://www.semanticweb.org/ont25# CarID_{id}> rdf:type :Car; :title {appearance}*

In target mapping, following placeholders are present in this model: a literal template, i.e., *appearance* describing one of the car attributes, and a URI template, i.e., *http://www.semanticweb.org/ont25#CarID_{id}*. The literal template placeholder is used to generate literal values, while URI template is used to create object URIs from the data in car database.

id	*name*
22	bmw3.0
23	acura_mdx

Table 3: query example

Meaning of a mapping axiom: The main objective of the mapping axioms in this model is to convert data in the specified data sources into a set of ABox assertions/RDF triples. Consider the following mapping about Appearance attribute:

mappingId: Appearance
source : SELECT id, name FROM carAppearanceTable
target: *<http://www.semanticweb.org/ont25# CarID_{id}> rdf:type :Car; :name {name}*

:hasCarAttriubtes "appearance"

The source query takes the mapping axioms and *Car_Ontology* as input and associate RDF triples set for each resultant target row. By substituting the placeholders in target ({id} and {name}) with different values from the row, more triples can be generated. For e.g., if the answer to the source query is shown in Table 3, then the given mapping would generate the following six RDF triples:
<http://www.semanticweb.org/ont25#CarID_{22}> rdf:type :Car;

   :name "bmw3.0"
   :hasCarAttriubtes "appearance".
<http://www.semanticweb.org/ont25#CarID_{23}> rdf:type :Car;

   :name "acura_mdx"
   :hasCarAttriubtes "appearance".

Here, each target row generates three triples, since the target in the mapping had three triple templates. Here, by replacing {id} in the URI template *<http://www.semanticweb.org/ont25#CarID_{22}>* by the value 22, we get an actual URI *<http://www.semanticweb.org/ont25#CarID_{23}>*, and by replacing {name} in the literal template {name}: *string* by the value *bmw3.0*, we obtain an actual literal value *"bmw3.0"*.

8 Comparison of FBSA for cars

The numbers of sentiment ranks of car attributes are obtained by querying in SPARQL. Here, five-star rating is calculated based on weighted mean or average using the following formula:

$$\frac{\sum_{i=1}^{5} wt_i \times r_i}{R} \qquad (2)$$

where wt_i is the weight of the ith-star rating, r_i is the number of reviews at that weight wt_i, R is the total number of reviews. In Table 4, 5, 6, 7, 5-star rating is available at edmund site. The FBSA using dictionary-based (DbFBSA) method is compared with the FBSA using lexical resources and ontology (LoFBSA) on the error-rate basis. Error (%) is computed by the absolute difference of experimental five-star rating from the observed five-star rating available at edmund site.

As we observe here that error (%) of FBSA using lexical resources and ontology is less than the dictionary-based method.

CarAttribute	5-star rating	LoFBSA	DbFBSA
Comfort	4.73	8.03%	15.22%
Interior	4.73	7.82%	15.22%
Performance	4.72	9.95%	15.04%
Reliability	4.77	9.22%	16%

Table 4: Comparison table for Acura_mdx

CarAttribute	5-star rating	LoFBSA	DbFBSA
Comfort	4.68	8.33%	15%
Interior	4.75	9.05%	15.37%
Performance	4.76	10.08%	15.54%
Reliability	4.78	10.46%	16.32%

Table 5: Comparison table for Acura_rdx

CarAttribute	5-star rating	LoFBSA	DbFBSA
Comfort	4.67	9.2%	14%
Interior	4.67	8.13%	13.9%
Performance	4.60	8.2%	13%
Reliability	4.67	8.1%	14.34%

Table 6: Comparison table for Acura_tl

CarAttribute	5-star rating	LoFBSA	DbFBSA
Comfort	4.53	6.84%	12%
Interior	4.57	6.56%	12.03%
Performance	4.71	10.10%	15%
Reliability	4.37	5.49%	8%

Table 7: Comparison table for Bmw_3series

9 Conclusions

The main objective of this work is to provide a better recommendation to a user based on the reviews given by the customers. The proposed system performs FBSA on car reviews using SentiWordNet with WSD and a domain ontology. The contributions of this paper are 1) FBSA using lexical resources and ontology of car, 2) the mappings of car attributes for query analysis to determine the five-star ratings. Performance of LoFBSA is better than DbFBSA (without WSD) since LoFBSA considers data preprocessing with WSD, slangs, reversing polarity in case of negation and conjunctions for feature extraction.

10 Acknowledgement

This project was supported by DST-SERB No. YSS/2015/000906.

References

Fellbaum and Christiane. 1998. Wordnet: An electronic lexical database mit press. *Cambridge MA*.

Thomas R Gruber et al. 1993. A translation approach to portable ontology specifications. *Knowledge acquisition*, 5(2):199–220.

Emitza Guzman and Walid Maalej. 2014. How do users like this feature? a fine grained sentiment analysis of app reviews. In *2014 IEEE 22nd international requirements engineering conference (RE)*, pages 153–162, Karlskrona, Sweden. IEEE.

Minqing Hu and Bing Liu. 2004. Mining and summarizing customer reviews. In *Proceedings of the Tenth ACM SIGKDD International Conference on Knowledge Discovery and Data Mining*, KDD '04, pages 168–177, New York, NY, USA. ACM.

Bing Liu. 2012. Sentiment analysis and opinion mining. *Synthesis lectures on human language technologies*, 5(1):1–167.

Roberto Navigli. 2009. Word sense disambiguation: A survey. *ACM Comput. Surv.*, 41(2):10:1–10:69, February.

obdaModel. 2009. ontop. `http://ontop.inf.unibz.it/`. [Online; accessed 23-June-2016].

Prabu Palanisamy, Vineet Yadav, and Harsha Elchuri. 2013. Serendio: Simple and practical lexicon based approach to sentiment analysis. In *proceedings of Second Joint Conference on Lexical and Computational Semantics*, pages 543–548, Atlanta, Georgia. Citeseer.

J Ramanathan and R Ramnath. 2010. Context-assisted sentiment analysis. In *The 25th Annual ACM Symposium on Applied Computing*, pages 404–413, Sierre, Switzerland.

Ankit Ramteke, Akshat Malu, Pushpak Bhattacharyya, and J Saketha Nath. 2013. Detecting turnarounds in sentiment analysis: Thwarting. In *Proceedings of the 51st Annual Meeting of the Association for Computational Linguistics*, pages 860–865, Sofia, Bulgaria. Association for Computational Linguistics.

Diego Reforgiato Recupero, Sergio Consoli, Aldo Gangemi, Andrea Giovanni Nuzzolese, and Daria Spampinato. 2014. A semantic web based core engine to efficiently perform sentiment analysis. In *European Semantic Web Conference*, pages 245–248. Springer.

Pratik Thakor and Sreela Sasi. 2015. Ontology-based sentiment analysis process for social media content. *Procedia Computer Science*, 53:199–207.

Thien Khai Tran and Tuoi Thi Phan. 2015. Constructing sentiment ontology for vietnamese reviews. In *Proceedings of the 17th International Conference on Information Integration and Web-based Applications & Services*, iiWAS '15, pages 36:1–36:5, Brussels, Belgium. ACM.

Deepali Virmani, Vikrant Malhotra, and Ridhi Tyagi. 2014. Aspect based sentiment analysis to extract meticulous opinion value. *arXiv preprint arXiv:1405.7519*.

Wei Wei and Jon Atle Gulla. 2010. Sentiment learning on product reviews via sentiment ontology tree. In *Proceedings of the 48th Annual Meeting of the Association for Computational Linguistics*, pages 404–413, Uppsala, Sweden. Association for Computational Linguistics.

Cross-lingual transfer parsing from Hindi to Bengali using delexicalization and chunking

Ayan Das, Agnivo Saha, Sudeshna Sarkar
Department of Computer Science and Engineering
Indian Institute of Technology, Kharagpur, WB, India
ayan.das@cse.iitkgp.ernet.in
agnivo.saha@gmail.com
sudeshna@cse.iitkgp.ernet.in

Abstract

While statistical methods have been very effective in developing NLP tools, the use of linguistic tools and understanding of language structure can make these tools better. Cross-lingual parser construction has been used to develop parsers for languages with no annotated treebank. Delexicalized parsers that use only POS tags can be transferred to a new target language. But the success of a delexicalized transfer parser depends on the syntactic closeness between the source and target languages. The understanding of the linguistic similarities and differences between the languages can be used to improve the parser. In this paper, we use a method based on cross-lingual model transfer to transfer a Hindi parser to Bengali. The technique does not need any parallel corpora but makes use of chunkers of these languages. We observe that while the two languages share broad similarities, Bengali and Hindi phrases do not have identical construction. We can improve the transfer based parser if the parser is transferred at the chunk level. Based on this we present a method to use chunkers to develop a cross-lingual parser for Bengali which results in an improvement of unlabelled attachment score (UAS) from 65.1 (baseline parser) to 78.2.

1 Introduction

Parsers have a very important role in various natural language processing tasks. Machine learning based methods are most commonly used for learning parsers for a language given annotated parse trees which are called treebanks. But treebanks are not available for all languages, or only small treebanks may be available. In recent years, considerable efforts have been put to develop dependency parsers for low-resource languages. In the absence of treebank for a language, there has been research in using cross-lingual parsing methods (McDonald et al., 2011) where a treebank from a related source language (SL), is used to develop a parser for a target language (TL). In such work, an annotated treebank in SL and other resources in are used to develop a parser model for TL. Most of the existing work assume that although annotated treebanks are not available for the target language TL, there are other resources available such as parallel corpus between the source and the target languages (Xiao and Guo, 2015; Rasooli and Collins, 2015; Tiedemann, 2015). However, developing a parallel corpus is also expensive if such parallel corpus is not available.

In this work, our goal is to look at methods for developing a cross-lingual transfer parser for resource poor Indian language for which we have access to a small or no treebank. We assume the availability of a monolingual corpus in target language and a small bilingual (source-target) dictionary.

Given our familiarity with Bengali and Hindi, and availability of a small treebank we aim to test our approach in Hindi-Bengali transfer parsing. We choose Hindi as the source language as it is syntactically related to Bengali and a Hindi treebank (Nivre et al., 2016) is freely available which can be used to train a reasonably accurate parser (Saha and Sarkar, 2016). We wish to use this Hindi treebank to develop a Bengali parser. Although our current work aims to develop a parser in Bengali from Hindi, this may be taken up as a general method for other resource poor languages. We also have access to a monolingual corpus in Bengali and a small bilingual (Hindi-

D S Sharma, R Sangal and A K Singh. Proc. of the 13th Intl. Conference on Natural Language Processing, pages 99–108,
Varanasi, India. December 2016. ©2016 NLP Association of India (NLPAI)

Bengali) dictionary.

Since the vocabulary of two languages are different, some of the work in the literature attempted to address this problem by delexicalizing the dependency parsers by replacing the language-specific word-level features by more general part-of-speech or POS-level features. Such methods have yielded moderate quality parsers in the target language (McDonald et al., 2011). However the number of POS features is small and may not contain enough information. In order to alleviate this problem some work have been proposed to incorporate word-level features in the form of bi-lingual word clusters (Täckström et al., 2012) and other bilingual word features (Durrett et al., 2012; Xiao and Guo, 2014).

Both Hindi and Bengali use the SOV (Subject-Object-Verb) sentence structure. However, there exist differences in the morphological structure of words and phrases between these two languages (Chatterji et al., 2014). Since the overall syntactic structure of the languages are similar, we hypothesize that chunk level transfer of a Hindi parser to Bengali may be more helpful than word-level transfer.

The rest of the paper is organized as follows. Section 2 discusses some of the existing related work. In Section 3 we state the objective of this work. In Section 4 we present in details the the dataset used, and in 5 we state in details our approach for cross-lingual parsing. In Section 6 we analyze the errors. Section 7 concludes the paper.

2   Related work

A variety of methods for developing transfer parsers for resource poor languages without any treebank have been proposed in the literature. In this section, we provide a brief survey of some of the methods relevant to our work.

2.1   Delexicalized parsing

Delexicalized parsing proposed by Zeman and Resnik (2008) involves training a parser model on a treebank of a resource-rich language in a supervised manner without using any lexical features and applying the model directly to parse sentences in target language. They built a Swedish dependency parser using Danish, a syntactically similar language. Søgaard (2011) used a similar method for several different language pairs. Their system performance varied widely (F1-score : 50%-75%) depending upon the similarity of the language pairs.

Täckström et al. (2012) used cross-lingual word clusters obtained from a large unlabelled corpora as additional features in their delexicalized parser. Naseem et al. (2012) proposed a method for multilingual learning to languages that exhibit significant differences from existing resource-rich languages which selectively learns the features relevant for a target language and ties the model parameters accordingly. Täckström et al. (2013) improved performance of delexicalized parser by incorporating selective sharing of model parameters based on typological information into a discriminative graph-based parser model.

Distributed representation of words (Mikolov et al., 2013b) as vector can be used to capture cross-lingual lexical information and can be augmented with delexicalized parsers. Xiao and Guo (2014) learnt language-independent word representations to address cross-lingual dependency parsing. They combined all sentences from both languages to induce real-valued distributed representation of words under a deep neural network architecture, and then use the induced interlingual word representation as augmenting features to train a delexicalized dependency parser. Duong et al. (2015a) followed a similar approach where the vectors for both the languages are learnt using a skipgram-like method in which the system was trained to predict the POS tags of the context words instead of the words themselves.

2.2   Cross-lingual projection

Cross-lingual projection based approaches use parallel data or some other lexical resource such as dictionary to project source language dependency relations to target language (Hwa et al., 2005). Ganchev et al. (2009) used generative and discriminative models for dependency grammar induction that use word-level alignments and a source language parser.

McDonald et al. (2011) learnt a delexicalized parser in English language and then used the English parser to seed a constraint learning algorithm to learn a parser in the target language. Ma and Xia (2014) used word alignments obtained from parallel data to transfer source language constraints to the target side.

Rasooli and Collins (2015) proposed a method to induce dependency parser in the target language using a dependency parser in the source language and a parallel corpus. Guo et al. (2015) proposed a CCA based projection method and a projection method based on word alignments obtained from parallel corpus.

2.3 Parsing in Hindi and Bengali

Hindi and Bengali are morphologically rich and relaively free word order languages. Some of the notable works on Indian languages are by Bharati and Sangal (1993) and Bharati et al. (2002). Also the works of Nivre (2005) and Nivre (2009) have been successfully applied for parsing Indian languages such as Hindi and Bengali. Several works on Hindi parsing (Ambati et al., 2010; Kosaraju et al., 2010) used data-driven parsers such as the Malt parser (Nivre, 2005) and the MST parser (Mcdonald et al., 2005). Bharati et al. (2009b) used a demand-frame based approach for Hindi parsing. Chatterji et al. (2009) have shown that proper feature selection (Begum et al., 2011) can immensely improve the performance of the data-driven and frame-based parsers.

Chunking (shallow parsing) has been used successfully to develop good quality parsers in Hindi language (Bharati et al., 2009b; Chatterji et al., 2012). Bharati et al. (2009b) have proposed a two-stage constraint-based approach where they first tried to extract the intra-chunk dependencies and resolve the inter-chunk dependencies in the second stage. Ambati et al. (2010) used disjoint sets dependency relation and performed the intra-chunk parsing and inter-chunk parsing separately. Chatterji et al. (2012) proposed a three stage approach where a rule-based inter-chunk parsing followed a data-driven inter-chunk parsing.

A project for building multi-representational and multi-layered treebanks for Hindi and Urdu (Bhatt et al., 2009)[1] was carried out as a joint effort by IIIT Hyderabad, University of Colorado and University of Washington. Besides the syntactic version of the treebank being developed by IIIT Hyderabad (Ambati et al., 2011), University of Colorado has built the Hindi-Urdu proposition bank (Vaidya et al., 2014) and a phrase-structure form of the treebank (Bhatt and Xia, 2012) is being developed at University of Washington. A part of the Hindi dependency treebank[2] has been released in which the inter-chunk dependency re-

lations (dependency links between chunk heads) have been manually tagged and the chunks were expanded automatically using an arc-eager algorithm.

Some of the major works on parsing in Bengali language appeared in ICON 2009 (http://www.icon2009.in/). Ghosh et al. (2009) used a CRF based hybrid method, Chatterji et al. (2009) used variations of the transition based dependency parsing. Mannem (2009) came up with a bi-directional incremental parsing and perceptron learning approach and De et al. (2009) used a constraint-based method. Das et al. (2012) compares performance of a grammar driven parser and a modified MALT parser.

3 Objective

We want to build a good dependency parser using cross-lingual transfer method for some Indian languages for which no treebanks are available. We try to make use of the Hindi treebank to build the dependency parser. We explore the use of the other resources that we have.

Due to our familiarity with Bengali language and availability of a small treebank in Bengali we aim to perform our initial experiments in Bengali to test our proposed method. We have a small Hindi-Bengali bilingual dictionary and POS taggers, morphological analyzers and chunkers for both these languages.

In such a scenario delexicalization methods can be used for cross-lingual parser construction. We wish to get some understanding of what additional resources can be used for general cross-lingual transfer parsing in this framework depending on the similarity and differences between the language pairs.

4 Resources used

For our experiments, we used the Hindi Universal Dependency treebank to train the Hindi parser (Saha and Sarkar, 2016; Chen and Manning, 2014). The Hindi universal treebank consists of 16648 parse trees annotated using Universal Dependency (UD) tagset divided into training, development and test sets. For testing in Bengali we used the test set of 150 parse trees annotated using Anncorra (Sharma et al., 2007) tagset. This small Bengali treebank was used in ICON2010[3]

---

[1]http://verbs.colorado.edu/hindiurdu/index.html
[2]http://ltrc.iiit.ac.in/treebank_H2014/

[3]http://www.icon2010.in/

contest to train parsers for various Indian languages. The parse trees in the test data were partially tagged with only inter-chunk dependencies and chunk information. We completed the trees by manually annotating the intra-chunk dependencies using the intra-chunk tags proposed by Kosaraju et al. (2012). We used the complete trees for our experiments.

Table 1 gives the details of the datasets used.

Table 1: Universal Dependency Hindi treebank.

Data	Universal Dependency treebank (Number of trees)	ICON Bengali treebank (Number of trees)
Training	13304	979
Development	1659	150
Test	1685	150

The initial Hindi and Bengali word embeddings were obtained by running word2vec (Mikolov et al., 2013b) on Hindi Wikipedia dump corpus and FIRE 2011[4] corpus respectively.

For Hindi-Bengali word pairs we used a small bilingual dictionary developed at our institute as a part of ILMT project[5]. It consists of about 12500 entries. For chunking we used the chunkers and chunk-head computation tool developed at our institute. The sentences in the Hindi treebank were chunked using an automatic chunker to obtain the chunk-level features. In case of disagreement between the output of automatic chunker and the gold standard parse trees we adhered to the chunk structure of the gold standard parse tree.

Before parsing the Hindi trees we relabeled the Hindi treebank sentences by Anncorra (Sharma et al., 2007) POS and morphological tags using the POS tagger (Dandapat et al., 2004) and morphological analyzer (Bhattacharya et al., 2005) as the automatic chunker requires the POS and morphological information in Anncorra format. Moreover, due to relabeling both the training and the test data will have the POS and morphological features in Anncorra format.

5 Our proposed Hindi to Bengali cross-lingual dependency parser

5.1 Baseline delexicalization based method

For the delexicalized baseline we trained the Hindi parser using only POS features. We used this model directly to parse the Bengali test sentences. It gives an UAS (Unlabelled Attachment Score) of 65.1% (Table 2).

We report only the UAS because the Bengali arc labels uses AnnCorra tagset which is different from Universal Dependency tagset. The dependency lables in the UD and ICON treebanks are different, with ICON providing a more fine-grained and Indian language specific tags. However, it was observed that the unlabelled dependencies were sufficiently similar.

5.2 Transferred parser enhanced with lexical features

When the parser trained using the lexical features of one language is used to parse sentences in another language the performance depends on the lexical similarity between the two languages.

We wish to investigate whether it is possible to use the syntactic similarities of the words to transfer some information to the Bengali parser along with the non-lexical information. We have used word embeddings (Mikolov et al., 2013b) for the lexical features in the hope that the word vectors capture sufficient lexical information.

Our work is different from that of (Xiao and Guo, 2014) and (Duong et al., 2015b) where the word vectors for both the languages are jointly trained. We observed that the work of (Xiao and Guo, 2014) is dependent on the quality and size of the dictionary and the training may not be uniform due to the difference in frequency of the words occurring in the corpus on which the vectors are trained. It also misses out the words that have multiple meanings in the other language.

Our method has the following steps;

Step 1 - Learning monolingual word embeddings : The monolingual word embeddings for Hindi and Bengali are learnt by training word2vec (Mikolov et al., 2013b) on monolingual Hindi and Bengali corpus respectively. The dimension of the learnt word embeddings are set to 50.

Step 2 - Training the Hindi monolingual dependency parser : To train the Hindi parser model using the Hindi treebank data we used the parser proposed by Chen and Manning (2014). The word embeddings were initialized by the ones learnt from monolingual corpus. Apart from the word embeddings, the other features are randomly initialized.

---

[4] http://www.isical.ac.in/ clia/2011/
[5] http://ilmt.iiit.ac.in/ilmt/index.php

Step 3 - Learning interlingual word representations using linear regression based projection:
For learning interlingual word representations we used all the cross-lingual word pairs from a Hindi-Bengali dictionary and dropped the Hindi words whose corresponding entry in Bengali is of multiple words. We used only those word pairs for which both the words are in the vocabulary of the corresponding monolingual corpora on which the word embeddings were trained. The linear regression method (Mikolov et al., 2013a) was used to project the Bengali word embeddings into the vector space of the Hindi embeddings obtained after training the parser on Hindi treebank data. The regressor was trained using the embeddings of the 3758 word-pairs obtained from the dictionary.

Subsequently, we attempted to compare the method proposed by Xiao and Guo (2014). In both the cases the parser performances were very similar and hence we report only the results obtained using linear regression.

Step 4 - Transfer of parser model from Hindi to Bengali : In the delexicalized version, the parsers are used directly to test on Bengali data. In the lexicalized versions, we obtained the Bengali parser models by replacing the Hindi word embeddings by the projected Bengali word vectors obtained in Step 3. The transformation is shown in figure 1.

Table 2: Comparison of 1) delexicalized parser model and 2) parser using projected Bengali vectors.

	Delexi-calized (Baseline)	Projected Bengali vectors
(Chen and Manning, 2014) parser	65.1	67.2

Table 2 compares the UAS of word-level transfer for the 1) delexicalized parser model (*Delexicalized*) and 2) the lexicalized Bengali parser model in which the Hindi word embeddings are replaced by Bengali word vectors projected onto the vector space of the Hindi word embeddings (*Projected Bengali vectors*). We observe that projected lexical features improves UAS over the delexicalized baseline from 65.1 to 67.2.

5.3 Chunk-level transfer for cross-lingual parsing

There exist differences in the morphological structure of words and phrases between Hindi and Bengali. For example, the English phrase "took bath" is written in Hindi as "*nahayA*" using a single word and the same phrase in Bengali is written as "*snan korlo*" "(bath did)" using two words. Similarly, the English phrase "is going" is written in Hindi as "*ja raha hai*" "(go doing is)" using three words and the same phrase in Bengali is written as "*jachhe*" using a single word.

This makes us believe that chunking can help to improve cross-lingual parsing between Hindi and Bengali languages by using the similarities in the arrangement of phrases in a sentence. Chunking (shallow parsing) reduces the complexity of full parsing by identifying non-recursive cores of different types of phrases in the text (Peh and Ann, 1996). Chunking is easier than parsing and both rule-based chunker or statistical chunker can be developed quite easily.

In figure 2 we present a Bengali sentence and the corresponding Hindi sentence. They are transliterated to Roman. The English gloss of the sentences are given. We indicate by parentheses the chunks of the sentences. We indicate by line the correspondence between the chunks. We see that the correspondence is at the chunk level and not at the word level.

The sentences are quite similar as far as the inter-chunk orientation is concerned as is evident from the Figure 3 and 4.

We have used Hindi and Bengali chunkers which identify the chunks and assign each chunk to its chunk type, chunk-level morphological features and the head words. For chunk level transfer we performed the following steps:

Step 1: We chunked the Hindi treebank sentences and extracted the chunk heads.

Step 2: We converted the full trees to chunk head trees by removing the non-head words and their links such that only the chunk head words and their links with the other head words are left.

Step 3: We trained the Hindi dependency parsers using the Hindi chunk head trees by the delexicalization method and the method described in section 5.2.

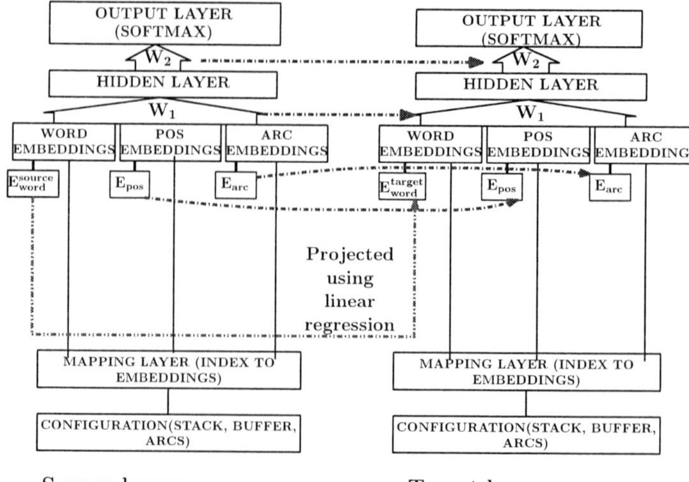

Figure 1: The neural network shares parameters like weights and POS, arc-label embeddings in source and target language parser models. Only the source language word embeddings replaced by projected target language word vectors. E_{word}^{source}, E_{word}^{target}, E_{POS}, E_{arc} are the embedding matrices from which the mapping layer gets the vectors by indexing.

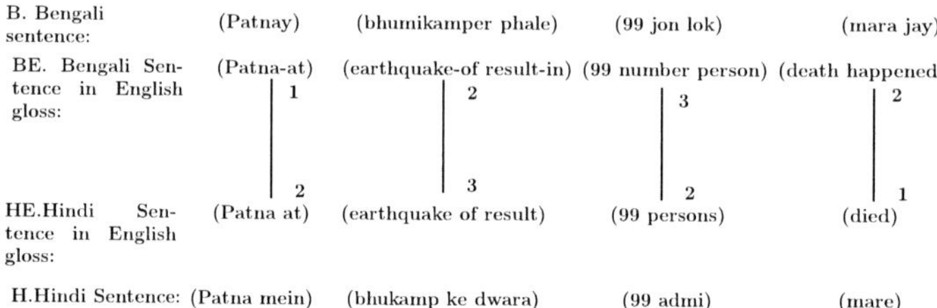

Figure 2: Chunk mapping between a Bengali and Hindi sentence that conveys the same meaning : "99 people died due to earthquake in Patna".

Figure 3: Word-level parse trees of the example Bengali and Hindi sentences (a) Bengali word-level parse tree (b) Hindi word-level parse tree

Figure 4: Chunk-level parse trees of the example Bengali and Hindi sentences (a) Bengali chunk-level parse tree (b) Hindi chunk-level parse tree

Step 4: This parser was transferred using the methods described in section 5.2 to get the delexi- calized parser for Bengali head trees.

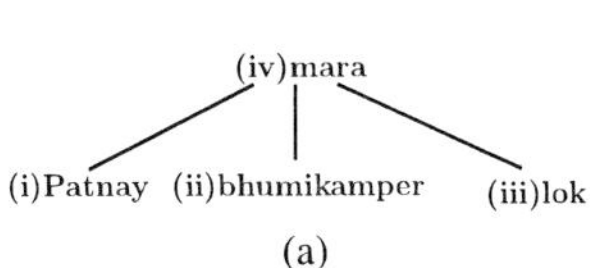 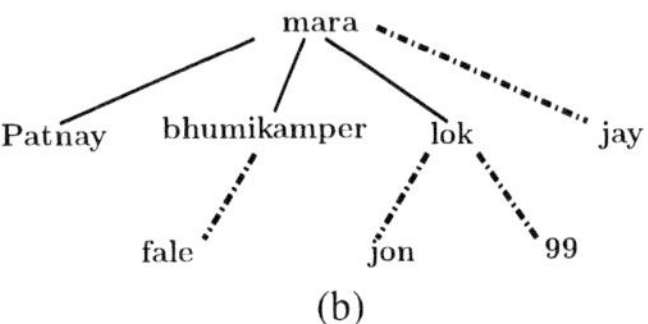

(a)   (b)

Figure 5: Chunk-level parse tree of the example Bengali sentence before and after expansion (a) Bengali chunk head parse tree (b) Bengali chunk head parse tree after expansion

Step 5: For testing, we parsed the Bengali test sentences consisting of only the chunk head words. The UAS score for head trees obtained by delexicalized method is 68.6.

Step 6: For intra-chunk expansion we simply attached the non-head words to their corresponding chunk heads to get the full trees (This introduces a lot of errors. In future we plan to use rules for chunk expansion to make the intra-chunk expansion more accurate.) The UAS score for trees after intra-chunk expansion is 78.2.

We observed that our simple heuristic for inter-chunk expansion increases accuracy of the parser. There are some rule-based methods and statistical approach for inter-chunk expansion (Kosaraju et al., 2012; Bharati et al., 2009a; Chatterji et al., 2012) in Hindi which may be adopted for Bengali.

Table 3: Comparison of word-level and chunk-level transfer of parse trees

	Delexicalized	Projected Bengali vectors
Trees after word-level transfer	65.1	67.2
Expanded chunk head trees after chunk-level transfer	78.2	75.8

Table 3 compares the UAS of baseline parsers for word-level transfer with chunk-level transfer followed by expansion. We found a significant increase of UAS score from 65.1 to 78.2 after parsing and subsequent intra-chunk expansion. However, while using common vector-based word representation had shown slight improvement when applied to the word level transfer it did not help when applied to chunk level transfer. This may be because we used only the vector embeddings of chunk heads for the chunk-level parsing. We wish to work further on vector representation of chunks which might capture more chunk-level information and help improve the results.

While chunking has been used with other parsers, we did not find any work that uses chunking in a transfer parser. The source (Hindi) delexicalized word-level parser gave an accuracy of 77.7% and the source (Hindi) delexicalized chunk-level parser followed by expansion gave an accuracy of 79.1% on the UD Hindi test data.

There is no reported work on cross-lingual transfer between Bengali and Hindi. But as a reference we will like to mention the type of UAS accuracy values reported for other transfer parsers based on delexicalization in the literature for other language pairs. Zeman and Resnik (2008)'s delexicalized parser gave a F-score of 66.4 on Danish language. Täckström et al. (2012) achieved an average UAS of 63.0 by using word clusters on ten target languages and English as the source language. They achieved UAS of 57.1 without using any word cluster feature. In their works, (Xiao and Guo, 2014) tried out cross-lingual parsing on a set of eight target languages with English as the source language and achieved a UAS of 58.9 on average while their baseline delexicalized MSTParser parser using universal POS tag features gave an UAS of 55.14 on average. Duong et al. (2015b) also applied their method on nine target languages and English as the source language. They achieved UAS of 58.8 on average.

6 Error analysis

We analyzed the errors in dependency relations of the parse trees obtained by parsing the test sentences. We analyze the results based on the number of dependency relations in the gold data that actually appear in the trees parsed by our parser. We report results of the ten most frequent dependency tags in table 4.

From table 4 we find that chunk-level transfer increases the accuracy of tree root identification. Chunk-level transfer significantly increases the ac-

105

Table 4: Comparison of errors for 12 dependency tags. The entries of column 3 to 6 indicates the number of dependencies bearing the corresponding tags in the gold data that actually appear in the parsed trees and the accuracy (in %).

	Actual Count of dependency relations	Delexicalized word-level transfer		Word-level transfer using projected Bengali vectors		Delexicalized chunk-level transfer		Chunk-level transfer using projected Bengali vectors	
k1 (doer/agent/subject)	166	111	(66.9)	104	(62.7)	133	(80.1)	118	(71.1)
vmod (Verb modifier)	111	71	(64.0)	78	(70.3)	85	(76.6)	71	(64.0)
main (root)	150	96	(64.4)	108	(72.5)	105	(70.5)	103	(69.1)
k2 (object)	131	100	(76.3)	92	(70.2)	104	(79.4)	88	(67.2)
r6 (possessive)	82	21	(25.6)	49	(59.8)	13	(15.9)	52	(63.4)
pof (Part of relation)	59	55	(93.2)	58	(98.3)	56	(94.9)	56	(94.9)
k7p (Location in space)	50	31	(62.0)	30	(60.0)	38	(76.0)	33	(66.0)
ccof (co-ordinate conjunction of)	47	1	(2.1)	4	(8.5)	1	(2.12)	2	(4.3)
k7t (Location in time)	40	25	(62.5)	20	(50.0)	31	(77.5)	15	(37.5)
k7 (Location elsewhere)	22	15	(68.2)	14	(63.6)	16	(72.7)	17	(77.3)
k1s (noun complement)	18	13	(72.2)	14	(77.8)	14	(77.8)	14	(77.8)
relc (relative clause)	12	1	(8.4)	1	(8.4)	0	(0.0)	0	(0.0)

curacy of identifying the relations with *k1*, *vmod*, *k2* and *k7* tags also.

Although delexicalized chunk-level parser gives the overall best result, the accuracy is lowest for the relation of type *r6* (possessive/genitive). We observed that in most of the erroneous cases, both the words that are expected to be connected by the *r6* dependency, are actually being predicted as modifiers of a common parent. We find that the accuracy of *r6* tag improves in case of delexicalized word-level transfer and the best accuracy on *r6* is achieved with the use of lexical features. Hence, the drop in performance may be due to the lack of sufficient information in the case of chunk-level transfer or the chunk expansion heuristic that we have used this work.

However, for all the methods discussed above the parser performs poorly in identifying the "conjuction of" (*ccof*) relations and relative clause (*relc*) relations. we observed that the poor result on *ccof* tag is due to the difference in annotation scheme of ICON and UD. In case of ICON data, the conjunctions are the roots of the trees and the corresponding verbs or nouns are the modifiers, while in UD scheme the conjunctions are the modifiers of the corresponding verbs of nouns. We need to investigate further into the poor identification of *relc* dependencies.

7   Conclusion

We show that knowledge of shallow syntactic structures of the languages helps in improving the quality of cross-lingual parsers. We observe that chunking significantly improves cross-lingual parsing from Hindi to Bengali due to their syntactic similarity at the phrase level. The experimental results clearly shows that chunk-level transfer of parser model from Hindi to Bengali is better than direct word-level transfer. This also goes to establish that one can improve the performance of pure statistical systems if one additionally uses some linguistic knowledge and tools. The initial experiments were done in Bengali. In future we plan to broaden the results to include other Indian languages for which open source chunkers can be found.

References

Bharat Ram Ambati, Samar Husain, Sambhav Jain, Dipti Misra Sharma, and Rajeev Sangal. 2010. Two methods to incorporate 'local morphosyntactic' features in Hindi dependency parsing. In *Proceedings of the NAACL HLT 2010 First Workshop on SPMRL*, pages 22–30, Los Angeles, CA, USA, June. Association for Computational Linguistics.

Bharat Ram Ambati, Rahul Agarwal, Mridul Gupta, Samar Husain, and Dipti Misra Sharma. 2011. Error detection for treebank validation. *Asian Language Resources collocated with IJCNLP 2011*, page 23.

Rafiya Begum, Karan Jindal, Ashish Jain, Samar Husain, and Dipti Misra Sharma. 2011. Identification of conjunct verbs in hindi and its effect on parsing accuracy. In *International Conference on Intelligent Text Processing and Computational Linguistics*, pages 29–40. Springer.

Akshar Bharati and Rajeev Sangal. 1993. Parsing free word order languages in the paninian framework. In *Proceedings of the 31st Annual Meeting on ACL*, ACL '93, pages 105–111, Stroudsburg, PA, USA. Association for Computational Linguistics.

Akshar Bharati, Rajeev Sangal, and T Papi Reddy. 2002. A constraint based parser using integer programming. *Proc. of ICON*.

Akshar Bharati, Mridul Gupta, Vineet Yadav, Karthik Gali, and Dipti Misra Sharma. 2009a. Simple parser for indian languages in a dependency framework. In *Proceedings of the Third Linguistic Annotation Workshop*, pages 162–165, Suntec, Singapore, August. Association for Computational Linguistics.

Akshar Bharati, Samar Husain, Meher Vijay, Kalyan Deepak, Dipti Misra Sharma, and Rajeev Sangal. 2009b. Constraint based hybrid approach to parsing indian languages. In *Proceedings of the 23rd PACLIC*, pages 614–621, Hong Kong, December. City University of Hong Kong.

Rajesh Bhatt and Fei Xia. 2012. Challenges in converting between treebanks: a case study from the hutb. In *META-RESEARCH Workshop on Advanced Treebanking*, page 53.

Rajesh Bhatt, Bhuvana Narasimhan, Martha Palmer, Owen Rambow, Dipti Misra Sharma, and Fei Xia. 2009. A multi-representational and multi-layered treebank for hindi/urdu. In *Proceedings of the Third Linguistic Annotation Workshop*, ACL-IJCNLP '09, pages 186–189, Stroudsburg, PA, USA. Association for Computational Linguistics.

Samit Bhattacharya, Monojit Choudhury, Sudeshna Sarkar, and Anupam Basu. 2005. Inflectional morphology synthesis for bengali noun, pronoun and verb systems. In *In Proceedings of the national conference on computer processing of Bangla (NCCPB*, pages 34–43.

Sanjay Chatterji, Praveen Sonare, Sudeshna Sarkar, and Devshri Roy. 2009. Grammar driven rules for hybrid bengali dependency parsing. *Proceedings of ICON09 NLP Tools Contest: Indian Language Dependency Parsing, Hyderabad, India*.

Sanjay Chatterji, Arnad Dhar, Sudeshna Sarkar, and Anupam Basu. 2012. A three stage hybrid parser for hindi. In *Proceedings of the Workshop on MT-PIL*, pages 155–162, Mumbai, India, December. The COLING 2012 Organizing Committee.

Sanjay Chatterji, Tanaya Mukherjee Sarkar, Pragati Dhang, Samhita Deb, Sudeshna Sarkar, Jayshree Chakraborty, and Anupam Basu. 2014. A dependency annotation scheme for bangla treebank. *Language Resources and Evaluation*, 48(3):443–477.

Danqi Chen and Christopher Manning. 2014. A fast and accurate dependency parser using neural networks. In *Proceedings of the 2014 EMNLP*, pages 740–750, Doha, Qatar, October. Association for Computational Linguistics.

S. Dandapat, S. Sarkar, and A. Basu. 2004. A hybrid model for part-of-speech tagging and its application to bengali.

Arjun Das, Arabinda Shee, and Utpal Garain. 2012. Evaluation of two bengali dependency parsers. In *Proceedings of the Workshop on MTPIL*, pages 133–142, Mumbai, India, December. The COLING 2012 Organizing Committee.

Sankar De, Arnab Dhar, and Utpal Garain. 2009. Structure simplification and demand satisfaction approach to dependency parsing for bangla. In *Proc. of 6th ICON tool contest: Indian Language Dependency Parsing*, pages 25–31.

Long Duong, Trevor Cohn, Steven Bird, and Paul Cook. 2015a. Cross-lingual transfer for unsupervised dependency parsing without parallel data. In *Proceedings of the Nineteenth Conference on CONLL*, pages 113–122, Beijing, China, July. Association for Computational Linguistics.

Long Duong, Trevor Cohn, Steven Bird, and Paul Cook. 2015b. Low resource dependency parsing: Cross-lingual parameter sharing in a neural network parser. *Volume 2: Short Papers*, page 845.

Greg Durrett, Adam Pauls, and Dan Klein. 2012. Syntactic transfer using a bilingual lexicon. In *Proceedings of the 2012 Joint Conference on EMNLP and CoNLL*, pages 1–11, Jeju Island, Korea, July. Association for Computational Linguistics.

Kuzman Ganchev, Jennifer Gillenwater, and Ben Taskar. 2009. Dependency grammar induction via bitext projection constraints. ACL '09, pages 369–377, Stroudsburg, PA, USA. Association for Computational Linguistics.

Aniruddha Ghosh, Pinaki Bhaskar, Amitava Das, and Sivaji Bandyopadhyay. 2009. Dependency parser for bengali: the ju system at icon 2009. In *Proc. of 6th ICON tool contest: Indian Language Dependency Parsing*, pages 7–11.

Jiang Guo, Wanxiang Che, David Yarowsky, Haifeng Wang, and Ting Liu. 2015. Cross-lingual dependency parsing based on distributed representations. In *Proceedings of the 53rd ACL and the 7th IJCNLP*, volume 1, pages 1234–1244.

Rebecca Hwa, Philip Resnik, Amy Weinberg, Clara Cabezas, and Okan Kolak. 2005. Bootstrapping parsers via syntactic projection across parallel texts. *Natural Language Engineering*, 11:11–311.

Prudhvi Kosaraju, Sruthilaya Reddy Kesidi, Vinay Bhargav Reddy Ainavolu, and Puneeth Kukkadapu. 2010. Experiments on indian language dependency parsing. *Proceedings of the ICON10 NLP Tools Contest: Indian Language Dependency Parsing*.

Prudhvi Kosaraju, Bharat Ram Ambati, Samar Husain, Dipti Misra Sharma, and Rajeev Sangal. 2012. Intra-chunk dependency annotation : Expanding hindi inter-chunk annotated treebank. In *Proceedings of the Sixth Linguistic Annotation Workshop*, pages 49–56, Jeju, Republic of Korea, July. Association for Computational Linguistics.

Xuezhe Ma and Fei Xia. 2014. Unsupervised dependency parsing with transferring distribution via parallel guidance and entropy regularization. In *Proceedings of the 52nd Annual Meeting of the ACL (Volume 1: Long Papers)*, pages 1337–1348, Baltimore, Maryland, June. Association for Computational Linguistics.

Prashanth Mannem. 2009. Bidirectional dependency parser for hindi, telugu and bangla. *Proceedings of ICON09 NLP Tools Contest: Indian Language Dependency Parsing, Hyderabad, India*.

Ryan Mcdonald, Fernando Pereira, Kiril Ribarov, and Jan Hajič. 2005. Non-projective dependency parsing using spanning tree algorithms. In *In Proceedings of HLT Conference and Conference on EMNLP*, pages 523–530.

Ryan McDonald, Slav Petrov, and Keith Hall. 2011. Multi-source transfer of delexicalized dependency parsers. In *Proceedings of the Conference on EMNLP*, EMNLP '11, pages 62–72, Stroudsburg, PA, USA. Association for Computational Linguistics.

Tomas Mikolov, Quoc V. Le, and Ilya Sutskever. 2013a. Exploiting similarities among languages for machine translation. *CoRR*, abs/1309.4168.

Tomas Mikolov, Ilya Sutskever, Kai Chen, Greg S Corrado, and Jeff Dean. 2013b. Distributed representations of words and phrases and their compositionality. In *NIPS 26*, pages 3111–3119. Curran Associates, Inc.

Tahira Naseem, Regina Barzilay, and Amir Globerson. 2012. Selective sharing for multilingual dependency parsing. In *Proceedings of the 50th Annual Meeting of the ACL: Long Papers - Volume 1*, ACL '12, pages 629–637, Stroudsburg, PA, USA. Association for Computational Linguistics.

Joakim Nivre, Marie-Catherine de Marneffe, Filip Ginter, Yoav Goldberg, Jan Hajic, Christopher D. Manning, Ryan McDonald, Slav Petrov, Sampo Pyysalo, Natalia Silveira, Reut Tsarfaty, and Daniel Zeman. 2016. Universal dependencies v1: A multilingual treebank collection. In *Proceedings of the Tenth International Conference on Language Resources and Evaluation (LREC 2016)*, may.

Joakim Nivre. 2005. Dependency grammar and dependency parsing. Technical report, Växjö University.

Joakim Nivre. 2009. Parsing indian languages with MaltParser. In *Proceedings of the ICON09 NLP Tools Contest: Indian Language Dependency Parsing*, pages 12–18.

Li-Shiuan Peh and Christopher Ting Hian Ann. 1996. A divide-and-conquer strategy for parsing. *CoRR*, cmp-lg/9607020.

Mohammad Sadegh Rasooli and Michael Collins. 2015. Density-driven cross-lingual transfer of dependency parsers. In *Proceedings of the 2015 Conference on EMNLP*, pages 328–338, Lisbon, Portugal, September. Association for Computational Linguistics.

Agnivo Saha and Sudeshna Sarkar. 2016. Enhancing neural network based dependency parsing using morphological information for hindi. In *17th CICLing*, Konya, Turkey, April. Springer.

D.M. Sharma, Sangal R., L. Bai, R. Begam, and K. Ramakrishnamacharyulu. 2007. Anncorra : Treebanks for indian languages, annotation guidelines (manuscript).

Anders Søgaard. 2011. Data point selection for cross-language adaptation of dependency parsers.

Oscar Täckström, Ryan McDonald, and Jakob Uszkoreit. 2012. Cross-lingual word clusters for direct transfer of linguistic structure. In *Proceedings of the 2012 Conference of the NAACL: HLT*, NAACL HLT '12, pages 477–487, Stroudsburg, PA, USA. Association for Computational Linguistics.

Oscar Täckström, Ryan T. McDonald, and Joakim Nivre. 2013. Target language adaptation of discriminative transfer parsers. pages 1061–1071.

Jörg Tiedemann. 2015. Improving the cross-lingual projection of syntactic dependencies. In *Proceedings of the 20th Nordic Conference of Computational Linguistics (NODALIDA 2015)*, pages 191–199, Vilnius, Lithuania, May. Linköping University Electronic Press, Sweden.

Ashwini Vaidya, Owen Rambow, and Martha Palmer. 2014. Light verb constructions with 'do'and 'be'in hindi: A tag analysis. In *Workshop on Lexical and Grammatical Resources for Language Processing*, page 127.

Min Xiao and Yuhong Guo. 2014. Distributed word representation learning for cross-lingual dependency parsing. In *Proceedings of the Conference on Natural Language Learning (CoNLL)*.

Min Xiao and Yuhong Guo. 2015. Annotation projection-based representation learning for cross-lingual dependency parsing. In *Proceedings of the Nineteenth Conference on Computational Natural Language Learning*, pages 73–82, Beijing, China, July. Association for Computational Linguistics.

D. Zeman and Philip Resnik. 2008. Cross-language parser adaptation between related languages. *NLP for Less Privileged Languages*, pages 35 – 35.

Constraint Grammar-based conversion of Dependency Treebanks

Eckhard Bick
University of Southern Denmark
Campusvej 55, DK-5230 Odense M, Denmark
eckhard.bick@gmail.com

Abstract

This paper presents a new method for the conversion of one style of dependency treebanks into another, using contextual, Constraint Grammar-based transformation rules for both structural changes (attachment) and changes in syntactic-functional tags (edge labels). In particular, we address the conversion of traditional syntactic dependency annotation into the semantically motivated dependency annotation used in the Universal Dependencies (UD) Framework, evaluating this task for the Portuguese Floresta Sintá(c)tica treebank. Finally, we examine the effect of the UD converter on a rule-based dependency parser for English (EngGram). Exploiting the ensuing comparability and using the existing UD Web treebank as a gold standard, we discuss the parser's performance and the validity of UD-mediated evaluation.

1   Introduction

Dependency parsers have become a standard module in language technology program pipelines, providing structural information for higher-level tasks such as Information Extraction (Gamallo & Garcia 2012) and Machine Translation (Xu et al. 2009). Dependency links are computationally easy to process because they are token-based, but they also provide a syntactic bridge for the assignment or approximation of semantic relations. In order to facilitate such a semantic interpretation of dependency trees, some descriptive conventions within dependency grammar have moved from syntactically motivated attachment to direct links between content words, regarding function words (prepositions, auxiliaries, subordinating conjunctions) as dependents - and never heads - of content words (nouns, verbs, adjectives). Such semantic dependencies are used, for instance, to link semantic roles in the tecto-grammatical layer of the Prague Dependency treebank (Böhmová 2013), and they are also an important design feature in Universal Dependencies (McDonald et al. 2013), a new standard for dependency annotation designed to facilitate the exchange of tools and data across languages.

In addition, being a descriptive rather than a procedural standard, the Universal Dependencies (UD) framework not only makes it easier to use a given tool with input from different languages, but also to use different tools for the same language in a comparable fashion, making the output interpretable across paradigms, and allowing higher-level applications to work independently of the dependency technology used. In order for this setup to work, however, interoperability is important, and the output from existing parsers (or, in machine learning, their input from training treebanks) has to be converted into the new formalism. Syntactic conversion tasks are not a new issue: For instance, many dependency treebanks are converted versions of constituent treebanks, usually employing hand-written rules (e.g. tregex patterns, Marneffe et al. 2006). In this paper, we describe a method for the conversion of syntactic Constraint Grammar (CG) dependencies, using the same type of rules (i.e.

D S Sharma, R Sangal and A K Singh. Proc. of the 13th Intl. Conference on Natural Language Processing, pages 109–114,
Varanasi, India. December 2016. ©2016 NLP Association of India (NLPAI)

CG) for the conversion as are used in the parser itself. This way, all contextual information can be integrated seamlessly, and unlike simple regular expressions, a CG conversion rule can make use of complex contextual constraints and relational information, such as propagated dependency links. Also, topological constraints (n-gram context or unbounded left- or right-searches) and non-topological constraints (dependencies) can be addressed at the same time, or even in the same rule. Since CG rules are run in modular batches and allow the use of environment variables or input-driven flags, language-specific conversion needs can be addressed in a flexible way within the same grammar..

2 CG Dependency rules

Constraint Grammar-rules are linguistically designed rules expressing linguistic truths in a contextual and procedural fashion. The open source CG3 formalism (Bick & Didriksen 2015), for instance, allows the grammarian to assign dependency relations based on POS context, syntactic function etc., and will even allow reference to other, already-assigned dependencies.

rule (a) SETPARENT (DET)
      TO (*1 N BARRIER NON-ADJ)

rule (b) SETPARENT (<mv>)
      TO (p <aux> + VFIN LINK p (*))

Thus, rule (a) is meant for "virgin" input without dependencies, and will attach a determiner (DET) to a noun (N) to the right (*1) with nothing but adjectives (NON-ADJ) in between. Rule (b), on the other hand, is an example of a format conversion rule, raising main verb attachment from the syntactic, finite verb auxiliary head (p=parent) to the latter's own head, whatever its type (*). With regard to punctuation, "virgin" rules were needed rather than conversion, because many parsers simply attach punctuation to either the top node or the preceding token. UD-style coordination, on the other hand, was achieved in a straight-forward fashion, since input treebank data followed the "Melczuk" tradition of sequential coordination, with a "Melczuk" flag[1] for live parses.

All in all, our conversion grammar contains 79 attachment rules in its general section. Rule order is important, and sometimes several steps are needed for one change, as in *"he wondered if David would be at the meeting"* (Fig. 1 and 2), where an object clause function has to be raised from an auxiliary to its main verb, then - if the latter is a copula - to the subject complement, and if this is a pp, yet another level to the pp's semantic head.

He [he] <masc> PERS 3S NOM @SUBJ> #1->2
wondered [wonder] <mv> V IMPF @FS-STA #2->0
if [if] <clb> KS @SUB #3->5
David [David] <hum> PROP S NOM @SUBJ> #4->5
would [will] <aux> V IMPF @FS-<ACC #5->2
be [be] <mv> V INF @ICL-AUX< #6->5
at [at] PRP @<SA #7->6
the [the] <def> ART S/P @>N #8->9
meeting [meeting] <occ> <def> N S NOM @P< #9->7

Fig. 1: CG dependency annotation[2]

1	He	he	PRON	2	nsubj
2	wondered	wonder	VERB	0	root
3	if	if	SCONJ	9	mark
4	David	David	PROPN	9	nsubj
5	would	will	AUX	9	aux
6	be	be	VERB	9	cop
7	at	at	ADP	9	case
8	the	the	DET	9	det
9	meeting	meeting	NOUN	2	ccomp
10	.	.	PU	2	punct

Fig. 2: UD annotation[3]

---

only the first of several coordinated direct objects to the verb, and treating the first object as the head of the others.

[2] In CG, a token has space-separated tag fields, such as word form, [lemma], <secondary tags>, POS & MORPHOLOGY, @SYNTACTIC_FUNCTION, #self-id->daughter-id. Tags used in Fig. 1 are: PERS=personal pronoun, MASC=male, 3S=third person singular, NOM=nominative, @SUBJ=subject, V=verb, IMPF=past tense, <mv>=main verb, KS=subordinating conjunction, @SUB=subordinator, PROP=proper noun, S=singular, <hum>=human, <aux>=auxiliary, @FS-<ACC=accusative [direct object] subclause, INF=infinitive, @ICL-AUX<=complement of auxiliary, PRP=preposition, @<SA=left-attached valency-bound adverbial, ART=article, <def>=definite, S/P=singular/plural, N=noun, @P<=argument of preposition

[3] Fig. 2 shows UD in CoNLL notation, here with the following TAB-separated fields: ID-nr., token, lemma, POS, head-id, edge label. There is also a field for fine-grained POS which in UD is filled with feature-attribute pairs. These are generated

---

[1] Coordination annotation following Melczuk attaches the second and all furhter conjuncts onto the first, e.g. attaching

Fig. 1 and 2 illustrate the substantial differences between a traditional dependency scheme, like EngGram's, and the UD convention. Thus, while the daughter of "wondered" (id 2) in Fig. 1 is an internally structured object subclause represented by its finite verb (id 5), it is a c-complement noun (9 meeting) in Fig. 2, with a shallow row of daughters, where the distinction between subordinator, subject, auxiliary, copula and preposition only resides in the so-called edge labels (mark, nsubj, aux, cop and - for prepositions - case), without any internal structure.

3   Function tag normalisation

Apart form the dependency structure itself, format conversion into the UD standard also involves the adaptation of syntactic function tags (or *edge labels*). In our scenario, this amounts to the conversion of one cross-language tag set (in our test scenario, the VISL[4] tag set) into another (UD), with a potential of being largely language-independent. Correspondences are not 1-to-1, however, with differences in granularity. Therefore, contextual rules are needed for this task, too. Rule (c), for instance, substitutes the existing edge label of an argument-of-preposition (@P<) with another label ($1 variable), harvested from the copula head of that preposition, implementing the UD principle "semantically" transparent.

```
rule (c) SUBSTITUTE (/¥.*/r) (VSTR:$⁵1)
         TARGET @P<
         (*-1 PRP LINK 0 @<SC OR @<SA)
         (p COPULA LINK 0 (/\(¥.*?\)$/r)) ;
```

In addition, some edge labels in the UD scheme are not purely syntactic, with conversion rules having to draw on morphological or semantic features from the input annotation, as for modifier edge labels that are named after the modifying POS, rather than its syntactic function with relation to the head. Thus, the VISL scheme distinguishes between free adverbials (ADVL), bound adverbials (SA), prepositional arguments (PIV) adnominal (>N, N<) and adject (>A, A<) modifiers, all of which will either be *nmod, amod* or *advmod* in the

UD scheme, depending on whether the dependent is a noun, adjective or adverb[6]. Our general UD-converter contains about 90 edge label rules, with optional additions for the normalization of POS and morphological features (mostly local rules) and English treebank-specific rules. Because our method performs tag conversion not by means of a simple replacement table, but through the use of context-dependent rule of (almost) arbitrary complexity, it is not limited to VISL-style tags and can handle complicated many-to-many tag conversion where the necessary category information is implicit only, and distributed over different constituents or across various levels of annotation.

4   Alignment-driven changes

Attachment and label conversion are enough to make an existing parser produce output compatible with UD guidelines, but for the sake of interoperability and evaluation, tokenization can be very important, too, as well as treebank-specific handling of the internal dependencies and edge labels of complex names and multi-word expressions (MWE). Thus, in order to make converted EngGram output compatible with the UD English Web Treebank (Silveira et al. 2014), we had to add another grammar module, handling MWEs such as names, compounds and complex function words. Among other adaptations, we introduced a new rule type designed to assign separate tags and attachments to input MWEs. Thus, (d) addresses 3-part proper nouns (with '=' as separation marker), creating 3 separate tokens, <NER1-3>, with word and lemma forms taken from regular expression variables in the target MWE. In the example, * indicates the part that inherits the original POS and function, while 1->3, 2->3 indicate rightward internal attachment[7] and c->p means that the last part inherits incoming (c, child) and outgoing (p, parent) dependencies from the MWE.

---

by our converter, but left out in the illustration for clarity.

[4] http://beta.visl.sdu.dk/tagset_cg_general.pdf

[5] http://beta.visl.sdu.dk/treebanks.html

[6] This reflects different parser designs of function-first (CG) vs. form-first (statistical parsing), where attachments are based on either syntactic function or POS, respectively

[7] This head-last name part attachment is treebank-specific and in conflict with UD guidelines that ask for head-first attachment:

http://universaldependencies.github.io/docs/u/dep/name.html

rule (d)   SPLITCOHORT:threepart
        ("<$1>"v "$1"v <NER1> PROP @>N
¥compound 1->3 "<$2>"v "$2"v <NER2> PROP
@>N ¥compound 2->3 "<$3>"v "$3"v <NER3> *
c->p) TARGET ("<([^=]+?)=([^=]+?)=([^=]+?)>"r
PROP) (NOT 0 (<e-word>)) ;

5   Evaluation

Though our method allows the formulation of conversion rules for any kind of dependency treebank, we chose UD conversion of two specific treebanks for testing - the Danish Arboretum treebank[8] (423.000 tokens) and the Portuguese Floresta treebank[9] (210.000 tokens, Afonso et al. 2002), both using the afore-mentioned VISL annotation style[10]. In this setting, conversion speed was about 25.000 tokens/sec on a single 4-core machine with a Linux OS. In a live parsing pipeline using rule-based parsers[11] this amounts to only a slight increase in CPU time.

5.1   Qualitative evaluaion: Floresta treebank

In the treebank conversion task, dependency arcs were changed for 52% of tokens for Danish, and 51% for Portuguese, reflecting the essential difference between "traditional" syntactic heads and UD's semantic heads. Especially affected were pp's, verb chains and predicatives. Specific UD edge labels could be assigned with a very high coverage (99.7%) for both treebanks.

In order to validate our claim that a format converter based on CG rules can be very accurately tailored to a given target annotation convention such as Universal Dependencies, we compared our own conversion of the Portuguese Floresta treebank (FlorestaUD) with the one published at the UD website for the CoNLL version of Floresta (HamleDT[12]), also based on automatic conversion (using Treex[13] and Interset[14]). Since Portuguese was added to the UD website *after* we developed

our converter, our rules reflect the general annotation guidelines of the UD project, and are not based on Portuguese examples from the UD website, and any differences can thus be used to illustrate how well - or not - the two versions match the UD target guidelines[15] at http://universaldependencies.org/u/overview/synta x.html and http://universaldependencies.org/u/dep/.

For the inspected sentences (914 tokens), our CG conversion and the HamleDT conversion differed in 13.6% of dependency arcs and 9.8% of edge labels:

UD guidelines conflicts	dependency arcs	edge labels
differences CG/Hamle	13.6 %	9.8 %
Hamle UD conflicts	12.1 %	6.2 %
CG UD conflicts	0.2 %	0.5 %
both in conflict (treebank errors)	0.7 %	0.3 %
both compatible (unclear/undecided)	0.5 %	1.2 %

Table 1: Conflicts with UD guidelines

As can be seen from Table 1, our CG-based conversion achieved a satisfactory match with UD guidelines, with almost no conflicts for dependency arcs, and 10-times fewer conflicts for edge labels than in the HamleDT version. A breakdown of conflict types revealed that the discrepancy was largest for punctuation, accounting for 47% of HamleDT''s dependency arc conflicts. Since the original Floresta treebank attaches all punctuation to the root node (0), while UD guidelines ask for true syntactic attachments (e.g. highest node in a subordinated unit for paired punctuation), this is an area where conversion actually *adds* information, and using complex contextual rules - such as CG rules - becomes an obvious advantage.

---

[8] Available through the ELRA Catalogue of Language Resources (catalog.elra.info)

[9] Available through the Linguateca project website (http://www.linguateca.pt/floresta/)

[10] The annotation style is described at http://visl.sdu.dk/treebanks.html#VISL_dependency_trees

[11] such as the ones listed on visl.sdu.dk/ constraint_grammar_languages.html

[12] http://ufal.mff.cuni.cz/hamledt

[13] http://ufal.mff.cuni.cz/treex

[14] http://ufal.mff.cuni.cz/interset

[15] Using the same annotation convention and thus making treebanks comparable across languages is the very core idea of UD, and while language-specific additions are possible, they only make sense for features not shared with the majority of languages, and none such additions are documented in the Portuguese section of the UD website.

Another systematic area of conflict were verb phrases (vp's): The UD scheme, in accordance with its semantics-over-syntax approach, sees auxiliaries as dependents of main verbs, but unlike our CG rules, HamleDT conversion seems to have no such effect on the Floresta treebank (which has syntactic dependency and auxiliaries as heads), causing on average two edge label discrepancies and two attachment discrepancies for each vp. Also, as a consequence of this conversion failure, HamleDT does not seem to be able to "see through" auxiliaries in connection with the otherwise UD-mandated copula switch[16], where both subject and copula verb become dependents of subject complements.

Edge label conflicts are fewer, but the HamleDT conversion appears to have more problems than the CG-based conversion, in particular where the change is not local/POS-based, but contextually motivated, as in the distinction between name relations and appositions, or the distinction between quantifying numerals (nummod) and others (e.g. year names or dates).

As a final topic of notorious difficulty in dependency annotations, we checked coordination ellipsis (e.g. 'he bought a hat for his wife, and a book for his daughter'), where UD suggests a 'remnant' edge label for the coordinated small clause, with dependency arcs between equivalent functions. This structure, while difficult for a live CG parse, could be correctly produced by our rules on the basis of Floresta treebank labels[17] and shallow verb attachment.

5.2   Quantitative evaluation: CG Parsing

Obviously, comparability of tools and data is a major motivation for UD conversion, so we tried to put this hypothesis to the test by going beyond an evaluation of just the conversion method, comparing live, *UD-converted* EngGram output against the English test section of the UD Web Treebank[18]. While UD-conversion did make a direct comparison possible, we also encountered a long list of unexpected problems even in the face of converted labels and attachments, caused in particular by conflicts between the publically available UD Web Treebank and official UD guidelines (e.g. name heads, punctuation attachment). Any such difference will look like a performance error in the evaluated system, while in reality it is a consistency error in the treebank. These problems were furhter aggravated by some lexicon-based "idiosyncratic" tokenization in both the UD treebank (e.g. some hyphenated words are split, some aren't) and the input parsers (that used closed-class MWEs). Forcing the latter to accept the tokenization of the former with the help of an additional preprocessor improved alignment, but at the price of potentially detrimental changes in rule performance, for instance where a contextual reference to a given MWE cannot be instantiated, because it has been split. Performance figures naturally reflect all of these issues on top of EngGram and conversion accuracy as such. In addition, the "as-is" run on force-tokenized raw test also includes errors from the morphosyntactic stage of EngGram, propagating into the dependency stage. Thus, providing the dependency stage with hand-corrected morphosyntactic input improved performance, providing a cleaner picture of structural and categorial conversion efficiency.

UD English Web Treebank test data	label failure[19]	UAS (dep)	LS (label)	LAS (both)
as is	0.3%	80.9	86.6	75.7
hand-corrected morphosyntactic input	0.2%	86.2	90.6	81.9

Table 2: Performance of Conversion Grammar

---

[16] Other, minor copula differences, albeit possibly intended ones, were that HamleDT extended the copula switch to clausal predicatives and that it seemed to derive copula status from the existence of a predicative argument, ending up with at least one extra copula ('ficar' - 'become'), while our own conversion implemented the general UD guidelines, with only one copula foreseen ('be'), and no switch for clausal predicatives..

[17] The Floresta treebank uses ordinary function labels for the constituents in coordination ellipsis - the same ones that would have been used in the presence of a - repeated - verb.

[18] This treebank uses the CoNLL format (Buchholz et al. 2006), for which EngGram has an export option.

[19] Cases where no rule could assign a specific UD edge label, resulting in the underspecified 'dep'.

The labelled attachment score (LAS) for dependency (81.9) matches the average in-domain system performance for English in the CoNLL 2007 shared task (80.95, Nivre et al. 2007), where the tagged input to the dependency parsers also had been hand-corrected[20]. In other words, our UD-conversion makes it possible to compare the output of a rule-based system (EngGram) to machine-learning (ML) parsers that also use the UD scheme. The converted EngGram output does fall short of CoNLL top-performance *in-domain* (89.61), but on the other hand LAS is similar to the best *cross-domain* CoNLL result (81.06), which arguably is a fairer comparison, because we are using an existing rule-based system without domain specificity as input for our UD conversion grammar. For such a system, everything is - so to say - cross-domain.

6   Perspectives

Although our method was employed and evaluated as a conversion extension for CG parsers and CG treebanks, the same type of conversion rules should in principle work for non-CG input, too, as long as dependencies and tags are expressed in a compatible fashion. Thus, similar rules could be used for linguistically transparent genre tuning of existing dependency parsers, or for adding depth and additional annotation layers to existing treebanks. Examples of the latter are missing punctuation attachment (as in the Floresta Treebank), secondary dependencies for relative pronouns and small clauses, or discourse-spanning long-distance dependencies.

References

Susana Afonso, Eckhard Bick, Renato Haber & Diana Santos. 2002. Floresta sintá(c)tica: a treebank for Portuguese, In Proceedings of LREC'2002, Las Palmas. pp. 1698-1703, Paris: ELRA

Eckhard Bick & Tino Didriksen. 2015. CG-3 - Beyond Classical Constraint Grammar. In: Beáta Megyesi: Proceedings of NODALIDA 2015, May 11-13, 2015, Vilnius, Lithuania. pp. 31-39. Linköping: LiU Electronic Press

Eckhard Bick. 2003. Arboretum, a Hybrid Treebank for Danish, in: Joakim Nivre & Erhard Hinrich (eds.), *Proceedings of TLT 2003 (2nd Workshop on Treebanks and Linguistic Theory, Växjö, November 14-15, 2003)*, pp.9-20. Växjö University Press

Alena Böhmová, Jan Hajič, Eva Hajičová and Barbora Hladká. 2003. The Prague Dependency Treebank, A Three-Level Annotation Scenario. In: Anne Abeillé (ed.): Treebanks - Building and Using Parsed Corpora. pp 103-127. Springer

Sabine Buchholz & Erwin Marsi. 2006. CoNLL-X Shared Task on Multilingual Dependency Parsing. Proceedings of the Tenth Conference on Computational Natural Language Learning (CoNLL-X), pages 149–164, New York City. Association for Computational Linguistics. http://www.aclweb.org/anthology/W06-2920.

Ryan McDonald, Joakim Nivre, Yvonne Quirmbach-Brundage, Yoav Goldberg, Dipanjan Das, Kuzman Ganchev, Keith Hall, Slav Petrov, Hao Zhang, Oscar Täckström, Claudia Bedini, Núria Bertomeu Castelló, and Jungmee Lee. 2013. Universal dependency annotation for multilingual parsing. In Proceedings of ACL 2013

Pablo Gamallo, Marcos Garcia & Santiago Fernández-Lanza. 2012. Dependency-Based Open Information Extraction. In: Proceedings of the Joint Workshop on Unsupervised and Semi-Supervised Learning in NLP. pp. 10-18. ACL

Marie-Catherine de Marneffe, Bill MacCartney, and Christopher D. Manning. 2006. Generating typed dependency parses from phrase structure parses. In: Proceedings of LREC, pp. 449-454

J. Nivre, J. Hall, S. Kübler, R. McDonald, J. Nilsson, S. Riedel, and D. Yuret. 2007. The CoNLL 2007 shared task on dependency parsing. In: Proceedings of the CoNLL Shared Task of EMNLP-CoNLL 2007, pp. 915-932

Natalia Silveira, Timothy Dozat, Marie-Catherinde de Marneffe, Samuel Bowman, Miriam Connor, John Bauer & Christopher D. Manning. 2014. A Gold Standard Dependency Corpus for English. In: Proceedings of LREC 2014.

Peng Xu, Jaeho Kang, Michael Ringgaard and Franz Och. Using a Dependency Parser to Improve SMT for Subject-object-verb-languages. In: Proceedings of NAACL '09. pp 245-253. ACL

---

[20]In the CoNLL task, linguist-revised treebanks were used to provide tagged input and dependency gold standards.

Meaning Matters: Senses of Words are More Informative than Words for Cross-domain Sentiment Analysis

Raksha Sharma, Sudha Bhingardive, Pushpak Bhattacharyya
Dept. of Computer Science and Engineering
IIT Bombay, Mumbai, India
{raksha,sudha,pb}@cse.iitb.ac.in

Abstract

Getting labeled data in each domain is always an expensive and a time consuming task. Hence, cross-domain sentiment analysis has emerged as a demanding research area where a labeled source domain facilitates classifier in an unlabeled target domain. However, cross-domain sentiment analysis is still a challenging task because of the differences across domains. A word which is used with positive polarity in the source domain may bear negative polarity in the target domain or vice versa. In addition, a word which is used very scarcely in the source domain may have high impact in the target domain for sentiment classification. Due to these differences across domains, cross-domain sentiment analysis suffers from negative transfer. In this paper, we propose that senses of words in place of words help to overcome the differences across domains. Results show that senses of words provide a better sentiment classifier in the unlabeled target domain in comparison to words for 12 pairs of source and target domains.

1 Introduction

Generally users do not explicitly indicate sentiment orientation (positive or negative) of the reviews posted by them on the Web, it needs to be predicted from the text, which has led to plethora of work in the field of Sentiment Analysis (SA) (Esuli and Sebastiani, 2005; Breck et al., 2007; Li et al., 2009; Prabowo and Thelwall, 2009; Taboada et al., 2011; Cambria et al., 2013; Rosenthal et al., 2014). Most of the proposed techniques for sentiment analysis are based on the availability of labeled train data considering that train data and test data belong to the same domain. Easy access

of internet has made the users to post their experiences with any product, service or application very frequently. Consequently, there is a high increase in number of domains in which sentimental data is available. Getting sentiment (positive or negative) annotated data manually in each domain is not feasible due to the cost incurred in annotation process.

Cross-domain SA provides a solution to build a classifier in the unlabeled target domain from a labeled source domain. But, due to the differences across domains, cross-domain SA suffers from negative transfer. A word which is used with positive polarity in the source domain may bear negative polarity in the target domain or vice versa. We call such words as *changing polarity* words. In most of the cases, the difference in polarity occurs due to the use of the word with different senses. Example of such changing polarity word is as follows:

1a. *His behavior is very **cheap**.* (Negative)

1b. *Jet airways provides very **cheap** flight tickets.* (Positive)

In the first case, the word *cheap* is used with the sense *of very poor quality*, while in second case the sense is *relatively low in price*. Use of *cheap* with different senses is making it to have opposite sentiment polarity. On the other hand, a word which is used very scarcely (low impact) in the source domain might be used very frequently (high impact) in the target domain for sentiment classification. We call such words as *missing* words. In most of the cases, this difference occurs due to the use of different synonymous words having the same sense. Example of such missing word is as follows:

2a. *This mobile phone has a **decent** battery.*

D S Sharma, R Sangal and A K Singh. Proc. of the 13th Intl. Conference on Natural Language Processing, pages 115–119,
Varanasi, India. December 2016. ©2016 NLP Association of India (NLPAI)

(Positive)

2b. *This place has **satisfactory** food options.* (Positive)

The words *decent* and *satisfactory* are synonyms of each other as per Princeton WordNet-3.1.[1] But, the domains of the sentences in 2a and 2b are different, in the first case it is the mobile domain, while in the second case it is the restaurant domain. The words *decent* and *satisfactory* can be used interchangeably to express positive opinion in different domains.

In this paper, we propose that use of senses in place of words helps to overcome the differences across domains for cross domain SA. A word like *cheap* which is negative for human behavior and positive for tickets can be identified with the correct polarity orientation in the domain if we use the respective sense of the *cheap* in place of the word *cheap*. On the other hand, if a word is missing in the source domain, but its synonym is present in the target domain then the weight learned by a supervised classifier for the synonym in the source domain can be transferred (reused) to the target domain. In this way, use of senses of words in place of words is overcoming the data sparsity problem. The exemplified words *satisfactory* and *decent* are holding the same polarity orientation, that is, positive. They can be represented by the same sense as they belong to the same synset in WordNet. Draught et al., 2012 gave the formal characterization of WordNet as follows.

WordNet: The WordNet is a network (N) of synsets. A synset is a group of words having the same sense. In other words, it groups synonymous words as they bear the same sense. The network N can be represented as a quadruple (W, S, E, f), where W is a finite set of words, S is a finite set of synsets, E is a set of undirected edges between elements in W and S, i.e., $E \subseteq W \times S$ and f is a function assigning a positive integer to each element in E. For an edge (w,s), f(w,s) is called the frequency of use of w in the sense given by s.

In WordNet each synset (sense) is assigned a unique synset-ID. Hence, two words which belong to the same sense will share the same synset-ID. On the other hand, if a word has two different senses, then their synset-IDs will be differ-

---

[1]Princeton WordNet is available at: `http://wordnetweb.princeton.edu/perl/webwn`.

ent. In this way, by use of synset-ID of a sense to which the word belongs, we can overcome the differences across domains for cross-domain SA.

In summary, use of senses (synset-IDs) of words in place of words reduces the amount of negative transfer from labeled source domain to unlabeled target domain to an extent, which in turn results into a more accurate classifier in the target domain. In this paper, we show the effectiveness of senses over words across four domains, *viz.,* DVD (D), Electronics (E), Kitchen (K), and Books (B). Results show that the sense-based classifier in the target domain is more accurate than word-based classifier for 12 pairs of the source and target domains.

2 Related Work

Sentiment analysis within a domain has been widely studied in literature, where the train and test datasets are assumed to be from the same domain (Pang et al., 2002; Turney, 2002; Ng et al., 2006; Kanayama and Nasukawa, 2006; Breck et al., 2007; Pang and Lee, 2008; Li et al., 2009; Taboada et al., 2011). This kind of sentiment analysis where the train and test data are from the same domain is known as in-domain SA. Balamurali et al., (2011) have shown that use of senses in places of words improves the performance of in-domain SA significantly. Though they did not explore senses as features for cross-domain SA. Performance of the sentiment analysis systems drops severely when the test data is from some other domain than the train domain. This drop in performance occurs due to the differences across domains. Hence, getting a high accuracy classifier in the unlabeled target domain from a labeled source domain is a challenging task.

Domain adaptation for cross-domain sentiment classification has been explored by many researchers (Jiang and Zhai, 2007; Ji et al., 2011; Saha et al., 2011; Xia et al., 2013; Bhatt et al., 2015; Zhou et al., 2014; Glorot et al., 2011). Most of the works have focused on learning a shared low dimensional representation of features that can be generalized across different domains. Glorot et al., (2011) proposed a deep learning approach which learns to extract a meaningful representation for each review in an unsupervised fashion. Zhou et al., (2014) also proposed a deep learning approach to learn a feature mapping between cross-domain heterogeneous features as well as a better feature representation for mapped data to reduce the bias issue caused by the cross-domain correspondences. Although, our approach also focuses on shared representation of the source and target, but it observes the senses of words instead of words to reduce the differences created by words across domains. Our approach can handle the use of a word with opposite polarity orientation between source and target domains. In addition, it can deal with words which are missing in the source domain, but significant for target domain. Identification of changing polarity words and missing words by the use of senses across domains makes our approach more robust. Our approach do not determine a low dimensional representation of features (words) mathematically, hence it is less computationally expensive. However, it uses a manually complied resource, that is, WordNet to obtain senses of words.

3 Dataset

In this paper, we have shown impact of word's sense in cross-domain SA for four domains, *viz.,* DVD (D), Electronics (E), Kitchen (K), and Books (B). Data for all four domains is taken from the amazon archive (Blitzer et al., 2007).[2] Each domain has 1000 positive and 1000 negative reviews. Table 1 shows the total number of reviews per domain and an average number of words per review in each domain.

Domain	No. of Reviews	Avg. Length
Electronics (E)	2000	110
DVD (D)	2000	197
Kitchen (K)	2000	93
Books (B)	2000	173

Table 1: Dataset Statistics

4 Experimental Setup

In all four domains, dataset is divided into two parts, train (80%) and test (20%). Classifier is trained on the train data from source domain and results are reported on the test data from the target domain. We use SVM algorithm (Tong and Koller, 2001) to train a classifier with all the source and target pairs reported in the paper.[3] We have

presented comparison between word-based cross-domain SA and sense-based cross-domain SA. In case of word-based SA, a set of unique words (unigrams) in the training corpus make a feature set. In case of sense-based cross-domain SA, a set of unique synset-IDs (senses) form a set of features. In order to annotate the corpus with senses, we have used IMS (It Makes Sense), which is a publicly available supervised English all-words word sense disambiguation (WSD) system.[4] There were a few instances of words which IMS failed to annotate with sense, for these instances we considered the word as feature.

5 Results

Total 12 pairs of source and target domains are possible with 4 domains. We have extensively validated our hypothesis that use of senses in place of words provides a more accurate sentiment classification system in an unlabeled target domain. We have shown results using 12 pairs of source and target domains. Figure 1 shows the classification accuracy obtained with word-based and sense-based systems in the target domain. The classification algorithm (SVM) and the training corpus are the same in both cases, though the difference lies in the representation of data. In case of word-based system, corpus is seen as a sequence of words, while in case of sense-based system, corpus is seen as a sequence of senses. In other words, in sense-based system words are replaced with their respective senses.

For all 12 pairs of source and target domains sense-based system performs better than word-based system. Though in case of $D \rightarrow E$ and $E \rightarrow D$, difference in accuracy is low. DVD and electronics are two very different domains unlike electronics and Kitchen, or DVD and books. DVD dataset contains reviews about music albums, while electronics dataset contains reviews about electronic products. This difference in types of reviews make them to share less number of words. Table 2 shows the percent (%) of common words among the 4 domains. The percent of common unique words are common unique words divided by the summation of unique words in the domains individually. However, consistent improvement in accuracy for all 12 pairs validates our hy-

---

[2]The dataset is available at: `http://www.cs.jhu.edu/mdredze/datasets/sentiment/index2.html`

[3]We use SVM package libsvm, which is available in java-based WEKA toolkit for machine learn-

ing: `http://www.cs.waikato.ac.nz/ml/weka/downloading.html`

[4]Available at: `http://www.comp.nus.edu.sg/-nlp/software.html`

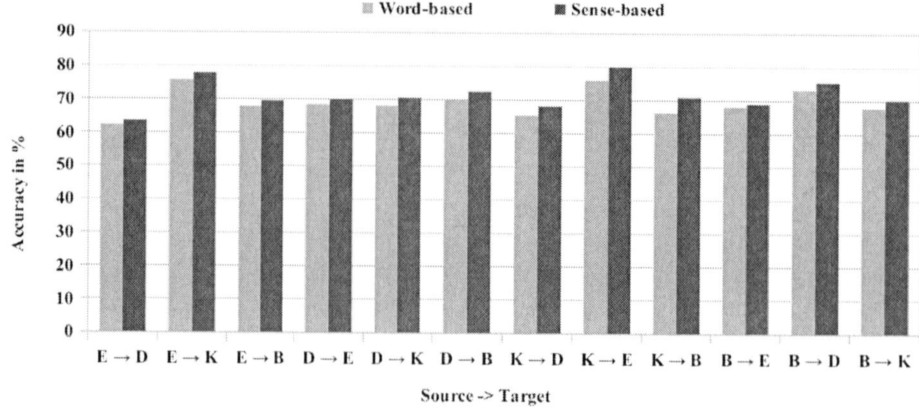

Figure 1: Accuracy obtained with word-based and sense-based systems in the target domain.

E - D	E - K	E - B	D - K	D - B	K - B
15	22	17	14	22	17

Table 2: Common unique words between the domains in percent (%).

Domain	Word-based	Sense-based
E	79	81.25
D	76.25	79
K	85	86
B	75.75	79

Table 3: In-domain sentiment classification accuracy in %.

pothesis that use of senses in place of words reduces the amount of negative transfer from source domain to the target domain, which in turn leads to a more accurate cross-domain sentiment analysis system.

Table 3 shows the in-domain sentiment classification accuracy obtained with words and senses as features. Here, the classification algorithm is the same for all four domains, but the train and test data are from the same domain. For example, if the classifier is trained in the electronics domain, the results are reported on the test data from the electronics domain only. Balamurali et al., (2011) have shown that senses are better features than words for in-domain SA. They have reported results in the tourism and health domains.[5] The results reported in Table 3 for electronics, DVD, kitchen and book domains also validate the hy-

pothesis proposed by Balamurali et al., (2011). We can consider the accuracies reported in the Table 3 as the upper bound for cross-domain SA. Though the gap in accuracy obtained under cross-domain (cf. Figure 1) settings and in-domain (cf. Table 3) settings is very high, yet use of senses tries to fill the gap to an extent.

6 Conclusion

Cross-domain sentiment analysis is a challenging task due to the differences across domains. Direct application of a classifier on a domain other than the domain of the training data degrades the classification accuracy. In this paper, we propose that use of senses of words in place of words helps to overcome the differences across domain to an extent, which in turn leads to a more accurate classifier in the target domain from a labeled source domain. Senses are able to assign correct weights to changing polarity words and missing words across domains under supervised classification settings. Results have shown that sense-based cross-domain system outperforms the word-based system by 3% on an average. We have shown impact of senses of words in comparison to words for 12 pairs of source and target domains using 4 domains. In future, senses of words can be combined with other features and techniques to reduce the gap between upper bound and the reported accuracy for cross-domain SA.

---

[5]Since the dataset in tourism (600 documents) and health (1000 documents) domains is very small in size, we have not reported results with these domains for cross-domain SA.

References

AR Balamurali, Aditya Joshi, and Pushpak Bhattacharyya. 2011. Harnessing wordnet senses for supervised sentiment classification. In *Proceedings of the Conference on Empirical Methods in Natural Language Processing*, pages 1081–1091. Association for Computational Linguistics.

Himanshu S. Bhatt, Deepali Semwal, and S. Roy. 2015. An iterative similarity based adaptation technique for cross-domain text classification. In *Proceedings of Conference on Natural Language Learning*, pages 52–61.

John Blitzer, Mark Dredze, Fernando Pereira, et al. 2007. Biographies, bollywood, boom-boxes and blenders: Domain adaptation for sentiment classification. In *Proceedings of Association for Computational Linguistics*, pages 440–447.

Eric Breck, Yejin Choi, and Claire Cardie. 2007. Identifying expressions of opinion in context. In *Proceedings of International Joint Conference on Artificial Intelligence*, pages 2683–2688.

Erik Cambria, Bjorn Schuller, Yunqing Xia, and Catherine Havasi. 2013. New avenues in opinion mining and sentiment analysis. *IEEE Intelligent Systems*, (2):15–21.

Andrea Esuli and Fabrizio Sebastiani. 2005. Determining the semantic orientation of terms through gloss classification. In *Proceedings of International Conference on Information and Knowledge Management*, pages 617–624.

Xavier Glorot, Antoine Bordes, and Yoshua Bengio. 2011. Domain adaptation for large-scale sentiment classification: A deep learning approach. In *Proceedings of the 28th International Conference on Machine Learning (ICML-11)*, pages 513–520.

Yang-Sheng Ji, Jia-Jun Chen, Gang Niu, Lin Shang, and Xin-Yu Dai. 2011. Transfer learning via multiview principal component analysis. *Journal of Computer Science and Technology*, 26(1):81–98.

Jing Jiang and ChengXiang Zhai. 2007. Instance weighting for domain adaptation in nlp. In *Proceedings of Association for Computational Linguistics*, pages 264–271.

Hiroshi Kanayama and Tetsuya Nasukawa. 2006. Fully automatic lexicon expansion for domain-oriented sentiment analysis. In *Proceedings of Conference on Empirical Methods in Natural Language Processing*, pages 355–363.

Tao Li, Yi Zhang, and Vikas Sindhwani. 2009. A nonnegative matrix tri-factorization approach to sentiment classification with lexical prior knowledge. In *Proceedings of International Joint Conference on Natural Language Processing*, pages 244–252.

Vincent Ng, Sajib Dasgupta, and SM Arifin. 2006. Examining the role of linguistic knowledge sources in the automatic identification and classification of reviews. In *Proceedings of the COLING/ACL on Main conference poster sessions*, pages 611–618. Association for Computational Linguistics.

Bo Pang and Lillian Lee. 2008. Opinion mining and sentiment analysis. *Foundations and Trends in Information Retrieval*, 2(1-2):1–135.

Bo Pang, Lillian Lee, and Shivakumar Vaithyanathan. 2002. Thumbs up?: sentiment classification using machine learning techniques. In *Proceedings of Conference on Empirical Methods in Natural Language Processing*, pages 79–86.

Rudy Prabowo and Mike Thelwall. 2009. Sentiment analysis: A combined approach. *Journal of Informetrics*, 3(2):143–157.

Sara Rosenthal, Preslav Nakov, Alan Ritter, and Veselin Stoyanov. 2014. Semeval-2014 task 9: Sentiment analysis in twitter. In *Proceedings of SemEval*, pages 73–80.

Avishek Saha, Piyush Rai, Hal Daumé III, Suresh Venkatasubramanian, and Scott L DuVall. 2011. Active supervised domain adaptation. In *Machine Learning and Knowledge Discovery in Databases*, pages 97–112.

Maite Taboada, Julian Brooke, Milan Tofiloski, Kimberly Voll, and Manfred Stede. 2011. Lexicon-based methods for sentiment analysis. *Computational Linguistics*, 37(2):267–307.

Simon Tong and Daphne Koller. 2001. Support vector machine active learning with applications to text classification. *Journal of machine learning research*, 2(Nov):45–66.

Peter D. Turney. 2002. Thumbs up or thumbs down?: Semantic orientation applied to unsupervised classification of reviews. In *Proceedings of Association for Computational Linguistics*, pages 417–424.

Rui Xia, Chengqing Zong, Xuelei Hu, and Erik Cambria. 2013. Feature ensemble plus sample selection: domain adaptation for sentiment classification. *IEEE Intelligent Systems*, 28(3):10–18.

Joey Tianyi Zhou, Sinno Jialin Pan, Ivor W Tsang, and Yan Yan. 2014. Hybrid heterogeneous transfer learning through deep learning. In *AAAI*, pages 2213–2220.

POS Tagging Experts via Topic Modeling

Atreyee Mukherjee
Indiana University
atremukh@indiana.edu

Sandra Kübler
Indiana University
skuebler@indiana.edu

Matthias Scheutz
Tufts University
matthias.scheutz@tufts.edu

Abstract

Part of speech taggers generally perform well on homogeneous data sets, but their performance often varies considerably across different genres. In this paper we investigate the adaptation of POS taggers to individual genres by creating POS tagging experts. We use topic modeling to determine genres automatically and then build a tagging expert for each genre. We use Latent Dirichlet Allocation to cluster sentences into related topics, based on which we create the training experts for the POS tagger. Likewise, we cluster the test sentences into the same topics and annotate each sentence with the corresponding POS tagging expert. We show that using topic model experts enhances the accuracy of POS tagging by around half a percent point on average over the random baseline, and the 2-topic hard clustering model and the 10-topic soft clustering model improve over the full training set.

1 Introduction

Part-of-speech (POS) tagging is the task of assigning word classes to lexical items and is often considered a solved problem. However, even though we can reach high accuracies on the Penn Treebank, POS taggers are sensitive to differences in genre (cf. e.g. (Khan et al., 2013; Miller et al., 2007; Søgaard, 2013)). In the current research, we investigate a novel way of adapting POS taggers to different genres, but also to specific lexical and syntactic characteristics of texts. We propose to use topic modeling, an unsupervised soft clustering method that clusters documents, or sentences in our case, into a distribution of individual topics. We interpret the topics as specialized training sets, which are used to train a POS tagging expert for each topic. Test sentences are also clustered into the same topics, and each test sentence is annotated by the corresponding POS tagging expert. We investigate different methods of converting topics into expert training sets.

Thus, our method is related to domain adaptation approaches (Khan et al., 2013; Miller et al., 2007) in that it focuses on adapting to specific characteristics of texts, but it is more generally applicable because it determines the domains and the experts automatically. It is also related to approaches of mitigating domain effects (e.g., (Søgaard, 2013)), but in contrast to those methods, we obtain individual experts that can be used and investigated separately.

Our results show that the topic modeling experts are sensitive to different genres (financial news vs. medical text) as well as to smaller differences between the Wall Street sentences. On average, the improvement over randomly selected subsets is around 0.5-1 percent point. Our results also show that one major difference between the POS tagging experts based on topics models concerns the treatment of unknown words. In the financial expert, such words have a much higher tendency to be assigned to the noun class. And even though names are one of the most difficult classes, the error rate for them is reduced in the POS experts based on topic models.

The remainder of the paper is structured as follows: Section 2 discusses our research questions in more detail. Section 3 discusses related work, and in section 4, we provide details about the data sets, the topic modeler, and the POS tagger. In section 5, we show the results, and in section 6, we draw our conclusions and discuss future extensions of our work.

D S Sharma, R Sangal and A K Singh. Proc. of the 13th Intl. Conference on Natural Language Processing, pages 120–128,
Varanasi, India. December 2016. ©2016 NLP Association of India (NLPAI)

2 Research Questions

Our investigation into creating POS tagging experts is based on the assumption that the data that we need to analyze is not homogeneous but rather a collection of different text types or even syntactic constructions. In one setting, we may have a mixed set of newspaper articles, research papers, financial reports, and weblogs to analyze. In a different setting, we may have texts that use specialized vocabulary, such as in the biomedical domain or in law texts, or we could have headlines with an elliptical sentence structure. For this reason, we assume that the POS tagger can reach a higher accuracy if we can split the data sets into more homogeneous subsets and then train individual expert POS taggers, specialized for individual subsets. We determine these homogeneous subsets by using topic modeling. Since topic modeling is unsupervised, the sentences will be divided into sets based on similarity. This similarity may be based on similarity of content, but it can also be based on similarity on the structural level. For example, if we use the Penn Treebank (Marcus et al., 1994), we could assume that one topic consists of sentences reporting changes of the stock market while another topic consists of sentences about the earthquake in San Francisco. Yet, another topic may consist of mostly questions.

Our current research concentrates on answering the four questions described below. In this investigation, we use a setting in which we perform topic modeling jointly on the training and test data. This is a simplification of the problem since this means that we would have to create new experts every time a new sentence needs to be tagged. We assume that we can rerun the topic modeling including test sentences and then match the new topics to the ones we obtained on the training set alone. Another approach would be to use the similarity metrics by Plank and van Noord (2011). We will test these hypotheses in the future.

2.1 Question 1: Do Topic Models Provide Information from which POS Tagging Experts can Profit?

The first question is concerned with determining whether the data splits we obtain from topic modeling are meaningful for creating POS tagging experts. In other words, do the topics that we can generate in an unsupervised manner provide a specialization that has an effect on POS tagging? In order to investigate this question, we manually generate a two-topic corpus by combining data from the Wall Street Journal (WSJ) section of the Penn Treebank (Marcus et al., 1994) and from the GENIA corpus (Tateisi and Tsujii, 2004). The WSJ covers financial news while GENIA uses Medline abstracts as its textual basis. As a consequence, we have sentences from two different genres, but also slight variations in the POS tagsets. The tagset used in GENIA is based on the Penn Treebank tagset, but it uses the tags for proper names and symbols only in very restricted contexts. This setup allows us to test whether the topic modeler is able to distinguish the two genres, and whether POS tagging experts can profit from this separation.

2.2 Question 2: Can we use Soft Clusters of the Topic Models?

The first set of experiments uses the topics as hard clusters, i.e., every sentence belongs to the topic with the highest probability. This is a simplification since a sentence can represent different topics to different degrees. Thus, we now investigate whether we can utilize the soft clustering information directly and add every sentence to every POS tagging expert, weighted based on the degree to which it represents the topic of this expert. This not only allows us to model topics in more detail, it can also help combating data sparsity since every sentence contributes to every POS expert. The risk is that we "diffuse" the expert knowledge too much by adding all sentences even if they are weighted.

2.3 Question 3: Can Topic Modeling Detect Micro-Genres?

While the previous sets of experiments used two very different genres, the current question focuses on data from within one genre. Can we use topic modeling within one genre, and do the resulting topics allow us to create POS tagging experts for "micro"-genres? To investigate this question, we exclusively use the WSJ data set. Our hypothesis is that the WSJ corpus contains different newspaper sections, which may use different styles. Since there is no information available from the Penn Treebank about those section, we cannot evaluate how well the topic modeler splits the sentences into topics, but we can evaluate whether the POS tagging experts are successful in adapting to those micro-genres.

2.4 Question 4: Which Specialization do the POS Tagging Experts Learn?

Here, we will take a closer look at the results from the first question to investigate where the improvements by the POS tagging experts come from. Are all the improvements based on lower rates of out-of-vocabulary words? For example, suppose we have two experimental settings, both using the same size of the training set, but in one setting, the majority of the training set is from GENIA while in the second setting, the training set is a mix of GENIA and WSJ. It is more likely that the former will contain a wider range of biomedical vocabulary than the latter. However, it is also possible that the experts will learn different regularities, for example with regard to how the proper name tags are used in the two corpora. Thus, we will look at the ratio of unknown words in the different experiments and at the error rates of known and unknown words. We will additionally look at the confusion matrices.

3 Related Work

We are not aware of any research that directly compares to the research presented here. The closest area is domain adaptation. For this reason, we will cover work on domain adaptation for POS tagging here. However, more work has been done on domain adaptation for parsing. The work in that area seems to fall into two categories: "frustratingly easy" when some annotated data from the target domain is available (Daumé III, 2007) and "frustratingly hard" if no such target data is available (Dredze et al., 2007).

For POS tagging, Clark et al. (2003) used the results of one POS tagger on unannotated data to inform the training of another tagger in a semi-supervised setting using a co-training routine with a Markov model tagger and a maximum entropy tagger. The authors tested both agreement-based co-training, where the sentences are added to training only if the taggers both agree, and naive co-training, where all sentences from one tagger are added to the training of the other, with no filter. Kübler and Baucom (2011) expanded on this method and used three different taggers to annotate additional data and then select those sentences for which the taggers agree. They found that adding not only complete sentences but also sequences of words where the taggers agree results in the highest gains. Khan et al. (2013) in-

vestigated the situation where some annotated target data is available. They focused on optimizing the balance between source and target sentences. They found that selecting sentences that are the most similar to the target data results in the highest gains. Blitzer et al. (2006) developed structural correspondence learning, which learns correspondences between two domains in settings where a small set of target sentences is available as well as in an unsupervised setting. They show an improved performance for POS tagging and for parsing when using the adapted POS tagger.

4 Experimental Setup

4.1 Data Sets

For our experiments, we use the Wall Street Journal (WSJ) section of the Penn Treebank (Marcus et al., 1994) and the GENIA Corpus (version 3.02) (Tateisi and Tsujii, 2004). Both corpora use the Penn Treebank POS tagset (Santorini, 1990) with minor differences, as described in section 2.1.

For the WSJ corpus, we extract the POS annotation from the syntactically annotated corpus. The GENIA Corpus comprises biomedical abstracts from Medline, and it is annotated on different linguistic levels, including POS tags, syntax, coreference, and events, among others. We use the POS tagged version. For WSJ, we use the standard data split for parsing: using sections 02-21 as training data and section 22 as our test set. We reserve section 23 for future parsing expert experiments.

For questions 1, 2, and 4, we need a balanced data set, both for the training and the test set. Since GENIA is smaller than WSJ and has no predefined data split, we have decided to use the same test set size (1 700 sentences), but now taking half of the sentences from WSJ and half from GENIA. The remaining GENIA sentences serve as half of the training set, and we extract the same number of sentences from WSJ. For GENIA, we consider the first 19 696 sentences as training set and the remaining 850 sentences as test set. For WSJ, the sentences are selected randomly out of the predefined training and test sets.

For question 3, we use the full WSJ training and test set, as described above. Table 1 gives an overview of the settings.

4.2 Topic Modeling

Probabilistic topic modeling is a class of algorithms which detects the thematic structure in a

Setting	Corpus	Training	Test
question 1, 2, 4	WSJ	19 696	850
	GENIA	19 696	850
question 3	WSJ	39 832	1 700

Table 1: Overview of the data sets.

large volume of documents. Topic modeling is unsupervised, i.e., it does not require annotated documents (Blei, 2012) but rather discovers similarity between documents. Latent Dirichlet Allocation (LDA) is one of the topic modeling algorithms. It is a generative probabilistic model that approximates the underlying hidden topical structure of a collection of texts based on the distribution of words in the documents (Blei et al., 2003).

We use the topic modeling toolkit MALLET (McCallum, 2002). The topic modeler in MALLET implements Latent Dirichlet Allocation (LDA), clustering documents into a predefined number of topics. As a result, it provides different types of information such as:

- Topic keys: The highest ranked words per topic with their probabilities;

- Document topics: The topic distribution for each document (i.e., the probability that a document belongs to a given topic); and

- Topic state: This correlates all words and topics.

For our experiments, we use sentences as documents. Based on the document topic information, we then group the sentences into genre topics. We collect all sentences from the training and test set, cluster them via the MALLET topic modeler, and determine for which expert(s) the sentence is relevant. There are several ways of determining the best expert, see below. Then, we separate the sentences for each expert into training and test sentences, based on the previously determined data splits (see above).

We can determine experts based on hard or soft clustering decisions: For question 1 and 3, the sentences are assigned to hard topics, based on the topic that has the highest probability in that sentence. I.e., if for sentence s_x, MALLET lists the topic t_1 as the topic with the highest probability, then s_x is added to the data set of topic t_1. In other words, the data set of topic t_1 consists of all sentences for which MALLET showed topic t_1 as

the most likely topic. This means that the data set sizes vary between topics.

For questions 2 and 3, we utilize the entire topic distribution of a sentence by weighting sentences in the training data based on their topic distribution. Since the POS tagger does not support the weighting of training examples and since we do not have access to the code of the POS tagger, we simulate weighting training sentences by adding multiple copies to the training files of the experts. Thus, for the 2-topic experiments, a sentence with 80% probability for topic 1 will be included 80 times in the expert for topic 1 and 20 times in the expert for topic 2. We repeat these experiments, adding a sentence per every 10%, but rounding up small percentages so that every sentence will be added to every expert at least once. Thus, we use a more fine grained topic model to mitigate data sparseness, but we risk adding non-typical or irrelevant sentences to experts.

4.3 POS Tagging

For part of speech tagging, we use the TnT (Trigrams'n'Tags) tagger (Brants, 2000). TnT is based on a second order Markov Model and has an elaborate model for guessing the POS tags for unknown words. We use TnT mainly because of its speed and because it allows the manual inspection of the trained models (emission and transition frequencies).

4.4 Baselines

We use two baselines. As the first baseline, we take the complete training set when no topic modeling is performed. Note that this is a very competitive baseline since the topic modeling experts have access to considerably smaller amounts of training data. In order to avoid differences in accuracy resulting from different training set sizes, we create a second baseline by splitting the sentences randomly into the same number of groups as the number of topics, while maintaining the equal distribution of WSJ and GENIA sentences where applicable. I.e., we assume the same number of random "topics", all of the same size. Thus, in the 2-topic setting with the the genres, we create two separate training sets, each containing half of the WSJ training set and half of the GENIA one. In this setting, we test all experts on the whole test set and average over the results.

T.	2 topics		5 topics		10 topics	
	% in train	%in test	% in train	%in test	% in train	% in test
1	91.06	99.61	99.33	99.64	93.04	100
2	8.74	9.70	17.71	21.00	94.17	98.64
3			99.44	98.78	94.49	98.72
4			93.84	98.75	4.24	2.92
5			0.20	0.19	5.15	5.41
6					95.42	99.16
7					4.40	5.24
8					96.26	100
9					3.59	5.43
10					63.10	80.85

Table 2: Distribution of sentences from the WSJ+GENIA data set given 2, 5, and 10 topics (showing the percentage of GENIA sentences per topic).

1	cells cell expression il nf activation human binding gene transcription protein kappa ab cd ti factor alpha activity induced
2	mr million ui year company market stock billion share corp years shares trading president time quarter sales government business

Table 3: Examples of words in topics for the 2-topic experiments on the WSJ+Genia corpus.

Setting	Accuracy		
	2 topics	5 topics	10 topics
Full training set	96.64	96.64	96.64
Random split	96.48	95.92	95.49
Topic model	**96.84**	96.54	96.34

Table 4: Comparing the topic model experts to the baselines on the WSJ+GENIA data set.

5 Experimental Results

5.1 WSJ+GENIA Experiments

In this set of experiments, we use the manually created corpus that contains WSJ and GENIA sentences in equal parts. A logical first setting is to have the topic modeler distinguish between two different topics, to see if these two topics correspond to the two gold topics, WSJ and GENIA. We repeat the experiment using 5 and 10 topics to see if a finer granularity improves results. We then use the trained POS tagging experts to annotate the test sentences based on their assigned topic.

Investigating the topic modeler splits. The distributions of sentences in the training set and test set resulting from topic modeling are shown in Table 2. In the case of the 2 clusters, we see a clear split. A vast majority of GENIA sentences are clustered into the first topic, and less than 10% are clustered into the second topic. In the case of 5 and 10 topics, the split is even clearer. For example. for the 10-topic setting, topics 4, 5, 7, and 9 represent WSJ topics while the others are GENIA topics. Here, the error rate is between 3% and 6%. Both sets have one outlier, topic 2 for

the 5-topic setting, and topic 10 for the 10 topics, which are most likely the topics for difficult to classify sentences. Thus, in all cases, we have good splits, which should allow the POS tagging experts to learn specifics of the two corpora. Table 3 shows example words from the 2-topic experiment, which show a clear separation of topics into biomedical and financial terms.

POS tagging experiments. The results of the POS tagging experiments for the 2-topic, 5-topic, and the 10-topic settings are shown in Table 4. The results show that the experts created by the topic models outperform the randomly split models in all cases: For the 2-topic setting, we see the smallest increase from 96.48% to 96.84%, while the 10-topic setting reaches the largest increase, from 95.49% to 96.34%. However, note that the results in the 5- and 10-topic settings are slightly lower than the ones in the 2-topic setting. This is due to the reduced training set size.

When we compare the topic modeling experts to the full training set, the 2-topic model reaches an improvement over the full training set. The accuracy of the 5-topic setting almost reaches that of the full training set. Thus, even with a fifth of the training set compared to the full set, the per-

Top.	Train. size	Test size	Accuracy
1	53 436	2 504	96.74
2	113 033	5 902	97.51
3	79 133	3 974	97.48
4	89 761	7 814	95.29
5	84 467	3 327	92.41
6	151 562	6 363	98.02
7	141 415	4 612	95.67
8	68 518	2 071	96.77
9	145 224	4 425	96.70
10	25 444	604	94.21

Table 5: Results for the individual topic model experts for the WSJ+GENIA data.

	Accuracy		
Copies	2 topics	5 topics	10 topics
1	**96.84**	96.54	96.34
10	96.73	**96.67**	**96.84**
100	96.04	96.54	96.73

Table 6: Results for soft clustering on 2, 5, and 10 topics experiments

Setting	Accuracy
Full training set	96.23
Random split	95.16
Topic model	95.53
Soft Clustering	**96.32**

Table 7: Comparing topic model experts to the baselines on WSJ data (10 topics).

formance of topic models is almost at par with the results on the full training set.

The results lead us to the conclusion that a higher number of topics results in better experts, as shown by the gains over the random baseline. However, the gain of a high number of experts is offset by the reduction of the training set.

Next, we investigate the results of the 10-topic setting more closely: Table 5 shows the results of this setting per topic. These results show that the individual topics vary considerably in size, from around 25 000 words (topic 10) to 150 000 words (topic 6). However, contrary to expectation, there is no direct correlation between training set size and accuracy: Topic 10 has the lowest number of sentences, but its expert performs better than the topic 5 expert, which had access to more than 3 times the amount of training sentences. There is also no clear correlation between accuracy and WSJ or GENIA topics. While the WSJ topics 4, 5, and 7 are at the lower end of the accuracy range, topic 9 has a higher accuracy than GENIA topics 1 and 10 and a similar performance to topic 8.

5.2 Using Soft Clustering Information

Now we investigate soft clustering information by adding 10 or 100 copies of the sentence to experts based on its topic distribution, in comparison to a hard clustering setting. Table 6 shows the results of these experiments. For the 2-topic experiments, the results indicate that the POS tagger does not benefit from utilizing the topic distribution as there is a slight drop in the accuracy. The reason is that for 2 topics, the separation between WSJ and GENIA into separate topics is very clear. I.e., a sentence generally has a very high proba-

bility for its corresponding topic and thus should only be added to that topic. Consequently, the advantage of using experts is largely outweighed by misclassified sentences that are added to the wrong expert. However, soft clustering with 5 or 10 topics shows improvements over the full training baseline since the topic distribution is more fine grained. Here, a sentence is more likely to be included in more than one topic. Using a sentence 10 times rather than 100 times seems to be a better fit. The 10-topics, 10 copies setting reaches the same accuracy as the hard clustering 2-topic setting, thus showing that expert knowledge is capable of combating data sparseness.

5.3 WSJ Experiments: Creating Micro-Topics

Here, we investigate whether we can also successfully use topic modeling to create POS tagging experts in cases where there is only one genre. That is, is topic modeling only sensitive towards genre differences or can it also detect smaller types of variation, and can those variations be translated into specialized POS tagging experts? We use the WSJ corpus for this set of experiments, and we compare an experiment with 10 topics to the two baselines. The results of these experiments are shown in Table 7. We see a positive effect of using experts based on the hard clustering topic models over the random split: Accuracy increases from 95.16% to 95.53%. Similar to the GENIA+WSJ 10-topic experiment, we also do not reach the baseline using all training data. Per topic, there are similar trends to the ones for the WSJ+GENIA set-

Data Set	Setting	Accuracy
standard	random split	95.16
standard	topic model	95.53
5-fold	topic model	95.70

Table 8: Comparing the standard data split to a random data split for WSJ data (10 topics).

Random split				Topic model			
split 1		split 2		topic 1		topic 2	
NN	335	NN	300	NN	387	CD	227
JJ	219	JJ	187	JJ	217	NNP	226
CD	151	CD	162	CD	70	NN	132
NNP	132	NNP	162	NNS	51	JJ	104
NNS	67	NNS	69	NNP	28	NNS	57
VBN	31	VBG	30	FW	13	VBN	32

Table 10: The 6 most frequent POS tags assigned to unknown words (2 topics).

ting, a large variation of topic sizes and no direct correlation of training set size and accuracy. However, the soft clustering results show that there is a 0.8 percent improvement over the topic models and a small improvement over the full training set. This reinforces the hypothesis that soft clustering can indeed handle the data sparseness issue even when the genres are not as clearly distinguishable as WSJ vs. GENIA.

The differences between topic models and a random split are less pronounced than in the case of the combined WSJ+GENIA corpus. One explanation for this may be that the topics are less different from each other than in the WSJ+GENIA setting so that the POS tagging expert are not very different from each other. Another possible explanation is that this is a consequence of the way we split the WSJ corpus into training and test sets: As described in section 4, we use the standard split with section 02-21 as training set and section 22 as our current test set. This means that the test set may contain different topics from the training set, which may generate problems in topic modeling. To test this hypothesis, we repeat the experiment with 10 topics, but this time, we perform a five-fold cross-validation for POS tagging on sections 02-22. I.e., we vary the test set across all sections, to create a more homogeneous data split. The results of this experiment, in comparison to previous results, are shown in Table 8. We reach slightly higher results in the 5-fold cross-validation; accuracy increases from 95.53% to 95.70%. This means that the training and test set in the standard setting are not optimally homogeneous. However, since the difference in accuracy is rather small, the differences between training and test set do not seem to impact the performance of our system.

5.4 What do the Experts Learn?

In this section, we investigate the differences between the models learned based on a random split as opposed to the models learned based on the topic models. We concentrate on the 2 topic models based on the WSJ+GENIA data set from section 5.1.

First, we take a closer look at the distribution of unknown words, and the POS taggers' accuracy on known and unknown words. Unknown words are defined as those words from the test set that do not occur in the training set. This means that the POS tagger needs to guess the word's possible tags without having access to its ambiguity class. The results for this investigation are listed in Table 9. These results show that the percentage of unknown words is higher by 0.76 percent points in the random split setting. This means that the two topic models acquire more specialized lexicons that allow the taggers to cover more words. A look at the accuracies shows that, as expected, the accuracy for known words is higher in the topic model setting. However, the results also show that the accuracy on unknown words is significantly higher in this setting, 85.22% for the topic model experts vs. 83.11% for the random splits. This means that the POS tagging models learned from the topic model data split has acquired better models of unknown words based on the word distribution from the training corpora.

We then investigate which POS labels are assigned to unknown words in the two settings. The 6 most frequent POS tags per setting and topic are shown in table 10. A comparison shows that for the random split, both subsets have a very similar distribution: Unknown words are assigned one of the following labels: noun (NN), adjective (JJ), cardinal number (CD), proper name (NNP), plural noun (NNS), past participle (VBN) or present participle (VBG). The distributions for the topic models show a visibly different picture: In the second topic (which is the WSJ topic, see table 2), cardinal numbers are the most frequent class for unknown words, followed closely by names. These two labels are three times and ten times more frequent than in topic 1. In contrast, topic 1 (GENIA)

Topic	Random split			Topic model		
	% Unknown	Known Acc.	Unknown Acc.	% Unknown	Known Acc.	Unknown Acc.
1	4.86	97.25	83.38	3.85	98.35	85.12
2	4.79	97.06	82.84	4.29	96.29	85.31
avg.	4.83	97.16	83.11	4.07	97.33	85.22

Table 9: Unknown word rates and accuracies for known and unknown words in the WSJ+GENIA experiment using 2 topics.

Random split			Topic model		
Gold	TnT	No.	Gold	TnT	No.
NN	JJ	141	NN	JJ	122
JJ	NN	111	JJ	NN	104
NNP	NN	93	VBD	VBN	82
VBD	VBN	88	NNP	NNPS	70
NN	NNP	66	RB	IN	64
IN	RB	65	IN	RB	61
RB	IN	62	NN	NNP	53
NNP	NNPS	53	VBG	NN	50

Table 11: The 8 most frequent confusion sets (2 topics).

is closer to the distribution of the models based on random sampling, but it has a higher number of foreign words (FW), which is an indication that some biomedical terms are not recognized as such and are then marked as foreign words. Examples of such cases are the words "aeruginosa" and "Leishmania". Overall, these results corroborate our hypothesis that the topic models learn individual characteristics of unknown words.

Finally, we consider the types of errors that the POS taggers make by looking at confusion sets. The 8 most frequent confusion sets under both conditions are shown in table 11. A closer look at the confusion sets of the two experiments shows that the categories in the random split setting are consistent with standard errors that POS taggers make: These POS taggers mostly confuse nouns (NN) with adjectives (JJ) and with names (NNP), past tense verbs (VBD) with participles (VBN), prepositions (IN) with adverbs (RB). One notable difference in the topic modeling setting is that the number of confusions between nouns (NN) and names (NNP) (in both directions) is almost reduced by half in comparison to the random split setting: 88 vs. 159 cases (note that the condition NN NNP is not among the 8 most frequent cases for the topic model as shown in table 11, it is the

12th most frequent confusion set). Names are generally difficult because they constitute an open set, and thus not all of them will be found in the training set. For example, names that were misclassified as nouns in the random split data set included "BART", "Jefferies", and "Tulsa". Thus, a reduction of these errors means that the topic model experts are learning characteristics that allow them to handle domain specific names better, even though the respective learned model files of the topic model setting contain considerably fewer lexical entries.

6 Conclusion and Future Work

In our research, we have investigated whether we can use topic modeling in order to create specialized subsets of POS annotated data, which can then be used to train POS tagging experts for the topic. Our results show that the POS tagging experts achieve higher accuracies both for a manually created mixed data set with financial news and medical texts and for a more homogeneous data set consisting only of financial news. The latter shows that our system is capable of adapting to nuances in the micro-genres within the Wall Street Journal texts. Our analysis also shows that a significant improvement is achieved, particularly, for proper names. The topic model experts are almost three times more likely to tag a name correctly than the random split models.

We have created a flexible and fully automatic methodology of POS tagging experts for different genres. These experts can be extracted from a heterogeneous text source, without the need of having to separate the genres manually. Additionally, we obtain individual experts, which can be used separately. Further applications for this kind of technology can be found in adapting POS taggers to characteristics of different speech or cognitive impediments but also to the characteristics of non-native speakers.

Our current experiments have used 2, 5, and 10

topic models. In theory, the number of topics can be set to a higher number, thus creating more subtle topics. However, as we have also shown, the higher the number of topics, the more severe data sparseness becomes. This can be mitigated by using training sentences for more than one topic, based on the distribution provided by the topic modeler. We plan on extending our work to syntactic parsing, for which the differences between genres will be more noticeable.

References

David M. Blei, Andrew Y. Ng, and Michael I. Jordan. 2003. Latent dirichlet allocation. *Journal of Machine Learning Research*, 3:993–1022.

David M. Blei. 2012. Probabilistic topic models. *Communications of the ACM*, 55(4):77–84.

John Blitzer, Ryan McDonald, and Fernando Pereira. 2006. Domain adaptation with structural correspondence learning. In *Proceedings of the Conference on Empirical Methods in Natural Language Processing (EMNLP)*, pages 120–128, Sydney, Australia.

Thorsten Brants. 2000. TnT–a statistical part-of-speech tagger. In *Proceedings of the 1st Conference of the North American Chapter of the Association for Computational Linguistics and the 6th Conference on Applied Natural Language Processing (ANLP/NAACL)*, pages 224–231, Seattle, WA.

Stephen Clark, James Curran, and Miles Osborne. 2003. Bootstrapping POS-taggers using unlabelled data. In *Proceedings of the Seventh Conference on Natural Language Learning (CoNLL)*, Edmonton, Canada.

Hal Daumé III. 2007. Frustratingly easy domain adaptation. In *Proceedings of the 45th Annual Meeting of the Association of Computational Linguistics*, pages 256–263, Prague, Czech Republic.

Mark Dredze, John Blitzer, Partha Pratim Talukdar, Kuzman Ganchev, João Graca, and Fernando Pereira. 2007. Frustratingly hard domain adaptation for dependency parsing. In *Proceedings of the CoNLL Shared Task Session of EMNLP-CoNLL 2007*, pages 1051–1055, Prague, Czech Republic.

Mohammad Khan, Markus Dickinson, and Sandra Kübler. 2013. Towards domain adaptation for parsing web data. In *Proceedings of the International Conference on Recent Advances in Natural Language Processing (RANLP)*, Hissar, Bulgaria.

Sandra Kübler and Eric Baucom. 2011. Fast domain adaptation for part of speech tagging for dialogues. In *Proceedings of the International Conference on Recent Advances in NLP (RANLP)*, Hissar, Bulgaria.

Mitchell Marcus, Grace Kim, Mary Ann Marcinkiewicz, Robert MacIntyre, Ann Bies, Mark Ferguson, Karen Katz, and Britta Schasberger. 1994. The Penn Treebank: Annotating predicate argument structure. In *Proceedings of the ARPA Human Language Technology Workshop, HLT 94*, pages 114–119, Plainsboro, NJ.

Andrew Kachites McCallum. 2002. Mallet: A machine learning for language toolkit. http://mallet.cs.umass.edu.

John Miller, Manabu Torii, and K. Vijay-Shanker. 2007. Adaptation of POS tagging for multiple biomedical domains. In *Proceedings of the Workshop on Biological, Translational, and Clinical Language Processing*, pages 179–180, Prague, Czech Republic.

Barbara Plank and Gertjan van Noord. 2011. Effective measures of domain similarity for parsing. In *Proceedings of the 49th Annual Meeting of the Association for Computational Linguistics: Human Language Technologies*, pages 1566–1576, Portland, OR.

Beatrice Santorini. 1990. Part-of-speech tagging guidelines for the Penn Treebank Project. Department of Computer and Information Science, University of Pennsylvania, 3rd Revision, 2nd Printing.

Anders Søgaard. 2013. Zipfian corruptions for robust POS tagging. In *Proceedings of the 2013 Conference of the North American Chapter of the Association for Computational Linguistics: Human Language Technologies*, pages 668–672, Atlanta, GA.

Yuka Tateisi and Jun'ichi Tsujii. 2004. Part-of-speech annotation of biology research abstracts. In *Proceedings of 4th International Conference on Language Resource and Evaluation (LREC)*, Lisbon, Portugal.

Graph theoretic interpretation of *Bangla* traditional grammar

Samir Karmakar
School of Languages and Linguistics
Jadavpur University
samirkrmkr@yahoo.co.in

Sayantani Banerjee
School of Languages and Linguistics
Jadavpur University
banerjeesayantni@gmail.com

Soumya Ghosh
School of Languages and Linguistics
Jadavpur University
ghosh.soumya73@yahoo.com

Abstract

The paper is an investigation into the graph theoretic interpretation of the *Bangla* traditional grammar to understand the way grammatical information is structurally encoded in language. The hierarchical and the linear structural principles of grammatical compositionality is discussed in terms of certain graph theoretic concepts like tree, subtree, inverse tree etc.

Translating linguistic structure into the tree structure is not new. In fact, the Transformational-Generative grammar, Tree adjoining grammar etc. have shown quite successfully how syntacto-semantic principles can be talked about in terms of tree structures. The present work differs in certain respects from the assumptions of TG grammarians, primarily because of the type of grammar and language it is dealing with.

1   Introduction

This paper seeks to investigate how substantially the structure of a language can be dealt with the aid of graph theory. Because of being qualified with the discrete structure, natural language can be represented and processed with graph-theoretic methods. Compositional nature of language makes it more viable to the concept of constituent hierarchies within the scope of which syntactic and semantic principles are operating. Under this situation, the graph theoretic interpretation provides excellent opportunities to explore the issues pertinent in structural composition. Certain contemporary models like head-driven phrase structure grammar, semantic networks etc. make good use of graph theoretic methods. WordNet, VerbNet etc. have also their deep connections with this branch of discrete mathematics. Under the influence of these approaches, the current paper seeks to investigate how grammatical regulations are crucial in imposing constraint on the structure with a special reference to the traditional *Bangla* grammar within the framework of graph theoretic enquiry.

Translating linguistic structure into the tree structure is not new. In fact, the Transformational-Generative (hereafter, TG) grammar has shown quite successfully how syntacto-semantic principles can be talked about in terms of tree structures. The present work differs in certain respects from the assumptions of TG grammarians, primarily because of the type of grammar and language it is dealing with. Not only the TG grammar, tree adjoining (hereafter, TA) grammar has also made a good use of the graph theory. Though both TG and TA have made use of the graph theory but definitely from the two different perspectives.

The current proposal resembles TA grammar more closely than the TG grammar; and as a result, the proposed model of language representation and processing can probably be classified in terms of weak generative capacity, a position between context free grammars and indexed grammars.

2   Research Objectives

Within the broader theoretical background as is discussed in Section (1), this paper will investigate the way grammatical structures of *Bangla* as is described in traditional *Bangla* grammar (Chatterji 1939) can be talked about in terms of graph theoretic assumptions. This is possibly the most salient point where the paper does differ even from its nearest kin TA grammar. Under this situation, following two questions will be investigated in this paper: (a) how the structural

D S Sharma, R Sangal and A K Singh. Proc. of the 13th Intl. Conference on Natural Language Processing, pages 129–136,
Varanasi, India. December 2016. ©2016 NLP Association of India (NLPAI)

complexity of the *Bangla* sentence can be talked about with respect to graph theoretic assumptions; and, (b) if it is possible to develop a theoretical scheme to capture the syntacto-semantic peculiarities of the individual constituents of a sentence.

3 Theoretical Background

Approaching the above mentioned research objectives seeks the setting of the theoretical framework which presumes some fundamental understanding of the graph theory and the knowledge of traditional *Bangla* grammar.

3.1 Tree as a Graph

Graphs are not used for some sheer illustrative purposes; In fact, they reveal hidden intricacies involved in complex structures. As a consequence, it is quite essential to concentrate on some basic concepts which are crucial in explaining the construal of graph in general: Mathematically, graph is defined as a set of sets – one of which contains the nodes and other, a set of ordered pairs or edges. For the purpose of this paper, a particular type of graph will be discussed, namely 'tree'. A tree is defined as a graph in which each pair of vertices is connected with a unique path. Tree is characterized as acyclic and directed (Liu, 2001). An example of tree is given in the figure below:

1.

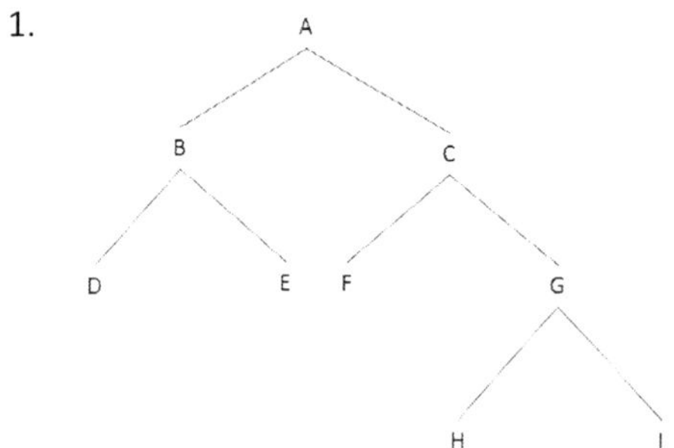

An alternative way to represent the graph of a tree is to follow the technique of embedded bracketing as is shown in (2). In this framework, the notion of hierarchical depth of a particular node can be interpreted in terms of its interiority in the bracketed representation. Furthermore, the concept of edge here in this case is inferred from an understanding of 'who embeds whom'.

2.   [A [B [D] [E]] [C [F] [G [H] [I]]]]

According to (1) and also (2), then, a graph of tree (= G_T) could be represented as $\{V_T, E_T\}$, where V_T is the set of vertices/nodes $\{A, B, C, D, E, F, G, H, I\}$ and E_T is a set of edges $\{AB, AC, BD, BE, CF, CG, GH, GI\}$. Each of the members of E_T can be defined as a relation defined over the set of vertices. As per this definition, then, an edge is an ordered pair. In other words, an edge could be conceived as a relation from one vertex to another non-identical vertex. A tree (= G'_T) will be called as the subtree of G_T, iff and only if $V'_T \subset V_T$ and $E'_T \subset E_T$. For example, the trees drawn in (3) are the subtrees of (1):

3.

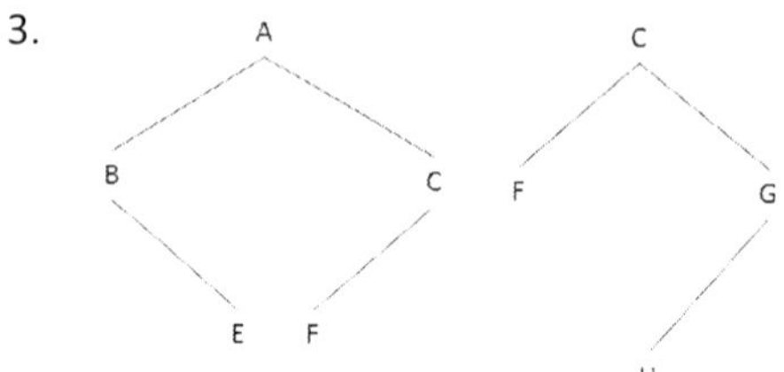

Two subtrees of a tree will be considered as inverse to each other if and only if their union can result into a tree of which they are the subtrees. Therefore, the following two subtrees are the inverse of each other because their union will produce the graph shown in (1):

4.

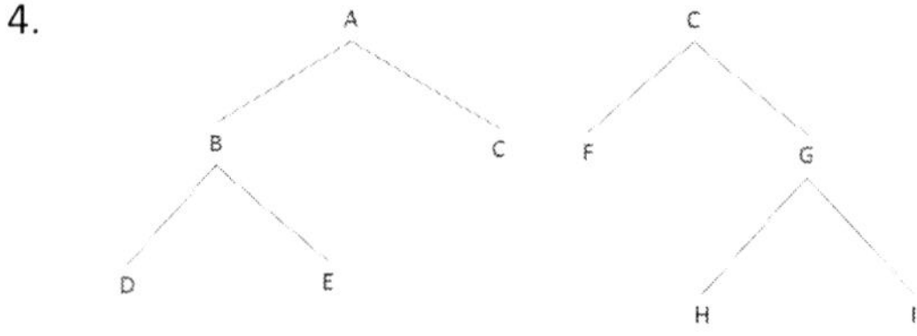

Just like the graph theory, traditional grammar of *Bangla* can also generate the trees. Therefore, it becomes quintessential to explore how and to what extent trees generated by the grammar of a language (here, *Bangla*) resemble the structural aspect of tree as the mathematical object.

3.2 Traditional *Bangla* Grammar

Likewise the western tradition, *Bangla* sentence (*bākya*) also has two distinct parts namely subject (*uddeśya*) and predicate (*bidheya*). Both subject and predicate can be modified; and, modifiers will be classified as elaborator (*samprasāraka*). As a result of elaboration, whatever is produced is classified again either as subject or as predicate. Elaborators are optional and they can appear in any numbers for finer grain specifications of the communicative intent. Unlike elaborators, predicate could have complement (*pūraka*). Complements are not optional; rather, they are the obligatory components of the predicates, and their numbers are often fixed by the semantic expectancy of the verbs. To capture the structural peculiarities of a sentence the notion of subject, predicate, elaborator and complement are extremely useful. In addition to this, the notion of *maximality* is proposed to incorporate the idea of the scope of complete interpretation for a particular structure. Within the maximal scope of a structure, syntactic and semantic necessities of a particular constituent are satisfied and beyond that scope these necessities have no role to play. Accordingly, the addition of complement to the verb in (5) makes their immediate dominator maximal in case of transitive *Bangla* verbs. Note this understanding of maximality is quite different than the one talked about by Chomsky. This issue will be picked up again in our successive discussions to exemplify the way maximality is instrumental in graph theoretic framework of language interpretation.

5.

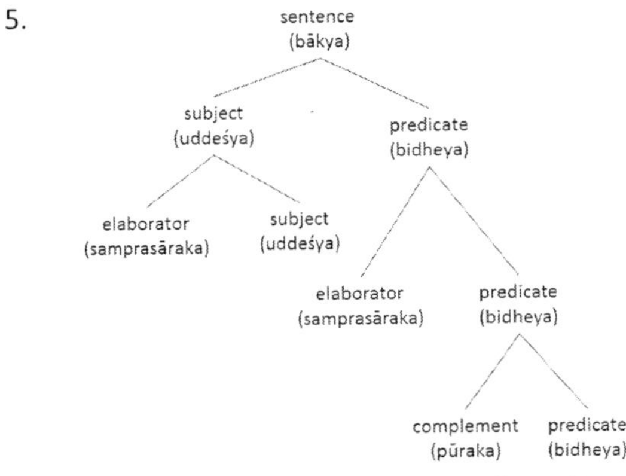

Note: A = sentence; B = subject; C = predicate; D = elaborator; E = subject; F = elaborator; G = predicate; H = complement; I = predicate

In addition to what is discussed earlier, we would like to incorporate the word-internal composition to understand the reach of the graph theoretic methods of language description. More importantly, studies solely depended on the morphology of English often fails to appreciate the linguistic intricacies involved in other vernaculars. Word internal morphological complexity is one such intricacy which demands our attention.

Morphological complexities of words in *Bangla* are more in case of nominal and verbal constituents of a sentence. Nominal and verbal – both

types of constituents can be decomposed in two major parts: (a) a part constitutive of core meaning, traditionally termed as *prātipadika*; (b) another part constitutive of relational meaning, traditionally classified as *bibhakti*. In case of nominal, relational meaning denotes case relations and has direct relevance with the core meaning of the verbal constituents; in case of verbal, the relational meaning denotes agreement with the nominal and also contain information about the time. The core meaning is constitutive of base form and the satellite. Depending on how the constituent is classified, base could be of two types: namely, (a) nominal base (*sajñā*) and (b) verbal base (*dhātu*). Both of these two bases are further decomposed into (a) root (*prakriti*) and (b) formative (*avayava*). According to the nature of the base, the formative could be of two types namely gender signifying and causative. In case of verbal constituent, satellite is constitutive of grammatical aspect and tense, whereas classifier has the status of formative in case of nominal.

6.

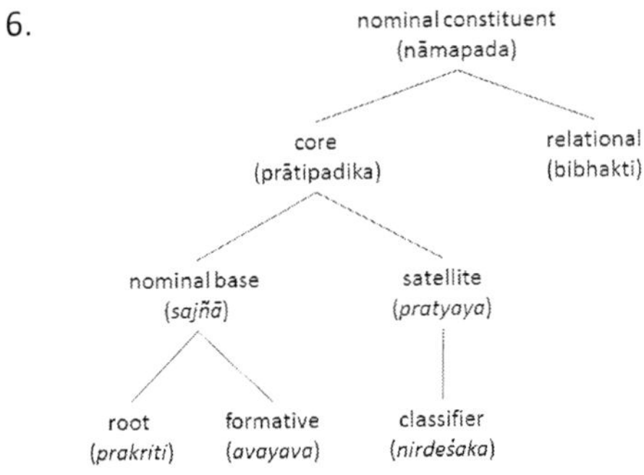

The terminal vertices of (5) – excepting one marked as predicate (= I) – will be further augmented by (6); whereas, terminal position 'I' will be augmented with (7):

7.

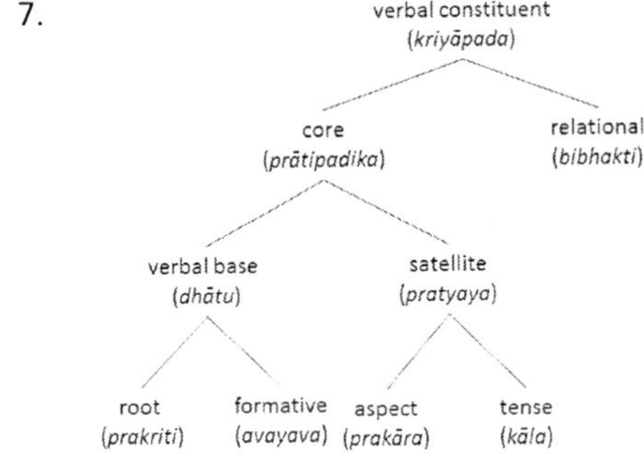

This will then lead us to a fully specified tree capable of representing sentences; however, without postposition (*anusarga*). Sentences containing postposition are kept aside keeping the scope of the paper in mind.

4 Discussion

After having the brief introductions of different theoretical tools, we will now investigate how graph theory and the traditional *Bangla* grammar interact with each other. In continuation to the above discussion, one can now suggest that instead of having a set of distinct vertices/nodes one can simply distinguish the non-identical vertices of (5) in terms of their respective 'maximality' – discussed earlier. Developing such mechanism can be done in two distinct stages: Firstly, to substitute the identical vertices with a single alphabet to indicate the similarities among them; and secondly, to capture the dissimilarities in terms of their respective syntactic and semantic properties certain conceptual measures have to be thought of. With the initiation of the first, (5) is simply transformed into (8):

8.

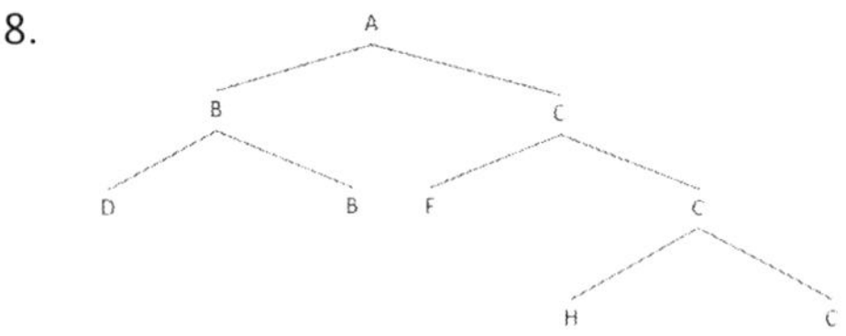

Similar vertices/nodes are reflecting their endocentric nature. In virtue of being endocentric, they are category preserving. Though the similarities of certain vertices are well-represented in (8), the dissimilarities are hardly traceable from this representation until the seemingly similar vertices are interpreted in terms of maximality. To understand this problem, consider the case of C: Are the three instances of C in (8) same? Are they similar type of 'predicate'? – A little attention will reveal the fact that they are not. Nonbranching C can license the verbal constituent only, when the intermediating one has the provisions for the complement(s) (i.e. the terminal vertex H) and the verbal constituents (i.e. the terminal vertex C). Finally, the topmost C is projected due to the addition of elaborator with the complement(s) and the verbal constituent. This simply compels us to import one another concept, namely *hierarchical depth* or *relative interiority*. Hierarchical depth can be translated in terms of certain constitutional scopes. Within a scope different types of syntactic and semantic expectancies are satiated. Under this situation

then it becomes essential to distinguish these three instances of Cs in terms of their respective scopes. This leads us to the following proposal: In (8), C of the non-branching vertex is the head. Being non-branching, the hierarchical depth or relative interiority of head C is more than the other Cs above it. Due to the successive projections, this head results into the appearances of C_{MAX} as maximal projection (hence, subscripted with 'MAX') and C_E as elaborated projection (hence, subscripted with 'E'). While getting projected maximally, complements are accommodated; whereas to get elaborated projection, elaborators are accommodated. The distinction between these two types of projections namely maximal and elaborated is instrumental in distinguishing complements from the adjunct. This solution is restricted not only to any specific subtree – rather it has some general appeal: Consider the case of multiple appearances of B. Following the general strategy, outlined above, non-branching B will be labeled as head. This is projected into a higher non-branching vertex B which has the status of elaborator (= D) and therefore must be represented as B_E. Since the elaborators are not the essential part of a lexeme, they are kept out side of the maximal projection in this proposal which is contrary to the basic claim of the X-bar theory where adjuncts are kept within the scope of the maximal projection (Chomsky, 1970). Therefore, (8) is further modified into (9):

9. $[A [B_E [D] [B]] [C_E [F] [C_{MAX} [H] [C]]]]$

What is of worth mentioning is that the identification of a vertex either as maximal or as elaborator has to do nothing with their relative hierarchies in a tree. Also, it does not mean that the maximal projection will be always embedded within the elaborated projection. Relative saliencies in terms of hierarchical depth or interiority of maximal and elaborated projections may vary in a language like *Bangla* on the basis of how they do appear in the body of a sentence: (9) can simply be rewritten as (10) if F and H changes their respective positions:

10. $[A [B_E [D] [B]] [C_{MAX} [H] [C_E [F] [C]]]]$

The specification of maximal will only serve the purpose of stating the fact that beyond it appearance of further complement is simply impossible. That means the verb – whose maximal projection it is – is completely saturated once it is maximally projected. This would simply exclude the provision for any intermediating projection to attain the status of maximal in virtue of not getting completely saturated.

Let us consider the case of (6) and (7) now. For the sake of brevity and abstraction, the technical terms of these two trees are replaced with the alphabets in (11) and (12). For the vertices of the tree representing nominal constituent, J-Q alphabets are used. Alphabets from R-Z are allotted to the vertices of the tree representing the verbal constituencies.

11.

12.

Unlike the structure of the sentence as is represented in (5), the structures of nominal and verbal constituents are well-demarcated in the sense that recurring use of same term is not noticeable. That does not mean that the intermediate projections are not there. Rather, it confirms the intermediating projections by adopting a strict demarcating policy.

Notion of subtree can be exploited in favor of syntactically and semantically independent expressions that the native speakers of *Bangla* encounter often in their linguistic world. Consider the following example: *br̥ddh-ā-ṭi-ke* means 'to the old lady', where *br̥ddh-* = O, *-ā-* = P, *-ṭi-* = Q, and *–ke* = L of (11). In case of (11), following expressions will be syntactically and semantically well-formed: (i) *br̥ddh-ā* (= M), (ii) *br̥ddh-ā-ṭi* (= K), and finally (iii) *br̥ddh-ā-ṭi-ke* (= J). This

leads to the classification of M, K and J as maximal however with reference to different types of grammatical compulsions: M is maximal because no formative can be added outside its scope; K would not permit the addition of any classifier beyond it; and, no more relational markers are licensed beyond the scope of J. This understanding then in turn justifies why certain trees with the roots M, K, and J are in the subtree relations with (11). Other subtrees of graph (11) other than the ones mentioned above are mathematically possible subtrees but linguistically are not plausible. Grammatically significant trees are represented in (13) with the marking of the concentric circles:

13.

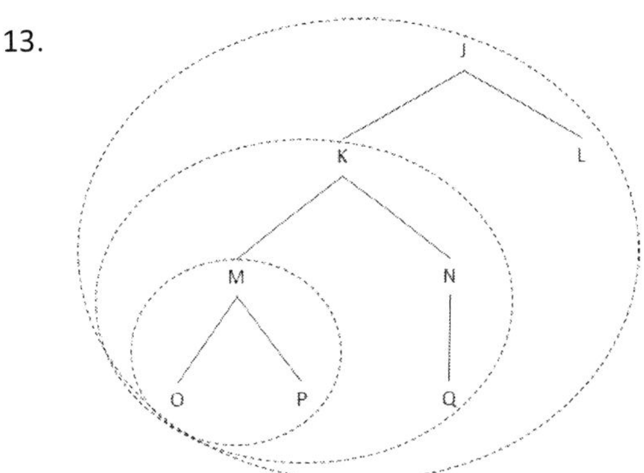

Contrariwise, in case of (12), except the entire tree (which is an improper subtree of itself), no proper (stand-alone) subtree can be identified in spite of the presence of different maximal nodes in different layers of structural hierarchies or interiorities as is evidenced in (14):

14.

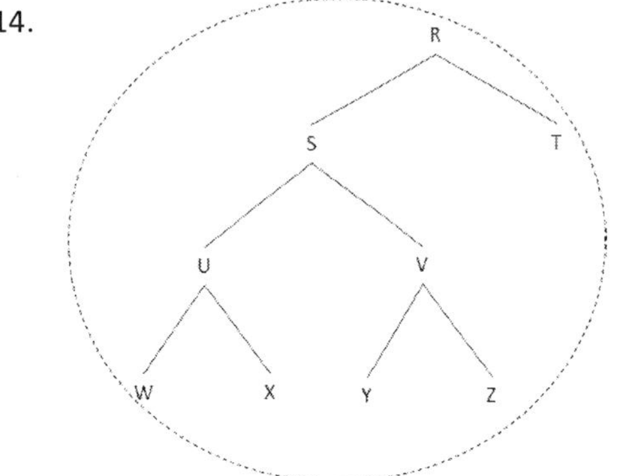

Therefore, in the context of linguistic structures, those subtrees are of immense significance which consist of maximally projected nodes as their roots – with the statutory precaution that all maximally projected nodes are not capable to perform the task of the root of a (sub)tree. It is also worthwhile to note that subtree without a root marked as maximal are optional in nature. Extending this discussion beyond the level of the words will also unveil similar type of findings. For example (9) contains subtrees with the root C_{MAX}, C_E, B_E, and A.

Having discussed this, time now is to look into the issues of the semantic import of the nodes constituting the tree. In other words, the question which will be delved into is 'what constitutes a node?' – As per the principle of compositionality, "the meaning of a complex expression is a function of the meanings of its parts and of the syntactic rules by which they are combined" (Partee, Meulen, and Wall 1990). Under the immediate influence of the compositionality principle then the task will be to explain what governs the combinatorial behavior of neighboring nodes of same hierarchy. Answer to this question must have some provisions for what we will call selectional restrictions. Selectional restriction which is a semantic function associated with each of the nodes remains instrumental in determining 'who can go with whom'.

As per the standard practices of lexical semantics like the one proposed by Jackendoff (1990), constitutive nodes should contain information about itself with a special reference to the structure which it is a part of. Since the constituent node has its connotations both at the levels of local and global structures the semantics of a node must contain information about (a) the subtree reflecting its immediate scope and (b) the subtree with a root node marked as maximal where the immediate scope is embedded. As per this proposal then the meaning of an expression, say for example O, will be the following:

15.

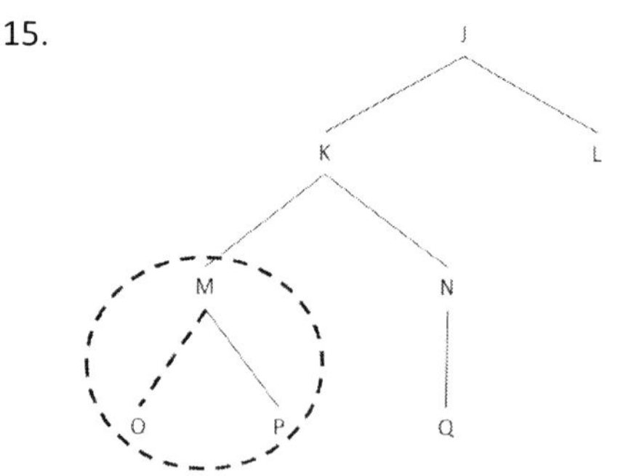

A subtree – like the one circled with dashed line in (15) marked with the presence of maximal

root – i.e. M, and is in inverse relation with the following tree:

16.

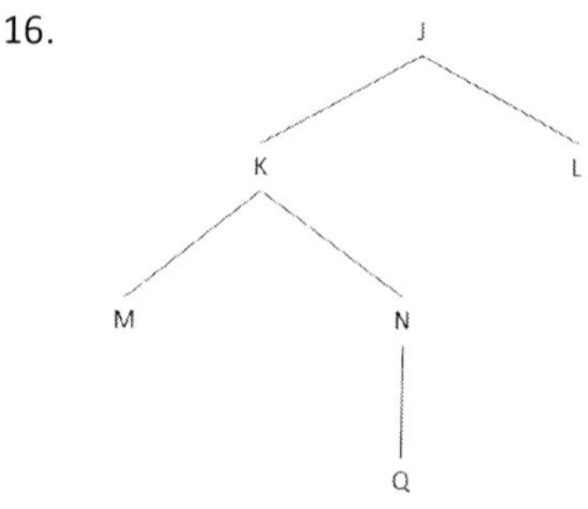

The traditional grammar of *Bangla*, then, can be conceptualized in terms of the following concepts:
i) a set of terminal symbols (= S_T); Here, terminal symbols are the representatives of different word classes;
ii) a set of non-terminal symbols (= S_{NT}); such that, $S_T \cap S_{NT} = \Phi$;
iii) Non-terminal symbols has a set of distinguished members (= D) capable of being marked either with MAX or with E resulting into two distinct partitions, namely D_{MAX} and D_E. Point to be noted $(D_{MAX} \cap D_E = D) \subset S_{NT}$;
iv) a highly distinguished member A which belongs to D;
v) A set of initial trees (T_I) whose interior nodes are labeled by nonterminal symbols. Nonterminal nodes of a particular tree at the bottom can be replaced by the distinguished members of it for further derivation. However, if the bottom consists of terminal symbols, no more replacement as well as further derivation is permitted;
vi) the appearance of lexical element in a tree will indicate the end of a particular path;

The graph theoretic approach to the traditional grammar of *Bangla* will be classified as lexical because each lexical item, in virtue of being the member of word classes belonging to the set of terminal symbols is associated with structural description which is functional is nature. In other words, the lexical constituents of a language must contain the functional descriptions for their respective distribution in a structure. In order to meet this structural goal, then, one needs to identify the information in two broad categories: (a) the information which is locally relevant and constitutes the core of the lexical properties, and (b) the information which is globally relevant and indicates the relation of the lexical core to its global sentential context within which it is grounded. This in one way address the classical problem of symbol grounding which is addressed by Harnard (1990).

As per the theoretical framework described above the structural meaning of classifier (CLS) with respect to (13) will be as follows:

17. | CLS
     | Q
     | [N[Q]]
     | [K[M][N]]

The first line of this representation is the grammatical classification of the node Q as classifier. Third line of the representation is a non-maximal subtree which is in inverse relation with the subtree mentioned in the fourth line. Subtree mentioned in the fourth line contains an intervening maximal projection K – which is already discussed in the context of (11) and (13), previously. Following the similar graph theoretic approach, a lexical grammar of simple *Bangla* sentence can be written with the help of graph-theoretic assumptions discussed earlier. In fact the graphical representations that we have illustrated in (5), (6), and (7) can produce the sentences which can be interpreted following the techniques of lexical grammar discussed above. One such sentence is represented in the Appendix of this article to show how rich the structural aspect of *Bangla* is. This paper will be concluded with an observation which we are interested of: Since CLS is a word class, the function mentioned in (17) will be finitely ambiguous in virtue of containing expressions like *-ṭi, -ṭā, -khāni, -khānā* etc. In order to exclude this type of problem, further investigation has to be initiated towards the finer grain analysis of different categories.

References

Barbara H. Partee, Alice ter Meulen, and Robert E. Wall. 1990. *Mathematical Methods in Linguistics*. Kluwer Academic Publishers, Dordrecht.

C.L. Lieu. 1985. *Elements of Discrete Mathematics*. Tata MCgraw-Hill Publishing Company Limited, New Belhi.

Harnard, S. (1990). The Symbol Grounding Problem, *Physica D* 42, 335-346.

Noam Chomsky. 1970. Remarks on nominalization. In: R. Jacobs and P. Rosenbaum (eds.) *Reading in English Transformational Grammar*, 184-221. Waltham, Ginn.

Ray Jackendoff. 1990. *Semantic Structure*. The MIT Press, Massachussets.

Suniti Kr. Chatterji. 1939. *Bhasha-Prakash Bangla Vyakarana*. Edition 2014. Rupa Publication India Ltd, New Delhi.

Appendix 1

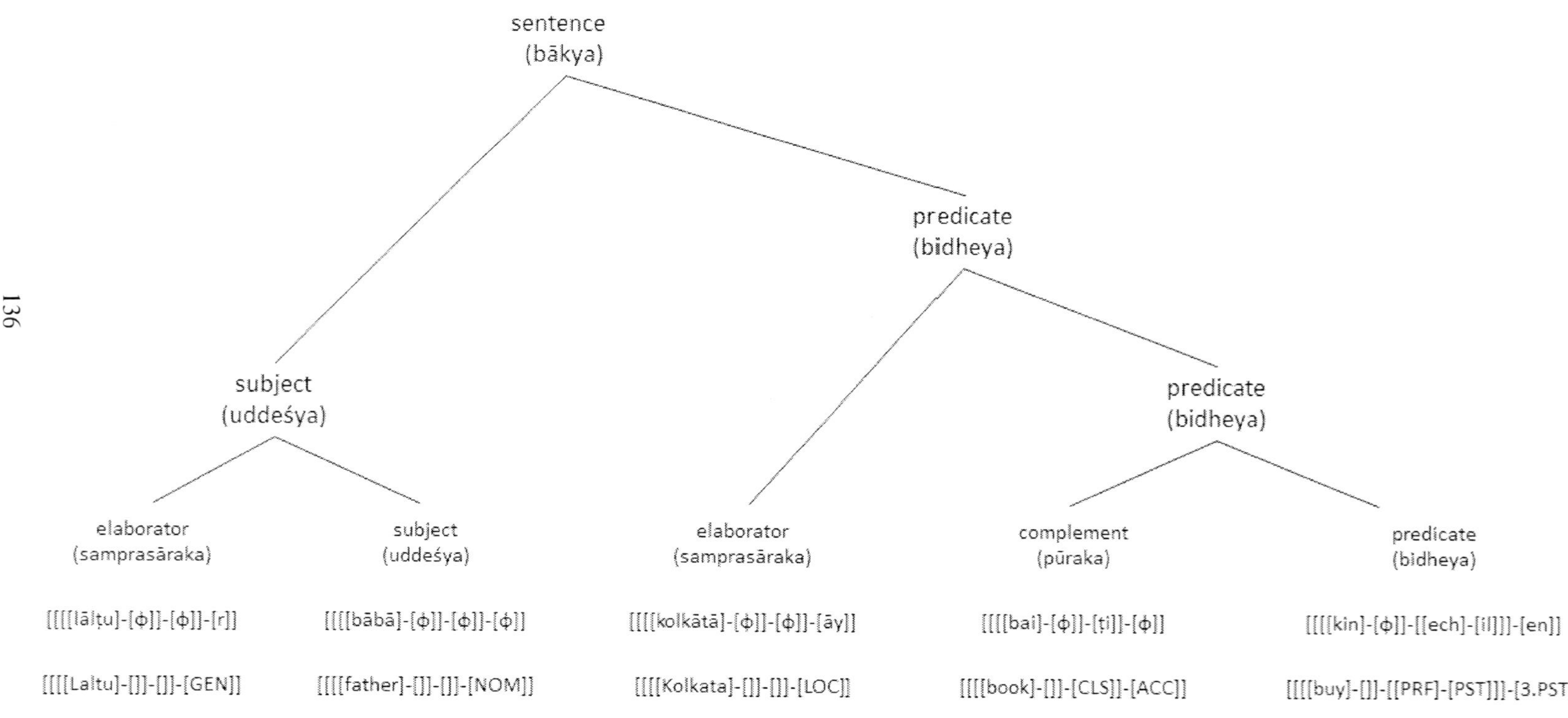

136

A method for Automatic Text Summarization using Consensus of Multiple Similarity Measures and Ranking Techniques

Mukesh Kumar Jadon
Department of Computer Science and Engineering
The LNM Institute of Information Technology
Jaipur, India
jadonmukesh30@gmail.com

Ayush Pareek
Department of Computer Science and Engineering
The LNM Institute of Information Technology
Jaipur, India
ayush.original@gmail.com

Abstract

In the era of information overload, text summarization can be defined as the process of extracting useful information from a large space of available content using traditional filtering methods. One of the major challenges in the domain of extraction based summarization is that a single statistical measure is not sufficient to produce efficient summaries which would be close to human-made 'gold standard', since each measure suffers from individual weaknesses. We deal with this problem by proposing a text summarization model that combines various statistical measures so that the pitfalls of an individual technique could be compensated by the strengths of others. Experimental results are presented to demonstrate the effectiveness of the proposed method using the TAC 2011 Multiling pilot dataset for English language and ROUGE summary evaluation tool.

1 Introduction

What is the need of text summarization? One of the major reasons is Information explosion. A study (Cho et al., 2015) by IBM in 2013 estimated that everyday 2.5 Quintillion bytes of new information were born on the internet. The velocity with which this is increasing can be estimated from the fact that 90 percent of total data on web at that time was created in the previous two years alone. Thus there is a progressing need to effectively extract useful content from big data and use streamlined filtering methods to make it comprehensible and non- redundant.

In this paper, we have introduced a novel technique for automatic single-document extraction-based text summarization. The proposed approach uses a number of statistical models such as Pearson Correlation Coefficient, Cosine Similarity and Jaccard Similarity (Huang and Anna, 2008) that compute multiple summaries of a text and combine them, using configurable consensus methods.

Finally, we stretch a step further and use machine-learning to make the summary domain-specific or personalized. Our basic focus is on designing a technique to improve the weighing constants in the consensus step by using a genre-specific training set.

2 Related Work

Most common methods of automatic text summarization are either based on abstraction or extraction. Abstraction based methods focus on creating an internal semantic representation of source text using Natural Language Processing and generating new sentences as the summary (Dragomir and Radev, 2004; Hahn and Romacker, 2001). In contrast, extraction-based summarization is based on extracting a subset of the original text as a summary (Gupta et al., 2010). The most common way to achieve this is through sentence ranking by associating a score with each sentence and greedily choosing the highest weighting sentences for the final summary up to the required compression ratio (Nenkova et al., 2012). In this way, locally optimal solutions enable global optimization which is presented as the final summary. Another approach is based on clustering of similar sentences and successively extracting those sentences which do not represent the redundant information (Huang, 2008; Aggarwal et al., 2012).

In both of these approaches, data regarding similarity of all pairs of sentences is essential for producing the rankings. Many useful measures have been

D S Sharma, R Sangal and A K Singh. Proc. of the 13th Intl. Conference on Natural Language Processing, pages 137–143,
Varanasi, India. December 2016. ©2016 NLP Association of India (NLPAI)

proposed like Cosine similarity, IR f-measure (Alguliev & Aliguliyev, 2007), Jaccard similarity (Mittal et. al, 2014) etc. But it has been experimentally (Alguliev & Aliguliyev, 2007) discovered that due to imperfections of any particular similarity measure, there could be significant prejudices in the scores which make the summarizer misjudge the importance of sentences. We have tried to overcome this problem by combining multiple algorithms so that erroneous rankings can be normalized.

3 Proposed Approach

Consider a document $\mathbf{D}$ containing a set of sentences $S = \{s_1, s_2, ..., s_m\}$ and a set of unique terms $T= \{t_1, t_2, ..., t_p\}$. The proposed framework for summarization of $\mathbf{D}$ consists of four phases as depicted in Figure 1.

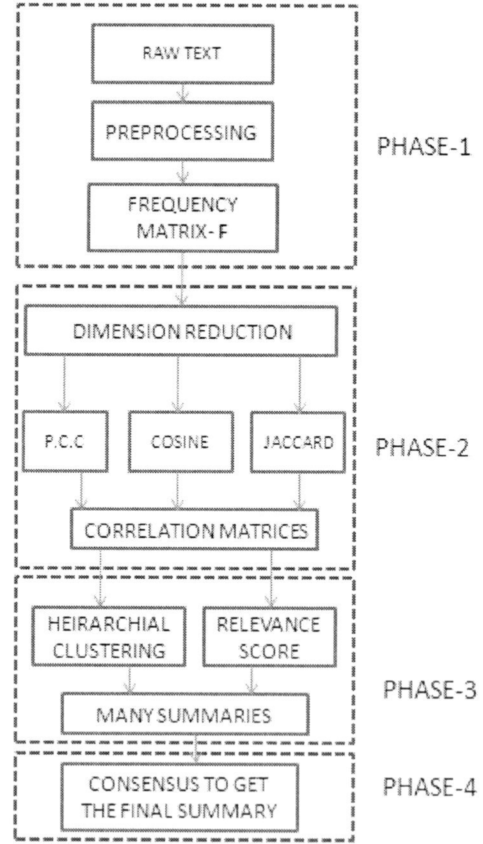

Figure 1. Framework for summarization process

3.1 Phase 1: Frequency Matrix Formation

Raw text contains noise in the form of stop words, punctuation marks, digits, special characters etc. which is not useful for our statistical analysis and increases the probability of exponential work in our process. Thus, we eliminated such terms using close-class word list (Buckley and Salton, 2013) and converted the remaining terms to lower-case. Next, we performed stemming using the Porter stemming algorithm (1980). It has been shown that this kind of preprocessing does not degrade the performance of extractive summarization (Ledeneva, 2008).

Finally, we created a frequency matrix $\mathbf{F}^{mxq}$ for $\mathbf{m}$ sentences and $\mathbf{q}$ distinct terms ($q<p$ since some terms have been eliminated) where element f_{ij} is the frequency of the term t_j in sentence s_i.

3.2 Phase 2: Getting Correlation and Similarity Matrices using Statistical Models

Application of text mining algorithms on matrix $\mathbf{F}^{mxq}$ with very high value of dimension $\mathbf{q}$ could be computationally costly. Hence, Zipf's law, based on Luhn's model (Luhn, 1958), could be used to eliminate terms with very high or very low cumulative frequency as shown in Figure 2. Formally, the cumulative frequency ($\mathbf{Cf}$) for a term t_j in $\mathbf{F}^{mxq}$ can be represented as-

$$Cf(t_j) = \sum_{i=1}^{q} f_{ij} \tag{1}$$

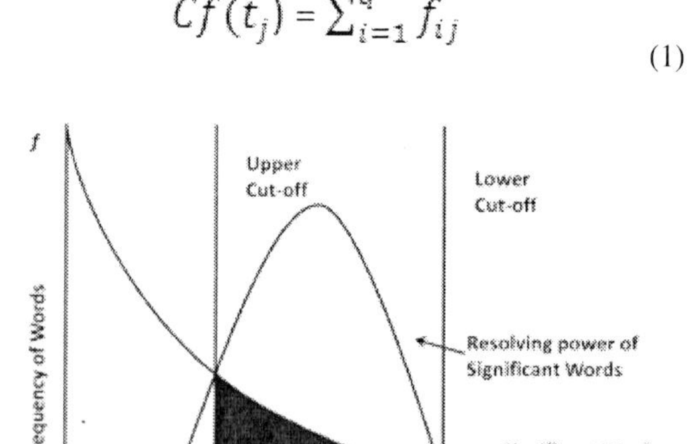

Figure 2. Zipf's Law dictates that words having rank (based on frequency) between the upper and lower cutoffs are most significant

Let n terms remain after application of Zipf's Law. We define sentence vector S_i on matrix F^{mxn} (where $n<q<p$) such that

$$S_i = [f_{i1}, f_{i2}, f_{i3}, ..., f_{in}] \qquad (2)$$

Finally, we generated three Correlation or Similarity matrices C_1^{mxm}, C_2^{mxm} and C_3^{mxm} by using the following statistical measures (Huang, 2008) respectively-

1. Pearson Correlation Coefficient

2. Cosine Similarity

3. Jaccard Similarity

Let $c_k(i, j)$ be an element in the matrix C_k^{mxm}.

Formally,

$$c_k(i,j) = Simlarity\left(S_i, S_j\right) \quad \forall \ k \in \{1,2,3\}$$

$$(3)$$

Figures 3, 4 and 5 show sample matrices C_1^{mxm}, C_2^{mxm} and C_3^{mxm} (with m=6) respectively.

	S_1	S_2	S_3	S_4	S_5	S_6
S_1	1	0.224	0.125	0.404	0.127	0.224
S_2	0.224	1	0.317	0.328	0.012	0.116
S_3	0.125	0.317	1	0.297	-0.092	-0.050
S_4	0.404	0.328	0.297	1	0.079	0.349
S_5	0.127	0.012	-0.092	0.079	1	-0.079
S_6	0.224	0.116	-0.050	0.349	-0.079	1

Figure 3. C_1^{6x6} using Pearson Correlation Coefficient

	S_1	S_2	S_3	S_4	S_5	S_6
S_1	1	0.452	0.029	0.172	0.035	0.221
S_2	0.452	1	0.167	0.278	0.032	0.196
S_3	0.029	0.167	1	0.284	0.002	0.010
S_4	0.172	0.278	0.284	1	0.079	0.169
S_5	0.035	0.032	0.002	0.079	1	0.093
S_6	0.221	0.196	0.010	0.169	0.093	1

Figure 4. C_2^{6x6} using Cosine similarity

	S_1	S_2	S_3	S_4	S_5	S_6
S_1	1	0.341	0.017	0.167	0.044	0.177
S_2	0.341	1	0.174	0.332	0.024	0.214
S_3	0.017	0.174	1	0.265	0.013	0.023
S_4	0.167	0.332	0.265	1	0.021	0.147
S_5	0.044	0.024	0.013	0.021	1	0.113
S_6	0.177	0.214	0.023	0.147	0.113	1

Figure 5. C_3^{6x6} using Jaccard similarity

3.3 Phase 3: Ranking Sentences using Relevance Score and Clustering Methods

The fundamental goal of this phase is to devise methods for ranking sentences using matrices C_1^{mxm}, C_2^{mxm} and C_3^{mxm} so that the summaries can be obtained using a subset of top ranked sentences. The size of the summaries would depend on user-given compression ratio.

3.3.1 Ranking through Relevance Score

We define **Relevance Score** or **RScore** of sentence s_i as the sum of its correlation magnitudes with all other sentences, except itself i.e.

$$RScore(s_i) = \sum_{j=1}^{n} c_k(i,j), \ i = 1,2,...,n.\ i \neq j$$

$$\forall k \in \{1,2,3\} \qquad (4)$$

In this method, we ranked sentences from highest to lowest based on decreasing order of their **RScores**. The sentences which have the highest **RScores** form a subset of S having high information content and low redundancy (Gong et al., 2001). We performed this process for all three matrices C_1^{mxm}, C_2^{mxm} and C_3^{mxm} obtained in phase 2 and generated three ranking orders of sentences - R_1, R_2 and R_3. Finally, we obtained summaries Sm_1, Sm_2 and Sm_3 by extracting the top ranking sentences from R_1, R_2 and R_3 respectively, until they satisfy the compression ratio.

3.3.2 Ranking through Hierarchical Clustering

Clustering is a form of unsupervised learning in which categorization is done based on highest similarity. The goal is to organize data into natural collections such that we obtain high intra-collection similarity and low inter-collection similarity (Huang, 2008). We have used pair wise hierarchical clustering of sentence vectors in matrices C_1^{mxm}, C_2^{mxm} and C_3^{mxm} to group together sentences which represent similar information. Detailed procedure is described as follows-

Let S_i and S_j be two sentence vectors clustered together in the matrix C_k^{mxm}. We define normalization of row vector S_i as replacing S_i with the mean of corresponding elements of S_i and S_j.

139

Formally,

$$N^{1 \times n}{}_{row}(S_i) = [\frac{c_{i,1} + c_{j,1}}{2}, \frac{c_{i,2} + c_{j,2}}{2}, \ldots \frac{c_{i,n} + c_{j,n}}{2}]$$

(5)

Similarly, we can define normalization of column vector S_i as-

$$N^{n \times 1}{}_{col}(S_i) = [\frac{c_{1,i} + c_{1,j}}{2}, \frac{c_{2,i} + c_{2,j}}{2}, \ldots \frac{c_{n,i} + c_{n,j}}{2}]$$

(6)

Let $R(S_i)$ denotes removing sentence vector S_i from the matrix $C^{m \times m}$ and thus reducing its dimensions to $(m-1) \times (m-1)$.

Also, define $c_k(x, y)$ as the maximum non-diagonal element in the matrix $C_k^{m \times m}$ i.e.

$$c_k(x,y) = \max(c_k(i,j)) \quad \forall (i,j) \; such\,that \; i \neq j$$

(7)

We extract ranking orders from correlation matrices as described in Algorithm 1.

INPUT: $\mathbf{Matrices}\ \boldsymbol{C_k}^{mxm} \forall\, k \in \{1, 2, 3\}$
OUTPUT: Ranking orders of sentences - $\boldsymbol{R_k} \forall\, \boldsymbol{k} \in \{1, 2, 3\}$

1.	$F(S_t)$: **Returns** the position of S_t in source text
2.	**Do for** $t = 1\ to\ k$
3.	**Do for** $l = m\ to\ 1$
4.	**If** $(m = 1)$ **Then**
5.	$R_t. append\,(F(S_1))$
6.	**Else**
7.	Find $c_k(x, y)$ //eq. 7
8.	Do $N_{row}(S_z)$ and $N_{col}(S_z)$, where $z = \max(x, y)$
9.	Do $R(S_w)$ where $w = \min(x, y)$
10.	$R_t. append\,(F(S_w))$
11.	**EndIf**
12.	**EndDo**
13.	**EndDo**

Algorithm 1. Pseudo-code for getting ranking orders from Correlation matrices

Summaries Sm_4, Sm_5 and Sm_6 are derived by extracting the top ranking sentences from R_1, R_2 and R_3 until they satisfy the compression ratio.

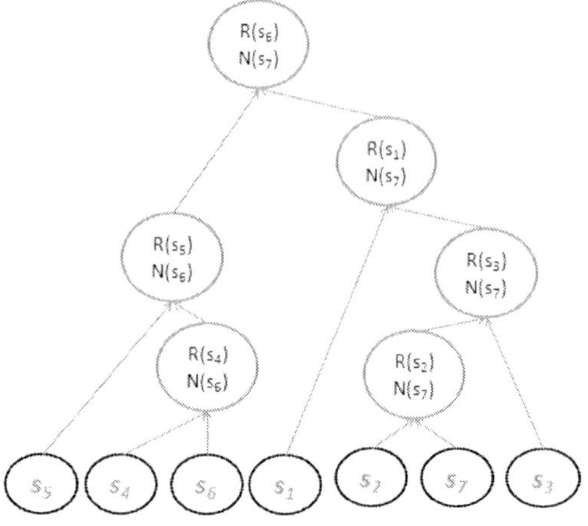

Figure 6. One of the possible clustering patterns by application of the ranking algorithm on seven sentences.

By forming clusters, we are essentially grouping together two sentences with similar information and using the sentence which occurs first, as its representation in the ranking order. We call the sentence vector which is removed from the cluster as 'representative sentence vector' of the cluster. The other sentence vector is normalized using eq.5 and eq.6. This is performed to improve the accuracy of similarity measure magnitudes for non-representative sentence vector by averaging its coefficients with those of the representative sentence vector, since they are found out to be the most similar among the sentence vectors that are present in the Correlation matrix.

3.4 Phase 4: Consensus Methods to get the final summary

At the end of Phase 3, we have six ranking orders , namely- R_1, R_2 , R_3 R_4, R_5 and R_6 .Given a compression ratio **r**, we can obtain six summaries from these rankings, namely-Sm_1, Sm_2 , Sm_3 ,Sm_4, Sm_5 and Sm_6 ,by extracting the top ranked sentences till **r** is satisfied and then sort in the order they appeared in the original text.

3.4.1 Generic Summaries

In this section, we will describe a method for getting a generic summary by giving equal importance to all the summaries obtained. Let us generalize the number of summaries we obtained from phase 3 as k.

Let weight W_i where $i \in \{1,2,..,k\}$ represents the importance given to the ith summary in deriving the final summary.
For generic summary,

$$W_i = \frac{1}{k} \ \forall \ i \ \in \{1,2,...,k\} \tag{7}$$

For all sentences S_i for which $\exists$ at least one summary Sm_j ($j \in \{1, 2, ..., k\}$) such that $S_i \in Sm_k$, we define the Final-Score as-

$$FScore(S_i) = \sum_{j=1}^{k} W_j B_j \tag{8}$$

where, $B_j = 1$ if the sentence S_i is present in the Summary j and $B_j = 0$, otherwise. To get the final summary, we arranged all sentences in summaries Sm_j ($j \in \{1, 2, ..., k\}$) in decreasing order of $FScore$ and extracted from the top till the compression ratio was satisfied. Then, the sentences were sorted in the original order of source text and finally presented as a generic-summary.

3.4.2 Query-based Summaries

Since we have k distinct summaries, their compatibility with user-given keywords or title of the text can be measured by calculating a query score based on the distribution of query terms and can be added to its Final-Score. To simplify this process, we propose using the 'cumulative frequency of keywords in a summary' as the primary metric for its relevance and calculate $FScore$ using this hypothesis. Moreover, sophisticated metrics giving weight age to keyword distribution can also be used in further research.
By defining F_j as the cumulative frequency of all keywords in summary j, we have-

$$W_j \ \propto F_j \tag{9}$$

Equation (8) in this case becomes,

$$FScore(S_i) = \sum_{j=1}^{k} F_j B_j \tag{10}$$

where, F_j = total frequency of keywords in j^{th} summary. As described in section 3.4.1, we arranged all sentences in Summaries Sm_i ($i \in \{1, 2, ..., k\}$) in decreasing order of Final-Score and extract from the top till the compression ratio is satisfied. Then the sentences were sorted in original order of source text and presented as final summary.

3.4.3 Domain-specific and Personalized Summaries

A Machine Learning based method for generating summaries which improve themselves using a certain training set is described as follows.

The *F-measure* represents the accuracy of test summary with respect to the ideal summary (Powers, 2011).

$$F = 2 \frac{precision.recall}{precision + recall} \tag{11}$$

The fundamental idea is to utilize a domain-specific training set with v documents to adjust the weights- $W_i \ \forall \ i \in \{1, 2, ..., k\}$ assigned to each summary, based on its *F-measure* with respect to the ideal summary. Then, the final summary is obtained using *FScores* (Equation 8). Hence, the performance of summarizer can be significantly improved when another document of similar domain is given as input. Let f_{js} ($s \in \{1, 2, ..., k\}$ be the *F-measure* of summary Sm_j ($j \in \{1, 2, ..., k\}$ obtained from document s using proposed approach. Let A_j be the algorithm used to derive Sm_j. We define the mean-*F-measure* for all summaries obtained using A_j
as-

$$F_{mean_j} = \frac{\sum_{s=1}^{v} f_s}{v} \tag{12}$$

For summarizing a document after training the summarizer, we followed the same approach till phase 3 but modified Equation (8) in section 3.4.1 as follows-

$$FScore(S_i) = \sum_{j=1}^{k} F_{mean_j} B_j \tag{13}$$

Rest of the approach is same as described in Section 3.4.1. Thus, we are using supervised learning to measure the mean performance of different algorithms on a domain-specific training set and using this knowledge to assign weights to the summaries derived by these algorithms. The final summary of a new document of the same domain will represent a consensus of these algorithms in proportion to their performance on the testing data.

For personalized summaries, a user profile is required, containing the keywords which will represent the interest of user. These keywords may be retrieved from online social media like LinkedIn or facebook, blogs etc. or they could be explicitly provided by the user. In this case, we will have **m** summaries namely $\mathbf{Sm_j}$ ($\forall\ j \in \{1, 2, ..., \mathbf{k}\}$) by following the same approach till phase 3. We define Summary Score as follows-

$$SumScore_j = M_j \quad \forall\ j \in \{1, 2, ..., k\} \tag{14}$$

where, $\mathbf{M_j}$ = metric to determine the amount of relevance a particular summary has with respect to the input keywords. To simplify this procedure, we could take the frequency measure of the keywords in the particular summary as a metric but much better metrics which take into account the distribution of these keywords can also be applied. We simply output the summary having the maximum *SumScore* as the final summary.

Another approach requires the user to train the summarizer by identifying ideal summaries with respect to his requirement, using data sets and their summaries which satisfy his specifications.
Hence, the summarizer is trained using personalized supervised learning to adjust its weights and adapt to the exposed configuration. This approach essentially converts a particular user's personalized configuration as a new domain and then follows the domain-specific approach discussed previously in Section 3.4.3.

4 Experiments

For testing our approach, we have used the following two datasets: (1) TAC 2011 Multiling pilot summarization task dataset (Giannakopoulos et al., 2011) which is derived from publicly available WikiNews (http://www.wikinews.org/). It is divided into ten collections with each collection containing ten documents. A single collection has all documents of the same topic. We have only tested on the English version of the documents. The dataset contains at least one "golden-summary" for comparison. (2) Six English News document collections retrieved for Summarization-research purpose in 2012 (http://dbdmg.polito.it/wordpress/research/document-summarization/). Each collection is made up of ten news documents of the same topic each. This data set was retrieved from Google News for research related to TAC2011 MultiLing Pilot Overview (Giannakopoulos et al., 2011).

We divided the ten documents in each collection into a training set and a testing test randomly with each set consisting of 5 documents. The upper limit of the summary size was kept to be 250 words. The widely used summary evaluation tool 'ROUGE' (Lin, 2004) was used to compare the results with several other summarizers. Our competitors consist of summarization methods that competed in the TAC 2011 conference (UBSummarizer and UoEssex), a widely used summarizer which is integrated with Microsoft-Word (auto-summarize) and the recently proposed Association Mixture Text Summarization (AMTS) (Gross et al., 2014). Test results the Recall, Precision and F-measure using ROUGE-2 and ROUGE-SU4 summary evaluation techniques that is shown in Table1 and Table 2 respectively.

Summarizer	ROUGE-2		
	Recall	Precision	F1
Our Summarizer	**0.0740**	0.1616	**0.1015**
UBSummarizer	0.0466	0.0952	0.0625
AMTS	0.0705	**0.1633**	0.0984
autosummarize	0.0425	0.0824	0.0560
U$_o$Essex	0.0712	0.1617	0.0988

Table 1: Test Results using ROUGE-2

Summarizer	ROUGE-SU4		
	Recall	Precision	F1
Our Summa-rizer	0.0838	**0.2080**	**0.1194**
UBSummarizer	0.0711	0.1652	0.0994
AMTS	**0.0843**	0.1994	0.1185
autosummarize	0.0684	0.1567	0.0952
U$_o$Essex	0.0839	0.1976	0.1177

Table 2: Test Results using ROUGE-SU4

5 Conclusion and Future Work

Based on different similarity measures and ranking procedures, we presented a model for performing consensus of multiple summarization algorithms that perform extraction-based text summarization. Experimental results reveal that our approach has significantly outperformed some of the widely used techniques. We have argued that this is due to the strength of combining various similarity measures to get rid of their individual weakness and also due to the 'domain-adaptive' nature of our summarizer.

For further research, we will add more similarity measures and ranking techniques in the model to make it more accurate.

References

Anastasios Tombros and Mark Sanderson. Advantages of Query Biased Summaries in Information Retrieval. In Research and Development in Information Retrieval, pages 2–10, 1998.

Anna Huang. "Similarity measures for text document clustering."Proceedings of the sixth new zealand computer science research student conference (NZCSRSC2008), Christchurch, New Zealand. 2008.

Charu C. Aggarwal, and ChengXiang Zhai. Mining text data. Springer Science & Business Media, 2012.

Chin-Yew Lin, "Rouge: A package for automatic evaluation of summaries. " Text summarization branches out: Proceedings of the ACL-04 workshop. Vol. 8. 2004.

Chris Buckley et al. "Automatic query expansion using SMART: TREC 3."NIST special publication sp (1995): 69-69.

David Martin Powers. "Evaluation: from precision, recall and F-measure to ROC, informedness, markedness and correlation." (2011).

G Erkan and Dragomir R. Radev, "LexRank: Graph-based Centrality as Salience in Text Summarization", Journal of Artificial Intelligence Research, Re-search, Vol. 22, pp. 457-479 2004.

George Giannakopoulos, Mahmoud El-Haj, Benoit Favre, Marina Litvak, Josef Steinberger, & Vasudeva Varma. (2011). TAC2011 MultiLing Pilot Overview. TAC 2011 Workshop. Presented at the TAC 2011, Gaithersburg, MD, U.S.A.

H. Luhn, "The automatic creation of literature abstracts. IBM Journal of Research and Development", 2(2), 139–145. The article is also included in H. P. Luhn: Pioneer ofInformation Science, 1958.

John Makhoul et al. "Performance measures for information extraction."Proceedings of DARPA broadcast news workshop. 1999.

Namita Mittal, et al. "Extractive Text Summarization." (2014).

R. Alguliev, and R. Aliguliyev. "Experimental investigating the F- measure as similarity measure for automatic text summarization." Applied and Computational Mathematics 6.2 (2007): 278-287.

Vishal Gupta, and Gurpreet Singh Lehal. "A survey of text summarization extractive techniques." Journal of emerging technologies in web intelligence2.3 (2010): 258-268.

Yihong Gong and Xin Liu. "Generic text summarization using relevance measure and latent semantic analysis." Proceedings of the 24th annual international ACM SIGIR conference on Research and development in information retrieval. ACM, 2001.

Yongwon Conrad Cho and Sunwhie Hwang. "Future Trends in Spatial Information Management: Suggestion to New Generation (Internet of Free-Open)." International Journal of Signal Processing Systems 3.1 (2015): 75-81.

Automatic Translation of English Text to Indian Sign Language Synthetic Animations

Lalit Goyal, Assistant Professor,
DAV College, Jalandhar.
goyal.aqua@gmail.com

Dr. Viahal Goyal, Associate Professor,
Punjabi University, Patiala.
vishal.pup@gmail.com

Abstract

This article presents the prototype for English Text to Indian Sign Language conversion system using synthetic animations in real domain. The translation system consists of parsing module which parses the input English sentence to phrase structure grammar representation on which Indian sign language grammar rules are applied to reorder the words of the English sentence (as the grammar of English language and Indian sign language is different). Elimination module eliminates the unwanted words from the reordered sentence. Lemmatization is applied to convert the words into the root form as the Indian sign language does not use the inflections of the words. All the words of the sentence are then checked into lexicon which contains the English word with its HamNoSys notation and the words that are not in the lexicon are replaced by their synonym. The words of the sentence are replaced by their counter HamNoSys code. In case the word is not present in the lexicon, HamNoSys code will be taken for each alphabet of the word. The HamNoSys code is converted into the SiGML tags and this SiGML tags are sent to animation module which converts the SiGML code into the synthetic animation using avatar.

The proposed system is innovative as the existing working systems uses videos rather than synthetic animations. Even the existing systems are limited to conversion of words and predefined sentences into Indian sign language whereas our proposed system converts the English sentences into Indian sign language in real domain.

1 Introduction

There are approximately 7105 known living languages in the world divided in 136 different language families. Sign language is one of these 136 families which is used by hearing impaired people to convey their message. This family of the language contains 136 sign languages all over the world depending upon the region of the world. Out of nearly 7 billion people on earth, nearly 72 million are deaf and hard of hearing. Out of such a big number approximately 4.3 million such people use Sign language. Rest of nearly 67 million deaf and hard of hearing people do not use any sign language to communicate. Thus nearly 90% deaf have a very limited or no access to education and other information [1, 2].

Sign language is used by hearing impaired people using hand shapes, fingers, face expressions, gestures and other parts of the body [1]. It is a **visual-spatial** language as the signer often uses the 3D space around his body to describe an event [5]. As sign languages do not have well defined structure or grammar therefore there is no or very less acceptability of these signs outside their small world. Sign languages until the 1960s were not viewed as bona fide languages, but just collections of gestures and mime. Dr. Stokoe's research on American Sign Language proved that it is a full-fledged language with its own grammar, syntax, and other linguistic attributes. To prove the same for other sign languages, there are some efforts including Indian Sign Language [3].

In spoken language, a word is composed of phonemes. Two words can be distinguished by

D S Sharma, R Sangal and A K Singh. Proc. of the 13th Intl. Conference on Natural Language Processing, pages 144–153,
Varanasi, India. December 2016. ©2016 NLP Association of India (NLPAI)

at least one phoneme (while speaking a pause and while writing a space). In SL, a sign is composed of cheremes (equivalent to phoneme in a spoken language) and similarly two signs can differ by at least one chereme [6]. A sign is a sequential or parallel construction of its manual and non-manual cheremes. A manual chereme can be defined by several parameters like Hand shape, Hand location, Hand Orientation, Hand Movements (straight, circular or curved). Non-manual chereme are defined by parameters like Facial expressions, Eye gaze and Head/body posture [5].

However, there exist some signs which may contain only manual or only non-manual components. For example the sign "Yes" is signed by vertical head nod and it has no manual component. SL signs can be generally classified into three classes: One handed, two handed, and non-manual signs. Figure shows the overall Indian sign hierarchy.

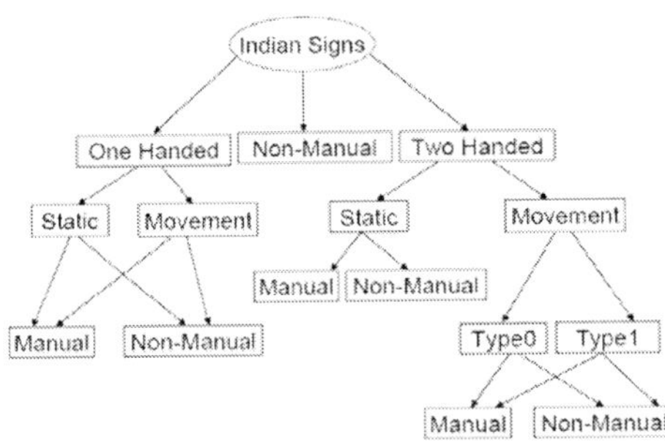

Figure 1. ISL Type Hierarchy

One Handed Signs: The one handed signs are represented by a single dominating hand. One handed signs can be either static or dynamic (having movements). Each of the static and movement signs is further classified into manual and non-manual signs. Figure shows examples of one handed static signs with non-manual and manual components.

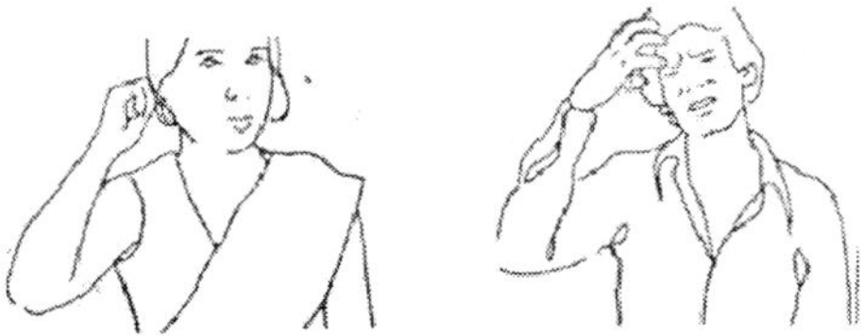

Figure 2. One Handed Static Manual Sign (Ear) and Non-Manual Sign (Headache)

Two Handed Signs: The two handed signs are represented by both the hands of the signer. As in the case of one handed signs, similar classification can be applied to two handed signs. However, two handed signs with movements can be further distinguished as: Type0 and Type1 signs.

Type0 signs are those where both hands are active

Type1 signs are those where one hand (dominant) is more active compared to the other hand (non-dominant) as shown below.

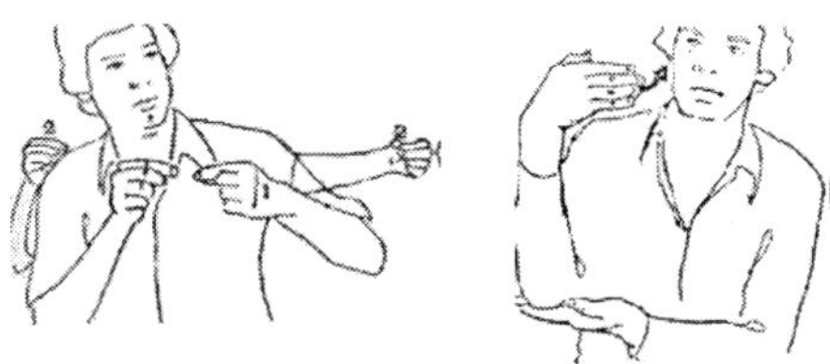

Figure 3. Two Handed Sign "long"(both the hands are moving) and "Flag" (only the dominant right hand is moving)

Communication for the hearing impaired people in common places like railway stations, bus stands, banks, hospitals etc. is very difficult because a hearing person may not understand the sign language used by the hearing impaired person to communicate. Also, a hearing person cannot convey any message to hearing impaired person as he/she may not know the sign language.

To make the communication between hearing impaired and hearing community, the language translation is must that may include,

Figure 4: Communication between Hearing and Hearing Impaired Community

This is worth mentioning here that Sign languages are not "Natural languages represented through signs" or not even **translated word to word** in signs. For example, the word light in English has different meanings. Light means not heavy, or

145

we say light color i.e. not dark or switch on the light. Here, we represent these different meanings in English with same word 'light' but in sign language, we will represent these different meanings with different signs. So, Sign language is not representation of word as it is but rather the meanings are represented using Sign language.

So we interpret that Sign language and **Signed Language** are different. Signed Language is any other natural language for which signs are created for every word. Signed English has word order of English only and every word of English is represented using signs. The problem with this approach is that it is very slow because signing every word takes time and if speech and the Signed English both are being communicated at the same time, Signed English will be much behind the actual words spoken in English [3]. Another type of sign mechanism exists, known as **Sign Supported English**. Sign Supported English does not display sign for each word and only signs are displayed for some important words of the speech and rest of the sentence is spoken only.

Yet another type is **Finger Spelling** where instead of having the symbols for words, fingers are used to show the letters, which make the word. This form is merged with any other form of Sign Language because of limited dictionary of Sign Language.

An alternative to Sign Language is **Cued Speech**. It uses hand shapes and placement with mouth movements to show the sounds. Considered to be visible counterpart of spoken language, cued speech works by combining visible hand and mouth movements to represent sound just like phonemes are combined in any other natural language. Cued speech represents the individual sounds of words via a system of visual phonetics where as sign language is used to represent a whole word. One advantage cued speech over sign language systems is that the number of different signs to remember is far less than in a sign language because only a few phonemes are to be represented using signs and rest all the words are made up of these phonemes' signs only [4].

2 Facts about Indian Sign language

Sign language is natural language which has some facts with which the people are not aware off. Some of the facts of the sign language are:

- NOT the same all over the world.
- NOT just gestures and pantomime, but do have their own grammar.
- Have much smaller dictionary than the other spoken natural languages.
- Finger-spelling for the unknown words.
- Words may be joined e.g. to represent dinner, one might show the sign of Night and then Food.
- Most of the sign languages put the adjective after the noun e.g. Car Red.
- Never use am/is/are/was/were/ (linking verbs).
- Never use word-endings/suffixes.
- Always sign in the Present Tense.
- Do not use articles. (a, an, some, the).
- Do not use I, but uses me.
- WH-questions are at the END e.g. "You go where?"
- Have no gerunds. (-ing).
- Use non-manual expressions as well e.g. use of eye brows, eye lids, facial expressions, head and shoulders movement.
- NOT been invented by hearing people.

3 Overview of Overall System

The success of the translation system from English text to Indian sign language required lexical and syntactic knowledge of Indian sign language. The lexicon has been created for English word – ISL sign as discussed in the next section. The overall architecture of the system is shown in the figure below. The system consists of 7 modules:

- *English parser for parsing the English text*
- *Sentence reordering module based on ISL grammar rules*

146

- *Eliminator for eliminating the unwanted words*
- *Lemmatization for getting the root word of each word and Synonym replacement module to replace the unknown word with its synonym counterpart*
- *Word to SiGML conversion using HamNoSys*
- *Synthetic Animation module.*

The input to the system is written English text which is parsed to get the phrase structure grammar representation of the sentence. The parsed sentence is then sent to the conversion module which reorders the words of the English sentence according to the rules of ISL grammar. Reordering is required as English uses SVO order where as ISL uses the SOV order along with some other variations for interrogative and negative sentences. After getting the sentence as per ISL grammar, unwanted words from the sentence are removed. This is because the ISL used only the words which have some meaning and all the helping words like linking verbs, articles etc are not used. The output is sent to the lemmatization module which converts the words in their root form. This is again because the sign language uses the root form of each word irrespective of other languages which uses suffixes, gerund, past and futures words in their sentences. Because of limited dictionary of ISL, the unknown words in the sentence are replaced with their synonym counterpart, in case the synonym is not available, finger spelling of the word is performed character by character. At this stage, the sentence is ready to animate. Each word of the sentence is replaced by its equivalent HamNoSys (Writing notation of the sign)[8] from the English Word-HamNoSys dictionary and the HamNoSys string is converted to SiGML (Signing gesture markup language) code using SiGML rules. This SiGML code is sent to SiGML animation tool which plays the synthetic animation.

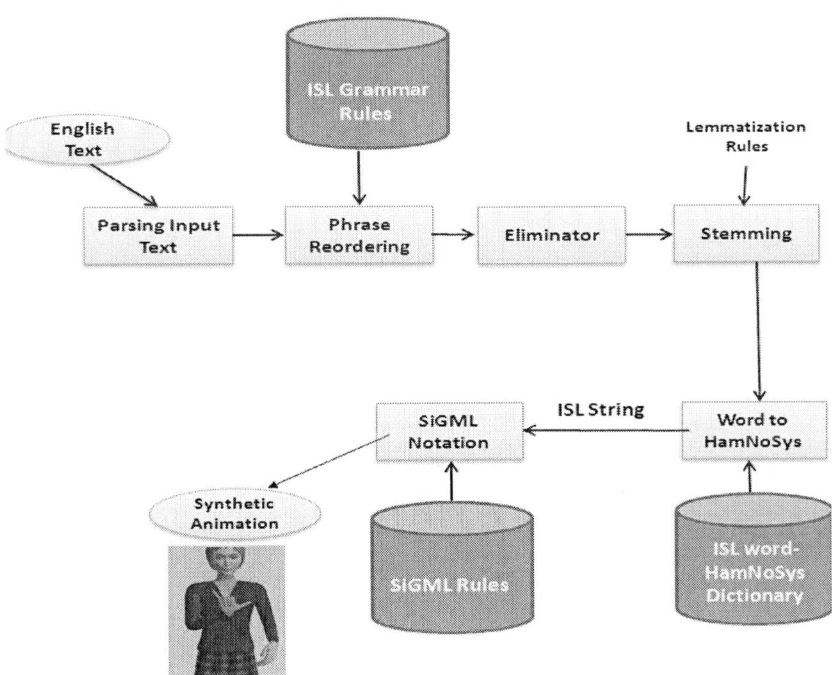

Figure 5: Architecture of English Text to ISL Synthetic Animation System

4 English-ISL Lexicon

Translating from a source language to target language requires a bilingual dictionary. Translating English text to ISL, bilingual dictionary of English and Indian Sign Language is created which contains the English word and its equivalent Indian sign. Here, the English word's counterpart Indian sign can be taken as the real human video, sign picture, coded sign language text, or synthetic animation. All the approaches have their own pros and cons but the synthetic animations are well suited for the translation of spoken language to sign language. A comparison of all the media has been given in the table as shown:

Table 1: Comparison of Different Media for Representing the Sign

Kind of Media	Pros	Cons
Video Signs	• Realistic • Easy to create	• Time consuming to create • High memory consumption • Not supported by translation system
Pictures	• Very less memory consumption	• Time consuming to create pictures • Not realistic as compared to videos • Not supported by translation system
Coded Sign Language Text	• Minimal Memory consumption • Supported by translation system as it is the written form and can be processed very easily	• Very difficult to read and understand • Required to be learnt
Synthetic Animations	• Very less memory consumption • Can be easily reproduced • Supported by translation system • Avatar can be made different according to choice	• Not as realistic as human videos.

Because synthetic animation is supported by the translation system are much realistic as compared to pictures and coded text so synthetic animations have been produced for corresponding English word in this translation system.

To create the animation of each English word, a written form of the sign is taken. Though a 3D sign cannot be written but researchers have put their efforts to create the notation system with which a 3D sign can be expressed in written form. Some of the written forms for 3D sign are Stokoe Notation[11], SignWriting[12], Hamburg notation System[8] etc. We have used HamNoSys (Hamburg Notation System)[8] notation for creating the dictionary. HamNoSys has an alphabet of about 200 symbols (Unicode of this notation system is available)[8] which covers almost all the hand shapes, Hand location, Hand/palm orientation, Hand movement, and non-Manual part of the sign. The basic structure of the HamNoSys is:

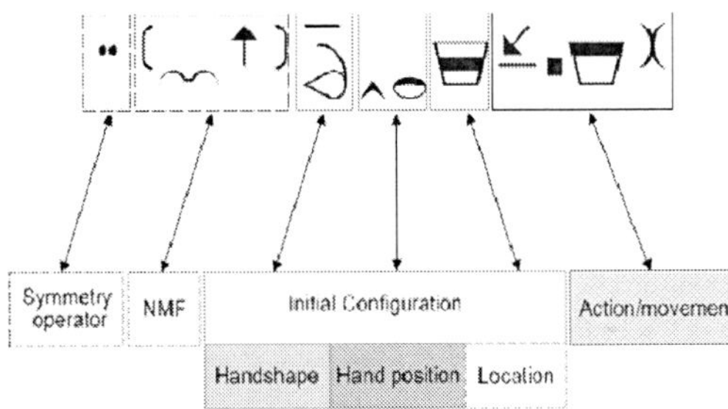

Figure 6: Structure of HamNoSys Code

Later this HamNoSys can be converted into SiGML code which can be animated by an animation tool using an Avatar as shown in the following architecture:

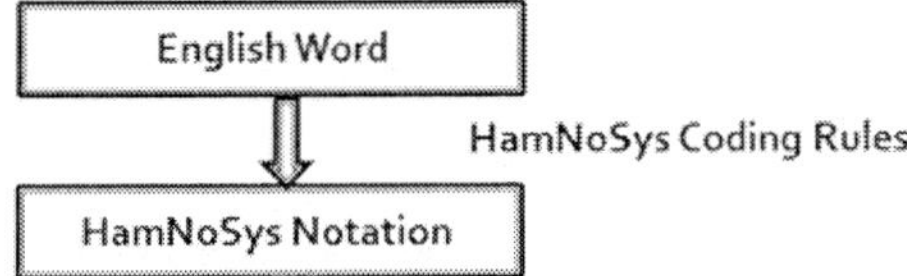

Figure 7: Architecture to produce the animation from English word.

A list of 1818 most commonly used English words[10] used by the differently abled people is taken for creating the bilingual dictionary of English word and HamNoSys notation. The words are categorized in part of speech and a count of 1510 words are coded into HamNoSys as shown in the table[10]:

Table 2: Statistics of Words Implemented

Word Category	No. of Words	No. of Words Implemented
Adjectives	185	177
Adverb	54	54
Conjunction	3	3
Determiner	12	12
Noun	1136	855
Preposition	32	32
Pronoun	33	32
Verb	359	333

5 Parsing of the Input English Sentence

For rule based conversion of one language to another language, grammatical structure of the source language is required so that the words of the source sentence can be reordered as per the grammar rules of the target language. Parsing is the answer to know the grammatical structure of the sentence. To get the grammatical structure of the sentences of English language, parsing is done using third party software. We have used the Stanford parser[7] for this purpose which uses unlexicalized PCFG(probabilistic context free grammar) with output accuracy of 86.36%. Probabilistic parser is trained on the hand-parsed sentences and the knowledge gained is used to parse the new sentences. Stanford parser is capable to produce three different outputs, part-of-speech tagged text, context free phrase structure grammar representation, and type dependency representation. Stanford parser uses Penn Tree tags for parsing the English sentence. In this project, we have used phrase structure grammar representation as in rule based approach, the grammatical structure of the English sentence was required to convert it into the sentence as per the grammatical structure of target language (Indian sign language).

6 Grammar Rules for Conversion of English Sentence to ISL Sentence

Translation of one spoken language to another spoken language is complex task if both the languages have different grammar rules. The complexity is increased many folds when source language is spoken language and the target language is sign language. For translating English text to Indian sign language, a comparison of grammar of both the languages is must:

Table 3: Comparison of Grammar of English and Indian Sign Language

English language grammar	Indian sign language grammar
English grammar is well structured and a lot of research work has been carried out to define the rules for it. English grammar follows the subject-verb-object order.	ISL is invented by deaf and a little work has been done to study the grammar of this language. The structure of sentences of ISL follows the subject-object-verb order[13].
English language uses various forms of verbs and adjectives depending upon the type of the sentence. Also, a lot of inflections of the words are used in English sentences.	ISL does not use any inflections (gerund, suffixes, or other forms), it uses the root form of the word.
English language has much larger dictionary	Indian sign language has a very limited dictionary, approximately 1800 words[10].
Question word in interrogative sentences is at the start in English	In Indian sign language, the question word is always sentence final[1].
A lot of helping verbs, articles, and conjunctions are used in the sentences of English	In Indian sign language, no conjunctions, articles or linking verbs are used

For conversion of English sentence to a sentence as per ISL grammar rules, all the verb patterns (20 patterns)[15] are studied and rules are formed to convert English sentence into ISL sentence. The parsed sentence is the input to this module where the noun phrase and the prepositional phrase are freezed but if there is any verb phrase present in the sentence, it is checked recursively because the verb phrase may further be composed of noun phrase, prepositional phrase, verb phrase or even the sentence. Some of the rules of conversion are given in the table:

Table 4: Examples of Grammatical Reordering of Words of English Sentence

Verb Pattern	Rule	Input Sentence	Parsed Sentence	Output Sentence
verb + object	VP NP	go school	(VP (VB Go) (NP (NN school)))	school go
subject + verb	NP V	birds fly	(NP (NNS birds)) (VP (VBP fly))	birds fly
subject + verb + subject complement	NP V NP	his brother became a soldier	(NP (PRP$ his) (NN brother)) (VP (VBD became) (NP (DT a) (NN soldier)))	his brother a soldier became
subject + verb + indirect object + direct object	NP V NP NP	i lent her my pen	(NP (FW i)) (VP (VBD lent) (NP (PRP her)) (NP (PRP$ my) (NN pen)))	i her my pen lent

subject + verb	subject + verb	show me your hands	(VP (VBP show) (NP (PRP me))) (NP (PRP$ your) (NNS hands))	me your hands show
subject + verb + direct object + preposition +prepositional object	NP V NP PP	she made coffee for all of us	(NP (PRP She)) (VP (VBD made) (NP (NN coffee)) (PP (IN for) (NP (NP (DT all)) (PP (IN of) (NP (PRP us))))))	she coffee for all of us made
subject + verb + indirect object + direct object	V NP PP	show your hands to me	(VP (VB show) (NP (PRP$ your) (NNS hands)) (PP (TO to) (NP (PRP me))))	your hands to me show
subject + verb + preposition prepositional object	NP V PP	we are waiting for suresh	(NP (PRP we)) (VP (VBP are) (VP (VBG waiting) (PP (IN for) (NP (NN suresh)))))	we for suresh are waiting

7 Elimination of Unwanted Words

Indian sign language sentences are formed of main words. All the words like linking verbs, suffixes, articles are not used. After applying the grammar rules, the ISL sentence is generated of which all the unwanted words are required to be removed. The part of speech which are not the part of ISL sentence are detected and eliminated from the sentence. Out of 36 POS tags, the various part of speech which do not form the part of ISL sentence are TO, POS(possessive ending), MD(Modals), FW(Foreign word), CC(coordinating conjuction), some DT(determiners like a, an, the), JJR, JJS(adjectives, comparative and superlative), NNS, NNPS(nouns plural, proper plural), RP(particles), SYM(symbols), Interjections, non-root verbs. These above mentioned unwanted words are removed from the ISL sentence. Below is the table of examples in which unwanted words are removed.

Table 5: Elimination of unwanted words

Input English Sentence	**Sentence after reordering**	**Output ISL Sentence(After elimination)**
go school	school go	go school
birds fly	birds fly	birds fly
his brother became a soldier	his brother a soldier became	his brother soldier become
i lent her my pen	i her my pen lent	i her my pen lent
show me your hands	me your hands show	me your hand show
she made coffee for all of us	she coffee for all of us made	she coffee all we made
show your hands to me	your hands to me show	your hand me show
we are waiting for suresh	we for suresh are waiting	we suresh waiting

8 Lemmatization & Synonym Replacement

Indian sign language uses the root words in their sentences. All the words used must not contain suffixes, gerund or it should not be an inflexion of a word. If a word in the ISL sentence is not root word, it is converted into the root word after passing it to the stemmer and applying lemmatization rules. The porter stemmer [16] is used for stemming.

After converting the inflections of the words to their respective root words, the ISL sentence contains only the root words. Now, each root word is checked for availability in the English-ISL dictionary. Though this dictionary contains only 1478 words, a list of synonyms is created to make the system robust and increase the hits in the dictionary. An indirect approach is used rather than creating a list of all the synonyms of English language. We have collected the synonyms of only 1478 words (the words which are in our bilingual dictionary) A total of approximately 4000 synonym words are included in our database. It was taken care to remove the duplicacy of the words as well the part of speech of each word was taken care. For example, the word *inaugural is an adjective*, its synonym is taken as *opening as adjective* otherwise the word *opening* is used as verb also. The word anger(v) has the synonyms irate, insense, enrage, infuriate which all are verbs. Also the word angry(n) has the synonyms as annoyance, irritation, fury, rage, resentment, antagonism which all are noun. In case, no word is found in the dictionary or synonym list, the word is spelled. Here, spelling the word means finger spelling i.e. each character of the word is taken whose sign will be produced. Signs of all the alphabets of English have also been maintained in the database increasing the dictionary size to approximately 6000 words. All the personal nouns(names of persons, buildings etc) are finger spelled.

9 Sign Animation using Avatar

After all processing done on the English sentence to convert to ISL sentence, it is ready to be animated. As already discussed, the synthetic animation(using a computer generated character known as Avatar) is best suitable for producing the sign. To animate the sentence, we have used an animation tool SiGML Player[17]. To generate the animation through this tool, the input must be the tags of SiGML(Signing Gesture Markup Language) and the output of this tool is animated character.

To get the SiGML tags, each word of the ISL sentence is replaced with its corresponding HamNoSys code. For the words which are not in the English-ISL dictionary database, each character (alphabet) of the word is replaced with the corresponding HamNosys code. Now, we have the HamNosys code of the whole ISL sentence. The HamNoSys code is now converted to SiGML tags using HamNoSys-SiGML conversion rules. As soon as we get the SiGML tags for the whole sentence, it is sent to the animation tool which plays it as the animated character.

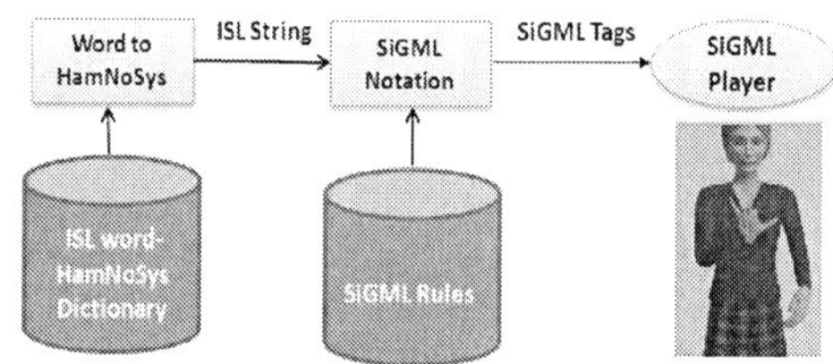

Figure 8: Architecture to produce the Animation from English word

10 Conclusion

In this paper, a translation system for English text to Indian sign language has been presented. The automatic system is the first ever translation system for Indian sign language in real domain. The major components of the system are conversion module(converts the English sentence to ISL sentence based on the grammatical rules), Elimination module(eliminates the unwanted words from the ISL sentence), Synonym and Lemmatization module(converts each word of the ISL sentence to root word), and Animation module(converts the ISL sentence to synthetic animation). Currently, the system has been created for context free conversion of English text to synthetic animations. A lot of time is consumed to create the dictionary of English word to Indian sign in which non-manual component of each sign is taken care as well as the lips of avatar are animated so that it a hard of hearing person can read the lips also. Overall conversion accuracy has been checked by demonstrating the system in various deaf schools. The work has been very much appreciated by the interpreters and students. In future, the dictionary of sign language can be enhanced adding more words in it. Also, the context can be taken care while converting the English sentence to ISL sentence.

References

1. Ethnologue: Languages of the World. (2015). Retrieved July 10, 2016, from http://www.ethnologue.com/

2. WFD | World Federation of the Deaf - World Federation of the Deaf, WFD, human rights, deaf, deaf people. (2015). Retrieved July 10, 2016, from https://wfdeaf.org/

3. Zeshan, U., Vasishta, M. N., & Sethna, M. (2005). Implementation of Indian Sign Language in educational settings. *Asia Pacific Disability Rehabilitation Journal, 16*(1), 16-40.

4. Setting Cued Speech Apart from Sign Language - Accredited Language Services. (2016). Retrieved March 21, 2016, from https://www.accreditedlanguage.com/2016/08/17/setting-cued-speech-apart-from-sign-language/

5. Zeshan, U. (2003). Indo-Pakistani Sign Language grammar: a typological outline. *Sign Language Studies, 3*(2), 157-212.

6. Stokoe, W. C. (2005). Sign language structure: An outline of the visual communication systems of the American deaf. *Journal of deaf studies and deaf education, 10*(1), 3-37.

7. Klein, D., & Manning, C. D. (2003, July). Accurate unlexicalized parsing. In *Proceedings of the 41st Annual Meeting on Association for Computational Linguistics-Volume 1* (pp. 423-430). Association for Computational Linguistics.

8. Hanke, T. (2004, May). HamNoSys-representing sign language data in language resources and language processing contexts. In *LREC* (Vol. 4).

9. Goyal, L., & Goyal, V. (2016). Development of Indian Sign Language Dictionary using Synthetic Animations. *Indian Journal of Science and Technology, 9*(32).

10. Dictionary | Indian Sign Language. (n.d.). Retrieved July 15, 2016, from http://indiansignlanguage.org/dictionary

11. Stokoe, W. C. (1978). Sign language structure.

12. Sutton, V. (1995). *Lessons in sign writing.* SignWriting

13. Sinha, S. (2003). A skeletal grammar of Indian sign language. *Unpublished master's diss., Jawaharlal Nehru University, New Delhi, India.*

14. Aboh, E., Pfau, R., & Zeshan, U. (2005). When a wh-word is not a wh-word: The case of Indian Sign Language. *The yearbook of South Asian languages and linguistics, 2005,* 11-43.

15. Wren, P. C., & Martin, H. (1999). High school English grammar and composition.

16. Porter, M. F. (2001). Snowball: A language for stemming algorithms.

17. JASigning. (2015). Retrieved june 15, 2016, from http://vh.cmp.uea.ac.uk/index.php/JASigning

Towards Deep Learning in Hindi NER: An approach to tackle the Labelled Data Scarcity

Vinayak Athavale*[1],Shreenivas Bharadwaj *[2],Monik Pamecha*[3],Ameya Prabhu[1] and Manish Shrivastava[1]

[1]International Institute of Information Technology, Hyderabad (India)

[2]National Institute of Technology, Tiruchirappalli , [3]Dwarkadas J. Sanghvi College of Engineering

{vinayak.athavale,ameya.prabhu} @research.iiit.ac.in

{vshreenivasbharadwaj} @gmail.com , {monik.pamecha}@djsce.edu.in

{m.shrivastava} @iiit.ac.in

Abstract

In this paper we describe an end to end Neural Model for Named Entity Recognition (NER) which is based on Bi-Directional RNN-LSTM. Almost all NER systems for Hindi use Language Specific features and handcrafted rules with gazetteers. Our model is language independent and uses no domain specific features or any handcrafted rules. Our models rely on semantic information in the form of word vectors which are learnt by an unsupervised learning algorithm on an unannotated corpus. Our model attained state of the art performance in both English and Hindi without the use of any morphological analysis or without using gazetteers of any sort.

1 Introduction

Named entity recognition (NER) is a very important task in Natural Language Processing. In the NER task, the objective is to find and cluster named entities in text into any desired categories such as person names (PER), organizations (ORG), locations (LOC), time expressions, etc. NER is an important precursor to tasks like Machine Translation, Question Answering , Topic Modelling and Information Extraction among others. Various methods have been used in the past for NER including Hidden Markov models, Conditional Random fields, Feature engineering approaches using Support Vector Machines, Max Entropy classifiers for finally classifying outputs and more recently neural network based approaches.

Development of an NER system for Indian languages is a comparatively difficult task. Hindi and many other Indian languages provide some inherent difficulties in many NLP related tasks. The structure of the languages contain many complexities like free-word ordering (which affect n-gram based approaches significantly), no capitalization information and its inflectional nature (affecting hand-engineered approaches significantly). Also, in Indian languages there are many word constructions that can be classified as Named Entities (Derivational/Inflectional constructions) etc and these constraints on these constructions vary from language to language hence carefully crafted rules need to be made for each language which is a very time consuming and expensive task.

Another major problem in Indian languages is the fact that we have scarce availability of annotated data for indian languages. The task is hard for rule-based NLP tools, and the scarcity of labelled data renders many of the statistical approaches like Deep Learning unusable. This complexity in the task is a significant challenge to solve. Can we develop tools which can generalize to other languages(unlike rule based approaches) but still can perform well on this task?

On the other hand, RNNs and its variants have consistently performed better than other approaches on English NER and many other sequence labelling tasks. We believe RNN would be a very effective method compared to fixed-window approaches as the memory cell takes much larger parts of the sentence into context thus solving the problem of sentences being freely ordered to a large extent. We propose a method to be able to model the NER task using RNN based approaches using the unsupervised data available and achieve good improvements in accuracies over many other models without any hand-engineered features or any rule-based approach. We would learn word-vectors that capture a large number of precise semantic and syntactic word relationships from a large unlabelled corpus and use them

---

* indicates these authors contributed equally to this work.

154

D S Sharma, R Sangal and A K Singh. Proc. of the 13th Intl. Conference on Natural Language Processing, pages 154–160,
Varanasi, India. December 2016. ©2016 NLP Association of India (NLPAI)

to initialize RNNs thus allowing us to leverage the capabilities of RNNs on the currently available data. We believe to the best of our knowledge, that this is the first approach capable of using RNN for NER in Hindi data. We believe learning based approaches like these could generalize to other Indian languages without having to handcraft features or develop dependence on other NLP related tools. Our model uses no language specific features or gazetteers or dictionaries. We use a small amount of supervised training data along with some unannotated corpus for training word embeddings yet we achieve accuracies on par with the state of the art results on the CoNLL 2003 dataset for English and achieve 77.48% accuracy on ICON 2013 NLP tools corpus for Hindi language.

Our paper is mainly divided into the following sections:

- In Section 1 we begin with an introduction to the task of NER and briefly describe our approach.

- In Section 2, we mention the issues with hindi NER and provide an overview of the past approaches to NER.

- In Section 3, we descibe our proposed RNN based approach to the task of NER and the creation of word embeddings for NER which are at the core of our model.

- In Section 4 We explain our experimental setup, describe the dataset for both Hindi and English and give results and observations of testing on both the datasets.

- In Section 5 We give our conclusions from the experiments and also describe methods to extend our approach to other languages.

2   Related Work

NER task has been extensively studied in the literature. Previous approaches in NER can be roughly classified into Rule based approaches and learning based approaches. Rule based approaches include the system developed by Ralph Grishman in 1995 which used a large dictionary of Named Entities (R. Grishman et al., 1995). Another model was built for NER using large lists of names of people, location etc. in 1996(Wakao et al., 1996). A huge disadvantage of these systems is that a huge list needed to be made and the output for any entity not seen before could not be determined. They lacked in discovering new named entities, not present in the dictionary available and also cases where the word appeared in the dictionary but was not a named entity. This is an even bigger problem for indian languages which would frequently be agglutinative in nature hence creation of dictionaries would be rendered impossible. People either used feature learning based approaches using Hand-crafted features like Capitalization etc. They gave these features to a Machine learning based classifier like Support Vector Machine (SVM)(Takeuchi et al., 2002), Naive Bayes (NB) or Maximum Entropy (ME) classifiers. Some posed this problem as a sequence labelling problem terming the context is very important in determining the entities. Then, the handcrafted series were used in sequences using Machine learning methods such as Hidden Markov Models (HMM)(Bikel et al., 1997), Conditional Random Field (CRF) (Das et al., 2013) and Decision Trees (DT)(Isozaki et al., 2001).

Many attempts have been made to combine the above two approaches to achieve better performance. An example of this is (Srihari et al., 2000) who use a combination of both handcrafted rules along with HMM and ME. More recent approaches for Indian language and Hindi NER are based on CRFs and include (Das et al., 2013) and (Sharnagat et al., 2013).

The recent RNN based approaches for NER include ones by (Lample et al., 2016). Also, there are many approaches which combine NER with other tasks like (Collobert et al., 2011) (POS Tagging and NER along with Chunking and SRL tasks) and (Luo et al., 2015) (combining Entity Linking and NER) which have produced state-of-the-art results on English datasets.

3   Proposed Approach

Owing to the recent success in deep learning frameworks, we sought to apply the techniques to Indian language data like Hindi. But, the main challenge in these approaches is to learn inspite of the scarcity of labelled data, one of the core problems of adapting deep-learning approaches to this domain.

We propose to leverage the vast amount of unlabelled data available in this domain. The recurrent neural networks RNN trained generally have

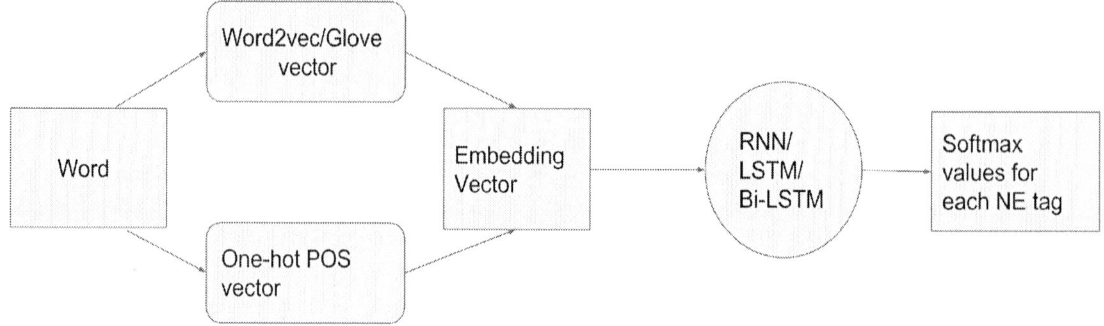

Figure 1: Our pipeline is illustrated above. Every word gets an embedding and a POS tag, which are concatentated to form the word embeddings of the word. It is then passed to recurrent layers and softmax over all classes is the predicted class.

to learn the recurrent layer as well as the embedding layer for every word. The embedding layer usually takes a large amount of data to create good embeddings. We formulate a two stage methodology to utilize the unlabelled data:

In the first stage we utilize unlabelled corpora. We learn Skip-gram (Mikolov et al., 2013) based embeddings and GloVe (Pennington et al., 2014) embeddings on those corpora. We use the Wikipedia corpus for Hindi as a source to train these models. By that, we get wordvectors which will be used in the second stage.

In the second stage, as illustrated in Figure 1, we use the deep-learning based models. We initialize their embedding layers with the wordvectors for every word. Then, we train the network end-to-end on the labelled data. As various approaches have proved, a good initialization is crucial to learning good models and train faster (Sutskever et al., 2013). We apply this approach to use word-vectors to counter the scarcity of labelled data. The idea behind this is that the models would require much lesser data for convergence and would give much better results than when the embeddings are randomly initialized.

To get both previous and subsequent context for making predictions we use Bi-Directional RNN (Schuster et al., 1997). We know that Vanilla RNN suffers from not being able to model long term dependencies (Bengio et al., 1994) Hence we use the LSTM variant of the RNN (Hochreiter et al., 1997)

which helps the RNN model long dependencies better.

3.1 Generating Word Embeddings for Hindi

Word2Vec based approaches use the idea that words which occur in similar context are similar. Thus, they can be clustered together. There are two models introduced by: (Mikolov et al., 2013) CBOW and Skipgram. The latter is shown to perform better on English corpuses for a variety of tasks, hence is more generalizable. Thus, we use the skip-gram based approach.

Most recent method for generating wordvectors was GloVe, which is similar in nature to that of Skipgram based model. It trains embeddings with local window context using co-occurrence matrices. The GloVe model is trained on the non-zero entries of a global co-occurrence matrix of all words in the corpus. GloVe is shown to be a very effective method, and is used widely thus is shown to be generalizable to multiple tasks in English.

For English language, we use the pretrained word embeddings using the aforementioned approaches, since they are widely used and pretty effective. The links for downloading the vectors are provided[1]. However, for Hindi language we train using above mentioned methods(Word2Vec and GloVe) and generate word vectors. We start with One hot encoding for the words and random

---

[1]Links for download note:webpage not maintained by us
https://github.com/3Top/word2vec-api

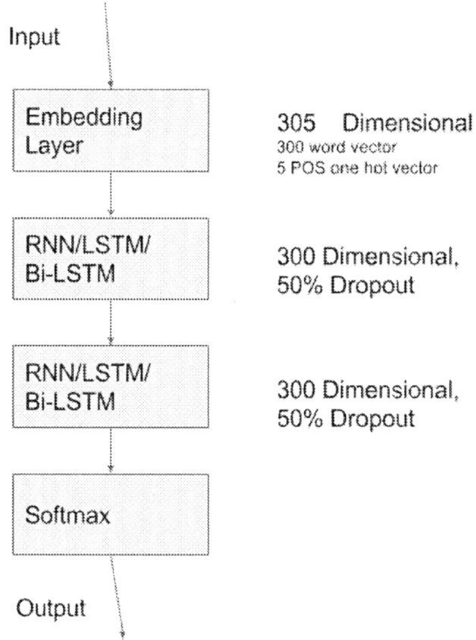

Figure 2: Architecture of the model

initializations for their wordvectors and then train them to finally arrive at the word vectors. We use the Hindi text from LTRC IIIT Hyderabad Corpus for training. The data is 385 MB in size and the encoding used is the UTF-8 format (The unsupervised training corpus contains 27 million tokens and 500,000 distinct tokens). The training Hindi word embeddings were trained using a window of context size of 5. The trained model is then used to generate the embeddings for the words in the vocabulary. The data would be released along with the paper at our website along with the wordvectors and their training code[2]. For a comparative study of performance of these methods, we also compare between the Skip-gram based wordvectors and GloVe vectors as embeddings to evaluate their performance on Hindi language.

3.2 Network Architecture

The architecture of the neural networks is described in Figure 2. We trained deep neural networks consisting of either one or two recurrent layers since the labelled dataset was small. In the architecture, we have an embedding layer followed by one or two recurrent layers as specified in the experiments followed by the softmax layer. We experimented with three different kinds of recurrent layers: Vanilla RNN, LSTM and Bi-directional LSTM to test which one would be the

most suitable for NER task. For the embedding layer, it is initialized with the concatenation of the wordvector and the one-hot vector indicating its POS Tag. The POS Tagging task is generally considered as a very useful feature for entity recognition, so it was a reliable feature. This hypothesis was validated when the inclusion of POS tags into the embedding improved the accuracy by 3-4%.

This setup was trained end-to-end using Adam optimizer (Kingma et al., 2015) and batch size of 128 using dropout layer with the dropout value of 0.5 after each of the recurrent layers. We have used dropout training (Srivastava et al., 2014) to reduce overfitting in our models and help the model generalise well to the data. The key idea in dropouts is to randomly drop units with their connections from the neural network during training.

4   Experiments

We perform extensive experimentation to validate our methodology. We have described the datasets we use and the experimental setup in detail in this section. We then present our results and provide a set of observations made for those results.

4.1   Datasets

We test the effectiveness of our approach on ICON 2013 NLP tools contest dataset for Hindi language, along with cross-validating our methodology on the well-established CoNLL 2003 English named entity recognition dataset (Sang et al., 2003) .

4.1.1   ICON 2013 NLP Tools Contest Dataset

We used the ICON 2013 NLP tools contest dataset to evaluate our models on Hindi. The dataset contains words annotated with part-of-speech (POS) tags and corresponding named entity labels in Shakti Standard Form (SSF) format (Bharti et al., 2009) . The dataset primarily contains 11 entity types: Organization (ORG), Person (PER), Location (LOC), Entertainment, Facilities, Artifact, Living things, Locomotives, Plants, Materials and Diseases. Rest of the corpus was tagged as non-entities (O). The dataset was randomly divided into three splits: Train, Development and Test in the ratios 70%, 17% and 13%. The training set consists of 3,199 sentences comprising 56,801 tokens, development set contains 707 sentences comprising 12,882 tokens and test set contains 571 sentences comprising of 10,396 tokens. We

---

use the F1-measure to evaluate our performance against other approaches.

4.1.2 CoNLL 2003 Dataset

We perform extensive experiments on the CoNLL 2003 dataset for Named Entity Recognition. The dataset is primarily a collection of Reuters newswire articles annotated for NER with four entity types: Person (PER), Location(LOC), Organization(ORG), Miscellaneous (MISC) along with non entity elements tagged as (O). The data is provided with a training set contains 15,000 sentences consisting of approximately 203,000 tokens, along with a development set containing 3466 sentences consisting of around 51,000 tokens and a test set containing 3684 sentences comprising of approximately 46,435 tokens. We use the standard evaluation scripts provided along with the dataset for assessing the performance of our methodology. The scripts use the F1-score to evaluate the performance of models.

4.2 Experimental Setup

We use this architecture for the network because of the constraint on the dataset size caused by scarcity of labelled data. We used a NVIDIA 970 GTX GPU and a 4.00 GHz Intel i7-4790 processor with 64GB RAM to train our models. As the datasets in this domain expand, we would like to scale up our approach to bigger architectures. The results obtained on ICON 2013 NLP Tools dataset are summarized in Table 2. We cross-validated our approach with English language using the CoNLL 2003 dataset. The results are summarized in Table 1, We are able to achieve state-of-the-art accuracies without using additional information like Gazetteers, Chunks along with not using any hand-crafted features which are considered essential for NER task as chunking provides us data about the phrases and Gazetteers provide a list of words which have high likelihood of being a named entity.

4.3 Observations

The neural networks which did not have wordvector based initializations could not perform well on the NER task as predicted. This can be attributed to the scarcity of the data available in the NER task. We also observe that networks consisting of one recurrent layer perform equally good or even better than networks having two recurrent layers. We believe this would be a validation to our hy-

Method	Embed.	Dev	Test
Bi-LSTM	Random	20.04%	6.02%
Bi-RNN	Skip-300	74.30%	70.01%
Collobert	-	-	89.59%
Luo (Gaz.)		–	89.9%
Ours: Bi-LSTM	Skip-300	93.5%	89.4%
Ours: Bi-LSTM	GloVe-300	93.99%	**90.32%**
Dyer	-	-	**90.94%**
Luo (Gaz. & Link)			**91.2%**

Table 1: Results on the CoNLL 2003 dataset. We achieve 90.32% accuracy without using any Gazetter information (Gaz.)

Method	Embed.	Dev	Test
RNN 1l	Skip-300	61.88%	55.52%
RNN 2l	Skip-300	59.77%	55.7%
LSTM 1l	Skip-300	65.12%	61.78%
LSTM 2l	Skip-300	61.27%	60.1%
Bi-RNN 1l	Skip-300	70.52%	68.64%
Bi-RNN 2l	Skip-300	71.50%	68.80%
Bi-LSTM 1l	Skip-300	73.16%	68.5%
Bi-LSTM 2l	Skip-300	74.02%	70.9%
Bi-LSTM 1l	GloVe-50	74.75%	71.97%
Devi et al CRF (Gaz.+Chu.)*	-	70.65%	**77.44%**
Bi-LSTM 1l	GloVe-300	**78.60%**	**77.48%**
Das et al CRF (Gaz.)*	-	-	**79.59%**

Table 2: Results on the ICON NLP Tools 2013 dataset. We achieve 77.48% accuracy without using any Gazetter information (Gaz.) or Chunking Information (Chu.).

pothesis that increasing the number of parameters can lead to overfitting. We could see Significant improvement in performance after using LSTM-RNN instead of Vanilla RNN which can be attributed to the ability of LSTM to model long dependencies. Also, the bidirectional RNN achieved significant improvement of accuracy over the others suggesting that incorporating context of words around (of both ahead and back) of the word is very useful. We provide only 1 layer in our best model to be released along with the paper. [3]

5 Conclusion

We show that the performance of Deep learning based approaches on the task for entity recognition can significantly outperform many other approaches involving rule based systems or hand-crafted features. The bidirectional LSTM incorporates features of varied distances providing a bigger context relieving the problem of free-

---

[3]Code available at: https://github.com/monikkinom/ner-lstm

158

Entity Type	Precision	Recall	F1
ARTIFACT:	86.04%	71.84%	78.3%
DISEASE:	52.5%	80.76%	63.63%
ENTERTAINMENT:	87.23%	84.16%	85.66%
FACILITIES:	56.47%	81.35%	66.66%
LIVTHINGS:	55.55%	47.61%	51.28%
LOCATION:	26.47%	42.85%	32.72%
LOCOMOTIVE:	60.60%	71.42%	65.57%
MATERIALS:	26.31%	71.42%	38.46%
ORGANIZATION:	83.33%	62.50%	71.42%
PERSON:	61.29%	61.29%	61.29%
PLANTS:	50.00%	59.99%	54.54%
Total:	75.86%	79.17%	77.48%

Table 3: Entity wise Precision, Recall and F1 scores on the ICON NLP Tools 2013 Hindi dataset (Test Set) for glove 300 size Embeddings and Bi-LSTM 1 layer deep model.

word ordering too. Also, given the scarcity of data, our proposed method effectively leverages LSTM based approaches by incorporating pre-trained word embeddings instead of learning it from data since it could be learnt in an unsupervised learning setting. We could extend this approach to many Indian Languages as we do not need a very large annotated corpus. When larger labelled datasets are developed, in the new system we would like to explore more deep neural network architectures and try learning the neural networks from scratch.[4]

References

Guillaume Lample,Miguel Ballesteros,Sandeep Subramanian,Kazuya Kawakami,Chris Dyer. 2016. Neural Architectures for Named Entity Recognition. *Proceedings of NAACL 2016,*.

Ronan Collobert,Jason Weston,Leon Bottou,Michael Karlen,Koray Kavukcuoglu,Pavel Kuksa. 2011. Natural Language Processing (almost) from Scratch. *Journal of Machine Learning Research, 12:2493-2537, 2011,*.

Tomas Mikolov, Ilya Sutskever, Kai Chen, Greg Corrado, Jeffrey Dean. 2013. Distributed Representations of Words and Phrases and their Compositionality. *Proceedings of Neural Information Processing Systems,*.

Jeffrey Pennington, Richard Socher, Christopher D. Mannin. 2014. GloVe: Global Vectors for Word Representation. *Empirical Methods in Natural Language Processing (EMNLP),*.

Sepp Hochreiter , Jrgen Schmidhuber. 1997. Long Short-Term Memory. *Journal Neural Computation archive Volume 9 Issue 8, November 15, 1997 ,*.

Diederik Kingma, Jimmy Ba. 2015. Adam: A Method for Stochastic Optimization. *International Conference for Learning Representations,*.

Mike Schuster and Kuldip K. Paliwal. 1997. Bidirectional Recurrent Neural Networks. *IEEE TRANSACTIONS ON SIGNAL PROCESSING, VOL. 45, NO. 11, NOVEMBER 1997,*.

Erik F. Tjong Kim Sang and Fien De Meulder. 2003. Introduction to the CoNLL-2003 Shared Task: Language-Independent Named Entity Recognition. *CoNLL-2003,*.

R Grishman. 1995. The NYU system for MUC-6 or Wheres the Syntax . *Sixth Message Understanding Conference (MUC-6) ,*.

Wakao T., Gaizauskas R. and Wilks Y. 1996. 1996. Evaluation of an algorithm for the Recognition and Classification of Proper Names. *proceedings of COLING-96,*.

Hideki Isozaki. 2001. Japanese named entity recognition based on a simple rule generator and decision tree learning. *proceedings of the Association for Computational Linguistics, pages 306-313.,*.

Koichi Takeuchi,Nigel Collier 2002. Use of Support Vector Machines in extended named entity recognition. *CoNLL-2002,*.

Daniel M. Bikel, Scott Miller, Richard Schwartz and Ralph Weischedel.. 1997. Nymble: a high performance learning name-finder . *Fifth conference on Applied natural language processing, pages 194-201,,*.

Dekang Lin and Xiaoyun Wu. 2009. Phrase clustering for discriminative learning.. *Proceedings of the Joint Conference of the 47th Annual Meeting of the ACL and the 4th International Joint Conference on Natural Language Processing of the AFNLP:,*.

Gang Luo, Xiaojiang Huang, Chin-Yew Lin, and Zaiqing Nie. 2015. Joint named entity recognition and disambiguation. *Proc. EMNLP,*.

Nitish Srivastava, Geoffrey Hinton, Alex Krizhevsky, Ilya Sutskever, Ruslan Salakhutdinov. 2014. Dropout: A Simple Way to Prevent Neural Networks from Overfitting. *Journal of Machine Learning Research,*.

Akshar Bharati, Rajeev Sangal, Dipti Misra Sharma. 2009. SSF: Shakti Standard Format Guide..

---

[4]* indicates that different training/test data is used. Our training data is significantly smaller than the one in consideration (4030 sentence in the original split v/s 3199 sentences in our split.). The original split was unavailable.

Arjun Das, Utpal Garain. 2013. CRF-based Named Entity Recognition @ICON 2013. *ICON-2013*,

Sobha Lalitha Devi, Malarkodi C S, Marimuthu K . 2013. Named Entity Recognizer for Indian Languages . *ICON-2013*,.

Srihari R., Niu C. and Li W. 2000. A Hybrid Approach for Named Entity and Sub-Type Tagging. *Proceedings of the sixth conference on applied natural language processing*,

Rahul Sharnagat and Pushpak Bhattacharyya 2013. Hindi Named Entity Recognizer for NER task of FIRE 2013. *FIRE-2013* ,

Ilya Sutskever,James Martens, George Dahl,Geoffrey Hinton. 2013. On the importance of initialization and momentum in deep learning. *Journal of Machine Learning Research*,

Yoshua Bengio, Patrice Simard, Paolo Frasconi 1994. Learning Long-Term Dependencies with Gradient Descent is difficult. *IEEE Transactions on Neural Networks* ,

Vaidya: A Spoken Dialog System for Health Domain

Prathyusha Danda   Brij Mohan Lal Srivastava Manish Shrivastava
International Institute Information and Technology, Hyderabad
{danda.prathyusha, brijmohanlal.s}@research.iiit.ac.in
m.shrivastava@iiit.ac.in

Abstract

In this paper, we introduce Vaidya, a spoken dialog system which is developed as part of the ITRA[1] project. The system is capable of providing an approximate diagnosis by accepting symptoms as free-form speech in real-time on both laptop and hand-held devices. The system focuses on challenges in speech recognition specific to Indian languages and capturing the intent of the user. Another challenge is to create models which are memory and CPU efficient for hand-held devices. We describe our progress, experiences and approaches in building the system that can handle English as the input speech. The system is evaluated using subjective statistical measure (Fleiss' kappa) to assess the usability of the system.

1   Introduction

Healthcare is a basic need of any sustainable society and has advanced many folds since the advent of technology. But effective medical diagnosis still remains inaccessible to the rural population in developing nations. The main reasons for this are scarcity of skilled healthcare staff in countries like India[2] and minimal Internet connectivity. Dialectal variations in rural areas render remote diagnosis methods like telemedicine, ineffective. Using spoken language technology, we can fill this gap and bring the state-of-the-art healthcare at the hand's reach of almost everyone. This paper presents a spoken dialog system which targets problems like understanding low-resource languages, inferring diagnosis from medical ontologies, capturing intent of the user and working with resources having limited memory and computational power such as a handheld devices.

Spoken dialog systems (SDS) have been an active area of research for the past few decades. But a large body of work has gone in developing SDS for English. There are several active systems currently in use for travel and healthcare in English. Research projects in India focus on understanding the linguistic structure of Indian languages and to make them easily representable in digital form. Structural analysis of languages coupled with SDS can create viable solutions for healthcare. There is a huge necessity of SDS in Indian healthcare systems since 1) medical knowledge is readily available through well-crafted disease ontologies which can be easily queried and 2) the mortality rate in rural areas is much higher due to lack of advanced diagnosis[3].

Most of the recent language technologies being developed currently are feasible on a standard computer with a good internet connectivity. Lately hand-held devices are gaining a lot of power both in case of memory as well as computation and are available at a reasonable cost. This has made these devices very handy to a large extent of population. Keeping the pervasive nature of mobile phones in mind, we can design solutions that are available to a large section of society. We can even penetrate the rural areas since the core technologies of dialog systems do not expect high literacy among its users and even work for languages that have no written form. Such interfaces where speech is used as underlying modality hold great promise as a preferred choice.

Main contributions of this paper are as follows:

- Domain-independent dialog flow structure built to scale to multiple languages and domains

- Low resource adaptation of Large Vocabulary

---

[1] Information Technology Research Academy http://itra.medialabasia.in/

[2] https://data.gov.in/catalog/rural-health-statistics-india-2014

[3] http://www.who.int/countries/ind/en/

D S Sharma, R Sangal and A K Singh. Proc. of the 13th Intl. Conference on Natural Language Processing, pages 161–166,
Varanasi, India. December 2016. ©2016 NLP Association of India (NLPAI)

Continuous Speech Recognition (LVCSR) to improve Indian language speech recognition

- Creation of healthcare domain ontology compatible with domain-independent dialog structure

This paper is organized as follows: The following section gives an overview of related literature. In section 3 we furnish the details of data that is collected as well as the open source data which is used to build different modules. In section 4 we describe the overall architecture of Vaidya with subsections describing the modules of the spoken dialog system. Section 5 that follows, concludes the paper and planned future directions are mentioned.

2 Related Works

Since early 1970s there have been several clinical decision support systems (CDSS), like Internist-I (Miller et al., 1982), Mycin (Shortliffe, 2012), etc. which help in clinical knowledge management and assist the healthcare providers to diagnose with desirable accuracy. But these systems are not directly accessible and operable by the patients. Bickmore (Bickmore and Giorgino, 2006) and Barahona (Rojas-Barahona, 2009) wrote a detailed account for creation of such systems and the methodologies involved that can be used for construction as well as evaluation. Sherwani (Sherwani et al., 2007) worked on the ideas similar to the current work where community health workers and dialog system technologies were collaboratively used in order to provide healthcare to the low-literate sections of Pakistan.

3 Data description

Medical knowledge is vital for the development of system hence we used the human disease ontology[4] created by Institute of Genome Sciences. This ontology is transformed into a domain-specific knowledge-base which coordinates with dialog manager to determine the state of the dialog and further actions. The ontology contains diseases as classes and relationships such as "has_symptom" which help create a knowledge-base of diseases and their corresponding symptoms. All those diseases which have minimum of three symptoms were taken into account with no

---

[4]http://disease-ontology.org/about/

constraint on upper limit. All the diseases which have two symptoms were segregated and were checked manually to see if any popular diseases are present and then were added to the ontology. The plural forms of the symptoms were replaced with the singular form to maintain consistency throughout the knowledge-base. E.g. lymph nodes → lymph node. Verb forms were replaced with the respective stems. E.g. coughing → cough. After these modifications the ontology consists a total of 560 diseases and 623 symptoms. This knowledge can also be used to create language models and in collection of relevant speech data.

In order to train the acoustic models with speech specific to Indian languages, we use single-speaker CMU Arctic database which is recorded in Indian English. We also collected speech samples for English, Telugu and Hindi (approx. 100 sentences each) from students of IIIT-H.

4 System Architecture

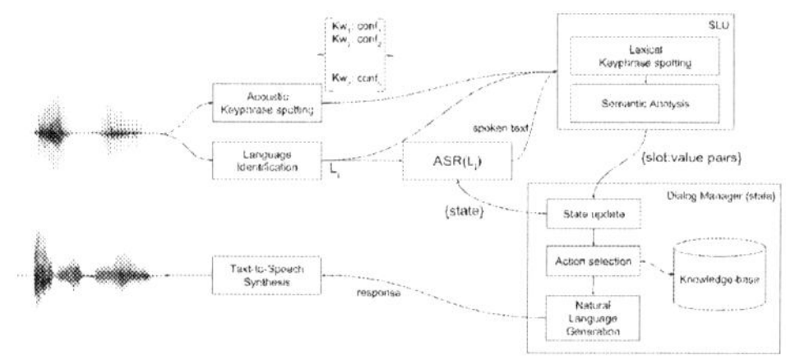

Figure 1: Vaidya architecture

The general framework of Vaidya is illustrated in Figure 1. It consists of modules like ASR, Dialog Manager, Natural Language Understanding, Knowledge-base and Text-to-Speech Synthesis. ASR is naturally the starting point of the dialog flow, where input is collected in form of speech signal and converted to text. This text is accepted by the dialog manager, which performs natural language understanding over it to understand the semantics of the spoken input. It queries the knowledge-base to check the state of the dialog flow and retrieves relevant information. Finally, a suitable response is generated by the text-to-speech synthesis module to let the user know the state of the dialog and prompts to expect required responses. During the development of the system, we encounter several challenges. One of them is speech recognition in Indian languages which can be implemented as keyword spotting using articulatory gestures as cardinal units (B. M. L. Srivastava et al., 2016). Currently the system focuses on building recognition engine for English with Indian accent by adapting the existing acoustic models towards Indian language speech. After recognition, the output is normalized and represented as a text which can be parsed by keyphrase spotter in order to interpret the embedded legal symptoms as per the ontology. These symptoms are queried against the knowledge-base and a list of probable diseases is generated. Additionally, the system also takes pictures from inbuilt camera on mobile as input and the future extension is to normalize them to legal symptoms. This input will help in classification of wounds or rashes.

4.1 Multilingual Automatic Speech Recognition (ASR)

Usually the knowledge is represented in form of concepts, specifically, structured text such as Resource Description Format (RDF) or as semantic networks of relations such as ontologies. Therefore in order to query this knowledge it is of paramount importance to convert spoken speech signal to lexical units. The final aim of this module is to convert speech signal spoken in any language to corresponding text. But each language follows its own set of sound units which vary largely based on geography. Hence it is not feasible to create a speech recognizer which understands all the languages perfectly. There have been several attempts to create a multilingual speech recognizer based on two approaches. A two-pass method where a language identification system (B. M. L. Srivastava et al., 2015) is followed by several ASR modules as shown in figure 2. This module segments the speech signal based on different languages present in the signal. Then each segment is fed to its corresponding ASR for transcription. Another approach (Figure 3) is to train the ASR over a multilingual speech corpus which covers most of the phones that are expected to be encountered in the test signal.

The performance of ASR can be improved by tuning the acoustic models, pronunciation dictionary and language models. In order to train acoustic models we used the phonetically tied model provided by Pocketsphinx (Huggins-Daines et al., 2006) as the base model and adapted it using rel-

evant domain-specific data. We used CMU Arctic database and the collected medical speech samples to adapt the model for Indian languages. The word error rate (WER) obtained when we adapted the model by different data is mentioned in Table 1.

Pronunciation dictionary is manually created for all the medical words that are expected to be encountered as speech input. We used US English phones to approximate the pronunciation of each word. Language modeling of the word sequences is important based on the context that is being discussed currently as part of that dialog. Therefore, three types of language models were constructed. 1) Generic trigram language model for free-form open ended conversation; 2) symptoms language model in JSpeech Grammar Format (JSGF); and 3) binary language model for affirmative / negative responses.

4.2 Dialog Manager

This module is the central part of the system which maintains consistency between the utterances. For each conversation, it creates a context object which stores several parameters needed to proceed with the dialog. These parameters are state-dependent. Current system works with 7 states namely,

- greet state
- ask_symptoms state
- diagnosis state
- disease_details state
- symptoms_details state
- disease_enquiry state
- first_aid state

Each of these states has a global set of flags which help the dialog manager to track the progress of dialog. They can also change the language model based on the requirement. E.g. a state which is expecting a boolean affirmative / negative response need not search in a huge generic language model. System successfully works on laptop as well as a low-end Android mobile and performs in real-time.

Initially, the greet state takes user input and determines the goal of the conversation. It finds out the domain which has to be selected and queried. This is for the purpose of scalability since there can be several other domains which can be integrated within the framework. It also determines out- of-domain utterances and rejects them. ask_symptoms state is selected when user

Acoustic model	Word Error Rate (WER %)
default model (en-us-ptm)	39.77
default + adapted using CMU Arctic	39.79
default + adapted using IIIT-H speech samples	**24.54**
default + adapted using CMU Arctic + IIIT-H speech samples	24.56

Table 1: WER for each acoustic model

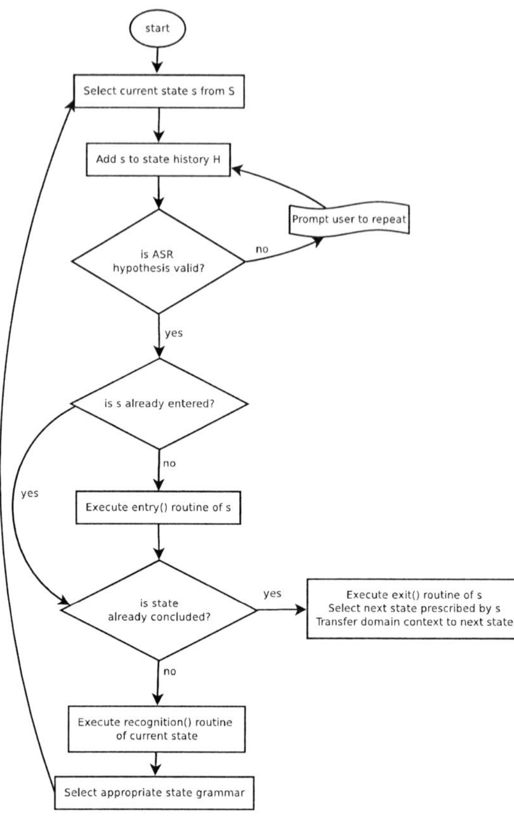

Figure 2: Domain-independent dialog flow

tem may prompt another query or give the diagnosis. The user has an option to ask what a particular symptom means, to which the the system will give information about the symptom by going to symptom_details state and then automatically goes back to diagnosis state to proceed with the diagnosis. We narrow down to one or zero disease by querying the user with that symptom, which we get from following Algorithm 1. The user is presented with the result of diagnosis. Finally the dialog enters disease_details state if the user wants to know more about the disease, else he is prompted with the greet state.

User can continue with other functionalities of the application which include first aid, disease inquiry and diagnosis. The first aid flow of the application requires the user to mention the type of help required. The system will then prompt the steps to be followed and guides the user through the interactive process of treatment where user can provide speech and images as input.

User can also inquire about a disease just by providing the disease name. The system will give the definition, symptoms and causes of the disease in form of text as well as speech for advanced accessibility. In another scenario, user may want to know if they have certain disease and the system will interactively find the symptoms and causes particular to that disease.

5 Evaluation & Results

We incorporate Fleiss' kappa statistical measure in order to assess the usability of submodules and the entire system. Evaluation is conducted by employing 10 subjects with varying age groups and gender. All the subjects are Indian non-native English speakers. Each subject was assigned 5 randomly selected diseases which are unique to them. Ratings were assigned by the subjects based on following five parameters.

1. Ease of use (1 - System is confusing and misleading, 5 - System is seamless and well-guided)

wants to describe their symptoms for diagnosis. This state accepts natural language speech and looks for symptoms that can be present in the transcribed text. Once the user has exhausted their list of symptoms, the system enters diagnosis state. This state queries the knowledge base and narrows down to a list of most probable diseases. This state further finds out the symptoms corresponding to these diseases and assigns a score to each one of them which measures the number of times each symptom occurs in the disease list. We follow the algorithm mentioned as Algorithm 1 in order to reduce the list down to one or zero disease. Depending on the user's response the sys-

---

Algorithm 1 Algorithm for diagnosis

1: **procedure** DIAGNOSIS
2: $\quad D \leftarrow (\, d_1, d_2, \dots, d_k\,)$
3: $\quad S \leftarrow (\, s_1 : n_1, s_2 : n_2, \dots, s_m : n_m\,)$
4: $\quad$**while** $len(D) > 1$ **do**
5:
$$\tilde{s}_i = \underset{\tilde{s}_i}{\arg\min}(len(D)/2 - n_i) \qquad (1)$$

6: $\qquad$prompt user to ask if he/she is observing $\tilde{s}_i$
7: $\qquad$mark $\tilde{s}_i$ based on user response
8: $\qquad$remove corresponding diseases from D
9: $\quad$**return** D

---

2. ASR performance (1 - Recognizes nothing correctly, 5 - Recognizes everything correctly). ASR performance is also quantitatively measured as fraction of correctly recognized utterances for objective analysis.

3. How often does the system digress from the main goal? This measure analyzes if the user is being interrupted by annoying information in the middle of dialog.

4. Success rate. This measures that how many times the system reaches correct goal.

5. Steps taken to reach the goal. The system is designed to optimize the total number of steps in order to complete the dialog. In ideal case, system must halve the disease search space with each question it asks, so it must converge to a disease in no more than $\log_2 N$ steps, N being total number of symptoms. Since the dialog flow does not follow the ideal scenario due to speech recognition errors and uneven distribution of diseases in symptom space, system may take more than $\log_2 N$ steps to converge. We objectively measure this and incorporate it into the evaluation criteria.

Table 5 shows the subjective evaluation results by 10 users pertaining to 5 measures. The rating is from 1 to 5 for each measure, 1 being the lowest rating and 5 being the highest. 86% of the dialogs led to successful completion with correct diagnosis. The last column of Table 5 refers to the average number of steps or questions asked by system in order to complete the diagnosis. Minimum number of steps to complete the diagnosis is

0 and maximum number of steps is 16. On average, system requires 3.8 number of steps to reach the diagnosis.

We compute the overall rating of the system using Fleiss' kappa measure (κ).

Overall agreement	0.50
Fixed marginal kappa	0.15
Free marginal kappa	0.37

Table 2: Kappa measures

6 Conclusion & Future Work

We described the general framework of Vaidya, which accepts speech as input from the user and guides her to diagnose symptoms and possible diseases. We further describe its various components and subsystems and the resources we used to build each of one them. The overall system successfully works on laptop as well as a low-end Android mobile and performs in real-time. This system will act as the baseline for further versions of Vaidya. There is scope for improvement at symptom recognition level and capturing the semantic invariance of user's intent in the framework. Extensive speech resources are being collected in form of medical conversations which will enable the system to improve and extend the recognition capability. These resources can also be used to model the dialogs and learn to adapt based on the dialog act history and the state which is currently active. We also need to formulate a general evaluation strategy which can provide objective as well as subjective measure of overall system performance.

Acknowledgments

Authors would like to thank ITRA for supporting the project financially.

References

T. Bickmore and T. Giorgino. 2006. Health dialog systems for patients and consumers. *TJournal of biomedical informatics*, 39(5):556–571.

D. Huggins-Daines, M. Kumar, A. Chan, A. W. Black, M. Ravishankar, A. Rudnicky. 2006. Pocketsphinx: A free, real-time continuous speech recognition system for hand-held devices. In *Acoustics, Speech and Signal Processing, 2006. ICASSP 2006 Proceedings. 2006 IEEE International Conference on*, volume 1, pages I–I.

User index	Ease of use	ASR performance	Consistency	Success rate	# Steps
1	4	5	4	5	4
2	4	4	4	5	4
3	4	3	4	5	4
4	4	5	5	5	5
5	3	4	4	5	5
6	5	4	5	5	5
7	4	4	5	5	5
8	5	4	5	5	4
9	5	4	3	5	4
10	3	2	4	5	4

Table 3: Subjective evaluation results over 50 diseases

R. A. Miller, H. E. Pople Jr, and J. D. Myers. 1982. Internist-i, an experimental computer-based diagnostic consultant for general internal medicine. *New England Journal of Medicine*, 307(8):468–476.

J. D. Osborne, S. Lin, W. Kibbe, L. Zhu, M. Danila, and C. Rex. 2007. Generif is a more comprehensive, current and computationally tractable source of gene-disease relationships than omim. *Bioinformatics Core, Northwestern University Technical Report.*

L. Rojas-Barahona. 2009. *Health care dialogue systems: practical and theoretical approaches to dialogue management.*PhD thesis, University of avia, Pavia, Italy

J. Sherwani, N. Ali, S. Mirza, A. Fatma, Y. Memon, . Karim, R. Tongia, and R. Rosenfeld. 2007. Healthline: Speech-based access to health information by low-literate users. *Information and Communication Technologies and Development, 2007. ICTD 2007. International Conference on*, pages 1–9. IEEE, 2007.

E. Shortliffe. 2012. Generif is a more comprehensive, current and computationally tractable source of gene-disease relationships than omim. *Computer-based medical consultations: MYCIN.*Elsevier.

B. M. L. Srivastava, H. K. Vydana, A. K. Vuppala, and M. Shrivastava. 2015. A language model based approach towards large scale and lightweight language identification systems.

B. M. L. Srivastava and M. Shrivastava. 2016. Articulatory gesture rich representation learning of phonological units in low resource settings. 4th SLSP 2016.

Cosmopolitan Mumbai, Orthodox Delhi, Techcity Bangalore: Understanding City Specific Societal Sentiment

Aishwarya N Reganti, Tushar Maheshwari, Upendra Kumar, Amitava Das

Indian Institute of Information Technology, Sri City, Andhra Pradesh, India
{aishwarya.r14, tushar.m14, upendra.k14, amitava.das}@iiits.in

Abstract

The paper reports work on investigating societal sentiment using the Schwartz values and ethics model, and applying it to social media text of users from 20 most populous cities of India to represent geo-specific societal sentiment map of India. For the automatic detection of societal sentiment we propose psycholinguistic analysis, that reveals how a user's social media behaviour and language is related to his/her ethical practices. India is a multi-cultural country, values and ethics of each Indian are highly diverse and dependent on the region or society s/he belongs to. Several experiments were carried out incorporating Linguistic Inquiry Word Count analysis, n-grams, topic modeling, psycholinguistic lexica, speech-acts, and non-linguistic features, while experimenting with a range of machine learning algorithms including Support Vector Machines, Logistic Regression, and Random Forests to identify the best linguistic and non-linguistic features for automatic classification of values and ethics.

1 Introduction

Indian sub-continent is known for its diversity and multiplicity, with 29 states and 7 union territories each region has a culture of its own. India's plethora of rich cultural diversity is reflected in the fact that each region is unique in terms of the values and ethics borne by the individuals belonging to these regions or society. For example, Punjabis are fun loving and energetic, South Indians are reserved and introverts as compared to North Indians, Mumbaikars and Delhiites are outgoing and socially confident etc. The main objective of this paper is to demonstrate that these regional ethics can be inferred from social media languages and behavior using statistical analysis.

In the last decade there have been significant efforts in opinion and sentiment mining as well as inferring emotion from text. Classical sentiment/emotion analysis systems classify text into either one of the classes positive, negative or neutral, or into Ekman's classes of happy, sad, anger, fear, surprise, and disgust. Personality models [John and Srivastava1999] can be seen as an augmentation to the basic definition of sentiment analysis, where the target is to understand sentiment/personality at person level rather than only at message level. Here in this paper our motivation is to augment to one more level i.e., to understand societal sentiment, i.e., values and ethics. To understand the societal sentiment we borrow the psychological values and ethics model introduced by schwartz1990toward, defines ten basic and distinct ethical values (henceforth only values). The definitions of these 10 values are as following. *Achievement*: sets goals and achieves them; *Benevolence*: seeks to help others and provide general welfare; *Conformity*: obeys clear rules, laws and structures; *Hedonism*: seeks pleasure and enjoyment; *Power*: controls and dominates others, controls resources; *Security*: seeks health and safety; *Self-direction*: wants to be free and independent; *Stimulation*: seeks excitement and thrill; *Tradition*: does things blindly because they are customary; *Universalism*: seeks peace, social justice and tolerance for all [Schwartz2012]. All these basic ten values can be further grouped into higher order (super class: SC) groups which respectively are: **Self-Enhancement** (SC1) {Achievement, Power, Hedonism}, **Openness to change** (SC2) {Stimulation, Self-directions, Hedonism}, **Self-Transcendence** (SC3) {Universalism, Benevolence}, **Conservation** (SC4) {Security, Tradition,

D S Sharma, R Sangal and A K Singh. Proc. of the 13th Intl. Conference on Natural Language Processing, pages 167–176,
Varanasi, India. December 2016. ©2016 NLP Association of India (NLPAI)

Conformity}. In addition to identifying the ten basic values, Schwartz' theory also explains how the values are interconnected and influenced with each other, since the pursuit of any of the values results in either an accordance with one another (e.g., Conformity and Security) or a conflict with at least one other value (e.g., Benevolence and Power). These ten basic values are related to various outcomes and effects of a person's role in a society [Argandoña2003, Agle and Caldwell1999, Hofstede et al.2010, Rokeach1973]. The values have also proved to provide an important and powerful explanation of consumer behaviour and how they influence it [Kahle et al.1986, Clawson and Vinson1978]. Moreover, there are results that indicate how values of workforce and ethical practices in organizations are directly related to transformational and transactional leadership [Hood2003]. We believe that these kind of models may become extremely useful in the future for various purposes like Internet advertising (specifically social media advertising), community detection, computational psychology, recommendation systems, sociological analysis (for example East vs West cultural analysis) over social media. Customized products can be crafted for specific regions of the country by analysing the collective values of that region. In order to experiment, a twitter corpus was collected and annotated with Schwartz values. A range of machine learning techniques were then utilized to classify an individual's ethical practices into Schwartz' classes by analyzing the user's language usage and behaviour in social media. The borders between the motivators are artificial and one value flows into another. Such overlapping and fuzzy borders between values make the computational classification problem more challenging.

The paper is organized in sections with Section 2 introducing related work in this area. The details of the corpora collection and annotation are given in Section 3. In Section 4 various experiments on automatic value detection are reported, Section 5 illustrates the results obtained for Indian cities and inferences that can be drawn while Section 6 discusses the performance of the psycholinguistic experiments and mentions possible future directions.

2   Related Works

The present day state-of-the-art sentiment analysis systems look at a fragment of text in isolation.

Therefore textual features and models proposed and discussed for such purposes is quite different than our current research need. Henceforth, we are focusing our discussion on the previous research on automatic personality analysis which is more closer to our research.

In the recent years, there have been a lot of research activities on automated identification of various personality traits of an individual from their language usage and behaviour in social media. One milestone in this area is the Workshop and Shared Task on Computational Personality Recognition in the year of 2013. Two corpora were released for this task. One was the Facebook corpus, which consisted of about 10,000 Facebook status updates of 250 users, plus their Facebook network properties, labelled with personality traits. markovikj2013mining and verhoeven2013ensemble achieved encouraging results on personality classification task. The following two paragraphs consolidate our discussion on various features and methods used by researchers in the workshop. Two kinds of features were put into use: linguistic and non-linguistic.

Linguistic Features: The participating teams tested several linguistic features. As a general fact, it is known that n-grams are the most famous and useful features for any kind of textual classification. Therefore, teams tested various features like unigrams, bigrams, and trigrams. We also noticed that Linguistic Inquiry Word Count (LIWC) features were used by all the teams as their baselines. LIWC [Pennebaker et al.2001] is a well developed hand-crafted lexicon. It has 69 different categorical words, specifically designed for psycholinguistic experiments. Another psycholinguistic lexicon called MRC [Wilson1988] was also used by a few teams. Lexicons like SentiWordNet [Baccianella et al.2010], WordNet Affect strapparava:369:2004:lrec2004, categorical features like part-of-speech (POS), a few other word level features like capital letters, repeated words were also used. Two more important textual features were discussed by the participating teams. Linguistic nuances introduced by tomlinson2013predicting, is the depth of the verbs in wordnet troponymy hierarchy. Speech act features have been discussed by appling2013towards. Authors manually annotated the given Facebook corpus with speech acts and reported their correlation with personality traits of the respective users.

Non-Linguistic Features: Facebook network properties including network size, betweenness centrality, density and transitivity, provided as a part of the released dataset, were used by all the teams.

Drawing inspiration from the learning of the above mentioned research, we have experimented with all the above mentioned linguistic and non-linguistic features and proposed a few new features. Effectiveness and performance impact of each feature on the classification result has been detailed and discussed in the section 4.

3 Corpus Acquisition

At the very beginning of this research, we asked ourselves very fundamental question - *if social media is a good proxy of the original society?* backetal2010 and GolbeckEA:11 provide empirical answers to this question. Their results respectively indicate that, in general, people do not use virtual desired/bluffed social media profiles to promote an idealized-virtual-identity and that a user's personality can be predicted from his/her social media profile. This does not mean that there are no outliers, but we grounded our corpus collection on the assumption that is true for a major portion of the population.

A standard method of psychological data collection is through self-assessment tests which are popularly known as psychometric tests. Self-assessments were obtained using a 50-question version of the Portrait Values Questionnaire (PVQ) [Schwartz et al.2001]. This questionnaire consists of questions where the participant's answer must be a score rating from 1-6 Likert scale. A rating of 1 means "not like me at all" which progressively changes to 6 meaning "very much like me". An example question is *"He likes to take risks. He is always looking for adventures."* where the user should answer while putting himself in the shoes of "He" in the question. Once all the questions in the PVQ have been answered, a value score is generated using an averaging formula for each value consisting of scores of the related questions.

3.1 Twitter Values Corpus

In the first quarter of 2016, the micro blogging service Twitter averaged 310 million monthly active users,[1] with around 6,000 tweets being posted every second. Unlike other popular social media like Facebook, Twitter provides open access to its data. Therefore, Twitter came as the natural choice for the data collection. The data collection was crowd-sourced using Amazon Mechanical Turk as a service, while ensuring that the participants came from various cultures and ethnic backgrounds: the participants were equally distributed, and consisted of Americans (Caucasian, Latino, African-American), Indians (East, West, North, South), and a few East-Asians (Singaporeans, Malaysian, Japanese, Chinese). The selected Asians were checked to be mostly English speaking.

The participants were requested to answer the 50-question version of PVQ and to provide their Twitter IDs, so that their tweets could be crawled. However, several challenges have to be addressed when working with Twitter, and a number of iterations, human interventions and personal communications were needed to resolve all the issues. For example, several users had protected Twitter accounts, so that their tweets were not accessible when using the Twitter API. In addition, many users had to be discarded since they had published less than 100 tweets, making them uninteresting for statistical analysis. The open source free Twitter API: Twitter4J[2] also has a limit of accessing only the current 3,200 tweets from any user. To resolve this issue, an open source Java application [Henrique2015] was used. At the end of the data collection process, data from 367 unique users had been gathered. The highest number of tweets for one user was 15K, while the lowest number of tweets for a user was a mere 100; the average number of messages per user in the Twitter corpus was found to be 1,608.

3.2 Geo-Specific Data for Indian Values Map

We started our data collection with a list of India's top 20 populous cities spanning almost the whole country i.e. North, South, East and West India. Names of those cities could be seen in the Table 3. Twitter GET geo/search API [Yamamoto2014] provides a facility of searching users based on latitude-longitude. We searched city specific users

---

[1]http://www.statista.com/statistics/282087/number-of-monthly-active-twitter-users/

[2] http://twitter4j.org/

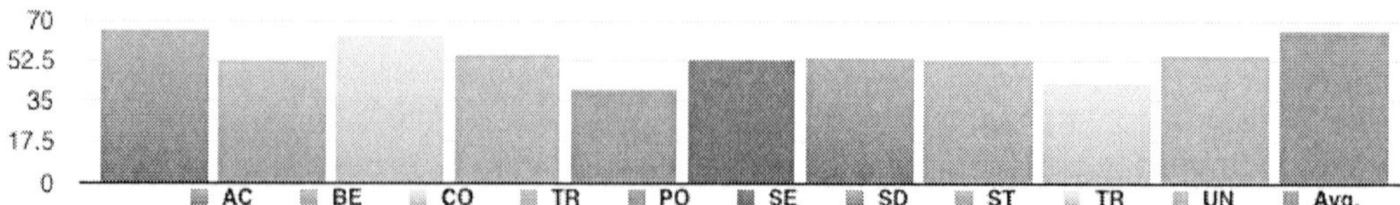

Figure 1: Values Ethics Class Distribution

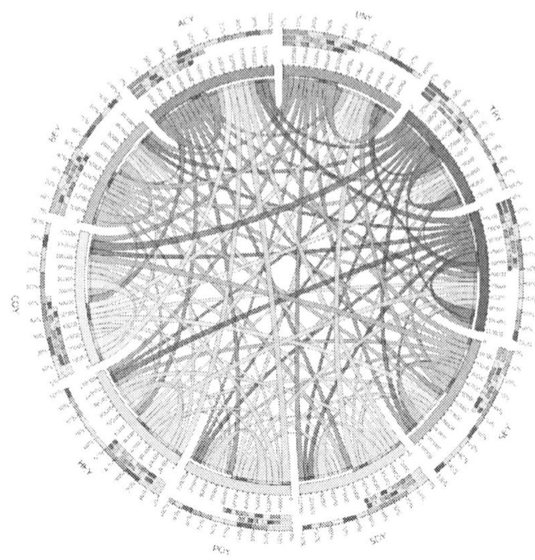

Figure 2: Values Ethics Fuzzy Class Distribution within latitude-longitude range of 0.5°*0.5° (i.e. approximately area of 55*55 sq.km).

3.3 Post-Processing and Corpus Statistics

The scores obtained from the questionnaire were in the range 1–6 and the corpus contain crowd sourced data, so we had no control over value type distributions. For example, the Schwartz value scores for the corpus were in the following ranges: Achievement [-4.12, 3.36], Benevolence [-1.56, 3.39], Conformity [-3.35, 3.01], Hedonism [-5.18, 4.35], Power [-6.12, 2.27], Security [-2.60, 2.40], Self-Direction [-1.61, 3.40], Stimulation [-5.0, 2.63], Tradition [-4.49, 3.35], Universalism [-3.33, 3.30]. The distribution of a particular value type over a corpus was analysed using the Bienaymé-Chebyshev Inequality [Bienaymé1853, Tchébichef1867], showing that, for example, most of the Achievement instances (89%) were in the range [-2.96, 2.84]. Therefore normalization was applied to obtain equilibrium in the obtained value ranges. For all the corpora, the range of each value type was rescaled to the range of [-1,1] using the formula: $\{x_{scaled} = \frac{2*(x-x_{min})}{x_{max}-x_{min}} - 1\}$. A 1 ('Yes') or 0 ('No') class was assigned to each Schwartz value. If the score was less than 0, the class was considered to be negative,. indicating absence of that value trait for the particular user, while scores $\geq$ 0 were considered to belong to the 'Yes' class, indicating the presence of that trait for the user.

Schwartz' model defines fuzzy membership, which means that an power-oriented individual can be achievement oriented as well, i.e., the values can overlap with each other. To understand this notion vividly, we have reported the fuzzy membership in the Figure 2 where it can be observed that the emerging bands signifies the fuzzy membership of other 9 values into one of the remaining values. For example, on careful investigation of Figure 2, we can observe that ACY oriented people's fuzzy membership is represented by outgoing red bands. The width of the bands represent the degree of membership ACY oriented people have in other values. Similarly, we can also observe that there are 10 incoming bands of 10 different colours towards ACY, which shows membership of each of the classes in ACY class.In each class, it can be observed that there is an self-arc which represents membership of each class with itself (i.e 100%). The self-arc can be used as reference in order to measure the degree of membership of each of the classes with other classes. The intricate structure of Circos (by Krzywinski18062009) figure rightly signifies how values are strongly connected with each other at societal level. Some of the interesting trends which can be observed from the Figure 2 are : power (POY) oriented people have highest overlap with achievement (ACY) oriented people, tradition oriented people have highest overlap with people high in conformity and hedonic (HEY) people have significant overlap with people seeking stimulation (STY).

LWC	Achieve	Benevol	Conform	Hedonism	Power	Security	Self-Direct	Stimulation	Tradition
PREPS	0.014	0.066	-0.006	-0.077	-0.113	-0.035	0.090	-0.037	-0.029
SPACE	-0.002	0.019	0.001	-0.001	-0.077	0.013	0.040	0.010	-0.003
UP	0.028	0.015	0.017	-0.008	-0.073	0.000	0.073	-0.015	0.033
TIME	-0.024	0.061	0.009	-0.084	-0.112	-0.018	0.078	0.007	0.062
OCCUP	0.042	-0.021	0.006	-0.078	-0.058	0.004	-0.011	-0.002	0.040
ACHIEVE	0.030	-0.014	-0.016	-0.066	-0.039	0.008	-0.010	0.008	0.037
INCL	-0.016	0.090	-0.001	0.091	0.107	-0.009	0.031	-0.056	0.008
SENSES	-0.020	0.066	-0.015	-0.049	-0.089	-0.038	0.063	-0.033	0.009
PAST	-0.021	0.075	0.022	-0.056	-0.087	-0.004	0.036	-0.033	0.010
PHYSCAL	-0.068	0.100	-0.019	-0.024	-0.073	-0.049	-0.012	0.017	0.029
EATING	-0.012	0.058	-0.013	-0.039	-0.049	0.005	0.059	-0.016	0.002
DOWN	-0.008	0.060	0.019	0.000	-0.048	-0.042	0.041	0.077	-0.019
EXCL	-0.011	0.093	-0.017	-0.029	0.128	-0.031	0.135	-0.013	-0.011
COGMECH	-0.015	0.069	-0.046	-0.058	-0.094	-0.046	0.090	-0.003	-0.052
DISCREP	-0.052	0.030	0.012	-0.013	0.005	0.014	0.015	0.015	-0.038
NUMBER	0.021	0.012	0.041	-0.022	-0.049	0.038	0.072	-0.004	0.034
CAUSE	0.004	-0.004	-0.046	-0.037	-0.049	-0.065	0.074	0.032	-0.036
NEGATE	-0.020	0.092	-0.026	-0.028	-0.077	-0.013	0.146	-0.029	-0.055
MONEY	-0.037	-0.016	-0.047	0.022	-0.021	0.055	0.047	-0.007	-0.034
AFFECT	-0.026	0.116	-0.006	-0.079	-0.122	-0.018	0.011	-0.037	0.003
NEGEMO	-0.037	0.034	-0.049	-0.055	-0.077	0.010	0.107	0.019	-0.026
SAD	-0.071	0.006	-0.019	-0.020	-0.073	-0.074	0.085	0.027	-0.016
INHIB	-0.001	-0.008	0.068	0.021	0.059	-0.021	0.059	0.025	0.091
ANGER	-0.001	0.031	-0.006	-0.074	0.075	0.035	0.093	-0.026	0.041
POSEMO	-0.017	0.120	0.013	-0.071	0.112	-0.025	-0.030	0.051	0.014
OPTIM	0.012	0.086	0.044	-0.098	-0.078	0.004	-0.024	-0.036	0.034
INSIGHT	-0.012	0.075	0.093	-0.078	0.123	-0.060	0.145	-0.015	0.084
PRESENT	0.014	0.093	-0.017	-0.031	-0.102	-0.016	0.080	-0.026	-0.008
ASSENT	-0.026	0.044	0.070	0.006	-0.035	0.090	0.057	0.072	-0.012
BODY	-0.104	0.060	-0.021	0.015	-0.033	0.004	0.055	0.035	-0.039
POSFEEL	-0.036	0.076	0.033	0.009	-0.065	0.072	-0.041	-0.014	0.001
ANX	0.020	0.055	-0.092	0.003	-0.008	0.007	0.006	0.074	-0.081
SOCIAL	-0.017	0.118	0.101	-0.066	-0.097	0.031	0.024	-0.087	0.021
COMM	0.039	0.115	0.053	-0.096	-0.082	-0.021	0.005	-0.016	0.002
CERTAIN	-0.030	0.126	0.089	-0.150	-0.096	0.048	0.013	-0.091	0.072
SWEAR	-0.060	0.031	-0.065	0.049	-0.039	-0.035	0.072	0.036	-0.050
JOB	0.035	-0.080	-0.015	-0.020	0.014	0.058	-0.009	0.007	-0.016
METAPH	0.015	0.100	0.186	0.179	-0.088	0.042	-0.139	0.131	0.326
RELIG	0.025	0.097	0.190	0.184	-0.088	0.046	-0.149	0.135	0.332
TENTAT	-0.040	0.124	-0.027	-0.001	0.092	-0.081	0.102	0.050	-0.037
SLEEP	-0.002	-0.012	-0.051	0.021	-0.028	-0.069	0.055	0.027	0.028
DEATH	-0.060	0.045	0.021	-0.015	-0.039	-0.020	0.030	-0.006	0.042
SEXUAL	-0.039	0.074	-0.014	-0.004	-0.053	-0.064	-0.092	0.030	0.054
SCHOOL	0.058	0.028	0.078	-0.060	-0.078	-0.053	-0.011	-0.029	0.041
LEISURE	0.029	0.042	0.066	0.012	-0.016	0.072	-0.036	-0.096	0.089
HOME	-0.005	0.027	0.078	0.006	-0.004	0.107	-0.083	-0.086	0.090
SMILES	0.006	0.050	-0.072	0.007	-0.025	-0.007	0.034	-0.070	-0.016
FEEL	-0.054	0.049	-0.066	-0.026	-0.073	-0.013	0.018	-0.036	-0.030
SPORTS	0.065	-0.021	-0.030	0.073	-0.015	-0.056	0.054	0.005	-0.041

Figure 3: Best LIWC feature selection (accuracy) for each of Schwartz' ten personality value types. The values in the 'Before Feature Ablation' row are based on the full feature set (69 features).

4 Experiments on Automatic Values Identification

We performed several experiments to get a better understanding of the most appropriate linguistic and non-linguistic features for the problem domain. The experiments were designed as a 20 class classification problem, with 'Yes' and 'No' classes for each of the ten Schwartz values. Ten different classifiers were trained, each for a particular value type. Each classifier predicts whether the person concerned is positively or negatively inclined towards the given Schwartz value. The versions implemented in WEKA [Witten and Frank2005] of three different machine learning algorithms were used in the experiments: Sequential Minimal Optimization (SMO; a version of Support Vector Machines, SVM), Simple Logistic Regression (LR), and Random Forests (RF). In all the mentioned experiments the corpora were pre-processed, i.e., tokenized by the CMU tokenizer [Gimpel et al.2011] and stemmed by the Porter Stemmer [Porter1980]. All the lexica were also stemmed in the same way before usage.

4.1 Linguistic Features

LIWC Analysis: LIWC [Pennebaker et al.2001] is a well developed hand-crafted lexicon. It has 69 different categories (emotions, psychology, affection, social processes, etc.) and almost 6,000 distinct words. The 69 categorical features were extracted as user-wise categorical word frequencies. As the text length (for the Essay corpus) or number of messages (Twitter and FB corpora) varies from person to person, Z-score normalization (or standardization) was applied using the equation: $\hat{x} = (x - \mu)/\sigma$, where x is the 'raw frequency count', μ and σ are respectively the mean and standard deviation of a particular feature. After normalizing, each feature vector value is centered around 0 and $\sigma = 1$. This normalization led to an increase in the accuracy figures in many of the cases.

To investigate how each LIWC feature contributes, feature ablation was performed and the Pearson correlations of LIWC features vs value types were analysed as reported in Figure3. The final classifiers were trained using only the features that were contributing for a particular value type. This resulted in a performance boost and also gave reduced time complexity (both model training and testing times). For example, the same accuracy (65.84%) for the Achievement class as obtained by using the full 69 feature set also can be obtained by using only 52 LIWC features. Moreover, the lowest obtained accuracy 53.06% for the Security class increased to 55.80% when considering only 47 features.

4.2 Topic Modeling

In order to find out the bag-of-words features for each value type, i.e., the vocabulary that a person uses more frequently, the MALLET [McCallum2002][3] topic modelling toolkit was used to extract a number of topics. MALLET uses Gibbs Sampling and Latent Dirichlet Allocation (LDA). In a pre-processing stage, stop words were removed and case was preserved. For the Twitter corpus, we tested with different number of topic clusters of sizes 10, 20, 50, 75, and 100, and observed that 50 was the most suitable number. Each of the 50 topics contained an average of 19 words, each with a specific weight attached. The top 5 topics were chosen for each value type, according to these weights, and the words of these topics were added as a new feature set along with the LIWC baseline features.

It was also observed that the rankings of the top 5 topics were almost similar for each Schwartz

---

[3]http://mallet.cs.umass.edu

| Values | Achievement | | | Benevolence | | | Conformity | | | Hedonism | | | Power | | |
Classifier	SMO	LR	RF	SMO	LR	RF	SMO	LR	RF	SMO	LR	RF	SMO	LR	RF
LIWC	80.93	80.93	80.10	78.75	78.75	77.38	73.02	72.48	77.93	77.11	76.84	76.02	54.77	50.68	52.59
+Topic	74.66	80.65	80.65	69.21	78.20	77.93	66.76	72.48	73.02	71.66	76.84	76.57	52.32	54.77	51.77
+Lexica	71.10	73.70	69.70	71.90	69.90	65.00	67.20	71.60	68.00	68.00	68.60	60.60	72.80	69.80	59.20
+Non-Linguistic	74.11	80.38	80.93	68.40	78.47	77.38	66.49	72.48	74.11	70.30	76.30	76.57	54.22	55.59	54.22
+Speech-Act	81.10	76.40	68.00	81.00	73.00	66.00	75.00	66.00	66.00	74.00	64.00	63.00	82.00	75.00	63.00

| Values | Security | | | Self-Direction | | | Stimulation | | | Tradition | | | Universalism | | | Average |
Classifier	SMO	LR	RF	SMO	LR	RF	SMO	LR	RF	SMO	LR	RF	SMO	LR	RF	
LIWC	76.29	75.75	74.11	83.38	83.38	75.20	73.57	72.48	70.84	58.04	55.31	55.86	82.02	81.47	80.65	**74.28**
+Topic	70.57	74.93	75.48	76.84	83.38	83.38	64.12	72.47	71.66	52.04	53.95	59.67	74.93	81.47	81.20	**73.70**
+Lexica	70.60	74.30	69.50	75.60	74.40	76.60	68.80	68.60	68.30	73.90	69.50	62.30	78.00	82.20	76.30	**73.38**
+Non-Linguistic	71.18	74.66	75.20	76.57	83.38	83.38	65.58	73.57	71.66	52.59	53.41	55.86	74.39	81.74	82.02	**73.57**
+Speech-Act	78.00	80.00	69.00	78.00	76.00	75.00	73.00	66.00	68.00	80.00	71.00	63.00	89.00	81.10	77.00	**80.00**

Table 1: Automatic Schwartz value detection (accuracy) on the Twitter corpora.

Speech Act	SNO	Wh	YN	SO	AD	YA	T	AP	RA	A	O	Avg.
Distribution	33.37	11.45	15.45	5.16	6.88	15.08	0.41	3.26	0.71	0.07	14.59	
F_1-score	0.45	0.88	0.88	0.72	0.45	0.60	0.72	0.60	0.12	0.77	0.12	0.69

Table 2: Speech act class distributions in the corpus (in %) and speech act classifier performance.

value. The accuracies obtained were almost similar to the accuracies obtained in the previous experiments. However, this time, since the dimension of the feature set is much smaller, the time complexity decreased by almost a factor of 10. Hence the topic modelling was repeated for the social media corpora from Facebook and Twitter, but resulting in a different number of topic clusters, namely 89. Added to the 69 LIWC features this thus resulted in a total of 158 features.

4.3 Psycholinguistic Lexica

In addition to the base feature set from LIWC, two other psycholinguistic lexica were added: the Harvard General Inquirer [Stone et al.1966] and the MRC psycholinguistic database [Wilson1988]. The Harvard General Inquirer lexicon contains 182 categories, including two large valence categories positive and negative; other psycholinguistic categories such as words of pleasure, pain, virtue and vice; words indicating overstatement and understatement, often reflecting presence or lack of emotional expressiveness, etc. 14 features from the MRC Psycholinguistic lexicon were included, namely, number of letters, phonemes and syllables; Kucera-Francis frequency, number of categories, and number of samples; Thorndike-Lorge frequency; Brown verbal frequency; ratings of Familiarity, Concreteness, Imagability and Age of acquisition; and meaningfulness measures using Colorado Norms and Pavio Norms. In order to get these MRC features a machine readable version of it has been used.[4] Fea-

ture ranking was done by evaluating the contribution of each feature in an SMO classifier. In addition, the sensorial lexicon Sensicon was used. It contains words with sense association scores for the five basic senses: Sight, Hearing, Taste, Smell, and Touch. For example, when the word 'apple' is uttered, the average human mind will visualize the appearance of an apple, stimulating the eye-sight, feel the smell and taste of the apple, making use of the nose and tongue as senses, respectively. Sensicon provides a numerical mapping which indicates the extent to which each of the five senses is used to perceive a word in the lexicon. We perform feature ablation and also analyze (Pearson) correlations of lexicon features vs values. Finally, classifiers are trained using only the features which are contributing for a particular value.

4.4 Non-Linguistic Features

Social network structure is very useful to predict any person's intrinsic value. For each user in the Twitter corpus, the total number of tweets or messages, total number of likes, average time difference between two tweets/messages, total number of favourites and re-tweets, and their in-degree and out-degree centrality scores on network of friends and followers were used as features adding to a total of 7 features along with the feature set used in the Topic Modelling experiment after observation of the structure of tweets and the previously done linguistic feature experiments. The degree centrality was calculated as of a vertex v, for a given graph $G(V,E)$ with $|V|$ vertices and $|E|$ edges, is defined as: $\{C_D = deg(v)\}$.

4.5 Speech Act Features

The way people communicate, whether it is verbally, visually, or via text, is indicative of Per-

---

[4]http://ota.oucs.ox.ac.uk/headers/1054.xml

sonality/Values traits. In social media, profile status updates are used by individuals to broadcast their mood and news to their peers. In doing so, individuals utilize various kinds of speech acts that, while primarily communicating their content, also leave traces of their values/ethical dimensions behind. By following the hypothesis of appling2013towards, we have applied speech act features in order to classify personalities/values. However, for this experiment we have restricted speech act classes into 11 major (avoiding 43 fine-grained speech act classes[5]) categories: Statement Non-Opinion (SNO), Wh Question (Wh), Yes-No Question (YN), Statement Opinion (SO), Action Directive (AD), Yes Answers (YA), Thanking (T), Appreciation (AP), Response Acknowledgement (RA), Apology (A) and others (O). A corpus containing 7K utterances was collected from Facebook and Quora pages, and annotated manually. Motivated by the work by [Li et al.2014], we used this corpus to develop an SVM-based speech act classifier using the following features: bag-of-words (top 20% bigrams), presence of "wh" words, presence of question marks, occurrence of "thanks/thanking" words, POS tags distributions, and sentiment lexica such as NRC Linguistic Database (mohammad2013nrc), SentiWordNet [Baccianella et al.2010], and WordNet Affect [Strapparava and Valitutti2004]. The categorical corpus distribution and the performance of the final classifier are reported in Table 2, showing an average F_1-score of 0.69 after 10-fold cross validation.

Automatic speech act classification of social media conversations is a separate research problem altogether, and hence out of scope of the current study. However, although the speech act clas-

sifier was not highly accurate in itself, the user specific speech act distributions could be used as features for the psycholinguistic classifiers (resulting in 11 additional features). Experiment on the Twitter Corpus, a noticable performance improvement of 6.12% (F-measure) was obtained.

5 Indian Values Map

Table 3 shows the percentage of the total population of the concerned cities which are inclined to the listed super classes. The percentages were further normalized (with an ε parameter) using the formula-

$$x_{norm} = \frac{x - x_{min} + \varepsilon}{x_{max} - x_{min} + \varepsilon} \times 100 \qquad (1)$$

We observe striking similarities to intuitive perception, i.e., the results obtained resemble our general perception about the city/town. For example, consider the class SC1 referring to Self-Enhancement, the percentage score of Mumbai is the highest which is expected as Mumbai is *"The city of dreams"* for people all over the country who move in to Mumbai to fulfill their ambitions. The huge population in Mumbai leads to immense competition, therefore, it is expected that people of Mumbai are hedonic, power, and achievement oriented. Other progressive cities like Chandigarh, Lucknow and Ahemdabad follow the same trend.

The values of SC2 (openness to change) are equally high for almost all cities, this is a consequence of the fact that a major population in cities are open to changes, they are self directed since they earn their own living and they are also stimulated as they have an active professional and personal life. It is also highly possible, that, since the data has been collected from social-media, the value of SC2 is high, as social-media users belong to the literate section of the society and possess

---

	AC	BE	CO	HE	PO	SE	SD	ST	TR	UN	SC1	SC2	SC4	SC3	MinT	MaxT	UsersT	AvgT
Ahemdabad	100.0	63.12	100.0	66.18	52.9	70.4	100.0	100.0	56.16	100.0	59.74	100.0	52.39	47.41	2.0	3249.0	136.0	1922
Amritsar	58.33	61.86	100.0	29.27	64.38	20.0	100.0	100.0	5.0	100.0	71.94	100.0	10.0	46.0	2.0	3250.0	201.0	2109
Bengalaru	19.16	81.5	100.0	40.72	50.74	42.0	100.0	100.0	16.36	100.0	31.85	100.0	21.59	73.55	2.0	3250.0	206.0	1846
Chandigarh	100.0	60.57	100.0	71.45	69.13	64.4	100.0	100.0	52.99	100.0	90.17	100.0	1.01	43.78	2.0	3250.0	113.0	1864
Chennai	58.33	63.36	100.0	56.36	49.01	100.0	100.0	100.0	50.23	100.0	33.28	100.0	53.34	47.75	1.0	3248.0	200.0	1698
Delhi	60.83	44.8	100.0	0.18	52.28	43.6	100.0	100.0	47.6	100.0	10.0	100.0	50.88	21.35	2.0	3249.0	212.0	1991
Goa	100.0	85.49	100.0	100.0	40.3	12.8	5.0	100.0	11.64	100.0	56.73	100.0	43.15	43.15	4.0	3248.0	91.0	1942
Guwahati	31.66	86.63	100.0	45.27	36.54	67.2	100.0	100.0	43.23	100.0	12.36	100.0	64.14	71.04	1.0	3250.0	121.0	1656
Hyderabad	60.0	76.99	100.0	22.72	44.44	60.8	100.0	100.0	17.5	100.0	5.0	100.0	19.63	64.58	1.0	3248.0	205.0	1880
Indore	100.0	62.64	100.0	40.72	49.19	100.0	31.19	100.0	48.28	100.0	28.05	100.0	51.51	46.73	1.0	3249.0	138.0	1634
Jaipur	100.0	59.15	100.0	11.09	54.32	100.0	100.0	100.0	50.23	100.0	9.66	100.0	53.34	41.77	22.0	3247.0	68.0	2161
Kanpur	100.0	39.03	100.0	5.0	100.0	100.0	100.0	100.0	34.81	100.0	75.27	100.0	46.52	25.97	2.0	3247.0	168.0	1920
Kolkata	100.0	86.42	100.0	54.18	54.93	100.0	100.0	100.0	57.71	100.0	54.35	100.0	60.35	80.22	1.0	3250.0	470.0	1702
Lucknow	100.0	5.0	100.0	54.54	80.37	56.8	100.0	100.0	61.75	100.0	86.37	100.0	52.27	10.0	3.0	3249.0	280.0	1940
Mumbai	**100.0**	100.0	100.0	**58.0**	68.39	41.6	55.04	100.0	33.87	100.0	**100.0**	100.0	34.91	**100.0**	8.0	3248.0	205.0	2032
Pune	100.0	94.59	100.0	58.0	53.7	5.0	100.0	100.0	29.36	100.0	70.68	100.0	27.71	92.56	2.0	3248.0	206.0	1915
Ranchi	5.0	58.61	100.0	33.09	48.58	52.0	100.0	100.0	34.81	100.0	19.8	100.0	38.88	41.0	4.0	3250.0	83.0	1710
Srinagar	37.5	44.47	100.0	25.45	70.8	70.0	100.0	100.0	58.24	100.0	58.32	100.0	60.85	20.88	2.0	3246.0	136.0	1715
Varanasi	100.0	48.91	100.0	71.63	54.25	100.0	100.0	100.0	100.0	100.0	78.28	**100.0**	100.0	27.21	2.0	3250.0	152.0	1557
Vizag	100.0	93.81	100.0	40.18	5.0	100.0	100.0	100.0	37.37	100.0	8.55	100.0	53.52	81.5	4.0	3247.0	68.0	1964

Table 3: City-Wise Indian Values

	AC	BE	CO	HE	PO	SE	SD	ST	TR	UN	SC1	SC2	SC4	SC3	MinT	MaxT	UsersT	AvgT
North India	37.83	15.0	100.0	15.0	100.0	45.53	100.0	100.0	100.0	100.0	100.0	100.0	100.0	33.0	2.0	3250.0	1466.0	1911
South India	15.0	91.36	100.0	22.58	15.0	93.75	100.0	100.0	15.0	100.0	33.0	100.0	10.0	89.96	1.0	3250.0	679.0	1824
East India	18.91	98.7	100.0	55.48	45.92	100.0	100.0	100.0	70.15	100.0	63.5	100.0	66.0	97.19	1.0	3250.0	674.0	1694
West/Central India	**100.0**	100.0	100.0	100.0	57.97	15.0	15.0	100.0	29.09	100.0	87.22	33.0	12.55	100.0	1.0	3249.0	640.0	1896

Table 4: Region-Wise Indian Values

a good educational background. As there is no differentiation of SC2 values we are not reporting the values of SC2 in Indian Values Map. In SC3, which refers to Self-Transcendence, Mumbai again scores the highest, with inhabitants from all over the country, Mumbaikars, are prone to be universal, since they accept people from all backgrounds. They also tend to be more benevolent and warm hearted, this trend can be observed in all other rapidly developing cities like Bangalore, Kolkata, Vizag, Indore etc. In the case of SC4, which refers to conservation, the temple town, Varanasi tops among others. This result can be easily anticipated since the Varanasi is high on tradition, individuals conform to rules in fear of god and yearn for a secure living. It can also be observed that rapidly-developing cities like Chandigarh, Bangalore, Hyderabad, Pune, Amritsar have low values, indicating the diminishing tradition and conformity to ancient rules and regulations in these cities. The trends have been visually demonstrated in Figure 4, indicating the location of each city and the respective percentage of population possessing the class of values as defined by the 4 super-groups.

For analysis of results at regional level, India can be broadly classified into four regions namely, North, South, East and West India. The region-wise results are aggregated and reported in the Table 4.

The results obtained at regional level are also close to general intuition about these regions which will be clear from the derived implications discussed next. One of the major implications is that West India tops in terms of achievement (AC) oriented and hedonistic (HE) people. In general, North Indians are among the most power (PO) oriented people. For example, majority of politicians and administrative officers are from North India as compared to other parts of India. In terms of traditional people, North India comes at top. This result can be attributed to the fact that the analysis of North India is based on more traditional cities like Srinagar, Kanpur, Lucknow and Varanasi. These trends are clearly reflected in Table 3 & 4.

6 Discussion and Conclusion

In this paper, we propose a computational Schwartz values model and applying to various Indian users and finally created a Indian values map.

As can be seen from the result that a few Schwartz values such as Self-Direction and Security are relatively difficult to identify, while on the other hand the accuracies for certain value types such as Power and Tradition are persistent and seem to be more salient. The results also indicate that social media text is difficult for automatic classification, which is obvious from its terse nature. A major limitation is that the collected social network corpus is skewed, therefore the results do not have much deviations from the majority baselines. Since the classes are imbalanced, the system is always statistically biased towards the major class. The expected solution is having more data, and we are collecting more data, aiming to reach data from 10,000 users. The collected data will be publicly released to the research community.

For the machine learners, closer analysis revealed that SMOs performance was irregular and random, which might be an indication of overfitting. On the other hand, the performance of the Random Forests classifier increased when the number of features was increased, resulting in a larger forest and hence for most value types Random Forests performed better than the other two classifiers with less over-fitting.

We are also very keen on the applied side of this kind of models. Presently we are analysing the community detection problem in social media in relation to values. Another interesting application could be comparative societal analysis between the Eastern and Western regions of the world. Relations among personality and ethics could also be explored.

References

[Agle and Caldwell1999] Bradley R. Agle and Craig B. Caldwell. 1999. Understanding research on values in business a level of analysis framework. *Business & Society*, 38(3):326–387.

[Argandoña2003] Antonio Argandoña. 2003. Fostering values in organizations. *Journal of Business Ethics*, 45(1–2):15–28.

[Baccianella et al.2010] Stefano Baccianella, Andrea Esuli, and Fabrizio Sebastiani. 2010. SentiWordNet 3.0: An enhanced lexical resource for sentiment analysis and opinion mining. In Nicoletta Calzolari, Khalid Choukri, Bente Maegaard, Joseph Mariani, Jan Odijk, Stelios Piperidis, Mike Rosner, and Daniel Tapias, editors, *Proceedings of the Seventh International Conference on Language Resources and Evaluation (LREC'10)*, Valletta, Malta, May. European Language Resources Association (ELRA).

[Bienaymé1853] Irénée Jules Bienaymé. 1853. Considérations à l'appui de la découverte de Laplace sur la loi de probabilité dans la méthode des moindres carrés. *Comptes Rendus de l'Académie des Sciences Paris*, 37:309–324.

[Clawson and Vinson1978] C. Joseph Clawson and Donald E. Vinson. 1978. Human values: A historical and interdisciplinary analysis. *Advances in Consumer Research*, 5(1).

[Gimpel et al.2011] Kevin Gimpel, Nathan Schneider, Brendan O'Connor, Dipanjan Das, Daniel Mills, Jacob Eisenstein, Michael Heilman, Dani Yogatama, Jeffrey Flanigan, and Noah A. Smith. 2011. Part-of-speech tagging for twitter: Annotation, features, and experiments. In *Proceedings of the 49th Annual Meeting of the Association for Computational Linguistics: Human Language Technologies: short papers-Volume 2*, pages 42–47. Association for Computational Linguistics.

[Henrique2015] Jefferson Henrique. 2015. https://github.com/jefferson-henrique/getoldtweets-java.

[Hofstede et al.2010] Geert Hofstede, Gert Jan Hofstede, and Michael Minkov. 2010. *Cultures and Organizations: Software of the Mind*. McGraw-Hill Education, 3 edition.

[Hood2003] Jacqueline N Hood. 2003. The relationship of leadership style and CEO values to ethical practices in organizations. *Journal of Business Ethics*, 43(4):263–273.

[John and Srivastava1999] Oliver P. John and Sanjay Srivastava. 1999. The big five trait taxonomy: History, measurement, and theoretical perspectives. volume 2, pages 102–138. Guilford, New York, NY.

[Kahle et al.1986] Lynn R. Kahle, Sharon E. Beatty, and Pamela Homer. 1986. Alternative measurement approaches to consumer values: The list of values (lov) and values and life style (vals). *Journal of Consumer Research*, pages 405–409.

[Li et al.2014] Jiwei Li, Alan Ritter, Claire Cardie, and Eduard Hovy. 2014. Major life event extraction from twitter based on congratulations/condolences speech acts. In *Proceedings of the 2014 Conference on Empirical Methods in Natural Language Processing (EMNLP)*, pages 1997–2007, Doha, Qatar, October. Association for Computational Linguistics.

[McCallum2002] Andrew Kachites McCallum. 2002. Mallet: A machine learning for language toolkit.

[Pennebaker et al.2001] James W. Pennebaker, Martha E. Francis, and Roger J. Booth. 2001. Linguistic inquiry and word count: LIWC 2001. *Mahway: Lawrence Erlbaum Associates*, 71:2001.

[Porter1980] M.F. Porter. 1980. An algorithm for suffix stripping. *Program*, 14(3):130–137.

[Rokeach1973] Milton Rokeach. 1973. *The nature of human values*. Free Press, New York, NY.

[Schwartz et al.2001] Shalom H. Schwartz, Gila Melech, Arielle Lehmann, Steven Burgess, Mari Harris, and Vicki Owens. 2001. Extending the cross-cultural validity of the theory of basic human values with a different method of measurement. *Journal of Cross-Cultural Psychology*, 32(5):519–542.

[Schwartz2012] Shalom H Schwartz. 2012. An overview of the Schwartz theory of basic values. *Online Readings in Psychology and Culture*, 2(1):11.

[Stone et al.1966] Philip J. Stone, Dexter C. Dunphy, and Marshall S. Smith. 1966. *The General Inquirer: A Computer Approach to Content Analysis*. MIT press.

[Strapparava and Valitutti2004] Carlo Strapparava and Alessandro Valitutti. 2004. WordNet Affect: an affective extension of WordNet. In *Proceedings of the Fourth International Conference on Language Resources and Evaluation (LREC-2004)*, Lisbon, Portugal. European Language Resources Association (ELRA).

[Tchébichef1867] Pafnuty Lvovich Tchébichef. 1867. Des valeurs moyennes (translated into French by N.V. Khanykov). *Journal de Mathématiques Pures et Appliquées*, 12(2):177–184.

[Wilson1988] Michael Wilson. 1988. MRC psycholinguistic database: Machine-usable dictionary, version 2.00. *Behavior Research Methods, Instruments, & Computers*, 20(1):6–10.

[Witten and Frank2005] Ian H. Witten and Eibe Frank. 2005. *Data Mining: Practical machine learning tools and techniques*. Morgan Kaufmann.

[Yamamoto2014] Yusuke Yamamoto. 2014. Twitter4j-a java library for the twitter api.

Keynote Lecture-2

Neural Models of Text Normalization for Speech Applications

Richard Sproat
Google, New York
Joint work with Navdeep Jaitly, Kyle Gorman and Ke Wu

In this talk, I will present our recent research on applying attention-based RNN's to the problem of text normalization for speech applications, in particular text-to-speech. In this task, we want to transform an input text, e.g. "A baby giraffe is 6ft tall and weighs 150lb", into a sequence of words that represents how that text would be read, e.g. "a baby giraffe is six feet tall and weighs one hundred fifty pounds". The state of the art for the complete text normalization problem to date still uses the 20-year-old technology of rule-based weighted finite-state transducers.

We show that RNNs provide an attractive data-driven approach, but that there are issues with it producing the occasional unacceptable error, such as reading "£" as "euro". We propose some possible solutions to those errors, and discuss future directions for this research.

D S Sharma, R Sangal and A K Singh. Proc. of the 13th Intl. Conference on Natural Language Processing, page 177,
Varanasi, India. December 2016. ©2016 NLP Association of India (NLPAI)

Wisdom of Students: A Consistent Automatic Short Answer Grading Technique

Shourya Roy[†] **Sandipan Dandapat**[‡] **Ajay Nagesh**[*] **Y. Narahari**[§]

[†]Xerox Research Centre India, Bangalore,
[‡]Microsoft India, Hyderabad,
[*]University of Massachusetts, Amherst,
[§]Indian Institute of Science, Bangalore

shourya.roy@xerox.com, sadandap@microsoft.com, ajaynagesh@gmail.com, hari@csa.iisc.ernet.in

Abstract

Automatic short answer grading (ASAG) techniques are designed to automatically assess *short* answers written in natural language having a length of a few words to a few sentences. In this paper, we report an intriguing finding that the set of short answers to a question, collectively, share significant lexical commonalities. Based on this finding, we propose an unsupervised ASAG technique that only requires sequential pattern mining in the first step and an intuitive scoring process in the second step. We demonstrate, using multiple datasets, that the proposed technique effectively exploits *wisdom of students* to deliver comparable or better performance than prior ASAG techniques as well as distributional semantics-based approaches that require heavy training with a large corpus. Moreover, by virtue of being independent of instructor provided model answers, our technique offers *consistency* by overcoming the limitation of undesired variability in performance exhibited by existing unsupervised techniques.

1 Introduction

Automatic grading systems have been in practice in the educational domain for many years now, but primarily for *recognition* questions where students have to choose the correct answer from given options such as multiple choice questions (MCQs). Prior research has shown that such recognition questions are deficient as they do not capture multiple aspects of acquired knowledge such as reasoning and self-explanation (Wang et al., 2008). In contrast, *recall* questions that seek students' constructed answers in natural language have been found to be more effective in assessing their ac-

quired knowledge. However, automating assessment of such answers is non-trivial owing to linguistic variations (a given answer could be articulated in different ways); subjective nature of assessment (multiple possible correct answers or no correct answer); lack of consistency in human rating (non-binary scoring on an ordinal scale within a range); etc. Consequently, this has remained a repetitive and tedious job for teaching instructors and is often seen as an overhead and non-rewarding. This paper is about a computational technique for automatically grading constructed student answers in natural language. In particular, we are interested in *short answers*: a few words to a few sentences long (everything in between fill-in-the-gap and essay type answers (Burrows et al., 2015)) and refer to the task as *Automatic Short Answer Grading* (ASAG). An example ASAG task is shown in Table 1.

Question	How are overloaded functions differentiated by the compiler?
Model Ans	Based on the function signature. When an overloaded function is called, the compiler will find the function whose signature is closest to the given function call.
Stud#1	It looks at the number, types, and order of arguments in the function call
Stud#2	By the number, and the types and order of the parameters.

Table 1: Example of question, model answer, and student answers from an undergraduate computer science course (Mohler and Mihalcea, 2009). These will be used as the running example through out the paper.

A large fraction of prior work in ASAG systems mostly comprises techniques that require extensive intervention from instructors (Roy et al., 2015; Burrows et al., 2015). In one group of such works, the instructors are expected to list key concepts (and their possible variations) to look for in student responses and grade them using *concept mapping* (Burstein et al., 1999; Leacock and Chodorow, 2003) and *information extraction*-based techniques (Bachman et al., 2002; Mitchell et al., 2002). These techniques are tedious and

D S Sharma, R Sangal and A K Singh. Proc. of the 13th Intl. Conference on Natural Language Processing, pages 178–187,
Varanasi, India. December 2016. ©2016 NLP Association of India (NLPAI)

unlikely to generalize and moreover tend to lead to a large number of false negatives owing to unspecified linguistic variations. The other group of techniques requires instructors to grade a fraction of student answers (typically ranging from half to three-quarter) to train *supervised learning algorithms* (Sukkarieh et al., 2011; Madnani et al., 2013) as training data for building classification or regression models. Unlike many applications where generation of labelled data is a one-time exercise, ASAG does not fit into *train-once-and-apply-forever* model. Every ASAG task is unique and would require ongoing instructor involvement to create labelled data. Requirement of such ongoing involvement of instructors limits the benefits of automation in practical and real-life applications.

The other broad group of work (*corpus-based* and *document similarity*-based techniques) uses various document similarity measures to grade student answers. These techniques largely reduce the need for human involvement. They do not require instructors to list all possible variations of model answers; rather rely on the measures to assess similarity between student and model answers. Unlike supervised techniques there is no ongoing instructor involvement as providing model answer is a one time task that does not depend on size of the student population. However, these techniques suffer from multiple other shortcomings. First, there is no standardization around how model answers are written across datasets or even within a dataset. The model answer in Table 1 is more detailed and self-contained than the model answer `` `Abstraction and reusability` `` for another question `` `What are the main advantages associated with object-oriented programming?` `` from the same dataset. This immediately hints at the fact that the same measure is unlikely to work for both questions. Second, variations in model answers can affect the performance of ASAG technique significantly. Using another valid model answer for the question in Table 1 `` `The compiler selects a proper function to execute based on number, types and order of arguments in the function call.` ``, causes correlation of ASAG scores with human scores vary significantly.[1] Finally, many similarity-based ASAG techniques require access to rich knowledge-bases which may not be available for all languages and all subject matters thereby limiting their applicability.

In this paper, we first report an intriguing finding that short answers to a question contain significant lexical overlap among them and such overlapping text are typically related to the correct answer to the question. We convert this finding into a technique assuming (and validating for datasets used) that such commonalities are characteristics of correct answers as typically there are fewer ways of expressing correct answers than incorrect ones.[2]

The proposed technique can be implemented in two steps. In the first step, we pose a variant of sequential pattern mining problem (Agrawal and Srikant, 1995) to identify sequential word patterns that are more common (than the rest of the patterns) among student answers. In the second step, based on our intuition driven hypothesis, that presence of such common patterns is indicative of correct answers, we deduce the scores using an intuitive scoring method (assigning weights to patterns by their length along with frequencies). The approach is truly unsupervised as it does not require human supervision in terms of pre-graded answers or manually crafted key concepts. Unlike similarity-based techniques, it does not suffer from non-standardization of model answers. Other than minimal pre-processing, we do not perform any feature engineering which is typical of ASAG solutions and thus our approach generalizes better. In the sequel, we use the words *approach*, *method* and *technique* synonymously.

Our contributions: The contributions and novelty of this work are summarized below.

- We report a novel and potentially surprising finding regarding the extent of lexical overlap between students' short answers to a question. Exploiting the finding, we propose a new ASAG technique which is completely unsupervised, consistent, and generalizable (§ 3).

---

[1] We will see evidence of such variations in Section 4.3.

[2] Before describing the technique, we acknowledge that this assumption may not be true for all questions. For example, occasionally instructors design difficult and tricky questions which mislead students to incorrect answers. Nonetheless, we empirically demonstrate that the proposed technique is comparable to existing document similarity based ASAG techniques on standard datasets and thereby providing a truly unsupervised strong baseline at the least. We provide additional discussion as future work in Section 5 towards leveraging the proposed technique for designing more practical ASAG techniques.

- We demonstrate with quantitative results on multiple datasets that the proposed technique delivers comparable or better performance than similarity-based ASAG techniques on various dimensions. In particular, it offers *consistency* by overcoming the limitation of performance variability exhibited by similarity-based techniques caused by switches to equivalent model answers(§ 4.2).
- We provide detailed qualitative analysis with examples from our datasets to portray how the proposed technique would work even under different scenarios such as when most student answers are not perfect or when there are multiple model answers (§ 4.4).
- We create and offer a new dataset on high-school English reading comprehension task in a Central Board of Secondary Education (CBSE) school in India. The dataset contains 14 questions answered by 58 students. The answers were graded by two human raters based on model answers and an optional scoring scheme (§ 4.1).

2 Prior Art

Two recently written survey papers by Roy et. al (2015) and Burrows et. al. (2015) provide comprehensive views of research in ASAG. Both of them have grouped prior research based on the types of approaches used as well as extent of human supervision needed. In this section, we review similarity-based ASAG techniques (e.g. lexical, knowledge-based, vector space etc.).

Similarity based ASAG techniques are premised on measuring similarity between model and student answers. Higher the similarity, higher the score a student answer receives and vice versa. Various types of similarity measures have been used in prior art of ASAG. Among the **lexical** measures, Evaluating Responses with BLEU (ERB) due to Pérez et al. (2004) is one of the earliest work. It adapted the most popular evaluation measure for machine translation, BLEU (Papineni et al., 2001) for ASAG with a set of Natural Language Processing (NLP) techniques such as stemming, closed-class word removal, etc. This work initially appeared as a part of an ASAG system, *Atenea* (Alfonseca and Pérez, 2004) and later as *Willow* (Pérez-Marín and Pascual-Nieto, 2011). Mohler and Mihalcea (2009) conducted a comparative study of different

semantic similarity measures for ASAG including **knowledge-based** measures using Wordnet as well as **vector space-based** measures such as Latent Semantic Analysis (LSA) (Landauer et al., 1998) and Explicit Semantic Analysis (ESA) (Gabrilovich and Markovitch, 2006). LSA has remained as a popular approach for ASAG and been applied in many variations (Graesser et al., 2000; Wiemer-Hastings and Zipitria, 2001; Kanejiya et al., 2003; Klein et al., 2011). Lexical and semantic measures have been combined to validate natural complementarity of syntax and semantics for ASAG tasks (Pérez et al., 2005). Combination of different string matching and overlap techniques were studied by Gütl on a small scale dataset (2008). Gomaa and Fahmy compared several lexical and corpus-based similarity algorithms (13 string-based and 4 corpus) and their combinations for grading answers in 0-5 scale (2012). Irrespective of the underlying similarity measure used, these techniques rely solely on the instructor provided model answer for scoring student answers. This central reliance on model answer leads to significant variation in performances even when the model answer is replaced by another equivalent model answer. Dzikovska et al. conducted a 5-way (non-ordinal scale) Student Response Analysis challenge as a part of SemEval-2013 (2013). However, the task had more emphasis on giving feedback on student answers possibly using textual entailment techniques.

3 Proposed Approach

In this section, we provide intuition and details of our proposed approach.

3.1 The Intuition: Wisdom of Students

In similarity-based ASAG techniques, every student answer is compared against the model answer **independently** to arrive at a score indicating the goodness of the student answer. These methods ignore the fact that student answers to a question, as a collection, is expected to share more lexical **commonalities** than any arbitrary collection of text snippets. While the extent of commonality varies, we observe such commonalities for almost all questions in the datasets we dealt with. An example is shown in "Sample Answers" to our running example question in Table 2.

We also empirically note that the correct student answers are expected to contain *more* of these commonalities than incorrect ones. For our running example, words such as *argument, number, order, execute, type* are among the most frequent ones and are related to the correct answer to the question ("Sample Patterns" in Table 2). If we can identify these commonalities from student answers, then we wondered, can the same be used to score them as well? We hypothesize that the correct student answers are expected to contain *more* of these commonalities than incorrect ones and propose an intuitive scoring technique based on such commonalities.

Sample Answers	The number and type of its parameters.
	The compiler selects the proper functions to execute based on number, types and order of arguments in the function call.
	It selects the proper function to execute based on number, types and order of arguments in the function call.
	The compiler selects proper function to execute based on number, types and order of arguments in the function call.
	Is based on number, types, and order of arguments in the function call.
	Compiler selects proper function to execute based on number, types and order of arguments in the function call.
Sample Patterns	(number, type, order, argument, call)
	(select, proper, execut, base, number)
	(base, number, type, order)
	(execut, base, number, type)
	(proper, execut, base)

Table 2: Illustration: A few student answers and a selection of sequential patterns of stemmed words identified for the question and model answer shown in Table 1.

3.2 Proposed Technique

We model the task of finding commonalities from student answers in a manner similar to the *sequential pattern mining* problem (Agrawal and Srikant, 1995). Sequential patterns in the context of text has been used to capture non-contiguous sequence of words for classification and clustering (Jaillet et al., 2006). Prior work has reported that for such tasks sequential patterns have more reliable statistical properties than commonly used lexical features e.g. n-grams in NLP domain (Sebastiani, 2002). For short answers too, our observation was that sequential patterns are more statistically significant and less noisy than n-grams.

The following two steps, namely, *mining sequential patterns* and *scoring answers* are repeated for all questions by making two passes over all students answers.

Step 1: Mining Sequential Patterns

The objective of this step is to extract commonly occurring patterns and quantify the notion of commonalities using *support*:

1. A student answer (s_i) is converted to a sequence of words $(w_1^i, w_2^i, \ldots, w_n^i)$ by removing stopwords and stemming content words to their respective base forms. We optionally remove words which appear in the corresponding question to avoid giving importance to *parrot answering*.

2. A sequential pattern (SP), p of length l, is a sequence of l tokens from s_i i.e. $p = w_{i_1}, w_{i_2}, \ldots, w_{i_l}$ such that $i_1 < i_2 < \ldots < i_l$.

3. Support of p is defined as $sup(p) = |\{s_i : p \in s_i\}|$ i.e. the number of student answers containing p. Connecting to our intuition, patterns with high support are commonalities among answers we are looking for. Lower part of Table 2 shows some of the common patterns obtained from all student answers for the question in Table 1.

4. While $sup(p)$ captures importance of a pattern, they ignore *lexical diversity* (Johansson, 2009) of student answers across questions. Consider two sequential patterns p_1 and p_2 with equal support t for two different questions q_1 and q_2. If we consider only support values then both p_1 and p_2 will contribute equally to score student answers. However, if student answers to q_1 are more *diverse* than q_2, then the fact that p_1 has a support of t is more significant than p_2 having the same support t. We quantify this factor by extending the well known measure *type-token ratio* (TTR) (Lieven, 1978) for lexical diversity. TTR values are in range [0,1] and higher values indicate higher diversity.

$$TTR(d) = \frac{\#\text{distinct patterns of length } d}{\#\text{patterns of length } d}$$

Step 2: Scoring Answers

In this step, we make a second pass over all answers and use the statistics gathered in the previous step to score them:

1. Again a student answer (s_i) is represented as a sequence of words $(w_1^i, w_2^i, \ldots, w_n^i)$ by doing the same pre-processing.

2. Building on our intuition, score of s_i is a function of support of all patterns $p \in s_i$. We realize that longer patterns will have (much) less support but their presence are stronger indications than presence of shorter patterns. Hence score of s_i ($Sc(s_i)$) should be a function of support of all patterns p in s_i weighed by respective pattern length. We tried different weighing schemes and found *exponential* weighing ($sup(p)^{len(p)}$) to work the best with respect to correlation with human scores. This indeed matches with our intuition that longer patterns are significantly more important than shorter ones.

3. Subsequently, we use lexical diversity values to bring down contribution of a pattern p if there is less diversity among student answers by modifying $Sc(s_i)$ as below :

$$Sc(s_i) = \sum_{p \in s_i} sup(p)^{len(p)} \times TTR(len(p))$$

4. $Sc(s_i)$ values are normalized using min-max normalization and scaled by maximum obtainable marks in a question.

3.3 Discussion on the Proposed Technique

Step-1 of the proposed technique is similar to the classical sequential pattern mining algorithm but with a couple of differences. Firstly, in our context a common support threshold does not make sense as support values of patterns vary widely across questions depending on nature of answers expected as well as their difficulty levels. Secondly, typically in the literature *closed* and *maximal* frequent patterns are of interest as they subsume smaller length frequent patterns(Tan et al., 2006). However, we consider all patterns to score answers in step-2 but differentially weigh them based on their length.

The basic intuition of the proposed technique can be traced back to the concept based systems of early days of ASAG (Burstein et al., 1998; Nielsen et al., 2008) where instead of (or along with) model answers, a list of concepts were specified. ASAG systems scored student answers based on presence or absence of listed concepts or variations thereof. However, those systems needed the concepts to be specified by the instructor, whereas our endeavour is to identify the important concepts in an unsupervised manner. Recently Ramachandran et al. demonstrated effectiveness of using student answers to a question to extract patterns for ASAG (Ramachandran et al., 2015). They used a graph based approach to extract patterns from groups of questions and their answers towards constructing regular expression alike patterns. While they use a supervised approach using the extracted patterns as features, our approach is completely unsupervised - hence easier to test on new datasets and deploy in real life. Secondly, we opine that regular expression based features can be constraining towards generalization and real life usage for free text answers.

4 Experimental Results

4.1 Experimental Protocols

Datasets: The recent survey papers referred to in Section 2 noted that rarely any ASAG work reported results on multiple (standard) datasets (Burrows et al., 2015; Roy et al., 2015). They emphasized the need for sharing of datasets and structured evaluations on them. Towards that, we evaluated the proposed technique and compared against multiple similarity-based baseline techniques on three datasets:

- **CSD:** This is one of the earliest ASAG datasets consisting of 21 questions with 30 student answers evaluated each on a scale of 0-5 from an undergraduate computer science course (Mohler and Mihalcea, 2009). Student answers were independently evaluated by two annotators and automatic techniques are measured against their average.
- **X-CSD:** This is an extended version of CSD with 81 questions by the same authors (Mohler et al., 2011).
- **RCD:** We created a new dataset on a reading comprehension assignment for Standard-12 students in Central Board of Secondary Education (CBSE) in India. The dataset contains 14 questions answered by 58 students. The answers were graded by two expert human raters based on model answers, again on a scale of 0-5.

All datasets have less than (total number of questions $\times$ total number of students) answers as presumably some students did not answer some questions. We mark such missing entries as "No Answer" and corresponding groundtruth scores as zero.

Metrics: A wide variety of evaluation metrics has been used in the literature for measuring goodness of ASAG techniques. We use Pearson's r in this paper as it has been one of the most popular metrics though its appropriateness have been questioned (Mohler and Mihalcea, 2009). For every question we compute Pearson's r between groundtruth and predicted scores and average across all questions are reported.

4.2 Quantitative Results

We compare the proposed technique against word similarity based ASAG techniques briefly described in Section 2. The basic premise of word similarity based ASAG techniques is: higher the similarity between the model and a student answer, higher the score the latter receives. Given two texts, model answer M and a student answer S, we conduct standard pre-processing operations such as stopword removal and stemming. The score of S with respect to M is then defined as:

$$asym(M,S) = \frac{1}{k} \sum_{i=1}^{k} \max_{\mathbf{s}_j \in S}(sim(\mathbf{m}_i, \mathbf{s}_j)) \quad (1)$$

where $\mathbf{m}_i$ and $\mathbf{s}_j$ are pre-processed n-grams of M and S respectively and k is the number of n-grams in M. For $n = 1$, $\mathbf{m}_i$ and $\mathbf{s}_j$ are words of M and S; and k is the length of M with respect to number of words. $sim(.,.)$ is a textual similarity measure of one of the following types:

- **Lexical**: In this category, we consider lexical overlap (**LO**) between model and student answers. It is a simple baseline measure which looks for exact match for every content word (post pre-processing e.g. stopword removal and stemming).
- **Knowledge based**: These measures employ a background ontology to arrive at word level semantic similarity values based on various factors such as distance between two words, lowest common ancestor, etc. Mohler and Mihalcea (2009) compared eight different knowledge-based measures to compute similarities between words in the model and student answers using Wordnet (Miller, 1995). We select the two best performing measures from their work viz. shortest path (**SP**) and the measure proposed by Jiang and Conrath (**JCN**) (Jiang and Conrath, 1997).
- **Vector space based**: In this category, we have chosen one of the most popular measures of semantic similarity, namely, Latent Semantic Analysis (**LSA**) (Landauer et al., 1998) trained on a Wikipedia dump. We also consider the recently popular word2vec tool (**W2V**) (Mikolov et al.,) to obtain vector representation of words which are trained on 300 million words of Google news dataset and are of length 300. Both LSA and W2V build on several related ideas towards capturing importance of context to obtain vector representation of words e.g. the distributional hypothesis "Words will occur in similar contexts if and only if they have similar meanings" (Harris, 1968). Similarity between words is measured as the cosine distance between corresponding word vectors in the resultant vector space using the well known dot product formula.

4.3 Results

In this section first we present comparative performance of the proposed technique against word similarity based ASAG techniques. Secondly, we expose a vulnerability of word similarity based ASAG techniques owing to their sole reliance on instructor provided model answer and thereby bringing out another benefit of the proposed technique.

Performance with respect to instructor provided model answers: Table 3 shows comparative performances of the proposed technique against unsupervised ASAG techniques for CSD. For each question as well as aggregate across all questions, winners are emphasized. In aggregate, the proposed technique performs comparatively and better than LO and knowledge based measures (JCN and SP) but a few points worse than LSA and W2V. Secondly, it is evident that, no one technique consistently outperforms others. In fact, the proposed technique has more question wise *winners* than LO, SP, JCN, and LSA. For example, for (Q19) (which is our running example in this paper), it has much better performance than the rest supporting our argument that leveraging student answer corpus is effective. Finally, variations across questions are significant - while high correlation is achieved for Q1, Q15 etc. but they remained low for Q12 and Q16. Considering such high variations across different questions, it is unlikely that any one method would perform the best across all types of questions in a general setting.

Table 4 shows the overall performance of the

Q#	Proposed	LO	JCN	SP	LSA	W2V
1	0.56	0.79	0.84	0.81	0.78	**0.85**
2	**0.55**	0.42	0.34	0.40	0.27	0.35
3	0.32	0.33	0.27	0.46	0.51	**0.62**
4	0.75	0.81	0.81	**0.86**	0.80	0.81
5	0.69	0.68	0.68	0.83	**0.84**	0.73
6	0.67	**0.82**	0.75	0.76	0.73	0.78
7	**0.71**	0.49	0.49	0.50	0.64	0.63
8	0.68	**0.79**	0.73	0.74	0.67	**0.79**
9	**0.58**	0.55	0.57	0.54	0.43	**0.58**
10	0.67	0.73	0.67	0.50	0.66	**0.75**
11	0.54	0.43	0.49	0.61	0.52	**0.64**
12	**0.46**	0.14	0.14	-0.10	0.24	0.30
13	0.70	0.57	0.75	0.69	**0.76**	0.67
14	0.52	0.48	0.52	0.45	**0.68**	**0.68**
15	0.56	0.55	0.80	0.69	**0.95**	0.84
16	0.05	**0.30**	**0.30**	**0.30**	0.24	0.29
17	0.68	0.83	**0.84**	0.81	0.71	0.76
18	0.23	0.55	0.17	0.33	**0.61**	0.46
19	**0.51**	0.37	0.43	0.50	0.43	0.44
20	**0.69**	0.55	0.51	0.35	0.61	0.50
21	0.76	0.78	0.76	0.68	0.75	**0.80**
Agg.	0.57	0.57	0.56	0.56	0.61	**0.63**

Table 3: Question wise Pearson's r of the proposed technique against unsupervised ASAG techniques.

proposed technique against word similarity based ASAG techniques. The top row of the table shows the inter-annotator agreement (IAA) for all datasets. For CSD and XCSD, performance of the proposed technique is respectively comparable and better than IAA. For both the datasets, its performance is comparable or better than lexical and knowledge-based methods but about 0.06 worse than the vector space methods.

	CSD	XCSD	RCD
IAA	0.59	0.54	0.67
LO	0.57	0.67	**0.56**
JCN	0.56	0.65	0.55
SP	0.56	0.67	0.38
LSA	0.61	**0.73**	0.47
W2V	**0.63**	**0.73**	**0.56**
Proposed	0.57	0.67	0.41

Table 4: Comparison of Pearson's r of unsupervised ASAG techniques against the proposed technique.

Variation with changes in model answers: The word similarity based ASAG techniques suffer from a surprising shortcoming. Variation in model answers can significantly affect their performance. Consider another possible model answer of our running exam-

ple "based on number, types and and order of arguments in the function call." Replacing the instructor provided model answer with this is not expected to change human evaluation of student answers. However doing so make unsupervised ASAG techniques exhibit significant change in performance (Pearson's r for LO, JCN, SP, LSA and W2V get changed by 43%, 23%, 2%, 19% and 20% respectively). Towards systematically exploring this, for each question we select those student answers which were graded as perfect 5/5 by the instructor with respect to the model answer. We consider each of them (and the instructor provided model answer) as a model answer in turn and grade remaining student answers. Resulting variation is shown in Table 5 in terms of minimum and maximum Pearson's r obtained as well as standard deviation of r values.[3] Careful observation of Table 5 reveals that all word similarity based ASAG technique show variation in performance for almost all questions. In some cases correlation with human provided groundtruth scores goes to a low minimum (even negative) and very high maximum correlation. Standard deviation values indicate high degree of variation in Pearson's r. On the other hand, the proposed technique due to its independence with model answers, does not exhibit *any* fluctuation. It is interesting to note that for all questions the minimum correlation obtained by all word similarity based ASAG techniques is worse than corresponding correlation of the proposed technique. In fact, for multiple questions the proposed technique performs comparably to the maximum correlation obtained by the word similarity based ASAG techniques. While further studies will be required to understand the root causes of these variation, it is unlikely that any one method would work the best for all questions.

4.4 Qualitative Analysis

In this section, we provide qualitative analysis to address a few questions which an intrigued reader might have:

- **Proposed technique will work only if all/most student answers are perfect**: No - even if most student answers are imperfect

---

[3]Owing to space constraint we show numbers for one representative technique from lexical, knowledge-based and vector space categories but we note similar variations for other techniques too.

Qs.	LO			JC			W2V			Proposed
	Min	Max	SD	Min	Max	SD	Min	Max	SD	
1	0.45	0.79	0.13	0.46	0.84	0.15	0.44	0.85	0.13	0.56
2	0.42	0.75	0.14	0.28	0.75	0.19	0.35	0.80	0.19	0.55
3	0.23	0.41	0.06	0.22	0.50	0.11	0.41	0.62	0.07	0.32
4	0.39	0.97	0.16	0.39	0.97	0.16	0.40	0.99	0.17	0.75
5	0.43	0.68	0.09	0.43	0.68	0.09	0.62	0.79	0.05	0.69
6	0.58	0.82	0.08	0.53	0.75	0.07	0.67	0.81	0.05	0.67
7	0.33	0.66	0.08	0.37	0.67	0.08	0.54	0.73	0.06	0.71
8	0.30	0.79	0.16	0.34	0.74	0.13	0.20	0.79	0.20	0.68
9	0.42	0.61	0.05	0.45	0.66	0.06	0.41	0.63	0.06	0.58
10	0.62	0.73	0.04	0.51	0.67	0.06	0.62	0.81	0.07	0.67
11	0.10	0.51	0.10	0.00	0.58	0.11	0.28	0.64	0.08	0.54
12	0.01	0.59	0.18	0.06	0.63	0.19	0.23	0.69	0.15	0.46
13	0.48	0.62	0.04	0.64	0.75	0.03	0.63	0.75	0.04	0.70
14	0.48	0.57	0.04	0.52	0.52	0.00	0.54	0.68	0.07	0.52
15	0.07	0.82	0.54	0.39	0.91	0.17	0.21	0.84	0.16	0.56
16	-0.09	0.30	0.11	-0.09	0.30	0.10	-0.02	0.29	0.09	0.05
17	0.37	0.83	0.11	0.53	0.84	0.09	0.51	0.81	0.10	0.68
18	0.15	0.72	0.18	0.02	0.74	0.23	0.03	0.74	0.20	0.23
19	0.22	0.58	0.09	0.34	0.56	0.06	0.17	0.57	0.10	0.51
20	0.22	0.79	0.13	0.33	0.84	0.13	0.29	0.83	0.15	0.69
21	0.32	0.81	0.12	0.45	0.80	0.09	0.42	0.83	0.10	0.76

Table 5: Fluctuation in performance (minimum (Min), maximum (Max) and standard deviation (SD)) of ASAG techniques with different model answers. The proposed technique does not exhibit any fluctuation.

the proposed technique could work well. This is because partially correct answers contribute towards boosting up support values of common patterns. For example, only 3 out of 31 students got perfect 5/5 in (Q2) of CSD: `` What stages in the software life cycle are influenced by the testing stage?''. In spite of that proposed method has significantly better correlation than all word similarity based ASAG techniques. It is obvious that the proposed technique would perform the best when all answers are correct in the same manner and worst if in an unlikely case all are wrong in the same manner.

- **This will not work if there are multiple correct answers**: As long as a large enough fraction of students have written a correct answer, the proposed technique would work. Among various types, example seeking questions would fall in this category. Consider Q4 of RCD: ``Give two examples of people who are most vulnerable to RSI.'' where proposed method (0.40) has a better correlation than W2V (0.26) and JC (0.33). In fact, similarity-based techniques would not work well, if correct examples are not semantically similar.

- **Instructors won't have any control on as-sessment**: True - while we do not see this as a major drawback, we are working on an extension which will offer teachers more control.

5 Conclusion and Future Work

In this paper, we present a novel and intuitive finding in ASAG and propose a truly unsupervised and simple technique. The proposed method intelligently exploits structure of the ASAG problem to offer comparable performance to knowledge-based measures which depend on human curated Wordnet built over years and vector space-based measures which are trained on an astronomically large corpora. While the proposed technique is based on the assumption of *wisdom of students*, we intend to work on validating its correctness in broader settings including non-English and Science subjects. We believe that the proposed technique would, at the least, serve as a strong baseline for future ASAG research. Noting the wide variation in performance of different measures across questions, we are working towards exploring to bring together the proposed technique with word similarity based techniques. Finally, we see ASAG as an important line of research with the growing popularity of Massive Online Open Courses (MOOCs) and their limited assessment capability based solely on recognition questions.

References

Rakesh Agrawal and Ramakrishnan Srikant. 1995. Mining Sequential Patterns. In *Proceedings of the Eleventh International Conference on Data Engineering*, pages 3–14.

Enrique Alfonseca and Diana Pérez. 2004. Automatic Assessment of Open Ended Questions with a Bleu-Inspired Algorithm and Shallow NLP. In *EsTAL*, volume 3230 of *Lecture Notes in Computer Science*, pages 25–35. Springer.

Lyle F. Bachman, Nathan Carr, Greg Kamei, Mikyung Kim, Michael J. Pan, Chris Salvador, and Yasuyo Sawaki. 2002. A Reliable Approach to Automatic Assessment of Short Answer Free Responses. In *Proceedings of the International Conference on Computational Linguistics (COLING)*.

Steven Burrows, Iryna Gurevych, and Benno Stein. 2015. The Eras and Trends of Automatic Short Answer Grading. *International Journal of Artificial Intelligence in Education*, 25(1):60–117.

Jill Burstein, Karen Kukich, Susanne Wolff, Chi Lu, and Martin Chodorow. 1998. *Computer Analysis of Essays*. Educational Testing Service.

Jill Burstein, Susanne Wolff, and Chi Lu. 1999. Using lexical semantic techniques to classify free-responses. In *Breadth and depth of semantic lexicons*, pages 227–244. Springer.

Myroslava O. Dzikovska, Rodney D. Nielsen, Chris Brew, Claudia Leacock, Danilo Giampiccolo, Luisa Bentivogli, Peter Clark, Ido Dagan, and Hoa T Dang. 2013. SemEval-2013 task 7: The Joint Student Response Analysis and 8th Recognizing Textual Entailment Challenge. Technical report, DTIC Document.

Evgeniy Gabrilovich and Shaul Markovitch. 2006. Overcoming the Brittleness Bottleneck using Wikipedia: Enhancing Text Categorization with Encyclopedic Knowledge. In *AAAI*, pages 1301–1306. AAAI Press.

Wael H. Gomaa and Aly A. Fahmy. 2012. Short Answer Grading Using String Similarity and Corpus-based Similarity. *International Journal of Advanced Computer Science and Applications (IJACSA)*, 3(11).

Arthur C. Graesser, Peter M. Wiemer-Hastings, Katja Wiemer-Hastings, Derek Harter, and Natalie K. Person. 2000. Using Latent Semantic Analysis to Evaluate the Contributions of Students in AutoTutor. *Interactive Learning Environments*, 8(2):129–147.

Christian Gütl. 2008. Moving Towards a Fully Automatic Knowledge Assessment Tool. *International Journal of Emerging Technologies in Learning*, 3(1):1–11.

Zellig Harris. 1968. *Mathematical Structures of Language*. John Wiley and Son, New York.

Simon Jaillet, Anne Laurent, and Maguelonne Teisseire. 2006. Sequential Patterns for Text Categorization. *Intelligent Data Analysis*, 10(3):199–214.

Jay J. Jiang and David W. Conrath. 1997. Semantic Similarity Based on Corpus Statistics and Lexical Taxonomy. In *Proceedings of the International Conference on Research in Computational Linguistics*, pages 19–33.

Victoria Johansson. 2009. Lexical Diversity and Lexical Density in Speech and Writing: A Developmental Perspective. *Working Papers in Linguistics*, 53:61–79.

Dharmendra Kanejiya, Arun Kumar, and Surendra Prasad. 2003. Automatic Evaluation of Students' Answers using Syntactically Enhanced LSA. In *Proceedings of the HLT-NAACL workshop on Building Educational Applications using Natural Language Processing*, pages 53–60.

Richard Klein, Angelo Kyrilov, and Mayya Tokman. 2011. Automated assessment of short free-text responses in computer science using latent semantic analysis. In *ITiCSE*, pages 158–162. ACM.

Thomas K Landauer, Peter W. Foltz, and Darrell Laham. 1998. An Introduction to Latent Semantic Analysis. *Discourse Processes*, 25:259–284.

Claudia Leacock and Martin Chodorow. 2003. C-rater: Automated Scoring of Short-answer Questions. *Computers and the Humanities*, 37(4):389–405.

Elena VM Lieven. 1978. *Conversations Between Mothers and Young Children: Individual Differences and their Possible Implication for the Study of Language Learning*.

Nitin Madnani, Jill Burstein, John Sabatini, and Tenaha O'Reilly. 2013. Automated Scoring of a Summary Writing Task Designed to Measure Reading Comprehension. In *Proceedings of the 8th workshop on innovative use of nlp for building educational applications*, pages 163–168.

Tomas Mikolov, Kai Chen, Greg Corrado, and Jeffrey Dean. Efficient Estimation of Word Representations in Vector Space. *arXiv preprint arXiv:1301.3781*.

George A. Miller. 1995. WordNet: A Lexical Database for English. *Communications of the ACM*, 38(11):39–41.

Tom Mitchell, Terry Russell, Peter Broomhead, and Nicola Aldridge. 2002. Towards Robust Computerized Marking of Free-Text Responses. In *Proceedings of International Computer Aided Assessment Conference (CAA)*.

Michael Mohler and Rada Mihalcea. 2009. Text-to-text semantic similarity for automatic short answer grading. In *Proceedings of the Conference of the European Chapter of the Association for Computational Linguistics (EACL)*, pages 567–575.

Michael Mohler, Razvan C. Bunescu, and Rada Mihalcea. 2011. Learning to Grade Short Answer Questions using Semantic Similarity Measures and Dependency Graph Alignments. In *Proceedings of the Conference of the Association for Computational Linguistics (ACL)*, pages 752–762.

Rodney D. Nielsen, Jason Buckingham, Gary Knoll, Ben Marsh, and Leysia Palen. 2008. A Taxonomy of Questions for Question Generation. In *Proceedings of the Workshop on the Question Generation Shared Task and Evaluation Challenge*.

Kishore Papineni, Salim Roukos, Todd Ward, and Wei-Jing Zhu. 2001. BLEU: a Method for Automatic Evaluation of Machine Translation. Technical report, IBM Research Report.

Diana Pérez, Enrique Alfonseca, and Pilar Rodríguez. 2004. Application of the BLEU Method for Evaluating Free-text Answers in an E-learning Environment. In *LREC*. European Language Resources Association.

Diana Pérez, Alfio Gliozzo, Carlo Strapparava, Enrique Alfonseca, Pilar Rodriguez, and Bernardo Magnini. 2005. Automatic Assessment of Students' Free-Text Answers Underpinned by the Combination of a BLEU-Inspired Algorithm and Latent Semantic Analysis. In *Proceedings of the International Florida Artificial Intelligence Research Society Conference (FLAIRS)*.

Diana Pérez-Marín and Ismael Pascual-Nieto. 2011. Willow: a system to automatically assess students free-text answers by using a combination of shallow NLP techniques. *International Journal of Continuing Engineering Education and Life Long Learning*, 21(2-3):155–169.

Lakshmi Ramachandran, Jian Cheng, and Peter Foltz. 2015. Identifying Patterns for Short Answer Scoring using Graph-based Lexico-semantic Text Matching. In *Proceedings of the Tenth Workshop on Innovative Use of NLP for Building Educational Applications*, pages 97–106.

Shourya Roy, Y. Narahari, and Om D. Deshmukh. 2015. A Perspective on Computer Assisted Assessment Techniques for Short Free-Text Answers. In *Proceedings of the International Conference on Computer Assisted Assessment (CAA)*, pages 96–109. Springer.

Fabrizio Sebastiani. 2002. Machine Learning in Automated Text Categorization. *ACM computing surveys (CSUR)*, 34(1):1–47.

Jana Z. Sukkarieh, Ali Mohammad-Djafari, Jean-Franc̨ois Bercher, and Pierre Bessie´re. 2011. Using a MaxEnt Classifier for the Automatic Content Scoring of Free-text Responses. In *Proceedings of the AIP Conference American Institute of Physics*, volume 1305, page 41.

Pang-Ning Tan, Michael Steinbach, Vipin Kumar, et al. 2006. *Introduction to data mining*, volume 1. Pearson Addison Wesley Boston.

Hao-Chuan Wang, Chun-Yen Chang, and Tsai-Yen Li. 2008. Assessing Creative Problem-solving with Automated Text Grading. *Computers and Education*, 51(4):1450–1466.

P. Wiemer-Hastings and I. Zipitria. 2001. Rules for Syntax, Vectors for Semantics. In *Proceedings of the 23rd Annual Conference of the Cognitive Science Society*, Mahwah, NJ. Erlbaum.

A Recurrent Neural Network Architecture for De-identifying Clinical Records

Shweta, Ankit Kumar, Asif Ekbal, Sriparna Saha, Pushpak Bhattacharyya
Indian Institute of Technology Patna
Bihar, India
{shweta.pcs14,ankit.cs13,asif,sriparna,pb}@iitp.ac.in

Abstract

Electronic Medical Records contains a rich source of information for medical finding. However, the access to the medical record is limited to only de-identified form so as to protect the confidentiality of patient. According to Health Insurance Portability and Accountability Act, there are 18 PHI categories that should be enclosed before making the EMR publicly available. With the rapid growth of EMR and a limited amount of de-identified text, the manual curation is quite unfeasible and time-consuming, which has drawn the attention of several researchers to propose automated de-identification system. In this paper, we proposed deep neural network based architecture for de-identification of 7 PHI categories with 25 associated sub-categories. We used standard benchmark dataset from i2b2-2014 de-identification challenge and performed the comparison with very strong baseline based on Conditional Random Field. We also perform the comparison with the state-of-art. Results show that our proposed system achieves significant improvement over baseline and comparable performance over state-of-art.

1 Introduction

Appreciable amount of information extracted from Electronic Medical Record (EMR) have flourished Medical Natural Language Processing in recent past. In general, the medical records are restricted according to Health Insurance Portability and Accountability Act (HIPAA)[1], 1996. Before making it publicly available, the medical records should be de-identified which refers to hiding the personal details. De-identification can be thus seen as the task of enclosing the private health information (PHI) while maintaining the exact sense of the record. According to the HIPAA standards, total of 18 PHI categories have to enclosed before making records publicly available. Taking into account, the vast size of available EMR, manual de-identification could be expensive and unfeasible. These motivate us to develop an automated de-identification system for this task.

De-identification shares the common property with the traditional named entity recognition which aims to identify the proper labeled sequence for the given input sequence. However, detection of PHI entities suffers from several challenges such as:

(1) Terminological variation and irregularities: PHI entities can occur within text in different variations, for example '3041023MARY' is the combination of two different PHI categories '3041023' which represents the MEDICALRECORD and 'MARY' which is another PHI category.

(2) Lexical variations: In EMR same entities are often written in different lexical form. For example, variation of the entities such as the '50 yo m', '50 yo M', '55 YO MALE'.

(3) Inter-PHI ambiguity: Ambiguity of PHI terms with the non-PHI terms. For e.g., 'Brown' can be identified as the PHI term 'Name (Doctor)' as well as non-PHI term.

(4) Intra-PHI ambiguity: Ambiguity of PHI terms with the other PHI terms. For e.g., '30s' can be identified as the PHI term (Age) as well as other PHI terms (Date).

Recently several shared tasks have been organized to solve the de-identification problem such as Center of Informatics for Integrating Biology (i2b2)[2].

---

[1] http://www.hhs.gov/hipaa

[2] https://www.i2b2.org/

D S Sharma, R Sangal and A K Singh. Proc. of the 13th Intl. Conference on Natural Language Processing, pages 188–197,
Varanasi, India. December 2016. ©2016 NLP Association of India (NLPAI)

The traditional de-identification system generally falls into three different categories *viz.* machine-learning-based system, rule based system and hybrid system (based on the machine learning and rule based). Rule based system depends on the patterns formed by the regular expressions and gazetteers which are developed by humans. Rule based techniques might be very successful for one domain but fail to show significant improvements when domain changes. To overcome these difficulties, supervised machine learning techniques were proposed to solve the de-identification task. The popular machine learning models were based on decision tree (Szarvas et al., 2006), support vector machine (Hara, 2006), (Guo et al., 2006), log-linear models and popular conditional random fields (Yang and Garibaldi, 2015; He et al., 2015). However, existing techniques based on machine learning suffer from the following drawbacks: (1) requirement of significant amount of labeled data, (2) involves an extensive feature engineering or rule generation step necessitating human effort. Hence, both the techniques require manual intervention for designing features and rules which are restricted to single domain and thus incur time and cost.

The introduction of deep learning technique has facilitated to learn effective features without any manual intervention i.e., there is no requirement of feature engineering. The models could learn implicitly relevant features by word in the form of vectors known as the word embedding. These embedding are jointly learned by other hyper-parameters which are initialized randomly or can be pre-trained on large unlabeled corpus. Pre-training is much beneficial in improving performance as it effectively captures the linguistic variations and patterns. Recently, there has been significant success of deep learning techniques in solving various natural language processing tasks such as text classification (Kim, 2014), language modeling (Mikolov et al., 2010), machine translation (Bahdanau et al., 2014), spoken language understanding (Mesnil et al., 2013) as well as named entity recognition (Collobert et al., 2011; Lample et al., 2016).

Motivated by the success of deep learning techniques, in this paper, we have adopted in particular Recurrent Neural Network (RNN) (Mikolov et al., 2010) architecture to capture PHI terms. RNN has shown advantages over other machine learning and rule based techniques. RNN unlike other techniques does not require features explicitly developed for the classifier learning. The virtue of system learning by itself makes the system adaptable and scalable. This work is an extension of our previous work (Shweta et al., 2016) where we identified only 7 PHI category (Patient, Doctor, Hospital, Location, Date, Age, ID) irrespective of subcategories using only i2b2-2014 training dataset. The current work provide comprehensive experimentation on i2b2-2014 challenge dataset to de-identify 7 categories and 25 subcategories. We have formulated this task as the sequence labeling problem and developed the baseline model using a supervised machine learning technique. Conditional random field (CRF) (Lafferty et al., 2001) along with a set of handcrafted features are used to build the base classifier.

In the current study, we performed comparative analysis with two different variants of RNN network model *viz* Elman-type networks (Elman, 1990; Mikolov et al., 2011) and Jordan-type networks (Jordan, 1997). A thorough comparison of these two RNN variants with strong baseline based on CRF is a part of the paper. The results obtained show the effectiveness of RNN over traditional CRF based model. We further compared our deep learning model with state-of-art results on de-identification task. We have shown that RNN achieves comparable results with the state-of-art using machine learning techniques.

2 Related Works

Since last decade, de-identification task has emerged as a fascinated research problem (Coorevits et al., 2013). Recently, various challenges have been organized for this task. Center of Informatics for Integrating Biology and the Bedside (i2b2) has organized several de-identification shared tasks. In i2b2 2006 shared task (Uzuner et al., 2007), Wellner et al.(2007) achieved the remarkable performance by adapting machine learning approach using CRF and SVM as the base classifiers with some lexical and semantic features. Szarvas et al.(2007) developed an iterative technique using machine learning based approach. They designed local features and used dictionaries for learning decision tree based classifier. Most of the submitted systems used Conditional Random Field (CRF) classifier (Wellner et al., 2007; Aramaki et al., 2006), while some systems had also used SVM (Hara, 2006). Most of the submissions focused on the machine learning techniques while some systems (Guillen, 2006) made use of rule based approaches for solving this task.

In 2014 I2b2 shared task, the task was relatively stricter than 2006 shared task. Here the challenge was to identify 8 PHI categories with the associated subcategories. Yang et al.(2015) developed best performing system. They adopted hybrid technique considering both machine learning and rule based techniques. They developed several features like linguistic, syntactic and various word surface oriented features with different regular expressions to capture PHI terms like date and ID. Dehghan et al.(2013) developed system using knowledge based and rule based approaches using CRF as classifier. Xu et al.(2010) utilized the biomedical dictionary for identifying the PHI terms. Literature survey shows that hybrid systems perform better over the rule based and machine learning based techniques.

3 De-identification of Electronic Medical Record

De-identification of EMR can be identified as a two phase task, where the first phase of the task deals with the extraction and classification of entities (PHI) from the medical records and second phase deals with the encryption of identified PHI terms. In the current study the first phase of the problem is formulated as a sequence labeling task while some of the existing systems treat this as a classification problem.

We visualize this task as the traditional named entity recognition task, where for the given word sequence W, the goal is to identify the best possible label sequence L with the maximum posterior probability represented as $P(L|W)$. In case of generative model framework, Bayes rule can be applied as

$$\hat{L} = argmax_L P(L|W)$$
$$= argmax_L P(W|L)P(L) \tag{1}$$

Thus for each W and L, joint probability $P(W|L)P(L)$ has to be maximized by the objective function of a generative model. Table-1 shows the input as word-sequence with its corresponding label sequence and the output as the de-identified sentence.

Several probabilistic models, like SVM, HMM and most popular CRF model, have been used for solving sequence labeling problem in the literature.

In this work, we have developed CRF based model as the baseline. Here, each patient note is first pre-processed which includes tokenization and feature generation for each corresponding token. During training, CRF parameter is optimized to maximize the posterior probability while during test phase, the best output label is predicted. Several systems based on CRF were introduced in i2b2-2014 challenge which performed well in de-identification task. Other discriminative models such as Support Vector Machines (SVM) (Cortes and Vapnik, 1995) are very popular where local probability functions are used. Other popular models include Hidden Markov Model (HMM) (Rabiner and Juang, 1986). However, these models require a good feature engineering which is mostly applicable for a single domain. This motivated us to use Recurrent Neural Network architecture for solving the patient de-identification task.

4 RNN Architecture for De-identification

We describe here recurrent neural network (RNN) architecture w.r.t de-identification of EMR.

4.1 Neural network based Word Representation: Word Embedding

Word embedding is real valued word representation in the form of a vector. This vector is provided as input to the RNN architecture. Word embedding thus have powerful capability to capture both semantic and syntactic variations of words (Mikolov et al., 2013). The vector initially can be generated randomly or can be pre-trained from the large unlabeled corpus in an unsupervised fashion using external resources such as Wikipedia, news article, bio-medical literature etc. Word embedding is learned through sampling word co-occurrence distribution. These techniques are useful to identify similar words which appear in close vicinity in vector space. There are several ways of generating the word-vectors using different architectures such as word2vec (Mikolov et al., 2013), shallow neural networks (Schwenk and Gauvain, 2005), RNN (Mikolov et al., 2010; Mikolov et al., 2011) etc. We learn our word embedding through three different ways such as random number initialization, RNN's word embedding and continuous bag-of-words (CBOW) based models. In case

Sentence	Discussed	this	case	with	Dr.	John	Doe	for	Mr.	Ness
Named Entity	O	O	O	O	O	B-DOCTOR	I-DOCTOR	O	O	B-PATIENT
De-identified Sentence	Discussed	this	case	with	Dr.	XYZ_DOCTOR		for	Mr.	XYZ_PATIENT

Table 1: Sample sentence (sequence of words with the corresponding labels using BIO notation) and its corresponding de-identified sentence

of random number initialization, we randomly generate vector of length 100 in the range -0.25 to $+0.25$ for each word. To exploit the significance of RNN, we have used the word embedding of dimension 80 for a word trained on Broadcast news corpus as provided by RNNLM [3]. In addition to these we have also generated 300 dimension vector for a word trained using CBOW technique (Mikolov et al., 2013) on news corpus.

4.2 Capturing Short term Dependency with Context Window

The input provided to feed forward neural network is the word embedding of a target word. However, just the target word lacks in effectively capturing the dependencies related to the target word. While, context words are very helpful in capturing short-term temporal dependencies. As such for each word, d dimensional word embedding is generated with the word-context window of size m. We generate the word vector as the ordered concatenation of $2m + 1$ word embedding vectors considering m previous words, m next words and current word as follows:

$$C_m(w_{i-m}^{i+m}) = v_{i-m}^d \oplus \ldots v_i^d \ldots \oplus v_{i+m}^d \quad (2)$$

Here, $\oplus$ is a concatenation operator where for each word w_i, the word embedding vector v_i is generated. Within the window size m, concatenation of dependent words is represented as follows:
$w_{i-m}^{i+m} = [w_{i-m} \ldots, w_i \ldots w_{i+m}]$ For the words in the beginning and end, padding is performed in order to generate m context window. Below shows an example for context window 2 generation for the target word 'Hess'

$$C(t) = [\text{for Clarence } Hess \text{ at BCH}] \quad (3)$$

$$C(t) \rightarrow x(t) = [v_{\text{for}}^d \; v_{\text{Clarence}}^d \; v_{Hess}^d \; v_{\text{at}}^d \; v_{\text{BCH}}^d]$$
Here, $C(t)$ represents context window of 2 words. v_{Hess} denotes the word embedding vector for the target word 'Hess' and the embedding vector dimension is provided by d. Similarly, for each sequence of word $w(t)$ at t time, their vector concatenation is represented by $C(t)$.

<hr>
[3] http://rnnlm.org/

4.3 Variant of RNN Model

Here we have used two different variants of RNN architecture for de-identification of patient notes. These are Elman-type RNN (Elman, 1990) and the Jordan-type RNN (Jordan, 1997). Architecture for both the models have been depicted in Figure-1. The neural network architecture is motivated from the biological neural network. The basic neural network is the feed forward neural network (NN) (Svozil et al., 1997) model. In contrast to the basic feed forward model, the connection formed in RNN is also through the previous layers. In Elman-type network, every state have the information of its previous hidden layer states through its recurrent connections. As such, the hidden layer $h(t)$ at the time instance t have the information of the previous $(t-1)^{th}$ hidden layer i.e., the output of $(t)^{th}$ hidden layer is dependent on the $(t-1)^{th}$ hidden layer $h(t-1)$ and context window $C_m(w_{t-m}^{t+m})$ as input. Below provide the mathematical expression for Elman-type network with H hidden layers

$$h^{(1)}(t) = f(\mathbf{W}^{(1)}C_m(w_{t-m}^{t+m}) + \mathbf{U}^{(1)}h^{(1)}(t-1) + \mathbf{b}) \quad (4)$$
$$h^{(H)}(t) = f(\mathbf{W}^{(H)}h^{(H-1)}(t) + \mathbf{U}^{(H)}h^{(H)}(t-1) + \mathbf{b}) \quad (5)$$

A non-linear sigmoid function as the activation unit of hidden layer has been used throughout the experiments.

$$f(x) = 1/(1 + e^{-x}) \quad (6)$$

The superscript represents the hidden layer depth and, $\mathbf{W}$ and $\mathbf{U}$ denote the weight connections from input layer to the hidden layer and hidden layer of last state to current hidden layer, respectively. Here, $\mathbf{b}$ is a bias term. The softmax function is later applied to the hidden states to generate the posterior probabilities of the classifier for different classes as given below:

$$P(y(t) = i | C_m(w_{t-m}^{t+m})) = g(\mathbf{V}h^{(H)}(t) + \mathbf{c}) \quad (7)$$

Here, $\mathbf{V}$ is weight connection from hidden to output layer, $\mathbf{c}$ is a bias term and g is the softmax function defined as follows:

$$g(z_m) = \frac{e^{z_m}}{\sum_{i=1}^{i=k} e^{z_k}} \qquad (8)$$

Jordan model is another variation of RNN architecture which is similar to the Elman model except inputs to the recurrent connections are through the output posterior probabilities:

$$h(t) = f(\mathbf{W}C_m(w_{t-m}^{t+m})+\mathbf{U}P(y(t-1))+\mathbf{b}) \quad (9)$$

where $\mathbf{W}$ and $\mathbf{U}$ denote the weight connection between input to hidden layer and output layer of previous state to current hidden layer, respectively, and $P(y(t-1))$ is the posterior probability of last word of interest. The sigmoid function described in Eq-6 is used as non-linear activation function f.

5 Dataset, Experiments and Results

In the current study, we have used the standard benchmark dataset of i2b2-2014 challenge (Stubbs et al., 2015) to evaluate our model. The challenge was part of 2014 i2b2/UTHealth shared task Track 1 (Stubbs et al., 2015). Total ten teams have participated in the shared task resulting in 25 different submissions. The i2b2-2014 dataset is the largest publicly available de-identification dataset collected from "Research Patient Data Repository of Partners Healthcare". A total of 1304 medical records of 297 patients were manually annotated which were divided into training and test set comprising of 790 and 514 records, respectively. There are $17,045$ and $11,462$ PHI instances in the training and test sets, respectively. This was manually annotated using seven types with twenty-five subcategories as: **(1)** Name (subtypes: Patient, Doctor, Username), **(2)** Profession, **(3)** Location (subtypes: Hospital, Department, Organization, Room, Street, City, State, Country, ZIP), **(4)** Age, **(5)** Date, **(6)** Contact (subtypes: Phone, Fax, Email, URL, IPAddress), **(7)** Ids (subtypes: Medical Record Number, Health Plan Number, Social Security Number, Account Number, Vehicle ID, Device ID, License Number, Biometric ID) Table-2 provides detailed distribution of PHI terms in both the sets.

5.1 Evaluation measures

For the evaluation of our model, we adopted similar evaluation metrics as used in i2b2 challenge such as recall (R), precision (P) and F-Measure

PHI category	Train	Test
NAME	2262	2883
PROFESSION	234	179
LOCATION	2767	1813
AGE	1233	764
DATE	7502	4980
CONTACT	323	218
ID	881	625

Table 2: Data set statistics: distribution of different classes in training and test sets.

(F). *recall* is defined as the ratio of total number of correctly predicted PHI terms by model with the total PHI terms available in gold data. Similarly *precision* is the ratio of correctly predicted PHI terms by model with the total number of PHI terms predicted my model. The *F-measure* is the harmonic mean of precision & recall. We have computed these values at the entity level across the full corpus. Micro-averaged F-measure is used as our primary metric. This helps in identifying how system performs compared to gold standard data. We have used the same i2b2 evaluation script to make comparative analysis with the existing systems.

5.2 Learning Methods: Fine tuning RNN hyper-parameter

We have trained our RNN model using stochastic gradient descent. RNN can be tuned with hyper-parameters such as number of hidden layers (H), context window size (m), learning rate (λ), dropout probability (p) and no of epochs. In order to fine tune our system, we have conducted experiments on development set which is 10 % of our training data. For training the RNN model, we have performed mini batch gradient descent approach considering only one sentence per mini batch, minimizing negative log-likelihood. We have initialized the embedding and weight matrices in the range of $[-1,1]$ following uniform distribution. Table-3 shows the optimized hyper-parameter values for both the RNN models.

5.3 Dropout Regularization

Over-fitting causes the degradation of system performance in RNN model. In order to prevent this, we have used recently proposed regularization technique know as dropout (Hinton et al., 2012). Dropout excludes some portion of hidden layers as well as the input vector from every

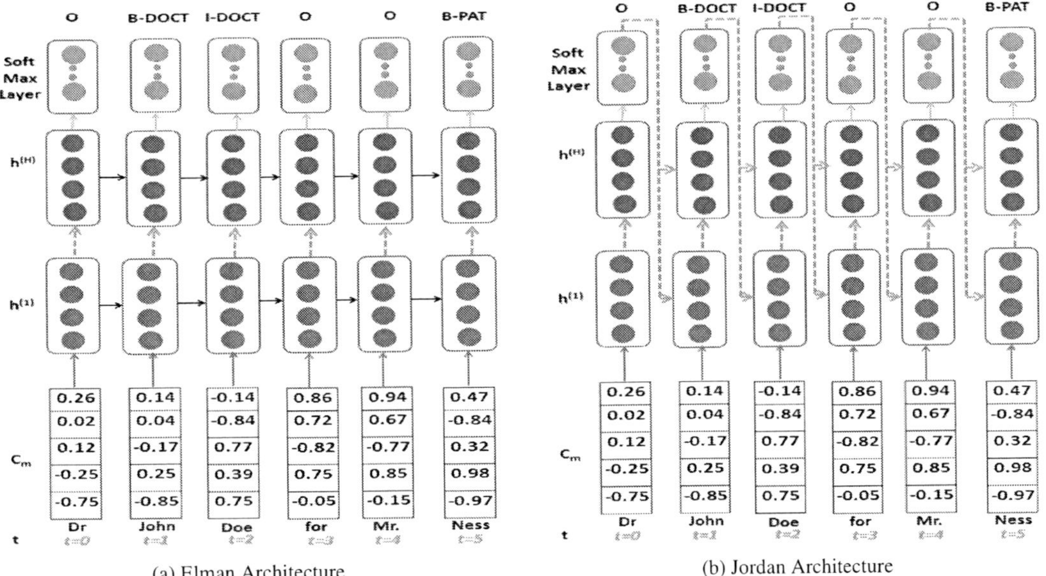

(a) Elman Architecture   (b) Jordan Architecture

Figure 1: Architecture of Recurrent Neural Network: Elman & Jordan type. In the network architecture C_m is context embedding of window size m, $h^{(1)}$ is the first hidden layer and $h^{(H)}$ is the last hidden layer in H hidden layer-sized network. In both the RNN architectures dotted arrow from $h^{(1)}$ to $h^{(H)}$ denotes the existence of multiple hidden connections between them. Similarly in Jordan network dotted arrow from softmax layer to hidden layer, represents the feeding of probability value to each hidden layer. **Note:** Here the hypothetical real value vector of size 5 is used to demonstrate the network.

Parameter's	E-RNN	J-RNN
Hidden layer size	100	150
learning rate	0.01	0.01
Dropout probability	0.5	0.5
no. of epochs	25	25
context window size	11	9

Table 3: Optimal hyper-parameter values for Elman and Jordan model

Word Embedding Techniques	dimension (d)	precision	recall	F-measure
Random Number	100	94.19	85.48	89.62
RNNLM	80	94.21	87.98	90.98
CBOW	300	97.09	90.52	93.68

Table 4: Impact of fine-tuned word embedding technique on PDI using Elman architecture. **RNNLM:** The word embedding obtained from RNN language modeling technique(Mikolov et al., 2010). **CBOW:** The continuous CBOW takes the context word as the input and tries to predict the target word.

training sample. Literature survey shows the performance improvements with the introduction of dropout. For both the RNN models, we set the value of dropout probability p as 0.5.

5.4 Results on Word Embedding Techniques

We have compared the impact of three word embedding techniques w.r.t Elman-type model as shown in Table-4. We have observed that CBOW outperform other two embedding models (RNNLM and Random Number) as it adapts distributional hypothesis while training. RNNLM obtained word vectors were very effective in capturing syntactic part because of its direct connection to the non-linear hidden layer. However, CBOW model was even better than RNNLM in identifying syntactic part and performs comparable on the semantic part.

5.5 CRF Model: Baseline

Literature survey shows that majority of the existing systems on patient de-identification learn the CRF based classifier with features such as Chunk, Part-of-Speech (POS), n-gram character etc. This motivated us to develop supervised machine learning model based on CRF classifier as our baseline. The classifier is trained with a standard set of hand-crafted features, which are chosen based

193

on the best system of i2b2 2014 challenge (Yang and Garibaldi, 2015):

1. Context word feature: Local context plays very important role in identifying the current word. We use current word and the local context spanning from the preceding three to the succeeding three words.

2. Bag-of-word feature: We generated unigrams, bi-grams and tri-grams features within window size of $[-2, 2]$ w.r.t current word.

3. Part-of-Speech (PoS) Information: POS information is very helpful in identifying the entity as most of the entities belong to noun phrases. Here, we have generated features for current word, previous two words and next two words. We have used Stanford tagger (Toutanova and Manning, 2000) to extract POS information.

4. Chunk Information: In identification of boundary of PHI-term, chunk information plays a very important role. We have used Chunk information as feature from *openNLP*[4].

5. Combined POS-token and Chunk-token Feature: We have generated the combined feature of PoS and chunk within the context window of $[-1, 1]$. This is represented as $[w_0p_{-1}, w_0p_0, w_0p_1]$ where w_0 represents the target word, and p_{-1}, p_0 and p_1 represent the previous, current and the next PoS or chunk tags, respectively.

6. Task-specific Feature: A task-specific list is generated which includes all US states names and acronyms, names of countries, names of all days in a week, month, season, US festival. Apart from this we also include lexical clues w.r.t each PHI category such as "Ms.", "Mr." for patient, "Dr.", "M.D." in case of doctor.

7. Regular Expression Patterns: Specific regular expression patterns are designed for identifying PHI related information such as date, ID, age, phone number, username, medical record.

CRF based model was developed using above-mentioned feature set. We performed experiments using the CRF implementation[5] of CRF^{++} using the default parameter. Table-5 provided the comprehensive results with the model build on CRF.

5.6 Results with Elman-RNN

We have implemented Elman RNN model as described in Subsection-4.3 to extract PHI terms from medical records. We have provided detailed

evaluation results in Table-5 describing overall F-Measure as well as F-Measure value for every PHI categories separately. Obtained results shows that E-RNN outperforms CRF based model in identifying PHI terms. We have further evaluated E-RNN on different word embedding techniques as discussed in Subsection-5.4. We have obtained an interesting observation as shown in Table 4 that CBOW based word embedding outperforms other embedding technique when provided as input to E-RNN.

5.7 Results with Jordan-RNN

We have also implemented second variant of RNN, Jordan RNN for exploiting the effectiveness in identifying PHI terms. Jordan like Elman also outperforms the strong baseline model based on CRF. We present the detailed comparative results in Table-5. Obtained results show the effectiveness of J-RNN over the other two models. J-RNN performs better than E-RNN in identifying 5 PHI categories.

5.8 De-Identification of PHI terms

The final stage after identification of PHI terms is to de-identify those terms. It is required in order to preserve the medical contents of the records for their applicability in further research. A basic template is used to convert all the identified PHI terms, e.g., *Patient, Hospital, Doctor* etc. are converted into a generic format like XYZ_Patient, XYZ_Hospital, XYZ_Doctor respectively, and all the dates into the format 00_00_Date. Similarly, we also de-identify all the PHONE numbers and IDs by representing all the identified IDs and PHONE numbers as NUM_ID and NUM_PHONE, respectively. This helps to capture the information required without compromising the personal details.

6 Error Analysis

The results presented in Table-5 show the success of RNN model over the CRF-based baseline model. Detailed investigation of the output produced by the system yields the following:

(1) RNN model significantly fails in showing sustainable results in case of *ID* which is correctly identified by the CRF-based model due to the use of well-defined regular expression patterns.

(2) Inter-PHI ambiguity: These errors occur mostly in case of *Doctor* and *Patient* categories. As the name-forms are quite similar to each other, these PHI terms are highly ambiguous. This error arises most of the times when the name consists of

---

[4]https://opennlp.apache.org/

[5]https://taku910.github.io/crfpp/

PHI Category	CRF Model			Elman			Jordan		
	P	R	F	P	R	F	P	R	F
NAME	97.82	95.01	96.39	98.92	94.94	96.88	98.95	95.29	97.08
PROFESSION	74.24	70.25	72.18	81.01	75.25	78.02	81.94	75.93	78.82
LOCATION	85.47	86.28	85.87	94.74	88.98	91.76	94.24	89.57	91.84
AGE	96.18	92.28	94.18	97.92	92.89	95.33	98.81	92.17	95.37
DATE	98.25	94.96	96.57	98.64	93.47	95.98	98.95	94.98	96.92
CONTACT	97.86	94.23	96.01	97.25	95.91	96.57	97.84	93.12	95.42
ID	98.04	98.17	98.10	97.26	94.26	95.73	97.17	94.89	96.01
Micro-averaged	**94.89**	**89.28**	**91.99**	**97.09**	**90.52**	**93.68**	**97.26**	**90.67**	**93.84**

Table 5: Performance of CRF and RNN based models for identifying PHI at entity level. CRF is the baseline model based on Conditional Random Field. Elman and Jordan are two variants of RNN model. Our system is evaluated w.r.t *recall(R), precision (P)* and *F-measure (F)*. All the values are reported in %

Systems	Features & Rules	Techniques	External Resources	F-Measure
Our model		Deep Learning: RNN	Word vectors	93.84%
Nottingham (Yang and Garibaldi, 2015)	Regular Expression template for e.g. DATE, USERNAME, IDNUM, AGE, PHONE, MEDICAL RECORD	CRF: Sentence level, contextual, orthographic, word-token	Dictionary for US states, countries, week, month	93.60%
Harbin-Grad (Liu et al., 2015)	Regular Expression for FAX, MEDICAL RECORD , EMAIL, IPADDR, PHONE	CRF: Part of Speech (PoS), bag-of-words,affixes, orthographic features, dictionary feature, section information, word shapes		91.24%
Manchester (Dehghan et al., 2015)	Orthographic, contextual, entity, pattern	CRF: semantic, lexical, positional,orthographic	Wikipedia, DEID, GATE	90.65%
Harbin (He et al., 2015)	Regular expression patterns for tokenization	CRF: lexical, syntactic, orthographic		88.52%
Kaiser (Torii et al., 2014)	Regular expression patterns for EMAIL, PHONE, ZIP	Standford NER, no feature mentioned	De-ID corpus	81.83%
Newfoundland (Chen et al., 2015)		Bayesian HMM: token, number and word token		80.55%

Table 6: Comparisons with the existing systems. The F-measure value reported is on micro-averaged entity based evaluation.

single word. For examples, "Glass", "Chabechird" etc.

(**3**) RNN models is seen to outperform CRF for detecting *PROFESSION* category. The main reason of RNN's success is due to semantic and syntactic property captured by word embedding models.

(**4**) RNN model was able to capture the variations in the wordforms, which most of the time, is predicted incorrectly by a CRF-based model such as misspelling, tokenization and short wordform. For e.g., "KELLIHER CARE CENTER", "KCC", "20880703" etc.

(**5**) RNN models are able to capture semantic variance, which CRF model is unable to capture properly. The systems learned through RNN are trained on a large unlabeled corpus which makes RNN suitable in capturing the context efficiently which would be significantly time consuming for generating the features for every possible context.

(**6**) CRF model is seen to be good at identifying the words included in the dictionary or gazetteers, for e.g., "Christmas". As "Christmas" never appears in the training set, RNN model fails to identify it. Whereas CRF identifies it properly because of its presence in the gazetteer list.

6.1 Discussion and Comparative Analysis

We have performed comprehensive study of two variants of RNN architectures, Elman and Jordan in identifying PHI terms. Both the RNN models outperform CRF based model which requires hand-crafted features. However, J-RNN was observed to be best model in identifying majority of the PHI categories. J-RNN adjusts the weights for current word considering output from both previous words and hidden layer not just from previous words unlike E-RNN. As a result of this, J-RNN was able to perform better on multi-word

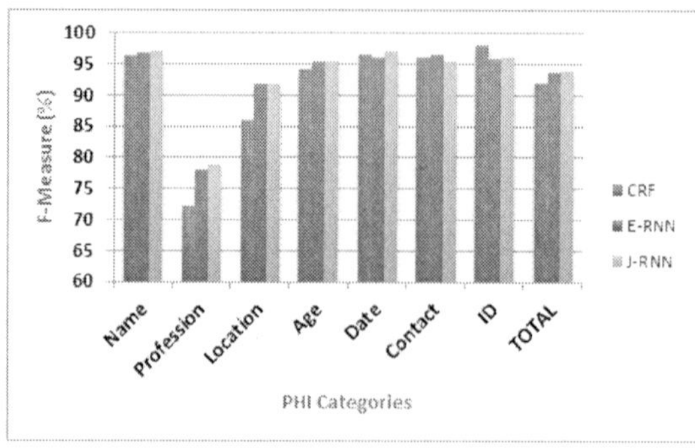

Figure 2: Comparison of CRF based model with Elman and Jordan models in term of F-Measures on 7 identified PHI categories

PHI terms[6]. We also compare with the state-of-art models as shown in Table-6. It shows that RNN model performs better compared to the machine learning based systems, including the best system of i2b2-2014 task (Yang and Garibaldi, 2015). Although the performance of our RNN based model is not tremendously high as compared to Nottingham system, it should be noted that their system was explicitly fine-tuned according to i2b2 dataset and evaluation framework. They performed post-processing on the identified PHI tokens. For e.g., changing "3041023MARY" to "304102" and "MARY", for term "MWFS" to "M", "W", "F", "S".

7 Conclusions

This paper presents the application of deep neural network architecture for solving de-identification task that is designed to identify and classify Protected Health Information (PHI) present in free-text medical records. We have systematically compared different variants of RNN architectures, including Elman, Jordan. We have also explored the effectiveness of using the word embedding for de-identification task. We observed the significant improvement of RNN type model over CRF based baseline. Experiments on the benchmark datasets over the baseline show the performance improvement of 1.69% and 1.85% with the Elman-type and Jordan-type network respectively. RNN based techniques also significantly outperforms the existing state-of-art systems. Future work will explore other effective learning methods for RNN such as Long Short term Memory (LSTM) as well

exploring some other word embedding technique. We would also like to perform experiments with word embedding trained on clinical data.

References

Eiji Aramaki, Takeshi Imai, Kengo Miyo, and Kazuhiko Ohe. 2006. Automatic deidentification by using sentence features and label consistency. In *i2b2 Workshop on Challenges in Natural Language Processing for Clinical Data*, pages 10–11.

Dzmitry Bahdanau, Kyunghyun Cho, and Yoshua Bengio. 2014. Neural machine translation by jointly learning to align and translate. *arXiv preprint arXiv:1409.0473*.

Tao Chen, Richard M Cullen, and Marshall Godwin. 2015. Hidden markov model using dirichlet process for de-identification. *Journal of Biomedical Informatics*, 58:S60–S66.

Ronan Collobert, Jason Weston, Léon Bottou, Michael Karlen, Koray Kavukcuoglu, and Pavel Kuksa. 2011. Natural language processing (almost) from scratch. *Journal of Machine Learning Research*, 12(Aug):2493–2537.

Pascal Coorevits, M Sundgren, GO Klein, A Bahr, B Claerhout, C Daniel, M Dugas, D Dupont, A Schmidt, P Singleton, et al. 2013. Electronic health records: new opportunities for clinical research. *Journal of internal medicine*, 274(6):547–560.

Corinna Cortes and Vladimir Vapnik. 1995. Support-vector networks. *Machine learning*, 20(3):273–297.

Azad Dehghan, Aleksandar Kovacevic, George Karystianis, John A Keane, and Goran Nenadic. 2015. Combining knowledge-and data-driven methods for de-identification of clinical narratives. *Journal of biomedical informatics*, 58:S53–S59.

Jeffrey L Elman. 1990. Finding structure in time. *Cognitive science*, 14(2):179–211.

R Guillen. 2006. Automated de-identification and categorization of medical records. In *i2b2 Workshop on Challenges in Natural Language Processing for Clinical Data*, volume 116.

Yikun Guo, Robert Gaizauskas, Ian Roberts, George Demetriou, and Mark Hepple. 2006. Identifying personal health information using support vector machines. In *i2b2 workshop on challenges in natural language processing for clinical data*, pages 10–11. Citeseer.

Kazuo Hara. 2006. Applying a svm based chunker and a text classifier to the deid challenge. In *i2b2 Workshop on challenges in natural language processing for clinical data*, pages 10–11. Am Med Inform Assoc.

---

[6]In multi-word NE, previous label provide effective information to predict the current word.

Bin He, Yi Guan, Jianyi Cheng, Keting Cen, and Wenlan Hua. 2015. Crfs based de-identification of medical records. *Journal of biomedical informatics*, 58:S39–S46.

Geoffrey E Hinton, Nitish Srivastava, Alex Krizhevsky, Ilya Sutskever, and Ruslan R Salakhutdinov. 2012. Improving neural networks by preventing co-adaptation of feature detectors. *arXiv preprint arXiv:1207.0580*.

Michael I Jordan. 1997. Serial order: A parallel distributed processing approach. *Advances in psychology*, 121:471–495.

Yoon Kim. 2014. Convolutional neural networks for sentence classification. *arXiv preprint arXiv:1408.5882*.

John Lafferty, Andrew McCallum, and Fernando Pereira. 2001. Conditional random fields: Probabilistic models for segmenting and labeling sequence data. In *Proceedings of the eighteenth international conference on machine learning, ICML*, volume 1, pages 282–289.

Guillaume Lample, Miguel Ballesteros, Sandeep Subramanian, Kazuya Kawakami, and Chris Dyer. 2016. Neural architectures for named entity recognition. *arXiv preprint arXiv:1603.01360*.

Zengjian Liu, Yangxin Chen, Buzhou Tang, Xiaolong Wang, Qingcai Chen, Haodi Li, Jingfeng Wang, Qiwen Deng, and Suisong Zhu. 2015. Automatic de-identification of electronic medical records using token-level and character-level conditional random fields. *Journal of Biomedical Informatics*, 58:S47–S52.

Grégoire Mesnil, Xiaodong He, Li Deng, and Yoshua Bengio. 2013. Investigation of recurrent-neural-network architectures and learning methods for spoken language understanding. In *INTERSPEECH*, pages 3771–3775.

Tomas Mikolov, Martin Karafiát, Lukas Burget, Jan Cernockỳ, and Sanjeev Khudanpur. 2010. Recurrent neural network based language model. In *Interspeech*, volume 2, page 3.

Tomáš Mikolov, Stefan Kombrink, Lukáš Burget, Jan Černockỳ, and Sanjeev Khudanpur. 2011. Extensions of recurrent neural network language model. In *2011 IEEE International Conference on Acoustics, Speech and Signal Processing (ICASSP)*, pages 5528–5531. IEEE.

Tomas Mikolov, Kai Chen, Greg Corrado, and Jeffrey Dean. 2013. Efficient estimation of word representations in vector space. *arXiv preprint arXiv:1301.3781*.

Lawrence Rabiner and B Juang. 1986. An introduction to hidden markov models. *ieee assp magazine*, 3(1):4–16.

Holger Schwenk and Jean-Luc Gauvain. 2005. Training neural network language models on very large corpora. In *Proceedings of the conference on Human Language Technology and Empirical Methods in Natural Language Processing*, pages 201–208. Association for Computational Linguistics.

Shweta, Asif Ekbal, Sriparna Saha, and Pushpak Bhattacharyya. 2016. Deep learning architecture for patient data de-identification in clinical records. In *Proceeding of Clinical Natural Language Processing Workshop (ClinicalNLP) at the 26th International Conference on Computational Linguistics (COLING 2016), Japan (accepted)*.

Amber Stubbs, Christopher Kotfila, and Özlem Uzuner. 2015. Automated systems for the de-identification of longitudinal clinical narratives: Overview of 2014 i2b2/uthealth shared task track 1. *Journal of biomedical informatics*, 58:S11–S19.

Daniel Svozil, Vladimir Kvasnicka, and Jiri Pospichal. 1997. Introduction to multi-layer feed-forward neural networks. *Chemometrics and intelligent laboratory systems*, 39(1):43–62.

György Szarvas, Richárd Farkas, and András Kocsor. 2006. A multilingual named entity recognition system using boosting and c4. 5 decision tree learning algorithms. In *International Conference on Discovery Science*, pages 267–278. Springer.

Manabu Torii, Jung-wei Fan, Wei-li Yang, Theodore Lee, Matthew T Wiley, Daniel Zisook, and Yang Huang. 2014. De-identification and risk factor detection in medical records. In *Seventh i2b2 Shared Task and Workshop: Challenges in Natural Language Processing for Clinical Data*.

Kristina Toutanova and Christopher D Manning. 2000. Enriching the knowledge sources used in a maximum entropy part-of-speech tagger. In *Proceedings of the 2000 Joint SIGDAT conference on Empirical methods in natural language processing and very large corpora: held in conjunction with the 38th Annual Meeting of the Association for Computational Linguistics-Volume 13*, pages 63–70. Association for Computational Linguistics.

Özlem Uzuner, Yuan Luo, and Peter Szolovits. 2007. Evaluating the state-of-the-art in automatic de-identification. *Journal of the American Medical Informatics Association*, 14(5):550–563.

Ben Wellner, Matt Huyck, Scott Mardis, John Aberdeen, Alex Morgan, Leonid Peshkin, Alex Yeh, Janet Hitzeman, and Lynette Hirschman. 2007. Rapidly retargetable approaches to de-identification in medical records. *Journal of the American Medical Informatics Association*, 14(5):564–573.

Hui Yang and Jonathan M Garibaldi. 2015. Automatic detection of protected health information from clinic narratives. *Journal of biomedical informatics*, 58:S30–S38.

Twitter Named Entity Extraction and Linking
Using Differential Evolution

Utpal Kumar Sikdar and **Björn Gambäck**

Department of Computer and Information Science
Norwegian University of Science and Technology
Trondheim, Norway
{sikdar.utpal,gamback}@idi.ntnu.no

Abstract

Systems that simultaneously identify and classify named entities in Twitter typically show poor recall. To remedy this, the task is here divided into two parts: i) named entity *identification* using Conditional Random Fields in a multi-objective framework built on Differential Evolution, and ii) named entity *classification* using Vector Space Modelling and edit distance techniques. Differential Evolution is an evolutionary algorithm, which not only optimises the features, but also identifies the proper context window for each selected feature. The approach obtains F-scores of 70.7% for Twitter named entity extraction and 66.0% for entity linking to the DB-pedia database.

1 Introduction

Twitter has established itself as one of the most popular social networks, with about 320 million active users daily generating almost 500 million short messages, *tweets*, with a maximum length of 140 characters (Twitter, 2016). The language used is very noisy, with tweets containing many grammatical and spelling mistakes, short form of the words, multiple words merged together, special symbols and characters inserted into the words, etc. Hence it is difficult to analyse and monitor all types of tweets, and the vast number of tweets: specific messages may need to be filtered out from millions of tweets. Named entity extraction plays a vital role when filtering out relevant tweets from a collection. It is also useful for pre-processing in many other language processing tasks, such as machine translation and question-answering.

The paper is organized as follows: Section 2 describes related work on Twitter named entity recognition and linking. The actual Twitter name identification methodology and different features used are presented in Section 3. Section 4 focuses on classification of the identified named entities and their linking to DBpedia. Experimental results and a discussion of those appear in Section 5 and Section 6, respectively, while Section 7 addresses future work and concludes.

2 Related Work

The noisiness of the texts makes Twitter named entity (NE) extraction a challenging task, but several approaches have been tried: Li et al. (2012) introduced an unsupervised strategy based on dynamic programming; Liu et al. (2011) proposed a semi-supervised framework using a k-Nearest Neighbors (kNN) approach to label the Twitter names and gave these labels as an input feature to a Conditional Random Fields, CRF (Lafferty et al., 2001) classifier, achieving almost 80% accuracy on their own annotated data. Supervised models have been applied by several authors, e.g., Ritter et al. (2011) who applied Labeled LDA (Ramage et al., 2009) to recognise possible types of the Twitter names, and also showed that part-of-speech and chunk information are important components in Twitter NE identification.

A shared task challenge was organized at the ACL 2015 workshop on noisy user-generated text (W-NUT) (Baldwin et al., 2015), with two subtasks: Twitter named entity identification and classification of those named entities into ten different types. Of the eight systems participating, the best (Yamada et al., 2015) achieved an F_1 score of 70.63% for Twitter name identification and 56.41% for classification, by combining supervised machine learning with high quality knowledge obtained from several open knowledge bases such as Wikipedia. Akhtar et al. (2015) used a strategy based on differential evolution, getting F_1 scores of 56.81% for identification and 39.84% for classification.

198

D S Sharma, R Sangal and A K Singh. Proc. of the 13th Intl. Conference on Natural Language Processing, pages 198–207,
Varanasi, India. December 2016. ©2016 NLP Association of India (NLPAI)

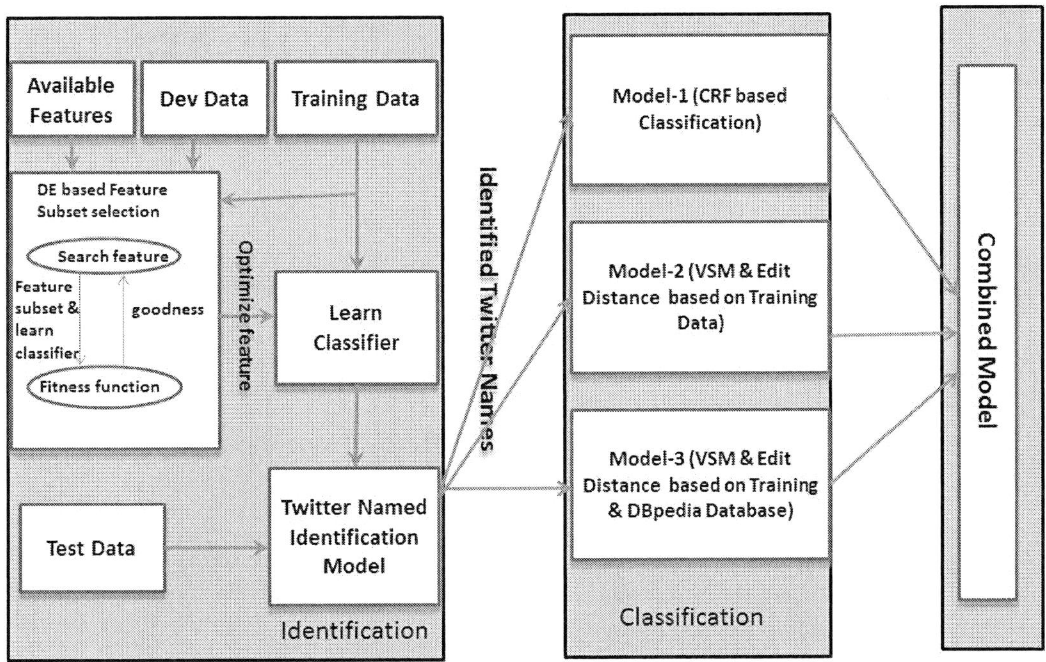

Figure 1: Twitter Named Identification and Classification system.

The challenge was repeated at W-NUT 2016 (Strauss et al., 2016), with ten participating teams. The best system (Limsopatham and Collier, 2016) used a bidirectional Long Short-Term Memory (LSTM) recurrent neural network model, obtaining F-scores of 65.89% for Twitter name identification and 52.41% for the classification task. Another system (Sikdar and Gambäck, 2016) utilized a CRF classifier built on a large feature set to get the second highest F-score on identification: 63.22%, but lower (40.06%) on classification.

A specific shared task on Twitter named entity recognition and linking (NEEL) to DBpedia was held at the #Microposts2016 workshop (Rizzo et al., 2016), with the problem defined as to identify named entities from the tweets (called 'Strong_typed_mention_match') and to link them to the DBpedia database ('Strong_link_match'). DBpedia extracts structured information from Wikipedia and links different Web data sets to Wikipedia data, allowing for sophisticated queries against Wikipedia. The DBpedia knowledgebase is available in 125 languages, with the English version describing 4.58 million items, out of which 4.22 million are classified in a consistent ontology.

Five teams participated in the #Microposts2016 NEEL challenge. However, most of the sys-tems suffered from very low recall values in the Twitter NE identification task and were actually unable to efficiently recognise Twitter names: Two knowledge-based approaches (Caliano et al., 2016; Greenfield et al., 2016) achieved F-scores of 26.7% and 31.9%, respectively, due to recall values of 18.8% and 24.0%. Two other systems (Ghosh et al., 2016; Torres-Tramón et al., 2016) produced recall values of 28.9% and 24.2%. The best system (Waitelonis and Sack, 2016) achieved recall, precision and F-measure values of 49.4%, 45.3% and 47.3%. In this system, each token is mapped to gazetteers that are developed from the DBpedia database. Tokens are discarded if they match with stop words or are not nouns.

To increase recall and F-score, we take a two-step approach to identifying and classifying named entities in noisy user-generated texts. In the first step, Twitter names are identified using CRF within the framework of Differential Evolution (Storn and Price, 1997). In step two, the named entities are classified into seven categories and linked to DBpedia using a vector space model and edit distance techniques. The identified named entities are also classified using CRF, and the outputs of the classification models are later combined. Figure 1 shows the system architecture.

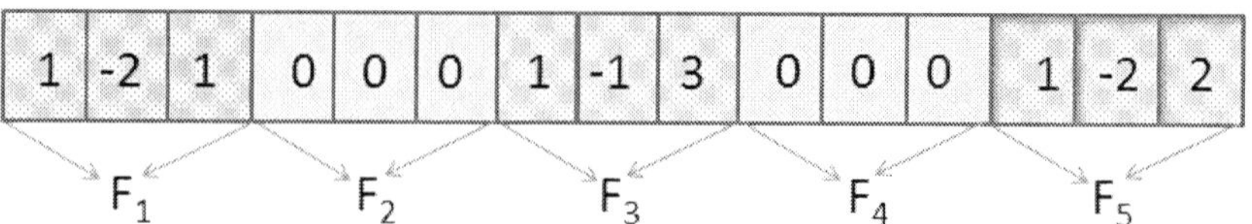

Figure 2: Chromosome representation of five available features; three are present and two absent.

3 Twitter Named Entity Identification

Twitter named entities are first extracted using a supervised machine learning approach, namely CRF in a Differential Evolution (DE) setting. However, Twitter names contain a lot of noise, making it difficult to identify them directly from the texts, so some words are segmented: words containing special characters (e.g., #, @, _), words containing a lower-case letter followed by a upper-case letter (e.g., 'realDonaldTrump' is split into real, Donald and Trump), letters followed by digits, etc. This section first briefly introduces Multi-objective Differential Evolution and then describes the DE-based Twitter name identification procedure (the left side of Figure 1).

3.1 Multi-objective Differential Evolution

Differential Evolution (Storn and Price, 1997) is a parallel direct search method over complex, large and multi-modal landscapes, and in general provides near-optimal solutions to an optimization problem. In DE, the parameters of the search space are encoded in the form of strings called chromosomes. A collection of N such strings is called a population, and is denoted by D-dimensional parameter vectors $X_{i,G} = [x_{1,i,G}, x_{2,i,G}, \ldots, x_{D,i,G}]$, $i = 1, 2, \ldots, N$ for each generation G. The initial vector population is chosen randomly, which covers different points in the search space.

For multi-objective optimization, more than one objective or fitness function is associated with each chromosome. These objective values represent the degrees of goodness of the string. DE generates new parameter vectors ("mutation") by adding the weighted difference between two population vectors to a third vector. The mutated vector's parameters are then mixed ("crossover") with the parameters of another predetermined vector, the target vector. For selection, these N trial vectors are merged with the current population, and the best N solutions are chosen from these $2 \times N$ candidate solutions based on domination, non-domination, and crowding distance. The processes of mutation, fitness computation, crossover and selection are executed for a pre-selected maximum number of generations.

3.2 DE-based Named Entity Extraction

When extracting named entities, suppose that there are a number of available features $F_1(-m, n), F_2(-m, n), \ldots F_K(-m, n)$, where K represents the total number of features, while m and n denote the preceding and succeeding context window lengths of each feature. Differential Evolution aims to find the relevant features along with proper context windows and learn a classifier using these features to optimize two objective functions: precision and recall.

Each DE chromosome represents the number of features along with their context windows, so the length of the chromosome is $D = K \times 3$. Each feature consists of one bit and two integer values: the bit represents presence or absence of a feature (1 or 0), two integer values denote the length of preceding and succeeding context windows (0–5). The algorithm proceeds as follows:

Chromosome Initialization: All chromosomes in the first population generation are initialized with random values within the search space. The bit position feature value of '0' indicates that the particular feature is not participating in constructing the classifier and '1' indicates that the feature is present in constructing the classifier using the context features. The chromosome initialization is shown in Figure 2, where features F_1, F_3 and F_5 are present, and features F_2 and F_4 are absent.

Fitness Computation: More than one fitness function can be associated with each chromosome. Suppose that k features are present in the chromosome and that the context window for each feature is denoted by $F_p(-m_p, n_p)$ where $1 \leq p \leq k$. In Figure 2, the preceding and succeeding context window lengths of F_1, F_3 and F_5 are respectively (2, 1), (1, 3) and (2, 2). The CRF classifier is

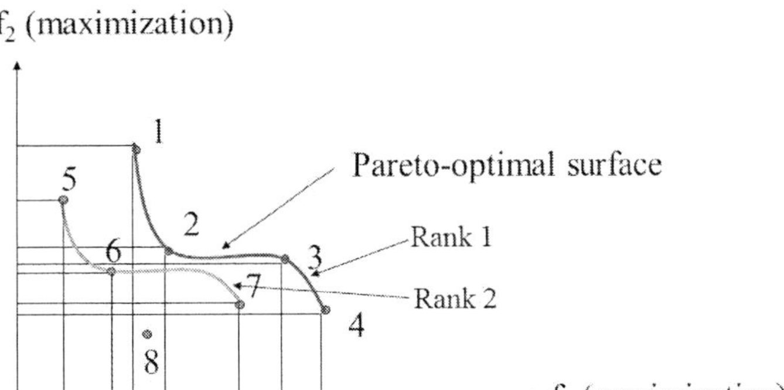

Figure 3: Dominated and non-dominated solutions. Here solutions 1, 2, 3 and 4 are non-dominating in relation to each other (rank 1). Solutions 5, 6 and 7 are also non-dominating to each other (rank 2), while solution 8 is dominated by at least one solution from rank 1 or rank 2.

trained on the k features along with their context features, and the DE search capability maximizes the two objective values precision and recall.

Mutation: A mutant vector $V_{i,G+1}$ is generated for each target vector X according to

$$V_{i,G+1} = X_{r1,G} + F_{mu} \times (X_{r2,G} - X_{r3,G})$$

where $\{r1, r2, r3\} \in \{1, 2, \ldots, N\})$ are randomly generated indices, $F_{mu} \in [0, 1]$ a mutation factor, and G resp. $G+1$ the current and next generations.

Crossover: Crossover is introduced to increase the diversity of the mutant parameter vector: the parameters of the mutant vector $V_{i,G+1}$ are mixed with the parameters of the target vector $X_{i,G}$ to generate a trail vector $U_{i,G+1}$:

$$U_{i,G+1} = (u_{i,1,G+1}, u_{i,2,G+1}, \ldots, u_{i,D,G+1})$$

where for $j = 1, 2, \ldots, D$,

$$u_{i,j,G+1} = \begin{cases} v_{i,j,G+1} & : rd_j \leq C_r \ or \ j = j_{rd} \\ x_{i,j,G} & : rd_j > C_r \ and \ j \neq j_{rd} \end{cases}$$

where $rd_j \in [0, 1]$ is a randomly generated floating point value, $C_r \in [0, 1]$ is the crossover constant, and $j_{rd} \in \{1, 2, \ldots, D\}$ a randomly chosen index ensuring that the trail vector gets at least one parameter from the mutant vector.

Selection: To select the N best chromosomes for the next generation $G + 1$, the trial population is merged with the current population. These $2 \times N$ solutions are ranked based on domination and non-domination relations in the objective function space. A solution non-dominated if at least one

of the objective values is better than another solution. If all objective values of a solution are better than another solution, the latter solution is dominated. All the non-dominated solutions form a Pareto-optimal front (Deb, 2001), as exemplified in Figure 3. The top ranked solutions are added to the next generation population until the total number of solutions is equal to N. If the number of solutions of a particular rank is $> N$, the crowding distance sorting algorithm (Deb, 2001) is applied to discard the excess solutions.

Termination Condition: The processes of mutation, crossover, fitness computation and selection are executed for G_{max} generations. A set of non-dominated solutions is obtained on the final Pareto optimal front from the last generation population. None of these solutions is better compared to the others, and each of them represents a set of optimal feature combinations. The last generation population contains rank 1 solutions where some are good with respect to recall and others with respect to precision. Here, the solutions with highest F-scores are selected, but any criterion can be used based on user preferences.

3.3 Twitter Named Entity Features

A range of different features are utilised to extract named entities from the noisy text. All features (except part-of-speech) are domain independent, and most of them are binary (yes/no) flags:

- Local context (F_1): The preceding and succeeding words of the current token.
- Word prefix (F_2) and suffix (F_3): Up to 4 leftmost/rightmost characters.

201

- Special character followed by token (F_4): If a special character (e.g., @, #) follows the token, this binary flag is set.
- Gazetteer list (F_5): A named entity list is extracted from the training data and F_5 indicates if the current token is on that list.
- Last (F_6) and first word (F_7): The token is the last/first word of the sentence.
- Alphanumeric (F_8), all digit (F_9): The token contains only alphanumerics or digits.
- Single capital (F_{10}), capital inner (F_{11}), initial capital (F_{12}), and all capital (F_{13}): The token contains only one single capital letter, any capital letter in inner position, starts with a capital letter, or contains only capitals.
- Stop word match (F_{14}): The current word matches with a stop word.
- Word normalization (F_{15}): Tokens with similar word shapes may belong to the same class. Word mapped to its equivalent class: each capital letter in the token is mapped to A, small letters to a, and digits to 0. Other characters are kept unaltered.
- Word frequency (F_{16}): Whether the word's frequency is greater than a certain threshold (the threshold values were set to 10 for training data and to 5 for development/test data).
- Word previously occurred (F_{17}): If the current word occurred earlier in the corpus.
- Word length (F_{18}): The word length is greater than some threshold (e.g., ≥ 5).
- Part-of-speech (F_{19}): Part-of-speech tags from the TweeboParser[1].
- Dynamic (F_{20}): The output label(s) of the previous token(s).

4 Twitter NE Classification and Linking

The previous section described how Twitter named entities are identified using CRF and Differential Evolution. In this section, the identified Twitter named entities are classified into seven predefined categories (Thing, Event, Character, Location, Organization, Person and Product) and linked to the DBpedia database. Three models are built for classification of Twitter names. The outputs of these three models are later merged using a priority-based approach (precision value). Finally, the classified Twitter names are linked to DBpedia.

The three Twitter named entities classification models are composed as follows.

Model-1: A CRF-based supervised classification technique is simply used to predict the classes of the Twitter names. All the extracted Twitter names from the DE-based approach are used as a feature in this model. So the model is developed with this feature along with the previous and next two context words of the current word.

Model-2: Model-2 is developed based on training datasets. Each type of training instances (Twitter names) is stored in a unique document whose class is one of the seven predefined categories. After removing all stop words and special characters from the tweets, the remaining non-entity words are stored in a separate document. Each extracted Twitter name from the DE-based approach is considered as a query (search keyword). The following steps are used to classify Twitter names.

1. Retrieve the top-100 documents for each query using a Vector Space Model (Salton et al., 1975) based on cosine similarity.
2. Calculate edit distance (also called Levenshtein distance) between the query and each of the retrieved documents.
3. Assign the closest document's class to the query, where the closest document is the one with minimum edit distance to the query. The class of an entity is retrieved using Lucene.[2]

Model-3: Model-3 is based on the DBpedia and training datasets. From the DBpedia ontology classes,[3] the datasets are mapped to the seven predefined categories and the same technique as described in Model-2 is applied. We extracted rdf-schema#label items from the csv files (e.g., African Volleyball Championship) and stored each in a unique document whose class is one of the seven predefined categories. In Model-3, the training data is merged with the DBpedia datasets.[4]

Combined Model: The extracted Twitter named entity classes are merged based on the priority of the above models. The priorities are given to the models based on the precision value of the development data. Suppose, for example, that Model-3 has the highest priority followed by Model-2 and Model-1. Voting in the ensemble is then carried out as follows: If Model-3 is unable to identify the

---

Dataset	Number of	
	Tweets	**Entities**
Training	4,073	8,665
Development	100	340
Test	296	1,022

Table 1: Statistics of the NEEL2016 datasets

class of an entity (i.e., if it identifies it as belonging to the 'not-Entity' document class), the entity is passed to Model-2. If Model-2 also fails to identity the class of the entity, the class of the entity is assigned by Model-1.

A knowledge-based technique is used to link the Twitter named entities to DBpedia database. In the training data, for each entity a link was provided. In DBpedia, for each rdf-schema#label, a link was assigned. When the class of an entity (Twitter name) is extracted using the above models, the corresponding link is maintained based on training or DBpedia datasets, and the link is assigned to that particular entity. If no link is found, a NIL link is assigned to the entity.

5 Experiments and Results

The approach was tested on the NEEL2016 datasets (Rizzo and van Erp, 2016). The statistics of the datasets are given in Table 1. This data was used to train a CRF-based classifier as baseline and then to build all the models of the full DE-based system, for Twitter named entity identification as well as for categorization and DBpedia linking, as described in turn below.

5.1 Baseline Model

To obtain a baseline model, the CRF-based machine learning approach was applied to identify and classify the Twitter named entities using the features described in Section 3.3 and the same evaluation scorer as in the NEEL2016 challenge.

After building a classifier on the training data, the recall (R), precision (P), and F_1-measure values of the development datasets were 36.20%, 69.9% and 47.7% (as also shown in the first row of Table 3 below). The low F-score is due to the poor recall. The baseline approach was also evaluated on the unseen test data, obtaining recall, precision and F_1 scores of 23.7%, 50.7% and 32.3%. The performance on the test data is similar to that on the development data because of the bad recall.

In order to increase the data for available for training the models, the development data was merged with the training data. This also increases the number of named entities in the gazetteer list (feature F_5) and the statistics that some of the other features are based on. When the same model is built by merging the training and development data, and evaluated on the test data, the results are improved considerably, with recall, precision and F-measure values of 55.6%, 69.7% and 61.9%.

5.2 Twitter NE Identification Experiments

To enhance recall and F-score, Twitter names are first identified using the multi-objective DE-based technique. In a second step, the identified Twitter named entities are classified using vector space modelling and edit distances.

A baseline model for identification of Twitter names was built using the features described in Section 3.3. When trained on the training data and evaluated on the development data, the model shows recall, precision and F_1-scores of 56.1%, 87.5% and 68.4%, respectively, as given in the 'Dev Data' column of Table 2.

To improve on these results, a Differential Evolution-based feature selection technique was used to identify named entities in noisy text. For Twitter named entity identification, the parameters of the DE were set as follows:

- N (population size) = 100,
- C_r (probability of crossover) = 0.5,
- G_{max} (number of generation) = 100, and
- F_{mu} (mutation factor) = 0.5.

The best feature set along with the context features was determined based on development data. The selected features along with context features are $F_1(-3,4)$, $F_5(-1,0)$, $F_6(0,1)$, $F_8(-1,0)$, $F_{11}(0,1)$, $F_{12}(-2,2)$, $F_{14}(-2,1)$, $F_{17}(-2,1)$, $F_{19}(-2,1)$ and $F_{20}(-1,0)$. This setup achieved recall, precision and F-measure values of 79.9%, 93.8% and 86.3% on the development data. The performance of the system increases almost 18 F-measure points over the baseline model.

To fairly evaluate the approach, it was applied to the unseen test data using the selected features along with the context features, giving the recall, precision and F_1-scores of 73.9%, 89.2% and 80.8%, respectively; also shown in Table 2 (the 'Test Data' column). The F-measure performance is increased by 20 points over the baseline.

Training set Test set Method	Training Data Dev Data			Test Data			Training + Dev Data Test Data		
	R	P	F_1	R	P	F_1	R	P	F_1
Baseline (CRF-based)	56.1	87.5	68.4	48.4	81.8	60.8	79.3	88.2	83.5
DE-based identification	79.9	93.8	86.3	73.9	89.2	80.8	81.3	90.8	85.7

Table 2: Twitter Named Entity Identification results

When merging the development data with the training data and building a model using selected features, the recall, precision and F-measure values are 81.3%, 90.8% and 85.7%, respectively, also improving on the scores obtained by the baseline model. The results show that the multi-objective DE-based approach efficiently identifies Twitter names from noisy text.

5.3 Twitter NE Classification Experiments

In the next step, the identified Twitter names extracted using the multi-objective DE-based approach were classified. Three models were built to classify the Twitter named entities into the seven categories described at the beginning of Section 4.

In the first model (Model-1), the identified Twitter named entities are passed through a CRF-based supervised classifier. The recall, precision and F-measure values given in Table 3 are 38.8%, 40.7% and 39.8%, respectively, showing that the recall is increased over the baseline model (Section 5.1), which simultaneously identifies and classifies the named entities.

Another Twitter named classification model (Model-2) was built using VSM and edit distance techniques based on training data, giving recall, precision and F-scores of 27.9%, 87.2% and 42.3%. The probable reason for the low performance is that sufficient examples (instances) may not be found in the training data.

When the Model-2 approach was applied to the DBpedia database (Model-3), the recall, precision and F-scores are 67.4%, 86.7% and 75.8%, respectively. Model-3 achieves one of the best results among all the models and also outperforms all existing approaches, as shown in Table 3.

All the models were blindly evaluated on the test data (the second set of R-P-F_1 scores given in Table 3). The Model-3 results show that its performance is far better than all other present state-of-the-art approaches. It achieves recall, precision and F-measure values of 50.8%, 76.1% and 60.9%, respectively. Even though the performance of Model-3 on the development data is

only slightly better than the best existing system, KEA (Waitelonis and Sack, 2016), the gap in performance on the test data is a lot larger, since the KEA system tries to increase the recall value as much as possible without controlling the precision value. As a result, KEA's performance on the test data is fairly bad.

In the last model (Combined Model), the outputs of the three models are merged, increasing the F-score almost 5 points compared to Model-3 on the test data. The precision, recall and F_1-scores of the Combined Model are 65.3%, 67.1% and 66.2%, respectively (see Table 3). Hence the Combined Model produces the best results compared to all the other models as well as to all the #Microposts2016 systems.

When merging the development data with the training data (the third set of R-P-F_1 scores in Table 3), the performances of Model-1 and Model-2 are better than Model-3 because many examples in the test data are seen in the development data and these two models are developed based on training instances, while Model-3 classifies the Twitter names based on the DBpedia database. Here, the Combined Model also achieves the best results among all the approaches, with precision, recall and F-score of 69.7%, 71.7% and 70.7%.

5.4 Twitter NE Linking Experiments

To link the classified Twitter names, we use a knowledge-based approach (utilizing either training data or the DBpedia database). The DBpedia links for Models 1 and 2 reported in Table 4 are based on training data. These models achieve better precision values than the state-of-the-art systems. In Model-3, the links are retrieved from the DBpedia database. The performance of Model-3 is better than the first and second models. The recall, precision and F-measure values of Model-3 on the test data are 26.9%, 67.1% and 38.4%.

The Combined Model performs best among our models and produces an F-measure value of 42.1%. All these models outperform the NEEL 2016 systems in terms of precision, but fail get

| Strong_typed_mention_match | Training data | | | | | | Training + Dev Data | | |
| | Dev Data | | | Test Data | | | Test Data | | |
	R	P	F$_1$	R	P	F$_1$	R	P	F$_1$
Baseline Model	36.2	69.9	47.7	23.7	50.7	32.3	55.6	69.7	61.9
Model-1	38.8	40.7	39.8	32.8	33.8	33.3	64.5	66.3	65.4
Model-2	27.9	**87.2**	42.3	27.8	**86.9**	42.2	49.3	**91.0**	64.0
Model-3	67.4	86.7	75.8	50.8	76.1	60.9	52.5	76.6	62.3
Combined Model	**75.3**	79.0	**77.1**	**65.3**	67.1	**66.2**	**69.7**	71.7	**70.7**
KEA (Waitelonis and Sack, 2016)	66.0	57.2	61.3	49.4	45.3	47.3	-	-	-
MIT Lincoln Lab (Greenfield et al., 2016)	28.7	58.7	38.6	24.0	47.4	31.9	-	-	-
JU (Ghosh et al., 2016)	35.3	41.1	38.0	28.9	33.8	31.2	-	-	-
UniMiB (Caliano et al., 2016)	17.8	54.5	26.8	18.8	46.2	26.7	-	-	-
Insight-centre@NUIG (Torres-Tramón et al., 2016)	35.5	33.4	34.4	24.2	24.9	24.6	-	-	-

Table 3: Twitter Named Entity Classification results ('Baseline Model': using all features)

| Strong_link_match | Training Data | | | | | | Training + Dev Data | | |
| | Dev Data | | | Test Data | | | Test Data | | |
	R	P	F$_1$	R	P	F$_1$	R	P	F$_1$
Baseline Model	18.4	85.5	30.3	13.5	**75.0**	22.8	46.9	74.4	57.5
Model-1	35.3	**90.9**	50.8	26.1	67.8	37.7	54.2	**78.1**	64.0
Model-2	29.0	90.2	43.9	19.2	65.9	29.7	49.3	77.4	60.2
Model-3	43.1	87.3	57.7	26.9	67.1	38.4	52.4	77.5	62.6
Combined Model	44.7	87.0	59.1	30.4	68.5	42.1	**57.2**	**78.1**	**66.0**
KEA (Waitelonis and Sack, 2016)	**86.2**	66.7	**75.2**	**56.0**	45.4	**50.1**	-	-	-
MIT Lincoln Lab (Greenfield et al., 2016)	41.8	79.9	54.9	28.5	64.6	39.6	-	-	-
JU (Ghosh et al., 2016)	16.1	58.6	25.2	21.7	29.0	24.8	-	-	-
Insight-centre@NUIG (Torres-Tramón et al., 2016)	32.4	49.1	39.0	16.7	25.7	20.2	-	-	-
UniMiB (Caliano et al., 2016)	38.7	45.2	41.7	13.9	35.4	16.2	-	-	-

Table 4: Twitter Named Entity Linking results ('Baseline Model': using all features)

a higher F-score than the KEA system (Waitelonis and Sack, 2016) due to lower recall. However, when development data are merged with the training data for the model building, the Combined Model again gives the best test data results among all the systems, achieving recall, precision and F-measure values of 57.2%, 78.1% and 66.0%.

6 Discussion

The task is divided into two parts: identification of Twitter named entities, and classification and linking to DBpedia. For the NE identification, a Conditional Random Fields classifier is used in a Differential Evolution framework. DE selects features randomly and lets the CRF classifier train on these features in order to optimize the feature selection based on fitness values on the development data. Hence, the CRF classifier runs many times based on the size of the population and the number of generation given as parameters to the Differential Evolution. So the learning time depends on the training data size, number of features, number of class, etc. Here, the training time is reduced since the training data size, number of features,

and number of classes are small. To increase the speed, a multi-threading approach was also used for CRF learning.

When running the CRF classifier for the identification task using all the features described in Section 3.3, the performance (baseline model) is low because the model fails to efficiently retrieve Twitter names. To enhance the performance on the identification task, the DE setting was used, since it identifies near optimal features based on its search capability.

The system output was analysed in order to understand the nature of the errors encountered: a significant number of entities were not correctly detected, resulting in low performance. A closer look reveals that many misclassifications are caused by common word(s) in both query and document. For example, 'LiberalPhenom' is annotated as a person name, but the system identifies it as a organization since the 'LiberalPhenom' (split as 'Liberal Phenom') query is closer to the document 'Liberal Forum'. In many cases, the system classifies an entity as a Twitter name even though it is not considered as an entity in the gold standard annotation. For example, 'InAbuDhabi' (split as 'In Abu Dhabi' which is closer to 'Abu Dhabi') is tagged as a location, but in gold annotation it is not considered to be a Twitter name.

The output of the entity linking to DBpedia was also analysed. The linking performance is not good because many entities with links are not in the DBpedia database. For example, 'TheForceAwakens' (split as 'The Force Awakens') is correctly identified as a Twitter named entity by the system, but that name along with a link is not in DBpedia (Release 2014). Another cause of errors is that many entities and their corresponding links simply are not identified at all by the system.

7 Conclusion

In this paper, we propose a system for Twitter named entity extraction and linking to DBpedia. Twitter names are first identified from the noisy texts using a multi-objective technique based on Differential Evolution and a range of different features. The most important features are identified along with their context features. In a second step, the identified Twitter named entities are classified and linked to the DBpedia database. For classification of Twitter names, a vector space model and edit distance techniques are used, achieving results outperforming both a tough baseline model and other state-of-the-art systems.

In the future, we will experiment with other datasets and try to collect more examples along with contextual information to reduce misclassifications. It would also be interesting to apply the approach described here to tweet named entity extraction for under-resourced languages, such as the languages of India.

Furthermore, we will develop other entity extraction models to perform ensemble classification using a multi-objective approach, and experiment with tree-based structured learning (Yang and Chang, 2015) for the task of linking Twitter named entities to DBpedia.

Acknowledgements

We are most grateful for some very useful comments from several anonymous reviewers, that helped to substantially improve the paper.

Many thanks also to the NEEL 2016 shared task organisers (Rizzo et al., 2016) for collecting, annotating and publishing the data.

References

Md Shad Akhtar, Utpal Kumar Sikdar, and Asif Ekbal. 2015. IITP: Multiobjective differential evolution based Twitter named entity recognition. In *Proceedings of the 53rd Annual Meeting of the Association for Computational Linguistics and the 7th International Joint Conference on Natural Language Processing*, pages 106–110, Beijing, China, July. ACL. Workshop on Noisy User-generated Text.

Timothy Baldwin, Marie Catherine de Marneffe, Bo Han, Young-Bum Kim, Alan Ritter, and Wei Xu. 2015. Shared tasks of the 2015 workshop on noisy user-generated text: Twitter lexical normalization and named entity recognition. In *Proceedings of the 53rd Annual Meeting of the Association for Computational Linguistics and the 7th International Joint Conference on Natural Language Processing*, pages 126–135, Beijing, China, July. ACL. Workshop on Noisy User-generated Text.

Davide Caliano, Elisabetta Fersini, Pikakshi Manchanda, Matteo Palmonari, and Enza Messina. 2016. UniMiB: Entity linking in tweets using Jaro-Winkler distance, popularity and coherence. In *Proceedings of the 6th Workshop on Making Sense of Microposts (#Microposts2016)*, pages 60–72, Montréal, Canada, April.

Kalyanmoy Deb. 2001. *Multi-objective Optimization Using Evolutionary Algorithms*. John Wiley & Sons, Chichester, England.

Souvick Ghosh, Promita Maitra, and Dipankar Das. 2016. Feature based approach to named entity recognition and linking for tweets. In *Proceedings of the 6th Workshop on Making Sense of Microposts (#Microposts2016)*, pages 74–76, Montréal, Canada, April.

Kara Greenfield, Rajmonda Caceres, Michael Coury, Kelly Geyer, Youngjune Gwon, Jason Matterer, Alyssa Mensch, Cem Sahin, and Olga Simek. 2016. A reverse approach to named entity extraction and linking in microposts. In *Proceedings of the 6th Workshop on Making Sense of Microposts (#Microposts2016)*, pages 67–69, Montréal, Canada, April.

John D. Lafferty, Andrew McCallum, and Fernando C. N. Pereira. 2001. Conditional Random Fields: Probabilistic models for segmenting and labeling sequence data. In *Proceedings of the 18th International Conference on Machine Learning*, pages 282–289, Williamstown, Maryland, USA, June.

Chenliang Li, Jianshu Weng, Qi He, Yuxia Yao, Anwitaman Datta, Aixin Sun, and Bu-Sung Lee. 2012. TwiNER: Named entity recognition in targeted Twitter stream. In *Proceedings of the 35th International Conference on Research and Development in Information Retrieval*, pages 721–730, Portland, Oregon, August. ACM SIGIR.

Nut Limsopatham and Nigel Collier. 2016. Bidirectional LSTM for named entity recognition in Twitter messages. In *Proceedings of the 26th International Conference on Computational Linguistics*, pages 145–152, Osaka, Japan, December. ACL. 2nd Workshop on Noisy User-generated Text.

Xiaohua Liu, Shaodian Zhang, Furu Wei, and Ming Zhou. 2011. Recognizing named entities in tweets. In *Proceedings of the 49th Annual Meeting of the Association for Computational Linguistics: Human Language Technologies*, volume 1, pages 359–367, Portland, Oregon, June. ACL.

Daniel Ramage, David Hall, Ramesh Nallapati, and Christopher D. Manning. 2009. Labeled LDA: A supervised topic model for credit attribution in multi-labeled corpora. In *Proceedings of the 2009 Conference on Empirical Methods in Natural Language Processing*, pages 248–256, Singapore, August. ACL.

Alan Ritter, Sam Clark, Mausam, and Oren Etzioni. 2011. Named entity recognition in tweets: An experimental study. In *Proceedings of the 2011 Conference on Empirical Methods in Natural Language Processing*, pages 1524–1534, Edinburgh, Scotland, August. ACL.

Giuseppe Rizzo and Marieke van Erp. 2016. Named Entity rEcognition and Linking (NEEL) challenge. `http://microposts2016.seas.upenn. edu/challenge.html`.

Giuseppe Rizzo, Marieke van Erp, Julien Plu, and Raphaël Troncy. 2016. Making sense of microposts (#Microposts2016) Named Entity rEcognition and Linking (NEEL) challenge. In *Proceedings of the 6th Workshop on Making Sense of Microposts (#Microposts2016)*, pages 50–59, Montréal, Canada, April.

Gerard Salton, A. Wong, and C. S. Yang. 1975. A vector space model for automatic indexing. *Communications of the ACM*, 18(11):613–620, November.

Utpal Kumar Sikdar and Björn Gambäck. 2016. Feature-rich Twitter named entity recognition and classification. In *Proceedings of the 26th International Conference on Computational Linguistics*, pages 164–170, Osaka, Japan, December. ACL. 2nd Workshop on Noisy User-generated Text.

Rainer Storn and Kenneth Price. 1997. Differential Evolution — a simple and efficient heuristic for global optimization over continuous spaces. *Journal of Global Optimization*, 11(4):341–359, December.

Benjamin Strauss, Bethany E. Toma, Alan Ritter, Marie Catherine de Marneffe, and Wei Xu. 2016. Results of the WNUT16 named entity recognition shared task: Twitter lexical normalization and named entity recognition. In *Proceedings of the 26th International Conference on Computational Linguistics*, pages 138–144, Osaka, Japan, December. ACL. 2nd Workshop on Noisy User-generated Text.

Pablo Torres-Tramón, Hugo Hromic, Brian Walsh, Bahareh R. Heravi, and Conor Haye. 2016. Kanopy4Tweets: Entity extraction and linking for Twitter. In *Proceedings of the 6th Workshop on Making Sense of Microposts (#Microposts2016)*, pages 64–66, Montréal, Canada, April.

Twitter. 2016. Company information, June. `https://about.twitter.com/company`.

Jörg Waitelonis and Harald Sack. 2016. Named entity linking in #tweets with KEA. In *Proceedings of the 6th Workshop on Making Sense of Microposts (#Microposts2016)*, pages 61–63, Montréal, Canada, April.

Ikuya Yamada, Hideaki Takeda, and Yoshiyasu Takefuji. 2015. Enhancing named entity recognition in Twitter messages using entity linking. In *Proceedings of the 53rd Annual Meeting of the Association for Computational Linguistics and the 7th International Joint Conference on Natural Language Processing*, pages 136–140, Beijing, China, July. ACL. Workshop on Noisy User-generated Text.

Yi Yang and Ming-Wei Chang. 2015. S-MART: Novel tree-based structured learning algorithms applied to tweet entity linking. In *Proceedings of the 53rd Annual Meeting of the Association for Computational Linguistics and the 7th International Joint Conference on Natural Language Processing*, volume 1, pages 504–513, Beijing, China, July. ACL.

Learning Non-Linear Functions for Text Classification

Cohan Sujay Carlos
Aiaioo Labs
Bangalore
India
cohan@aiaioo.com

Geetanjali Rakshit
IITB-Monash Research Academy
Mumbai
India
geet@cse.iitb.ac.in

Abstract

In this paper, we show that generative classifiers are capable of learning non-linear decision boundaries and that non-linear generative models can outperform a number of linear classifiers on some text categorization tasks.

We first prove that 3-layer multinomial hierarchical generative (Bayesian) classifiers, under a particular independence assumption, can only learn the same linear decision boundaries as a multinomial naive Bayes classifier.

We then go on to show that making a different independence assumption results in nonlinearization, thereby enabling us to learn non-linear decision boundaries.

We finally evaluate the performance of these non-linear classifiers on a series of text classification tasks.

1 Introduction

Probabilistic classifiers predict a *class* c given a set of *features* F of the data point being classified, by selecting the most probable class given the features, as shown in Equation 1.

$$\arg\max_{c} P(c|F) \qquad (1)$$

Bayesian classifiers, also known as generative classifiers, are those that learn a model of the joint probability $P(F, c)$ of the inputs F and labels $c \in C$ (Ng and Jordan, 2001), and use the *Bayes rule* (2) to invert probabilities of the features F given a class c into a prediction of the class c given the features F.

$$P(c|F) = \frac{P(F|c) \times P(c)}{P(F)} \qquad (2)$$

2-layer classifiers such as the perceptron and the naive Bayes classifier are only capable of learning linear decision boundaries (Minsky and Papert, 1988) passing through the origin (if learning a multinomial probability distribution), or quadratic decision boundaries (with a Gaussian probability distribution or kernel).

The multilayer perceptron, a 3-layer classifier with an input layer, a hidden layer and an output layer, is capable of learning non-linear decision boundaries (Cybenko, 1989; Andoni et al, 2014). It is therefore only to be expected that 3-layer generative models should also be capable of learning the same. However, it turns that under certain conditions, 3-layer generative models for classification are only as powerful as 2-layer models, and under other conditions, are capable of learning non-linear decision boundaries.

In this paper, we study 3-layer hierarchical multinomial generative models, and define the conditions under which their decision boundaries are linear or non-linear. The main contributions of the paper are the following:

- We prove that a certain set of independence assumptions results in linear decision boundaries and identical classification performance to a naive Bayes classifier.

- We demonstrate that a different set of independence assumptions makes models with the same parameters capable of learning non-linear decision boundaries and certain non-linear functions, for instance, a scaled and shifted XOR function.

- We show through experiments that such **non-linear hierarchical Bayesian models** can outperform many commonly used machine learning models at certain text classification tasks.

D S Sharma, R Sangal and A K Singh. Proc. of the 13th Intl. Conference on Natural Language Processing, pages 208–218,
Varanasi, India. December 2016. ©2016 NLP Association of India (NLPAI)

2 Related Work

Deep learning is a term used to describe any method of machine learning involving the use of multiple processing layers to learn representations of data (LeCun et al., 2015; Bengio, 2009).

2.1 Neural Network Models

Two machine learning algorithms used in deep learning are the multilayer perceptron (Rumelhart et al, 1986) and the autoencoder (Alex et al, 2011), both of which are neural networks (Wang and Yeung, 2016).

2.2 Probabilistic Graphical Models

Probabilistic graphical models are concise graph-based representations of probability distributions over possibly complex and high-dimensional spaces, with the nodes representing variables of interest and various properties of the graph representing functions interpretable as probabilities (Koller and Friedman, 2009). Probabilistic graphical models are usually of one of two types, depending on whether their edges are directed or undirected.

Undirected probabilistic graphical models (also known as Markov random fields) have undirected edges and are models of probability distributions whose factorization is a function of the cliques in the graph (Wainwright and Jordan, 2008). They represent discriminative classifiers, which learn the probability of the labels given the features $P(c|F)$ directly (Ng and Jordan, 2001) without first learning $P(F|c)$ and then applying Bayesian inversion. Two machine learning models used in deep learning - Boltzmann machines (Ackley et al, 1986) and restricted Boltzmann machines (Smolensky, 1986) - are both undirected probabilistic graphical models (Fischer and Igel, 2012).

Directed probabilistic graphical models (also known as Bayesian networks) are on the other hand directed acyclic graphs where the factorization of the probability distribution is a function of the parent-child relationships in the graph.

2.3 Directed Probabilistic Graphical Models

For each vertex $i \in 1 \ldots n$ in a directed probabilistic graphical model and the set of ancestor vertices $a(i)$ of i (vertices with a sequence of directed edges leading to i), the random variables x_1, x_2 $\ldots x_n$ attached to the nodes represent a family of probabilistic distributions that factorise according to Equation 3.

$$P(x_1, x_2 \ldots x_n) = \left(\prod_{1 \leq i \leq n} P(x_i | x_{a(i)}) \right) \quad (3)$$

In this paper, we focus on a subset of directed probabilistic graphical models known as hierarchical Bayesian models (Wainwright and Jordan, 2008).

2.4 Hierarchical Bayesian Models

Hierarchical Bayesian models are directed probabilistic graphical models in which the directed acyclic graph is a tree (each node that is not the root node has only one immediate parent). In these models the ancestors $a(i)$ of any node i do not contain any siblings (every pair of ancestors is also in an ancestor-descendent relationship). The factorization represented by a hierarchical Bayesian model is just a special case of Equation 3 (Wainwright and Jordan, 2008). Such models naturally lend themselves to classification tasks because the root node can be used to represent the set of classes C and the leaf nodes the set of features F.

The naive Bayes classifier is a special case of a hierarchical Bayesian classifier because it consists of a tree that is only two layers deep (a root node and a layer of leaf nodes). So, for the naive Bayes classifier, Equation 3 reduces to Equation 4.

$$P(F, c) = P(F|c)P(c) = \prod_{f \in F} P(f|c)P(c) \quad (4)$$

Naive Bayes classifiers are easy to train because all the nodes in the directed graph representation of a naive Bayes classifier are visible nodes. Since all the edge probabilities that need to be estimated in the learning step are between visible variables, they are easy to estimate.

With hierarchical Bayesian models, there are also "hidden" nodes which do not correspond to either labels or features in the data used in training. The estimation of the probabilities involving such hidden nodes requires the use of a training method such as Gibbs' sampling, variational method or expectation maximization (which is described below).

Though hierarchical support vector machine models (Sun and Lim, 2001) and hierarchical neural networks (Ruiz and Srinivasan, 2002) have been explored in hierarchical text categorization tasks, there has been relatively little work on hierarchical generative models. There have been evaluations of the performance of hierarchical generative models on hierarchical classification tasks (Veeramachaneni et al., 2005), on images (Liao and Carneiro, 2015) and also on text classification tasks (Vaithyanathan et al., 2000). But none of the earlier papers attempt formal characterization of the linear and non-linear aspects of hierarchical generative models. So, to our knowledge, there has been no earlier study establishing the conditions for linearity and non-linearity in such models along with a demonstration of superior performance in a typical text categorization task.

2.5 Expectation Maximization

The *expectation maximization* (EM) algorithm is an iterative algorithm for estimating the parameters of a directed graphical model with hidden variables. It consists of two steps: *expectation* (E-step) and *maximization* (M-step) (Dempster et al., 1977).

The parameters of the directed graphical model are at first randomly initialized. In the E-step, expected counts of features are calculated at each hidden variable using the current estimate of the parameters conditional on the observations. These expected counts are then used to re-estimate the parameters, which is the M-step. The E-step and M-step are iteratively computed until convergence (Do and Batzoglou, 2008).

Let X be the observations and Z be the underlying hidden variables. EM tries to solve for the parameters θ that maximize the log likelihood of the observed data.

$$log\ P(X|\theta) = log \sum_{z} P(X, Z|\theta) \qquad (5)$$

In the E-step, the algorithm finds a function that lower bounds $log P(X|\theta)$ (Jordan and Bishop, 2004).

E-Step:

$$Q(\theta|\theta^{(t)}) = E_{P(Z|X,\theta^{(t)})}[log\ P(X, Z|\theta)] \qquad (6)$$

The M-step calculates the new parameters from the maximized Q function in Equation 6.

M-Step:

$$\theta^{(t+1)} = argmax_\theta\ Q(\theta|\theta^{(t)}) \qquad (7)$$

2.6 Repeated Expectation Maximization

Since the objective function optimized by the expectation maximization algorithm is non-convex, expectation maximization can lead to suboptimal learning on account of local maxima. The accuracy of any resultant model consequently varies widely. Since the final state reached depends on the initial set of parameters used (Laird et al, 1987), repeating expectation maximization with different initial parameters (selected at random) and selecting the best performing models (using a validation set) yields better overall accuracy and lowers the variance of the same (Zhao et al., 2011).

3 Three-Layer Models

In a 3-layer model, the root node represents the set of class labels $C = \{c_1, c_2 \ldots c_k\}$ and the leaf nodes represent the set of features $F = \{f_1, f_2 \ldots f_i\}$. And sandwiched between the two is a set of hidden nodes $H = \{h_1, h_2 \ldots h_j\}$.

$P(F|c)$ can be obtained from $P(F, H|c)$ by marginalizing over the hidden nodes, as follows.

$$P(F|c) = \sum_{h} P(F, h|c) \qquad (8)$$

The chain rule gives us the following equation.

$$P(F, h|c) = P(F|h, c) \times P(h|c) \qquad (9)$$

Substituting Equation 9 in Equation 8, we get Equation 10.

$$P(F|c) = \sum_{h} P(F|h, c)P(h|c) \qquad (10)$$

The corresponding rule for individual features[1] can be similarly derived.

$$P(f|c) = \sum_{h} P(f|h, c)P(h|c) \qquad (11)$$

By substituting Equation 10 in Equation 2, we arrive at Equation 12.

$$P(c|F) = \sum_{h} P(F|h, c)P(h|c)\frac{P(c)}{P(F)} \qquad (12)$$

So the parameters that need to be learnt for classification are $P(F|h, c)$, $P(h|c)$ and $P(c)$. $P(F)$

---

[1] In the rest of the paper, we use capital letters to denote sets of variables (features, hidden nodes and classes), and lowercase letters for a specific variable (a feature, a hidden node or a class).

does not need to be learnt as it is independent of the class c and so is merely a normalization constant.

Once these parameters have been learnt, the probability of a class c given the features F can be computed in one of two ways:

1. Product of sums.

2. Sum of products.

We prove below that using the product of sums to compute $P(c|F)$ in a directed 3-layer multinomial hierarchical model trained using expectation maximization yields a linear decision boundary whereas using the sum of products results in a non-linear decision boundary.

3.1 Product of Sums

If you assume that each feature f is independent of every other feature conditional on a class c, then the joint probability of a set of features F given a class c can be written as a product of probabilities of individual features given the class.

$$P(F|c) = \prod_f P(f|c) \qquad (13)$$

Substituting Equation 11 into Equation 13, we get Equation 14.

$$P(F|c) = \prod_f \sum_h P(f|h, c)P(h|c) \qquad (14)$$

Substituting the above for $P(F|c)$ in Equation 2, we get

$$P(c|F) = \prod_f \left(\sum_h P(f|h, c)P(h|c) \right) \frac{P(c)}{P(F)} \qquad (15)$$

3.2 Proof of Naive Bayes Equivalence

In this subsection, we show that expectation maximization over any data-set results in the learning of multinomial parameters that when combined using Equation 15 yield a classifier with the same classification performance as a multinomial naive Bayes classifier trained on the same data-set.

The equation for $P(c|F)$ for a naive Bayes classifier can be obtained by dividing both sides by $P(F)$ in Equation 4.

$$P(c|F) = P(F|c)\frac{P(c)}{P(F)} \qquad (16)$$

By inspection of Equation 16 and Equation 15, we see that the right hand sides of these equations must be equal for both classifiers (the 3-layer hierarchical Bayesian and naive Bayes classifiers) to perform identically.

By equating the right sides of Equation 16 and Equation 15, we obtain Equation 17[2].

$$P_{nb}(F|c) = \prod_f \left(\sum_h P_{hb}(f|h, c)P_{hb}(h|c) \right) \qquad (17)$$

By substituting Equation 13 in Equation 17 we get Equation 18.

$$\prod_f P_{nb}(f|c) = \prod_f \left(\sum_h P_{hb}(f|h, c)P_{hb}(h|c) \right) \qquad (18)$$

Equation 18 is satisfied if each of the factors on the right hand side is equal to each of the corresponding factors on the left hand side, as shown in Equation 19.

$$P_{nb}(f|c) = \sum_h P_{hb}(f|h, c)P_{hb}(h|c) \qquad (19)$$

So, to prove that the multinomial "product of sums" hierarchical Bayes classifier is equivalent to the multinomial naive Bayes classifier (and therefore is only capable of learning a linear hyperplane separator between classes), all we have to establish is that Equation 19 holds for a given learning procedure.

Let the count of a feature f in a class c be $C(f)$, and let the distribution learnt be a multinomial distribution. For any class c and features $\phi \in F$, the class-conditional feature probability learnt by a naive Bayes classifier is that given by the maximum likelihood estimator as shown in Equation 20.

$$P_{nb}(f|c) = \frac{C(f)}{\sum_{\phi \in F} C(\phi)} \qquad (20)$$

---

[2] The subscripts in P_{nb} and P_{hb} indicate that these were probabilities estimated for the naive Bayes and the hierarchical Bayesian classifiers respectively.

For the hierarchical Bayesian classifier, the expectation maximization algorithm learns P_{hb} differently depending on whether hard expectation maximization or soft expectation maximization is used.

3.2.1 Hard Expectation Maximization

In hard expectation maximization, each data point is assigned to one of the hidden nodes $h \in H$ in the E-step. Let $C_h(f)$ of a feature $f \in F$ denote the count of the feature in the data points assigned to a hidden node h of a class c, and the set F_h denote the set of features assigned to that hidden node.

For any feature f, $C(f)$ and $C_h(f)$ are related as follows.

$$C(f) = \sum_{h \in H} C_h(f) \qquad (21)$$

It is now possible to write P_{hb} in terms of $C(f)$ as shown in Equation 22 and Equation 23.

$$P_{hb}(h|c) = \frac{\sum_{\theta \in F_h} C_h(\theta)}{\sum_{\phi \in F} C(\phi)} \qquad (22)$$

$$P_{hb}(f|h,c) = \frac{C_h(f)}{\sum_{\theta \in F_h} C_h(\theta)} \qquad (23)$$

By plugging Equation 22 and Equation 23 into the right hand side of Equation 19 we get

$$\sum_h P_{hb}(f|h,c)P_{hb}(h|c) = \sum_h \frac{C_h(f)}{\sum_{\phi \in F} C(\phi)} \qquad (24)$$

Since the sum of counts $C_h(f)$ over hidden nodes $h \in H$ is equal to $C(f)$ (Equation 21), the above equation is equal to

$$\sum_h P_{hb}(f|h,c)P_{hb}(h|c) = \frac{C(f)}{\sum_{\phi \in F} C(\phi)} \qquad (25)$$

Since the right hand sides of Equation 20 and Equation 25 are equal, we have proved that Equation 19 holds when the probabilities P_{nb} and P_{hb} are learnt using hard expectation maximization.

3.2.2 Soft Expectation Maximization

In soft expectation maximization, each data point is shared by all of the hidden nodes $h \in H$ of a class c in the E-step, with each hidden node's share of ownership being $m_h(d)$. Since $m_h(d)$ represents a probability distribution over h, ($m_h(d) =$

$P(h|d, \Theta)$ where Θ are the parameters of the model), the sum of $m_h(d)$ over all hidden nodes is 1.

$$\sum_{h \in H} m_h(d) = 1 \qquad (26)$$

Let $C_d(f)$ of a feature $f \in F_d$ denote the count of the feature f in data point d belonging to a class c, where F_d is the set of features in data point d.

Now the probabilities P_{hb} can be computed as follows.

$$P_{hb}(h|c) = \frac{\sum_d \left(m_h(d) \sum_{\theta \in F_d} C_d(\theta) \right)}{\sum_{\phi \in F} C(\phi)} \qquad (27)$$

$$P_{hb}(f|h,c) = \frac{\sum_d m_h(d) C_d(f)}{\sum_d \left(m_h(d) \sum_{\theta \in F_d} C_d(\theta) \right)} \qquad (28)$$

By plugging Equation 27 and Equation 28 into the right hand side of Equation 19 we get

$$\sum_h P_{hb}(f|h,c)P_{hb}(h|c) = \sum_h \frac{\sum_d m_h(d) C_d(f)}{\sum_{\phi \in F} C(\phi)} \qquad (29)$$

Taking the summation over h inside the summation over d we obtain Equation 30.

$$\sum_h P_{hb}(f|h,c)P_{hb}(h|c) = \frac{\sum_d \sum_h m_h(d) C_d(f)}{\sum_{\phi \in F} C(\phi)} \qquad (30)$$

Since $\sum_h m_h(d) = 1$ (26), the above equation reduces to Equation 31.

$$\sum_h P_{hb}(f|h,c)P_{hb}(h|c) = \frac{\sum_d C_d(f)}{\sum_{\phi \in F} C(\phi)} \qquad (31)$$

However, $\sum_d C_d(f) = C(f)$, so we obtain

$$\sum_h P_{hb}(f|h,c)P_{hb}(h|c) = \frac{C(f)}{\sum_{\phi \in F} C(\phi)} \qquad (32)$$

Since the right hand sides of Equation 20 and Equation 32 are equal, we have proved that Equation 19 holds when the probabilities P_{nb} and P_{hb} are learnt using soft expectation maximization.

Thus we have proved that a hierarchical Bayes classifier that computes $P(c|F)$ by taking the product of the sums of $P_{hb}(f|h,c) \times P_{hb}(h|c)$ is equivalent to a naive Bayes classier and is therefore, like a naive Bayes classifier, only capable of learning a linear decision boundary.

3.3 Sum of Products

If you assume that each feature f is independent of other features conditional on any hidden node h belonging to any class c of the set C, then the joint probability of a set of features F given a hidden node h and its class c, denoted as $P(F|h,c)$, can be written as a product of probabilities of individual features given the hidden node and class.

$$P(F|h,c) = \prod_f P(f|h,c) \qquad (33)$$

Substituting Equation 33 for $P(F|h,C)$ in Equation 12, we get Equation 34.

$$P(c|F) = \sum_h \left(\prod_f P(f|h,c) \right) P(h|c) \frac{P(c)}{P(F)}$$

$$(34)$$

Equation 34 allows you to compute the posterior probability $P(c|F)$ by taking the sum over the hidden nodes of the products of $P(f|h,c)$.

We show below that this method of computing the posterior probability allows a multinomial hierarchical Bayesian classifier to learn a non-linear decision boundary.

3.4 Demonstration of Non-Linearity

When the XOR function is scaled by 4 and shifted by 1 unit along the x and y axes, the resultant function maps the tuples $(x = 5, y = 5)$ and $(x = 1, y = 1)$ to 0 and the tuples $(x = 5, y = 1)$ and $(x = 1, y = 5)$ to 1 as shown in Figure 1.

We can verify by observation that the convex hulls around the data points in each of the categories intersect. The convex hull around category 1 is the line between $\{5, 1\}$ and $\{1, 5\}$. The convex hull around category 0 is the line between $\{1, 1\}$ and $\{5, 5\}$. These lines intersect at $\{3, 3\}$, and therefore the categories are not linearly separable.

Since the categories are not linearly separable, if a classifier is capable of learning (correctly classifying the points of) this XOR function it must be a non-linear classifier.

In this subsection, we demonstrate experimentally that a 3-layer multinomial hierarchical Bayesian classifier with a "sum-of-products" posterior and 4 hidden nodes (2 per class) can learn this function.

Figure 2 shows the outputs of various classifiers trained on the XOR function described in Figure 1 when run on random points in the domain of the

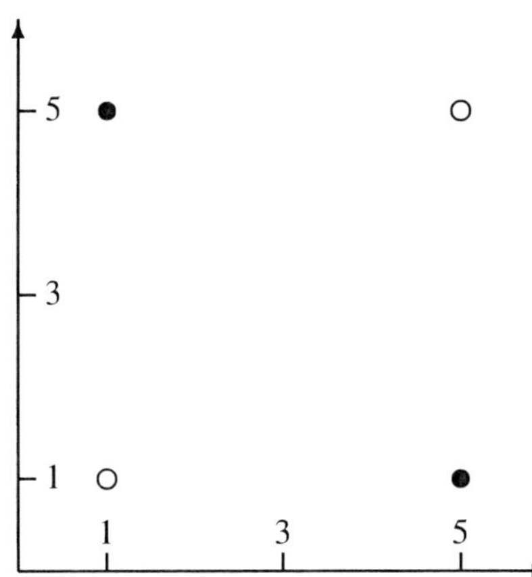

Figure 1: A 2-D plot of the shifted and scaled XOR function, where the filled circles stand for points that map to 1 and the unfilled circles for points that map to 0.

function. The small dots were placed at all points classified as 1.

3.4.1 Naive Bayes

It can be seen from Figure 2a that the boundary learnt by the naive Bayes classifier is a straight line through the origin.

It can be seen that no matter what the angle of the line is, at least one point of the four will be misclassified.

In this instance, it is the point at $\{5, 1\}$ that is misclassified as 0 (since the clear area represents the class 0).

3.4.2 Multinomial Non-Linear Hierarchical Bayes

The decision boundary learnt by a **multinomial non-linear hierarchical Bayes classifier** (one that computes the posterior using a sum of products of the hidden-node conditional feature probabilities) is shown in Figure 2b.

The boundary consists of two straight lines passing through the origin. They are angled in such a way that they separate the data points into the two required categories.

All four points are classified correctly since the points at $\{1, 1\}$ and $\{5, 5\}$ fall in the clear conical region which represents a classification of 0 whereas the other two points fall in the dotted region representing class 1.

Therefore, we have demonstrated that the multinomial non-linear hierarchical Bayes classifier can learn the non-linear function of Figure 1.

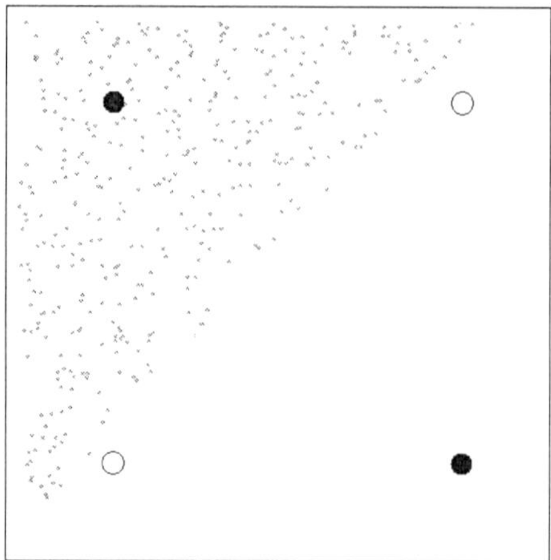

(a) Naive Bayes

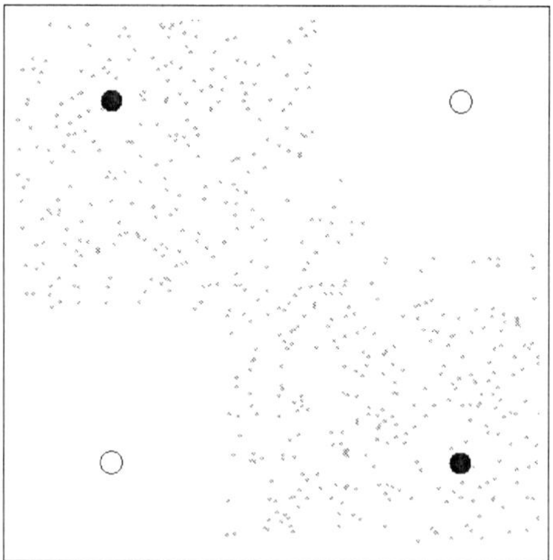

(b) Multinomial Non-Linear Hierarchical Bayes

(c) Gaussian Non-Linear Hierarchical Bayes

Figure 2: Decision boundaries learnt by classifiers trained on the XOR function of Figure 1. The dotted area represents what has been learnt as the category 1. The clear area represents category 0.

3.4.3 Gaussian Non-Linear Hierarchical Bayes

The decision boundary learnt by a **Gaussian** non-linear hierarchical Bayes classifier is shown in Figure 2c.

The boundary consists of two quadratic curves separating the data points into the required categories.

Therefore, the Gaussian non-linear hierarchical Bayes classifier can also learn the function depicted in Figure 1.

Thus, we have demonstrated that 3-layer hierarchical Bayesian classifiers (multinomial and Gaussian) with a "sum-of-products" posterior and 4 hidden nodes (2 per class) can learn certain non-linear functions.

3.5 Intuition on Learning Arbitrary Non-Linear Functions

Non-linear hierarchical Bayesian models based on the multinomial distribution are restricted to hyperplanes that pass through the origin. Each hidden node represents a linear boundary passing through the origin. Models based on the Gaussian distribution are not so restricted. Each hidden node in their case is associated with a quadratic boundary.

Assuming that the hidden nodes act as cluster centroids and fill the available hyperspace of a given class (for a suitable probability distribution), one might expect the dominance of the closest hidden nodes - dominance of one hidden node for text datasets is likely on account of extreme posterior probabilities (Eyheramendy et al, 2003) - to result in the piece-wise reconstruction of arbitrary boundaries in the case of Gaussian models. The dominance of the nearest hidden nodes (in terms of angular distances) is likely to result in appropriate radial boundaries in the case of multinomial models.

We now demonstrate empirically that a classifier capable of learning non-linear boundaries can outperform linear classifiers on certain text and tuple classification tasks.

4   Experimental Results

We conducted four sets of experiments to evaluate the performance of non-linear hierarchical Bayesian classifiers trained using repeated soft expectation maximization. In the first three experiments, the multinomial version was used and in

214

the last, the Gaussian version was used.

With both the naive Bayes classifier and the hierarchical Bayesian models, the smoothing used was Laplace smoothing. The SVM classifier used a linear kernel.

4.1 Large Movie Review Dataset

The first experiment was run on the large movie review dataset (Maas et al, 2011) which consists of $50,000$ movie reviews labelled as either positive or negative (according to whether they expressed positive or negative sentiment about a movie).

The training set size was varied between $5,000$ and $35,000$ in steps of $5,000$ (with half the reviews drawn from positively labelled data and the other half drawn from negatively labelled data). Of the remaining data, we used $5,000$ reviews ($2,500$ positive and $2,500$ negative) as a validation set. The rest were used as test data.

The accuracies for different training set sizes and hidden nodes are as shown in Figure 3. The accuracies obtained when training on $25,000$ reviews and testing on $20,000$ (with the remaining 5000 documents of the test set used for validation) are shown in Table 1 .

Classifier	Accuracy
Naive Bayes	0.7964 ± 0.0136
MaxEnt	0.8355 ± 0.0149
SVM	0.7830 ± 0.0128
Non-linear Hierarchical Bayes	$\mathbf{0.8438} \pm 0.0110$

Table 1: Accuracy on the movie reviews dataset when trained on 25,000 reviews.

4.2 Single-Label Text Categorization Datasets

We tested the performance of the various classifiers (the hierarchical Bayes classifier was configured with 2 hidden nodes per class) on the Reuters R8, R52 and 20 Newsgroups datasets preprocessed and split as described in (Cardoso-Cachopo, 2007). 10% of the training data was held back for validation. The results are shown in Table 2.

4.3 Query Classification Dataset

For this experiment, we used a smaller corpus of 1889 queries classified into 14 categories (Thomas Morton, 2005). Five different random orderings of

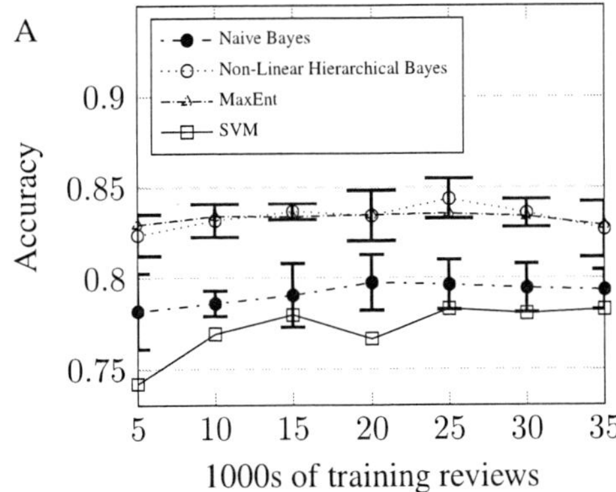

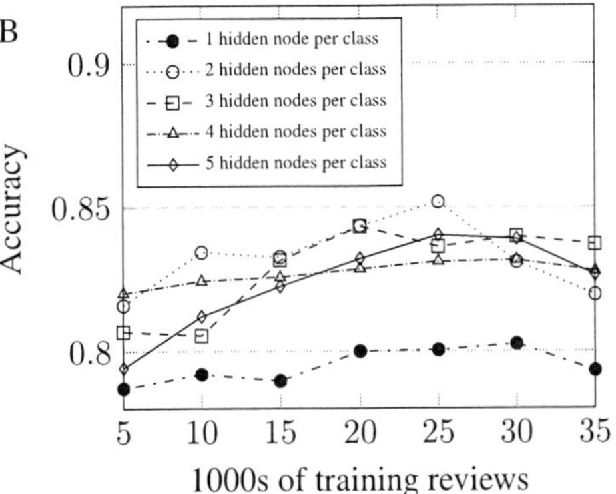

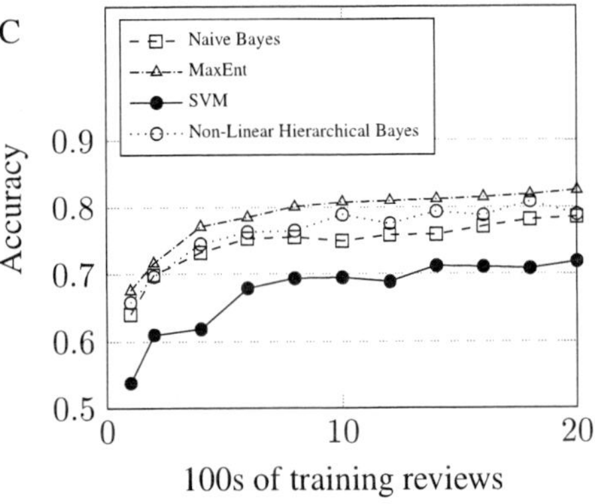

Figure 3: Evaluations on the movie reviews dataset. Plot A shows the performance of various classifiers on the dataset (the multinomial non-linear hierarchical Bayes classifier being configured with 2 hidden nodes per class and trained using 50 repetitions of 4 iterations of soft expectation maximization). Plot B compares the accuracies of multinomial non-linear hierarchical Bayes classifiers with different numbers of hidden nodes. Plot C charts the performance of the classifiers on much smaller quantities of data than in plot A (the 2-hidden-node multinomial non-linear hierarchical Bayes classifier being trained with 10 repetitions of 5 expectation maximization iterations).

Classifier	R8	R52	20Ng
Naive Bayes	0.955	0.916	0.797
MaxEnt	0.953	0.866	0.793
SVM	0.946	0.864	0.711
Non-Lin Hier Bayes	**0.964**	**0.921**	**0.808**

Table 2: Accuracy on Reuters R8, R52 and 20 Newsgroups.

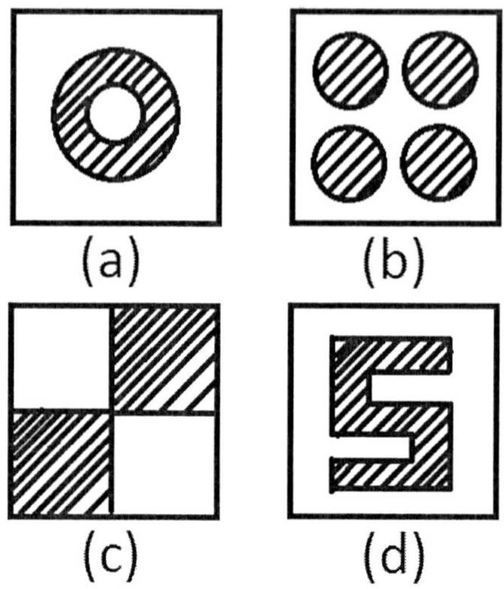

Figure 4: Artificial 2-dimensional dataset: a) ring b) dots c) XOR d) S

the data in the corpus were used, each with 1400 training, 200 validation and 289 test queries.

The accuracies of different classifiers (including a hierarchical Bayes classifier with 4 hidden nodes per class trained through 50 repetitions of 10 iterations of expectation maximization) on the query dataset are as shown in Table 3. The error margins are large enough to render all comparisons on this dataset devoid of significance.

Classifier	Accuracy
Naive Bayes	0.721 ± 0.018
MaxEnt	0.667 ± 0.028
SVM	0.735 ± 0.032
Non-Linear Hier Bayes	0.711 ± 0.032

Table 3: Accuracy on query classification.

4.4 Artificial 2-Dimensional Dataset

A total of 2250 points were generated at random positions (x, y) inside a square of width 500.

Those falling inside each of the four shaded shapes shown in Figure 4 were labelled 1 and the rest of the points (falling outside the shaded areas of the square) were labelled 0.

For each shape, 1000 of the points were used for training, 250 as the validation set and the remaining 1000 as the test set. Naive Bayes and non-linear hierarchical Bayes classifiers that assumed the Gaussian distribution were used.

The Gaussian naive Bayes (GNB) classifier and the non-linear Gaussian hierarchical Bayes (GHB) classifier (10 hidden nodes per class), trained with 10 repetitions of 100 iterations of expectation maximization were tested on the artificial dataset. Their accuracies are as shown in Table 4.

Shape	GNB	GHB
ring	0.664	0.949
dots	0.527	0.926
XOR	0.560	0.985
S	0.770	0.973

Table 4: Accuracy on the artificial dataset.

4.5 Discussion

We see from Table 1 that the multinomial non-linear hierarchical Bayes classifier significantly outperforms the naive Bayes and SVM classifiers on the movie reviews dataset. We see from Table 2 that its performance compares favourably with that of other classifiers on the Reuters R8, the Reuters R52 and the 20 Newsgroups datasets.

We also observe from Plot B of Figure 3 that multinomial non-linear hierarchical Bayes classifiers with 2, 3, 4 and 5 hidden nodes outperform 1 hidden node on that dataset.

Finally, we observe that the artificial dataset is modeled far better by a Gaussian non-linear hierarchical Bayes classifier than by a Gaussian naive Bayes classifier.

5 Conclusions

We have shown that generative classifiers with a hidden layer are capable of learning non-linear decision boundaries under the right conditions (independence assumptions), and therefore might be said to be capable of deep learning. We have also shown experimentally that multinomial non-linear hierarchical Bayes classifiers can outperform some linear classification algorithms on some text classification tasks.

References

Aixin Sun and Ee-Peng Lim. 2001. Hierarchical Text Classification and Evaluation. In *Proceedings of the 2001 IEEE International Conference on Data Mining*, ICDM '01, 521–528.

Andrew L. Maas, Raymond E. Daly, Peter T. Pham, Dan Huang, Andrew Y. Ng, and Christopher Potts. 2011. Learning Word Vectors for Sentiment Analysis. In *Proceedings of the 49th Annual Meeting of the Association for Computational Linguistics: Human Language Technologies, ACL-HLT2011*, 142–150.

Alex Krizhevsky, and Geoffrey E. Hinton. 2011. Using very deep autoencoders for content-based image retrieval. *ESANN*.

Alexandr Andoni, Rina Panigrahy, Gregory Valiant, and Li Zhang. 2014. Learning polynomials with neural networks. *ICML*.

Ana Cardoso-Cachopo. 2007. Improving Methods for Single-label Text Categorization. *PhD Thesis, Instituto Superior Tecnico, Universidade Tecnica de Lisboa*.

Asja Fischer and Christian Igel. 2012. An Introduction to Restricted Boltzmann Machines. *Progress in Pattern Recognition, Image Analysis, Computer Vision, and Applications*, 17th Iberoamerican Congress, CIARP 2012, Buenos Aires, Argentina, September 3-6, 2012. Proceedings, 7441:14–36.

Andrew Y. Ng and Michael I. Jordan. 2001. On discriminative vs. generative classifiers: A comparison of logistic regression and naive bayes. In *Advances in Neural Information Processing Systems 14 (NIPS'01)*, 841–848.

Arthur P. Dempster, Nan M. Laird, and Donald B. Rubin. 1977. Maximum likelihood from incomplete data via the EM algorithm. *Journal of the royal statistical society. Series B (methodological)*. 1–38. JSTOR.

Chuong B. Do, and Serafim Batzoglou. 2008. What is the expectation maximization algorithm?. *Nature biotechnology*. 26(8):897-899. Nature Publishing Group.

Daphne Koller and Nir Friedman. 2009. *Probabilistic graphical models: principles and techniques*. MIT Press, Cambridge, MA.

David E. Rumelhart, Geoffrey E. Hinton, and R. J. Williams. 1986. Learning Internal Representations by Error Propagation. In *Parallel distributed processing: explorations in the microstructure of cognition*. 1:318-362. MIT Press, Cambridge, MA.

David H. Ackley, Geoffrey E. Hinton, Terrence J. Sejnowski. 1985. A learning algorithm for Boltzmann machines. In *Cognitive science*. 9(1):147-169.

George Cybenko. 1989. Approximation by superpositions of a sigmoidal function. In *Mathematics of control, signals and systems*. 2(4):303–314

Hao Wang and Dit-Yan Yeung. 2016. Towards Bayesian Deep Learning: A Survey. *CoRR*.

Martin J.Wainwright and Michael I. Jordan. 2008. Graphical models, exponential families, and variational inference. *Foundations and Trends® in Machine Learning*, 1(1-2):1–305.

Marvin Minsky and Seymour Papert. 1988. *Perceptrons: an introduction to computational geometry (expanded edition)*. MIT Press, Cambridge, MA.

Michael I. Jordan, and Chris Bishop. 2004. *An introduction to graphical models*. Progress.

Miguel E. Ruiz, and Padmini Srinivasan. 2002. Hierarchical Text Categorization Using Neural Networks. In *Information Retrieval*, 5(1):87–118.

Nan Laird, Nicholas Lange, and Daniel Stram. 1987. Maximum likelihood computations with repeated measures: application of the EM algorithm. *Journal of the American Statistical Association*, 82(397):97–105.

Paul Smolensky. 1986. Chapter 6: Information Processing in Dynamical Systems: Foundations of Harmony Theory. *Parallel Distributed Processing: Explorations in the Microstructure of Cognition, Volume 1: Foundations*, 1:194281. MIT Press, Cambridge, MA.

Susana Eyheramendy, David D. Lewis, and David Madigan. 2003. On the Naive Bayes Model for Text Categorization. In *9th International Workshop on Artificial Intelligence and Statistics*.

Thomas Morton. 2005. Using semantic relations to improve information retrieval. *Dissertations available from ProQuest*. Paper AAI3197718.

Qinpei Zhao, Ville Hautamaki, and Pasi Franti. 2011. RSEM: An Accelerated Algorithm on Repeated EM. *2011 Sixth International Conference on Image and Graphics (ICIG)*. IEEE.

Shivakumar Vaithyanathan, Jianchang Mao, and Byron Dom. 2000. Hierarchical Bayes for Text Classification. *PRICAI Workshop on Text and Web Mining*, 36-43.

Sriharsha Veeramachaneni, Diego Sona, and Paolo Avesani. 2005. Hierarchical Dirichlet Model for Document Classification. In *Proceedings of the 22Nd International Conference on Machine Learning*, ICML '05, 928–935.

Yann LeCun, Yoshua Bengio, and Geoffrey Hinton. 2015. Deep learning. *Nature*, 521:436-444.

Yoshua Bengio. 2009. Learning deep architectures for AI. *Foundations and trends in Machine Learning*, 2(1):1-127.

Zhibin Liao and Gustavo Carneiro. 2015. The use of deep learning features in a hierarchical classifier learned with the minimization of a non-greedy loss function that delays gratification. *2015 IEEE International Conference on Image Processing (ICIP)*, IEEE.

A computational analysis of Mahabharata

Debarati Das
UG student,Dept. of CSE
PES
Institute of Technology
Karnataka, India
Debarati.d1994
@gmail.com

Bhaskarjyoti Das
PG Student, Dept. of CSE
Visvesvaraya
Technological University
Karnataka, India
Bhaskarjyoti01
@gmail.com

Kavi Mahesh
Dean of Research and Director
KAnOE-Center for Knowledge Analytics
and Ontological Engineering
PES University, Bangalore
Drkavimahesh
@gmail.com

Abstract

Indian epics have not been analyzed computationally to the extent that Greek epics have. In this paper, we show how interesting insights can be derived from the ancient epic Mahabharata by applying a variety of analytical techniques based on a combination of natural language processing, sentiment/emotion analysis and social network analysis methods. One of our key findings is the pattern of significant changes in the overall sentiment of the epic story across its eighteen chapters and the corresponding characterization of the primary protagonists in terms of their sentiments, emotions, centrality and leadership attributes in the epic saga.

1 Introduction

Large epics such as the Mahabharata have a wealth of information which may not be apparent to human readers who read them for the fascinating stories or spiritual messages they contain. Computational analysis of large texts can unearth interesting patterns and insights in the structure, flow of stories and dynamics of the numerous characters in the intricate stories that make up the epics. Unfortunately, not much attention has been paid to applying natural language processing and other related techniques to carry out computational analyses of Indian epics. In this work, we attempt to carry out detailed analyses of the Mahabharata epic.

Sentiment and social network analyses have been applied mainly to structured texts such as tweets, emails etc. to discover user sentiments or important personalities. Comparatively literary works are less subjected to computational analysis as there are no immediate business incentives. However,similar techniques can be adopted

towards appreciating the literary work, to understand underlying social network and to find or validate literary truths. As literary text is built around a social backdrop, it reflects the society the author lives in and reveals a lot about the contemporary social setting.

Unlike SMS and tweets, genre is important in literary text. Amongst the past and recent literary genres, epics and novels have seen most of the work in the Digital Humanity community as the scope is typically large in terms of time, number of events and characters to facilitate computational analysis. The Greek epics Iliad and Odyssey, the English epic Beowulf, novels such as Victor Hugo's Les Miserable and works of William Shakespeare are some of the examples. However, there is no major existing work around Indian epics such as Ramayana and Mahabharata. Hence we have chosen Mahabharata as the target text for a computational analysis effort.

2 Related work

The first important step in computational analysis of a literary text is to identify the protagonists. Next the relatedness of the protagonists can be computed to form the underlying social network. There are essentially two methods to capture social network from a literary text. One option is to capture all social events such as conversations assuming that all characters participating in a social event are socially related. This method does not work well for narrative intensive text. The other method assumes that all characters appearing in a given co-occurrence window have some kind of social relations. This approach ends up considering even insignificant characters but works better for narrative based texts such as epics. Newman and Girvan's work (2004) to detect the communities in Victor Hugo's Les Miserable is the first major effort to find the social network from narratives. Sack (2012) deduced

D S Sharma, R Sangal and A K Singh. Proc. of the 13th Intl. Conference on Natural Language Processing, pages 219–228,
Varanasi, India. December 2016. ©2016 NLP Association of India (NLPAI)

the plot from network by using concepts of structural balance theory. Elson et al.(2010) proposed dialogue based method to extract social network. Jayannavar et al. (2015) updated Elson's approach by broadening the scope of conversation to social events. Rydberg-Cox (2011) extracted social networks from Greek tragedies. Agarwal et al.(2012) showed that a dynamic network analysis can present more subtle facts. Beveridge and Shan (2016) built the underlying social network for the third book ("A storm of swords") of the TV series "Game of Thrones" with a co-occurrence window of 15 words. Stiller et al. analyzed ten of Shakespeare's plays (2003) also based on the co-occurrence logic. Carron and Kenna (2012) provided a quantitative approach to compare networks. Mac Carron et al.(2014) did a structural analysis of Iliad, English poem Beowulf and Irish epic Tain Bo Cuailnge. P. J. Miranda et al.(2013) has done a structural analysis of underlying social network of Homer's Odyssey. Alberich et al.(2002) have built a social network from Marvel comics.

As Mahabharata is an epic, we must mention Poetics by Aristotle and an excellent commentary provided by Lucas (1968). Aristotle defined literary genres such as poetry, tragedy, comedy and epic. Poetry mimics life. Tragedy is a type of poetry that showcase noble men and their noble qualities as well as values. Epics such as Mahabharata are a type of tragedy and are built around noble men in the form of narratives. A tragedy typically has a plot with a beginning, a middle and an end and other constituents of the text are secondary to the plot. The beginning of the plot typically is a scenario of stability which gets disturbed by some events. The middle is where the disequilibrium comes in along with lot of events and actions by the characters. All the events and actions are towards achieving the end where the problem gets resolved and stability sets in again. Plots have various constituents i.e. suffering, reversal, recognition of new knowledge, surprise. An epic is different from a more recent literary genre like a novel and will have lot of negative sentiment across its breadth but in spite of that conveys a noble theme in the minds of its audience.

One can measure sentence polarity by referring to some standard thesaurus where polarity measures are preassigned by researchers.This approach uses a resource like SentiWordnet

(http://sentiwordnet.isti.cnr.it/). Alternatively, in a supervised classification approach labelled data sets from similar domains are utilised. However, this approach works where the training dataset from similar domain is available and this method is not suitable for sentiment analysis for an epic. Emotion analysis finds causes of sentiment. Robert Plutchik(1980) defined the eight basic emotion types. Mohammad and Turney (2010) created the NRC emotion lexicon which is an association of a list of words with these eight basic types of emotion and two types of sentiment. Mohammad (2011) presented an emotion analyzer as a visualization exercise of these emotions in literary text.

Table 1: Key Attributes of Mahabharata Text

Attributes	Value	Remarks
Size in bytes	15,175 K	English translation
Size in bytes	13,947 K	After removing comments
Number of words	28,58,609	Using NLTK
Number of unique words	32,506	Using NLTK
Number of sentences	1,18,087	Using NLTK
Number of chapters	18	"parva"
Number of characters	210	appearing at least 10 times

For our research, we have used the English translation of Mahabharata available at Project Gutenberg site (http://www.gutenberg.org/ebooks/7864). This is a translation by Kisari Mohan Ganguli done between 1883-1896. Mahabharata is larger than Iliad and Odyssey together, compiled many years ago. This has 18 "parva"s or chapters and each "parva" has many sections.

3   The methodology

Mahabharata is not dialogue heavy and is mostly narrative. So, identifying relations between characters is done using co-occurrence algorithm with window size of a sentence.The method we devised for a comprehensive computational analysis of the Mahabharata epic is as follows:

1. Pre-processing

    - Filter out supporting texts such as tables of content, publisher details and chapter summaries.
    - Separate the text into chapters (called "parva") using suitable regular expressions.
    - Separate each "parva" into sections based on the structural elements in the text.

2. Identifying characters

    - Identify all proper nouns using POS tagging
    - Input a list of known characters of the Mahabharata story (widely available on the internet).
    - Input a thesaurus of equivalent names for the characters (also widely known, e.g. Draupadi=Panchali, Arjuna=Phalguni etc.) to merge equivalent names.
    - Filter out a list of known place names in ancient India and its neighbouring regions.
    - Apply a threshold to retain names whose frequency is above a minimum value (resulting in 210 characters for the Mahabharata story).
    - Retain only those characters which are in the top 30 percent of characters mentioned in a given parva (resulting in about 70 characters overall). Same logic is followed for both individual and cumulative analysis of each parva.

The following steps are carried out separately for each "parva" and also for the entire text.

3. Co-occurrence analysis

    - Compute a co-occurrence matrix for the identified characters using sentence boundaries as windows of co-occurrence.
    - Build a social graph from the co-occurrence matrix.

4. Network analysis

    - Various network metrics are computed for the social graph for each of the 18 "parva"s in both cumulative and standalone way viz. betweenness centrality, closeness centrality, degree centrality, size of maximal cliques, number of detected communities, size of ego networks for main nodes, core periphery analysis, density of the core and overall network etc.
    - Additionally various structural metrics are computed for social graph viz. degree assortativity, percentage size of giant component,average clustering coefficient, average shortest path length etc.

5. Overall sentiment analysis

    - Using syntactic meta data, phrases containing noun, adjective, verb and adverbs are identified.
    - The above text is tokenized using standard NLP techniques.
    - The tokens are POS (parts of speech) tagged and tagged tokens are mapped to synsets in Wordnet in a word sense disambiguation process.
    - The sentiment scores are picked up from SentiWordnet for each synset.
    - Overall sentiment of the parva is derived from these values by summing the constituent sentiment scores.

6. Sentiment analysis for main characters

    - Similarly sentiment analysis of each protagonist is done by extracting the sentences where the protagonist appears. This is done for each parva.

7. Emotion analysis

    - Emotion analysis for the full text and each of the protagonists is done with the help of NRC word-emotion association lexicon. After extracting the relevant part of the corpus,the score is calculated for each POS (part of speech) tagged token for each emotion and finally summed up. The obvious limitation with any lexicon based approach is the limitation imposed by the size of the lexicon itself and this limitation does apply to our analysis as well.

We have used the Python, NLTK(Natural Language Toolkit), various open source libraries (TextBlob, Networkx, Stanford SNAP, Gephi) and data analytics/visualization software Tableau in our work.

4 Analysis of results

4.1 The protagonists

We have tried out 3 different approaches to identify the protagonists.

- **Most frequently mentioned character:** As shown in Figure.1a, this method finds the most frequent characters. However this misses out the protagonists who are unfortunately low on frequency but may be important otherwise.

- **Size of the ego network:** Size of ego network (number of nodes directly connected) calculated from Mahabharata social network produces different results. As shown in Figure.1b, Kripa who is a teacher of the princes, is topping the list. Chieftains like Shalya, Virata, Drupada come towards the top in this list. Kunti(mother of Pandavas), Indra (the king of gods) and Narada (the sage) are also in this list being well connected!

- **Centrality metrics:** The betweenness, eigenvector, closeness and degree centrality are compared. Few observations can be made out of this from Figure.2:

    - Betweenness centrality differentiates the main protagonists whereas other centrality metrics are mostly equivalent.
    - Arjuna, Karna, Krishna, Yudhisthira, Bhisma, Kunti and Drona are the top few in terms of all four centrality. They are the most important protagonists.
    - Some of the personalities with very large ego network are having very low betweenness centrality and not making into the top list (Kripa, Shalya, Drupada, Virata etc.) because their influence is limited to one camp i.e. Kaurava or Pandava. Their importance is mostly local.

- Amongst the princesses and queen mothers, Kunti turns out to be the understated (in the existing literary analysis) power behind the scene (having a large ego network and high centralities). Her low eigenvector centrality leads to false perception that she is not important. Other main lady characters (Gandhari, Madri, Draupadi) are low on betweenness as their influence is limited to one camp.

4.2 The words say a lot

Word clouds show a marked difference between the protagonists as shown in Figure.3a to Figure.3d. These are drawn by extracting adjectives from respective corpus.

- Both Arjuna and Bhima are "mighty" and "warrior". But Arjuna has words like "great", "excellent", "capable", "celestial" whereas Bhima has "terrible", "fierce" etc. So Arjuna is the best in his class whereas Bhima is a mighty warrior with "terrible" anger.

- Bhisma has "invincible", "principal", "virtuous" whereas Krishna has "celestial", "beautiful", "illustrious". So, Bhisma sounds more like an invincible warrior famous for his virtue, whereas Krishna is almost godly.

- For Duryodhana, "wicked", "terrible" etc. stand out whereas for Yudhisthira, "virtuous" and "righteous" are key words. Both are leaders of their respective camps but they are poles apart.

4.3 Sentiments across the text

Mahabharata takes the readers through a roller coaster ride of sentiment as shown in Figure.4. "Aadi parva"(1) starts on a positive note but the "Sabha parva" (2) brings lot of negativity with the game of dice. "Vana parva"(3) is again positive as Panadavs in spite of being in exile, make lot of friends and have achievements. "Virat parva"(4) is negative as the Pandavas have to live in disguise doing odd jobs. "Udyog Parva" (5) is again positive with both sides are very hopeful of winning war. After that as elders and leaders get killed in the battle, it is a downward slide of sentiment with Duryodhana's death bringing in positive emotion in "Shalya parva"(9). In "Stri parva" (11), the destruction is complete and sentiment reaches the

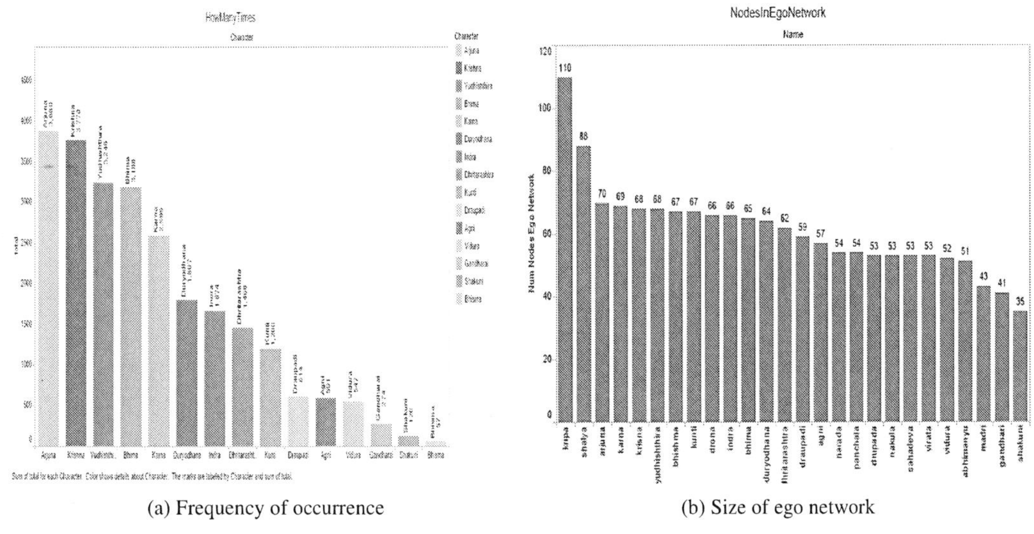

(a) Frequency of occurrence
(b) Size of ego network

Figure 1: Finding protagonists by number of mention and ego network

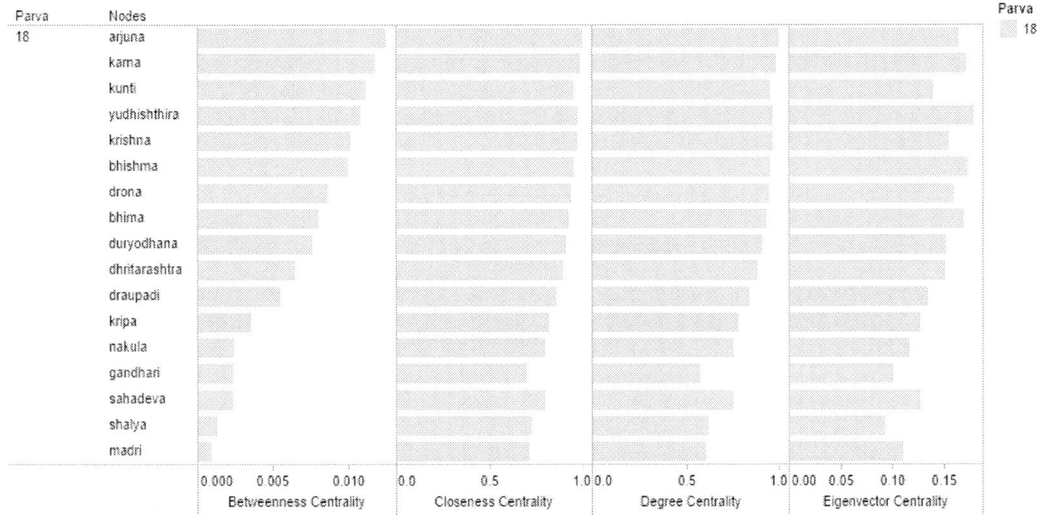

Figure 2: Finding protagonists by comparing centrality metrics

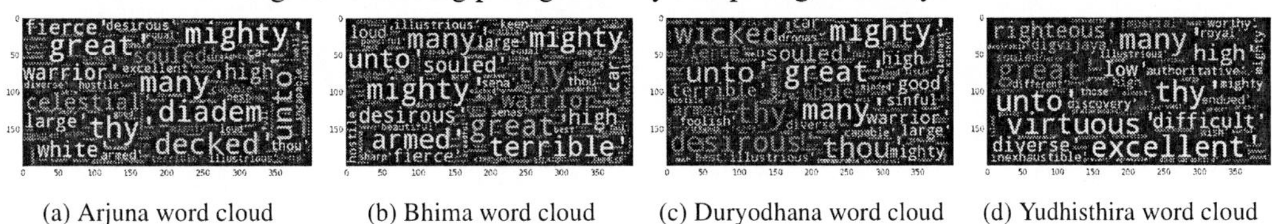

(a) Arjuna word cloud
(b) Bhima word cloud
(c) Duryodhana word cloud
(d) Yudhisthira word cloud

Figure 3: Words say a lot

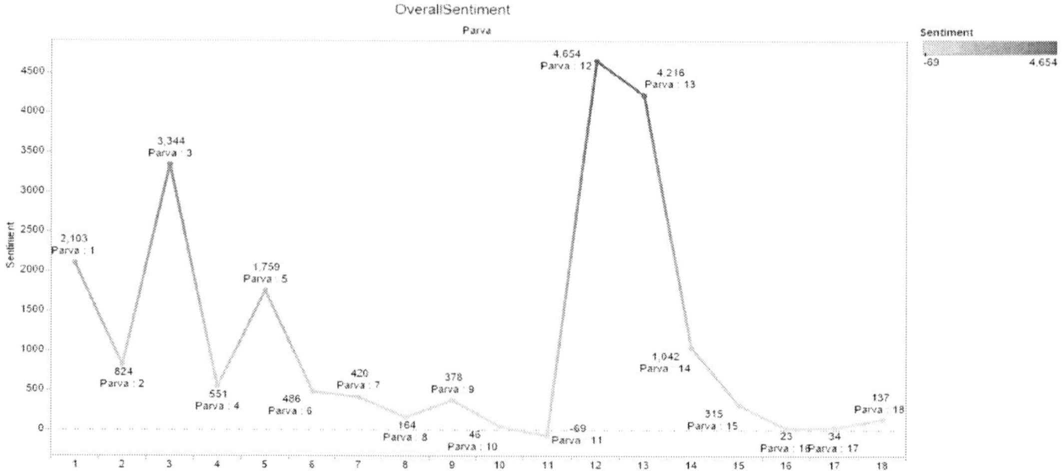

Figure 4: Sentiment across "parvas" of Mahabharata

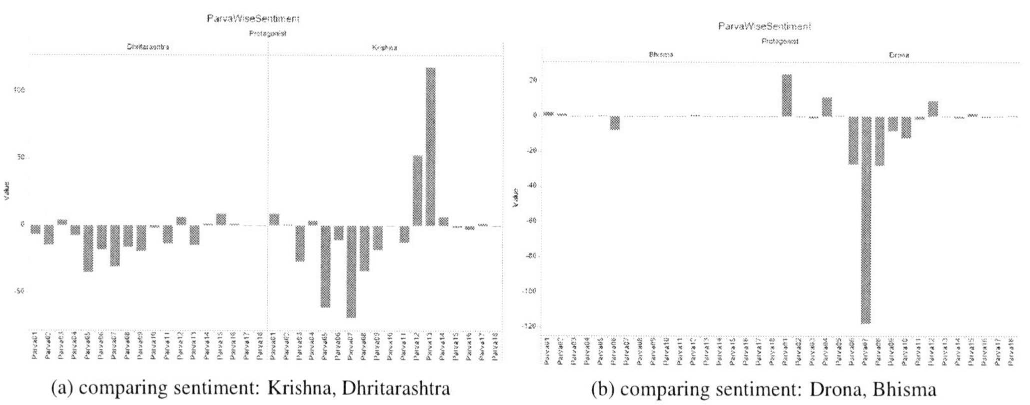

(a) comparing sentiment: Krishna, Dhritarashtra

(b) comparing sentiment: Drona, Bhisma

Figure 5: Comparing the sentiments

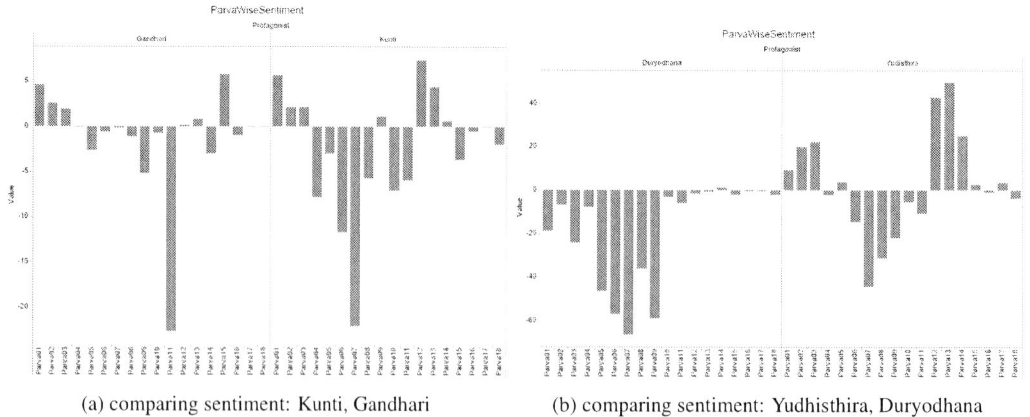

(a) comparing sentiment: Kunti, Gandhari

(b) comparing sentiment: Yudhisthira, Duryodhana

Figure 6: Comparing the sentiments

224

lowest level. The "Shanti parva" (12) brings in peak of positive sentiment with coronation of Yudhisthira and many achievements. After that, it is again a downward slide of sentiments with many deaths and even death of Lord Krishna. The sentiment sees an uptick in the last two "parva"s when Pandavas leave for Himalayas and finally attain divine status. Figure.5a to Figure.6b depict the net sentiment of the main protagonists according to the "parva". It leads to some interesting observations.

- Warriors like Arjuna and Bhima have lot of negativity around them.

- The leaders of the two warring camps Duryodhana and Yudhisthira are clear contrast as Yudhisthira has lot of positive sentiment around him.

- The gods like Indra and Agni have mostly positivity around them as they are mostly neutral on the ground.

- The eldest warrior, Bhisma is mostly neutral whereas Drona is committed to one camp and so is surrounded by negativity. Dhritarashtra, though elder, is mostly surrounded by negative sentiments.

- The two queen mothers Gandhari and Kunti are the sources of positive energy in both camps. Though understated they play pivotal roles. Compared to them, Draupadi is surrounded by negative sentiment.

- Lord Krishna, when he is in the thick of war, has negativity around him but once the battle gets over and larger senses prevail, he brings in sense of karma and lot of positive sentiments.

4.4 The emotions

We have analyzed the emotions both at the global and the protagonist level as shown in Figure.7 to Figure.9. Out of the eight basic emotion types, anger and trust are the key ones as expected in a tragedy that has an epic battle as the mainstay. Anticipation, disgust, fear, sadness come in almost equal proportion. In the scheming world of Mahabharata, there is not much of surprise and joy is kind of overshadowed by the other negative emotions. If we consider the emotions for some of the main protagonists, interesting conclusions can be drawn.

- Amongst the key ladies, Kunti stands out by the richness of positive emotion (trust and joy) and is the bedrock of strength for the Pandavas when they go through all their reversals of fate. Gandhari is relatively low key whereas Draupadi displays all the negative emotions that are key ingredients of a tragedy.

- Amongst the Pandava and Kaurava leaders (Duryodhana and Yudhisthira), Yudhisthira displays trust and joy more than any other emotion. Probably that is why he is perceived as a leader though there are many others with much more bravery and heroics. The contrast between Duryodhana and Yudhisthira is telling.

- Bhima and Duryodhana are very similar in emotions i.e. anger, trust and fear. Arjuna is quite unique and ambidextrous i.e. he displays enough of anger and fear and also large quantity of trust and joy.

- Amongst the elders, Bhisma is a detached persona and he does not show much of emotion. Drona is more attached to one camp and comparatively shows anger more than any other emotion.

- Krishna shows tremendous amount of trust, anticipation and joy in spite of all the tragedies and it is no wonder that he is called an incarnation of god.

4.5 Leadership analysis

We searched for leaders using two criteria viz. high in positive sentiments and high in centrality (degree and/or betweenness) as shown in Figure.10. Our assumption is leaders are not only centrally connected but they also show lot of positivity.

- It becomes very clear why Krishna is supreme as he is the only one who is in the high corner of this target quadrant.

- Closely following Krishna is Yudhisthira. That explains why in spite of not being a great warrior and known addiction for gambling, Yudhisthira is so well respected.

- Going by the same yardstick for leadership, Arjuna, Bhima, Drona, Karna are more of achievers or doers rather than leaders.

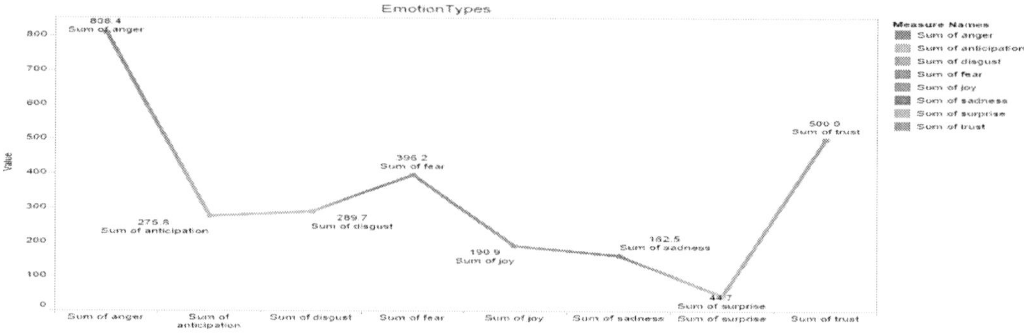

Figure 7: Emotions across the text

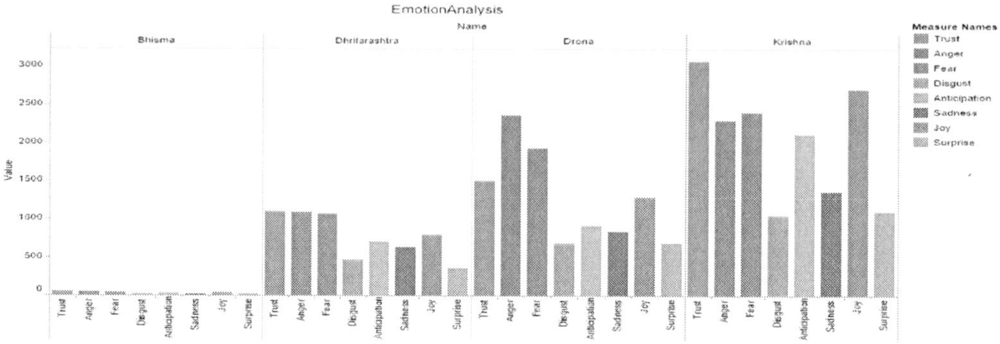

Figure 8: Emotion Analysis of Bhisma, Dhritarashtra, Drona and Krishna

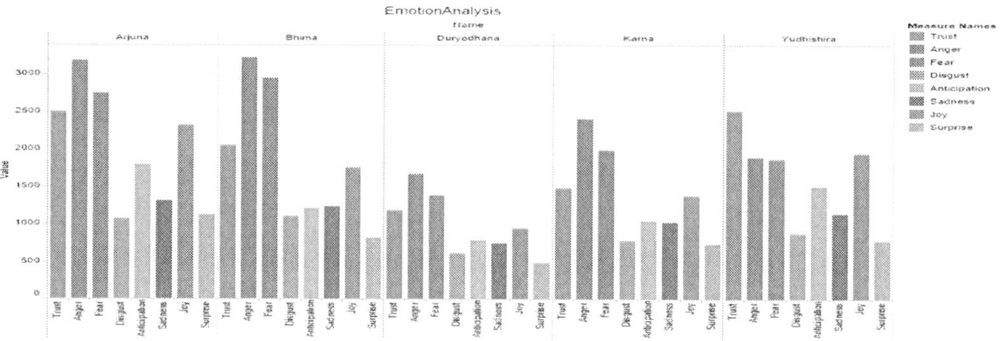

Figure 9: Emotion Analysis of Arjuna, Bhima, Duryodhana, Karna, Yudhisthira

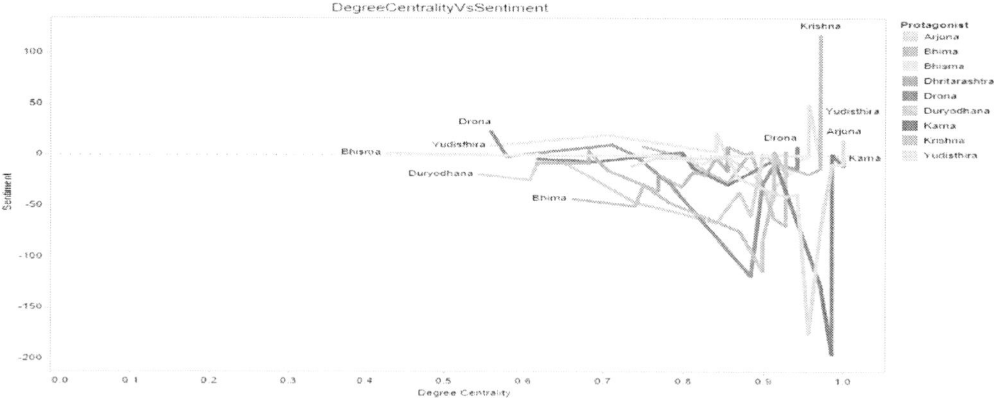

Figure 10: Leadership

226

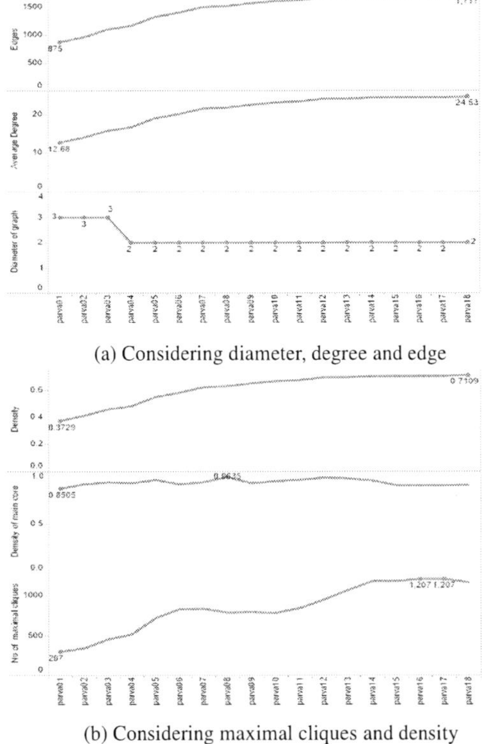

(a) Considering diameter, degree and edge

(b) Considering maximal cliques and density

Figure 11: Evolution of social network across parvas

- Bhisma is neither great in centrality nor in positivity. He is more of a helpless spectator apart from his hard to find commitment to whatever promise he makes.

- Clearly Kaurava camp lacks in leadership. Duryodhana, the Kaurava leader, shows the lack of it and it is somewhat compensated by the combined effort of the achievers in his camp.

4.6 The social network of Mahabharata

- The "core periphery analysis" of the social network reveals a core of size 52 and consistently high density that remains comparable to the overall density of the network i.e. the plot is built around these members of the core.

- Mahabharata is also the story of three camps as proved by community detection techniques using Louvain algorithm (Blondel et al., 2008). They are the Kauravas, Pandavas and the gods/sages who remained somewhat neutral.

- The story of Mahabharata encompasses many years before the battle, 18 days of battle and around thirty six years after the battle. The evolving social network of Mahabharata across the parvas is analyzed using various structural metrics viz. degree, average degree, number of edges, number of maximal cliques and density of the main core as well as overall density. As shown in Figure.11a and Figure.11b, various structural metrics of the underlying social network tend to stabilize towards the end after becoming destabilised initially following Aristotelian framework of stability-instability-stability.

- Mahabharata network comes out as a small world network(small average shortest path and large clustering coefficient). Transitivity measured is comparable to other random graph of similar size such as Barabassi Albert model. However, modularity is found to be low (mostly 3 communities detected) compared to some real world networks. Also the high positive correlation coefficients for each centrality pair, large giant component and negative degree assortativity indicate large fictional component in Mahabharata.

5 Discussion and conclusion

In this work, we have applied various Natural Language Processing and Social Network Analysis techniques to come up with a computational analysis of the "Mahabharata". We have not only validated what the literary critics have unearthed about the epic but also augmented their findings by discovering subtle facts. Protagonists are identified and analyzed using both statistical and social network parameters such as centrality and ego network. The trajectory of sentiment and various emotions across the length of the text for each protagonist are examined. The findings validate what the literary critics have already found. Additionally this analysis brings out some subtle facts i.e. Kunti is understated in the existing literary analysis but is seen to be playing a pivotal role as displayed by the sentiments, emotions, centrality and large ego network size. We figured out the influence category of various protagonists in terms of local or global influence.

The leadership analysis explains why Yudhisthira is described in such glorious terms in spite of his many weaknesses. We have also looked at leadership quotient of various protagonists by considering their position in the centrality-positivity quadrants and have brought out the leadership contrast between the warring camps in this epic.

The analysis also helps to explain why Mahabharata is an epic. Apart from the sheer number of characters, events, diversity of emotion and sentiment, it is found to conform to the Aristotelian definition of epics having the stability-instability-stability transitions. The analysis of the structural metrics also indicate that Mahabharata is not purely factual and has a large fictional component.

Clearly computational analysis of a literary text does not make the literary analysis redundant. But this provides an additional tool set for the students of literature to validate and augment their findings. The methods used can be easily replicated for other texts.

As a next step, we plan to extend similar analysis to the Indian epic Ramayana and perform similar structural analysis of the underlying social networks.

Acknowledgement

This work is supported in part by the World Bank/Government of India research grant under the TEQIP programme (subcomponent 1.2.1) to the Centre for Knowledge Analytics and Ontological Engineering (KAnOE http://www.kanoe.org) at PES University, Bangalore, India.

References

Apoorv Agarwal, Augusto Corvalan, Jacob Jensen, and Owen Rambow. 2012. Social network analysis of alice in wonderland. In *Workshop on Computational Linguistics for Literature*, pages 88–96.

Ricardo Alberich, Joe Miro-Julia, and Francesc Rosselló. 2002. Marvel universe looks almost like a real social network. *arXiv preprint cond-mat/0202174*.

Poetics Aristotle. 1968. Introduction, commentary and appendixes by dw lucas. *Oxford*, 125:16.

Andrew Beveridge and Jie Shan. 2016. Network of thrones. *Math Horizons*, 23(4):18–22.

Vincent D Blondel, Jean-Loup Guillaume, Renaud Lambiotte, and Etienne Lefebvre. 2008. Fast unfolding of communities in large networks. *Journal of statistical mechanics: theory and experiment*, 2008(10):P10008.

David K Elson, Nicholas Dames, and Kathleen R McKeown. 2010. Extracting social networks from literary fiction. In *Proceedings of the 48th annual meeting of the association for computational linguistics*, pages 138–147. Association for Computational Linguistics.

Prashant Arun Jayannavar, Apoorv Agarwal, Melody Ju, and Owen Rambow. 2015. Validating literary theories using automatic social network extraction. *on Computational Linguistics for Literature*, page 32.

Pádraig Mac Carron and Ralph Kenna. 2012. Universal properties of mythological networks. *EPL (Europhysics Letters)*, 99(2):28002.

P Mac Carron and R Kenna. 2014. Network analysis of beowulf, the iliad and the táin bó cúailnge. In *Sources of mythology: Ancient and contemporary myths. Proceedings of the Seventh Annual International Conference on Comparative Mythology (15–17 May 2013, Tübingen)*, pages 125–141.

Pedro J Miranda, Murilo S Baptista, and Sandro E de S Pinto. 2013. Analysis of communities in a mythological social network. *arXiv preprint arXiv:1306.2537*.

Saif M Mohammad and Peter D Turney. 2010. Emotions evoked by common words and phrases: Using mechanical turk to create an emotion lexicon. In *Proceedings of the NAACL HLT 2010 workshop on computational approaches to analysis and generation of emotion in text*, pages 26–34. Association for Computational Linguistics.

Saif Mohammad. 2011. From once upon a time to happily ever after: Tracking emotions in novels and fairy tales. In *Proceedings of the 5th ACL-HLT Workshop on Language Technology for Cultural Heritage, Social Sciences, and Humanities*, pages 105–114. Association for Computational Linguistics.

Mark EJ Newman and Michelle Girvan. 2004. Finding and evaluating community structure in networks. *Physical review E*, 69(2):026113.

Robert Plutchik. 1980. A general psychoevolutionary theory of emotion. *Theories of emotion*, 1:3–31.

Jeff Rydberg-Cox. 2011. Social networks and the language of greek tragedy. In *Journal of the Chicago Colloquium on Digital Humanities and Computer Science*, volume 1.

Graham Sack. 2012. Character networks for narrative generation. In *Intelligent Narrative Technologies: Papers from the 2012 AIIDE Workshop, AAAI Technical Report WS-12-14*, pages 38–43.

James Stiller, Daniel Nettle, and Robin IM Dunbar. 2003. The small world of shakespeares plays. *Human Nature*, 14(4):397–408.

Use of Features for Accentuation of *ghañanta* Words

Samir Janardan Sohoni
IIT Bombay
Powai, Mumbai 400076
India
sohoni@hotmail.com

Malhar A. Kulkarni
IIT Bombay
Powai, Mumbai 400076
India.
malharku@gmail.com

Abstract

Sanskrit is an accented language. The accent is very prominent in Vedic Sanskrit but classical Sanskrit does not make use of it. Accent is a disambiguation device which can help to understand the correct sense of a word.

Words in Sanskrit tend to fall in certain grammatical categories like *ghañantas*, vocatives etc. Words in a category tend to have an accent governed by either a general or a special rule of accentuation. Pāṇini's special (*apavāda*) rules of accentuation for a specific category of words can be studied along with the general (*utsarga*) rules of accentuation for the same class. The resulting body of rules states all the conditions necessary for accentuation of words from that class. The conditions reveal a set of features which can be used for determining the correct accent. If the features of accentuation for a class of words is understood, computers can be trained to accentuate unaccented words from that class. This paper discusses some features of *ghañanta* words and how the features can be used to restore accent on unaccented *ghañanta* words.

1 Introduction

Broadly, Sanskrit has two streams – Vedic and Classical. The latter is known as *bhāṣā*, the commonly spoken language which is the main focus of Pāṇini's grammar. The former is indicated in Pāṇini's grammar by terms like *mantre* and *chandasi*. Accentual contrasts are one distinctive feature of Vedic. During the time Pāṇini developed his Sanskrit grammar, accentuation must have been a feature of the language. Pāṇini has made provision for accents in the morphological machinery of Sanskrit – the roots (*dhātus*) and suffixes (*pratyayas*). The Aṣṭādhyāyī lays out the mechanisms for production of Vedic forms as well as those in bhāṣā using the same morphological framework. Accent was destined to vanish from written form of classical texts – none of the Sanskrit classics use accent. Classics would not have been able to use certain *alaṅkāras* if accentual contrasts were in force[1].

Accent plays an important role in ascertaining the senses of words. For example, the word *jyeṣṭháḥ*[2] means *elder* when pronounced with an acute final syllable. If pronounced as *jyéṣṭhaḥ*[3], which has an acute initial syllable, it means *praiseworthy*. Both forms are created by adding the superlative suffix *iṣṭhan*. Another example is the base *arya* which means *honourable*, *lord* or someone earning a living by doing business. If the word is pronounced as *aryá*[4] it strictly means a lord. If pronounced as *árya* it can take other meanings.

Although classical Sanskrit lacks tonal contrasts, marking plain text with correct accents can lower ambiguity and thereby contribute to high-quality translations of classical Sanskrit texts. Marking plain text with correct accents can help to reduce ambiguity by narrowing down senses of words. Low ambiguity can result in high-quality translations.

Pāṇinian grammar is generative – initial

---

[1] Devasthali (1967) pp 1 note 1 – *kāvyamārge svaro na gamyate*

[2] The derivation begins as *vṛddha + iṣṭhan*. See Aṣṭādhyāyī rule *jya ca* (A. 5.3.61). The accent is by *phiṭhsūtras*, see *jyeṣṭhakaniṣṭhayoḥ vayasi* (P. 1.23).

[3] The derivation begins as *praśasya + iṣṭhan*. See Aṣṭādhyāyī rule *vṛddhasya ca* (A. 5.3.62). The accent is by *ñnityādirnityam* (A. 6.1.197).

[4] See *aryasya svāmyākhyā cet* (P. 1.18) and *aryaḥ svāmivaiśyayoḥ* (A. 3.1.103).

D S Sharma, R Sangal and A K Singh. Proc. of the 13th Intl. Conference on Natural Language Processing, pages 229–238,
Varanasi, India. December 2016. ©2016 NLP Association of India (NLPAI)

conditions coupled with the rules from the Aṣṭādhyāyī lead to the final accented form. This might be the only way Pāṇinian grammar is designed to work. How, then, can accent be marked on unaccented words, such as those found in classical texts, using the Pāṇinian process? It seems that words have features due to which they are accentuated a certain way. If these features are learned and superimposed on unaccented words, they can be given the correct accent.

2 Notion of Compositionality

The meaning and accent of a sentence are composed of the meaning and the accent of words. Similarly, the meaning and accent of a word are composed of the meaning and the accent of morphological elements like roots and terminations. Kulkarni et al. (2015) have shown that sentences are based on the notion of compositionality.

An example of this notion of compositionality is shown in figure 1. Unlike sentential meaning, sentential accent is not cumulative. Sentential accent is not simply a concatenation of accented words. Accented words such as *gopāláḥ* (an agent), *grāmám* (an object) and *gácchati* (a verb) can be combined to form a sentence which means 'Gopāla goes to town.' However, the concatenated form *gopāláḥ grāmám gácchati* is not a correctly accented sentence. The correct rendering[5] is *gopāláḥ grāmám gacchati* because the rule *tiṅ atiṅaḥ* (A. 8.1.28) makes all syllables of a finite verb low-pitched when it follows something other than a finite verb. Just like *tiṅ atiṅaḥ* provides special syntactic conditions for accentuation of finite verbs, other rules lay down semantic, syntactic and lexical conditions for accentuation of many classes of words.

The accent on finite verbs is subject to several sentence-level syntactic considerations (See sections 8.1 and 8.2 of the Aṣṭādhyāyī). The rule *tiṅ atiṅaḥ* (A. 8.1.28) happens to be one rule among many which regulates verbal accent. This rule looks at the internal structure of adjacent words to decide if a verb follows a non-verb. Some rules governing accent on compounds also look at

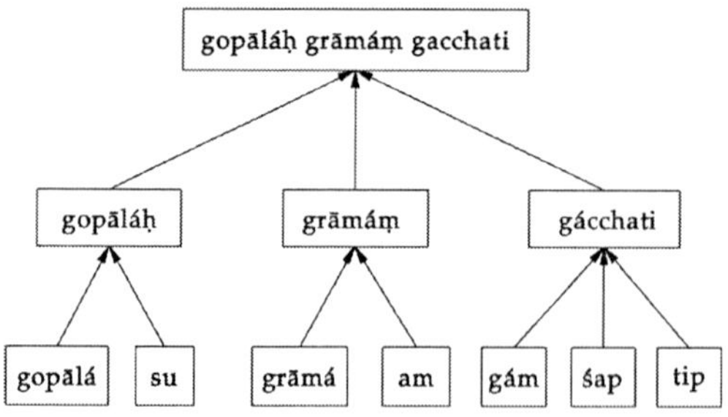

Figure 1: An example of how sentential accent develops

internal structure of words. For example, the compound *mudga-cūrṇam* (paraphrased as *mudgasya cūrṇam*) is accentuated by the rule *cūrṇādīnyaprāṇiṣaṣṭhyāḥ* (A. 6.2.134). The genetive suffix *sya* is elided in the process of compound formation. The rule A. 6.2.134 needs to know if the first word of the compound had a genetive suffix. Thus, the internal structure of words is important.

3 The Deep Structure of Words

The surface form of a word is the sequence of phonemes, which are represented by graphic letters. The word *rājā* is made up of the string of letters $r + \bar{a} + j + \bar{a}$. The surface form is the final form used in language.

For accentuation, meta information used by Pāṇinian rules is required. The form of the word which contains this meta information can be called the deep structure of the word. The meta information annotated in the deep structure is of two kinds. One kind represents the *saṃjñās* and the second kind represents the transformations of morphological elements.

3.1 The *saṃjñā* Labels

As a word is derived using Pāṇinian rules, several *saṃjñās* are applied to various parts of the word. These are Pāṇinian labels used in grammar to identify morphologicial elements so that operations can be applied to those elements. These labels, such as *dhātu* (root), *pratyaya* (suffix), etc. are pieces of meta information that belong to the deep structure of the word. Any keyword, which is important for a rule of accentuation, can be annotated onto the corresponding substring of the word in the deep structure.

3.2 The Transformations

In Pāṇinian grammar, the derivation of a word begins from an initial set of morphological affixes. The morphological elements undergo a transformation to become bits and pieces of the final form of the word. Often, a rule of accentuation specifies accent on an affix and that accent is honoured even if the affix is transformed later in the derivation. For instance, in the third person singular *lṛṭ* (second future) form *bhaviṣyáti* (will become), the typical suffix *sya* is introduced by the rule *syatāsī lṛluṭoḥ* (A. 3.1.33) and it has an acute initial syllable due the rule *ādyudāttaḥ ca* (A. 3.1.3). Subsequently, *sya* transforms into *ṣya* due to the rule *ādeśapratyayayoḥ* (A. 8.3.59), but retains the acute of the original suffix *sya*.

In general there are six different types of transformations in Pāṇinian grammar as shown in Figure 2. The initiation operation (fig. (a)) refers to the first use (*upadeśa*) of any kind of phonetic entity such as a root or suffix. Carrying forward a phonetic entity without any modification whatsoever is retention (fig. (b)). In retention the label *upadeśa* is not applicable. In modification (fig. (c)), several substitutions (*ādeśas*) can modify phonetic units as the derivation progresses. Deletion (fig. (d)) refers to Pāṇinian operations that elide phonetic units due to *lopa, luk, ślu* or *lup*. In disintegration (fig. (e)) *āgamas* (inserted elements) split the original phonetic unit into multiple units. Combination consists of combining multiple phonetic units into a single one due to operations such as *ekādeśa*.

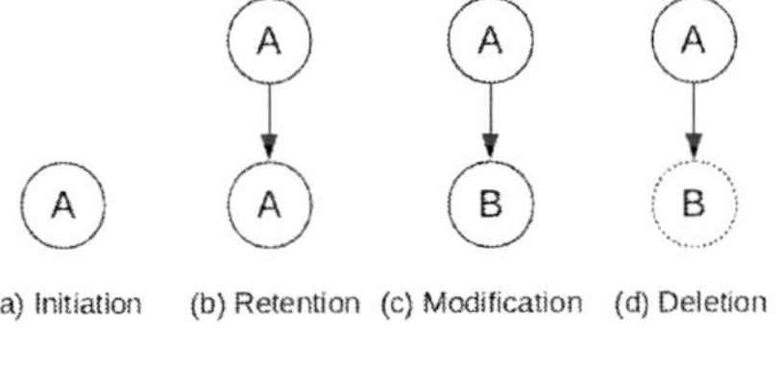

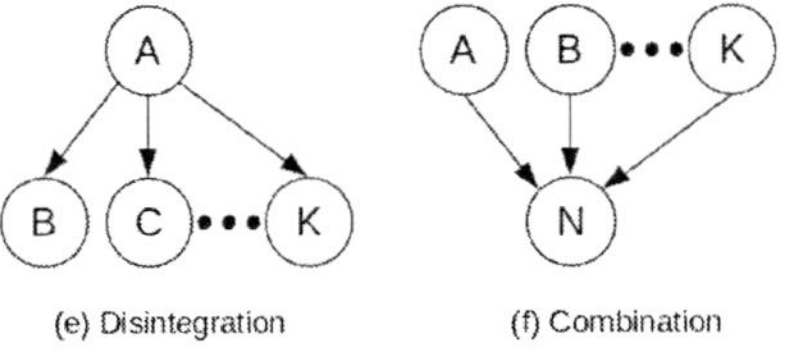

Figure 2: Types of transformations

3.3 Notation of Deep Structure

The transformations are shown using the left arrow. The keywords are shown in square brackets and apply to the immediate phonetic unit on the left. If such a phonetic unit is an aggregate having its own internal deep structure, parentheses are used around it.

As a matter of convention for easy reading, the Devanāgarī script is mixed with Latin script in the annotations of the deep structure. The latter is used only to mark the *saṃjñās*.

The deep structure of the word *bhaviṣyáti* is shown below.

```
(
   (भ् (अव् <- औ <- ऊ) [udātta])[dhātu]
   ( इ ट्[lopa, it]
   ((ष् <- स्)
   य्
   अ [udātta, active])
   ) [ārdhadhātuka, pratyaya]
   (ति प्[lopa, it]) [pratyaya]
)
```

4 Words Ending in *sup* Suffixes

A sentence is made of words. The string of words is not usually punctuated by spaces in between. Old manuscripts show sentences written with no spaces between words. In Sanskrit there are very few punctuation marks. Perhaps the *daṇḍa* and the double *daṇḍa*, which appear at the end of a half and full verse, are the most commonly seen punctuations. The *daṇḍas* are ubiquitous because there are no morphological markers for end of the sentence or quarter of a verse.

The rich inflectional morphology of Sanskrit supplies explicit (but non-unique) nominal termintions in seven cases and three numbers per case. The rule *svaujasamauṭ...* (A. 4.1.2) lists these suffixes in their raw form. Together the collection is known as *sup* suffixes. A nominal base can be used only after it is inflected. Such an inflection is called a word (*pada*)[6]. However, due to some mechanisms[7] the *sup* suffixes may vanish blurring the word boundary. However, the status of being a word is retained in spite of this by virtue of rule *pratyayalope pratyayalakṣaṇam* (A. 1.1.62).

---

[6]Whatever ends in *sup* or *tiṅ* suffixes is a word, cf. *suptiṅghantam padam* (A. 1.4.14)

[7]The rule *halṅyābbhyoḥ dīrghāt sutisyaprktam hal* (A. 6.1.68) deletes the *su* in words like *rājā*.

Thus, the *sup* suffixes are an important feature which helps to establish the word boundary of nominals. The feature can be marked on words as shown in the examples below.

1) (राजा(सु[luk,pratyaya])) [...]
2) (विवेक
   (((((: <- र्) उ[lopa,it]) <- स) उ[lopa,it]
)[pratyaya]
) [...]
3) (पर्ण(आत् <- ङसि[pratyaya]))[...]

5 Rules for *ghañ*-ending Words

Words ending in the suffix *ghañ* (*ghañantas*) are formed by adding the *ghañ* suffix to the verbal roots. The rules A. 3.3.16-55 of the Aṣṭādhyāyī make *ghañanta* words possible. These rules apply the *ghañ* suffix under coocurrence (*upasarga + dhātu*) and semantic conditions. For example, the rule *bhāve* (A. 3.3.18) states that the *ghañ* suffix comes after a root to show pure action regardless of doership. The rule *akartari ca kārake saṃjñayam* (A. 3.3.19) states that it *ghañanta* words indicate appellatives in which an entity is coupled with the action in a non-agentive manner. The rule *parimāṇākhyāyāṃ sarvebhyaḥ* (A. 3.3.20) allows any verbal root to receive the *ghañ* suffix in order to show a measure of quantity.

The following rules control the accent[8] of *ghañanta* words.

1. *ññityādirnityam* (A. 6.1.197)
   This rule causes words to have acute initial syllables when they are formed using such suffixes that are *ñit* or *nit*. *ghañ* being a *ñit* suffix[9] will make the initial syllable acute unless other rules override the provision of this general rule.

2. *karṣātvato ghaño'nta udāttaḥ* (A. 6.1.159)
   A. 6.1.159 overrides A. 6.1.197 and states that *karṣa* (a *ghañanta* stem derived from the verbal root √*kṛṣā* of the *bhvādi* group, not the *tudādi* one) and other *ghañanta* words that contain *ā* have a acute final syllable. The words formed using the *ghañ* suffix are nominal bases (*prātipadikas*) and get case inflection suffixes.

---

[8]In showing accent, the grave and acute diacritical marks are used for *svarita* and *udatta* respectively.
[9]The ñ is a marker that gets elided during derivation.

Examples:
a) *karṣá* = √*kṛṣā* (*bhvādi*) + *ghañ*
b) *pāká* = √*dupacaṣ* (*bhvādi*) + *ghañ*

3. *vṛṣādīnāṃ ca* (A. 6.1.203)
   The words that are part of the *vṛṣādigaṇa* have an acute initial syllable. *Vṛṣādigaṇa* contains *ghañanta* words as well as others that are differently derived. The three *ghañanta* words are *kāma*, *yāma* and *pāda*.

Example:
pắda = √*padā* (*divādi*) + *ghañ*, Gaṇa: *vṛṣādi*

4. *tyāgarāgahāsakuhaśvaṭhakrathānām* (A. 6.1.216)
   The words *tyāga*, *rāga*, *hāsa*, *kuha*, *śvaṭha* and *kratha* have an acute initial syllable as an option in addition to their natural accents which happens to be an acute final syllable. Thus, there is an optional accent in the case of *ghañantas* viz *tyāga*, *rāga*, *hāsa*.

Example:
tyāgá, *tyắga* = √*tyajā* (*bhvādi*) + *ghañ*.

5. *thāthaghañktājabitrakāṇām* (A. 6.2.144)
   This rule is from the domain of compounds. When a *ghañanta* word appears second in a compound, the rule *gatikārakopapadāt kṛt* (A. 6.2.139) would have retained its default (*prakṛti*) accent. One thing stated in rule A. 6.2.144 is that a *ghañanta* word appearing second in any compound, such as *bhéda* in the tatpuruṣa compound *kāṣṭa-bhedá*, will have an acute final syllable.

Example:
kāṣṭhabhedá = *kāṣṭha* + (√*bhidir* + *ghañ*)

6 Outlay of *ghañanta* words

Figure 3 shows a small window in the universe of words. It captures the outlay of all *ghañanta* words according to the rules listed above. The text in italics refers to actual words that the rules treat. Regular text only mentions the categories that can be gathered by a simple analysis of the rule text. The category called *ñidantaḥ* contains such words that end in *ñit* suffixes stated in *ññityādirnityam* (A.

6.1.197). *ghañantaḥ* is a sub-category of *ñi-dantaḥ* containing such words that end in suffix *ghañ*. The rule *karṣātvato ghaño'nta udāttaḥ* (A. 6.1.159) treats *ghañanta* words having *ā* and the *bhvādi ghañanta karṣa* specially, therefore words from the Having-ā class become another subclass of words within *ghañantaḥ* and *karṣa* is a special *ghañanta* word from the verbal root √*kṛṣā* which appears in the *bhvādi* and *tudādi* compilations of verbal roots (gaṇas). The words *tyāga*, *rāga* and *hāsa* are *ghañantas* but are specially treated in *tyāgarāgahāsakuhaśvaṭhakrathānām* (A. 6.1.216) so they form a subgroup within the Having-ā class of words in addition to the subgroup of *vṛṣādigaṇa* members *kāma*, *yāma* and *pāda*.

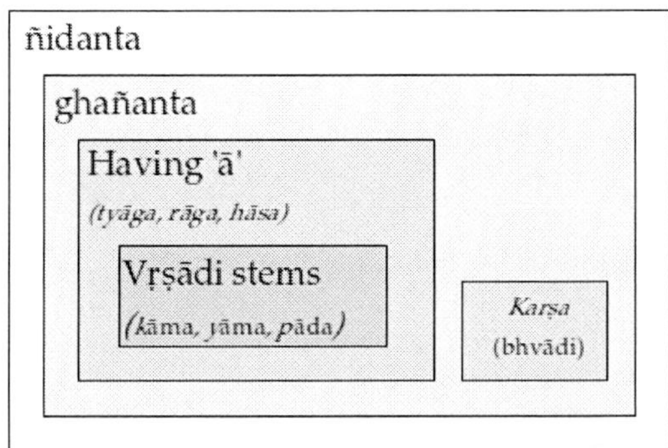

Figure 3: The outlay of *ghañanta* words.

syllable as stated in *vṛṣādīnāṃ ca* (A. 6.1.203). There are only three *ghañanta* stems viz *kāma*, *yāma* and *pāda* that are members of the *vṛṣādi* group of words. The class called 'Without-ā' contains *ghañantas* that do not have the syllable *ā*. Finally, the words *tyāga*, *rāga* and *hāsa* are optionally accentuated on the first syllable due to *tyāgarāgahāsakuhaśvaṭhakrathānām* (A. 6.1.216), in addition to being accentuated like the GaYantas in the 'Having-ā' class.

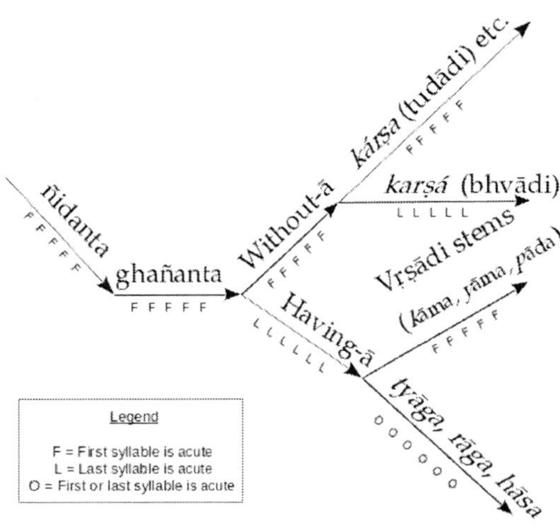

Figure 4: Accents on *ghañanta* words.

7 Accentuation of *ghañantas*

Figure 4 shows the accent that each class of *ghañantas* from figure 3 has. A string of 'F's indicates that words in that class have an acute initial syllable. A string of 'L's indicates that the corresponding words have an acute final syllable. A string of 'O's indicates that the words from that class optionally have an initial or a final acute syllable. A *ñidanta* (ñit-ending word form) has an acute initial syllable due to *ñit* accent of rule *ñnityādirnityam* (A. 6.1.197). A *ghañanta* also has an acute initial syllable because suffix *ghañ* is a *ñit* suffix. The class of *ghañantas* called 'Having-ā' has an acute final syllable according to *karṣātvato ghaño'nta udāttaḥ* (A. 6.1.159). The specific word *karṣa*, too, is accented by A. 6.1.159 provided that it is not derived from the verbal root √*kṛṣā* belonging to the tudādi group. The members of *vṛṣādi* group of words have an acute initial

8 Features for Accentuation of *ghañantas*

Section §7 shows how *ghañantas* are accentuated using Pāṇini's rules. A derivation starts from a set of initial conditions which enjoins the *ghañ* suffix after a verbal root. Over the course of a derivation, some of the rules apply at the right juncture to produce the correct accent. In case of A. 6.1.159, Pāṇini assumes that being *ghañanta* is a feature of a word and that this feature be made known. Similarly, if a *ghañanta* contains '*ā*', that too, is a feature and must be made known so that A. 6.1.159 may apply. Thus, *features* are necessary for proper accentuation. All the features necessary for accentuation of *ghañantas* are discussed in this section.

In figure 4, each line segment is a feature. Starting from the left hand side, the class *ñidanta* implies that *ñit* is a feature of the word.

233

The next segment implies that suffix *ghañ* is a feature too. The property of a word to have the vowel *a* is also a feature. Being a member of the *vṛṣādi* group is also a feature of a word. Since the rules explicitly treat specific words like *karṣa*, *tyāga*, *rāga* and *hāsa* these words also become features by themselves. If all these features are noted on a plain-text word, correct accent can be produced.

Though the set of features discussed above cannot be compromised upon, all the features need not be explicitly noted on the plain text, for some can be deduced. The suffix *ghañ* is a *ñit* suffix so *ñit* feature inheres and need not be explicitly noted. Similarly, we need not explicitly note that the words contain *a*. Finally, the words *tyāga*, *rāga* and *hāsa* will be dealt with in their respective rules and need not be explicitly mentioned. Since A. 6.1.159 deals with the word *karṣa* which is derived from the verbal root √*kṛṣā* in the bhvādi list, it becomes necessary to include the conjugational class of a verbal root (*dhātugaṇa*) as a feature.

Table 1 summarizes the features that must be noted on *ghañantas* for accentuation. The contents within braces are meant to suggest an option. The vertical bar separates the alternatives.

SN.	Feature	Rule	Rqd.
1	Suffix *ghañ*	6.1.159	Yes
2	Verb Group	6.1.159	Yes
3	Surface form has ā	6.1.159	No
4	Suffix *ñit*	6.1.197	No
5	*vṛṣādigaṇa* list	6.1.203	Yes
6	{*tyaga* | *rāga* | *hāsa*}	6.1.216	No
7	2nd word in a compound	6.2.144	Yes

Table 1: Features of *ghañantas*

SN.	Word	Annotation
1	*karṣa*	a) √*kṛṣā* (1) + *ghañ* b) √*kṛṣā* (6) + *ghañ*
2	*pāda*	√*padā* (4) + *ghañ*, *vṛṣādi*
3	*hāsa*	√*hasẽ* (1) + *ghañ*
4	*veda*	√*vidā* (2) + *ghañ*
5	*lekha*	√*likhā* (2) + *ghañ*
6	*kāṣṭhabheda*	*kāṣṭha* + (√*bhidir*(7) + *ghañ*)

Table 2: Examples of annotations on *ghañanta* words

8.1 Represenation of Sense

The rules A. 3.3.18-20 (§5) discussed that *ghañantas* are formed under three conditions – (i) *bhāve* (pure action), (ii) *saṃjñāyām akartari kārake* (a non-agentive term) and (iii) *parimāṇe* (a measure of quantity). Although, these are semantic conditions of formation and not accentuation of *ghañantas*, they still need to be represented in the deep structure of *ghañantas*. The sense that these conditions represent can be referred to by synset IDs from IndoWordNet[10]. The synset ID is a reference number assigned to a set of synonymns. The sense can be annotated as synset=<SynsetID> in the deep structure. The senses and synset IDs are discussed below.

bhāve The sense of *bhāva* is represented by the synset ID 12149 which is glossed as *kāraṇasya kārye parivartanasya avasthā* (state in which a cause produces an effect).

saṃjñāyām akartari kārake The word *saṃjñā* can be represented by synset ID 8150 which is glossed as *vyākaraṇaśāstre prayujyamānaḥ saḥ śabdaḥ yaḥ vāstavikam kalpitam vā vastu bodhayati* (that word used in grammar which conveys a real or imaginary thing). For a purpose such as this, the idea of *akartari kārake* can be captured by negating the meaning of the word *kartā* (an agent) represented by the synset ID 11886 and glossed as *vyakaraṇaśāstranusāreṇa tat kārakam yat dhātvarthasya vyāpārasya āśrayaḥ* (according to grammar, that role, upon which the action of the verb totally depends - an independent agent)

parimāṇe The sense of the word *parimāṇa* is given by synset ID 10743 which is glossed as *bhāraghanaphalādīnāṃ māpanam yena bhavati* (that by which weight, volume etc. are measured)

8.2 Artificial *saṃjñās*

The synset annotation is not a Pāṇinian *saṃjñā*, yet the deep structure can be anno-

---

[10]http://www.cfilt.iitb.ac.in/indowordnet

tated with it. The term *active*, used to indicate the one active *udātta* among potential ones, is another instance of a non-Pāṇinian *saṃjñā*. It is used in the deep structure of the word *bhaviṣyáti* in Section 3.3. It is not necessary that only formally defined *saṃjñās* be used in the deep structure. Pāṇini makes use of terms such as *pūrvapadam* and *uttarapadam*, without formally defining them, when discussing *samāsas* (compounds). A fabricated *saṃjñā* can also be used if it has a use.

8.3 Example of Deep Structure

Table 2 shows a few examples of *ghañanta* *prātipadikas* (nominal bases). The examples below show deep structure of masculine, nominative singular inflections of some of the words from Table 2.

1. *pādaḥ*
   ((प् (आ[udaatta,active] <- अ) द् अँ[lopa,it]
)[gana=4]

   (घ्[lopa,it] अ[udaatta] ञ[lopa,it]
) [pratyaya]

   (((((: <- र्) उ[lopa,it]) <- स्) उ[lopa,it]
)[pratyaya]
) [vrshaadigana, synset=!11886 & 8150]

2. *hāsaḥ*
   Due to optional accent there are two forms – *hắsaḥ* and *hāsáḥ*. The following is the deep structure of *hắsaḥ* produced by the rule *tyāgarāgahāsa...* (A. 6.1.216).

   ((हू (आ[udaatta,active] <- अ) स् पँँ[lopa,it]
)[gana=1]

   (घ्[lopa,it] अ[udaatta] ञ[lopa,it]
) [pratyaya]

   (((((: <- र्) उ[lopa,it]) <- स्) उ[lopa,it]
)[pratyaya]
) [synset=12149]

   The deep structure below is for the form *hāsáḥ* produced by the rule *karṣātvato...* (A. 6.1.159).

   ((हू (आ[udaatta] <- अ) स् पँँ[lopa,it]
)[gana=1]

   (घ्[lopa,it] अ[udaatta,active] ञ[lopa,it]
) [pratyaya]

   (((((: <- र्) उ[lopa,it]) <- स्) उ[lopa,it]
) [pratyaya]
) [synset=12149]

3. *lekhaḥ*
   ((ल् (ए[udaatta] <- इ) ख् अँ[lopa,it]
)[gana=2]

   (घ्[lopa,it] अ[udaatta,active] ञ[lopa,it]
) [pratyaya]

   (((((: <- र्) उ[lopa,it]) <- स्) उ[lopa,it]
)[pratyaya]
) [synset=10743]

9 Deep Morphological Analysis

Sanskrit morphological analyzers are available online on websites of JNU[11] and the Dept. of Sanskrit Studies (Univ. of Hyderabad)[12]. A Sanskrit segmenter is also available at the Sanskrit Heritage Site[13]. Given an unaccented input such as *lābhaḥ*, these morphological analyzers correctly analyse it as a masculine form and produce the stem *lābha* and nominative singular suffix. However, they do not produce a deeper analysis of the stem *labha* in terms of derivational morphology to show that it is derived from the suffix *ghañ*. Such analysis is required for accentuation of *ghañanta* words. JNU has a separate *kṛdanta* analyzer which gives a deep analysis in terms of the root √*dulabhaṣ*, *kṛt* suffix *ghañ* and the nominative singular case.

Some of Pāṇini's rules, such as A. 3.3.18-20 (Section 5), create *kṛdantas* in specific senses. For semantic processing of *kṛdantas* which may happen upstream in a stack of NLP applications, it would be good to provide deep analysis of words along with senses that Pāṇini intended. In the case of *ghañanta* words, various features, including the accent, senses and *gaṇa* membership, can be embedded in the deep structure. For example, the word *lābhás* (a

[11] http://sanskrit.jnu.ac.in/morph/analyze.jsp
[12] http://sanskrit.uohyd.ac.in/scl/
[13] http://sanskrit.inria.fr/DICO/reader.fr.html

pre-final form of the *ghañanta* word *lābhaḥ*) is shown below.

```
( ( ड़ू[lopa,it]
    उ[lopa,it]
    ऌ
    (आ <- अ)[udaatta]
    भ्
    अ[lopa,it]
    ष्[lopa,it]
  ) [dhaatu, group=1]

  ( घ्[lopa,it]  अ[udaatta,active] ञ्[lopa,it]
  ) [pratyaya]

  ( स्‌उ[lopa,it]
  ) [pratyaya]
)[synset=!11886 & 8150]
```

The deep structure shown above can be produced by a morphological analyzer created using the Stuttgart Finite State Transducer (SFST[14]). The following snippet[15] shows the FST mapping[16] from the string *lābhas* to the corresponding deep structure. In the mapping various portions of the word, namely *lābh*, *a* and *s*, are mapped to different portions of the deep structure using the language of the SFST (see constructs having pattern x:y). These portions correspond to the basic elements such as the verbal root √*ḍulabhaṣ* from the first (*bhvādi*) group, the suffix *ghañ*, and the nominative singular inflectional suffix *su*.

```
< ( (q[lopa,it]
     u[lopa,it]
     l (A<-a)[udaatta]
     B a[lopa,it]
     z[lopa,it]
    )[dhaatu,group=1]>:{lAB}

  < (G[lopa,it] a[udaatta,active] Y[lopa,it]
    )[pratyaya]>:a

  < (s u[lopa,it])[pratyaya]
    )[synset=!11886 & 8150]>:s
```

When a string such as *lābhas* is given to the transducer, the following output is produced

which can be parsed as the deep structure of *lābhas*.

```
< ( (q[lopa,it]
     u[lopa,it]
     l (A<-a)[udaatta]
     B a[lopa,it]
     z[lopa,it]
    )[dhaatu,group=1]>

  < (G[lopa,it] a[udaatta,active] Y[lopa,it]
    )[pratyaya]>

  < (s u[lopa,it])[pratyaya]
    )[synset=!11886 & 8150]>
```

10 Prioritization of Features

In a traditional derivation, the maxim *paranityāntraghgāpavādānām uttarotaraṃ balīyaḥ* is used to decide which one of the many applicable rules should apply. In the case of accentuation of a ready word, such as *tyāgaḥ*, that opportunity does not arise. Most features in table 1 apply to *tyāgaḥ*. Which rule should be used for accentuation?

The *utsarga-apavāda* nature of rules discussed in section 5 allows a prioritization tree to be created as shown in figure 5. A solid arrow points from a high priority rule to a low priority rule. In the case that a high priority rule applies, it debars all the low priority rules up the chain. For example, in accentuating the compound *kāṣṭhabhedá*, the rule A. 6.2.144 will debar the other rules. A dotted arrow shows an optional rule. The rule A. 6.1.216 is an optional rule. It does not debar A. 6.1.159 but provides an option to it. Accordingly, the words *tyāgaḥ*, *rāga* and *hāsa* will be accentuated in two ways (See example in Section 8.3 item 2).

The priority of the rules from figure 5 allows a prioritization of the features to be created as shown in figure 6. Accordingly, a feature towards the bottom of the figure debars the ones above it when connected using solid arrows. A feature connected using a dotted arrow allow an option. When a high priority feature is found on a word, the corresponding rule noted in the parenthesis should be used for accentuation. In case a high priority feature is not found the next level of features should be checked and so on. If none of the special fea-

---

[14]http://www.cis.uni-muenchen.de/ schmid/tools /SFST

[15]Snippet is actually a concatenated string, here it is formatted for easy reading.

[16]The mapping uses the Sanskrit Library Phonetic (SLP1) encoding.

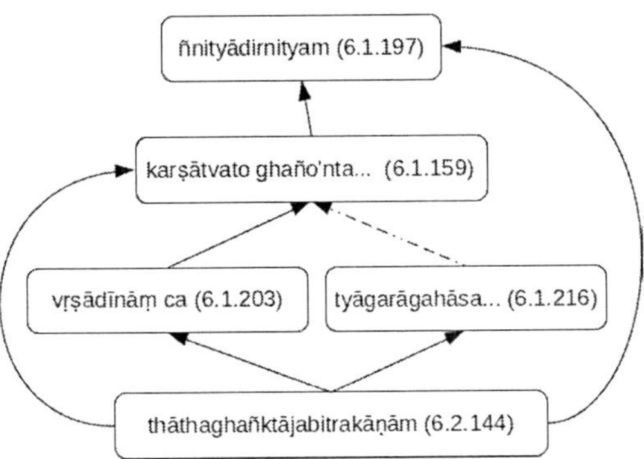

Figure 5: The priority of accent rules for *ghañanta* words

tures exist on a *ghañanta* word, it should be accentuated by the rule *ñnityādirnityam* (A. 6.1.197) due to the feature *ghañ*.

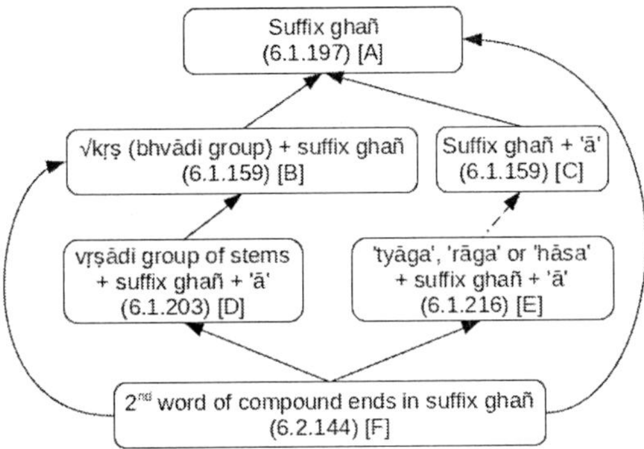

Figure 6: The priority of conditions for accentuation of *ghañanta* words

11 The Feature Arrays

All *ghañanta* words must have one or more primitive features from Table 1. Each of the prioritized conditions in figure 6 refers to a bundle of features. The letter in the square brackets indicates a bundle of features produced on a *ghañanta* word when the corresponding condition is true. A bundle of features can be translated into an array containing serial numbers of the corresponding primitive feature from Table 1. Referring to figure 6, condition [A] can be represented by the array '[1]'. Similarly the condition [E] can be represented by the feature array '[1, 3, 6]'.

Table 3 shows the feature array corresponding to each bundle of features. The ellipsis in the array for cumulative feature [F] is meant

to show that other features can coexist but are ignored because only features 1 and 7 are the important in the context of compounds.

The primitive feature numbers may occur only once in the feature array. They need not occur more than once because their repetition will not convey more information than what is conveyed by using them once.

Indicator	Array	Acute Accent On
A	[1]	First syllable
B	[1, 2]	Last syllable
C	[1, 3]	Last syllable
D	[1, 3, 5]	First syllable
E	[1, 3, 6]	First or last syllable
F	[1, 7, ...]	Last syllable

Table 3: Possible feature arrays for *ghañanta* words

12 The Process of Restoration of Accent

A morphological analysis, which containis elements of derivational morphology, is necessary for restoration of accent. A morphological analyzer built on principles discussed in Section 9 will be able to show accent in the deep structure. However, some morphological anaylzers, such as JNU's *kṛdanta* analyzer, produce derivational details but do not provide accent information. Depending upon the availability of accents in morphological analysis, there are two methods to restore accent on plain *ghañanta* words.

In the case that derivational morphology of a word is available without accent information, a computer program can produce a feature array using prioritized conditions shown in Figure 6. Given the feature array, accentuation of the surface form can happen according Table 3. If accent information is available, the accent from the deep structure can be simply copied onto the surface form.

A compound can be split using a Sanskrit compound analyser into *pūrvapada* and *uttarapada* constituents. These words can further be morphologically analysed to check if the second one is a *ghañanta*. For example, *kasthabheda* can be split into *kastha* + *bheda*. *bheda* is a *ghañanta*. A program can assigin '[1, 7]' as a feature array to the entire commpound and accentuate it using Table 3.

13 Conclusion and Future Work

The class of *ghañanta prātipadikas*[17] was examined. *utsarga* and *apavāda* rules of accentuation for suffix *ghañ* were studied. At least seven features used to accentuate *ghañanta* words were found. Thus, it is possible to create a set of structural, semantic and accent-related features for a specific morpheme by studying the *utsarga-apavāda* rules related to that morpheme.

Words in Sanskrit can be thought to have a grammatical deep structure, different from the surface form. The deep structure of words contains structural elements like roots and morphological suffixes. It also notes transformations of structural elements leading upto the final form. In addition, it can contain other features of the word such as senses and *gaṇa* membership, if any. Synset IDs from IndoWordNet are a good way to assign a certain sense to words for computational purpose. In this paper, the deep structure for *ghañanta* words was created by looking at some *utsarga-apavāda* rules. A general deep structure can be induced by a thorough study of Pāṇini's rules and how they interact with one another.

The deep structure shows the complete formation of a word, including its accent. Therefore, it can be used to build a morphological analyzer that analyzes the derivational morphology of words in addition to inflectional morphology.

To mark accent on unaccented *ghañantas* from classical texts, words will have to be morphologically decomposed. Existing morphological analyzers, such as JNU's *kṛdanta* analyzer, can be used or new faster ones can be developed using FST techniques. For restoring accent on compounds having *ghañantas* for final words, compound analyzers or segmenters like the Sanskrit Heritage Site, will have to be used.

Pāṇinian entities, such as the *vṛṣādigaṇa*, can be turned into computational resources for accentution.

References

Kāśīnātha Vāsudevaśāstrī Abhyankara. 2001. *Svaraprakriyā of Ramacandrapaṇḍita.* Ānandāśrama Publication, Pune, India.

Pushpak Bhattacharyya. 2010. Indowordnet. In *In Proc. of LREC-10*. Citeseer.

Raj Dabre, Archana Amberkar, and Pushpak Bhattacharyya. 2012. Morphological analyzer foraffix stacking languages: A case study of marathi.

G. V. Devasthali. 1967. *Phiṭsūtras of Śāntanava.* Publications of the Centre of Advanced Study in Sanskrit Class C No. 1. University of Poona, Pune, India.

Huet Gérard. 2003. Lexicon-directed segmentation and tagging of sanskrit. In *XIIth World Sanskrit Conference, Helsinki, Finland, Aug,* pages 307–325. Citeseer.

Gérard Huet. 2009. Sanskrit segmentation. *South Asian Languages Analysis Roundtable XXVIII, Denton, Ohio (October 2009).*

Brahmadatt Jigyasu. 1979. Ashtadhyayi (bhashya) prathamavrtti, three volumes. *Ramlal Kapoor Trust Bahalgadh,(Sonepat, Haryana, India)(In Hindi).*

Malhar Kulkarni, Chaitali Dangarikar, Irawati Kulkarni, Abhishek Nanda, and Pushpak Bhattacharyya. 2010. Introducing sanskrit wordnet. In *Proceedings on the 5th Global Wordnet Conference (GWC 2010), Narosa, Mumbai,* pages 287–294.

Malhar Kulkarni, Samir Sohoni, and Nandini Ghag. 2015. Compsitionality in Pāṇinian grammar. In *Journal Gaurigauravam. Department of Sanskrit, University of Mumbai.,* pages 90–94. Mohiniraj Enterprise.

Peter Scharf, Pawan Goyal, ANUJA AJOTIKAR, and Tanuja Ajotikar. 2015. Voice, preverb, and transitivity restrictions in sanskrit verb use. In *Sanskrit Syntax, Selected papers presented at the seminar on sanskrit syntax and discouse structures,* pages 157–202.

Srisa Chandra Vasu. 1891. *The Ashtadhyayi of Panini. 2 Vols.* Motilal Banarsidass Publishers Private Limited, New Delhi.

---

[17] *kṛttaddhitasamāsāḥ ca* (A. 1.2.46)

Learning to Identify Subjective Sentences

Girish K. Palshikar, Manoj Apte, Deepak Pandita
TCS Research, Tata Consultancy Services
Pune 411013
{gk.palshikar, manoj.apte, deepak.p7}@tcs.com

Vikram Singh
M. Tech., Computer Science & Engineering
Indian Institute of Technology, Patna
vikramsinghiitp@gmail.com

Abstract

Subjective sentences describe people's opinions, points-of-view, interpretations, comparisons, sentiments, judgments, appraisals or feelings toward entities, events and their properties. Identifying subjective sentences is the basis for opinion mining and sentiment analysis and is important in applications like political analysis, social media analytics and product review analytics. We use standard classifiers to build models of SUBJECTIVE vs. NON-SUBJECTIVE sentences and demonstrate that they outperform the approaches reported in the literature on several interesting datasets. We discuss two novel applications of this work: prevalence of subjective sentences in performance appraisal text and scientific papers. We demonstrate that scientific papers also contain a substantial fraction of subjective sentences. We compare the nature of subjective sentences in performance appraisals text and scientific papers, and observe *different* reasons why some sentences in these domains are subjective. We propose the need to further investigate the linguistic and semantic basis for subjective sentences across different domains.

1 Introduction

Documents contain a mixture of facts, opinions and other kinds of sentences, such as questions or instructions. Factual sentences include *objective expressions* about entities, events and their properties. Opinion sentences usually include *subjective expressions* that describe people's sentiments, judgments, appraisals or feelings toward entities, events and their properties (Liu, 2010). Objective information is typically fact-based, measurable, observable and verifiable. For example, (S1) (Table1) is a factual sentence. In contrast, most opinion sentences express some sentiment, usually having a positive or negative polarity. However, some opinion sentences are *neutral* i.e., they do not explicitly express any particular sentiment. For example, (S2) is an opinion sentence that expresses some sentiment (mostly positive), whereas (S3), (S4) and (S5) are opinion sentences that do not express any particular sentiment. Some factual sentences may be *mixed* i.e., they may also contain subjective expressions, with or without the presence of an explicit sentiment polarity. Sentences (S6) and (S7) are mainly factual, but (S6) contain an opinion along with a positive sentiment whereas (S7) expresses an opinion without much sentiment. Any expression about the private (internal) state of mind of a person is, by definition, a subjective sentence; e.g., (S8). Opinion sentences often contain subjective expressions other than sentiments, such as opinions, points of view (S4), judgements (S5), predictions (S9), interpretations, comparisons (S10) etc.

In this paper, we are interested in automatically identifying *subjective* sentences, which contain subjective expressions, but which may or may not contain explicit sentiment markers. We are also interested in detecting mixed sentences, which contain both facts and opinions. In this paper, we include mixed sentences in the class of subjective sentences. The remaining sentences (i.e., of the other class) either express pure facts or they may express neither facts nor opinions (e.g., they may be instructions or questions).

Categorization of sentences as subjective or

D S Sharma, R Sangal and A K Singh. Proc. of the 13th Intl. Conference on Natural Language Processing, pages 239–248,
Varanasi, India. December 2016. ©2016 NLP Association of India (NLPAI)

S1	On April 24, 1975, the West German embassy in Stockholm was seized by members of the RAF; two of the hostages were murdered as the German government under Chancellor Helmut Schmidt refused to give in to their demands.
S2	Windows 7 is quite simply faster, more stable, boots faster, goes to sleep faster, comes back from sleep faster, manages your files better and on top of that it's beautiful to look at and easy to use.
S3	More than 98 bank entities are expected to be serviced under the Web based PaySys application.
S4	With Spy Kids 2, the Spy Kids franchise establishes itself as a part of the movie landscape for children.
S5	The security cover for deputy ministers can be reduced.
S6	The ninth seed Sindhu took 40 minutes to dismantle the eighth seeded Tai and gave her medal chances a boost in her maiden Olympic appearance.
S7	Google Duo isn't much different from the other video chatting services, except that it gives a glimpse at who is making the call, helping the recipient decide whether to answer.
S8	John found his sorrow receding in the cool breeze.
S9	The Independence Day holiday will boost the film's biz further.
S10	The Mi 5 camera in performs better in most outdoor situations than OnePlus 3.
S11	Baseball writer Bill James, in the The New Bill James Historical Baseball Abstract, ranked Robinson as the 32nd greatest player of all time strictly on the basis of his performance on the field, noting that he was one of the top players in the league throughout his career.

Table 1: Some example sentences.

non-subjective has many practical applications. Information extraction, question-answering and document summarization are often interested in factual sentences, and hence would use the classification of sentences to remove subjective sentences, which can improve the system performance and effectiveness. Some real-life applications explicitly need to mark and summarize sentiments and opinions (which are inherently subjective); for example, identifying features facing criticism from product reviews, identifying extreme positions from political views, and marketing oriented anaysis of web contents.

Classification of sentences from different perspectives is a well-explored problem. Syntactically, a sentence is typically classified into classes such as DECLARATIVE, IMPERATIVE, INTERROGATIVE, EXCLAMATIVE, COMMUNICATIVE, INFORMATIVE etc., with further sub-classes. Other structurally-oriented sentence classes include MAJOR (has subject and predicate), MINOR (without a finite verb; e.g., The more, the merrier.), PERIODIC (meaning is not complete until the final clause or phrase; e.g., Silent and soft, and slow, descends the snow.) etc. Semantically classifying sentences (based on the sentence's purpose) is a much harder task, and is gaining increasing attention from linguists and NLP researchers (Zhou et al., 2004), (Wang et al., 2005), (McKnight and Srinivasan, 2003), (Cohen et al., 2004), (Corston-Oliver et al., 2004),

(Ivanovic, 2006), (Khoo et al., 2006), (Yamamoto and Takagi, 2005), (Hachey and Grover, 2004), (He et al., 2006), (Naughton et al., 2010), (Kadoya et al., 2005), (Momtazi and Klakow, 2009). Most work in this area has used supervised learning approaches (e.g., using SVM, decision trees, maximum entropy based classifier, naive Bayes etc.), with the exception of (Ito et al., 2004) (semi-supervised) and (Teufel and Moens, 1998), (Ibekwe-SanJuan et al., 2008) (knowledge-based) and (Deshpande et al., 2010) (rule-based). Sentence classification has been applied to tasks such as summarization, information extraction, IR, automatic ontology creation (Hearst, 1998) and text entailment (Zanzotto and DellArciprete, 2009). Sentence classification has been used on documents in several practical application domains such as biomedical papers, legal judgements, product reviews, customer complaints in help-desk, emails etc. The sentences classes have also been more domain dependent (Table 2).

In this paper, we use a variety of standard classifiers to build models of SUBJECTIVE vs. NON-SUBJECTIVE sentences. We demonstrate that some of the standard classifiers outperform the approaches reported in the literature on several interesting datasets, including one real-life dataset from us[1]. We discuss two novel applications of this work, which have not been reported in the literature to our knowledge. We perform predic-

---

[1] Please contact the authors for obtaining this dataset.

tive identification (and a subsequent analysis) of the prevalence of subjective sentences in two interesting domains: the first in performance appraisal text and the other in scientific papers.

The rest of the paper is organized as follows. We review the related work in Section 2. Then, we describe the features used for a classification based approach to identify subjective sentences in Section 3. The experiments performed and the results are described in Section 4. In Section 5 we apply the classifiers learned earlier to identify subjective sentences in two novel domains: (i) performance appraisal text; and (ii) scientific papers. Finally, we discuss the conclusions of our work and identify some further work in Section 6.

2   Related Work

There has been a considerable amount of research work in the field of Sentiment Analysis and Opinion Mining. We focus here on predictive identification of subjective text, which can be done at document, sentence and phrase level by using features like presence of a pronoun, adjective, semantic orientation etc. Often the other class is objective or factual text (as against a general non-subjective class, as in this paper).

(Yu and Hatzivassiloglou, 2003) presented a Bayesian classifier for discriminating between Opinion or Factual articles. Then, three approaches to classify opinions from facts at the sentence level were proposed. The first approach was based on the similarity of the given sentence to the opinion or fact documents. In the second approach, a Naive Bayes classifier was trained using the sentences in opinion and fact documents. The features included words, bigrams, trigrams and the parts of speech, as well as the presence of semantically oriented words combined with the polarity information and the average semantic orientation of the words in a sentence. In the third approach multiple Naive Bayes classifiers were trained using iterative training process relying on different set of features.

In a classic paper (Pang and Lee, 2004), the authors have used Naive Bayes and SVM to detect subjective sentences and used these sentences for sentiment analysis and proposed a novel graph-cut based method for assigning the overall polarity to a document, based on the sentiments in these individual sentences.

(Kim and Hovy, 2005) developed a collec-tion of opinion bearing and non-opinion bearing words using multiple collections like Wordnet, WSJ Data, Columbia wordlist and then combined these lists into a single collection with averaging the score of individual lists. Score of a sentence was computed using these scores in two ways. In the first approach the scores of all the words in the sentence were added and in second approach presence of a single strong valence word was used as the score.

(Stepinski and Mittal, 2007) classified news articles into facts and opinions by training a classifier on opinion/fact stories. Sentences in an article were labeled as factual and opinion and an overall score was computed as the average of these labels. Label was weighed based on the confidence of the classification. Then a Passive-Aggressive algorithm (Crammer et al., 2006) was trained on unigram, bigram and trigram features. An iterative training process in which a classifier is trained using a subset of the desired features was used. Based on the results of classifying the training set with the classifier, the misclassified sentences were removed and the classifier was trained again using a larger set of features.

(Kim and Myaeng, 2007) introduced a lexical information based methodology for opinion analysis. The task of classifying sentences into Subjective or Objective was done by using a combination of rule-based approach and a machine learning based method. First, a training set was obtained using the rules based on lexical clues and then a SVM-based classifier was trained on the same. Polarity or semantic orientation of the subjective sentences was determined and the opinion holders were also found by using Named-Entity Recognition with extracted lexical clues.

(Godbole et al., 2007) use co-occurrence of an entity and a sentiment word in the same sentence to mean that the sentiment is associated with that entity. Mentioning that it can lead to inaccuracies they claim that due to the volume text that is processed by them enables them to generate accurate sentiment words. They create two scores for each entity polarity score and subjectivity score. Polarity indicates percentage of positive sentiment references among total sentiment references, while Subjectivity indicates proportion of sentiment to frequency of occurrence.

(Pak and Paroubek, 2010) have presented a method for automatic collection of corpus that can

Domain	Sentence Classes
research papers	BACKGROUND, TOPIC, RELATED-WORK, PURPOSE/PROBLEM, HYPOTHESIS, AIM, SOLUTION/METHOD, RESULT, CONCLUSION/CLAIM, FUTURE-WORK (Yamamoto and Takagi, 2005), (Ibekwe-SanJuan et al., 2008), (Teufel and Moens, 1998), (McKnight and Srinivasan, 2003)
movies	OPINIONATIVE, FACTOID (Momtazi and Klakow, 2009)
product reviews	RECOMMEND, NOT-RECOMMEND (Wang et al., 2005)
help-desk	REQUEST, QUESTION, APOLOGY, INSTRUCTION, SUGGESTION, STATEMENT, SPECIFICATION, THANKS, APOLOGY, RESPONSE-ACK (Khoo et al., 2006)
legal	FACT, PROCEEDINGS, BACKGROUND, FRAMING, DISPOSAL (Hachey and Grover, 2004)
emails	REQUEST, PROPOSE, AMEND, DELIVER, COMMIT, MEETING, DATA, TASK, CHITCHAT, FAREWELL (Cohen et al., 2004), (Corston-Oliver et al., 2004)
biography	BIO, FAME, PERSONALITY, SOCIAL, EDUCATION, NATIONALITY, SCANDAL, PERSONAL, WORK (Zhou et al., 2004)

Table 2: Examples of Sentence Classes (modified from (Deshpande et al., 2010)).

be used to train a sentiment classifier. The corpus contains both positive and negative sentiments as well as objective text (no sentiments). For positive and negative sentiments help was taken from emoticons used in the tweets and for objective text the messages from twitter accounts of popular newspapers and magazines were considered. They first conduct basic statistical analysis of the collected corpus and then run multinomial naive based classifier that uses N-Gram and POS Tags as features on the data collected.

3 Classification of Subjective Sentences

We adopt a feature-based classification approach to classify the sentences into facts and opinions. We extract several features from each sentences and thus represent each sentence as a numeric feature vector. We then use several standard classifiers for the task of classifying a sentence as SUBJECTIVE or NON-SUBJECTIVE and compare their results.

Number of adjectives: An interesting relation between presence of adjectives in a sentence and its subjectivity has been explored in the literature (Wiebe et al., 1999), (Hatzivassiloglou and Wiebe, 2000), (Wiebe, 2000). (Wiebe et al., 1999) demonstrated that adjectives are statistically significantly, and positively correlated with subjective sentences in the corpus on the basis of the log-likelihood ratio. The probability that a sentence is subjective, given that there is at least one adjective in the sentence, is 0.545, even though there are more objective than subjective sentences in the corpus. Therefore, we use number of adjectives in a sentence as a feature. Note that if the same adjective occurs multiple times in a sentence, then we count each occurrence separately.

Number of nouns: (Riloff et al., 2003) reported the effectiveness of nouns for identification of subjective sentences. Hence, we use number of nouns, including proper nouns, as a feature.

Word count: Opinions and subjective sentences tend to be more elaborate and hence longer. So we use number of words in the sentences, excluding stop words and punctuations, as a feature.

Number of strongly subjective words: Most of the systems developed for subjectivity classification and sentiment analysis, such as (Liu, 2010), (Syed et al., 2010), use a lexicon of opinion-bearing words. Two of the most commonly used lexicons are the SentiWordNet (Baccianella et al., 2010) and the Subjectivity Lexicon (Wilson et al., 2005b). The Subjectivity Lexicon classifies a word as strongly subjective (e.g., `beautiful`) or weakly subjective (e.g., `benefit`). We use the number of strongly subjective words from the Subjectivity Lexicon present in a sentence divided by word count as a feature. We also use the number of words from SentiWordNet (having either nonzero positive polarity score or nonzero negative polarity score) present in a sentence divided by word count as another feature.

Number of named entities: A commonly observed characteristics of a factual or objective sentence is then it tends to use more number of named entities. Hence we use number of named entitied present in a sentence as a feature. We use Stanford NER tool for this purpose.

Number of comparatives: This feature represents the number of comparative words (e.g., `faster`) used in the sentence.

Number of superlatives: This feature refers to the number of superlative words (e.g., `fastest`) used in the sentence.

Dataset	#Sentences	#SubjSent	#NonSubjSent
D1	2074	1130	944
D2	10000	5000	5000
D3	293	135	158
D4	613	281	332

Table 3: Dataset Description

Tense: Sentences in future tense tend to be more subjective. Hence we use the major tense (past, present or future) of the sentence as a feature.

Number of adverbs: This feature represents the number of adverbs (e.g., `simply, back`) in the sentence.

Number of date, time and numbers: The intuition behind this is that the factual information generally has lots of dates and numeric data. Such a sentence has a higher probability of being non-subjective than subjective. Therefore, we use number of date, time and number entities present in the sentence as a feature.

As an example, the feature vector for the non-subjective sentence S11 is $[3, 18, 25, 0.08, 0.32, 2, 0, 1, 0, 1, 1]$. This sentence has number of adjectives = 3 (`Historical, 32nd, top`), number of nouns = 18, word count = 25, fraction of strongly subjective words as per Subjectivity Lexicon = $2/25 = 0.08$ (`greatest, strictly`), fraction of sentiment words as per SentiWordNet = $8/25 = 0.32$, number of named entities = 2 (`Bill James, Robinson`), number comparatives = 0, number of superlatives = 1 (`greatest`), tense = 0 (past), number of adverbs = 1 (`strictly`), number of date, time and numbers = 1 (`one`).

4 Experiments and Results

4.1 Datasets

Table 3 lists the datasets we have used in this paper. Dataset D1 contains 1130 subjective sentences taken from the opinosis dataset (Ganesan et al., 2010), to which we added 944 non-subjective sentences that contain factual information about various domains like science, history, sports etc. Dataset D2 is the subjectivity dataset published in (Pang and Lee, 2004), and contains 5000 subjective and 5000 non-subjective sentences. Dataset D3 and D4 are explained later.

4.2 Results

We train a number of classifiers from the WEKA toolset on dataset D2, using 10-fold cross validation. For stacking-based classification, we use Logistic as a meta-classifier (combiner of base classifiers). In Stacking1, we used Naive Bayes, SVM, MultilayerPerceptron and Random Forest as base classifiers. In Stacking2, we use Naive Bayes, SVM, Logistic regression, MultilayerPerceptron and Random Forest as base classifiers. In Stacking3, we used MultilayerPerceptron + bagging, Logistic + AdaBoost as base classifiers.

For comparison, we use OpinionFinder and TextBlob. OpinionFinder is a system that automatically identifies subjective sentences, as well as various aspects of subjectivity within sentences, including agents who are sources of opinion, direct subjective expressions and speech events, and sentiment expressions. OpinionFinder has two classifiers for subjectivity classification, one is rule-based and the other is a model trained on MPQA corpus (Wilson et al., 2005a), (Riloff and Wiebe, 2003), (Wiebe and Riloff, 2005), (Wilson et al., 2005b), (Riloff and Wiebe, 2003). TextBlob is a Python library for processing textual data and provides an API for common natural language processing (NLP) tasks such as part-of-speech tagging, noun phrase extraction and sentiment analysis (`https://textblob.readthedocs.io/en/dev/`).

The results given by various classifiers trained on dataset D2 using 10-fold cross validation are shown in Table 4. As seen, Stacking3 shows the best F-measure on D2, which is much better than the baselines of both the OpinionFinder subjectivity classifiers and TextBlob. The F-measure of Stacking2 and MLP + bagging classifier on D2 is also quite close to Stacking3. We then use the classifiers trained on D2 and apply them to D1 as the test dataset. Once again, Stacking3 shows the best F-measure on D1, which is much better than the baselines of both OpinionFinder subjectivity classifiers but, is very close to TextBlob. The F-measures of the MLP + bagging and Logistic + Bagging on D1 are also quite close to Stacking3.

5 Applications

5.1 Performance Appraisal Text

Performance appraisal (PA) is a crucial HR process that enables an organization to periodically measure and evaluate every employee's perfor-

Classifier	D1			D2			D3			D4		
	P	R	F	P	R	F	P	R	F	P	R	F
J48	0.727	0.683	0.677	0.666	0.666	0.666	0.675	0.669	0.659	0.622	0.622	0.622
Logistic regression	0.748	0.699	0.692	0.684	0.683	0.683	0.681	0.672	0.66	0.671	0.672	0.67
MultilayerPerceptron (MLP)	0.736	0.694	0.688	0.681	0.681	0.681	0.685	0.679	0.67	0.66	0.656	0.656
Naive Bayes (NB)	0.726	0.688	0.682	0.666	0.664	0.663	0.696	0.693	0.687	0.655	0.656	0.651
Random Forest (RF)	0.65	0.62	0.614	0.645	0.645	0.644	0.646	0.642	0.629	0.611	0.613	0.611
SVM	0.719	0.685	0.68	0.685	0.684	0.684	0.655	0.652	0.643	0.638	0.63	0.63
J48 + AdaBoost	0.708	0.662	0.654	0.656	0.656	0.656	0.621	0.618	0.602	0.633	0.635	0.631
Logistic + AdaBoost	0.748	0.699	0.692	0.684	0.683	0.683	0.681	0.672	0.66	0.671	0.672	0.67
MLP + AdaBoost	0.739	0.696	0.69	0.681	0.681	0.681	0.69	0.683	0.673	0.663	0.659	0.66
NB + AdaBoost	0.726	0.688	0.682	0.666	0.664	0.663	0.696	0.693	0.687	0.655	0.656	0.651
RF + AdaBoost	0.664	0.628	0.62	0.647	0.647	0.647	0.636	0.631	0.617	0.626	0.628	0.624
SVM + AdaBoost	0.719	0.675	0.668	0.676	0.676	0.676	0.688	0.672	0.656	0.652	0.653	0.652
J48 + bagging	0.696	0.649	0.64	0.667	0.667	0.667	0.682	0.662	0.641	0.638	0.638	0.63
Logistic + bagging	0.751	0.7	0.693	0.684	0.684	0.684	0.686	0.676	0.664	0.673	0.674	0.671
MLP + bagging	0.752	0.702	0.694	0.688	0.688	0.687	0.71	0.693	0.679	0.663	0.664	0.661
NB + bagging	0.728	0.688	0.682	0.665	0.663	0.662	0.696	0.693	0.687	0.664	0.664	0.658
RF + bagging	0.684	0.641	0.632	0.656	0.656	0.656	0.639	0.631	0.613	0.618	0.62	0.615
SVM + bagging	0.716	0.684	0.68	0.682	0.682	0.682	0.647	0.645	0.637	0.647	0.638	0.638
Stacking1	0.733	0.69	0.684	0.685	0.685	0.685	0.694	0.683	0.671	0.671	0.67	0.671
Stacking2	0.74	0.696	0.689	0.687	0.687	0.687	0.7	0.686	0.673	**0.677**	**0.677**	**0.677**
Stacking3	**0.757**	**0.719**	**0.715**	**0.688**	**0.688**	**0.688**	**0.718**	**0.71**	**0.702**	0.665	0.666	0.665
OpinionFinder rule-based	0.37	0.423	0.311	0.371	0.388	0.367	0.364	0.454	0.374	0.42	0.498	0.404
OpinionFinder classifier	0.722	0.599	0.559	0.58	0.577	0.572	0.625	0.604	0.563	0.704	0.643	0.595
TextBlob	0.712	0.713	0.712	0.599	0.595	0.591	0.597	0.59	0.591	0.642	0.643	0.642

Table 4: Results (Precision, Recall and F-Measure) of various classifiers on different datasets.

mance and also to drive performance improvements. While the use of IT-based PA systems is fairly common in modern organizations, the use of text-mining techniques to derive insights from PA data is relatively less explored in academic research (Apte et al., 2016), (Ramrakhiyani et al., 2016). In most PA processes, the communication contains 2 major steps: (i) in *self-appraisal*, where an employee records his/her achievements, activities, tasks handled etc.; and (ii) in *feedback*, where the supervisor provides the criticism, appreciation, judgement, evaluation and suggestions for improvement of performance etc.

We have selected a small set of sentences from feedback step in a real performance appraisal in a large IT organization. This dataset D3 has 293 sentences, which were manually tagged by two people independently. We trained the classifier Stacking3 on Dataset D2 and applied the learned model to test on this dataset D3. The results are shown in Table 4.

One may expect many sentences in the PA dataset to be subjective, full of opinions and sentiments, since these sentences are related to the evaluation of one person's work by another person. However, that does not quite seem to be the case - only 46% sentences are marked as SUBJECTIVE by annotators. Further, the human annotators seem to be using a somewhat broader notion of subjectivity here. Note that the annotators have marked 135 sentences as SUBJECTIVE whereas the classifier has predicted only 98 sentences as SUBJECTIVE. Moreover, out of 135 sentences marked as SUBJECTIVE by annotators, the classifier has marked 61 as NON-SUBJECTIVE.

The main observations from an analysis of the results are as follows. First, many sentences are suggestions or recommendations made by the supervisors, which might be inherently considered as subjective (A1, A2 in Table 5). Human annotators have marked 52 sentences as suggestions, out of which they have marked 48 as SUBJECTIVE. On the other hand, the classifier identified only 19 sentences (out of these 52) as SUBJECTIVE, indicating that it is weak in identifying suggestions. This may be because the training dataset (D2) did not have too many suggestions (the sentences are from movie reviews). Thus we might improve the accuracy by adding a Boolean feature, regarding whether a sentence is a suggestion or not. Work such as (Pawar et al., 2015) may be useful to compute this feature automatically.

Second, several sentences contain ambiguous fragments, such as `very good team player`, `very large teams`, `constantly engaged`, `the right stakeholders` etc.; see also sentences A3, A4 in Table 5. These text fragments are ambiguous in the sense that the extent of quantification is not clear, or may even be impossible. However, human annotators seem to be tolerant of such ambiguities, and many sentences which they have marked as NON-SUBJECTIVE contain such ambiguous fragments. However, the classifier has marked many such sentences as SUBJECTIVE, indicating that the role of ambiguous text in subjective sentences needs to be explored more from a linguistic perspective.

5.2 Scientific Abstracts

Factual observations and objective descriptions are important in scientific literature, and hence it is expected that it would not contain much subjectivity. To validate this hypothesis, we downloaded 1440 abstracts for biomedical literature taken from Medline (`www.ncbi.nlm.nih.gov/pubmed`). Total number of sentences in these abstracts is 18261. Average number of words per sentence is 19 and the average number of words per abstract is 239. Our dataset D4 consists of 613 sentences taken randomly from these abstracts and labeled manually. There were 281 (46%) SUBJECTIVE sentences and 332 (54%) NON-SUBJECTIVE sentences. Some of the SUBJECTIVE sentences are shown in Table 6. Table 4 shows the results for various classifiers on this dataset D4. Stacking2 classifier seem to give the best results. We then applied the Stacking3 classifier (trained on Dataset D2 where it gives the best results) to all the 18261 (unlabeled) sentences in the abstracts. It classified 3532 (19.3%) sentences as SUBJECTIVE. Thus preliminary results show that there is a significant prevalence of SUBJECTIVE sentences in scientific literature, contrary to popular belief. We now look closely at these SUBJECTIVE sentences.

Some sentences seem to be comments, judgements, opinions or evaluations (of some experiments, say), which are inherently subjective; see B1, B4, B7. Suggestions are another class of sentences often marked as SUBJECTIVE by our classifier; see B3, B4. The third class of marked SUBJECTIVE sentences is about conclusions or predictions; see B5, B6. Some sentences, such as B8, seem to be classified as SUBJECTIVE because of the use of ambiguous expressions such as `possible`, `common`, `potential`. A common scenario where the classifier seems to be going wrong is when sentences (e.g., B2) include words like `significant`, which actually refer to rigorous notion of statistical significance and not to any vague ideas about significance of something.

In the PA dataset D3, we naturally expect a high fraction of sentences to be SUBJECTIVE; D3 had 46% SUBJECTIVE sentences. Surprisingly,

the scientific abstracts also seem to contain a fairly high fraction (19.3%) of SUBJECTIVE sentences. We have also observed that the context and domain play an important role in terming a sentences as SUBJECTIVE or NON-SUBJECTIVE. A single sentence can be termed as SUBJECTIVE when it is taken as an isolated sentence. However the context, i.e. accompanying sentences and domain, can be used to interpret the sentence as NON-SUBJECTIVE. For example, B1 is marked as SUBJECTIVE as an isolated sentence. The paragraph in which it appears is as follows: `The mucocele decreased in size and the postoperative course was uneventful. No recurrence was observed at 6 months' follow-up.` A possible reasons why this sentence is marked as subjective is because of vague word like `uneventful`. The next sentence provides a more objective basis, which can make this sentence NON-SUBJECTIVE.

6   Conclusion

Subjective sentences describe people's opinions, points-of-view, interpretations, comparisons, sentiments, judgments, appraisals or feelings toward entities, events and their properties. Identifying subjective sentences is the basis for opinion mining and sentiment analysis, and is important in practical applications such as political position analysis, social media analytics for marketing and product review analytics. Identifying subjective sentences is particularly challenging for neutral sentences i.e., when there is no particular sentiment expressed. Sentimentally neutral, but still subjective, sentences occur in many practical documents such as scientific papers, patents, financial reports and news. The notion of subjective expression or subjective communication is also crucial in philosophy of art. While there is much work in identifying sentiments and their polarity, there is relatively less work in identifying subjective sentences. In this paper, we used a variety of standard classifiers to build models of SUBJECTIVE vs. NON-SUBJECTIVE sentences. We demonstrated that some of the standard classifiers outperform the approaches reported in the literature on several interesting datasets. We discussed two novel applications of this work, which have not been reported in the literature to our knowledge: understanding the prevalence of subjective sentences in (i) performance appraisal text; and (ii)

ID	Actual	Predicted	Sentence
A1	S	NS	The assets can be extended to larger infra led offerings and cloud migration offerings.
A2	S	NS	He also needs to accept and bring changes in his team to suit evolving needs of the account.
A3	NS	S	Is able to effectively collaborate across the organisational groups for achieving the desired objective.
A4	NS	S	Being well organised and having done multiple roles in xyzxyz – Delivery, Presales, Domain Consulting – he can run a small mid size unit quite comfortably.

Table 5: Some example sentences from Dataset D3.

B1	The mucocele decreased in size and the postoperative course was uneventful.
B2	Significant differences were detected in bacterial community structures and co-occurrence patterns between the wet and dry seasons.
B3	New epidemiological and genetic studies are needed to identify possible common risk factors.
B4	Findings suggest that specific types of stressors may influence eating behaviors differently.
B5	This approach should be of special interest to those concerned about the impact of the presence of low-volatility organic liquids in waters of environmental and biological systems.
B6	Hence, this may provide a new insight into understanding the mechanism of DR pathogenesis, as well as a potential therapeutic target for proliferative DR.
B7	Some patients may experience a short term pain response.
B8	This review is an up-to-date compilation on its traditional uses in context to phytochemical and pharmacological perspectives.

Table 6: Examples sentences from scientific abstracts.

scientific papers. Rather surprisingly, we found that scientific papers also seem to contain a substantial fraction of subjective sentences. Finally, we compared the nature of subjective sentences in the human-centric text (such as performance appraisals) and scientific papers, and reported that there seem to be *different* reasons why some sentences in these domains are subjective.

For further work, we are developing additional techniques for subjectivity detection, based on co-training and label propagation. We are also exploring detection of subjectivity in different domains, such as financial reports and political news. It is already known, and we have also found in our work, that there is substantial variation and disagreement in the human annotators' perception of subjective sentences. That is, the basis of subjectivity may itself be subjective! It would be interesting to explore the nature of subjective expressions by taking into account context and human psychological factors. To get a deeper understanding of the notion of subjectivity, we propose the need to further investigate the linguistic and semantic basis for subjective sentences, and their variations across different domains.

References

M. Apte, S. Pawar, S. Patil, S. Baskaran, A. Shrivastava, and G.K. Palshikar. 2016. Short text matching in performance management. In *Proc. 21st Int. Conf. on Management of Data (COMAD)*, pages 13–23.

Stefano Baccianella, Andrea Esuli, and Fabrizio Sebastiani. 2010. Sentiwordnet 3.0: An enhanced lexical resource for sentiment analysis and opinion mining. In *Proc. LREC*, pages 2200–2204.

W.W. Cohen, V.R. Carvalho, and T.M. Mitchell. 2004. Learning to classify email into "speech acts". In *Proc. Empirical Methods in Natural Language Processing (EMNLP-04)*, pages 309–316.

S. Corston-Oliver, E. Ringger, M. Gamon, and R. Campbell. 2004. Task-focused summarization of email. In *Proc. ACL-04 Workshop on Text Summarization Branches Out*, pages 43–50.

Koby Crammer, Ofer Dekel, Joseph Keshet, Shai Shalev-Shwartz, and Yoram Singer. 2006. Online passive-aggressive algorithms. *Journal of Machine Learning Research*, 7:551–585.

S. Deshpande, G.K. Palshilkar, and G. Athiappan. 2010. An unsupervised approach to sentence classification. In *Proc. Int. Conf. on Management of Data (COMAD)*, pages 88–99.

Kavita Ganesan, ChengXiang Zhai, and Jiawei Han. 2010. Opinosis: a graph-based approach to abstractive summarization of highly redundant opinions. In *Proc. 23rd Int. Conf. Computational Linguistics*, pages 340–348.

Namrata Godbole, Manja Srinivasaiah, and Steven Skiena. 2007. Large-scale sentiment analysis for news and blogs. In *Proc. ICWSM*, pages 219–222.

B. Hachey and C. Grover. 2004. Sentence classification experiments for legal text summarisation. In *Proc. 17th Annual Conference on Legal Knowledge and Information Systems (Jurix-2004)*, pages 29–38.

Vasileios Hatzivassiloglou and Janyce M. Wiebe. 2000. Effects of adjective orientation and gradability on sentence subjectivity. In *Proc. 18th Int. Conf. Computational Linguistics*, pages 299–305.

Q. He, K. Chang, and E.-P. Lim. 2006. Anticipatory event detection via sentence classification. In *Proc. IEEE Int. Conf. on Systems, Man and Cybernetics (SMC-06)*, pages 1143–1148.

M. A. Hearst. 1998. Automated discovery of wordnet relations. In *in C. Fellbaum (Ed.), WordNet: An Electronic Lexical Database and Some of its Applications*. MIT Press.

F. Ibekwe-SanJuan, S. Fernandez, E. SanJuan, and E. Charton. 2008. Annotation of scientific summaries for information retrieval. In *Proc. ESAIR-08*.

T. Ito, M. Shimbo, T. Yamasaki, and Y. Matsumoto. 2004. Semi-supervised sentence classification for medline documents. *IEIC Technical Report*, 104(486):51–56.

E. Ivanovic. 2006. Using dialogue acts to suggest responses in support services via instant messaging. In *Proc. 2006 Australasian Language Technology Workshop (ALTW2006)*, pages 159–160.

Y. Kadoya, K. Morita, M. Fuketa, M. Oono, E.-S. Atlam, T. Sumitomo, and J.-I. Aoe. 2005. A sentence classification technique using intention association expressions. *Int. J. Computer Mathematics*, 82(7):777–792.

A. Khoo, Y. Marom, and D. Albrecht. 2006. Experiments with sentence classification. In *Proc. 2006 Australasian Language Technology Workshop (ALTW2006)*, pages 18–25.

Soo-Min Kim and Eduard Hovy. 2005. Automatic detection of opinion bearing words and sentences. In *Proc. Int. Joint Conf. Natural Language Processing (IJCNLP)*, pages 61–66.

Youngho Kim and Sung-Hyon Myaeng. 2007. Opinion analysis based on lexical clues and their expansion. In *Proc. NTCIR-6*, pages 347–354.

Bing Liu. 2010. Sentiment analysis and subjectivity. In *Handbook of natural language processing, vol. 2*, pages 627–666.

L. McKnight and P. Srinivasan. 2003. Categorization of sentence types in medical abstracts. In *Proc. American Medical Informatics Association Annual Symposium*, pages 440–444.

S. Momtazi and D. Klakow. 2009. Language model-based sentence classification for opinion question answering systems. In *Proc. International Multi-conference on Computer Science and Information Technology*, pages 251–255.

M. Naughton, N. Stokes, and J. Carthy. 2010. Sentence-level event classification in unstructured texts. *Information Retrieval*, 13(2):132–156.

Alexander Pak and Patrick Paroubek. 2010. Twitter as a corpus for sentiment analysis and opinion mining. In *Proc. LREC*, pages 1320–1326.

Bo Pang and Lillian Lee. 2004. A sentimental education: Sentiment analysis using subjectivity summarization based on minimum cuts. In *Proc. 42nd annual meeting on Association for Computational Linguistics*, page 271.

S. Pawar, N. Ramrakhiyani, G. K. Palshikar, and S. Hingmire. 2015. Deciphering review comments: Identifying suggestions, appreciations and complaints. In *Proc. 20th Int. Conf. Applications of Natural Language to information Systems (NLDB), LNCS 9103*, pages 204–211.

N. Ramrakhiyani, S. Pawar, G.K. Palshikar, and M. Apte. 2016. Aspects from appraisals! a label propagation with prior induction approach. In *Proc. 21st Int. Conf. Applications of Natural Language to information Systems (NLDB), LNCS 9612*, pages 301–309.

Ellen Riloff and Janyce Wiebe. 2003. Learning extraction patterns for subjective expressions. In *Proc. Conf. on Empirical methods in natural language processing (EMNLP)*, pages 105–112.

Ellen Riloff, Janyce Wiebe, and Theresa Wilson. 2003. Learning subjective nouns using extraction pattern bootstrapping. In *Proc. 7th Conf. Natural Language Learning (HLT-NAACL)*, pages 25–32.

Adam Stepinski and Vibhu Mittal. 2007. A fact/opinion classifier for news articles. In *Proc. 30th ACM Conf. Research and development in information retrieval (SIGIR)*, pages 807–808.

Afraz Z. Syed, Muhammad Aslam, and Ana Maria Martinez-Enriquez. 2010. Lexicon based sentiment analysis of urdu text using sentiunits. In *Proc. Mexican Int. Conf. on Artificial Intelligence*, pages 32–43.

S. Teufel and M. Moens. 1998. Sentence extraction and rhetorical classification for flexible abstracts. In *Proc. AAAI-98*.

C. Wang, J. Lu, and G. Zhang. 2005. A semantic classification approach for online product reviews. In *Proc. IEEE/WIC/ACM International Conference on Web Intelligence*, pages 276–279.

Janyce Wiebe and Ellen Riloff. 2005. Creating subjective and objective sentence classifiers from unannotated texts. In *Proc. Int. Conf. Intelligent Text Processing and Computational Linguistics*, pages 486–497.

Janyce M. Wiebe, Rebecca F. Bruce, and Thomas P. O'Hara. 1999. Development and use of a gold-standard data set for subjectivity classifications. In *Proc. 37th annual meeting of the Association for Computational Linguistics*, pages 246–253.

Janyce Wiebe. 2000. Learning subjective adjectives from corpora. In *Proc. AAAI/IAAI*, pages 735–740.

Theresa Wilson, Paul Hoffmann, Swapna Somasundaran, Jason Kessler, Janyce Wiebe, Yejin Choi, Claire Cardie, Ellen Riloff, and Siddharth Patwardhan. 2005a. Opinionfinder: A system for subjectivity analysis. In *Proc. Conf. on Human Language Technology and Empirical Methods in Natural Language Processing interactive demonstrations*, pages 34–35.

Theresa Wilson, Janyce Wiebe, and Paul Hoffmann. 2005b. Recognizing contextual polarity in phrase-level sentiment analysis. In *Proc. Conf. on Human Language Technology and Empirical Methods in Natural Language Processing*, pages 347–354.

Y. Yamamoto and T. Takagi. 2005. Experiments with sentence classification: A sentence classification system for multi biomedical literature summarization. In *Proc. 21st International Conference on Data Engineering Workshops*, pages 1163–1168.

Hong Yu and Vasileios Hatzivassiloglou. 2003. Towards answering opinion questions: Separating facts from opinions and identifying the polarity of opinion sentences. In *Proc. Conf. on Empirical methods in natural language processing (EMNLP)*, pages 129–136.

F.M. Zanzotto and L. DellArciprete. 2009. Efficient kernels for sentence pair classification. In *Proceedings of the 2009 Conference on Empirical Methods in Natural Language Processing (EMNLP-09)*, pages 91–100.

L. Zhou, M. Ticrea, and E. Hovy. 2004. Multi-document biography summarization. In *Proc. Empirical Methods in Natural Language Processing (EMNLP-04)*, pages 434–441.

Opinion Mining in a Code-Mixed Environment: A Case Study with Government Portals

Deepak Gupta, Ankit Lamba, Asif Ekbal and Pushpak Bhattacharyya
Department of Computer Science & Engineering
IIT Patna, Patna
Bihar, India
{deepak.pcs16,ankit.cs12,asif,pb}@iitp.ac.in

Abstract

With the phenomenal growth in social media, citizens are coming forward to participate more in discussions on socially relevant topics including government policies, public health etc. India is not an exception to this, and the website *mygov.in* launched by the Government of India acts as a platform for discussion on such topics. People raise their viewpoints as comments and blogs on various topics. In India, being a diverse country, citizens write their opinions in different languages, which are often in mixed-languages. Code-Mixing refers to the mixing of two or more languages in speech or in a text, and this poses several challenges. In this paper, we propose a deep learning based system for opinion mining in an environment of code-mixed languages. The insights obtained by analyzing the techniques lay the foundation for better lives of citizens, by improving the efficacy and efficiency of public services, and satisfying complex information needs arising within this context. Moreover, understanding the deep feelings can help government to anticipate deep social changes and adapt to population expectations, which will help building Smart city.

1 Introduction

The report as published by Statista shows that there has been a phenomenal growth in the use of social media and messaging applications. It has grown 203 percent year-on-year in 2013, with overall application use rising 115 percent over the same period. This implies that 1.61 billion people are now active in social media around the world and this is expected to rise to 2 billion users in 2016, led by India. The research also reveals that users daily spend approximately 8 hours on digital media including social medias and and mobile internet usages.

At the heart of this interest is the ability for users to create and share contents via a variety of platforms such as blogs, microblogs, collaborative wikis, multimedia sharing sites, social networking sites etc. The unprecedented volume and variety of user-generated contents, as well as the user interaction networks constitute new opportunities for understanding social behavior and building socially intelligent systems. Therefore, it is important to investigate tools and methods for knowledge extraction from social media data.

In social media, contents are often written in mixed-languages, and this phenomenon is known as code-mixing. Code-Mixing or code-switching is defined as the embedding of linguistic units such as phrases, words and morphemes of one language into an utterance of another language. This phenomenon is prevalent among bi-lingual and multilingual individuals. This is a well-known trait in speech patterns of the average bilingual in any human society all over in the world. With the phenomenal growth in social media, people from different dialects participate on web portals to showcase their opinions. This diversity of users contributes to the non-uniformity in texts and as a result the data generated lead to code-mixed. There is also a tendency among the users to write in their own languages, but in transliterated forms. Transliteration is the process of converting a text from one form to the other. Transliteration is not merely a task of representing sounds of the original characters, ideally it should be done accurately and unambiguously. Hence, we must have a way to convert transliterated text into its own original script for effective analysis. One of the crucial

D S Sharma, R Sangal and A K Singh. Proc. of the 13th Intl. Conference on Natural Language Processing, pages 249–258,
Varanasi, India. December 2016. ©2016 NLP Association of India (NLPAI)

issues in code-mixed languages is to identify the origin of a text for further processing. Hence, we must have a way to discriminate texts written in different scripts. Given a text, the task is to identify the origin of a text, i.e. the language in which it belongs to. In this paper we propose an approach based on deep learning for sentiment analysis[1] of the user comments written in a well-known public portal, namely mygov.in, where citizens express their opinions on different topics or government schemes. This will facilitate urban informatics (for building Smart Cities), where the goal is to analyze the opinions that lay the foundation for improving the lives of citizens, by improving the efficacy and efficiency of public services, and satisfying complex information needs arising within this context. Moreover, understanding the deep feelings can help government to anticipate deep social changes and adapt to population expectations, which will help building smart city. The first task that we address is a classification problem, where each word has to be labeled either with one of the two classes, either Hindi or English[2]. We propose a technique for language identification, which is supervised. We also do back-transliteration whenever necessary. The final step is to find the opinion expressed in each comment. We propose a deep convolutional neural network (CNN) based approach to solve this particular problem.

Most existing work on sentiment analysis makes use of handcrafted features for training of the supervised classifier. This process is expensive and requires significant effort to extract features. Moreover, handcrafted features which are generally specific to any particular domain requires to be altered once we focus on a different domain. Our proposed model does not use any handcrafted features for sentiment classification, and hence can be easily adapted to a new domain and language. The contributions of the present research can be summarized as follows: (i). we propose a deep learning based approach for opinion mining from a code-mixed data (ii). we develop a system that could be beneficial for building a smart city by providing useful feedback to the govt. bodies (iii). we create resources for sentiment analysis involving Indian language code-mixed data.

The rest of the paper is structured as follows:

---

[1]Here we use the terms opinion mining and sentiment analysis interchangeably

[2]Here, we consider that our contents are mixed in nature that contains either English or Hindi or both.

Comments	Language Identification	Back-Transliteration	Opinion
Swachh bharat is a good *initiative to unite every one.* *i wish our PM for the same*	E E E E E E E E E E. E E E E E E E	Not-Required	Positive
jab tak puri tarh se polithin *ke prayog band nhi hoga swatch* *bharat abhiyan kabhi pura nhin hoga*	H H H H H H H H H H H H H H H H H H	जब तक पूरी तरह से पार्लीथिन के प्रयोग बन्द नही होगा स्वच्छ भारत अभियान कभी पूरा नही होगा	Negative

Table 1: Examples of comments along with the output at various steps of the proposed approach. Langage identification **E**: English, **H**: Hindi.

In Section 2 we present a brief literature overview. Pre-processing, annotation and statistics of the resources that we created are described in Section-3. Section-7 gives the details of our proposed convolutional network model to identify opinion from comments. The experimental setup along with the details of external data are described in Section-8. The obtained results, key observations and error analysis are discussed in Section-9. Finally, we conclude in Section-10.

2 Related Works

Nowadays deep learning models are being used to solve various natural language processing (NLP) problems. Usually, the input to any deep learning based model is the word representation. Some of the commonly used word representation techniques are word2vec (Mikolov et al., 2013), Glove (Pennington et al., 2014), Neural language model (Mikolov et al., 2010), etc. Distributed representation of a word is one of the popularly used models (Hinton, 1984; Rumelhart et al., 1988). Similarly recurrent neural network (Liu et al., 2015) has been used for modeling sentence and documents. The numeric vectors, used to represent words are called word embedding. Word embedding has shown promising results in variety of the NLP applications, such as named entity recognition (NER) (dos Santos et al., 2015), sentiment analysis (Socher et al., 2013b) and parsing (Socher et al., 2013a; Turian et al., 2010). The convolutional neural network(CNN) (LeCun et al., 1998) was originally proposed for computer vision. The success of CNN has been seen in few of the NLP applications such as sentence modeling (Kalchbrenner et al., 2014), semantic parsing for question answering (Yih et al., 2014), query retrieval in web search (Shen et al., 2014), sentence classification (Kim, 2014; Socher et al., 2013b) etc. Collobert (Collobert et al., 2011) has also claimed the effectiveness of CNN in traditional NLP task such as PoS tagging, NER etc. Deep learning based architectures have shown success for sentiment classification of tweets, such as (Tang et al., 2014; dos Santos and Gatti, 2014). The domain adaption for large scale sentiment classification has been handled through deep learning model (Glorot et al., 2011). In social media contents, code-mixing where more than one language is mixed is very common that demands special attention. Significant characteristics of code mixing have been pointed out in some of the works such as (Milroy and Muysken, 1995; Alex, 2007; Auer, 2013). In a multi-lingual country like India, code-mixing poses a big challenge to handle the contents in social media. Chinese-English code mixing in Macao (San, 2009) and Hong Kong (Li, 2000) indicated that linguistic constructions predominantly trigger code mixing. The work reported in (Hidayat, 2012) showed that Facebook users tend to mainly use inter-sentential switching over intra-sentential. A code-mixed speech corpus of English-Hindi on student interviews is presented in (Dey and Fung, 2014). It shows analysis and motivations of code mixing, and discusses in what grammatical contexts code mixing occurs (Dey and Fung, 2014) . To the best of our knowledge we do not see the use of any deep learning that addresses the problem of sentiment analysis in a code-mixed environment.

In our current work we discuss the scope for text analysis based on deep learning architecture on government data / citizen views which can very well frame a new concept of better e-governance.

3 Resource Creation

We design a web-crawler to crawl user comments from *mygov.in* portal. We consider the comments written for the section of 'cleanliness in school curriculum' under *Swachh Bharat Abhiyaan*. In total 17,155 cleaned[3] comments were crawled from the web [4]. The contents are mixed in nature containing both *English* and *Hindi*. Hence, it poses several challenges to extract meaningful information.

3.1 Pre-processing

We pre-process the crawled data in order to effectively extract opinion from the comments. Since we extract the comments from an open platform where anyone has the freedom to give their opin-

___
[3]this number is after the Pre-processing of comments
[4]https://mygov.in/group-issue/cleanliness-school-curriculum/

ions the way they want, there was a necessity to pre-process the data before its use. We perform the following steps:

- First we manually remove comments which are neither in English script nor in Devanagari (Hindi). For e.g., अधार्मिकाः यदा धर्मं वदन्ति स्वार्थसाधने । ते धर्मं दूषयन्त्येव

- While analyzing the comments, we noticed that some of the comments having shorter length do not contain any vital opinion. Therefore, we removed all the comments which have less than 5 words. For e.g. *Clean India, Swachh Bharat Abhiyan* etc.

- We define regular patterns to discard the strings containing html symbols, e.g. *', ", €, &trade*.

- We remove all webpage and HTML references from the data by using proper regular expressions. For e.g. `https://www.youtube.com/watch?v=wP1bmk`.

- We also observe that there are quite a few cases where the comments are duplicated. We remove all the duplicates and keep only one copy for each comment.

3.2 Data Annotation

In order to test the effectiveness of our method we manually annotate a portion of the data. It is to be noted that we perform language identification to identify the origin of written text. Thereafter, we distribute the data into two groups, one containing comments in English and the other containing comments in Hindi. We manually annotate 492 Hindi and 519 English comments using two sentiment classes, positive or negative. Sample examples are given in Table-1. The data were annotated by two experts. In order to assess the quality of a annotations by both annotators we calculate inter-rater agreement. We compute Cohen's Kappa coefficient (Kohen, 1960) agreement ratio that showed the agreements of 95.32% and 96.82% for Hindi and English dataset, respectively. We present a brief statistics of our crawled-data in Table-2.

4 Language Identification(LI)

The problem of language identification concerns with determining the origin of a given word. The task can be modelled as a classification problem, where each word has to be labeled with one of the two classes, *Hindi* or *English*. Our proposed

# of comments	17155
# of sentences	54568
Average No. of sentence/comments	3
No. of identified English Coments	14096
No. of identified Hindi Coments	3059
Total no. of tokens	$10, 26, 612$

Table 2: Statistics of crawled data from *mygov.in*

method for language identification is supervised. In particular we develop the systems based on four different classifiers, *random forest, random tree, support vector machine* and *decision tree*. For faster computation, we use Sequential Minimal Optimization (Platt, 1998) implementation of SVM. Random tree (Breiman, 2001) is basically a decision tree, and in general used as a weak learner to be included in some ensemble learning method. Random forest (Breiman, 2001) is a kind of ensemble learner. We use the Weka implementations[5] of these classifiers. In order to further improve the performance we construct an ensemble by combining the decisions of all the classifiers using majority voting. We use the Character n-gram, word normalization and gazetteer based features as used in (Gupta et al., 2014) to build our model. The accuracy of this model on a gold standard test set was 87.52%. A public comment is a sequence of sentences, which are made up of several word-level tokens. Each token of a sentence is labeled with one of the classes (denoting English or Hindi) that correspond to its original script. Based on the classes assigned at the token-level we classify the sentence based on the majority voting. The sentence is classified to belong to that particular class which appears most in the sentence. Mathematically, it can be defined as follows:

$$S = \{x | x \in lang(t), \forall t \in T\}$$

$$Lang(comments) = \operatorname*{argmax}_{s \in S}(f(s)) \quad (1)$$

where $f(s)$ is cardinality function, $x \in \{$Hindi, English$\}$ $lang(t)$ is the language of a token t; and T denotes all the tokens in a comment.

5 Transliteration

Most of Hindi comments are in their transliterated forms. In order to train an effective word embedding model we need to have enough data. We have

abundant of data sources from Hindi Wikipedia. We back-transliterate the roman script into Devanagari script. A transliteration system takes as input a character string in the source language and generates a character string in the target language as output. The transliteration algorithm (Ekbal et al., 2006) that we used here can be conceptualized as two-levels of decoding: (a) segmenting source and target language strings into transliteration units (TUs); and (b). defining appropriate mapping between the source and target TUs by resolving different combinations of alignments and unit mappings. The TU is defined based on a regular expression. For a given token belonging to 'non-native' script X[6] written in English Y as the observed channel output, we have to find out the most likely English transliteration Y that maximizes $P(Y|X)$. The Indic word(Hindi) is divided into TUs that have the pattern C^+M, where C represents a vowel or a consonant or conjunct and M represents the vowel modifier or matra. An English word is divided into TUs that have the pattern C^*V^*, where C represents a consonant and V represents a vowel (Ekbal et al., 2006). The most appropriate mappings between the source and target TUs are learned automatically from the bilingual training corpus. The transliteration of the input word is obtained using direct orthographic mapping by identifying the equivalent target TU for each source TU in the input and then placing the target TUs in order. We have used three types of statistical model to obtained transliterated output. **Model-I**: This is a kind of monogram model where no context is considered, i.e.

$$P(X,T) = \Pi_{i=1}^{k} P(< x, t >_i) \quad (2)$$

Model-II: This model is built by considering next source TU as context.

$$P(X,T) = \Pi_{i=1}^{k} P(< x, t >_i | x_{i+1}) \quad (3)$$

Model-III: This model incorporates the previous and the next TUs in the source and the previous target TU as the context.

$$P(X,T) = \Pi_{i=1}^{k} P(< x, t >_i | < x, t >_{i-1}, x_{i+1})$$
$$(4)$$

The overall transliteration process attempts to produce the best output for the given input word

---

[5]http://www.cs.waikato.ac.nz/ml/weka/

[6]Denotes Indian languages written in roman script and mixed with English language

using Model-III. If the transliteration is not obtained then we consult Model-II and then Model-I in sequence. If none of these models produces the output then we consider a literal transliteration model developed using a dictionary. The accuracy of this model on a gold standard test set was 83.82%.

6 Baseline Models for Sentiment Analysis

In this section we describe the baseline model that we build for sentiment analysis.

6.1 Representation of comments

An effective representation of comment is important to uncover the opinion associated with a comment. Since we deal with a code-mixed environment, it is not very straightforward to represent the tokens. Here, we describe the representation techniques used only for our baseline input. The input to the CNN based sentiment analysis model is discussed in Section-7.

Representation of English comments: We use the well-known *word2vec*[7] tool to generate the word vectors of each token. We use freely available Google news word embedding model trained on news data. A comment is finally represented by a vector composed of the word vectors of the individual tokens. The vector is generated as follows:

$$Reps(comment) = \frac{\sum_{t_i \in Comment(T)} Reps(t_i)}{number\ Of\ Lookups}$$

$$(5)$$

Here, $Reps(t)$ is the token representation obtained by Google news word embedding and *number of lookups* is equal to the number of tokens from the comments present in the word embedding model.

Representation of Hindi comments: For Hindi we build our own word embedding model. For training we use the data sets obtained from the Hindi Wikipedia and some other sources (Joshi. et al., 2010; Al-Rfou et al., 2013) including all the comments that we crawled. We use *skip-gram* representation (Mikolov et al., 2013) for the training of *word2vec* tool. Further, we use Eq-5 to obtain the representations of Hindi comments. We set dimension to 200 and window size as 5. After we represent the comments in terms of vectors, we develop two baselines to compare with our proposed approach.

---

[7]https://code.google.com/archive/p/word2vec/

6.2 Baseline-1

The hypothesis behind this baseline being the fact that, if two comments have the same sentiments (positive or negative) then the similarity between them would be higher than any other comments having different sentiments. We use the IMDB movie reviews data sets (Maas et al., 2011) containing 2K positive and 2K negative reviews for English and Hindi movie reviews, and tourism data (Joshi. et al., 2010) to compare the opinions represented in our Hindi comments. This algorithm takes as input a comment and the source documents (i.e. datasets that we collected). Each comment and all the documents belonging to a particular set (positive set: containing all the positive comments and negative set: containing all the negative comments) are represented as vectors following the representation techniques that we discussed in Subsection-6.1. We compute the cosine similarity of a given comment with respect to all the documents present in a 'positive set' or 'negative set'. Based on the dominance of average cosine similarity, we assign the opinion. We sketch the steps in Algorithm-1.

6.3 Baseline-2: SVM based Model

We construct our second baseline using SVM that classifies the comments into positive and negative. The model is trained with the word-embedding representations as discussed in Subsection-6.1. For English, we use the IMDB movie review dataset for training. For Hindi, we use Hindi movie reviews and tourism datasets which were used in building the first baseline. In order to perform the experiment we use SVM implementation *libsvm* (Chang and Lin, 2011) with linear kernel.

7 Sentiment Analysis using CNN

We propose a method for sentiment analysis using convolutional neural network (CNN). Our model is inspired by the network architectures used in (Kim, 2014; Kalchbrenner et al., 2014) for performing various sentence classification tasks. Typically, a CNN is composed of *sentence representation matrix, convolution layer, pooling layer* and *fully connected layer*. Our proposed system architecture is shown in Fig-1. Now We describe each component of CNN in the following:

Input: A comment C, Positive reviews data, Negative reviews data

Output: Sentiment of a comments $Sent(C)$

n_P= no. of Positive reviews data

n_N=no. of Negative reviews data

begin

   Calculate the cosine similarity of comment with every positive review

   for $i = 1$ *to* n_P **do**

$$sim(C, P_i) = \frac{\vec{Reps}(C) \cdot \vec{Reps}(P_i)}{\|Reps(C)\|\|Reps(P_i)\|}$$

   end

   Calculate the average positive similarity $AvgPoS(C)$ of comment C as follows:

$$AvgPoS(C) = \frac{\sum_{i=1}^{n_P} sim(C, P_i)}{n_P}$$

   Calculate the cosine similarity of comment with every negative review.

   for $i = 1$ *to* n_N **do**

$$sim(C, N_i) = \frac{\vec{Reps}(C) \cdot \vec{Reps}(N_i)}{\|Reps(C)\|\|Reps(N_i)\|}$$

   end

   Calculate the average positive similarity $AvgNeg(C)$ of comment C as follows:

$$AvgNeg(C) = \frac{\sum_{i=1}^{n_N} sim(C, N_i)}{n_N}$$

   if $AvgPoS(C) > AvgNeg(C)$ **then**

     | $Sent(C) = Positive$;

   else

     | $Sent(C) = Negative$;

   end

   return $Sent(C)$

end

Algorithm 1: Sentiment of comments using benchmark data sets

7.1 Sentence Representation Matrix

The input to our model is a comment C having 'n' words. Each token $t_i \in C$ is represented by its distributed representation $\mathbf{x} \in \mathbb{R}^k$. The distributed representation $\mathbf{x}$ is looked up into the word embedding matrix $\mathbf{W}$. We build a sentence representation matrix $\mathbf{C}$ by concatenating the distributed representation x_i for every i^{th} token in the comment C. The sentence representation matrix $x_{1:n}$ can be represented as:

$$x_{1:n} = x_1 \otimes x_2 \ldots \otimes x_n \tag{6}$$

where $\otimes$ is concatenation operator. After this step, network learns to capture low-level features of words from word embedding, and then project to the higher levels. In the next step network performs the series of operations on the matrix that we obtained.

7.2 Convolution

In order to extract the common patterns throughout the training set, we use convolution operation on the sentence representation matrix. A convolution operator is applied on sentence representation that involves a filter $\mathbf{F} \in \mathbb{R}^{m \times k}$, which is applied to a window of m words and produces a new feature c_i. A feature c_i is generated from window of word $x_{i:i+m-1}$ as follows.

$$c_i = f(\mathbf{F}.x_{i:i+m-1} + b) \tag{7}$$

where f is non-linear function and b is a bias term. The feature c_i is the result of element-wise product between a filter matrix $\mathbf{F}$ and column of $x_{i:i+m-1}$, which is then summed to a single value in addition of bias term b. This filter $\mathbf{F}$ can be applied to each possible window of a word in comment C. This generates a set of features which are also called as *feature map*. More formally possible window of m words in a comment C having size n would be $\{ x_{1:h}, x_{2:h+1}, \ldots, x_{n-m+1:n} \}$. A feature map $\mathbf{c}$ can be generated by applying each possible window of word.

$$\mathbf{c} = [c_1, c_2, \ldots, c_{n-h+1}] \tag{8}$$

The process described above is able to extract on feature map with one filter matrix. In order to form a deeper representation of data, deep learning models apply a set of filters that work in parallel generating multiple feature maps.

7.3 Pooling

The aim of pooling layer is to aggregate information and reduce representation. The output of convolution layer is fed into the pooling layer. There are several ways to apply pooling operations on the output of convolution layer. The well-known pooling operations are: *max pooling, min pooling, average pooling, and dynamic pooling*. We apply max pooling operation (Collobert et al., 2011) over the feature map and take the maximum value as the feature corresponding to this particular filter **F**.

7.4 Fully Connected Layer

Finally, the output of pooling layers p is subjected to a fully connected softmax layer. It computes the probability distribution over the given labels (positive or negative):

$$P(y = j | c, p, a) = softmax_j(p^T \mathbf{w} + a)$$
$$= \frac{e^{p^T w_j + a_j}}{\sum_{k=1}^{K} e^{p^T w_k + a_k}} \quad (9)$$

where b_k and w_k are the bias and weight vector of the kth labels.

8 Datasets and Experimental setup

8.1 Datasets

Our language identification system is trained on FIRE-2014 (Choudhury et al., 2014) Hindi-English query word labeling data sets. We back-transliterate FIRE-2013 (Roy et al., 2013) data sets. Detailed statistics of training and test data used in our experiment are shown in Table-4.

8.2 Regularization

In order to overcome the effect of overfit of network, we apply dropout on the penultimate layer of the network with a constraint on l_2-norms of the weight vectors (Hinton et al., 2012). Dropout prevents feature co-adaptation by randomly setting to zero a portion of hidden units during the forward propagation when passing it to the softmax output layer.

8.3 Network Training and Hyper-parameters

We use the rectified linear units (Relu) throughout training as a non-linear activation function. However, we also experiment with *sigmoid* and *tanh* but it could not perform better than *Relu*. For English, we use 15% of training data of English movie reviews as the development data to fine-tune the hyper-parameters of CNN. Similarly, we use 10% of training data of Hindi reviews as the development data to tune the hyper-parameter of CNN. The stochastic gradient descent (SGD) over mini-batch is used to train the network and backpropagation algorithm (Hecht-Nielsen, 1989) is used to compute the gradients. The Adadelta

(Zeiler, 2012) update rule is used to tune the learning rate. A brief details of hyper-parameters are listed in Table-5.

Parameter	Parameter Name	English CNN	Hindi CNN
d^x	Word embedding dimension	300	200
n	Maximum length of comments	50	50
m	Filter window sizes	3,4,5,6	3,4,5,6
c	Maximum feature maps	100	100
r	Dropout rate	0.5	0.5
e	Maximum epochs	50	60
mb	Mini-batch size	50	50
λ	Learning rate	0.2	0.2

Table 5: Neural network hyper-parameters

9 Results and Discussion

Results of our proposed model based on deep CNN are shown in Table-3. The first baseline model which is based on cosine similarity measure does not perform well. We observe that this is biased towards a specific class. However, the second baseline performs well to identify the opinions for both Hindi and English. Performance of our proposed CNN based model is encouraging for both the languages. We experiment with different filter sizes for both the languages. The effect of varying window size is shown in Fig-2. From further analysis of the system outputs, we come up with the following observations:

- Performance of the proposed model for Hindi is not at par with English. One possible reason could be the less amount of data that we use to train the network. The amount of data on which the word embedding model is trained is also less for Hindi.
- Results show that, for Hindi, the system performs better for the negative opinion. This may be due to the un-equal distribution (1035 vs.559 of negative vs. positive) of training instances.
- Model performance depends upon the size of filter window being used to train the network. It is clearly shown in Fig-2. The system performs well with window size combination {3,4,5} for Hindi. The best suited window size(s) for English is {4,5,6}.

9.1 Error Analysis

We analyze the system outputs to understand the shortcomings of the proposed system. We observe the following:

1. We observe that many errors were due to incorrect classification of positive comments

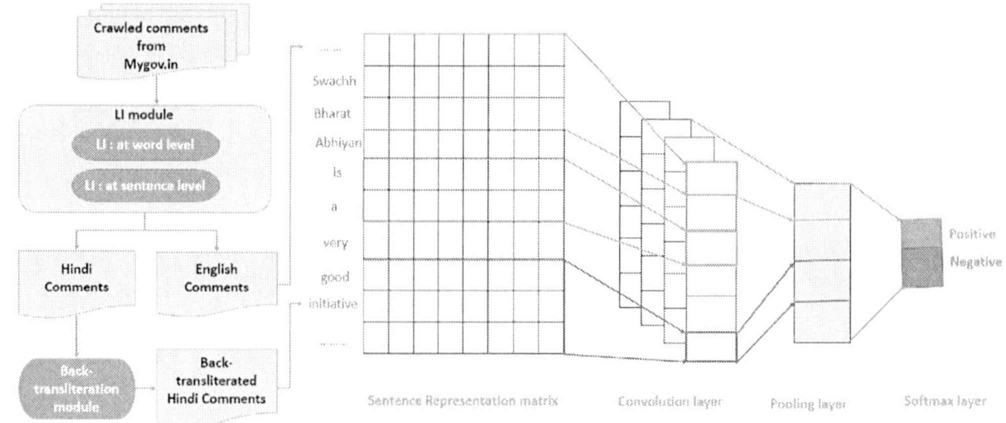

Figure 1: Proposed system architecture

Model	English Data				Hindi Data				Overall			
	R	P	F	Acc	R	P	F	Acc	R	P	F	Acc
Baseline-1	58.75	70.89	50.01	56.06	51.05	54.73	36.77	44.71	54.90	62.81	43.38	50.38
Baseline-2	67.21	67.73	67.25	67.82	57.70	70.5	54.30	57.72	62.45	69.11	60.77	62.77
Code-mixed-CNN	71.90	71.80	71.66	71.68	65.21	68.71	60.68	61.58	68.56	70.25	66.17	66.63

Table 3: Results of baselines and the proposed model. The best results obtained from the window size combination {3,4,5} with feature maps size 100 are reported here. Here, **R** : Recall, **P**: Precision, **F**: F-score and **Acc**: Accuracy

Language	Train			Test		
	Sources	# Positive instances	# Negative instances	Sources	# Positive instances	# Negative instances
English	IMDB movie Review(Maas et al., 2011)	2000	2000	Our crawled data	279	240
Hindi	Tourism Review(Joshi. et al., 2010)	98	100	Our crawled data	282	210
	Movie Review(Joshi. et al., 2010)	127	125			
	SAIL(Patra et al., 2015)	334	810			
	Total	559	1035			

Table 4: Training and test data statistics used in our experiments

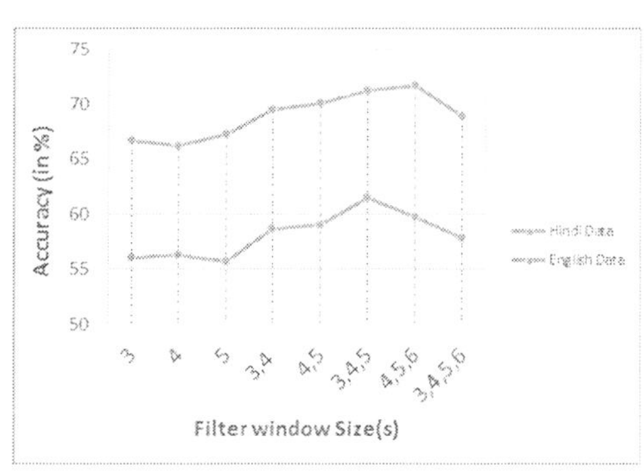

Figure 2: Effect of varying window size on accuracy in CNN model on both languages

into negative. The possible reason is that the comments seem to have conflicting opinions. For e.g., *"The scheme is fantastic but it would not be successful until polybag get banned...."*

2. Some positive comments were mis-classified as negative due to the presence of strong negative triggeres in context of suggestion, but not in the context of government scheme[8]. For e.g.

" इस अभियान से बहुत खुष हूँ पर आप ऐसा कानून लाईये जिससे जो गन्दगी करे उसे पैसे भरने पड़े और दंड हो "

(*very happy with the campaign but implement a law so that those who litter get penalized and punished.*) In this example, opinion is positive about the scheme, but user has given some suggestions with negative opinion bearing words such as पैसे भरने and दंड .

3. A number of errors were also due to annotations of suggestive comments as positive. Our proposed approach often fails to classify the suggestive comments properly due to the presence of negative triggers such as *should not, should also, does no mean, very few,*

---

[8]Suggestion is given with respect to any government scheme.

*but, at least, should be added etc.. "Swach bharat abhiyaan **should also** include cleaning of polluted rivers"*

(iv). The model could not perform well to classify the comments which are conditional in nature. For e.g., *"unless we make judicial system fair, fast, economical and secure we won't see good days I bet my life on it."* System predicts this comment as positive, but actual opinion should be negative.

10   Conclusion

In this paper we propose a deep learning based opinion miner that could be beneficial for urban informatics, where the goal is to work for the betterment of human lives through social media networks. We build this model based on the user comments crawled from *Mygov*.in portal where users write comments on various topics related to govt schemes. We create our own resources in order to build the model. One of the major challenges was to handle the code-mixed cases where the language of more than one script is mixed. We have developed algorithms to solve three crucial problems, *viz.* language identification, machine transliteration and opinion mining. Experiments on Hindi and English show encouraging results for the tasks. Further we would like to enhance the size of the corpus, build deep CNN models utilizing hand-crafted features and study the effectiveness of the proposed model.

Acknowledgment

We acknowledge Salam Amitra Devi (lexicographer, IIT Patna) for contributing in annotation of dataset.

References

Rami Al-Rfou, Bryan Perozzi, and Steven Skiena. 2013. Polyglot: Distributed word representations for multilingual nlp. In *Proceedings of the Seventeenth Conference on Computational Natural Language Learning*, pages 183–192, Sofia, Bulgaria, August. Association for Computational Linguistics.

Beatrice Alex. 2007. *Automatic detection of English inclusions in mixed-lingual data with an application to parsing*. Ph.D. thesis, University of Edinburgh.

Peter Auer. 2013. *Code-switching in conversation: Language, interaction and identity*. Routledge.

Leo Breiman. 2001. Random forests. *Machine Learning*, 45(1):5–32.

Chih-Chung Chang and Chih-Jen Lin. 2011. LIBSVM: A library for support vector machines. *ACM Transactions on Intelligent Systems and Technology*, 2:27:1–27:27. Software available at `http://www.csie.ntu.edu.tw/~cjlin/libsvm`.

M Choudhury, G Chittaranjan, P Gupta, and A Das. 2014. Overview and datasets of fire 2014 track on transliterated search. In *Pre-proceedings 6th workshop FIRE-2014*.

Ronan Collobert, Jason Weston, Léon Bottou, Michael Karlen, Koray Kavukcuoglu, and Pavel Kuksa. 2011. Natural language processing (almost) from scratch. *Journal of Machine Learning Research*, 12(Aug):2493–2537.

Anik Dey and Pascale Fung. 2014. A hindi-english code-switching corpus. In *LREC*, pages 2410–2413.

Cícero Nogueira dos Santos and Maira Gatti. 2014. Deep convolutional neural networks for sentiment analysis of short texts. In *COLING*, pages 69–78.

Cicero dos Santos, Victor Guimaraes, RJ Niterói, and Rio de Janeiro. 2015. Boosting named entity recognition with neural character embeddings. In *Proceedings of NEWS 2015 The Fifth Named Entities Workshop*, page 25.

Asif Ekbal, Sudip Kumar Naskar, and Sivaji Bandyopadhyay. 2006. A modified joint source-channel model for transliteration. *Proceedings of the COLING/ACL*, pages 191–198.

Xavier Glorot, Antoine Bordes, and Yoshua Bengio. 2011. Domain adaptation for large-scale sentiment classification: A deep learning approach. In *Proceedings of the 28th International Conference on Machine Learning (ICML-11)*, pages 513–520.

Deepak Kumar Gupta, Shubham Kumar, and Asif Ekbal. 2014. Machine learning approach for language identification & transliteration. In *Proceedings of the Forum for Information Retrieval Evaluation*, pages 60–64. ACM.

Robert Hecht-Nielsen. 1989. Theory of the backpropagation neural network. In *Neural Networks, 1989. IJCNN., International Joint Conference on*, pages 593–605. IEEE.

Taofik Hidayat. 2012. An analysis of code switching used by facebookers (a case study in a social network site). *Student essay for the study programme Pendidikan Bahasa Inggris (English Education) at STKIP Siliwangi Bandung, Indonesia*.

Geoffrey E Hinton, Nitish Srivastava, Alex Krizhevsky, Ilya Sutskever, and Ruslan R Salakhutdinov. 2012. Improving neural networks by preventing co-adaptation of feature detectors. *arXiv preprint arXiv:1207.0580*.

Geoffrey E Hinton. 1984. Distributed representations.

Aditya Joshi., Balamurali A. R., and Pushpak Bhattacharyya. 2010. A fall-back strategy for sentiment analysis in a new language: a case study for hindi. In *International Conference on Natural Language Processing*, pages 1081–1091.

Nal Kalchbrenner, Edward Grefenstette, and Phil Blunsom. 2014. A convolutional neural network for modelling sentences. *arXiv preprint arXiv:1404.2188*.

Yoon Kim. 2014. Convolutional neural networks for sentence classification. *arXiv preprint arXiv:1408.5882*.

Jacob Kohen. 1960. A coefficient of agreement for nominal scale. *Educ Psychol Meas*, 20:37–46.

Yann LeCun, Léon Bottou, Yoshua Bengio, and Patrick Haffner. 1998. Gradient-based learning applied to document recognition. *Proceedings of the IEEE*, 86(11):2278–2324.

David Li. 2000. Cantonese-english code-switching research in hong kong: A y2k review. *World Englishes*, 19(3):305–322.

Pengfei Liu, Xipeng Qiu, Xinchi Chen, Shiyu Wu, and Xuanjing Huang. 2015. Multi-timescale long short-term memory neural network for modelling sentences and documents. In *Proceedings of the Conference on Empirical Methods in Natural Language Processing, Lisbon*, pages 2326–2335. Citeseer.

Andrew L Maas, Raymond E Daly, Peter T Pham, Dan Huang, Andrew Y Ng, and Christopher Potts. 2011. Learning word vectors for sentiment analysis. In *Proceedings of the 49th Annual Meeting of the Association for Computational Linguistics: Human Language Technologies-Volume 1*, pages 142–150. Association for Computational Linguistics.

Tomas Mikolov, Martin Karafiát, Lukas Burget, Jan Cernockỳ, and Sanjeev Khudanpur. 2010. Recurrent neural network based language model. In *INTERSPEECH 2010, 11th Annual Conference of the International Speech Communication Association, Makuhari, Chiba, Japan, September 26-30, 2010*, pages 1045–1048.

Tomas Mikolov, Kai Chen, Greg Corrado, and Jeffrey Dean. 2013. Efficient estimation of word representations in vector space. *arXiv preprint arXiv:1301.3781*.

Lesley Milroy and Pieter Muysken. 1995. *One speaker, two languages: Cross-disciplinary perspectives on code-switching*. Cambridge University Press.

Braja Gopal Patra, Dipankar Das, Amitava Das, and Rajendra Prasath. 2015. Shared task on sentiment analysis in indian languages (sail) tweets-an

overview. In *International Conference on Mining Intelligence and Knowledge Exploration*, pages 650–655. Springer.

Jeffrey Pennington, Richard Socher, and Christopher D. Manning. 2014. Glove: Global vectors for word representation. In *Empirical Methods in Natural Language Processing (EMNLP)*, pages 1532–1543.

John Platt. 1998. Sequential minimal optimization: A fast algorithm for training support vector machines. Technical Report MSR-TR-98-14, Microsoft Research, April.

Rishiraj Saha Roy, Monojit Choudhury, Prasenjit Majumder, and Komal Agarwal. 2013. Overview and datasets of fire 2013 track on transliterated search. In *FIRE-13 Workshop*.

David E Rumelhart, Geoffrey E Hinton, and Ronald J Williams. 1988. Learning representations by back-propagating errors. *Cognitive modeling*, 5:3.

Hong Ka San. 2009. Chinese-english code-switching in blogs by macao young people.

Yelong Shen, Xiaodong He, Jianfeng Gao, Li Deng, and Grégoire Mesnil. 2014. Learning semantic representations using convolutional neural networks for web search. In *Proceedings of the 23rd International Conference on World Wide Web*, pages 373–374. ACM.

Richard Socher, John Bauer, Christopher D Manning, and Andrew Y Ng. 2013a. Parsing with compositional vector grammars. In *In Proceedings of the ACL conference*. Citeseer.

Richard Socher, Alex Perelygin, Jean Y Wu, Jason Chuang, Christopher D Manning, Andrew Y Ng, and Christopher Potts. 2013b. Recursive deep models for semantic compositionality over a sentiment treebank. In *Proceedings of the conference on empirical methods in natural language processing (EMNLP)*, volume 1631, page 1642. Citeseer.

Duyu Tang, Furu Wei, Bing Qin, Ting Liu, and Ming Zhou. 2014. Coooolll: A deep learning system for twitter sentiment classification. In *Proceedings of the 8th International Workshop on Semantic Evaluation (SemEval 2014)*, pages 208–212.

Joseph Turian, Lev Ratinov, and Yoshua Bengio. 2010. Word representations: a simple and general method for semi-supervised learning. In *Proceedings of the 48th annual meeting of the association for computational linguistics*, pages 384–394. Association for Computational Linguistics.

Wen-tau Yih, Xiaodong He, and Christopher Meek. 2014. Semantic parsing for single-relation question answering. In *ACL (2)*, pages 643–648. Citeseer.

Matthew D Zeiler. 2012. Adadelta: an adaptive learning rate method. *arXiv preprint arXiv:1212.5701*.

Use of Semantic Knowledge Base for Enhancement of Coherence of Code-mixed Topic-Based Aspect Clusters

Kavita Asnani
Computer Engineering Dept
Goa College of Engineering
Goa
India
kavita@gec.ac.in

Jyoti D Pawar
Computer Science and Technology Dept
Goa University
Goa
India
jyotidpawar@gmail.com

Abstract

In social media code-mixing is getting very popular due to which there is enormous generation of noisy and sparse multilingual text which exhibits high dispersion of useful topics which people discuss. Also, the semantics is expressed across random occurrence of code-mixed words. In this paper, we propose code-mixed knowledge based LDA (cmk-LDA), which infers latent topic based aspects from code-mixed social media data. We experimented on FIRE 2014, a code-mixed corpus and showed that with the help of semantic knowledge from multilingual external knowledge base, cmk-LDA learns coherent topic-based aspects across languages and improves topic interpretibility and topic distinctiveness better than the baseline models . The same is shown to have agreed with human judgment.

1   Introduction

The huge amount of social media text available online is becoming increasingly popular thereby providing an additional opportunity of mining useful information from it. Therefore, most of the research on social media text has concentrated on English chat data or on multilingual data where each message as a component is monolingual. In social media, people often switch between two or more languages, both at conversation level and at message level (Ling et al., 2013). However, majority of conversational data on social networking forums is informal and occurs in random mix of languages (Das and Gambäck, 2014). When this code alternation occurs at or above the utterance level, the phenomenon is referred to as code-switching; when the alternation is utterance internal, the term code-mixing is common (Gambäck

and Das, 2016). Thus, code-mixing while chatting has become prevalent in current times. However, exponentially increasing large volumes of short and long code-mixed messages contain lot of noise and has useful information highly dispersed. Unfortunately, it is not an easy task to retrieve useful knowledge from such data as code-mixing occurs at different levels of code-complexity and imposes fundamental challenges namely:

1. Code-mixed social media data is multilingual, usually bilingual (San, 2009). Therefore, semantics is spread across languages.

2. Social media data do not have specific terminology (Eisenstein, 2013).

Therefore, using training data from parallel or comparable corpora will not be useful in this context. Also, availability of pre annotated corpora for all language pairs used in social media may practically be very difficult to obtain. Our objective is to model unsupervised aspect extraction using topics, from the code-mixed context to obtain useful knowledge. Probabilistic Latent Semantic Analysis (pLSA) (Hofmann, 1999) and Latent Dirichlet Allocation (LDA)(Blei et al., 2003) are popularly recommended unsupervised topic modeling methods for this purpose; but a shortcoming with them is that they result in extracting some incoherent topics (Chang et al., 2009).This is due to the occurrence of some irrelevant and polysemous terms in extraction (Chang et al., 2009), which is likely to get aggregated in multilingual content. Therefore, in code-mixed context extraction of incoherent topics are highly likely to occur. In order to cross over the word level language barrier and augment each word with its semantic description we propose to leverage knowledge from external multilingual semantic knowledge base such as Babel-Net v3.0 [1] (Navigli et al., 2012) which is created

---

[1]http://babelnet.org

259

D S Sharma, R Sangal and A K Singh. Proc. of the 13th Intl. Conference on Natural Language Processing, pages 259–266,
Varanasi, India. December 2016. ©2016 NLP Association of India (NLPAI)

from integration of both Wikipedia and WordNet (Miller, 1995).

Our approach of incorporating semantic knowledge in LDA topic model has resemblance with General Knowledge based LDA (GK-LDA)(Chen et al., 2013) model. However, their sets were monolingual and were constructed using Word-Net. They called their semantic sets as Lexical Relation Sets(LR-sets) and were comprising of synonym, antonym and adjective relations. They addressed the problem of multiple senses using synonyms and antonyms in LR-Sets. However, in their work since semantic knowledge is augmented at word level not all LR-sets resulted in correct context knowledge. They handled this problem by using explicit word-correlation matrix and also fixed the wrong knowledge explicitly. But we take a different approach. In a single step, we obtain disambiguated synsets for a code-mixed message, retrieving correct multilingual synsets appropriate to the context across languages. This also resolves language related multiple senses issue. As per our knowledge, our proposed model is the first model to exploit semantic knowledge from BabelNet in topic models for producing coherent topics from code-mixed data.

The remaining part of the paper is organized as follows: Section 2 presents related work, Section 3 describes our proposed work, Section 4 gives implementation details, Section 5 presents experimental results and Section 6 states the conclusion.

2   Related Work

Code-switching and code-mixing are popularly been observed on social networking forums, especially in highly multilingual societies. In this paper, we will use the term code-mixing to refer to both of these situations. In general, multilingual users communicate in two or more languages. In (Barman et al., 2014) study was performed on code-mixed content by collecting data from Facebook posts, code-mixed in three languages Bengali(BN)-English(EN)-Hindi(HI). However, in (Bali et al., 2014), the analysis of code-mixed bilingual English-Hindi data showed significant amount of code-mixing and proved that most of the active users on facebook are bilingual. Out of 43,012 words on facebook chat, 38,144 were written in Roman script and 2661 in Devanagari script. They claimed that the deeper analysis of such data requires dis-

course linguists. We first briefly describe survey studies addressing characteristics of code-mixed text content which are affected by linguistic challenges. Linguistic processing of code-switched data was done by (Vyas et al., 2014) (Sequiera et al., 2015)(Solorio and Liu, 2008)(San, 2015) and they concluded that natural language processing tools are not equipped to resolve all issues related to pre-processing of code-mixed text. (Vyas et al., 2014) created multi-level annotated corpus of Hindi-English code-mixed text from Facebook forums. The annotations were attributed across three levels representing POS tags, language identification and transliteration respectively. They proved that POS tagging of code-mixed text cannot be done by placing two or more monolingual POS taggers together. They identified that it is complex to deal with code-mixed data due to spelling variation. (Sequiera et al., 2015) experimented with joint modeling of language identification and POS tagging. (San, 2015) used Random Forest based method on 400 code-mixed utterances from Facebook and Twitter and reported 63.5% word level tagging accuracy. Their work also illustrates challenge in POS tagging and need for transliteration.

Thus, code-mixed social media data suffer from its associated linguistic complexities which make the semantic interpretation of such high dimensional content very challenging. Also, content analysis in social media containing Twitter posts where training and evaluation is concerned, is done using supervised models in machine learning and NLP (Ramage et al., 2010). They claimed that this requires good prior knowledge about data. Such supervised approaches are not feasible in the context of code-mixed chat data as such data is generated randomly in any language and availability of parallel or comparable corpora for training in certain language pairs is difficult. Also, the use of machine translators is very challenging and not feasible in social media context as the volume of the data is large, inconsistent and translation is required to be done at the word-level. Using a shallow parser (Sharma et al., 2016), our proposed approach first addresses noise elimination and need for normalization. Then, we were motivated to model appropriate unsupervised topic based aspect extraction to discover useful knowledge offering significant information to the administrator or end user. Therefore, we turned to unsupervised topic models, as our goal is to use large collection of code-mixed documents and convert it into aspects of the text in the form of clusters of similar themes together called as topics.

(Peng et al., 2014) proposed code-switched LDA (cs-LDA) which is used for topic alignment and to find correlations across languages from code-switched social media text. They used two code-switched corpora (English- Spanish Twitter data and English-Chinese Weibo data) and performed per topic language-specific word distribution and per word language identification. They showed that cs-LDA improves perplexity over LDA, and learns semantically coherent aligned topics as judged by the human annotators. In addition, as code-mixed social media data involve words occurring in random mix of languages, very few languages have word-level language identification systems in place.

In this paper, we propose utilizing information from large multilingual semantic knowledge base called BabelNet (Navigli et al., 2012) as it provides the same concept expressed in many different languages; which can be used to augment information to code-mixed words, thereby dropping the language barrier. BabelNet (Navigli et al., 2012) offers wide coverage of lexicographic and encyclopedic terms. BabelNet provides multilingual synsets where each synset is represented by corresponding synonymous concepts in different languages. BabelNet v3.0 offers coverage for 271 languages with 14 million entries comprising of 6M concepts, 745M word senses and 380M semantic relations.The knowledge incorporated from BabelNet is used to guide our proposed cmk-LDA topic model.

In order to handle wrong knowledge (injected due to multiple senses), Babelfy (Moro et al., 2014) is used to obtain disambiguated code-mixed words across the message. Babelfy leverages information from BabelNet for its joint approach to multilingual word sense disambiguation and entity linking. It performs semantic interpretation of an ambiguous sentence using a graph and then extracts the densest subgraph as the most coherent interpretation. In order to discover knowledge from social media (Manchanda, 2015) investigated to find new entities and disambiguation as a joint task on short microblog text. They aimed to improve the disambiguation of entities using linked datasets and also discovery of new entities from tweets, thus improving the overall accuracy

Input Text: "you know we always right, चाहे सही चाहे गलत."

```
START Of The Program
Synset ID know#v#3
Synset ID bn:00114251r
always#r#2
Synset ID bn:00109849a
right#a#4
Synset ID bn:00067808n
right#n#2
End Of The Program
```

Output Code to Text: "know जानना right सही right सही"

Figure 1: An Example

of the system.

3   Our Proposed Work

In this section we introduce our proposed work. We first present how we addressed random occurrence of words in different languages in a code-mixed message.   For this purpose, we utilize knowledge from BabelNet which helps augment semantic interpretations of code-mixed words across languages in the form of **m**ultilingual **k**nowledge **S**ets (mulkSets).   We propose a new knowledge based LDA for code-mixed data, which we have called **c**ode-**m**ixed **k**nowledge based LDA (cmk-LDA). In order to automatically deal with random words occurring in different languages we add a new latent variable k in LDA, which denotes the mulkSet assignment to each word. We initially tried to construct mulkSets by directly obtaining synsets from BabelNet. But for each code-mixed word it resulted in retrieval of large number of synsets. This is due to all the possible multilingual senses assigned at the word level. Therefore, for correct semantic interpretation we had to ensure that code-mixed words sharing the same context should share similar sense in their mulkSets. Hence, we constructed mulkSet with disambiguated synsets using BabelFy [2]. Such disambiguated synsets address the shared context across languages. An example is presented in Figure 1. Our disambiguated set therefore contains the revised vocabulary having three words. We found this knowledge to be beneficial to our proposed cmk-LDA topic model as each topic is a multinomial distribution over mulkSets. Thus, cmk-LDA model finds co-occuring words automatically in a language independent manner. For the purpose of demonstration at the sentence level we illustrate two instances in the Figure 3. The

---

[2]http://babelfy.org

first sentence in Figure 3 is an input code-mixed sentence to Babelfy and the second sentence is the disambiguated output further augmented with synsets across languages from BabelNet. Based on this knowledge, cmk-LDA model further generates topic-based aspects across sentences by processing probability distribution over mulkSets.

3.1 The cmk-LDA Model

Given a collection of code-mixed messages
$$M = \{ m_1^L, m_2^L, m_3^L, ..., m_n^L \}$$
where n denotes number of code-mixed messages in $L = l_1, l_2, l_3, ..., l_l$ languages where l denotes number of languages in which code-mixing has occurred.

The code-mixed message is represented as

$$m_i^L = \{ w_{i1}^L, w_{i2}^L\ w_{i3}^L ..., w_{iN_i}^L \}$$

where N_i denotes number of words in the ith message and w_{ij} denotes j^{th} word of the ith message.

Figure 2 shows graphical representation for our proposed cmk-LDA model. Each circle node indicates a random variable and the shaded node indicates w, which is the only observed variable. We introduce new latent variable k, which assigns mulkSet to each word. Assume that there are K mulksets in total. Therefore, language independent code-mixed topics across the chat collection are given as: $Z = \{ z_1, z_2, z_{3,...}, z_k \}$

Each code-mixed message is thus considered as a mixture of K latent code-mixed topics from the set Z. These topic distributions are modeled by probability scores $P(\,z_k \mid m^i)$ Thus, M is represented as set Z of latent concepts present in M.

We have presented the generative process in Algorithm 1.

We performed approximate inference in cmk-LDA model using the block Gibbs sampler as followed typically in LDA. Gibbs sampling constructs Markov chain over latent variables, by computing the conditional distribution to assign a topic z and the mulkSet k to the word. The conditional distribution for sampling posterior is given in Equation 1.

$$P(z_i, k_i \| z^{-i}, k^{-i}, w, \alpha, \beta, \gamma) \propto$$
$$\frac{n_{-i}^{z,m} + \alpha}{n_{-i}^m + z\alpha} \times \frac{(n^{k,z})_{-i} + \beta}{n_{-i}^k + K\beta} \times \frac{(n^{z,k,w_i})_{-i} + \gamma}{n_{-i}^{z,k} + W\gamma}$$

$$(1)$$

1. **foreach** *topic* $z \in Z$ **do**
   Draw mulkSet distribution
   $\varphi \sim \mathrm{Dir}(\beta)$
   foreach *mulkSet* $k \in \{\ 1, ..., K\ \}$ **do**
     Draw mulkSet distribution over words
     $\psi_{z \times k} \sim \mathrm{Dir}(\gamma)$
     end
end

2. **foreach** *code-mixed message* $m \in M$ **do**
   Draw topic distribution $\theta_m \sim \mathrm{Dir}(\alpha)$
   foreach *code-mix word*
   $w_{m,n}^l$ *where language* $l \in L$ *and* $L = \{$
   $l_1, l_2, l_{3,...}, l_l\ \}$ *and* $n \in \{\ 1...N_m\ \}$ **do**
     Draw a topic $z_{m,n} \sim \theta_m$
     Draw a k-mulkSet $k_{m,n} \sim \varphi_{zm,n}$
     Draw a topic $w_{m,n} \sim \psi_{zm,n,km,n}$
     end
end

Algorithm 1: cmk-LDA Generative Process

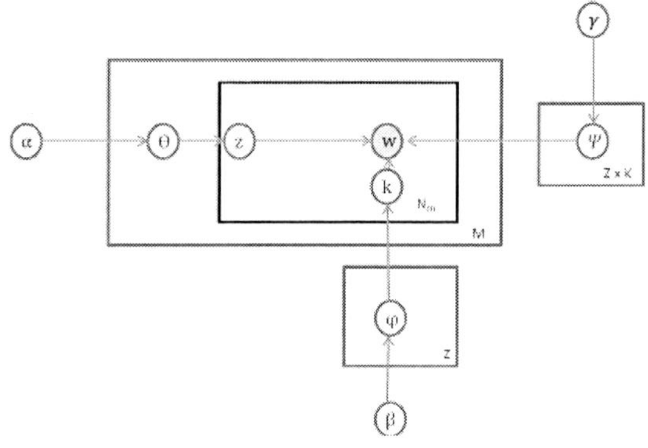

Figure 2: cmk-LDA Plate Notation

Example 1

Example 2

Figure 3: Example Sentences

Figure 6 shows the sample clusters generated by cmk-LDA.

4 Implementation Details

We have evaluated the proposed cmk-LDA model and compare it with the two baselines pLSA (Hofmann, 1999) and LDA(Blei et al., 2003). In our experiments, our proposed cmk-LDA model can deal with words randomly sharing context in either of the two languages Hindi or English. We compared the models by measuring coherence of aspect clusters. For evaluating semantic coherence of topics we used two evaluation metrics; topic coherence(UMass) and KL-Divergence to measure topic interpretability and topic distinctiveness respectively. We performed experiments on four models based on use of external semantic knowledge. The two baselines are addressed as *wek-PLSA* and *wek-LDA* where wek indicates models without external knowledge. We perform testing with different number of topics k and we made sure that we compare topic aspect clusters of the same size.

4.1 Dataset Used

We performed experiments on FIRE 2014[3](Forum for IR Evaluation) for shared task on transliterated search. This dataset comprises of social media posts in English mixed with six other Indian languages.The English-Hindi corpora from FIRE 2014 was introduced by (Das and Gambäck, 2014). It consists of 700 messages with the total of 23,967 words which were taken from Facebook chat group for Indian University students. The data contained 63.33% of tokens in Hindi. The overall code-mixing percentage for English-Hindi corpus was as high as 80% due to the frequent slang used in two languages randomly during the chat (Das and Gambäck, 2014).

4.2 Code-mixed data pre-processing

In our proposed cmk-LDA topic model we believe that a topic is semantically coherent if it assigns high probability scores to words that are semantically related irrespective of the language in which they are written. In the pre-processing phase, we used Shallow parser (Sharma et al., 2016) for our purpose to obtain normalized output. (Sharma et al., 2016) experimented on the same code-mixed English-Hindi FIRE 2014 dataset as we did and

---

[3]http://www.isical.ac.in/ fire/

Table 1: Cohens Kappa for inter-rater agreement

Index	1	2	3	4	5
k	3	6	9	12	15
Precision@k	0.899	0.798	0.876	0.712	0.766

they reported the accuracy on parsing as 74.48% and 75.07% respectively. Basically noise was eliminated by removal of stop-words [4] for Hindi and English.

4.3 Code-Mixed Message as a Document

Topic models are applied to documents to produce topics from them (Titov and McDonald, 2008). The key step in our method is to determine context and for that we address the code-mixed words co-occurring in same context. Such words with similar probabilities belong to the same topic and rejects words that have different probabilities across topics. Therefore, we treat each code-mixed message independently. Although, relationship between messages is lost, the code-mixed words across the language vocabulary within the code-mix message contribute to the message context. This representation is fair enough as it is suitable to obtain relevant disambiguated sets from Babelfy as it resolves context at the message level.

5 Experimental Results

5.1 Measuring Topic Quality by Human Judgement

We followed (Mimno et al., 2011)(Chuang et al., 2013) to evaluate quality of each topic as (good, intermediate, or bad). The topics were annotated as good if they contained more than half of its words that could be grouped together thematically, otherwise bad. Each topic was presented as a list in the steps of 5, 10, 15 and 20 code- mixed aspects generated by cmk-LDA model and sorted in the descending order of probabilities under that topic. For each topic, the judges annotated the topics at word level and then we aggregated their results to annotate the cluster. Table 1 reports the Cohens Kappa score for topic annotation, which is above 0.5, indicating good agreement. We observed a high score at k=3 due to few aspect topics with context highly dispersed resulting in strong agreement on low quality clusters. According to the scale the Kappa score

---

[4]https://sites.google.com/site/kevinbouge/stopwords-lists

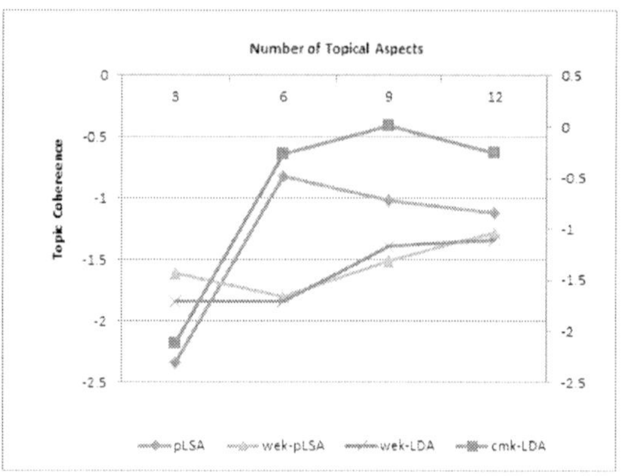

Figure 4: Topic Interpretibility Comparison

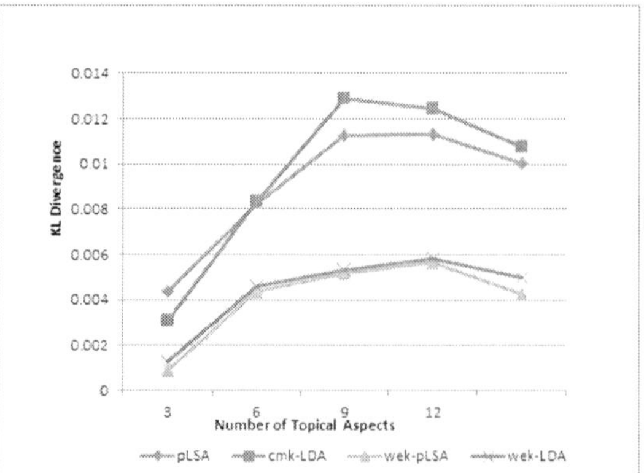

Figure 5: Topic Distinctivity Comparison

increases with more number of topic-based aspect clusters as the topics get semantically stronger. Relatively high agreement at k=9 points to the likely generation of good quality aspect topics.

5.2 Measuring Topic Interpretability

The UMass measure uses a pairwise score function introduced by (Mimno et al., 2011). The score function is not symmetric as it is an increasing function of the empirical probability of common words. Figure 4 shows testing for topic interpretability of topic based aspect clusters for comparison of all models with and without external knowledge. We see from the trend generated by cmk-LDA relative to the other models, generates rise indicating enhancement in coherence of topic distributions. Since most of the topics across languages indicate common context, such high probability topics in a cluster seem to be contributing to high UMass coherence. Both pLSA and cmk-LDA offer better topic interpretibility of clusters. These results confirm that incorporating multilingual external semantic knowledge in code-mixed data find higher quality topics offering better interpretation.

5.3 Measuring Topic Distinctiveness

The Kullback Leibler (KL) divergence measure (Johnson and Sinanovic, 2001) is a standard measure for comparing distributions. We apply symmetrical version of KL Divergence and average it across the topics. Higher KL divergence score indicates that the words across the topics are distinct and are considered to generate higher topic

distinctiveness. From the Figure 5, we can see that initially at k=3, cmk-LDA is lower because the context is wide and therefore words are common across the clusters. While KL scores of pLSA model closely follow cmk-LDA, topics at k=9 have generated higher KL score for cmk-LDA. This suggests that though the interpretibility of topics gains is as high in cmk-LDA, the topics are more distinct as well.

6 Conclusion and Future Work

In order to enhance coherence of topic-based aspects discovered from code -mixed social media data, we proposed a novel unsupervised cmk-LDA topic model which utilizes semantic knowledge from external resources. Such knowledge resolves semantic interpretations across random mix of languages. Our evaluation results show that cmk-LDA outperforms the baselines. We state that our proposed framework supports the utility of lexical and semantic knowledge freely available in external multilingual resources which can drop the language barrier and can help discover useful aspects.

We have not addressed mixed-script in our experiments. In our future experiments we will explore methods to perform term matching and spelling variation modelling the terms across the scripts.

References

David M Blei, Andrew Y Ng, and Michael I Jordan. Latent dirichlet allocation. *Journal of machine Learning research*, 3(Jan):993–1022, 2003.

Jonathan Chang, Sean Gerrish, Chong Wang, Jor-

Topic 1		Topic 2		Topic 3	
cmk-LDA	LDA	cmk-LDA	LDA	cmk-LDA	LDA
बयान 2.232033425e-02	ओर 2.040209203e-02	nickel 2.128407897e-02	अब 1.161278305e-02	Yé-yé 3.005151087e-02	Yé-yé -0.00826076693
लव 2.030074598e-02	you 9.566015083e-03	लड़की 1.433439870e-02	प्यार 1.152999829e-02	confession 1.234810178e-02	confessions 8.234011731
confession 1.565942252e-02	पर 7.971330765e-03	लॉग 1.432539903e-02	friend 9.907712946e-03	आदमी 9.324393775e-03	बद 6.254071239e-03
gid 1.357400234e-02	बस 7.968040771e-03	life 1.193675210e-02	your 8.265343356e-03	शरम 9.232991336e-03	देते 6.251607548e-03
चाहते_हैं 1.345637668e-02	male 7.937751536e-03	people 9.711018821e-03	चल 6.738929867e-03	जाति 9.232991336e-03	च्स 6.251607548e-03
महाविद्यालय 1.345637668e-02	मेरे 6.465273241e-03	परवेश 9.599584565e-03	हु 6.694215122e-03	कम 6.301562733e-03	लो 6.227501521e-03
बस 9.097880608e-03	तेरे 6.418388007e-03	इंतजार 9.599584565e-03	इतने 6.662849180e-03	उत्तर 6.293646760e-03	admin 4.282347564e-03
break 9.049881015e-03	लगा 6.383325233e-03	वाचक 7.262119658e-03	लड़की 5.071191812e-03	good 6.257993226e-03	आशिकी 4.220665853e-03
माता_पिता 9.049881015e-03	confessor 6.3833253e-03	caste 7.262119658e-03	ppl 5.071191812e-03	समसया 6.257993226e-03	thought 4.220665853e-03
कॉल 9.049881015e-03	part 6.383325233e-03	पते 7.262119658e-03	आएगा 5.040151602e-03	बात 6.257993226e-03	मने 4.220665853e-03

Figure 6: Sample Topics with Probability (Top n probability aspects comprise topics)

dan L Boyd-Graber, and David M Blei. Reading tea leaves: How humans interpret topic models. In *Advances in neural information processing systems*, pages 288–296, 2009.

Amitava Das and Björn Gambäck. Identifying languages at the word level in code-mixed indian social media text. 2014.

Jacob Eisenstein. What to do about bad language on the internet. In *HLT-NAACL*, pages 359–369, 2013.

Thomas Hofmann. Probabilistic latent semantic indexing. In *Proceedings of the 22nd annual international ACM SIGIR conference on Research and development in information retrieval*, pages 50–57. ACM, 1999.

Wang Ling, Guang Xiang, Chris Dyer, Alan W Black, and Isabel Trancoso. Microblogs as parallel corpora. In *ACL (1)*, pages 176–186, 2013.

Roberto Navigli and Simone Paolo Ponzetto. Babelnet: The automatic construction, evaluation and application of a wide-coverage multilingual semantic network. *Artificial Intelligence*, 193:217–250, 2012.

Hong Ka San. Chinese-english code-switching in blogs by macao young people. *Master's thesis, The University of Edinburgh, UK*, 2009.

Utsab Barman, Amitava Das, Joachim Wagner, and Jennifer Foster. Code mixing: A challenge for language identification in the language of social media. *EMNLP 2014*, 13, 2014.

Anupam Jamatia, Björn Gambäck, and Amitava Das. Part-of-speech tagging for code-mixed english-hindi twitter and facebook chat messages. *Recent Advances in Natural Language Processing, Bulgaria*, page 239–248, 2015.

Nanyun Peng, Yiming Wang, and Mark Dredze. Learning polylingual topic models from code-switched social media documents. In *ACL (2)*, pages 674–679, 2014.

Daniel Ramage, Susan T Dumais, and Daniel J Liebling. Characterizing microblogs with topic models. *ICWSM*, 10:1–1, 2010.

Royal Sequiera, Monojit Choudhury, and Kalika Bali. Pos tagging of hindi-english code mixed text from social media: Some machine learning experiments. *ICON 2015*

Kalika Bali Jatin Sharma, Monojit Choudhury, and Yogarshi Vyas. i am borrowing ya mixing? an analysis of english-hindi code mixing in facebook. *EMNLP 2014*, page 116, 2014.

Thamar Solorio and Yang Liu. Part-of-speech tagging for english-spanish code-switched text. In *Proceedings of the Conference on Empirical Methods in Natural Language Processing*, pages 1051–1060. Association for Computational Linguistics, 2008.

Yogarshi Vyas, Spandana Gella, Jatin Sharma, Kalika Bali, and Monojit Choudhury. Pos tagging of english-hindi code-mixed social media content. In *EMNLP*, volume 14, pages 974–979, 2014.

Arnav Sharma, Sakshi Gupta, Raveesh Motlani, Piyush Bansal, Manish Srivastava, Radhika Mamidi, and Dipti M Sharma. Shallow parsing pipeline for hindi-english code-mixed social media text. *arXiv preprint arXiv:1604.03136*, 2016.

Andrea Moro, Alessandro Raganato, and Roberto Navigli. Entity linking meets word sense disambiguation: a unified approach. *Transactions of the Association for Computational Linguistics*, 2:231–244, 2014.

Björn Gambäck, and Amitava Das. Comparing the Level of Code-Switching in Corpora. *LREC*, 2016.

Zhiyuan Chen, Arjun Mukherjee, Bing Liu, Meichun Hsu, Malu Castellanos, and Riddhiman Ghosh. Discovering coherent topics using general knowledge. In *Proceedings of the 22nd ACM international conference on Information & Knowledge Management*, pages 209–218. ACM, 2013.

Jason Chuang, Sonal Gupta, Christopher D Manning, and Jeffrey Heer. Topic model diagnostics: Assessing domain relevance via topical alignment. In *ICML (3)*, pages 612–620, 2013.

Don Johnson and Sinan Sinanovic. Symmetrizing the kullback-leibler distance. *IEEE Transactions on Information Theory*, 2001.

George A Miller. Wordnet: a lexical database for english. *Communications of the ACM*, 38(11):39–41, 1995.

Pikakshi Manchanda. Entity linking and knowledge discovery in microblogs. *ISWC-DC 2015 The ISWC 2015 Doctoral Consortium*, page 25, 2015.

Ivan Titov and Ryan McDonald. Modeling online reviews with multi-grain topic models. In *Proceedings of the 17th international conference on World Wide Web*, pages 111–120. ACM, 2008.

David Mimno, Hanna M Wallach, Edmund Talley, Miriam Leenders, and Andrew McCallum. Optimizing semantic coherence in topic models. In *Proceedings of the Conference on Empirical Methods in Natural Language Processing*, pages 262–272. Association for Computational Linguistics, 2011.

Genetic Algorithm (GA) Implementation for Feature Selection in

Manipuri POS Tagging

Kishorjit Nongmeikapam
Department of Computer Sc. & Engg.
Indian Institute of Information Technology (IIIT)
Manipur, India
kishorjit@iiitmanipur.ac.in

Sivaji Bandyopadhyay
Department of Computer Sc. & Engg.
Jadavpur University
Kolkata, India
sivaji_cse_ju@yahoo.com

Abstract

Feature selection is a major hurdle for the CRF and SVM based POS tagging. The features are of course listed which will have a very good impact with the identification of POS. Among the listed features, the feature selection is purely a manual effort with hit and trail methods among them. The best way for better output is to design a system where the system itself identifies the best combination of features. A Genetic Algorithm (GA) system is design so that the best possible combination can be sort out instead of a manual hit and trail method in feature selection. The system shows a Recall of **80.00%**, Precision (**P**) of **90.43%** and F-score (**F**) of **84.90%**.

1 Introduction

The Part of Speech (POS) tagging labels each word or token in a sentence with its appropriate syntactic category of a human language called part of speech. POS plays an important role in the language syntactic structure. It tells us the basic elements of the syntactic governing rules of a language that is the grammar of a human language. In general the POS tagging identifies the types of noun, pronoun, verb, adjective, determiner, etc.

The Manipuri language is one type of Tibeto-Burman language. Tibeto-Burman languages are generally agglutinative in nature. The Manipuri language is not simply agglutinative but one can observe that it is highly agglutinative like Turkish. Manipuri language or otherwise known as the

Meeteilon by the locals is a lingua franca language spoken in the state of Manipur, which is in the North Eastern part of India.

This paper is organized with the related works in Section 2, concepts of CRF in Section 3 followed by the concepts of GA in Section 4, the experimental design, experiment and evaluation is discussed in Section 5 and Section 6 respectively. The last but not the least Section 8 draws the conclusion of this work.

2 Related works

POS tagging forms one of the basic Natural Language Processing (NLP) work. Several works are reported for different languages. To list some among them, the POS tagger for English is reported with a Simple Rule-based based in (Brill, 1992). Also a transformation-based error-driven learning based POS tagger in (Brill, 1995), maximum entropy methods based POS tagger in (Ratnaparakhi, 1996) and Hidden Markov Model (HMM) based POS tagger in (Kupiec, 1992). The works of Chinese language are also reported which ranges from rule based (Lin et al., 1992), HMM (Chang et al., 1993)to Genetic Algorithms (Lua, 1996). For Indian languages like Bengali works are reported in (Ekbal et al., 2007a), (Ekbal et al., 2007b) (Ekbal et al., 2008c), (Anthony et al., 2010) for Malayalam and for Hindi in (Smriti et al., 2006).

CRF based Manipuri POS tagging is reported in (Kishorjit et al., 2012a) and also reported that an improvement is done using reduplicated multiword expression in (Kishorjit et al., 2012b). Manipuri

D S Sharma, R Sangal and A K Singh. Proc. of the 13th Intl. Conference on Natural Language Processing, pages 267–274,
Varanasi, India. December 2016. ©2016 NLP Association of India (NLPAI)

being resource poor language it is reported in (Kishorjit et al., 2012a) that a transliterated model is adopted.

3 Conditional Random Field (CRF)

Conditional Random Field is a very popular topic for the researcher to classify the classes through probabilistic model. Conditional Random Field (Lafferty et al., 2001) is developed in order to calculate the conditional probabilities of values on other designated input nodes of undirected graphical models. CRF encodes a conditional probability distribution with a given set of features. It is an unsupervised approach where the system learns by giving some training and can be used for testing other texts.

The conditional probability of a state sequence $X=(x_1, x_2,..x_T)$ given an observation sequence $Y=(y_1, y_2,..y_T)$ is calculated as :

$$P(Y|X) = \frac{1}{Z_X} \exp(\sum_{t=1}^{T}\sum_{k}\lambda_k f_k(y_{t-1},y_t,X,t)) \quad ---(1)$$

where, $f_k(y_{t-1},y_t, X, t)$ is a feature function whose weight λ_k is a learnt weight associated with f_k and to be learned via training. The values of the feature functions may range between $-\infty \ldots +\infty$, but typically they are binary. Z_X is the normalization factor:

$$Z_X = \sum_{y} \exp\sum_{t=1}^{T}\sum_{k}\lambda_k f_k(y_{t-1},y_t,X,t)) \quad ---(2)$$

which is calculated in order to make the probability of all state sequences sum to 1. This is calculated as in Hidden Markov Model (HMM) and can be obtained efficiently by dynamic programming. Since CRF defines the conditional probability $P(Y|X)$, the appropriate objective for parameter learning is to maximize the conditional likelihood of the state sequence or training data.

$$\sum_{i=1}^{N} \log P(y^i \mid x^i) \qquad ---(3)$$

where, $\{(x^i, y^i)\}$ is the labeled training data. Gaussian prior on the λ's is used to regularize the training (i.e., smoothing). If $\lambda \sim N(0,\rho^2)$, the objective function becomes,

$$\sum_{i=1}^{N} \log P(y^i \mid x^i) - \sum_{k} \frac{\lambda_i^2}{2\rho^2} \qquad ---(4)$$

The objective function is concave, so the λ's have a unique set of optimal values.

4 Genetic Algorithm (GA)

The use of genetic algorithm in the world of Computer science and engineering become very popular. John Holland in 1975 developed the idea of Genetic Algorithm, which is a probabilistic search method. Genetic Algorithm implements the idea of the real world for natural selection, mutation, crossover and production of the new offspring. The basic steps or algorithm in GA which is also mention in (Kishorjit et al., 2011) are as follows.

Algorithm: *Genetic Algorithm*

Step 1: Initialize a population of chromosomes.

Step 2: Evaluate each chromosome in the population or chromosome pool.

Step 3: Create offspring or new chromosomes by mutation and crossover from the pool.

Step 4: Evaluate the new chromosomes by a fitness test and insert them in the population.

Step 5: Check for stopping criteria, if satisfies return the best chromosome else continue from step 3.

Step 6: End

The flowchart in Figure 1 explains the above algorithm. The Genetic Algorithm have five basic components, they are:

1. Chromosome representations for the feasible solutions to the optimization problem.

2. Initial population of the feasible solutions.

3. A fitness function that evaluate each solution.

4. A genetic operator that produce a new population from the existing population.

5. Control parameter like population size, probability of generic operators, number of generations etc.

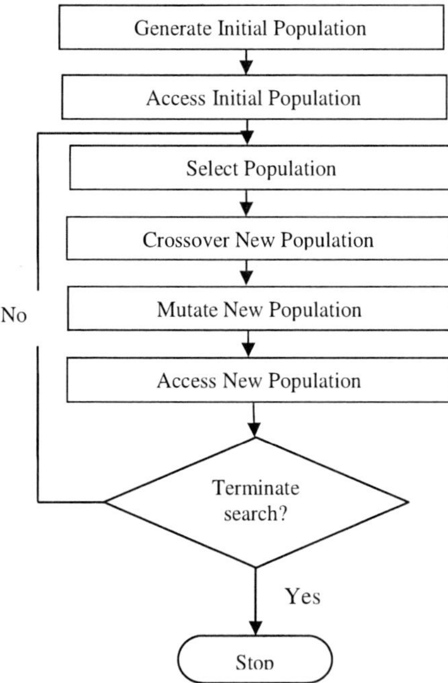

Figure 1. Flow chart of Genetic Algorithm.

5 System Design

The backbone of this system is the CRF model. The CRF based POS tagging model requires to pay much attention in the listing of the feature candidates. In the next step a careful selection of the combinations of the features is required. In much of the cases it is observed that the selection of the feature combination is a manual effort. In each run of the system, one has to select or drop a feature candidate in order to get the best output. In short it's a hit and trail method for the best combinations of the candidate features. One stops the experiment when it reached a good output but it may not be the best.

The work in this paper solves the problem of manual selection of candidate features for the best combination. This is achieved with the use of the Genetic Algorithm technique. So, the system design here is a combination of CRF and supported by the GA in the feature selection.

5.1 The CRF Model

One of the most popular CRF run toolkit for the POS tagging is used. A readily available C++ based CRF++ 0.53 package[1] which is as open source for segmenting or labeling sequential data is used. The CRF model for Manipuri POS tagging (Figure 2) consists of mainly data training and data testing. Cleaning of corpus is important to yield a better result. By cleaning it means to make the corpus error free from spelling, grammar, etc. Linguistic experts are employee for manual tagging. This manually POS tag data is used for the experimental purpose. Also the corpus is a domain based one. This work is done in the newspaper based corpus domain.

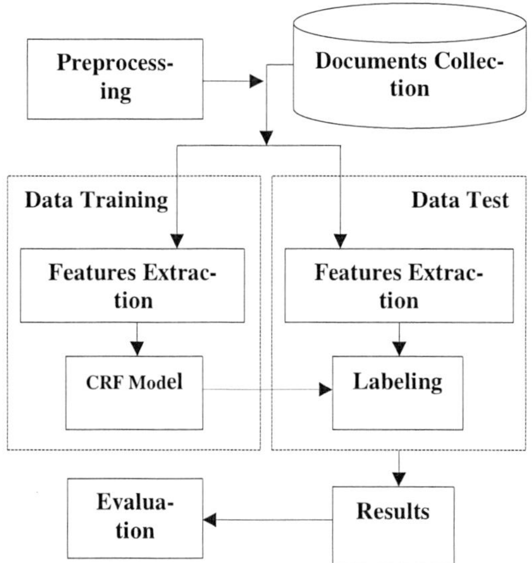

Figure 2. CRF Model of POS tagging

5.2 The Candidate Features

While dealing with the concept of CRF in Section 3 it is mentioned that there is a feature function. Various carefully selected candidate features are to be listed. This candidate features are listed with an aim that it will directly or indirectly influence the tagging of the POS. The candidate features details that have been applied for Manipuri POS tagging are as follows:

Current and adjoining words: The word and the adjoining words may play a crucial role in deciding the POS of the word. The grammatical rule shows an influence among the adjacent words thus current and adjoining words are considered as a feature.

---

[1] http://crfpp.sourceforge.net/

Root word: In order to get the stem word stemming is done as mentioned in (Kishorjit et al., 2011). Root word is considered as another feature. The root word itself sometimes tells the POS specially the noun and verb.

Adjoining root words: The preceding and following root words of a particular word sometimes influence the present word in case of POS.

Acceptable suffixes: As mention in (Nonigopal 1981) 61 suffixes have been manually identified in Manipuri and the list of suffixes is used as one feature. The language is highly agglutinative so ten columns separated by space for each word to store each suffix present in the word is adopted. A "0" notation is being used in those columns when the word consists of less or no acceptable suffixes.

Acceptable prefixes as feature: Also based on (Nonigopal 1981) 11 prefixes have been manually identified in Manipuri and the list of prefixes is used as a feature. For every word the prefix is identified and a column is created mentioning the prefix if it is present, otherwise the "0" notation is used.

Binary notation for suffix(es) present: The suffixes play an important role in Manipuri since it is a highly agglutinative language. For every word if suffix(es) is/are present during stemming a binary notation '1' is used, otherwise a '0' is stored.

Number of acceptable suffixes as feature: For every word the number of suffixes is identified during stemming, if any and the number of suffixes is used as a feature.

Binary notation for prefix(es) present: The prefixes play an important role in Manipuri since it is a highly agglutinative language. For every word if prefix(es) is/are present during stemming a binary notation '1' is used, otherwise a '0' is stored.

Binary Notation of general salutations/preceding word of Name Entity: In order to identify the NE salutations like Mr., Miss, Mrs, Shri, Lt., Captain, Rs., St., Date etc. that precede the Name Entity are considered as a feature. A binary notation of '1' if used, else a '0' is used.

Binary notation of general follow up words of Name Entity: Name Entities are generally MWEs. The following word of the current word can also be considered as a feature since a name may have ended up with clan name or surname or words like 'organization', 'Lup' etc for organization, words like 'Leikai', 'City' etc for places and

so on. A binary notation of '1' if used else a '0' is used.

Digit features: Date, currency, weight, time etc are generally digits. Thus the digit feature is an important feature. A binary notation of '1' is used if the word consists of a digit else a '0' is used.

Length of the word: Length of the word is set to 1 if it is greater than 3 characters. Otherwise, it is set to 0. Very short words are generally pronouns.

Word and surrounding word frequency: A range of frequencies for words in the training corpus are identified: those words with frequency <100 occurrences are set to the value 0, those words which occurs >=100 times but less than 400 times are set to 1. The determiners, conjunctions and pronouns frequently use.

Surrounding POS tag: The POS of the surrounding words are considered as an important feature since the POS of the surrounding words influence the current word POS.

Symbol feature: Symbols like $,% etc. are meaningful in textual use, so the feature is set to 1 if it is found in the token, otherwise 0. This helps to recognize Symbols and Quantifier number tags.

Multiword Expression (MWE): In order to avoid ambiguity or misinterpretation the MWE as a feature is important.

Reduplicated Multiword Expression (RMWE): (RMWE) are also considered as a feature since Manipuri is rich of RMWE. Identification is done using (Kishorjit et al, 2010).

5.3　Corpus preparation

A Manipuri newspaper corpus text document is used as an input file. The training and test files consist of multiple tokens. In addition, each token consists of multiple (but fixed number) columns where the columns are used by a template file. The template file gives the complete idea about the feature selection. Each token must be represented in one line, with the columns separated by white spaces (spaces or tabular characters). A sequence of tokens becomes a **sentence**. Before undergoing training and testing in the CRF, the input document is converted into a multiple token file with fixed columns and the template file allows the feature combination and selection.

An example of the template file which consists of feature details for two example stem words before the word, two stem words after the word, current word, the suffixes (upto a maximum of 10 suffixes), binary notation if suffix is present, number of suffixes, the prefix, binary notation of prefix is present, binary notation if digit is present, binary notation if general list of salutation or preceding word is present, binary notation if general list of follow up word is present, frequency of the word, word length, POS of the current word, POS of the prior two word, POS of the following two word details is as follows:

যুনিভর্সিটিশিংদা যুনিভর্সিটি দা শিং 0 0 0 0 0 0 0 0 1 2 0 0 0 0 0 1 0 NLOC
লুরক্কবা লুরক্ক বা 0 0 0 0 0 0 0 0 0 1 1 0 0 0 0 0 1 0 VN
মতাঙদা মতাঙ দা 0 0 0 0 0 0 0 0 0 1 1 ম 1 0 0 0 1 1 RB
মমালোন্দা মমালোন্ দা 0 0 0 0 0 0 0 0 0 1 1 ম 1 0 0 0 1 0 NN
তক্করিবা তক্করি বা 0 0 0 0 0 0 0 0 0 1 1 ভ 1 0 0 0 1 0 VN
অসিনা অ না সি 0 0 0 0 0 0 0 0 1 2 0 0 0 0 0 1 3 PR

Figure 3. Example Sample Sentence in the Training and the Testing File

To run the CRF generally two standard files of multiple tokens with fixed columns are created: one for training and another one for testing. In the training file the last column is manually tagged with all those identified POS tag. In the test file we can either use the same tagging for comparisons and evaluation or only 'O'.

5.4 The Chromosome and Features

The representation of chromosome is discussed in this section. The chromosome pool or population is developed as mentioned in Section 4. Each chromosome consists of genes, which is binary valued. When the gene value is '1' then the feature is selected and when it is '0' the feature is not selected. Figure 4 demonstrates the feature representation as a chromosome. In figure 4, $\mathbf{F_n}$ represents the features.

Feature:

$\mathbf{F_1}$	$\mathbf{F_2}$	$\mathbf{F_3}$	...	$\mathbf{F_{n-2}}$	$\mathbf{F_{n-1}}$	$\mathbf{F_n}$

Chromosome:

1	0	1	...	0	1	0

Selected Feature subset = {F1, F3,..., Fn-1}

Figure 4. Example Feature encoding using GA

From the Chromosome pool or initial population, first of all initial selection of chromosome is done. A randomly selected crossover point is marked and **crossover** is executed. During crossover, the sub parts of genes are exchanged from the two chromosomes at the crossover point.

The **mutation** is also done in random so that the chromosomes are not repeated. The objective of mutation is restoring the lost and exploring variety of data. The bit value is changed at a randomly selected point in the process of mutation.

Three fold cross validation technique is used as a **Fitness function**. By three fold cross validation we mean dividing the corpus into 3 nearly equal parts for doing 3-fold cross-validation (use 2 parts for training and the remaining part for testing and do this 3 times with a different part for testing each time).

After fitness test the chromosomes which are fit are placed in the pool and the rest of the chromosomes are deleted to create space for those fit ones.

5.5 Model File after training

In order to obtain a model file we train the CRF using the training file. This model file is a ready-made file by the CRF tool for use in the testing process. In other words the model file is the learnt file after the training of CRF. We do not need to use the template file and training file again since the model file consists of the detail information of the template file and training file

5.6 Testing

The test file is created with feature listed for each word. The last column is tag with the respective POS otherwise 'O' is assigned for those words which are not MWEs. This file has to be created in the same format as that of the training file, i.e., fixed number of columns with the same fields as that of training file.

The output of the testing process is a new file with an extra column which is POS tagged. The new column created by the CRF is the experimental output of the system.

271

6   Experiment and Evaluation

The experiment is to identify the best combination of features among the feature list. Feature selection is purely based on the Genetic Algorithm (GA) where the features are considered as chromosomes. In each experimental run the selected chromosome is feed as the feature for the CRF system. The out is verified with a three-fold cross validation.
Manipuri corpus are collected from a newspaper domain which is freely available on internet. The correction and filtration of the errors are done by linguistic experts. In the corpus some words are written in English, such words are rewritten into Manipuri in order to avoid confusion or error in the output. The corpus we have collected includes 45,000 tokens which are of Gold standard created by the linguistic experts.

Evaluation is done with the parameters of Recall, Precision and F-score as follows:

Recall,

$$R = \frac{No\ of\ correct\ ans\ given\ by\ the\ system}{No\ of\ correct\ ans\ in\ the\ text}$$

Precision,

$$P = \frac{No\ of\ correct\ ans\ given\ by\ the\ system}{No\ of\ ans\ given\ by\ the\ system}$$

F-score,

$$F = \frac{(\beta^2 + 1)\ PR}{\beta^2 P + R}$$

Where β is one, precision and recall are given equal weight.

A number of problems have been faced while doing the experiment due to typical nature of the Manipuri language. The Manipuri language is a tonal language so sometimes its ambiguity creates lots of problem in annotating the POS by the linguist. In Manipuri, word category is not so distinct. The verbs are also under bound category. Another problem is to classify basic root forms according to the word class. Although the distinction between the noun class and verb classes is relatively clear; the distinction between nouns and adjectives is often vague. Distinction between a noun and an adverb becomes unclear because structurally a word may be a noun but contextually it is adverb. Further a part of root may also be a prefix, which leads to wrong tagging. The verb morphology is more complex than that of noun. Sometimes two words get fused to form a complete word.

6.2   Experiment for selection of best feature

A 3-fold cross validation is adopted in this experiment, the corpus is divided into 3 nearly equal parts for doing 3-fold cross-validation (use 2 parts for training and the remaining part for testing). A total of 45,000 words are divided into 3 parts, each of 15000 words.

The features are selected using the GA and experiments are performed in order to identify the best feature. The best features are those which gave the best accurate POS tag in a given text. The experiment is stopped with 60 generations since the output doesn't show significant change in the F-score.

In each run of the CRF tool the feature template are changed according to the chromosome selected. Figure 5 shows the chart in terms of Recall (**R**), Precision (**P**) and F-score (**F**).

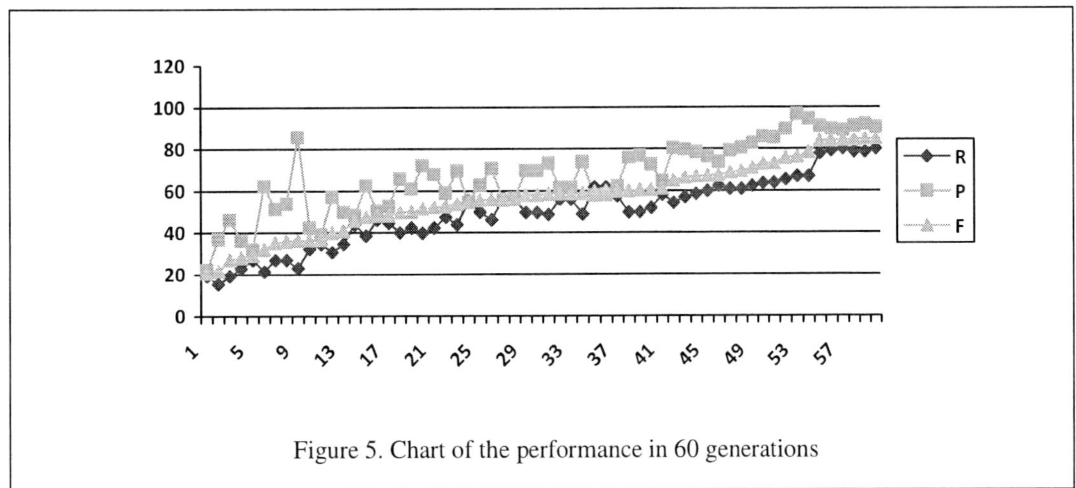

Figure 5. Chart of the performance in 60 generations

The System stops running when the F-Score shows no change in the F-score, i.e., which shows the output is exhausted.

6.3 The Best Feature

The best result for the Manipuri POS so far reported in (Kishorjit et al. 2012) is the Recall (**R**) of **80.20%**, Precision (**P**) of **74.31%** and F-score (**F**) of **77.14%**.

The work here shows the best result for the CRF based POS tagging with the Recall (**R**) of **80.00%**, Precision (**P**) of **90.43%** and F-score (**F**) of **84.90%**. This shows that the F-score is improved from the previous claim of 77.24% to 84.90%.

The implementation of GA could identify the best combination of features. This happens with the following feature set:
F= { W $_{i-1}$, W$_i$, W $_{i+1}$, W $_{i+2}$, RW$_{i-1}$, RW$_i$, RW$_{i+1}$, RW$_{i-2}$, no. of acceptable standard suffixes, no. of acceptable standard prefixes, acceptable suffixes present in the word, NE salutations, NE, POS$_{i-1}$, POS$_i$, POS$_{i+1}$word length, word frequency, digit feature, symbol feature, MWE, reduplicated MWE}

In the above feature list **W$_i$** represents current and surrounding words, **RW$_i$** represents root words, NE represents the name entity, POS represents the part of speech and MWE represents the multiword expression.

The use of GA for the feature selection stretches the best combination among the listed features. Apart from the best combination it also helps in improving the overall F-score from 77.24% to 84.90%. This means there is best combinations which manual selection missed.

The selection of the feature is done with the application of GA and the F-score can be improved by some 7.66%.

7 Conclusion

Among the works of CRF based POS tagging, this papers comes up with a new method of feature selection through genetic algorithm (GA). This approach reduces the manual effort of hit and trial. The tonal nature of the language sometimes create ambiguity so may be in future it may have to frame some rule or design a system to overcome the ambiguity.

The work is done on a newspaper based corpus, so it has scope to check in other domain and it may differ in other domain.

References

Antony. P.J.: Mohan. S.P.: Soman. K.P.:SVM Based Part of Speech Tagger for Malayalam. In the Proc. of International Conference on Recent Trends in Information. Telecommunication and Computing (ITC), pp. 339 – 341, Kochi, Kerala, India (2010).

Brill, Eric.: A Simple Rule-based Part of Speech Tagger. In the Proceedings of Third International Conference on Applied NLP, ACL, Trento, Italy (1992).

Brill, Eric.: Transformation-Based Error-Driven Learning and Natural Language Processing: A Case Study in POS Tagging, Computational Linguistics, Vol. 21(4), pp543-545, (1995).

Chang, C. H.& Chen, C. D.: HMM-based Part-of-Speech Tagging for Chinese Corpora, In the Proc.

of the Workshop on Very Large Corpora, Columbus, Ohio, pp40-47(1993).

Ekbal, Asif, Mondal, S & Sivaji Bandyopadhyay: POS Tagging using HMM and Rule-based Chunking, In the Proceedings of SPSAL2007, IJCAI, pp25-28, India (2007).

Ekbal, Asif, R. Haque & & Sivaji Bandyopadhyay: Bengali Part of Speech Tagging using Conditional Random Field, In the Proceedings 7th SNLP, Thailand (2007).

Ekbal, Asif, Haque, R. & & Sivaji Bandyopadhyay: Maximum Entropy based Bengali Part of Speech Tagging, In A. Gelbukh *(Ed.)*, Advances in Natural Language Processing and Applications, Research in Computing Science (RCS) Journal, Vol.(33), pp67-78 (2008).

Ekbal, Asif, Mondal, S & Sivaji Bandyopadhyay: Part of Speech Tagging in Bengali Using SVM, In Proceedings of International Conference on Information Technology(ICIT), pp. 106 – 111, Bhubaneswar, India (2008)

Ratnaparakhi, A. :A maximum entropy Parts- of-Speech Tagger, In the Proceedings EMNLP 1, ACL, pp133-142(1996).

Kishorjit, N., Bishworjit, S., Romina, M., Mayekleima Chanu, Ng. and Sivaji, B., 2011. *A Light Weight Manipuri Stemmer*, In the Proceedings of Natioanal Conference on Indian Language Computing (NCILC), Chochin, India

Kishorjit, N., Nonglenjao, L., Nirmal .Y, and Sivaji B., "Improvement of CRF Based Manipuri POS Tagger by Using Reduplicated MWE (RMWE)", In: Proceedings of First International Conference on Information Technology Convergence and Services (ITCS 2012), Bangalore, India, pp. 55-69, January 4, 2012.

Kishorjit, N., Nonglenjao, L., Nirmal Y., and Sivaji B., "Reduplicated MWE (RMWE) Helps In Improving The CRF Based Manipuri POS Tagger", International Journal of Information Technology and Computer Science (IJITCS) Vol 2, No 1, ISSN: 2231-1939. DOI: 10.5121/ijitcs.2012.2106, pp. 45-59, Feb 2012.

Kishorjit, N. and Sivaji B., "A Transliterated CRF Based Manipuri POS Tagging", In: Proceedings of 2nd International Conference on Communication, Computing & Security (ICCCS 2012), Elsevier Publication, NIT Rourkela, India

Kishorjit, N., & Sivaji Bandyopadhyay. Identification of Reduplicated MWEs in Manipuri: A Rule based Approached. In the Proc. of 23rd ICCPOL-2010, San Francisco; 2010, p. 49-54.

Kishorjit, N. and Sivaji, B.," Genetic Algorithm (GA) in Feature Selection for CRF Based Manipuri Multiword Expression (MWE) Identification". International Journal of Computer Science & Information Technology (IJCSIT) Vol 3, No 5, ISSN : 0975 – 3826, pp. 53-66, Oct 2011.

Kupiec, R.: Part-of-speech tagging using a Hidden Markov Model, In Computer Speech and Language, Vol 6, No 3, pp225-242(1992).

Lin, Y.C., Chiang, T.H. & Su, K.Y.: Discrimination oriented probabilistic tagging, In the Proceedings of ROCLING V, pp87-96(1992).

Lua, K. T.: Part of Speech Tagging of Chinese Sentences Using Genetic Algorithm, In the Proceedings of ICCC96, National University of Singapore, pp45-49 (1996).

Nonigopal Singh, N: A Meitei Grammar of Roots and Affixes, A Thesis, Unpublish, Manipur University, Imphal (1987)

Smriti Singh, Kuhoo Gupta, Manish Shrivastava, & Pushpak Bhattacharya: Morphological Richness offsets Resource Demand –Experiences in constructing a POS tagger for Hindi, In the Proceedings of COLING- ACL, Sydney, Australia (2006).

Effect of Syntactic Features in Bangla Sentence Comprehension

Manjira Sinha
Xerox Research Center
India[1]
manjira87@gmail.com

Tirthankar Dasgupta
TCS Innovation Lab,
New Delhi[1]
gupta.tirthankar@tcs.com

Anupam Basu
IIT Kharagpur
anupambas@gmail.com

Abstract

Sentence comprehension is an integral and important part of whole text comprehension. It involves complex cognitive actions, as a reader has to work through lexical, syntactic and semantic aspects in order to understand a sentence. One of the vital features of a sentence is word order or surface forms. Different languages have evolved different systems of word orders, which reflect the cognitive structure of the native users of that language. Therefore, word order affects the cognitive load exerted by a sentence as experienced by the reader. Computational modeling approach to quantify the effect of word order on difficulty of sentence understanding can provide a great advantage in study of text readability and its applications. Plethora of works have been done in English and other languages to address the issue. However, Bangla, which is the fifth mostly spoken languages in the world and a relatively free word order language, still does not have any computational model to quantify the reading difficulty of a sentence. In this paper, we have developed models to predict the comprehending difficulty of a simple sentence according to its different surface forms in Bangla. In the course of action, we have also established that difficulty measures for English do not hold in Bangla. Our model has been validated against a number of user survey.

1 Introduction

Complexity of a sentence is the amount of effort a user needs to put in order to understand or comprehend the sentence. Sentence complexity is an important factor in accessing text readability, language acquisition and language impairment. When a reader scans (generally left to right) a sentence, she first processes the syntax (structure and word organization) and semantics (meaning represented by the words) and then reduces them to a semantic whole to store in the memory (Levy, 2013). The short-term memory of the reader engages in real time comprehension of a sentence. While processing a sentence, the short-term memory encounters two types of costs (Oya, 2011): storage cost of the structure built in memory so far and the integration cost due to the proper insertion of the current word into that structure. Therefore, the integration complexity depends upon the relative positions of the entities to be connected, i.e., word order of the sentence.

One of the important grammatical information for sentence interpretation is the word order as it determines the organizations of different grammatical features. It has great impact on the sentence complexity (Meltzer et al., 2010) as it influences both the storage and integration cost and expectation load. Different languages follow different construction rules to build sentences and thus different word orders. Research has been performed to the study effect of word ordering in sentence comprehension in languages like English, Finnish, German (SWINNEY, 1998; Weyerts et al., 2002; Kaiser and Trueswell, 2004). In this paper, the language concerned is Bangla. Bangla is a descendant of the Eastern Indo-Aryan language family 2 . Typologically, it is an inflexional analytic language. Syntax or Sentence structure of Bangla differs from English in many aspects. Bangla is a head final language where the

---

[1] The work was done during the authors stay at IIT Kharagpur

[2] http://en.wikipedia.org/wiki/Bengali_language

275

D S Sharma, R Sangal and A K Singh. Proc. of the 13th Intl. Conference on Natural Language Processing, pages 275–284,
Varanasi, India. December 2016. ©2016 NLP Association of India (NLPAI)

principle word order is subject-object-verb (SOV). It is also a relatively free word-order language as it permits free word order in its constituent chunk or local word group level. Intra-chunk reordering of words is not always permitted; different surface forms of the same sentence are possible, which are grammatically correct; some surface forms are easy to comprehend and some are difficult. Therefore, even simple sentences in Bangla (Chatterji, 1926) can have different surface forms with different comprehending complexities. Till date, there is no prominent study to computationally model the cognitive load associated with different word orders in Bangla.

In this study, our objective is to develop models to quantify the influence of the syntactic and lexical properties of a sentence in sentence comprehension. We have considered simple sentences i.e. sentences having one finite verb[3]. Simple sentences in Bangla can contain many language specific constructs. We have explored the underlying factors responsible for the differences in complexity among different surface forms, such as relative order of subject(s) and object(s) with respect to the verb and organization of non-finite structures. First, we have conducted an empirical user survey, and then we have developed and enhanced our model to reflect the comprehending difficulty experienced by the readers efficiently. In the due course, we have demonstrated that although average dependency distance measure (ADD) (Oya, 2011) works well for English, it is not a good estimator of sentence difficulty in Bangla. Our proposed model takes into account both the relative position and number of unprocessed dependencies at an instant; it is unprocessed dependencies that give rise to expectation gaps in user's cognition. Thus, it models both storage and integration costs on reader's short-term memory in processing a sentence based on different surface forms. We have found high correlation among user preferences and model predictions.

The paper is organized as follows: In Section 2 we have presented the related works in the area of sentence comprehension. In section 3 we have discussed the empirical experiments on Bangla sentence comprehension. Section 4 presents the model building and result analysis. Finally, in Section 5 we conclude the paper.

2   Related Works

A handful of researches have been performed on sentence complexity and word order preference in sentence comprehension. Some approaches are based on dependencies such as placement of verbs in a sentence, position of subject and auxiliary verb in a sentence etc. Several psycholinguistic experiments have been performed to study the role of word order in sentence comprehension.

Research on sentence comprehension difficulty have focused on aspects such as T-unit analysis based on (Bardovi-Harlig, 1992), graph-based approach such as average dependency distance (Oya, 2011), effect of referential processing, subject related clause (SRC) and object related clause (ORC) (Gordon et al., 2001), noun phrases (Gordon et al., 2004), singly nested versus doubly nested structures(Gibson, 2000; Vasishth and Lewis, 2006), effect of semantic context (Tyler and Marslen-Wilson, 1977), influence of hierarchy (Bornkessel et al., 2005), memory interference during language processing like expectation and surprisal (Levy, 2008; Hale, 2006).

The study on comprehension of garden-path sentences started in 1970 (Bever, 1970). Emphasis has also been given on the relationship between linguistic structures in a sentence and language learning (Lachter and Bever, 1988). Within a decade, Bayesian approach towards sentence comprehension based on probabilistic context free grammar (PCFG) (Jurafsky, 1996; Jurafsky, 2002) and competition integration model arrived (Spivey and Tanenhaus, 1998). A different version of competition-integration model was proposed later (Hare et al., 2003) to account for effects of semantic contexts and verb sense effects in sentential complement ambiguity resolution.

Dependency Locality Theory (DLT) (Gibson, 2000) has suggested that during sentence processing, working memory experiences two types of costs. A storage cost to keep in memory what has been encountered so far and an integration cost to assemble sentence components appropriately in order to understand the meaning. The more the distance between an upcoming word and the head it belongs too, the more are the costs. The theory explained the lower comprehension difficulty of SRC than ORC, difficulty of multiple center-embedded structures, ease of cross-referential processing in center-embedded

---

[3] http://en.wikipedia.org/wiki/Simple_sentence

structure, heaviness effect and sentential ambiguities that were earlier explained using Active Filler Hypothesis (Clifton Jr and Frazier, 1989). Inspired from DLT, average dependency distance based sentence complexity metric has been effective in English and Japanese (Oya, 2011).

Notable works on Sentence comprehension in Hindi have been done in recent times (Vasishth and Lewis, 2006). With the help of SPRT, it has been demonstrated that contrary to the findings in English that center embedding sentences always hinders sentence comprehension speed and efficiency, in certain cases for Hindi, a center embedded doubly nested structure can be beneficial to sentence comprehension depending on the nature of intervening discourse particle between a noun and corresponding verb such as adverb or prepositional phrase. The phenomenon has been termed as anti-locality effect. The word by word reaction time in sentence comprehension has been modeled by spreading activation theory (Anderson, 1983). A study on word by word reading pattern in Hindi has revealed that in head final structures like Hindi, strong expectation overcome the locality effect but not weak expectation (Husain et al., 2014).

3 Empirical user study

Given the subjective nature of text difficulty perception, in order to understand how the different cognitive processes vary across different user groups, two categories of users have been considered for each user study. The choice of participants represents average Indian population. Group 1 consists of 25 native users of Bangla in the age range 21-25 years, who are pursuing college level education and group 2 consists of 25 native users in the age range 13 to 17 years. The former is referred to as the *adult* group and the latter is termed the *minor* group(refer to table 1.1).In this thesis, only the variations in age and years of education have been taken into account. Therefore, I have not fixated on a specific social background and have considered a distribution over a moderate range. The Socio-Economic Classification (SEC) guideline by the Market Research Society of India (MRSI) [4] has been primarily used to determine the social background of the participants. MRSI has defined 12 socio-economic strata: A1 to E3 in the decreasing order.

The appropriate class index against a household is assigned by the output of a survey questionnaire collecting data on household items and the education level of the chief wage earner of the family. As can be viewed from the SEC distribution pie-chart (refer to figure 1.5) below, our user group ranges from classes B2 to D2 with only 3 persons from E1 section. The range represent medium to low social-economic sections. The monthly household income ranges from Rs. 4500 to Rs. 15000. To capture the first-language skill, each native speaker was asked to rate his/her proficiency in Bangla on a 1-5 scale (1: very poor and 5: very strong). The distribution has been presented in figure1.4. A significant section of the participants poses medium to poor native language skill. In the backdrop of a country like India it is not exceptional that a person pursuing graduation or higher education is from a medium to low economic background (primarily due to the comparatively low cost of education and a well in place reservation policy) and is not so proficient in the native language.

Type	Background	Mean age (Standard deviation)
Group 1 (adult): 25 native speakers of Bangla	Education: pursuing graduation	22.8 (1.74)
	Socio Economic Classification: B2-D2	
Group 2 (minors): 25 native speakers of Bangla	Education: pursuing school education	15 (1.24)
	Socio Economic Classification: B2-D2	

Table 1.1: User details

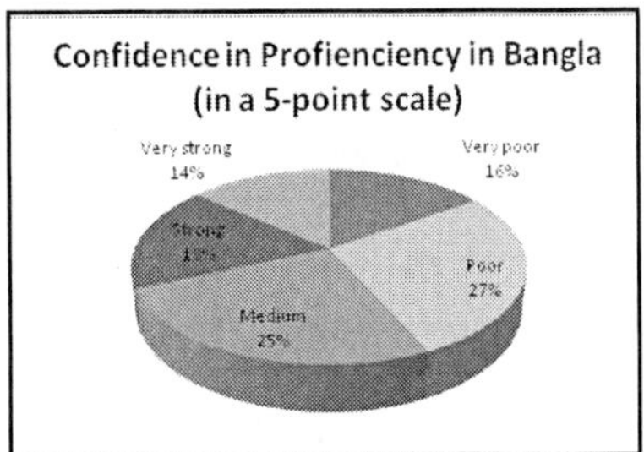

Figure1.1: Proficiency in Bangla

4   http://imrbint.com/research/The-New-SEC-system-3rdMay2011.pdf

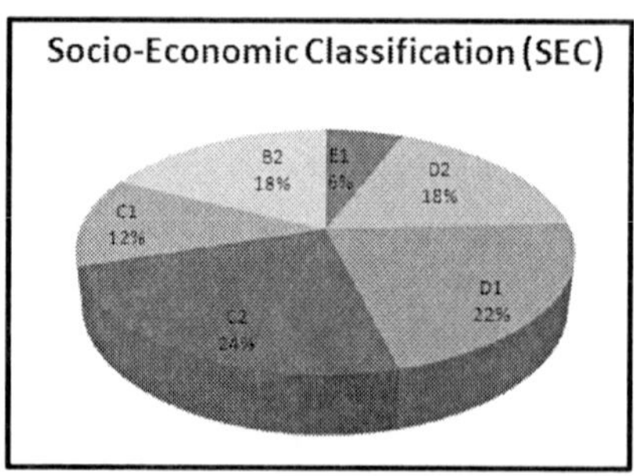

Figure 1.2: Social and economic background of the users.

No.	Feature	Code
1	**Average Dependency Distance** [Total distance among the dependencies in a sentence divided by number of dependencies]	**(ADD)**
2	**Total Word Length** [total length of words in a sentence in terms of visual units (*akshars*)]	**(WLN)**
3	**Syllable Count** [total syllable count in a sentence]	**(SLC)**
4	**Sentence Length** [length of the sentence in terms of words]	**(SLN)**
5	**Number of Dependencies** [number of dependencies in a sentence]	**(DCT)**
6	**Average Word Length** [total word length divided by sentence length]	**(AWL)**
7	**Average number of Syllables** [syllable count divided by sentence length]	**(ASW)**
8	**Number of Polysyllabic Words** [number of words in a sentence with more than two syllables]	**(PSW)**
9	**Number of Juktakshars** [number of consonant conjuncts in a sentence]	**(JUK)**
10	**Number of Clauses** [total number of dependent and independent clauses in a complex sentence]	**(CLU)**

Table 1.2: Sentence features studied with respect to users' perception

300 Bangla sentences (both simple and complex) were selected from a Bangla corpus of size 30 million words. The selection was done in a manner to accommodate many varieties of sentence constructions, such as the organization of nouns and verbs within a sentence, lexical combinations within the sentence such as presence of uncommon words that may be perceived as difficult to comprehend by the user, number of non-finite structures in a sentence, number of clauses etc. The sentence lengths vary from 5 to 25 words per sentence.

The participants were asked to perform the following two tasks for each of the 300 sentences. Each participant was allowed maximum 2 minutes time to rate each sentence. Rs.100/- were offered to each of them as a token of appreciation.

- Rate the sentence on a ten point scale (1=easiest, 10=hardest) depending on its overall comprehension difficulty as perceived by the reader.

- Mark words and phrases perceived as *hard* by the reader.

Inter-annotator agreement was measured by Krippendorf's alpha and it was found to be more than 0.7 for to each group. A paired t-test revealed significant difference ($p<0.05$) between the rating of two user groups.

The primary sentence attributes studied with respect to the user ratings has been given below in table 1.3. features like, average dependency distance and number of dependencies have been studied due to their importance in sentence comprehension.

4   Result analysis

In the first step, we have studied the Spearman rank correlation coefficients between sentence features and user ratings. The coefficients have been shown in figure 1.3.

From the above chart, it can be observed that total word length (in akshars), total syllable count and sentence length is highly correlated with the user ratings. However, the average word length and syllable distribution do not follow the same trend as user ratings. The same is true for dependencies in a sentence; while total number of dependencies posses a high correlation with user data, average dependency distance does not. These may be indicative of the fact that at sentential level, the overall syntactic nature of a sentence is important to the extent of effort required in comprehension rather than the average distribution of the features in a sentence. As expected, in Bangla, number of consonant conjuncts or jukta-akshars has a high correlation with user perception of difficulty. For complex sentences, user ratings for sentences vary strongly with the number of clauses in the sentence as is evident from the correlation coefficient.

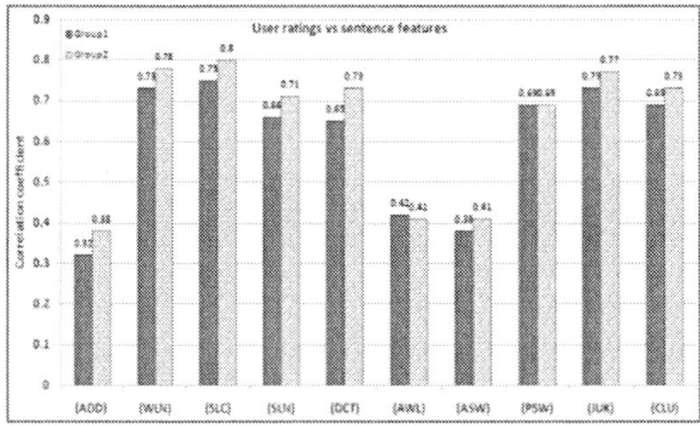

Figure 1.2: User rating versus sentence features

From the above chart, it can be observed that total word length (in akshars), total syllable count and sentence length is highly correlated with the user ratings. However, the average word length and syllable distribution do not follow the same trend as user ratings. The same is true for dependencies in a sentence; while total number of dependencies posses a high correlation with user data, average dependency distance does not. These may be indicative of the fact that at sentential level, the overall syntactic nature of a sentence is important to the extent of effort required in comprehension rather than the average distribution of the features in a sentence. As expected, in Bangla, number of consonant conjuncts or jukta-akshars has a high correlation with user perception of difficulty. For complex sentences, user ratings for sentences vary strongly with the number of clauses in the sentence as is evident from the correlation coefficient.

4.1 Models and regression

In the next step, the effects of sentence attributes have been investigated with regression. At first, detail views of the effects of certain sentence attributes on comprehension difficulty have been shown with graphs from figure 1.4 to figure1.8. Only group 1 data has been shown as group 2 data also follow similar trends.

From figure 1.3, it can be observed that the total word length in a sentence is highly correlated with the user feedback; in figure 1.4 below, we have plotted of word length of a sentence versus user rating and fitted the least square regression line. From the plot, it can be observed that user ratings have approximately a linear relationship with the total word length of a sentence and for a given value of word length the corresponding user ratings are scattered over a very small region around the mean. The regression line therefore has a high R^2 value signifying its goodness of fit. Figure 1.5 represents the relation between sentence length (x-axis) and user ratings (y-axis). It can be observed from the figure that for a given sentence length, the user ratings deflects heavily on both sides of the mean; this may be an indication that although sentence length is an important factor determining sentence comprehension complexity, but at the same time other factors also influence the comprehension load. We have explained the phenomena in the following section with some examples. The plot of average word length and average syllable length versus user ratings (figure 1.6 and 1.7) demonstrates that there is apparently no structured relation between these two features and user ratings. This corroborates the poor correlation coefficients obtained in figure 1.3. Another important attribute of a sentence is the average dependency distance (ADD). Although ADD has been found to explain the order of sentence complexity in English in different cases (Oya, 2011), here, the plot of ADD versus user ratings (refer to figure 1.8) demonstrates no apparent relation between these two; the regression equation in figure 1.8 posses a low R^2 value signifying a poor fit.

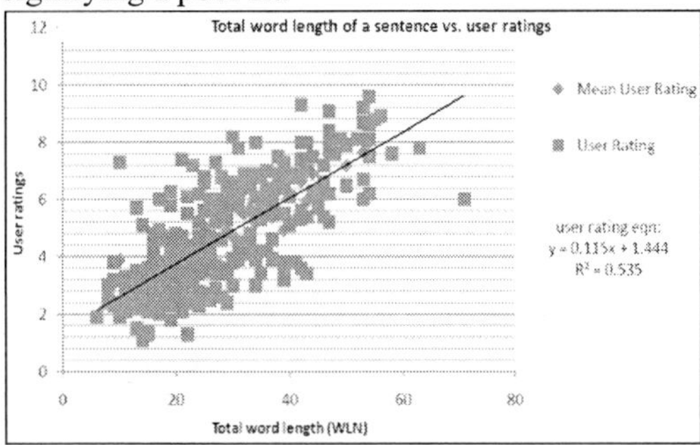

Figure 1.3: Relationship between total word length of sentence and user ratings for Group 1

In the figure 1.4 below, the x-value of a point (represents a sentence) is the total word length and y-value is the user rating of the particular sentence. The similar description also applies for other figures.

Next, we have considered different combinations of the features for predicting sentence complexity using regression with 225 sentences for training and 75 for testing. Results corresponding to the optimal subsets have been presented below in the table 1.2.

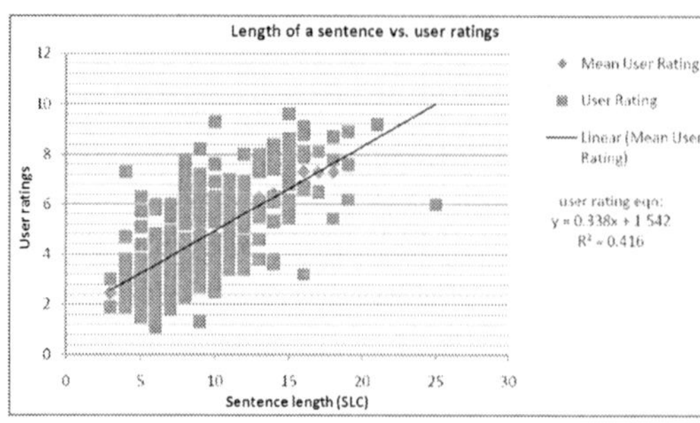

Figure 1.4: Relationship between sentence length and user ratings for Group 1

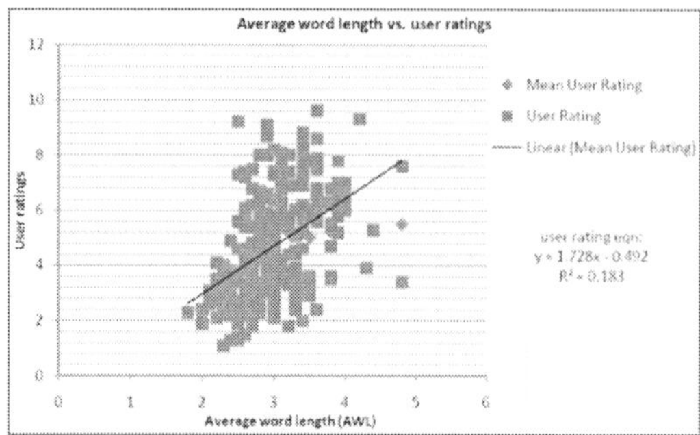

Figure 1.5: Relationship between average word length of sentence and user ratings for Group 1

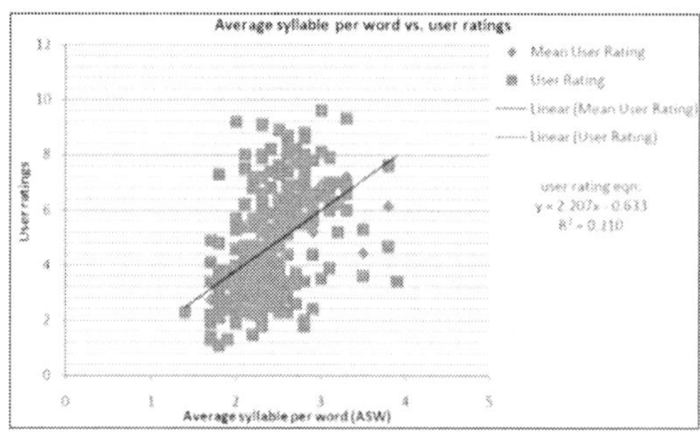

Figure 1.6: Relationship between average syllable per word and user ratings for Group 1

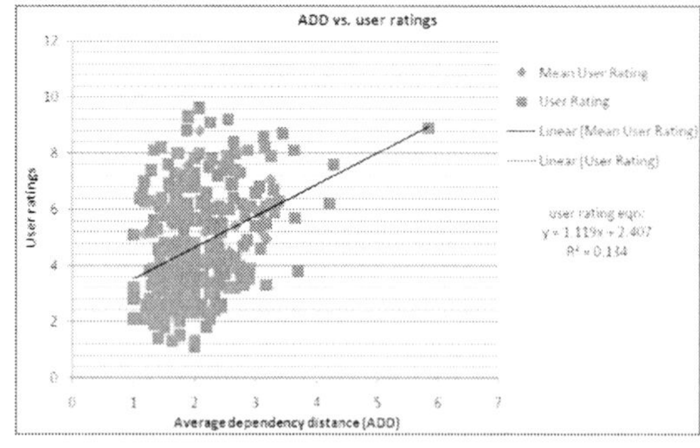

Figure 1.7: Relationship between average dependency distance of sentence and user ratings for Group 1

Below in table 1.3 are the RMSE values for model performances on the training data. From table 1.2 and table 1.3, it can be observed that model 4 for group 1 and model5 for group 2 have relative low error values and higher goodness of fit. Therefore, these models for the two groups can be used as predictive models for sentence complexity for the respective groups given the sentence features. Moreover, these two models have number of dependencies (DCT), total word length (WLN), total syllable length (SLC), number of consonant conjuncts (JUK) and number of clauses (CLU) as independent variables, these features have also found to posses high correlation with user data, therefore, the regression models further assert their contributory roles in sentence comprehension difficulty.

4.2 Effect of lexical and grammatical choice

Apart from the above mentioned syntactic and lexical features of a sentence, the difficulty of individual words also affects the comprehension complexity. To capture this aspect, participants were asked to mark the *hard* words in each sentence during experiment. Now, two outcomes are possible: the hard words will make the sentences difficult to comprehend and therefore they will get relatively higher user ratings than sentences having parameters such as same sentence length and word length; on the other hand, if the reader is able to infer the meaning from the context then the sentences will not be perceived as very difficult to comprehend. Examples of each of the two cases have been provided below in table 1.4 and 1.5 respectively.

In table 1.4, some example sentences with hard words as marked by the readers (shown in bold), have been presented along with user ratings, sentence length and total word length. It can be observed that for both the groups these sentences have user ratings higher than the other sentences with the same sentence length and word length (for a correspondence of group 1 data please refer to figure 1.4 and 1.5 above, group 2 data also follow similar trend).

In table 1.5 below, information about hard words such as their corpus frequency, akshar length, syllable length, number of consonant conjuncts and frequency of their commonly used synonym has been shown. It is apparent that all these words have significantly less corpus presence than their frequent synonyms and therefore are unfamiliar to the general readers. In table 1.5 below is another sets of sentences with hard words marked by the users (shown in bold), but they did not get high user ratings within the same sentence length or word length groups.

Upon further enquiry, it has been revealed that in these sentences, the meaning of the hard words can be resolved from the sentential contexts (the supporting contexts has been underlined).

Model –Expression		Group 1		Group 2	
		R^2	Err	R^2	Err
Model 1	-0.033*DCT + 0.106*JUK+ 0.104*WLN + 1.185	0.57	0.97	0.55	1.10
Model 2	0.114*DCT + 0.225*JUK + 0.137*SLN+ 1.312	0.59	0.81	0.63	0.92
Model 3	**-0.073*DCT -0.025*SLN + 0.081*WLN + 0.071*SLC - 0.015*PSW+ 1.120**	**0.61**	**1.2**	**0.59**	**1.10**
Model 4	0.097*JUK -0.051*SLC + 0.077*WLN + 0.044*CLU - 0.010*DCT+ 1.221	0.67	0.91	0.60	1.30
Model 5	**-0.051*DCT + 0.095*JUK + 0.077*WLN + 0.103*CLU -0.008*SLC + 1.165**	**0.61**	**1.1**	**0.65**	**0.87**

Table 1.2: Regression equations involving sentence features and user ratings (Err means RMSE (root mean square error)

Model	Model 1	Model 2	Model 3	Model 4	Model 5
Group 1 RMSE	1.2	1.1	0.97	0.79	0.85
Group 2 RMSE	1.1	0.89	1.3	0.91	0.81

Table 1.3: RMSE values for regression testing

No.	Sentence (difficult words in bold)	Rating		Sentence length	Word length
		Gr 1	Gr 2		
1.	উভয়ে রোদন **সম্বরণ** করিয়া চক্ষু মুছিলেন *ubhYe rodana **sambaraNa** kariYA cakShu muchilena* (Both of them hold their tears and wipe their eyes.)	5.9	5.5	6	19
2.	**ধাত্রীক্রোড়স্থ** শিশু মার সঙ্গে সঙ্গে কাঁদিতে কাঁদিতে গেল ***dhatrIkroRastha** shishu mAra sange sange k.NAdite k.NAdite gela* (Child went with the mother while crying in her nanny's lap)	6.8	6.5	8	21
3.	কিন্তু কালক্রমে সেই **আগলও** ভেঙেছে ধনতন্ত্রের **দুর্বার** চাপে *Kintu kAlakrame sei **Agalao** bhe.neche dhanatantrera **durbAra** cApe* (That obstacle too has collapsed with time by the mounting pressure of capitalism)	6.5	6.8	8	23
4.	ইতিহাসের বাঁকে কখনো কখনো সেই **সন্ধিক্ষণের** মুখোমুখি হলে আমরা তাকে সহজেই রূপান্তরের লগ্ন বলে চিনতে পারি *Itihasera b.NAke kakhano kakhano sei **sandhikShaNera** mukhomukhi hale AmrA tAke sahajei rupAntarera lagna bale cinathe pAri* (We can easily identify the beginning of change when we encounter that juncture in the turn of history)	8	8.5	16	50

Table 1.4: Sentences with difficult words and their ratings

Sentence	Rating		Sentence length	Word length
	Group 1	Group 2		
বাদল জড়ভরতের মত ঠায় সেই ভাবে বসিয়া আছে *(bAdala jaRabharatera mata thAYa sei bhAbe basiYA Ache)* **Badal has been sitting still ever since.**	2.5	2.7	8	22
গোরার ওষ্ঠপ্রান্তেঈষং একটু কঠোর হাসি দেখা দিল *(GorAra oShthaprAnte IShat ekatu kathora hAsi dekhA dila)* **A brief and cruel smile appeared at the corners of Gora's lips.**	2.9	3.2	8	22
বৃক্ষলতাকন্টক ভেদ করিয়া কল্যাণী বনমধ্যে প্রবেশ করিতে লাগিলেন *(brrikShalatAkanTaka bheda kariYA kalyANI banamadhye probesh karate lAgilena)* **Kalyani started entering the forest penetrating the thorny bushes.)**	4	3.4	8	29
কিন্তু একটি দ্বারেও কপাট বা অর্গলনাই *(kintu ekaTi dbAreo kapATa bA argala nAi)* **(No door has any knob or locking meachanism.**	2.6	2.1	7	17
শুদ্ধা চারী ব্রাক্ষ্মণ বাঘকে খাঁচায় আটক দেখেছিল *(shuddhAcArI brAkShmaNa bAghake kh.NAcAYa ATaka dekhechila)* **The pious bramhin saw the tiger locked in a cage.**	2.5	2.7	6	20

Table 1.5: Sentences with difficult words where contextual resolve is possible

Word	CF	AL	SL	N1	N2
সম্বরণ(*sambaraNa*)	160	4	3	1	আটকানো(*ATkAno*) 603
ধাত্রীক্রোড়স্থ (*dhatrIkroRastha*)	1	5	5	3	কোলে(*kole*) 1728
আগলও(*Agalao*)	59	4	3	0	বাঁধ, বাঁধা, বাঁধন(*b.Nadh/b.NdhA/b.Ndhana*) 510
দুর্বার (*durbAra*)	140	3	2	2	প্রবল, প্রচণ্ড(*prabala/ praconDa*) 5053/3093
সন্ধিক্ষণ(*sandhikShaNa*)	16	4	3	2	সঙ্গে(*sa.nYage*) 147
জড়ভরতের (*jaRabharatera*)	2	6	6	1	স্থির(*sthira*) 4700
ওষ্ঠপ্রান্তে (*oShthaprAnte*)	8	4	4	4	ঠোঁটে(*Th.NoTe*)42
বৃক্ষলতাকন্টক (*brrikShalatAkanTaka*)	1	7	6	4	কাঁটাবন, কাঁটাঝোপ,কাঁটাগুল্ম,কাঁটাগাছ,কাঁটাতরু *(k.NATAbana, k.NATAjhopa, k.NATAgulma, k.NATAgAcha, k.NATAtaru)*

অর্গল (*argala*)	27	3	2	1	খিল*(khila)* 131
শুদ্ধাচারী (*shuddhAcArI*)	23	4	4	4	ধার্মিক*(dhArmika)* 135

Table 1.6: Information about the difficult words (CF: Corpus frequency, AL: Akshar length, SL: Syllable length, N1: Number of jukta-akshars/ vowel diacritic, N2: Frequency of commonly used synonym)

Sentences	Rating		Sentence length	Word length
	Group 1	Group 2		
চুরি করা মহা পাপ (*curi karA mhApApa*) [Stealing is a grave sin/To steal is a grave sin]	1.2	1.5	3	8
পড়ার চেয়ে লেখা কঠিন (*paRAra ceYe lekhA kathina*) [Writing is harder than reading]	1.9	1.3	4	10
আমরা জিনিস বহন করার জন্য ব্যাগ ব্যবহার করি (*AmrA jinisa bahana karARra janYa bYAga bYabahAra kari*) [we use a bag to carry things]	2.4	3.2	8	22
দয়া করে ঘুমিয়ে থাকা শিশুকে জাগিয়ো না (*daYA kare ghumiYe thAkA shishuke jAgiYo nA*) [please, do not awake the sleeping baby]	1.8	2.2	7	16

Table 1.7: Sentences with different intransitive

In these cases also the relevant information about the hard words has been provided in table 1.6.

In English, non-finite structures have been found to have effect on sentence comprehension **(Error! Reference source not found.)**. Non-finite structures are infinitive, gerund, participle, nonfinite complement, nonfinite adjunct etc. In Bangla, no such nonfinite structures like gerund, participle or infinitive exists. Verbs are used in different grammatical formats to serve the purpose of nonfinite forms (Thompson, 2012). To examine the effect of such grammatical properties on sentence comprehension in Bangla, some sentences with such non-finite verbs were included in the experimental data group (shown in table 1.7). However, no significant variations in user ratings have been observed against these sentences as compared to sentences with same length and word length.

5   Conclusion

This paper has presented studies on sentence comprehension in Bangla. In the first part of the paper, relations between sentence features and user ratings have been studied. Subsequently regression formulae based on sentence syntactic and lexical attributes have been developed for both user groups for predicting sentence comprehension difficulty in Bangla. In addition, case by case study of effect of difficult words and presence of non-finite structures on sentence comprehension has also been studied. It has been observed that the way difficult to understand words in a sentence affect the sentence comprehension complexity depends on whether a contextual resolve of the meaning of the sentence is possible or not. Non-finite structures have been found to have no significant effect on sentence comprehension difficulty in Bangla. However, due to the small size (1200 sentences) of dependency annotated corpus in Bangla, the set of possible dependencies is not exhaustive and the probability values for the dependency rules may not always accurately represent the familiarity encountered in practice. This is a limitation of the present approach. Moreover, dependency rules are not formulated as recursive productions in a PCFG, therefore, a hierarchical relation between the increase or decrease in probabilities from one word to other in a sentence has not possible.

In future, it will be interesting to examine whether the accessibility hierarchy (Keenan and Comrie, 1977), observed to be true for English sentence comprehension, also holds in case for

Bangla. Another important path of investigation will be the relative differences in reading behavior among sentences with different relative ordering of noun and verb. Lastly, the word by word reading time study has to be extended for other user groups as well. With this, the study overall sentence readability in Bangla ends; the next and also the last contributory paper in sentence complexity will present study on influence of word ordering of a sentence comprehension in Bangla.

Reference

1. Chatterji, S.-K. (1926). *The origin and development of the Bengali language*, volume 2. Calcutta University Press.
2. Levy, R. (2013). Memory and surprisal in human sentence comprehension.
3. Meltzer, J. A., McArdle, J. J., Schafer, R. J., and Braun, A. R. (2010). Neural aspects of sentence comprehension: syntactic complexity, reversibility, and reanalysis. *Cerebral cortex*, 20(8):1853–1864.
4. Oya, M. (2011). Syntactic dependency distance as sentence complexity measure. In *Proceedings of the 16th International Conference of Pan-Pacific Association of Applied Linguistics*, pages 313–316.
5. SWINNEY, D. A. (1998). The influence of canonical word order on structural processing. *Syntax and semantics*, 31:153–166.
6. Weyerts, H., Penke, M., Münte, T. F., Heinze, H.-J., and Clahsen, H. (2002). Word order in sentence processing: An experimental study of verb placement in german. *Journal of Psycholinguistic Research*, 31(3):211–268.
7. Bardovi-Harlig, K. (1992). A second look at t-unit analysis: Reconsidering the sentence. TESOL quarterly, 26(2):390–395.
8. Oya, M. (2011).Syntactic dependency distance as sentence complexity measure. In Proceedings of The 16th Conference of Pan-Pacific Association of Applied Linguistics.
9. Gordon, P. C., Hendrick, R., and Johnson, M. (2001).Memory interference during language processing.Journal of Experimental Psychology: Learning, Memory, and Cognition, 27(6):1411.
10. Gibson, E. (2000). The dependency locality theory: A distance-based theory of linguistic complexity. Image, language, brain, pages 95–126.
11. Vasishth, S. and Lewis, R. L. (2006). Argument-head distance and processing complexity: Explaining both locality and antilocality effects. *Language*, pages 767–794.
12. Tyler, L. K. and Marslen-Wilson, W. D. (1977).The on-line effects of semantic context on syntactic processing.*Journal of Verbal Learning and Verbal Behavior*, 16(6):683–692.
13. Bornkessel, I., Zysset, S., Friederici, A. D., von Cramon, D. Y., and Schlesewsky, M. (2005). Who did what to whom? the neural basis of argument hierarchies during language comprehension. *Neuroimage*, 26(1):221–233.
14. Hale, J. (2006). Uncertainty about the rest of the sentence.*Cognitive Science*, 30(4):643–672.
15. Levy, R. (2008).Expectation-based syntactic comprehension.*Cognition*, 106(3):1126–1177.
16. Bever, T. G. (1970). The cognitive basis for linguistic structures.*1970*, pages 279–362.
17. Lachter, J. and Bever, T. G. (1988). The relation between linguistic structure and associative theories of language learning—a constructive critique of some connectionist learning models. *Cognition*, 28(1):195–247.
18. Jurafsky, D. (1996). A probabilistic model of lexical and syntactic access and disambiguation.*Cognitive Science*, 20(2):137–194.
19. Jurafsky, S. N. D. (2002). A bayesian model predicts human parse preference and reading times in sentence processing. *Advances in neural information processing systems*, 14:59.
20. Spivey, M. J. and Tanenhaus, M. K. (1998). Syntactic ambiguity resolution in discourse: modeling the effects of referential context and lexical frequency. *Journal of Experimental Psychology: Learning, Memory, and Cognition*, 24(6):1521.
21. Hare, M., McRae, K., and Elman, J. L. (2003). Sense and structure: Meaning as a determinant of verb subcategorization preferences. *Journal of Memory and Language*, 48(2):281–303.
22. Clifton Jr, C. and Frazier, L. (1989).Comprehending sentences with long-distance dependencies. In *Linguistic structure in language processing*, pages 273–317. Springer.
23. Kaiser, E. and Trueswell, J. C. (2004).The role of discourse context in the processing of a flexible word-order language.*Cognition*, 94(2):113 – 147.

A New Feature Selection Technique Combined with ELM Feature Space for Text Classification

Rajendra Kumar Roul
Dept of Computer Science and
Information System
BITS,Pilani-K.K.Birla Goa Campus
Zuarinagar
Goa-403726
rkroul@goa.bits-pilani.ac.in

Pranav Rai
Dept of Electrical and
Electronics Engineering
BITS,Pilani-K.K.Birla Goa Campus
Zuarinagar
Goa-403726
pranavrai95@gmail.com

Abstract

The aim of text classification is to classify the text documents into a set of pre-defined categories. But the complexity of natural languages, high dimensional feature space and low quality of feature selection become the main problem for text classification process. Hence, in order strengthen the classification technique, selection of important features, and consequently removing the unimportant ones is the need of the day. The Paper proposes an approach called Commonality-Rarity Score Computation *(CRSC)* for selecting top features of a corpus and highlights the importance of ML-ELM feature space in the domain of text classification. Experimental results on two benchmark datasets signify the prominence of the proposed approach compared to other established approaches.

Keywords: Classification; ELM; Feature selection; ML-ELM; Rarity

1 Introduction

With the increase in number of documents on the Web, it has become increasingly important to reduce the noisy and redundant features which can reduce the training time and hence increase the performance of the classifier during text classification. Large number of features, produces feature vector with very high dimensionality and hence, different methods to reduce the dimension can be used such as Singular Value Decomposition (SVD) (Golub and Reinsch, 1970), Wavelet Analysis (Lee and Yamamoto,), Principle Component Analysis (PCA)(Bajwa et al., 2009) etc. The algorithms used for feature selection are broadly classified into three categories: *filters, wrapper and embedded methods*. Filter methods use the properties of the dataset to select the features without using any specific algorithm (Kira and Rendell, 1992), and hence preferred over wrapper methods. Most filter methods give a ranking of the best features rather than one single set of best features. Wrapper methods use a predecided learning algorithm i.e. a classifier to evaluate the features and hence computationally expensive (Kohavi and John, 1997). Also, they have a higher possibility of overfitting than filter methods. Hence, large scale problems like text categorization mostly do not use wrapper methods (Forman, 2003). Embedded methods tend to combine the advantages of both the aforementioned methods. The computational complexity of the embedded methods, thus, lies in between that of the filters and the wrappers. Ample research work has already been done in this domain (Qiu et al., 2011)(Lee and Kim, 2015)(Meng et al., 2011)(Novovičová et al., 2007)(Yang et al., 2011)(Aghdam et al., 2009)(Thangamani and Thangaraj, 2010)(Azam and Yao, 2012)(Liu et al., 2005).

Selection of a good classifier plays a vital role in the text classification process. Many of the traditional classifiers have their own limitations while solving any complex problems. On the other hand, Extreme Learning Machine (ELM) is able to approximate any complex non-linear mappings directly from the training samples (Huang et al., 2006b). Hence, ELM has a better universal approximation capability than conventional neural networks based classifiers. Also, quick learning speed, ability to manage huge volume of data, requirement of less human intervention, good generalization capability, easy implementation etc. are some of the *salient features* which make ELM more popular compared to other traditional classifiers. Recently developed Multilayer ELM which is based on the architecture of deep learning is an extension of ELM and have more than one hidden layer.

D S Sharma, R Sangal and A K Singh. Proc. of the 13th Intl. Conference on Natural Language Processing, pages 285–292,
Varanasi, India. December 2016. ©2016 NLP Association of India (NLPAI)

In this paper, we propose an approach for feature selection called Commonality-Rarity Score Computation (*CRSC*) by means of three parameters (*Alpha* (measures weighted commonality), *Beta* (measures extent of occurrence of a term) and *Gamma* (average weight of term per document)), computes the score of a term in order to rank them based on their relevance. The top m% features are selected for text classification. The proposed approach is compared with traditional feature selections techniques such as Chi-Square (Manning and Raghavan, 2008), Bi-normal separation (BNS) (Forman, 2003), Information Gain (IG)(Yang and Pedersen, 1997) and GINI (Shang et al., 2007). Empirical results on 20-Newsgroups and Reuters datasets show the effectiveness of the proposed approach compared to other feature selection techniques.

The paper is outlined as follows: Section 2 discussed the architecture of ELM, ML-ELM and ML-ELM extended feature space. The proposed approach is described in Section 3. Section 4 covers the experimental work and finally, the paper is concluded in Section 5.

2 Background

2.1 ELM in Brief

Given an input feature vector $\mathbf{x}$ of N documents and L hidden neurons, the output function of ELM for one node (Huang et al., 2006b) is

$$y(\mathbf{x}) = h(\mathbf{x})\beta = \sum_{i=1}^{L} \beta_i h_i(\mathbf{x}) \qquad (1)$$

Here, $h_i(\mathbf{x}) \leftarrow g(w_i.x_j + b_i), \forall j \in N,$
$w_i \leftarrow$ input weight vector,
$b_i \leftarrow i^{th}$ hidden node biases,
$\beta \leftarrow$ the output weight vector between the hidden and output layer nodes.
The input feature vector and biases of the hidden layer nodes are selected randomly. The activation function $g(\mathbf{x})$ maps the input feature vector to an L dimensional hidden layer space called ELM feature space (Figure 2). The reduced form of equation 1 where Y and H output and hidden layer matrix, respectively can be written as

$$H\beta = Y \qquad (2)$$

2.2 Brief on Multilayer ELM

Multilayer ELM suggested by (Kasun et al., 2013) is based on the architecture of of deep learning and

is shown in the Figure 1. It combines bot ELM and ELM-autoencoder (ELM-AE) together, and hence contains all features of ELM.

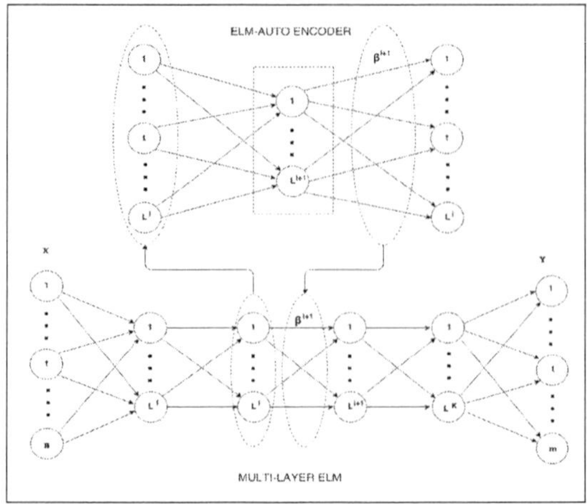

Figure 1: Architecture of Multiayer ELM

The design and architecture of ELM-AE is same as ELM except few differences are exist between them such as

1. In ELM, input weights and biases of hidden layer are randomly assigned where as in ELM-AE, both are orthogonal i.e.

$$w^T \cdot w = I \ and \ b^T \cdot b = 1$$

2. ELM is supervised in nature where the output is class labels. But ELM-AE is unsupervised in nature and the output is same as the input.

3. Computing β in ELM-AE is different then ELM and can be done using the following equations depending on the relationship between n and L.

   i. *Compress representation* $(n > L)$:

   $$\beta = \left(\frac{I}{C} + H^T H\right)^{-1} H^T X \qquad (3)$$

   where, C is is scaling parameter used to adjusts the structural and experiential risk.

   ii. *Dimension of equal length* $(n = L)$:

   $$\beta = H^{-1} X \qquad (4)$$

   iii. *Sparse representation* $(n < L)$:

   $$\beta = H^T (\frac{I}{C} + H H^T)^{-1} X \qquad (5)$$

According to (Huang et al., 2006a)(Huang et al., 2012), by increasing the number of nodes in the hidden layer compared to the input layer, the input feature vector become much simpler and thus linear separable in the extended space. Multilayer ELM uses the properties of *ELM feature mapping* and thus classify the features in a better manner which enhance its performance compared to other traditional classifiers.

The following equation is used to pass the data from one layer to another till it reaches the $(n-1)^{th}$ hidden layer.

$$H^n = g((\beta^n)^T H^{n-1}) \quad (6)$$

At the end, the final output matrix is generated by using the regularized least squares technique in order to calculate the results between the output and $(n-1)^{th}$ hidden layer.

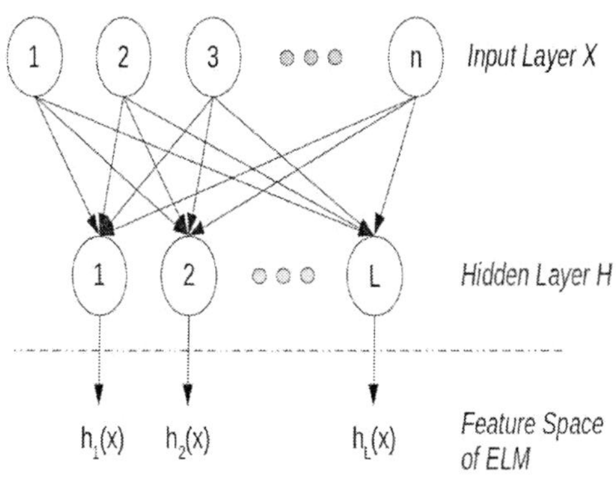

Figure 2: ELM feature space

3 Proposed Approach

The aim of a good feature selection technique is to effectively distinguish between terms that are relevant and those that are not. For this purpose, the meaning of 'relevance' needs to be considered clearly. Some methods understand 'relevance' on the basis of the relation of the term to a particular class. Other feature selection methods rely on probabilistic or statistical models to select the appropriate terms. For Commonality Rarity Score Computation (*CRSC*), a term is 'relevant' if it has the following attributes:

   i. It does not appear very frequently in the corpus, as it would then be unsuitable as a differentiator between documents.

   ii. It's frequency in the corpus is not very low, as it would then be unsuitable to be used for grouping similar documents.

   iii. In the documents in which the term appears, it should be reasonably frequent.

   iv. It needs to be a good discriminator at the document level.

In order to apply these properties to a mathematical definition of relevance, we propose three parameters, whose combination would provide a score to each term. If the score of a term would be higher then its its relevance is higher. The parameters mentioned above are alpha (α(t)), beta (β(t)) and gamma (γ(t)), each of which will be considered in detail in the next section.

3.1 Alpha

The parameter alpha ($\alpha(t)$), is a mathematical representation of the weighted commonality of the term t and is defined as

$$\alpha(t) = (\frac{1}{\overline{idf}} * y) + (\overline{idf} * (1 - y)) \quad (7)$$

where,

$$y = \frac{a}{N}$$

and

$$\overline{idf} = \sum_t^N \frac{idf(t)}{N}$$

Here, 'a' represents the number of documents with the term t and N represents total number of documents in the corpus. The IDF of a term indicates the rarity of the term in the corpus.

$$IDF(t) = 1 + log_{10}(\frac{N}{a})$$

The average IDF ($\overline{idf}$) denotes the average rarity of the corpus.

Since we are weighting y by $1/\overline{idf}$, y can be seen as being weighted by the commonality constant of the corpus. Therefore the term $1/\overline{idf} * y$ increases the value of $\alpha(t)$ iff the term t is common and the average commonality of the terms in the corpus is high. Similarly, the term $(1-y)$, which indicates the fraction of documents in the corpus without the term t, is weighted by the rarity constant $1/\overline{idf}$. Therefore the term $1/\overline{idf} * (1-y)$ increases the value of $\alpha(t)$ iff the term t is rare and the average rarity of the terms in the corpus is high. Thus, the equation for $\alpha(t)$ provides a method to compute a commonality-rarity of a term in the corpus. Since idf of a term is always greater than 1, therefore, $\overline{idf}$ will be more than 1. Also, if a term is very rare, it's (1-y) value will be high which makes the value of $\alpha(t)$ for that term as high. Hence, rare terms tend to have higher values for $\alpha(t)$. This feature is used to filter the unimportant terms, as explained in section 3.4.

3.2 Beta

The parameter beta $(\beta(t))$, is a mathematical representation of the frequency of appearance of the term t in the documents and can be given by

$$\beta(t) = y_1(t) + y_2^2(t) + y_3^3(t) + ...$$

where

$$y_i(t) = \frac{a_i}{N} \tag{8}$$

where $a_i \leftarrow$ number of documents where frequency of $t \geq i$. The term $\beta(t)$ therefore provides information regarding the prevalence of the term t in the corpus by considering the fraction of documents containing the term t and also taking into account the frequency of appearance of the term in each document. Terms which appear frequently in several documents will have a higher beta value. Also, the contribution of y_i to $\beta(t)$ decreases with increasing value of i. Therefore, very high frequency of occurrence of a term t in a particular document does not significantly increase its $\beta(t)$. This is done mathematically by giving each y_i as an exponent i.

3.3 Gamma

Gamma $(\gamma(t))$ is obtained by summing over all documents d in the corpus of $\gamma(t, d)$ and can be written as

$$\gamma(t, d) = \frac{\text{TF}(t, d)}{\text{maximum TF in } d} \tag{9}$$

$\gamma(t, d)$ gives an indication of the relative weight of the term t in the document d, by comparing the frequency of the term t to the highest frequency term in d. $\gamma(t)$ quantitatively denotes the average weighted frequency of the term per document in the corpus.

3.4 Score

Finally, using the above three parameters, a total score is assigned to each term in the corpus as an indication of its relevance. The score of a term t is given by

$$score(t) = \beta(t) * min(\gamma(t), 1/\gamma(t)) - \alpha(t) \tag{10}$$

A higher value of score(t) indicates a higher relevance of the term t to the corpus. As elaborated previously, $\beta(t)$ indicates the overall frequency of a term in the corpus, and the term $\gamma(t)$ indicates the average frequency of the term in each document in the corpus. A high value for $\beta(t)$ indicates that very frequently t is present in most of the documents, whereas a high value for $\gamma(t)$ suggests that the term t is frequent in those documents where it is present, and therefore a good discriminator for the same. For a term t to be a good differentiator among documents, not only must it be frequent in the corpus, but it must also be important for differentiating between documents. For this, $\gamma(t)$ should necessarily not be very low for a term, which is to be selected as part of the reduced feature space to classify the documents. However, a direct product of $\beta(t)$ and $\gamma(t)$ can result in common terms that appear in almost all documents given very high scores, despite them not being relevant per our earlier definition. In order to eliminate such terms, we instead use a product of $\beta(t)$ and the minimum of $\gamma(t)$ and $1/\gamma(t)$. With this product, terms which are very frequent, and as a result have a high value for $\beta(t)$, will result in the $\beta(t)$ value being divided by their equally large $\gamma(t)$ value, reducing their score, and preventing such terms being considered as important. The term $\alpha(t)$, which takes high values for rare terms, is subtracted from the previous product to produce the score. This eliminates those terms that are very rare from being considered as important.

The formula for score therefore eliminates terms that are both very frequent and very rare, leaving behind only those terms that are moderately rare, sufficiently good document level discriminators and sufficiently frequent in the documents in which they appear. score(t) therefore provides an accurate mathematical representation of the definition of relevant stated earlier, and helps to select relevant terms based on their commonality-rarity both at the document and corpus level.

3.5 Algorithm

Proposed approach of *CRSC* is discussed below.

Step 1. *Documents pre-processing and vector representation*:

The documents $d = \{d_1, d_2, ..., d_m\}$ of all classes of a corpus are collected and pre-processed by using a pre-processing algorithm. Then, all the documents are converted into vectors using the formal Vector Space Model (VSM)(Salton et al., 1975).

Step 2. *Formation of clusters*:

Traditional k-means clustering algorithm (Hartigan and Wong, 1979) is run on the corpus to generates k term-document clusters, $td_i, i = 1, ..., k$.

Step 3. *Important features selection*:

Now, for each term $t \in td_i$, $\alpha(t)$, $\beta(t)$ and $\gamma(t)$ are calculated and then the total score using equation 10 is computed.

Step 4. *Training ML-ELM and other conventional classifiers*:

Based on the total score, all the terms of a cluster are ranked and top m% terms from each cluster are selected which constitute the training feature vector.

4 Experimental Analysis

20-Newsgroups[1] and Reuters[2] datasets are used for experimental purpose. The classifiers which are used for comparison purpose are Support Vector Machine (LinearSVC), Decision Tree (DT), SVM linear kernel (LinearSVM), Gaussian Naive Bayes (GNB), Random Forest (RF), Nearest Centroid (NC), Adaboost, Multinomial Naive-Bayes (M-NB) and ELM. In all the tables bold indicates the highest F-measure obtained by *CRSC* using the corresponding classifier. The algorithm was tested on hidden layer nodes of different size both for ELM and ML-ELM and the best results are obtained when the number of nodes of hidden layer are more than the nodes in the input layer. In the k-means clustering, k (the number of clusters) was set as 8 (decided empirically) for both the datasets. The following parameters are used to measure the performance.

[1] http://qwone.com/~jason/20Newsgroups/
[2] www.daviddlewis.com/resources/testcollections/reuters/

Precision (P):

$$P = \frac{(\text{relevant}_{documents}) \cap (\text{retrieved}_{documents})}{\text{retrieved}_{documents}}$$

Recall (R):

$$R = \frac{(\text{relevant}_{documents}) \cap (\text{retrieved}_{documents})}{\text{relevant}_{documents}}$$

F-Measure (F): It combines both precision and recall and can be defined as follows:

$$F = \frac{2 \, (P \times R)}{(P + R)}$$

4.1 20-Newsgroups Dataset

20-Newsgroups is a very popular machine learning dataset generally used for text classification and having 7 different categories. For experimental purpose, approximately 11300 documents are used for training and 7500 for testing. The results can be summarized as follows:

- *top 1% features*: CRSC using ML-ELM and Multinomial naive-bayes has obtained the best results. Classifier wise, ML-ELM generates the maximum average F-measure for *CRSC* (Table 1).

- *top 5% features*: ML-ELM and LinearSVM generate the best results. Classifier wise, maximum average F-measure is obtained using ML-ELM (Table 2).

- *top 10% features*: CRSC has obtained best results using ML-ELM and Random Forest. Classifier wise *CRSC* obtained the highest average F-measure of 0.9602 using ML-ELM (Table 3).

Table 1: F-measure on top 1% features (20-NG)

Classifier	CHI2	BNS	IG	GINI	CRSC
Linear SVC	0.8812	0.8616	0.8636	0.8794	0.8651
Linear SVM	0.8925	0.8896	0.8915	0.8945	0.8842
NC	0.8458	0.8278	0.8338	0.8516	0.8222
Gaussian-NB	0.8726	0.8530	0.8599	0.8651	0.8078
M-NB	0.8532	0.8286	0.8279	0.8479	**0.8766**
Adaboost	0.8632	0.8731	0.8738	0.8747	0.8634
Decision Tree	0.8499	0.8484	0.8490	0.8324	0.8458
Random Forest	0.8867	0.8660	0.8764	0.8723	0.8676
ELM	0.9070	0.9023	0.8951	0.9066	0.9080
ML-ELM	0.9261	0.9143	0.9123	0.9233	**0.9262**

Table 2: F-measure on top 5% features (20-NG)

Classifier	CHI2	BNS	IG	GINI	CRSC
LinearSVC	0.9246	0.9187	0.9181	0.9315	0.9245
LinearSVM	0.9337	0.9241	0.9279	0.9337	**0.9359**
NC	0.8895	0.8756	0.8848	0.8859	0.8690
Gaussian-NB	0.9257	0.8787	0.8925	0.9187	0.8515
M-NB	0.9212	0.8914	0.9060	0.9151	0.8819
Adaboost	0.8876	0.8736	0.8526	0.8613	0.8682
Decision Tree	0.8499	0.8527	0.8481	0.8476	0.8461
Random Forest	0.8942	0.8702	0.8922	0.8842	0.8771
ELM	0.9287	0.9288	0.9366	0.9358	0.9374
ML-ELM	0.9345	0.9432	0.9378	0.0.9452	**0.9450**

Table 3: F-measure on top 10% features (20-NG)

Classifier	CHI2	BNS	IG	GINI	CRSC
LinearSVC	0.9374	0.9273	0.9368	0.9437	0.9392
LinearSVM	0.9428	0.9355	0.9364	0.9465	0.9353
NC	0.8947	0.8858	0.8886	0.8951	0.8858
Gaussian-NB	0.9297	0.9011	0.9235	0.9293	0.8613
M-NB	0.9282	0.9134	0.9227	0.9273	0.9093
Adaboost	0.8727	0.8526	0.8534	0.8625	0.8568
Decision Tree	0.8537	0.8392	0.8560	0.8491	0.8464
Random Forest	0.8829	0.8825	0.8740	0.8827	**0.8857**
ELM	0.9467	0.9388	0.9257	0.9484	0.9596
ML-ELM	0.9515	0.9422	0.9367	0.9521	**0.9602**

Table 4: F-measure on top 1% features (Reuters)

Classifier	CHI2	BNS	IG	GINI	CRSC
LinearSVC	0.9236	0.9137	0.9196	0.9297	0.8954
LinearSVM	0.9424	0.9391	0.9414	0.9495	0.9196
NC	0.8238	0.8242	0.8215	0.8283	0.8045
Gaussian-NB	0.8544	0.8453	0.8434	0.8434	0.8414
M-NB	0.8620	0.8318	0.8483	0.8503	0.8352
Adaboost	0.6300	0.6405	0.6435	0.7625	**0.7798**
Decision Tree	0.8816	0.8785	0.8804	0.8858	0.8548
Random Forest	0.9123	0.9195	0.9136	0.9124	0.8995
ELM	0.9444	0.9467	0.9468	0.9579	0.9161
ML-ELM	0.9531	0.9484	0.9522	0.9590	0.9178

Table 5: F-measure on top 5% features (Reuters)

Classifier	CHI2	BNS	IG	GINI	CRSC
LinearSVC	0.9412	0.9378	0.9408	0.9445	0.9376
LinearSVM	0.9529	0.9586	0.9568	0.9555	0.9449
NC	0.8327	0.8272	0.8364	0.8359	0.8298
Gaussian-NB	0.8196	0.8628	0.8476	0.8439	0.8387
M-NB	0.8945	0.8853	0.8932	0.9017	0.8766
Adaboost	0.6283	0.6484	0.6187	0.6648	**0.6834**
Decision Tree	0.8928	0.8962	0.8937	0.8935	0.8867
Random Forest	0.9184	0.9134	0.9238	0.9066	0.9075
ELM	0.9539	0.9588	0.9487	0.9587	0.9598
ML-ELM	9604	0.9643	0. 9512	0.9609	**0.9646**

4.2 Reuters Dataset

Reuters is a widely used dataset, predominantly utilized for text mining. It has 5485 training documents and 2189 testing documents classified into 8 classes, where all class documents are considered for evaluation. Out of 17512 features from all documents, 12345 features are considered for training. The results are summarized as follows:

- *top 1% features*: *CRSC* using Adaboost has obtained the best results. Classifier wise, LinearSVM generates the maximum average F-measure for *CRSC* (Table 4).

- *top 5% features*: Adaboost and ML-ELM generate the best results. Classifier wise, maximum average F-measure is obtained using ML-ELM (Table 5).

- *top 10% features*: *CRSC* has obtained the best results using ML-ELM and Adaboost. Classifier wise *CRSC* obtained the highest average F-measure of 0.9598 using ML-ELM (Table 6).

4.3 Discussion

Figure 3 - 5 show the performance comparison of different classifiers on top m% features using *CRSC* feature selection technique. Comparison of ELM with other traditional classifiers on *CRSC* are shown in Table 7. It is evident from all the results that ML-ELM outperforms other well known classifiers.

Table 6: F-measure on top 10% features (Reuters)

Classifier	CHI2	BNS	IG	GINI	CRSC
LinearSVC	0.9473	0.9417	0.9443	0.9469	0.9447
LinearSVM	0.9548	0.9568	0.9568	0.9581	0.9578
NC	0.8355	0.8332	0.8326	0.8354	0.8351
Gaussian-NB	0.7852	0.8372	0.8248	0.8019	0.7814
M-NB	0.8907	0.8955	0.8981	0.8997	0.8769
Adaboost	0.6270	0.6387	0.6248	0.6342	**0.6432**
Decision Tree	0.8955	0.8885	0.8968	0.8894	0.8965
Random Forest	0.9090	0.9069	0.9090	0.9098	0.9007
ELM	0.9472	0.9489	0.9477	0.9432	0.9588
ML-ELM	0.9566	0.9654	0.9645	0.9678	**0.9598**

Table 7: F-measure comparisons on *CRSC*

Classifier	20- NG (F-Measure-%)			Reuters (F-Measure-%)		
	1%	5%	10%	1%	5%	10%
LinearSVC	86.51	92.45	93.92	89.54	93.76	94.47
Linear SVM	88.42	93.59	93.53	**91.96**	94.49	95.78
NC	82.22	86.90	88.58	80.45	82.98	83.51
G-NB	80.78	85.15	86.13	84.14	83.87	78.14
M-NB	87.66	88.19	90.93	83.52	87.66	87.69
Adaboost	86.34	86.82	85.68	77.98	68.34	64.32
DT	84.58	84.61	84.64	85.48	88.67	89.65
RF	86.76	87.71	88.57	89.95	90.75	90.07
ELM	90.80	93.74	95.96	91.61	95.98	95.88
ML-ELM	**92.62**	**94.5**	**96.02**	91.78	**96.46**	**95.98**

5 Conclusion

The paper proposed a new feature selection technique called *CRSC*, where three parameters (Alpha, Beta and Gamma) are computed for each term of a document. Finally, a score for each term is calculated using these three parameters values. Then the terms are ranked in each cluster based on the assigned scores and top m% features are selected as the important features which are used to train the classifiers. 20-Newsgroups and Reuters datasets are used for experimental purpose. Empirical results show that *CRSC* is either better or comparable with the traditional feature selection

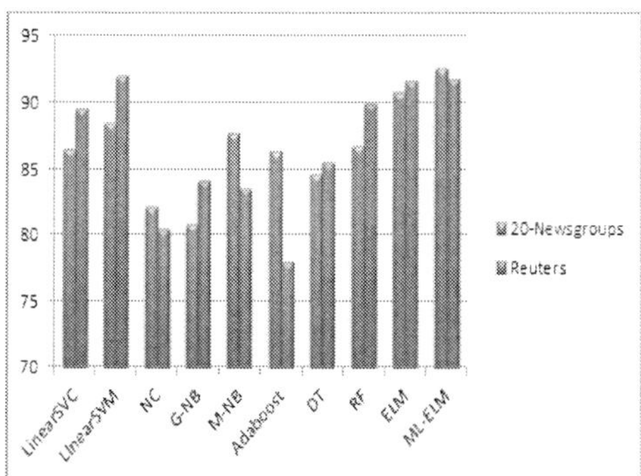

Figure 3: F-measure of *CRSC* for top-1%

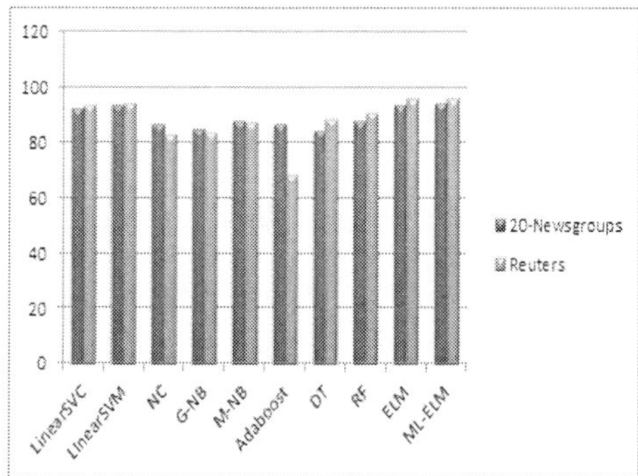

Figure 4: F-measure of *CRSC* for top-5%

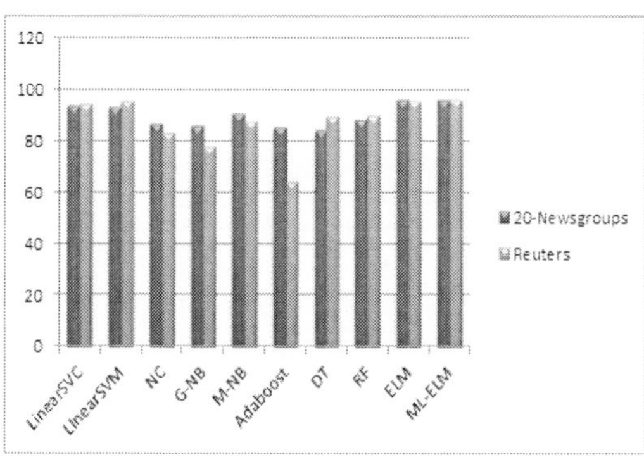

Figure 5: F-measure of *CRSC* for top-10%

techniques. The results obtained by ML-ELM which uses the ELM feature mapping technique by which makes the features linearly separable in the extended space, dominated all other state-of-the-art classifiers.

References

[Aghdam et al.2009] Mehdi Hosseinzadeh Aghdam, Nasser Ghasem-Aghaee, and Mohammad Ehsan Basiri. 2009. Text feature selection using ant colony optimization. *Expert systems with applications*, 36(3):6843–6853.

[Azam and Yao2012] Nouman Azam and JingTao Yao. 2012. Comparison of term frequency and document frequency based feature selection metrics in text categorization. *Expert Systems with Applications*, 39(5):4760–4768.

[Bajwa et al.2009] Imran S Bajwa, M Naweed, M Nadim Asif, and S Irfan Hyder. 2009. Feature based image classification by using principal component analysis. *ICGST Int. J. Graph. Vis. Image Process. GVIP*, 9:11–17.

[Forman2003] George Forman. 2003. An extensive empirical study of feature selection metrics for text classification. *The Journal of machine learning research*, 3:1289–1305.

[Golub and Reinsch1970] Gene H Golub and Christian Reinsch. 1970. Singular value decomposition and least squares solutions. *Numerische mathematik*, 14(5):403–420.

[Hartigan and Wong1979] John A Hartigan and Manchek A Wong. 1979. Algorithm as 136: A k-means clustering algorithm. *Journal of the Royal Statistical Society. Series C (Applied Statistics)*, 28(1):100–108.

[Huang et al.2006a] Guang-Bin Huang, Lei Chen, Chee Kheong Siew, et al. 2006a. Universal approximation using incremental constructive feed-forward networks with random hidden nodes. *IEEE Transactions on Neural Networks*, 17(4):879–892.

[Huang et al.2006b] Guang-Bin Huang, Qin-Yu Zhu, and Chee-Kheong Siew. 2006b. Extreme learning machine: theory and applications. *Neurocomputing*, 70(1):489–501.

[Huang et al.2012] Guang-Bin Huang, Hongming Zhou, Xiaojian Ding, and Rui Zhang. 2012. Extreme learning machine for regression and multiclass classification. *IEEE Transactions on Systems, Man, and Cybernetics, Part B (Cybernetics)*, 42(2):513–529.

[Kasun et al.2013] Liyanaarachchi Lekamalage Chamara Kasun, Hongming Zhou, Guang-Bin Huang, and Chi Man Vong. 2013. Representational learning with extreme learning machine for big data. *IEEE Intelligent Systems*, 28(6):31–34.

[Kira and Rendell1992] Kenji Kira and Larry A Rendell. 1992. The feature selection problem: Traditional methods and a new algorithm. In *AAAI*, volume 2, pages 129–134.

[Kohavi and John1997] Ron Kohavi and George H John. 1997. Wrappers for feature subset selection. *Artificial intelligence*, 97(1):273–324.

[Lee and Kim2015] Jaesung Lee and Dae-Won Kim. 2015. Mutual information-based multi-label feature selection using interaction information. *Expert Systems with Applications*, 42(4):2013–2025.

[Lee and Yamamoto] Daniel TL Lee and Akio Yamamoto. Wavelet analysis: theory and applications. *Hewlett Packard journal*, 45:44–44.

[Liu et al.2005] Luying Liu, Jianchu Kang, Jing Yu, and Zhongliang Wang. 2005. A comparative study on unsupervised feature selection methods for text clustering. In *Natural Language Processing and Knowledge Engineering, 2005. IEEE NLP-KE'05. Proceedings of 2005 IEEE International Conference on*, pages 597–601. IEEE.

[Manning and Raghavan2008] Christopher Manning and Prabhakar Raghavan. 2008. Introduction to information retrieval.

[Meng et al.2011] Jiana Meng, Hongfei Lin, and Yuhai Yu. 2011. A two-stage feature selection method for text categorization. *Computers & Mathematics with Applications*, 62(7):2793–2800.

[Novovičová et al.2007] Jana Novovičová, Petr Somol, Michal Haindl, and Pavel Pudil, 2007. *Progress in Pattern Recognition, Image Analysis and Applications: 12th Iberoamericann Congress on Pattern Recognition, CIARP 2007, Valparaiso, Chile, November 13-16, 2007. Proceedings*, chapter Conditional Mutual Information Based Feature Selection for Classification Task, pages 417–426. Springer Berlin Heidelberg, Berlin, Heidelberg.

[Qiu et al.2011] Xipeng Qiu, Jinlong Zhou, and Xuanjing Huang. 2011. An effective feature selection method for text categorization. In *Advances in Knowledge Discovery and Data Mining*, pages 50–61. Springer.

[Salton et al.1975] Gerard Salton, Anita Wong, and Chung-Shu Yang. 1975. A vector space model for automatic indexing. *Communications of the ACM*, 18(11):613–620.

[Shang et al.2007] Wenqian Shang, Houkuan Huang, Haibin Zhu, Yongmin Lin, Youli Qu, and Zhihai Wang. 2007. A novel feature selection algorithm for text categorization. *Expert Systems with Applications*, 33(1):1–5.

[Thangamani and Thangaraj2010] M Thangamani and P Thangaraj. 2010. Integrated clustering and feature selection scheme for text documents 1.

[Yang and Pedersen1997] Yiming Yang and Jan O Pedersen. 1997. A comparative study on feature selection in text categorization. In *ICML*, volume 97, pages 412–420.

[Yang et al.2011] Jieming Yang, Yuanning Liu, Zhen Liu, Xiaodong Zhu, and Xiaoxu Zhang. 2011. A new feature selection algorithm based on binomial hypothesis testing for spam filtering. *Knowledge-Based Systems*, 24(6):904–914.

On Why Coarse Class Classification is a Bottleneck for Noun Compound Interpretation

Girishkumar Ponkiya
Dept. of CSE,
IIT Bombay, India
girishp@cse.iitb.ac.in

Pushpak Bhattacharyya
Dept. of CSE,
IIT Bombay, India
pb@cse.iitb.ac.in

Girish K. Palshikar
TCS Research,
Tata Consultancy Services, India
gk.palshikar@tcs.com

Abstract

Sequences of long nouns, i.e., noun compounds, occur frequently and are productive. Their interpretation is important for a variety of tasks located at various layers of NLP. Major reasons behind the poor performance of automatic noun compound interpretation are: (a) lack of a well defined inventory of semantic relations and (b) non-availability of sufficient, annotated, high-quality dataset.

Tratz and Hovy (2010) presented an inventory of semantic relations. They compared existing inventories with their two-level hierarchy, and created a large annotated dataset.

We performed both theoretical as well as data-driven analysis of this inventory. Theoretical analysis reveal ambiguities in the coarse relations. Data-driven analysis report similar performance for coarse as well as fine relations prediction. Our experiments show that improving the coarse classification accuracy can improve the performance of fine class predictor by 13 to 30 points in F-score.

1 Introduction

An important characteristic of a language is the process of creating new words by means of compounding. Especially, in English, technical and scientific literature produces long sequences of nouns, such as *laptop screen, Internet connection, colon cancer symptoms*, etc. Following Downing (1977)'s definition (for English language), these long sequences of nouns, acting as single noun, are known as *noun compounds* (NCs). NLP tasks cannot ignore such long sequences of nouns as they are abundant and productive type of compounds in English.

Most noun compounds appear only once in a large corpus. Baldwin and Tanaka (2004) analyzed the BNC corpus and found that 63.4% of total noun compounds appear only once in the corpus. In addition to the productive nature, noun compounds are compositional. These characteristics of the noun compounds make them a special case, and demand a special treatment.

The conventional approach to tackle this problem is a pipeline of three steps: (1) find noun compounds from text, (2) parse them if required, and (3) extract the semantic relationships between components of the noun compounds. The task of extracting semantic relations between components of a noun compound, or paraphrasing it using verbs and/or prepositions is known as interpretation of noun compound (or noun compound interpretation).

Our primary interest resides in interpretation of two-word noun compounds using predefined semantic labels as classes. The labels have been arranged in a two level hierarchy - coarse classes and fine classes. In this paper, we report the technical and linguistic challenges that we faced while performing classification task. Particularly, we discuss the challenges with coarse level classification.

The rest of the paper is organized as follows: Section 2 covers the related work. Section 3 discusses our approach, the experiments and results for the same are shown in Section 4. Section 5 discusses the results, which is followed by conclusion and future work.

2 Related Work

In computational domain, most work uses either of two representations for semantic relations: (1) set of abstract relations, or (2) paraphrasing a noun compound. Among these two, the former is most popular; repositories of such relations are generally proposed by the linguists.

2.1 Semantic Relations

Researchers have used sets of abstract relations as a preferred choice for semantic relation representation (Levi, 1978; Warren, 1978; Tratz and Hovy, 2010). Levi (1978)'s theory categorizes noun compounds based on the compounding process as: (1) predicate deletion, where a predicate between the components is simply dropped to create a compound, and (2) predicate nominalization, where the head is nominalized form of a verb and modifier is argument of the verb. They proposed a set of abstract predicates for the former category, but no labels for the later category. Later Ó Séaghdha (2007) revised this inventory, and proposed a two level hierarchy of semantic relations.

D S Sharma, R Sangal and A K Singh. Proc. of the 13th Intl. Conference on Natural Language Processing, pages 293–298,
Varanasi, India. December 2016. ©2016 NLP Association of India (NLPAI)

	Method	Relations	Examples	Performance
Wermter (1989)	Neural network	7	108	81.5% Accuracy
Lauer (1995)	Various Methods	8	385	47% Accuracy
Rosario et al. (2002)	Rule Based (medical)	18	1660	60% Accuracy
Girju et al. (2005)	WordNet bases rule learning and SVM	35	4205	64% Accuracy
Kim and Baldwin (2005)	WordNet Similarity (k-NN)	20	2169	53% Accuracy
Séaghdha and Copestake (2013)	SVM and String Kernels	6	1443	65% Accuracy
Tratz and Hovy (2010)	MaxEnt / SVM	43	17509	79.4% Accuracy
Dima and Hinrichs (2015)	Deep neural network	43	17509	77.70% F1-score

Table 1: Performance of past approaches for noun compound interpretation. Note that (almost) all methods use different relation inventory and different dataset making it difficult to compare performance.

Levi (1978)'s study is purely based on linguistics. On the other hand, Warren (1978) analyzed the Brown corpus and proposed a four-level hierarchy of semantic relations. Nastase and Szpakowicz (2003) extended Warren (1978)'s approach. Their proposed set of relations is also based on Barker and Szpakowicz (1998)'s semantic relations.

Vanderwende (1994) proposed a set of 13 relations based on the syntactical category and types of questions. Girju et al. (2005) provided another inventory of semantic relation based on Moldovan et al. (2004) for semantic relation in noun phrases.

Finally, Tratz and Hovy (2010) compared and consolidated most of these theories and proposed a two level hierarchy of 43 semantic relations, which are grouped in 9 coarse relations. This inventory of relations was iteratively refined to improve inter-annotator agreement. Tratz and Hovy (2010) used crowd sourcing for the iterative process. We have used this relation repository for our experiments and analysis.

2.2 Automatic Interpretation

Researchers have proposed various methods for automatic interpretation (Wermter, 1989; Nakov, 2013; Dima and Hinrichs, 2015). Unfortunately, these methods have been tested on different relation inventories and datasets, which makes it hard to compare their performance. Table 1 summarizes various methods for automatic interpretation.

All these methods can be categorized in two categories based on how it models the relation: (1) model the relation using only component features (Kim and Baldwin, 2005, 2013), or (2) directly modeling the relation based on how components of a compound can interact in real world (Nakov and Hearst, 2008). A system based on the latter approach should ideally perform better. But, generalization of such information needs large annotated data and a Web scale resource for paraphrase searching.

2.3 Word Embeddings

For classification task, we need to represent a given noun compound as a feature vector. One way is to concatenate the word embeddings of its constituent words. Mathematically, a word embedding is a function $V : D \rightarrow R^n$, where D is a dictionary of the words in a language and R^n is an n-dimensional real space.

Word embeddings are based on the distributional hypothesis. So, the words which occur in similar context have similar vectors. As word vector captures the context, the embedding technique approximates the interaction of a word with other words. This intuition can help us in modeling semantic relation using vectors of the components only.

Dima and Hinrichs (2015) has shown that the noun compound interpretation using only word embeddings, without any feature engineering, gives results comparable to the state-of-the-art. For our experiments, we used Google's pre-trained word embeddings[1] (Mikolov et al., 2013a,b).

3 Approach

Our aim is to classify a given noun compound into one of fine classes. The classes are arranged in two level hierarchy. We want to exploit the hierarchy to improve the system.

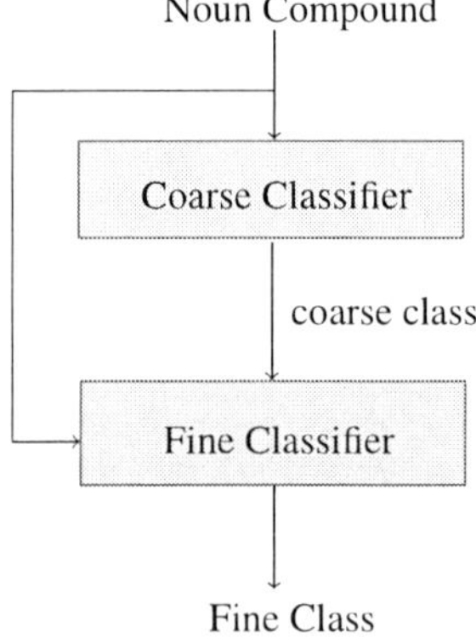

Figure 1: Pipeline architecture

If the coarse class of a noun compound is known, then inter coarse class confusion can be avoided. We try to leverage this fact by proposing a pipeline architecture (refer Figure 1) for the classification task. We

---

[1]https://code.google.com/archive/p/word2vec/

System Type	Input	Output	Remark
Type-1	vectors of the components + 1-hot presentation of a coarse relations	43 fine relations	
Type-2	vectors of the components + coarse class number	43 fine relations	
Type-3	vectors of the components only	9 coarse relations	Coarse Classification
Type-4	vectors of two components only	43 fine relations	End-to-end

Table 2: System types based on input features and output classes/relations.

define various systems based on the input and output to experiment with.

4 Experiments and Results

In this section we explain dataset creation, experiment setup, and the results. An analysis of experiments is discussed in the next section.

4.1 Dataset Pre-processing

For our experiment, we used Tratz and Hovy (2010)'s relation inventory and dataset. This inventory has 43 fine relations, grouped under 9 coarse relations. In this dataset, each example has been labeled with one of 43 fine semantic relations. We can get coarse class label indirectly as each fine relation belongs to exactly one coarse relation.

There are totally 19036 examples of noun-noun compounds in the Tratz and Hovy (2010)'s dataset. Some examples in the dataset contain more than one word as a component, e.g., *health-care legislation, real-estate speculation*. We eliminated such examples. We also eliminate examples for which at least one components has no word vector. This result in 18857 examples. We used Google's pre-trained word vectors to create feature vectors. For example, feature vector of *passenger traffic* is concatenation of two vectors: vector of *passenger* and vector of *traffic*.

We shuffled our dataset, and split it into three disjoint sets: train set (65%), validation set (15%), and test set (20%). The system was trained on the train set. The validation set was used for validation and hyperparameter searching. The system was evaluated on the test set.

4.2 Experimental Setup

To check our hypothesis, we defined four types of systems. Table 2 defines system types based on the input feature vector and the output classes. Given the word embeddings of a noun compound, Type-3 and Type-4 systems predict a coarse relation and a fine relation, respectively.

Type-1 and Type-2 systems are modeled as follows: given a noun compound and true coarse relation, predict a fine relation. The sole difference between them is how coarse-class information is represented. It is represented as 1-hot encoding in Type-1 system, whereas as a single numeric value in Type-2.

We used the following classifiers for our experiment with the above mentioned four types of settings:

- Naive Bayes

- k-nearest neighbor (kNN)

- SGD: Various linear classifiers with standard loss functions and stochastic gradient descent optimization (implemented as SGD in scikit-learn (Pedregosa et al., 2011))

- Decision tree (ID3 algorithm)

- Support vector machine (SVM)

- Deep neural network (DNN) (similar to Dima and Hinrichs (2015)'s architecture)

In addition to the above four types of systems and the classifiers, we use a pipeline architecture (proposed in Section 3), where predicted output of Type-3 system (coarse relation predictor) was fed to the Type-1 or Type-2 system.

For all of these multi-class classifications, we used one-vs-one and one-vs-rest techniques. Performance of the system in both sets of techniques are very similar.

4.3 Results

Figure 2 summarizes the results of various classifiers with different settings. SVM with polynomial kernel (degree=2, and soft margin constant C=10) outperforms all classifiers for all the mentioned systems. SVM results are separately shown in Table 3.

System Type	Precision	Recall	F1-score
Type-1	0.93	0.93	0.93
Type-2	0.92	0.92	0.92
Type-3	0.84	0.85	0.84
Type-4	0.81	0.81	0.80
Pipeline	0.79	0.8	0.79

Table 3: SVM (polynomial, degree 2, C 10) Results for all system types.

There are some interesting patterns across all classifiers. Most important patterns are: (a) performance of Type-3 (coarse predictor) and Type-4 (fine predictor) are almost same for most classifiers, (b) when coarse relation information was fed to a classifier in addition to word vectors (Type-1 or Type-2), performance of the system boosts up by 13 to 30 points in F-score.

For pipeline architecture, overall system performance degrades slightly compared to Type-4 system.

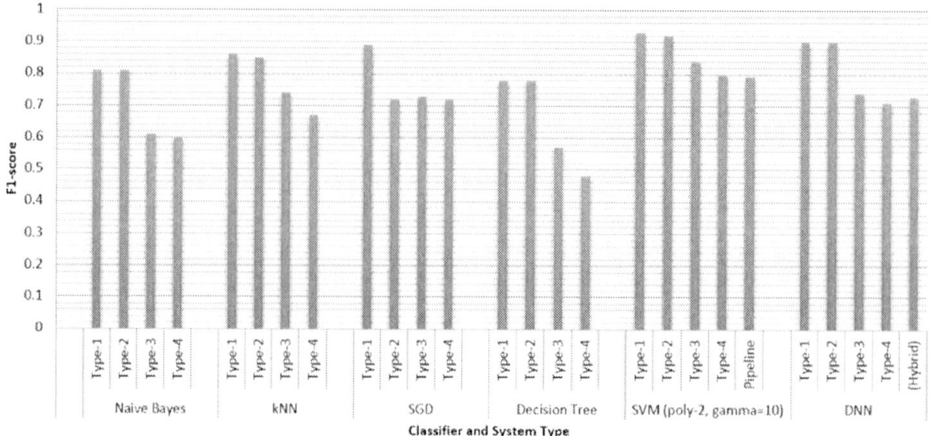

Figure 2: Performance (**F-score**) of combination of classifiers and system types. The system types are defined in Table 2.

Results for pipeline architecture (with SVM classifier) are shown in Figure 2. Similarly, slightly less F-scores are observed for other classifiers.

5 Discussions

Typically, it is expected that prediction among fine classes is difficult compared to prediction among coarse classes. A fine class predictor requires more information/samples compared to coarse class predictor. Particularly, the number of required training examples increases as the number of parameter to be estimated increases. We have the same number of examples for coarse and fine prediction. So, coarse classification is supposed to outperform fine classification. Despite such expectation, there is no significant difference in Type-3 (coarse predictor) and Type-4 (fine predictor) with most classifiers.

To check whether a better coarse class predictor can help the system in predicting the fine class, we used true coarse class labels as features in the fine class predictor (Type-1 and Type-2). Additional coarse class information boosts the performance of fine class predictor by 13 to 30 points in F1-score. This is evident from the difference in performance of Type-1 and Type-2 systems as compared to Type-4 system shown in Figure 2.

We analyzed the semantic relations and annotated dataset to understand the main reasons behind the poor performance of coarse relation predictor. Following are some important observations:

- The definition of OTHER is too vague. There are two fine relations under this coarse relation: *Other* and *Fixed Pair / Special / Lexicalized*. For '*Other*' subcategory, the annotator guideline says "*relationship between the two words is fairly clear, but no category seems appropriate*."

	Precision	Recall	F1-score	# Test Sample
C1	0.79	0.78	0.79	217
C2	0.84	0.91	0.88	1275
C3	0.78	0.78	0.78	361
C4	0.89	0.84	0.86	95
C5	0.79	0.72	0.76	258
C6	0.79	0.77	0.78	232
C7	0.89	0.90	0.90	867
C8	0.90	0.84	0.87	393
C9	0.55	0.14	0.23	77

Table 4: Confusion matrix for the coarse class predictor (Type-3) using SVM. (**C1**: "Causal Group", **C2**: "Function / Purpose Clusters", **C3**: "Ownership, Employment, and Use", **C4**: "Time", **C5**: "Location & Whole+Part", **C6**: "Composition / Containment", **C7**: "Topical", **C8**: "Coreferential / Attributive", **C9**: "Other")

	C1	C2	C3	C4	C5	C6	C7	C8	C9
C1	170	20	11	0	5	2	9	0	0
C2	15	1166	19	3	13	12	32	7	8
C3	10	38	281	1	8	6	11	6	0
C4	1	7	1	80	0	0	2	4	0
C5	4	18	18	0	187	9	19	3	0
C6	2	31	5	0	5	179	4	6	0
C7	6	43	13	5	8	4	781	6	1
C8	4	21	6	0	8	12	12	330	0
C9	3	38	4	1	3	3	8	6	11

Table 5: Confusion matrix for the coarse class predictor (Type-3) using SVM. For the labels, refer Table 4.

- PURPOSE/ACTIVITY GROUP has overlap with most of the coarse classes. This is also seen in the confusion matrix (ref. 2nd column and 2nd row in Table 5). In proportion to the total examples in this class, column values are small. But, as this class covers 33% of the total examples, a "small" value in C2 column can penalize the recall of other classes heavily (like C9). The same holds true for the row.

- *Fixed Pair / Special / Lexicalized* are multiword expressions, and such expressions should be handled separately. Typically, we can interpret compositional compounds only. If we feed a multiword expression to a system which is trained to interpret noun-noun compounds, then the system will try to predict the semantic relation based on semantics of the components. This was clear from error analysis and the confusion matrix. The last row (ref. Table 5) is heavy as compared to last column.

- *Partial Attribute/Feature/Quality Transfer*, belonging to ATTRIBUTIVE AND COREFERENTIAL coarse relation, is defined as "*The {attribute2} is metaphorically (but not literally) a/the/made_of {attribute1}.*" Like multiwords, the interpretation of metaphoric noun compounds cannot be inferred from the composition of the semantics of its components.

6 Conclusion and Future Work

In this paper, we claimed that the main bottleneck in noun compound interpretation task is the ambiguity between coarse classes. We analyzed an inventory of semantic relations and annotated data to understand such ambiguities. In addition, we also used a data driven approach to show that coarse relation prediction is a major bottleneck in the system. Experiment results also show that if one can improve coarse predictor, then overall system will improve significantly.

The SVM classifier with polynominal kernel (degree=2, and C=10) outperforms Tratz and Hovy (2010) and Dima and Hinrichs (2015) by a small margin. The salient points of our system are: 1) our system uses only word vectors, and 2) our system does not rely on computationally complex algorithms and resources.

To solve the ambiguity in semantic relation, we observe two possible directions:

1. Separate interpretable semantic relations from the rest, and define (or reshape) the coarse relation boundary accordingly.

2. Refining the definitions by adding more information. Such revised definitions may help the researcher in clarifying the class boundary. Such information can later be used to make the system more robust.

Acknowledgments

We thank CFILT members at IIT Bombay for their valuable comments and suggestions. This work is funded by Tata Consultancy Services Limited (TCS) under NGIE (Next Generation Information Extraction) with project code 13TCSIRC001.

References

Baldwin, T. and Tanaka, T. (2004). Translation by machine of complex nominals: Getting it right. In *Proceedings of the Workshop on Multiword Expressions: Integrating Processing*, pages 24–31. Association for Computational Linguistics.

Barker, K. and Szpakowicz, S. (1998). Semi-automatic recognition of noun modifier relationships. In *Proceedings of the 17th international conference on Computational linguistics-Volume 1*, pages 96–102. Association for Computational Linguistics.

Dima, C. and Hinrichs, E. (2015). Automatic noun compound interpretation using deep neural networks and word embeddings. *IWCS 2015*, page 173.

Girju, R., Moldovan, D., Tatu, M., and Antohe, D. (2005). On the semantics of noun compounds. *Computer speech & language*, 19(4):479–496.

Kim, S. N. and Baldwin, T. (2005). Automatic interpretation of noun compounds using wordnet similarity. In *Natural Language Processing–IJCNLP 2005*, pages 945–956. Springer.

Kim, S. N. and Baldwin, T. (2013). A lexical semantic approach to interpreting and bracketing english noun compounds. *Natural Language Engineering*, 19(03):385–407.

Lauer, M. (1995). Corpus statistics meet the noun compound: some empirical results. In *Proceedings of the 33rd annual meeting on Association for Computational Linguistics*, pages 47–54. Association for Computational Linguistics.

Levi, J. N. (1978). *The syntax and semantics of complex nominals*. Academic Press New York.

Mikolov, T., Chen, K., Corrado, G., and Dean, J. (2013a). Efficient estimation of word representations in vector space. *arXiv preprint arXiv:1301.3781*.

Mikolov, T., Yih, W.-t., and Zweig, G. (2013b). Linguistic regularities in continuous space word representations. In *HLT-NAACL*, pages 746–751.

Moldovan, D., Badulescu, A., Tatu, M., Antohe, D., and Girju, R. (2004). Models for the semantic classification of noun phrases. In *Proceedings of the HLT-NAACL Workshop on Computational Lexical Semantics*, pages 60–67. Association for Computational Linguistics.

Nakov, P. (2013). On the interpretation of noun compounds: Syntax, semantics, and entailment. *Natural Language Engineering*, 19(03):291–330.

Nakov, P. and Hearst, M. A. (2008). Solving relational similarity problems using the web as a corpus. In *ACL*, pages 452–460. Citeseer.

Nastase, V. and Szpakowicz, S. (2003). Exploring noun-modifier semantic relations. In *Fifth international workshop on computational semantics (IWCS-5)*, pages 285–301.

Ó Séaghdha, D. (2007). Annotating and learning compound noun semantics. In *Proceedings of the 45th Annual Meeting of the ACL: Student Research Workshop*, pages 73–78. Association for Computational Linguistics.

Pedregosa, F., Varoquaux, G., Gramfort, A., Michel, V., Thirion, B., Grisel, O., Blondel, M., Prettenhofer, P., Weiss, R., Dubourg, V., Vanderplas, J., Passos, A., Cournapeau, D., Brucher, M., Perrot, M., and Duchesnay, E. (2011). Scikit-learn: Machine learning in Python. *Journal of Machine Learning Research*, 12:2825–2830.

Rosario, B., Hearst, M. A., and Fillmore, C. (2002). The descent of hierarchy, and selection in relational semantics. In *Proceedings of the 40th Annual Meeting on Association for Computational Linguistics*, pages 247–254. Association for Computational Linguistics.

Séaghdha, D. O. and Copestake, A. (2013). Interpreting compound nouns with kernel methods. *Natural Language Engineering*, 19(03):331–356.

Tratz, S. and Hovy, E. (2010). A taxonomy, dataset, and classifier for automatic noun compound interpretation. In *Proceedings of the 48th Annual Meeting of the Association for Computational Linguistics*, pages 678–687. Association for Computational Linguistics.

Vanderwende, L. (1994). Algorithm for automatic interpretation of noun sequences. In *Proceedings of the 15th conference on Computational linguistics-Volume 2*, pages 782–788. Association for Computational Linguistics.

Warren, B. (1978). Semantic patterns of noun-noun compounds. *Acta Universitatis Gothoburgensis. Gothenburg Studies in English Goteborg*, 41:1–266.

Wermter, S. (1989). Learning semantic relationships in compound nouns with connectionist networks. In *Program of the Eleventh Annual Conference of the Cognitive Science Society*, pages 964–971.

Verbframator: Semi-Automatic Verb Frame Annotator Tool with Special Reference to Marathi

Hanumant Redkar, Sandhya Singh, Nandini Ghag, Jai Paranjape, Nilesh Joshi,

Malhar Kulkarni, Pushpak Bhattacharyya

Center for Indian Language Technology,
IIT Bombay, Mumbai, India
{hanumantredkar,sandhya.singh,samskritkanya,jai.para20,joshinilesh60}@gmail.com,
malhar@iitb.ac.in, pb@cse.iitb.ac.in

Abstract

The sentence is incomplete without a verb in a language. A verb is majorly responsible for giving the meaning to a sentence. Any sentence can be represented in the form of a verb frame. Verb frames are mainly developed as a knowledge resource which can be used in various semantic level Natural Language Processing (NLP) activities. This paper presents the *Verbframator* – a verb frame annotator tool which automatically extracts and generates verb frames of example sentences from Marathi wordnet. It also helps in generating Shakti Standard Format (SSF) files of the given example sentences. The generated verb frames and SSF files can be used in the dependency tree banking and other NLP applications like machine translation, paraphrasing, natural language generation, *etc.*

1 Introduction

Verb is one of the most important part-of-speech (POS) category in any language. It plays a major role in understanding or defining a sentence. Sentences in any language can be represented in the form of verb frames. *Verb frame* is made of verbal propositions and arguments of words around a given verb. It is required for creating dependency relations which leads to the development of a knowledge resource. These kinds of resources are always required for semantics related Natural Language Processing (NLP) applications like machine translation, natural language generation, paraphrasing, *etc.* Development and analysis of verb frames

for Indian languages is an emerging research topic in the field of NLP and computational linguistics.

This paper presents a verb frame generator tool to semi-automatically annotate and generate verb frames using example sentences from wordnet. Marathi wordnet is used as a reference wordnet for this purpose. Marathi[1] is an Indo-Aryan language spoken prominently in Maharashtra, India. Marathi wordnet[2] comes under the umbrella of IndoWordNet[3] which currently has around 32183 synsets and 43834 words, of which 3047 are verbs. The objective is to generate verb frames for these verbs using examples from Marathi wordnet.

The paper covers explanation of the concept, working of verb-frame tool, advantages and disadvantages of the tool and its applications. The immediate application of the output of this tool is to study Marathi sentences and their structures with the help of its generated verb-frames. This study will lead to development of rules and guidelines for verb-frame annotation process.

In computational linguistics and natural language processing, only few efforts have been taken to create this kind of resource for Indian languages. And in spite of Marathi being a morphologically rich, with sufficient resource availability, no remarkable work has been found.

In this paper, section 2 briefs the related work. Section 3 defines the verb frame. Section 4 discusses the work flow of verb frame annotator tool. Section 5 lists features and limitations of the tool. Section 6 concludes the paper with scope for improvement in the tool, followed by references.

---

[1] https://en.wikipedia.org/wiki/Marathi_language

[2] http://www.cfilt.iitb.ac.in/wordnet/webmwn/

[3] http://www.cfilt.iitb.ac.in/indowordnet/

D S Sharma, R Sangal and A K Singh. Proc. of the 13th Intl. Conference on Natural Language Processing, pages 299–304,
Varanasi, India. December 2016. ©2016 NLP Association of India (NLPAI)

2   Related Work

Verb POS easily represents the activity, state or action in a text which can lead to its semantic interpretation. This property of verb is useful in creating the necessary knowledge base required for NLP applications. Though, for English language, there is a substantial amount of work which has been done regarding the development and analysis using verb frames, but only limited work can be seen for Indian languages. This can be seen in the following research work.

Begum et al. (2008) discussed their experience with the creation of verb frames for Hindi language. These frames are further classified based on Paninian grammar framework using 6 karaka relations. The method followed by the authors considers the morphology, syntactic variations and semantics of the verb to divide it into different classes. This resource focuses on NLP related activities for Hindi language.

Based on similar approach, Ghosh (2014) created a resource for verb frames for compound verbs in Bengali language. The objective of the paper was to investigate if the vector verb from the compound verb is able to retain its case marking properties and argument structure or not. And also the knowledge and syntax associated with verb frames can be utilized for categorizing and analyzing the verb words for various NLP applications.

Soni et al. (2013) explored the application of verb frames and the conjuncts in sentence simplification for Hindi language. The method proposed by the authors includes usage of conjuncts as a first level of sentence simplification. This is followed by using verb frames enhanced with tense, aspect and modality features. It is a rule based system and its output was evaluated manually and automatically using BLEU score for the ease of readability and simplification.

Other related work by Schulte (2009), Theakston et al. (2015) has also explored verb frames for English language.

After reviewing these papers, the need for such kind of resource for Indian languages and a tool which can assist in the creation of this type of resources became more apparent. Also, apart from English, language specific verb-frame analysis has been done for few Indian languages such as Hindi and Bengali. However, no attempt has been made for Marathi language in the domain of verb-frame creation and analysis. This paper aims to fill the gap in the literature by providing verb-frame tool for the study of verb frames.

3   What is a Verb Frame?

In any language, verb is a major part-of-speech category. Verbs are used to define actions, activities and states. The potential of verbs to choose their complements (arguments/adjuncts) is referred to as 'verb sub-categorization' or 'verb valency' and a combination of functional components that are evoked by a verb is called as *verb frames*.

Verb frame typically is made of verbal propositions and arguments of words around a verb in a given sentence. Each of the propositional word in a verb frame has arguments such as an arc-label or semantic role label, its necessity in a frame, *vibhakti* (i.e. case marker), lexical type, relation with head verb, position with respect to head verb, *etc*. These verb frames are developed to generate dependency tree structures in a given language. Figure 1 shows a typical verb frame for a Marathi word घड (*ghaDa*, to happen).

```
Verb::घड
SID::
Verb Sense::
Eng_Gloss::
Verb Class::
Verb_in_Same_Class::
TAM for the verb root::हे
Frames::

Example::त्यांच्या देवघरात समर्पणी उद्धवस्वामींना दिलेली निशीवालय रामाची दुर्मिळ , ऐतिहासिक मूर्ती , भनौछे श्रै यंत्र आणि अभाच काही दुर्मिळ मूर्तींचे दर्शन घडले .
Frequency::1

FRAME_ID::1
--------------------------------------------------------------------
arc_label      necessity      Vibhakti       LexType       posn      reln
--------------------------------------------------------------------
k2             m              0              n             1         c
k7p            c              0              n             1         c
--------------------------------------------------------------------
```

Figure 1: Typical verb frame for a word घड

4   Verb Frame Annotator : *Verbframator*

Verb frame annotator interface or *Verbframator* is an online tool developed to extract the verb frames of example sentences from wordnet. It also generates the Shakti Standard Format (SSF) (Bharati et al., 2007) files for these example sentences.

The *Verbframator* is a semi-automatic tool which is developed in PHP and data is stored and maintained in MySQL *verbframe* database. The user input interface of *Verbframator* can be seen in figure 2.

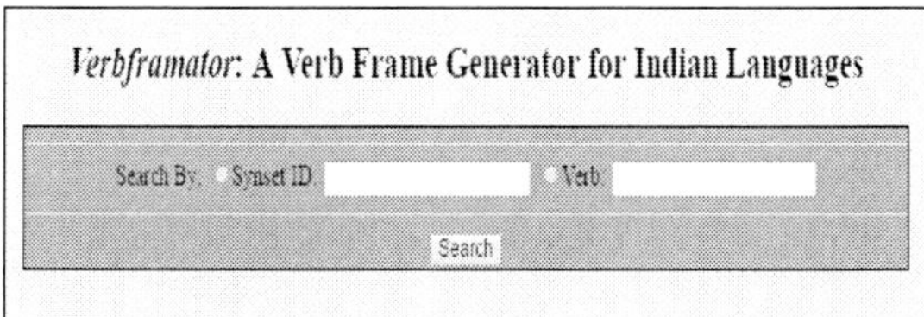

Figure 2: A *Verbframator* user input interface

4.1 Work Flow of *Verbframator*

The *Verbframator* is designed to generate verb frames of the example sentences from wordnet. In this study we have used Marathi wordnet. The work flow of this tool is shown in figure 3. Following are the steps used by *Verbframator* to generate verb frames:

(1) Take wordnet data as an input - synset id or verb:
The *Verbframator* starts with the user input in the form of either verb's synset id or a verb itself. The system is uses example sentences from wordnet for the verb frame annotation process. As shown in figure 2 above, search can be done by entering synset id or a verb in Marathi language.

(2) Extract example sentence(s):
(a) If the user enters verb synset id then system checks if the verb is present in the context of the example sentence and extract the corresponding example sentence.

(b) If the user enters verb itself there are two possibilities: (i) if there is only one synset for the input verb then the system extracts examples of that synset and (ii) if there are more than one synset then the system extracts all the synsets of the input verb. Here user selects synsets one by one and each synset is processed at a time.

In both the cases (a) and (b) above, the examples are extracted only if verb is present in the example sentence, else it will show corresponding error message. Also, if synsets have more than one example sen-

tence then the system extracts only those examples in which the input verb appears.

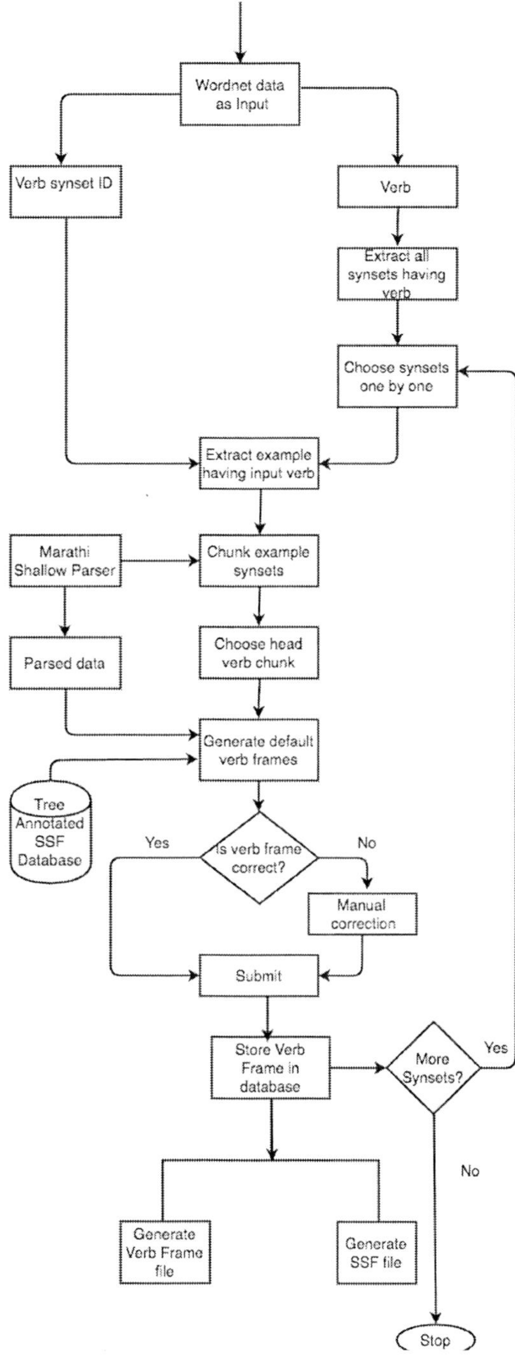

Figure 3: Work flow diagram of *Verbframator*

(3) Chunk example sentence(s):

The input example sentence processed through the Marathi shallow parser[4] which gives the chunked phrases of the input sentence. This chunked output is manually validated by a lexicographer. This can be seen in figure 4. Once the chunking is done the annotator decides and marks the head verb chunk and clicks on 'Extract Verb Frames' button to extract verb frames.

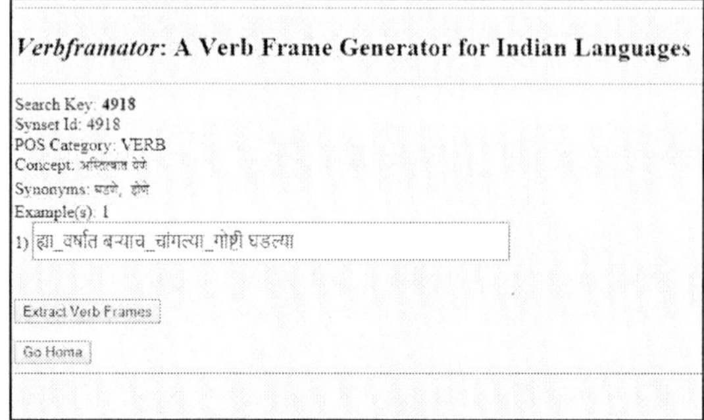

Figure 4: *Verbframator* sentence chunked output

(4) Generate default verb frame(s):

Once the chunking is done, the system automatically generates the default verb frame for an input example.

Figure 5: *Verbframator* - default frame generator

The method to automatically generate the default verb frames is explained in detail in the next section. The default verb frame generated for a verb घडणे (*ghaDaNe*, to happen, to occur) can be seen in figure 5.

(5) Validate extracted verb frame(s):

The annotator manually validates the generated verb frame. Here, user has to do minimal validation as most of the fields in the verb frame are already entered by the system automatically. Once the validation is done by an annotator, user can store the verb frame, generate the verb frame or/and generate the SSF file.

(6) Store the verb frame(s) data:

Verb frames are stored in the *verbframe* database by using button 'Store Verb Frames'.

(7) Generate verb frame(s):

We can generate the verb frames using button 'Generate Verb Frames'. The verb frame(s) of the processed verb frame is generated in the standard verb frame format. The extracted verb frame can be seen in figure 6.

Figure 6: Extracted verb frame for a verb घड

(8) Generate SSF file:

We can also generate SSF file of the processed example sentence by clicking on 'Generate SSF File'.

The process is repeated if there are more synsets for an input verb.

---

[4]http://ltrc.iiit.ac.in/showfile.php?filename=downloads/shallow_parser.php

4.2 Method to Generate Default Verb Frames

The default verb frames are automatically generated using (i) the tree annotated data and (ii) Marathi shallow parser output. While extracting verb frame features the *Verbframator* first checks if chunks are already present in the SSF tree annotated database. If chunks are present then the corresponding arc label is extracted from the database else the arc label is extracted from the shallow parser output data.

In extract features using *tree annotated data approach*, we automatically extract verb frame arguments from the tree annotated files. These files are already annotated by the human experts and are available in SSF format. Currently, the system has used about 92 tree annotated SSF files having 5536 sentences, 74476 words and 50813 chunks. This data continuously changes and new annotated data is appended to the existing data. Our offline system preprocesses this tree annotated data and features like arc labels, lex type and other necessary information are extracted from this annotated data. The SSF tree annotated data and extracted features are stored in the *verbframe* database. This is an ongoing process where the feature extraction is done on tree annotated data as and when new tree annotated data is added to the offline preprocessing system.

In extract features using *Marathi shallow parser approach*, if the required features are not available in *verbframe* database then the Marathi shallow parser tool is used to extract these features. The verb frame features such as *vibhakti's* and lexical type can be extracted using the output of the shallow parser tool. The extracted output can be mapped to get the *vibhakti's*. This can be seen in table 1, 2, and 3.

Marathi *Vibhakti* Table					
Sanskrit	**English**	**Sanskrit**	**English**	**Singular Suffixes**	**Plural Suffixes**
Ordinal Number	Ordinal Number	Case Description	Case Description	(एकवचन)	(अनेकवचन)
prathamā (प्रथमा)	First	kartā (कर्ता)	Nominative case	–	-ā (आ)
dwitīyā (द्वितीया)	Second	karma (कर्म)	Accusative case	-sa (-स), -lā (-ला), -te (-ते)	-sa (-स), -lā (-ला), -nā (ना), -te (-ते)
trutīyā (तृतीय)	Third	karaṇa (करण)	Instrumental case	-nī (नी), e (ए), shī (शी)	-nī (नी), -hī (ही), e (ए), shī (शी)
caturthī (चतुर्थी)	Fourth	sampradāna (सम्प्रदान)	Dative case	-sa (-स), -lā (-ला), -te (-ते)	-sa (-स), -lā (-ला), -nā (ना), -te (-ते)
pancamī (पञ्चमी)	Fifth	apādāna (अपादान)	Ablative case	-ūna (-ऊन), -hūna (-हून)	-ūna (-ऊन), -hūna (-हून)
shhashhthī (पष्ठी)	Sixth	sambandh (संबंध)	Genitive case	-chā (-चा), -chī (-ची), -che (-चे)	-ce (-चे), -cyā (-च्या), -cī (-ची)
saptamī (सप्तमी)	Seventh	adhikaran (अधिकरण)	Locative case	-ta (-त), -i (-इ), -ā (-आ)	-ta (-त), -ī (-ई), -ā (-आ)
sambhodan (संवोधन)	Vocative case	–	Vocative case	–	-no (-नो)

Table 1: *Vibhakti's* in Marathi

The attribute values for noun & pronoun								
	1	2	3	4	5	6	7	8
sample words	lex	cat	gend	num	pers	case	vib	tam
मनाच्या	मन	n	n	sg		o	च्या	'○ा_च्या'
मनाने	मन	n	n	sg		o	ने	'○ा_ने'
पर्यटनाची	पर्यटन	n	n	sg		o	ची	'○ा_ची'
दुष्परिणामापासून	दुष्परिणाम	n	m	sg		o	पासून	'○ा_पासून'
पर्यटकाला	पर्यटक	n	m	sg		o	ला	'○ा_ला'
सौंदर्याने	सौंदर्य	n	n	sg		o	ने	'○ा_ने'
लोकांसाठी	लोक	n	m	pl		o	साठी	'○ां_साठी'
त्यांच्यासाठी	तो	pn	m	pl		o	साठी	'○्यां_च्या_साठी'
ह्यांचे	हा	pn	m	pl		o	चे	'○्यां_चे'

Table 2: The attribute values for Noun & Pronoun

Vibhakti to Number Conversion		
Vibhakti's (7)		Numerical Form
Singular Suffixes	Plural Suffixes	
(एकवचन)	(अनेकवचन)	
–	आ	1
स ला ते	स ला ना ते	2
नी ए शी	नी ही ए शी	3
स ला ते साठी करिता	स ला ना ते साठी करिता	4
ऊन हून मुळे पासून	ऊन हून मुळे पासून	5
चा ची चे	चे च्या ची	6
त इ आ	त ई आ	7
–	नो	8

Table 3: *Vibh/akti* to Number Conversion

5 *Verbframator*: Features and Limitations

Salient features of *Verbframator*:

- *Verbframator* reduces the manual effort of creating verb frames.

- Verb frames are automatically extracted which requires minimal validation.

- It also generates SSF files of the input verb sentences.

- Helps in analyzing the generated verb frames and constructing similar patterns for a given verb.

- *verbframe* database stores verb frame and trained data in a systematic and classified manner.

Limitations of *Verbframator*

- Although *Verbframator* generates verb frames and SSF files automatically, it still requires manual intervention to complete some tasks.

- In wordnet, not all verbs in a synset are explained using an example sentence. Only first frequently used verb appears in the example sentence. The example sentence is not available for rest of the verbs in a given synsets. Hence, verb frame for such sentences cannot be developed.

- The *Verbframator* extracts examples having input verbs only.

- Quality of verb frames depends upon annotators understanding in annotating verb frames. Hence, inter-annotator-agreement should be of high value which can lead to better quality resource.

- Quality of verb frames also depends upon the quality of trained data or gold data.

- Currently *Verbframator* can be applicable only for wordnet sentences. It cannot be used for general corpus.

6 Conclusion and Future Scope

Verb is an important POS category for any language. Verb frames are created to generate dependency tree structures in a given language. This paper introduces an online tool *Verbframator* which semi-automatically extracts and generates verb frames using example sentences from Marathi wordnet. *Verbframator* also generates SSF formatted files of the given example sentences. These resources can be used in the dependency tree banking. In future, this verb frame annotator tool is to be made fully automatic. Also, this tool is to be expanded for other Indian languages under the umbrella of IndoWordNet. Sentences from other corpus are also to be included in the *Verbframator*.

References

Bharati, Akshar, Rajeev Sangal, and Dipti M. Sharma. 2007. "*Ssf: Shakti standard format guide.*" Language Technologies Research Centre, International Institute of Information Technology, Hyderabad, India (2007): 1-25.

Begum, Rafiya, Samar Husain, Lakshmi Bai, and Dipti Misra Sharma. 2008 "*Developing Verb Frames for Hindi." In LREC*. LREC 2008.

Ghosh, Sanjukta. 2014. "Making Verb Frames for Bangla Vector Verbs" ICON 2014.

Ghosh, Sanjukta. 2014. "*Noun Classification from the Verb Frames of Conjunct Verbs.*" Forthcoming in Journal of Advanced Linguistic Studies. Bahri Publications, New Delhi.

Schulte im Walde, Sabine. 2009. "*The induction of verb frames and verb classes from corpora.*" Corpus linguistics. an international handbook. Berlin: Mouton de Gruyter (2009): 952-972.

Soni, Ankush, Sambhav Jain, and Dipti Misra Sharma. 2013. "*Exploring Verb Frames for Sentence Simplification in Hindi."* In IJCNLP, pp. 1082-1086.

Theakston, Anna L., et al. 2015. "*Productivity of noun slots in verb frames.*"Cognitive science 39.6 (2015): 1369-1395.

Towards Building A Domain Agnostic Natural Language Interface to Real-World Relational Databases

Sree Harsha Ramesh, Jayant Jain, Sarath K S, and Krishna R Sundaresan
Surukam Analytics
Chennai
{harsha,jayant,sarath,krishna}@surukam.com

Abstract

In this paper we present Surukam-NLI —
a novel system of building a natural language interface to databases, which composes the earlier work on using linguistic syntax trees for parsing natural language queries with, the latest advances in natural language processing such as distributed language embedding models for semantic mapping of the natural language and the database schema. We will be evaluating the performance of our system on a sample online transaction processing (OLTP) database called as Adventure-WorksDB and show that we achieve partial domain independence by handling queries about three different scenarios — Human Resources, Sales & Marketing and Product scenarios. Since there is no baseline for query performance on OLTP databases, we report f-measure statistics on an internally curated query dataset.

1   Introduction

Natural language interfaces to databases (NLIs) are front-ends to a database which help casual users query the database even without knowing the schema of the database or any specialised query languages like Structured Query Language (SQL). This is especially useful for people in decision making roles who largely depend on analysts for their daily dose of reports. For reasons that we'll see in the following sections, we are still far from building a truly domain agnostic system that converts any natural language query successfully into SQL, given just the information about the database schema.

1.1   Background

Building a natural language interface to relational databases is almost as old as the concept of relational databases itself. Codd (1970) defined relational database as a digital database whose organization is based on the relational model of data in his seminal paper of 1970, while the earliest documented Natural Language Interface(NLI) is the Lunar Sciences Natural Language Information System (LSNLIS), (Woods et al., 1972). It was a question answering system built in 1972, that enabled lunar geologists to query the data collected during the Apollo missions.

Despite there being many NLIs since the LSNLIS such as PRECISE, PARLANCE, NaLIR, SEEKER and TEAM (Popescu et al., 2003; Bates, 1989; Li and Jagadish, 2014; Smith et al., 2014; Grosz et al., 1987), there has not been an encouraging adoption of this technology in the software industry, probably because of lengthy configuration phases and domain portability issues. SQL is still the preferred mode of querying relational databases which have highly complex architecture and for sensitive operations like inserting, updating and deleting data.

For a broad class of semantically tractable natural language questions, PRECISE described in (Popescu et al., 2003) is guaranteed to map each question to the corresponding SQL query. PRECISE determines whether a question is semantically tractable using max-flow algorithm and outputs the corresponding SQL query. It collects max-flow solutions corresponding to possible semantic interpretations of the sentence and discards the solutions that do not obey syntactic constraints and generates SQL queries based on remaining solutions. PRECISE is only effective on semantically tractable questions in which sentence tokenization results in distinct tokens which contain

D S Sharma, R Sangal and A K Singh. Proc. of the 13th Intl. Conference on Natural Language Processing, pages 305–314,
Varanasi, India. December 2016. ©2016 NLP Association of India (NLPAI)

at-least one wh-word[1]. So, queries like *list the highest selling product* and *show me all the goods purchased in the past week* would not be handled due to lack of wh-words.

Li and Jagadish (2014) present NaLIR which is an interactive natural language query interface for relational databases. The system contains a query interpretation part, an interactive communicator and a query tree translator. The query interpretation part is responsible for interpreting the natural language query and representing the interpretation as a linguistic parse tree. By communicating with the user, interactive communicator ensure that the interpretation process is correct. The query tree, possibly verified by the user, is translated into an SQL statement in the query tree translator and is then evaluated against an RDBMS. Although, this NLI correctly interprets complex natural language queries across a range of domains, the use of a conversational agent in the pipeline, in order to resolve the ambiguities in linguistic parse trees and query interpretation, precludes casual users who do not have the knowledge of the underlying schema and linguistic representation, from using the tool.

The approach described in (Pérez, 2016) proposes a semantically-enriched data dictionary called as Semantic Information Dictionary (SID) which stores the information necessary for the NLI to correctly interpret a query. The performance of the interface depends on the quantity and quality of semantic information stored in the domain dictionary. A translation module, which consists of components for lexical analysis, syntactic analysis, semantic analysis generates the SQL representation of the natural language query. This approach has a lengthy customization phase where a proficient customizer would need to fine-tune the NLI using the domain editor provided with the tool, similar to the approach adopted by Access ELF (Elf, 2009), one of the few surviving commercial NLIs. Yet another NLI that requires a domain and linguistic expert for configuring the NLI is C-Phrase (Minock, 2010). C-Phrase is a natural language interface system that models queries in an extended version of Codds tuple calculus, which are then automatically mapped to SQL. The NLI author would have to use synchronous context free grammars with lambda-expressions to represent semantic grammars. The given grammar rules may be used in the reverse direction to achieve paraphrases of logical queries by configuring the parser and generator to associate phrases with database elements.

As detailed in (Androutsopoulos et al., 1995), NLIs have an ambiguous linguistic coverage and are prone to tedious and lengthy configuration phases. Sometimes, they also have an additional requirement of having a highly specialized team of domain experts and skilled linguists who are capable of creating grammar rules. Motivated by the lack of an easily configurable tool that handles multiple domains with reasonable accuracy we propose Surukam-NLI[2], a domain-agnostic NLI that has an automatic configuration phase that uses a word embedding model trained on the Google News data-set and the entity-relationship details about the database.

1.2 Organization

In section 2, we describe the architecture of Surukam-NLI which includes a discussion on the parsing phase which identifies the entities and constraints, the schema generation phase which generates a dictionary using word-embeddings that is subsequently used for generating SQL and the mapping phase that maps entities and constraints to SQL clauses and columns. Section 3 contains a description of the AdventureWorks [3] database and an evaluation of our system's performance across multiple domains of the database. Section 4 contains some observations about our system's limits and compares our approach with the other approaches of building NLIs to databases.

2 Surukam-NLI Architecture

In this section we describe the pipeline of steps involved in translating the natural language query into a SQL query. This has also been outlined in Figure 1. Firstly, an intermediate dictionary which has tokens classified into entities and attributes using the parse tree output and named entities, is generated. Secondly, the intermediate output is mapped to the database schema using a combination of word-embeddings and database look-ups to generate the various components of a complete SQL query such as SELECT, FROM, WHERE

---

[1]They are function words used to ask a question, such as what, when, where, who, whom, why, and how.

[2]This system was developed at Surukam Analytics.

[3]https://technet.microsoft.com/en-us/library/ms124825(v=sql.100).aspx

and JOIN. We would be using the following query as the running example throughout this section:

total sales by year in Southeast Asia after 2001

2.1 Terminology

Let us formalize some terminology first - *entity* refers to the "target"of the user query, and hence the target of the SQL query. These typically map to SELECT statements in the final query, but may also contain other information — the "total" in the running example gives clues about aggregation and grouping. Information along with the entities usually tends to be about ordering, limits and aggregate functions viz. SUM, AVG and math operations viz., MAX, MIN. Any such supplementary information is considered a *modifier*.

The *constraints* refer to other conditions specified in the user query. Most constraints map to WHERE, GROUP and ORDER clauses. They typically correspond to NN phrases combined with PP phrases and CD values. Within a constraint, the *terms* come from noun phrases and the *condition* from prepositional phrases. Each entry in *terms* can be mapped to either a database column, relation, function or a value in a column, whereas the *condition* corresponds to either an operator or a clause.

2.2 Entity & Constraint Recognizer

In the first step of the pipeline, the natural language query is transformed into a dictionary of entities and constraints based on some rules applied on the parse tree output and the named entities.

2.2.1 Named Entity Recognition (NER)

The natural language query is run through the named entity recognizer (Finkel et al., 2005) which classifies the named entities in text into predefined categories such as the names of persons, organizations, locations, expressions of times, quantities, monetary values and percentages. This information is used to deduce the constraint attribute from the NER tags of the constraint values. For e.g., in the syntax tree shown in figure 2, *Southeast Asia* is classified as location and *2001* is classified as date which would help in adding country/territory/region and year/date as the constraint attributes.

2.2.2 Syntactic Parse Tree

Parse trees are syntactic representations of a sentence that convey the part of speech (POS) for each word of a sentence and also denote patterns of useful relationships such as subject-verb-object. POS tags are assigned to a single word according to its role in the sentence. Traditional grammar classifies words based on eight parts of speech: the verb (VB), the noun (NN), the pronoun (PR+DT), the adjective (JJ), the adverb (RB), the preposition (IN), the conjunction (CC), and the interjection (UH). The tag set is based on the Penn Treebank Tagging Guidelines (Santorini, 1990). Figure 2 shows the syntax tree representation of the running example query. Next, we explain how the patterns of relationships are exploited to classify a token into entities and constraints.

2.2.3 Generate dictionary of entities and constraints

These are some rules we have used in extracting entities and constraints from the syntax tree.

1. In the syntactic parse tree, the prepositional phrase (PP) which comes under a prepositional phrase node is classified as a constraint, while nouns (NN*) are classified as attribute, cardinal numbers (CD) as value, and adjectives (JJ) as conditions on attribute.

2. The first noun phrase (NP), which is not a subtree of a prepositional phrase (PP) is classified as a candidate for an entity chunk. All the nouns under this noun phrase (NP) belong to entity list, with adjectives (JJ) as modifier and cardinal numbers(CD) as value. All the tokens with the POS tag as CD (cardinal numbers) but have a word representation are converted into numerical form, to generate valid SQL queries.

3. There are queries which do not have an entity-item explicitly mentioned. In such cases, the domain to which the query belongs is considered as an entity. The contextual or semantic relation between query and domain is inferred with the help of attribute words of all the constraints. For inferring the domain name from the set of tokens identified as attributes in the query, WordNet (Miller et al., 1990) is used. WordNet is a large lexical database for English, that collects a network of meaningfully related words into a *SynSet*. For example, in the query — *who has the highest salary in last twenty years*, the wh-word who is resolved into the domain

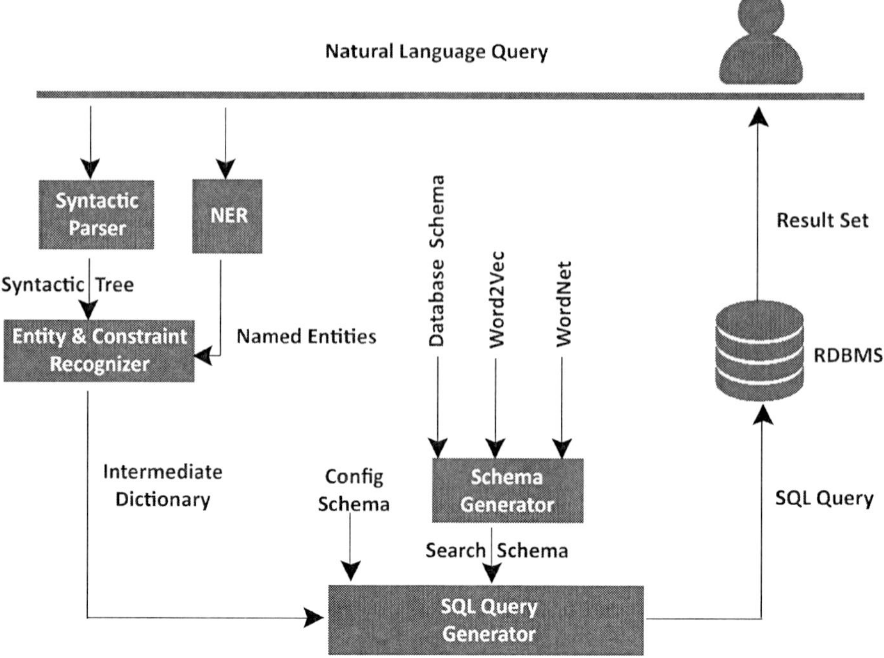

Figure 1: Surukam-NLI System Architecture

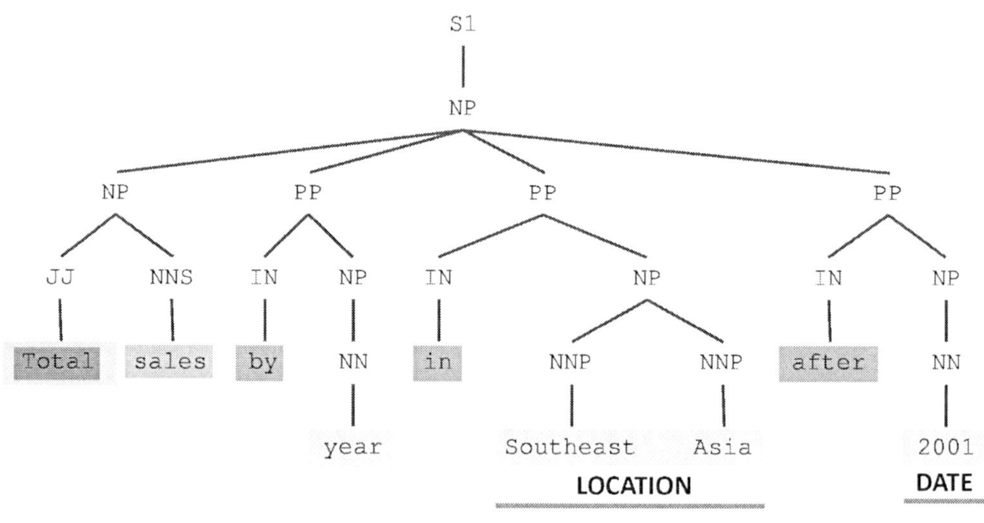

Figure 2: Syntax Tree and NER Output

employee based on the constraint term *salary* which is semantically related to the domain name *employee*, and the token *employee* is added as an entity for this query.

In our running example query — *total sales by year in Southeast Asia after 2001*, the tokens - *total* and *sales* would belong in entities with *sales* being the entity term and *total* being the entity modifier. In the same query, the tokens such as *after*, *2001*, *Southeast*, *Asia*, *by* and *year* would be classified as constraint phrases. The constraints would be further classified as: *after* into condition and *2001* as its corresponding value along with the implicit constraint term *year*, because of the NER tag. Similarly, *Southeast Asia* is classified into a constraint term which would be resolved into attribute name and value respectively, in Section 2.3.2.

2.3 SQL Query Generator

This section describes the process of mapping the output of the parsing stage to the correct columns, relations and clauses part of the final generated SQL statement. The basic structure of the output from the parse tree module is shown in Figure 3. The generation of the SQL query from the output of the syntactic parsing stage broadly involves two distinct parts - Schema Generation and Mapping.

```
{
  "entities":[
      {
        "terms"    :"sales",
        "modifiers":{
              "terms":"Total",
              "value":null
            }
      }
    ],
  "constraints":[
      {
        "terms":["year"],
        "condition":"by"
      }
      {
        "terms"    :["Southeast Asia"],
        "condition":"in"
      },
      {
        "terms"    :["2001"],
        "condition":"after"
      }
    ]
}
```

Figure 3: Intermediate representation of the parse tree output which has classified tokens into entities and constraints

2.3.1 Schema Generation

The goal of this module is to generate a search schema containing an expanded set of candidate database column and relation tokens. The expanded set of tokens is generated by making use of stemming, word embeddings and lexical ontologies to determine syntactically as well as semantically similar tokens.

Word stemming is an important feature present in modern day indexing and search systems. The main idea is to improve recall by reducing the words to their word roots, at both index time and query time. Recall is increased without compromising on the precision of the documents fetched, since the word roots typically represent similar concepts as the original word. Stemming is usually done by removing any attached suffixes and prefixes (affixes) from index terms before the actual assignment of the term to the index. We make use of the Snowball stemming algorithm in our implementation (Porter, 2001), which is an improved version of the Porter stemmer (Porter, 1980). Although, Lancaster stemmer (Paice, 1990) is marginally faster than Snowball, it has significantly lower precision.

Word embeddings are dense, distributed vector representations of words which try to capture semantic information about the word. Distributed representations of words in a vector space help learning algorithms to achieve better performance in natural language processing tasks by grouping similar words, and by solving the sparsity problem present in n-gram based models. Word representations computed using neural networks are especially interesting because the learned vectors explicitly encode many linguistic regularities and patterns. Semantically similar words can be found by determining cosine similarities between the word vectors. We use the skip-gram word2vec model (Mikolov et al., 2013a; Mikolov et al., 2013c) for training of word representations.

Pre-trained embeddings released as part of (Mikolov et al., 2013b) have been used. The word embeddings were trained on a Google News corpus consisting of 100 billion tokens with a vocabulary of 3 million unique words.

A lexical database is a source of lexical information that can be used effectively by modern computing methods. A lexical database often stores information about a large variety of semantic relations, such as synonymy, antonymy, hyponymy and entailment. These semantic relations can be made use of to generate additional tokens for database column and relation tokens. The WordNet lexical database is used in our paper to determine such tokens.

The set of additional tokens is generated by making use of the above - Snowball stemming, word2vec similarity, and WordNet synsets. Some preprocessing of the original database tokens based on simple pattern matching rules commonly relevant to database column and relation names - pascal cased tokens (eg: SalespersonName), camel cased tokens (eg: territoryID) and punctuation (eg: salesperson_id) - is also performed to obtain better tokens. Finally, the generated tokens are stored in a reverse index to facilitate easy search and retrieval, and this reverse index is called the search schema.

In addition to this, a config schema is also created which contains mappings between terms and certain SQL operators, functions and clauses. (eg: greater: >, top: ORDER BY ASC). These mappings are seeded with initial values manually, and then the same approach as the one used for creating the search schema is applied. Note that SQL function names are dependent on the version and type of database used, and hence this config schema is made to be configurable by the database administrator.

2.3.2 Mapping

The aim of the mapping module is to map each of the elements in both entities and constraints to a clause and column. This also includes applying any possible operators to values and aggregate functions to database columns. The mapping module makes use of the parse tree output from the syntactic parsing stage, and the search and config schemas generated in the schema generation module.

The mapping is done by first doing a direct lookup on the search schema, and in case that fails, by determining a similarity score between the terms in the user query elements and keys of the search schema. A combination of Levenshtein distance (Levenshtein, 1966), and semantic similarity is used to compute this similarity.

Levenshtein distance is a commonly used distance metric between two strings given by counting the minimum number of operations required to transform one string into the other. It is a commonly used metric for spelling error correction.

Semantic similarity is calculated from word embeddings by taking their cosine similarity. In case the word is out of vocabulary, ie there is no word embedding present for the word, simply the Levenshtein distance is used.

The mapping process is made configurable by a database administrator in case of special cases where Levenshtein distance and semantic similarities are not applicable, or in case the database administrator wishes to manually override any similarity based mapping. The manual configuration option is provided only for systems intended to run in production environments, and no manual configuration has been done to generate the results in this paper.

There are also cases where an explicit column term is not specified and simply a value is given in the query. The running example query *total sales by year in Southeast Asia after 2001*, does not specify year specifically, it simply mentions *after 2001*. This is known as ellipsis. To handle such cases, the mapper maintains a reverse index of all value tokens mapped to the column they belong to. Search query tokens that are not mapped to any candidate column or relation are checked against this reverse index to see if they can be mapped to a column.

In addition to tokens that map to values, certain tokens may also correspond to aggregate functions. This search is performed on the previously generated config schema with common terms for such functions being generated automatically. The config schema is also manually configurable and allows adding of custom terms for aggregate functions.

Taking the example of the intermediate representation in Figure 3, the constraint with the term *Southeast Asia* gets mapped to only the *SalesTerritory* relation, since no other table contains *Southeast Asia* as either a value token or a relation or column token. For the constraints with *by year* and *after 2001*, a number of candidate columns and relations are generated, since date objects are common in a lot of relations.

Once the list of possible columns and relations has been generated, a subset of the relations is taken such that -

1. Each token has a candidate mapped column or relation that belongs to the chosen subset of relations.

2. Schema constraints imposed by foreign keys

are satisfied. This involves creating a graph of the relations in the database by making use of foreign key information.

3. The sum of the size of the subset of relations and the number of joins required between the relations multiplied by the average token dissimilarity score is minimized. The dissimilarity score is simply calculated by subtracting the similarity score from 1.

For the given intermediate representation, the *SalesTerritory* and *SalesOrderHeader* relations are chosen, with *total sales* mapped to *SUM(salesorderheader.TotalDue)*, *by year* to *GROUP BY YEAR(salesorderheader.OrderDate)*, *in Southeast Asia* to *WHERE salesterritory.name = Southeast Asia*, and *after 2001* to *WHERE YEAR(salesorderheader.OrderDate) = 2001*.

Mapping of the condition term in constraints and the modifier term in entities is again done with the use of the config schema. Generation of the config schema makes use of semantic similarity computed using word embeddings, as well as WordNet synsets, after it has been manually seeded with initial values.

3 Experiments and Evaluation

Evaluation of the performance of our system has been done on a sample online transaction processing (OLTP) database called AdventureWorksDB, which is modeled very much along the lines of an Enterprise Resource Planning (ERP) solution.

AdventureWorksDB is an open database released as part of Microsoft's SQL Server and it has also been ported to MySQL [4]. It contains data about a fictitious bicycle manufacturing company called Adventure Works Cycles. There are five different scenarios covered in this database:

1. **Sales & Marketing Scenario** - It covers the customers and sales related information of Adventure Works Cycles. Typical queries include *show me all the individual customers who purchased goods worth greater than 100 dollars in the last year*

2. **Product Scenario** - It contains tables related to the product information like the cost of production, product description and product models, that is represented in the database.

A typical query would be — *Which was the most expensive product manufactured in Southeast Asia*

3. **Human Resources Scenario** - It contains employee-related information such as the salary, joining date and manager details. Typical query — *Which employee had the highest salary in 2001?*

We create a manual dataset of 100 Natural Language queries each for three domains in the AdventureWorks DB - Sales, Product and Human Resources. The different domains have been picked to evaluate if the system is domain independent enough to handle queries for different scenarios without manual configuration.

The performance of the system is evaluated by running each of the natural language queries in the dataset through the parsing and mapping system. In case the system successfully generates a query, the resulting query is executed on the database, and the results of the query are compared to the gold standard.

The evaluation metrics are computed as described in (Minock et al., 2008). The precision is defined as the percentage of successfully generated SQL queries that result in the correct output, and the recall is defined as the percentage of natural language queries that successfully generate an SQL query.

$$precision = \frac{\# \ of \ correct \ queries}{\# \ of \ sql \ queries \ generated}$$

$$recall = \frac{\# \ of \ sql \ queries \ generated}{\# \ of \ natural \ language \ queries}$$

$$f1\text{-}score = \frac{2 \cdot precision \cdot recall}{precision + recall}$$

4 Results

Figure 4 depicts the results of the query translation by Surukam-NLI across all the three domains we have considered in this paper and we observe similar performance throughout. The relatively small variations in precision and recall can easily result from randomness due to small sample sizes.

---

[4]https://sourceforge.net/projects/awmysql/

Domain	Query	SQL Generated	SQL Correct
Sales	Who had the highest sales in 2003?	Yes	Yes
	Which country had the highest sales in 2000?	Yes	Yes
	What are the total sales by region in the last five years?	Yes	Yes
	Who were the top 5 salesmen of 2001 by total sales?	Yes	Yes
	List top 10 orders by item price in Southwest.	Yes	No
Human Resources	Average employee salary by year over the past 10 years?	Yes	Yes
	What is the average salary by department?	Yes	Yes
	How many employees are over the age of 30?	No	-
	How many employees does the sales department have?	Yes	Yes
	What were the average vacation hours in 2002?	Yes	Yes
Product	What were the top rated 5 products in 2001?	Yes	Yes
	How many transactions took place in 2001?	Yes	Yes
	What is the average cost of products in x category?	Yes	No
	List the number of transactions by country in last 10 years?	Yes	Yes
	Number of purchases of amount 200 in the last month	No	-

Table 1: Results on sample queries

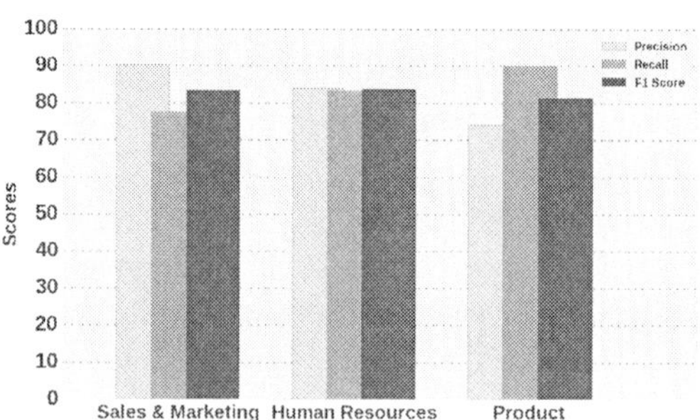

Figure 4: Histogram of Precision / Recall / F - measure for each domain.

Listed in Table 1 are a sample of the queries from each domain, whether they were successfully mapped to an SQL statement, and if the results of executing the query match the gold standard.

Delving deeper into a sample of queries for each domain, we can find some patterns in the queries that fail either in the mapping phase or in the execution phase.

1. Some complex operations require a deeper understanding of the query and the db schema. Example -

    (a) *Employees over the age of 30* - This requires the system to understand that the age of the employee can be calculated from subtracting the *BirthDate* from the current date.

2. Ambiguity in a query token leading to incorrect mapping. Example -

    (a) *What is the average cost of products of 'x' category?* - The *Products* table contains *ListPrice* and *StandardCost*, and the user intends to query on the basis of *ListPrice*, whereas *StandardCost* is the column chosen by our similarity matching algorithm

3. Ambiguity in the language of the query. Example -

    (a) *Top salesmen in 2001* - *Top* usually maps to an ORDER BY clause on a column directly mapped to the term right after top, however here in the context, *top* can refer to either amount of sales or number of sales. Without additional information, the system has no way of resolving such ambiguity.

    (b) *List top 10 orders by item price* - *by* in this context should map to an ORDER BY clause rather than a GROUP BY clause. This requires a deeper understanding of the query beyond the syntactic parsing.

4. Very similar database columns corresponding to query token. Example -

    (a) *How many sales have occurred in the last month?* - Here *last month* is meant to be compared against *OrderDate*. The similarity matcher is confused by the presence of *DueDate* and *ShipDate* and is unable to resolve the ambiguity correctly.

5. Sensitivity of the parser to grammar and spelling. Example -

   (a) *How many purchases of amount 200 took place in the last month?* - The incorrect grammar of the sentence causes the dependency parser to generate an incorrect parse tree, as a result of which the mapper is unable to generate a query

6. Sensitivity of Named Entity Recognition to case information. Example -

   (a) *Sales last year in the region southeast asia* - both the dependency parser and the NER system fail to recognize *southeast asia* as a proper noun or Named Entity, and hence the term is not included in the constraints.

5 Conclusions and Future Work

In this paper, we have described a novel natural language interface to real world databases built using syntactic parse trees for query parsing and a similarity model composed of word-embeddings, WordNet and database schema rules for mapping the tokens to SQL.

By choosing a real-world database like AdventureWorks which has 67 tables spanning across 5 scenarios, our evaluation is much closer to industry requirements than a simple geological fact database like GeoBase that has 8 tables in all.

Since many NLIs like C-Phrase, Elf, and the Spanish NLI described in (Pérez, 2016) have bench-marked their performance against Atis2 (Garofolo et al., 1993), Geobase and Geo-Query250 [5] , we would like to evaluate our results against these datasets in future.

We have also shown that we were able to handle queries about three different domains without manual configuration changes, because we leveraged a very generic word embedding model that was trained on the Google News corpus, and a WordNet thesaurus to resolve the tables of a given domain. In future, we would also be enriching the

auto-configuration phase by using word embedding enriched SynSets (Rothe and Schütze, 2015).

We are improving our system by adding support for complex SQL queries like nested queries and we also plan to make it a dialog system that is able to handle state and context. A typical conversation that we would like to handle in the future is :

Q: *Who were the top 10 salesmen of 2002?*

A: This query lists the top 10 salesmen with the highest sales.

Q: *Sort them by their department*

A: This query resolves the coreference *their* to the *top 10 salesmen* and them by their respective departments. This information would be fetched by creating an SQL JOIN operation on the *employee* table.

References

Ana-Maria Popescu, Oren Etzioni, and Henry Kautz. *Towards a theory of natural language interfaces to databases.* Proceedings of the 8th international conference on Intelligent user interfaces. ACM, 2003.

Barbara J. Grosz, Douglas E. Appelt, Paul A. Martin, and Fernando CN Pereira. *TEAM: an experiment in the design of transportable natural-language interfaces.* Artificial Intelligence 32, no. 2 (1987): 173-243.

Beatrice Santorini *Part-of-speech tagging guidelines for the Penn Treebank Project (3rd revision).* 1990

Chris D Paice *Another stemmer.* SIGIR Forum, 24(3), 56-61, 1990.

Edgar F Codd *A relational model of data for large shared data banks.* Communications of the ACM 13.6 (1970): 377-387.

Elf *Natural-language database interfaces from elf software co.* http://www.elfsoft.com. Accessed 25 Aug 2016

E. V. Smith, K. Crockett, A. Latham, and F. Buckingham. *SEEKER: A Conversational Agent as a Natural Language Interface to a relational Database.* Proceedings of the World Congress on Engineering 2014 Vol I, WCE 2014, July 2 - 4, 2014, London, U.K.

Fei Li, and H. V. Jagadish *Constructing an interactive natural language interface for relational databases.* Proceedings of the VLDB Endowment 8.1 (2014): 73-84.

---

[5]http://www.cs.utexas.edu/users/ml/nldata/geoquery.html

George A. Miller, Richard Beckwith, Christiane Fellbaum, Derek Gross, and Katherine J. Miller. *Introduction to WordNet: An on-line lexical database.* International journal of lexicography 3, no. 4 (1990): 235-244.

Ion Androutsopoulos, Graeme D. Ritchie, and Peter Thanisch. *Natural language interfaces to databasesan introduction.* Natural language engineering 1.01 (1995): 29-81.

Jenny Rose Finkel, Trond Grenager, and Christopher Manning. *Incorporating Non-local Information into Information Extraction Systems by Gibbs Sampling.* Proceedings of the 43nd Annual Meeting of the Association for Computational Linguistics (ACL 2005), pp. 363-370.

Joaquín Pérez *Comparative study on the customization of natural language interfaces to databases.* SpringerPlus 5.1 (2016): 1

John Garofolo et al. *ATIS2 LDC93S5.* Web Download. Philadelphia: Linguistic Data Consortium, 1993.

Madeleine Bates *Rapid porting of the parlance natural language interface.* Proceedings of the workshop on Speech and Natural Language. Association for Computational Linguistics, 1989.

Martin F. Porter *An algorithm for suffix stripping.* Program 14.3 (1980): 130-137.

Martin F. Porter *Snowball: A language for stemming algorithms.* 2001

Michael Minock *C-Phrase: A system for building robust natural language interfaces to databases.* Data & Knowledge Engineering 69, no. 3 (2010): 290-302.

Michael Minock, Peter Olofsson, and Alexander Nslund. *Towards building robust natural language interfaces to databases.* In International Conference on Application of Natural Language to Information Systems, pp. 187-198. Springer Berlin Heidelberg, 2008

Sascha Rothe, and Hinrich Schütze. *Autoextend: Extending word embeddings to embeddings for synsets and lexemes* Proceedings of the 53rd Annual Meeting of the Association for Computational Linguistics and the 7th International Joint Conference on Natural Language Processing, pages 17931803, Beijing, China, July 26-31, 2015.

Tomas Mikolov, Kai Chen, Greg Corrado, and Jeffrey Dean. *Efficient estimation of word representations in vector space.* arXiv preprint arXiv:1301.3781 (2013).

Tomas Mikolov and Jeffrey Dean. *Distributed representations of words and phrases and their compositionality.* Advances in neural information processing systems (2013).

Tomas Mikolov, Wen-tau Yih, and Geoffrey Zweig. *Linguistic Regularities in Continuous Space Word Representations.* In Proceedings of NAACL HLT, 2013a.

Vladimir I. Levenshtein *Binary codes capable of correcting deletions, insertions and reversals.* In Soviet physics doklady, vol. 10, p. 707. 1966.

W. Woods, R. Webber Kaplan. B. *The Lunar Sciences Natural Language Information System.* Final Report, Bolt Beranek and Newman Inc., Cambridge, Massachusetts. No. 2378. BBN Report, 1972.

Experimental Study of Vowels in Nagamese, Ao and Lotha: Languages of Nagaland

**Joyanta Basu, Tulika Basu, Soma Khan,
Madhab Pal, Rajib Roy**

Centre for Development of Advanced Computing
(CDAC), Kolkata
Salt Lake, Sector – V, Kolkata, India
{joyanat.basu,tulika.basu, soma.khan,
madhab.pal, rajib.roy}@cdac.in

Tapan Kumar Basu

Department of Electrical Engineering,
Academy of Technology
Aedconagar, Hooghly, West Bengal, India
basutk06@rediffmail.com

Abstract

This paper describes the vowels characteristics of three languages of Nagaland namely Nagamese, Ao and Lotha. For this study, nucleus vowel duration, formant structure (1st and 2nd formant i.e. F1 and F2) and intensity of vowels are investigated and analyzed for these languages. This paper includes the nasal context for different vowels and tries to examine its importance in different languages. A detailed analysis is carried out for six vowels namely /i/, /e/, /a/, /ə/, /o/, /u/ for readout speech of Nagamese, Ao and Lotha. Result shows that the vowel duration and formants play important roles in differentiating vowels characteristics. On the other hand, intensity of vowels do not play significant role in the characteristics of the vowels across the languages is observed. This initial study unveil the importance of vowels characteristics and may help to do research and development in the area of language identification, synthesis, speech recognition of three north-eastern languages of Nagaland.

1 Introduction

Culture and language diversity is one of the interesting phenomena in North-Eastern states of India. The seven states (i.e. Arunachal Pradesh, Assam, Meghalaya, Manipur, Nagaland, Mizoram and Tripura) except Sikkim of north-east India cover an area of 255,511 square kilometers (98,653 sq mi) i.e. about seven percent of India's total area. As of 2011 they had a population of 44.98 million, about 3.7 percent of India's total population. Although there is great ethnic and religious diversity within the seven states, they bear similarities in the political, social and economic spheres (Wikipedia, 2015). According to the 1971 census there are about 220 languages spoken in these states, belonging mainly to three language families, namely Indo Aryan, Sino-Tibetan and Austro-Asiatic. The Indo-Aryan is represented mainly by Asamiya and Bangla, Austro-Asiatic is represented mainly by Khasi and the Sino-Tibetan family of languages is represented by Tani group of languages (Apatani, Galo, Nyishi etc.), Angami, Chakesang, Kuki, Manipuri, Mizo, Kokborak etc.

The entire North-east India is enclosed by major international borders of Bhutan, Nepal and China in the North and North-East, Bangladesh in South and West and Myanmar in East. This region is therefore very sensitive from the point of view of national security and national integrity.

Among the eight states of north-east India, the states that share far east international borders with Myanmar i.e. Manipur and Nagaland are getting much importance now-a-days due to unrest social and political situations. Since the last decade, spread of recent communication mediums like mobiles, telephones and VoIP are supporting spoken communication in regional north-east languages. Speech data in these communications has become

D S Sharma, R Sangal and A K Singh. Proc. of the 13th Intl. Conference on Natural Language Processing, pages 315–323,
Varanasi, India. December 2016. ©2016 NLP Association of India (NLPAI)

necessary for surveillance purposes. But detailed analysis on any speech data depends largely on pre-defined knowledge on the spoken language and availability of language resources. Unfortunately very little prior works have been done on the languages of Nagaland and Manipur.

In this study, we are mainly concentrating on major languages of the Nagaland state. These are Nagamese, Ao and Lotha. Apart from the basic language grammar, phonetic reader and dictionary very few linguistic resources are available for study and research purposes. Among the previous resources of Ao language, an important and detail study has been reported on the phonetic and phonological description of the Mongsen dialect of Ao (Alexander R. Coupe, 2003). The study is well supported by experimental findings as well as author's personal insights on the studied language. Lotha language is very rarely studied till date. Different aspects of Lotha language has been documented in (Chiang Chen Shan, 2011) which is the only available study on this language. Nagamese, the communication language (lingua franca) of Nagaland is quite well studied since 1921 by J.H. Hutton. The first ever linguistic study of Nagamese has been reported by M. V. Sreedhar (1974) in "Naga Pidgin: A Sociolinguistic Study of Interlingual Communication Pattern in Nagaland". This was followed by "Standardized Grammar of Naga Pidgin" by Sreedhar himself in 1985. B K Boruah's "Nagamiz Kothalaga Niyom - A Primary Grammar on Nagamese" (1985) and "Nagamese: The Language of Nagaland" (1993) are also some relevant studies to understand the basic structure and nature of Nagamese language. The last reported study on Nagamese language is "The structure of Nagamese the contact language of Nagaland" (2003) by Ajii Kumar Baishya of Assam University.

However, the three languages Ao, Lotha and Nagamese were never studied together to frame out similarities or differences in phoneme characteristics. Moreover except Ao language, unfortunately very little work on acoustic analysis has been done so far in two other languages.

2 Purpose of the Study

Main purpose of the study is to find out vowels characteristics of the major languages of Nagaland i.e. Nagamese, Ao and Lotha. Vowels possess one of the defining structures of any language in the world. Their numbers, acoustic characteristics, particularly timbral ones need to be well defined for technology development (Tulika Basu and Arup Saha, 2011). For this work we have considered three important parameters of vowels like Formants, Nucleus Vowel Duration and Intensity. Nucleus vowel is defined as the steady state of the vowel along with the two transitions (Rajib Roy, Tulika Basu, Arup Saha, Joyanta Basu, Shyamal Kr Das Mandal, 2008) as in figure 1.

One way to objectively differentiate vowels is to examine the first two formant frequencies, namely 1st formant (F1) and 2nd formant (F2), which roughly correlate with tongue height and tongue position respectively (G. E. Peterson and H. L. Barney. 1952). In general high first formant is associated with narrow tongue constriction near the glottis. Similarly second formant frequency is increased as the constriction moves forward (K. N. Stevens and A. S. House. 1961). Using F1 and F2 it is possible to properly place them in a vowel diagram.

This study will help further for different applications like speech synthesis, language identification, speech recognition etc. in the target languages.

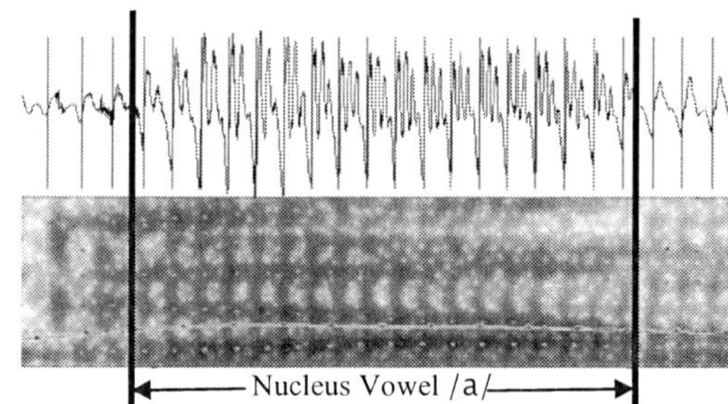

Figure 1. Nucleus Vowel Duration

3 Languages of Nagaland

Nagaland is a state in Northeast India. It borders the state of Assam to the west, Arunachal Pradesh and part of Assam to the north, Myanmar to the east and Manipur to the south. The state capital is Kohima, and the largest city is Dimapur. It has an area of 16,579 square kilometres (6,401 sq mi) with a population of 1,980,602 as per the 2011 Census of India. Nagaland is the home to 16 indigenous tribes namely Ao, Angami, Chang, Konyak, Lotha, Sumi, Chakhesang, Khiamniungan, Dimasa Kachari, Phom, Rengma, Sangtam,

Yimchunger,Kuki, Zeme-Liangmai (Zeliang) and Pochury as well as a number of sub-tribes. Each tribe is unique in character with its own distinct customs, language and dress. Nagaland is one of three states in India where most of the population is Christian (Wikipedia Nagaland).

As per Grierson's classification system, Naga languages can be grouped into three groups-Western, Central and Eastern Naga Groups. The Western Group includes Angami, Chokri and Kheza. The Central Naga group consists of Ao, Lotha and Sangtam, whereas Eastern Group comprises of Konyak and Chang. In addition, there are Naga-Bodo group illustrated by Mikir language, and Kuki group of languages illustrated by Sopvama (also called Mao Naga) and Luppa languages. These languages belong mostly to the Sino-Tibetan language family. Since most of these languages are mutually unintelligible, people depend on a pidgin language called Nagamese for communication. English has been used as the official language of the Nagaland state and it is quite popular among the educated mass of Nagaland. But Nagamese is used as the lingua franca among the various ethnic groups in the state. The languages of Nagaland state are not included in the scheduled list of twenty two languages in India, many of them spoken by dwindling number of speakers. This section presents a brief profile of major languages of the state. Figure 2 shows the languages map of Nagaland in different districts. Though, other dialects also exist in those districts, but from majority perspective they are not shown in the map.

Figure 2. Languages of Nagaland in different districts

For this study we have selected three important languages of Nagaland i.e. Nagamese, Ao and Lotha.

3.1 About Ao Language

Ao is one of the important languages in Nagaland. Ao is spoken by a large number of people in the state. Mongsen, Chungli, Chanki etc. are prominent among the Ao dialects. Among all the dialects, Chungli is the widely spoken one and people of other Ao dialects can speak Chungli Ao but not vice versa. The inhabitants of the Mokokchung district mainly converse in this language. The vowel inventory of Chungli Ao is like this: /i/, /e/, /ɨ/, /a/, /ə/, /u/ (Bruhn Daniel, 2009). Nasality is not phonemic in Ao. It is a tonal language with 3 contrasting lexical tones: high, mid and low. All are register tones.

3.2 About Lotha Language

The Lotha language is part of the Sino-Tibetan language family, spoken by approximately 166,000 people in Wokha district, west-central Nagaland, India. It is centered in the small district of Wokha. This district has more than 114 villages such as Pangti, Maraju (Merapani), Englan, Baghty (Pakti) and others, where the language is widely spoken and studied. It is a medium of education up to the post-graduate level in the state of Nagaland. It is also the language in which the church sermons are preached. Lotha has seven dialects. They are Live, Tsontsu, Ndreng, Kyong, Kyo, Kyon and Kyou (Chiang Chen Shan. 2011). Lotha language has six vowels namely /i/, /e/, /a/, /ə/, /o/, /u/. Nasality is not phonemic in Lotha. Like other Tibeto-Burman languages it is a tonal language with three register tones (Low, Mid, and High).

Sl. No.	Nagamese Vowels	Ao Vowels	Lotha Vowels
1	/i/	/i/	/i/
2	/e/	/e/	/e/
3	/a:/	/a/	/a/
4	/ə/	/ə/	/ə/
5	/o/	NA	/o/
6	/u/	/u/	/u/
7	NA	/ɨ/	NA

Table 1. List of Vowels of Nagamese, Ao and Lotha

Above Table 1 shows the list of vowels in three languages.

4 Experimental Data Set

The present study aims at finding out acoustic characteristics of vowels of different languages of Nagaland from readout text for different applications of speech processing in respective languages. For this purpose, text material in each of the three languages has been prepared including digits, numbers, units and paragraphs on different topics. The text material contains around 120 words and 60 sentences of different length. The text is read out by 15 native speakers from Nagaland in the age group between 20 to 40 years with 2 repetitions. All speakers are male speakers and English as their medium of primary education. Table 2 shows the detail Meta data of informants participated in this study.

Sl. No	Informant	Native-Language	Edu-Qualification	Age (in yr)
1	Speaker 1	Nagamese	Secondary	30
2	Speaker 2	Nagamese	Secondary	24
3	Speaker 3	Nagamese	Secondary	35
4	Speaker 4	Nagamese	Secondary	32
5	Speaker 5	Nagamese	Secondary	31
6	Speaker 6	Ao	Secondary	32
7	Speaker 7	Ao	Secondary	30
8	Speaker 8	Ao	Secondary	32
9	Speaker 9	Ao	Secondary	30
10	Speaker 10	Ao	Higher-Secondary	35
11	Speaker 11	Lotha	Secondary	34
12	Speaker 12	Lotha	Higher-Secondary	32
13	Speaker 13	Lotha	Graduate	26
14	Speaker 14	Lotha	Primary	37
15	Speaker 15	Lotha	Secondary	33

Table 2. Speakers' Meta data Information

5 Experimental Procedure

Steps for experimental procedure are as follows:

5.1 Data Collection

For the experiment purpose, speech data has been collected from native speakers of Nagamese, Ao and Lotha. To avoid disfluencies in reading, informants are instructed to read out the text material several times before final recording. Near about 3 hrs of speech data has been collected using Praat (Praat Website, 2016) software. Speech data is being recorded in a less noisy studio environment with 16 bit 22050 Hz digitization format.

5.2 Data Transcription:

Above collected speech data has been transcribed into phone level using Praat tool. It is worth mentioning here that tone is not considered in the present study. For the present study, only Vowel (V) phonemes (like /u/, /o/, /ə/, /a/, /e/, /i/) have been marked by the transcribers. For simplification and ease of understanding, following symbols are used by transcribers during transcription. Those are '*u*', '*o*', '*ac*', '*a*', '*e*', '*i*' respectively. Transcribers are also instructed to mark the nasal contexts (N) of vowel occurrences. If a vowel is preceded by nasal consonants like /m/, /n/, /ŋ/ etc. then it is marked as N_V and if vowel is followed by nasal consonants then it is marked as (V_N). Then all phone level transcription files are saved as .TextGrid file format. Figure 3 shows the sample transcribed speech data using Praat tool. From the figure three panes can be observed. First one shows the time domain signal, second one shows the spectrographic view of time domain signal and final tier shows the phone level (only vowels) transcription boundary marked manually by transcribers. Transcribers need to zoom in and zoom out the signal and play it repeatedly to perceptually identify the vowels.

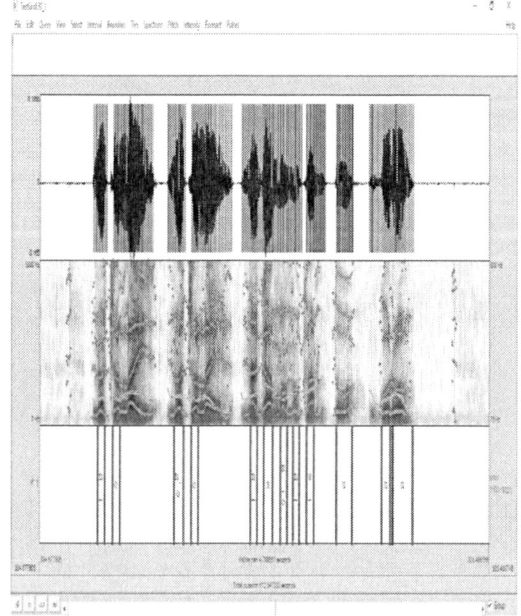

Figure 3. Transcription using Praat Tool

5.3 Extraction of duration, formants and intensity of vowels

Nucleus vowel duration, 1st formant (F1), 2nd formant (F2) and intensity are calculated using Praat scripts for further analysis. All vowels are segmented automatically using transcription output file i.e. from TextGrid file. These segmented files are required to test the perceptual appropriateness of different vowels by listeners.

6 Result and Discussion

Table 3 presents the number of vowel segments collected for analysis after transcriptions have been done. It has been observed that within our experiment data, occurrence of vowel /a/ is highest in Nagamese. Similarly vowel /u/ in Ao and vowel /o/ in Lotha language has the highest occurrence.

Sl. No.	Vowels	Nagamese	Ao	Lotha
1	/u/	448	694	405
2	/o/	569	NA	782
3	/ə/	578	670	605
4	/a/	809	527	525
5	/e/	576	579	576
6	/i/	735	547	623

Table 3. Vowel count in three languages under analysis

6.1 Analysis of Nucleus Vowel Duration

For present study on vowel duration, six vowels are considered including all vowel phonemes of Nagamese, Ao and Lotha languages. Those vowels (V) are /u/, /o/, /Ə/, /a/, /e/, /i/ i.e. *'u', 'o', 'ac', 'a', 'e'* and *'i'* respectively. Using Praat scripts, nucleus vowel durations are extracted from transcription files. Vowels in Nasal context V_N and N_V are also analyzed in this study.

6.1.1 Vowel duration in Nagamese

Figure 4 shows the mean and +/- standard deviation of duration for each vowel in Nagamese including all contexts. It has been observed that nucleus vowel duration of Nagamese vowel /e/ i.e. *'e'* is higher than other vowels and on the other hand duration of vowel /ə/ i.e. *'ac'* is lesser than the others.

In Figure 5, nucleus vowel durations in preceding and succeeding nasal contexts are shown separately. It has been found that duration of vowels followed by nasal consonants i.e. V_N is always lesser than that of N_V and V. In all cases, duration of /ə/ i.e. *'ac'* is less irrespective of nasal context. Duration of /e/ i.e. *'e'* is highest in V and N_V cases. But duration of vowel /e/ i.e. *'e'* is smaller than duration of /a/ i.e. *'a'* in V_N.

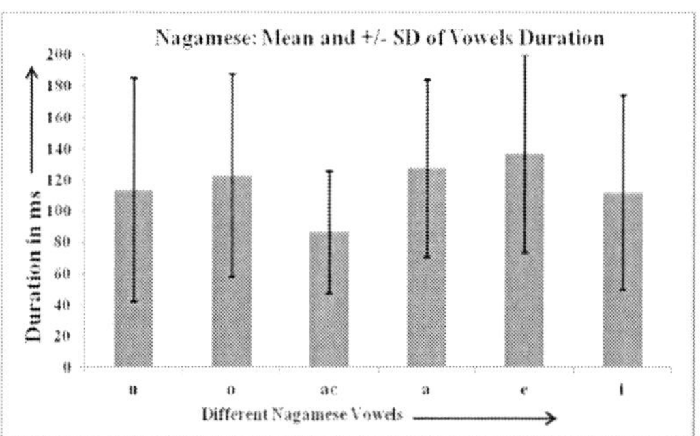

Figure 4. Nucleus vowel duration of Nagamese

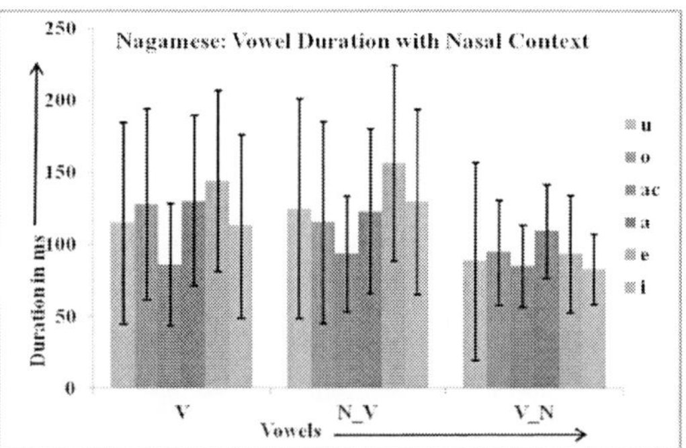

Figure 5. Nucleus Vowel Duration of Nagamese with nasal context

6.1.2 Vowel duration in Ao

Vowel inventory of Ao consists of /i/, /e/, /ɨ/, /a/, /ə/, /u/. But the speech data which have used in this study does not contain any /ɨ/ vowel. It is also interesting to note that though /o/ vowel is not included in the vowel inventory of Ao (be it in Chungli or Mongsen), in course of transcription /o/ vowel is found corresponding the grapheme 'u' like in words "tuko" which is pronounced sometimes as /tuko/ and sometimes as /toko/ by the native speakers of Chungli AO. This phenomenon is further supported by the previous study on AO language where it has been mentioned that vowel /u/ and /o/ are in free variation in AO language (Alexander R. Coupe, 2003).

From figure 6 it has been observed that nucleus vowel duration of Ao vowel /a/ i.e. '*a*' is higher than other vowels and on the other hand duration of vowel /ə/ i.e. '*ac*' is smaller than others.

Vowel duration of Ao with nasal context has been shown in figure 7. All vowels followed by nasal consonants i.e. V_N are lesser in duration than that of N_V and V.

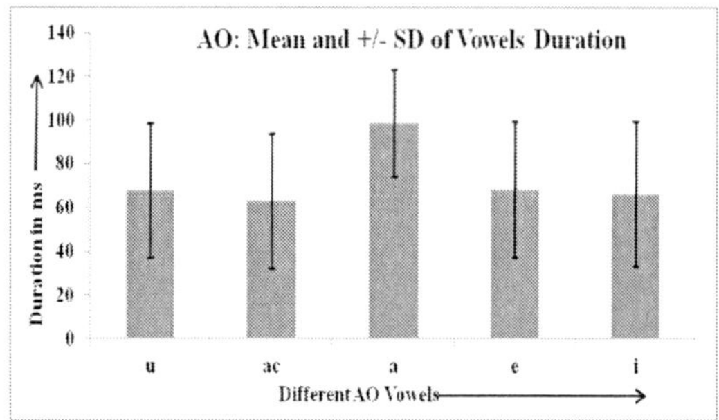

Figure 6. Nucleus Vowels Duration of Ao

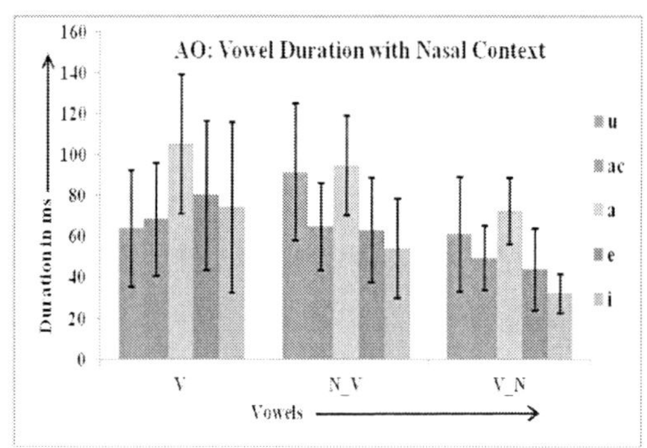

Figure 7. Nucleus Vowel Duration of Ao with nasal context

6.1.3 Vowel duration in Lotha

From figure 8 it has been observed that nucleus vowel duration of Lotha vowel /a/ i.e. '*a*' is higher than other vowels like Ao language and on the other hand duration of vowel /ə/ i.e. '*ac*' is smaller than others like Nagamese language.

From figure 9, it has been found that duration of vowel followed by nasal consonants i.e. V_N are smaller than duration of N_V and V except /e/ i.e. '*e*'. And in all the cases duration of /u/ i.e. '*u*' is smaller irrespective of nasal context.

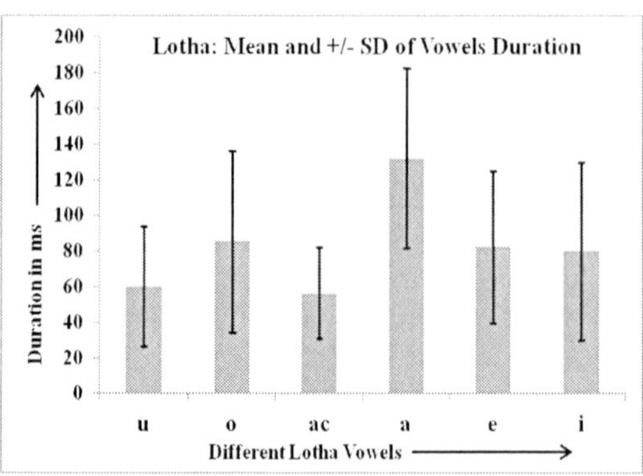

Figure 8. Nucleus Vowels Duration of Lotha

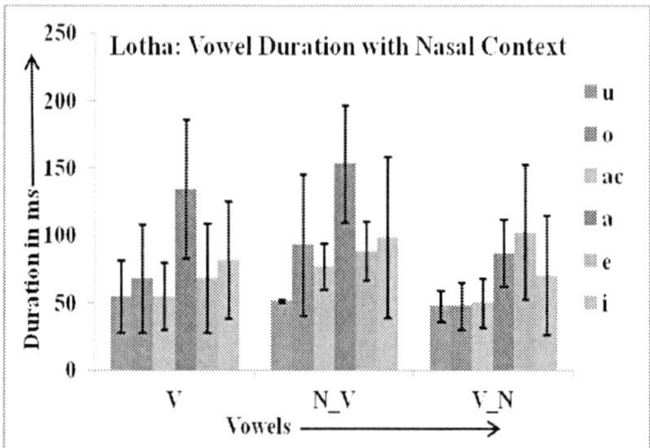

Figure 9. Nucleus Vowel Duration of Lotha with nasal context

6.2 Analysis of Vowel Formants

Formant analysis of the vowels in the three languages has been done including all contexts of their occurrence.

6.2.1 Vowel Formants in Nagamese

Figure 10 shows the F1 vs. F2 plot for Nagamese vowels. Six vowels have been observed and they are clustered in different zones. Zones of vowels /ə/ and /a/ are overlapped. But value of F1 for vowel /a/ is higher than the F1 value of /ə/. Some portion of /u/ and /o/ are also overlapped. But from then diagram it has been clearly identified the vowels like /i/ from /u/ or /e/ from /ə/ etc.

320

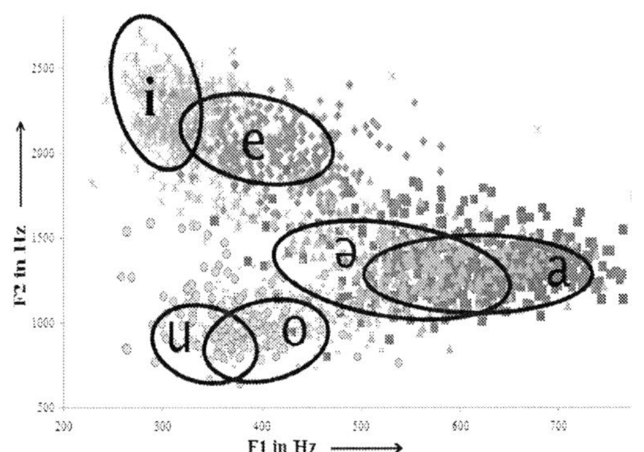

Figure 10. F1 vs. F2 of Nagamese vowels

6.2.2   Vowel Formants in Ao

Figure 11 shows the general F1 vs. F2 plot of different vowels in Ao language. It has been observed that there is a great amount of overlap in both the formant frequencies of vowel /u/ and /o/. So in this study these two vowels are merged together and analyzed as a single vowel /u/.

From the F1 vs. F2 plot it has been clearly identified the vowels like /i/, /ə/, /a/ and /u/. Values of /e/ and /ə/ are overlapped to some extent.

6.2.3   Vowel Formants in Lotha

Figure 12 shows the F1 vs. F2 plot of different vowels in Lotha language. In Lotha, six vowels have formed well separable clusters and thus they can be identified by F1 and F2 values. Only some cases it creates confusion for identifying the vowels /e/ and /ə/. In Lotha /u/ and /o/ vowels can be clearly identified by their values.

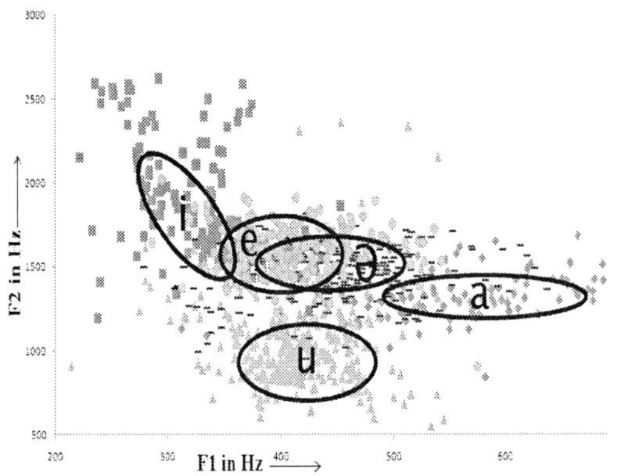

Figure 11. F1 vs. F2 of Ao vowels

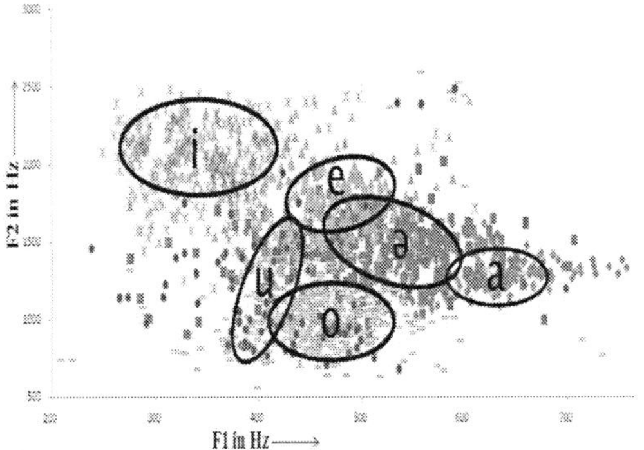

Figure 12. F1 vs F2 of Lotha vowels

Figure 13 shows overall comparison of F1 vs. F2 values of different vowels in Nagamese, Ao and Lotha languages. In the three languages (Nagamese, Ao and Lotha) F2 values have varied significantly for vowels /i/ and /e/ and mean F2 value of Nagamese is higher than that of Ao and Lotha.

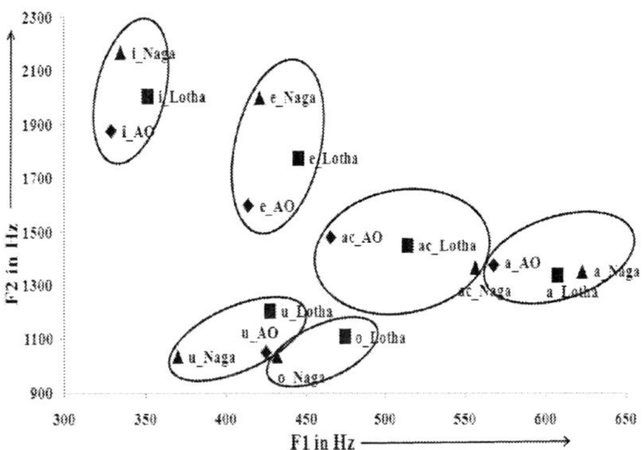

Figure 13. Comparison of F1 vs. F2 for Nagamese, Ao and Lotha vowels

On the other hand, F1 values have varied significantly for vowels '*ac*' and '*a*'. From this F1 vs. F2 comparison figure, all major vowels can be clearly identified by respective F1 and F2 values.

Changes in vowel formant characteristics for nasal context are also studied. Figure 14 and Figure 15 is showing the occurrence frequency distribution of F1 and F2 values respectively for different vowels in Nagamese. It has been observed from figure 14 that, there is no significant change of vowel 1st formant F1 with V_N and N_V context. But some changes of vowel 2nd formant F2 can be observed in figure 15 for V_N and N_V context. F2 values for vowels /ə/, /e/ and /i/ are showing different frequency distribution with two or three major peaks. After careful observations from data it has been found that these peaks are coming due to nasal contexts of vowels. Frequency distribution of F1 and F2 for the other two languages Ao and Lotha has also been calculated and similar pattern has been found in those cases. No effect of nasal context on F1 has been observed for Ao and Lotha also. But F2 plays important role in nasal context. F2 of Ao vowels /u/ and /i/ is found to be affected for nasal context. Similarly F2 of /e/ is affected in Lotha.

6.3 Analysis of Vowel Intensity

During this study intensity of different vowels of Nagamese, Ao and Lotha are analyzed. Figure 16 shows the intensity wise graph of different vowels.

It has been observed that there is no significant change in intensity of different vowels of the three languages. Intensity of some Ao vowels like *u, o, ax, ac, a, i* is smaller than that of Nagamese and Lotha.

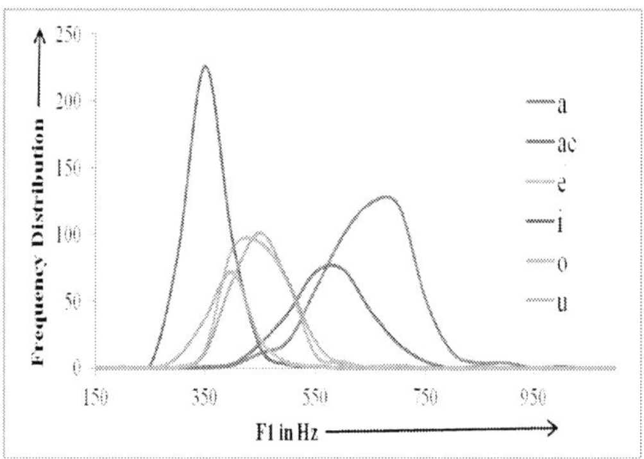

Figure 14. F1 of Nagamese Vowels with Nasal Context

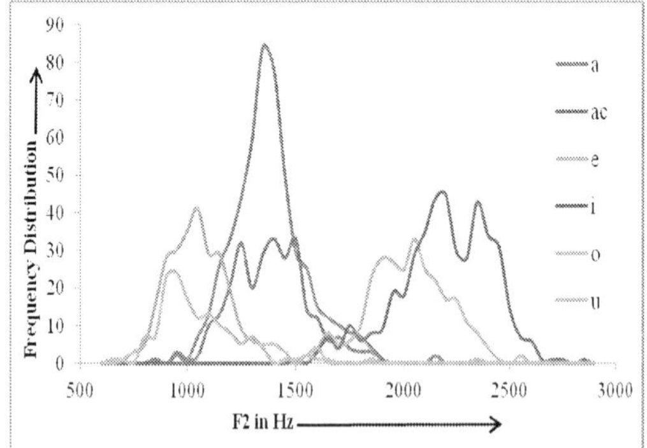

Figure 15. F2 of Nagamese Vowels with Nasal Context

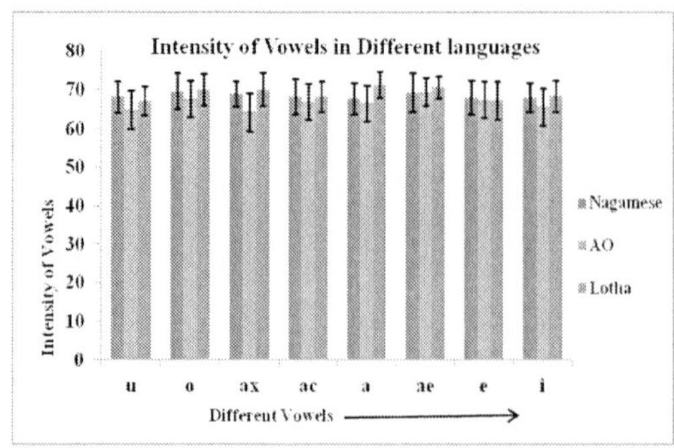

Figure 16. Intensity of Different Vowels of three languages of Nagaland

7 Conclusion

In this paper we have reported characteristics of vowels of three languages of Nagaland namely Nagamese, Ao and Lotha and carried out experimental study to find out language specific features. In this paper nucleus vowel duration, formant (F1 and F2) of vowels and intensity has been observed. The present study tried to find out significant influence on the nucleus vowel in presence of adjacent nasal phoneme i.e. preceding and succeeding nasal phoneme in all three languages.

In conclusion, the following points can be summarized for three languages of Nagaland:

- Nucleus vowel duration of vowel /e/, /a/ and /a/ is higher for Nagamese, Ao and Lotha respectively. The duration of /e/ in Nagamese is highest than the others may be due to the fact that most of the Nagamese verbs end with 'e' vowel and the speakers try to lengthen it to indicate the clause boundary.

- Similarly, duration of vowel /ə/, /u/ and /ə/ is smaller for Nagamese, Ao and Lotha respectively.

- In most of the cases duration of vowels followed by nasal consonants i.e. V_N is lesser than duration of N_V and V.

- In overall comparison of mean F1 vs. F2 all vowels are well separated in Nagamese, AO and Lotha.

- Vowels /u/ and /o/ are in free variation in Ao language because in F1-F2 plane they overlapped. Therefore samples of the two vowels are merged together and analyzed as a single vowel /u/ in Ao language.

322

- In case of nasal context i.e. V_N and N_V no significant influence of F1 has been observed for all three languages. But F2 plays important roles in nasal context. In frequency distribution of F2 of all vowels multiple peaks have been observed due to nasal context.
- No significant changes in intensity for different vowels are observed in all three languages.

However, there is scope of further study on vowels characteristics with respect to other different context like fricative, sibilants, plosives etc. This study may help the researches in the area of language identification, duration modeling for synthesis system as well as speech recognition on languages of Nagaland.

Acknowledgments

This work is a part of ongoing initiatives on "Deployment of Automatic Speaker Recognition System on Conversational Speech Data for North-Eastern states" under CDAC North-East grant. The authors are thankful to CDAC, Kolkata, India for necessary financial and infrastructural support. Authors like to thank user agency for enabling them to collect speech data on different languages under controlled environment at single place from a number of native speakers. They also like to thank Ms. Sushmita Nandi for her efforts in manual verification of recorded speech data and transcriptions.

References

Alexander R. Coupe. 2003. *A Phonetic and Phonological Description of Ao: A Tibeto-Burman Language of Nagaland North-East India* (Pacific Linguistics, 543), Publisher: The Australian National University (2003), ISBN-10: 0858835193, ISBN-13: 978-0858835191

Baishya, Ajit Kumar. 2004. *The structure of Nagamese: The contact language of Nagaland*, Silchar: Assam University (Doctoral dissertation).

Bhim Kanta Boruah. 1993. *Nagamese: the Language of Nagaland*, Mittal Publications, New Delhi, India

Boruah B.K.1993. *Nagamese: The Language of Nagaland*, Mittal Publications, New Delhi.

Bruhn Daniel. 2009. *The Tonal Classification of Chungli AO Verbs*, UC Berkeley Phonology Lab Annual Report

Chiang Chen Shan. 2011. *Language Documentation of Different Aspects of Lotha, a Tibeto-Burman language of Nagaland, north-east India, Division of Linguistics and Multilingual Studies*, Nanyang Technological University

G. E. Peterson and H. L. Barney. 1952. *Control Methods used in Study of Vowels*, Journal of the Acoustical Society of America, vol. 24, no. 2, pp. 175-184

K. N. Stevens and A. S. House. 1961. *An Acoustical theory of vowel production and some of its Implications*, Journal of Speech and Hearing Research, vol.4

Praat Website. 2016. *http://www.fon.hum.uva.nl/praat/*

Rajib Roy, Tulika Basu, Arup Saha, Joyanta Basu, Shyamal Kr Das Mandal. 2008. *Duration Modeling for Bangla Text to Speech Synthesis System*, International Conference on Asian Language Processing 2008, Chiang Mai, Thailand, November 12-14, 2008

Tulika Basu and Arup Saha. 2011. *Qualitative And Quantitative Classification Of Bangla Vowel*, O-COCOSDA 2011

Wikipedia Nagaland. *https://en.wikipedia.org/wiki/Nagaland*

Wikipedia. 2015. *https://en.wikipedia.org/wiki/Seven_Sister_States*

Perception of Phi-Phrase boundaries in Hindi

Somnath Roy
Center for Linguistics
Jawaharlal Nehru University
New Delhi-110067
somnathroy86@gmail.com

Abstract

This paper proposes an algorithm for finding phonological phrase boundaries in sentences with neutral focus spoken in both normal and fast tempos. A perceptual experiment is designed using Praat's experiment MFC program to investigate the phonological phrase boundaries. Phonological phrasing and its relation to syntactic structure in the framework of the end-based rules proposed by (Selkirk, 1986), and relation to purely phonological rules, i.e., the principle of increasing units proposed by (Ghini, 1993) are investigated. In addition to that, this paper explores the acoustic cues signalling phonological phrase boundaries in both normal and fast tempos speech. It is found that phonological phrasing in Hindi follows both end-based rule (Selkirk, 1986) and the principle of increasing units (Ghini, 1993). The end-based rules are used for phonological phrasing and the principle of increasing units is used for phonological phrase restructuring.

1 Introduction

A phonological phrase (ϕ-phrase) is a short breathe group, which speakers sometimes shorten or elongate (Ohala, 1978). The phonological rules which apply across words are covered under the domain of ϕ-phrase. Two important theories of ϕ-phrasing—end-based theory (Selkirk, 1986) and relation-based theory (Nespor and Vogel, 1986) are the base works in this area. (Ghini, 1993) proposed purely phonological rules for ϕ-phrasing while the phrasing rules in (Hayes and Lahiri, 1991) are based on c-command relation.

The idea of Selkirk's end based rule is based on the syntactic constituents. According to which, the right edge of each syntactic XP coincides with the right edge of a ϕ-phrase. A syntactic XP is a phrase where X represents the head of that phrase. In short, end-based rule is written as Align(XP, R, ϕ, R), i.e., the right edge of each XP must be aligned to the right edge of ϕ-phrase (Truckenbrodt, 1995). See the following examples from (Truckenbrodt, 1995)

1.

a. [V NP]$_{VP}\to$ (V NP)ϕ
e.g., (ingile mtana:ni)ϕ /entered the room/
b. [V PP]$_{VP}\to$ (V PP)ϕ
e.g., (mapendo ya maski:ni)ϕ /the love of a poor man/
c.[N AP]$_{NP}\to$ (N AP)ϕ
e.g., (nthi:-khavu) / dry land/
2. [NP V] $\to$ (NP)ϕ (V)ϕ
e.g., (maski:ni ha:tali) /a poor man does not choose/
3. For complex sentence having more than one NP following phrasing pattern is applied.

a. [NP V NP] $\to$ (NP)ϕ (V NP)ϕ
b. [NP NP] $\to$ (NP)ϕ (NP)ϕ
c. [V NP NP] $\to$ (V NP)ϕ (NP)ϕ

(Ghini, 1993) proposed purely phonological rules for ϕ-phrasing in Italian. He preferred binary branching over n-ary branching as proposed in Nespor and Vogel. His claims are based on the following observations.

a. ϕ-phrasing is related to the concept of branching. The branching XPs are never restructured with its preceding branching phrases, because the branching XPs are longer and contain more phonological material than the non-branching XPs.

D S Sharma, R Sangal and A K Singh. Proc. of the 13th Intl. Conference on Natural Language Processing, pages 324–330,
Varanasi, India. December 2016. ©2016 NLP Association of India (NLPAI)

b. The XPs use concept of weight, like a branching XPs are heavy and non-branchings are light. The heavy XPs contain more number of words than the light XPs.

c. The ϕ-phrasing is purely phonological. A string should be parsed into same length ϕs. By increasing and decreasing the tempo the ϕ-phrase is increased and decreased by one word respectively.

d. He has proposed the concept of phrasing based on increasing unit (prosodic word) in a phrase, which is called principle of increasing units. According to this principle, a preceding ϕ-phrase should not have higher weight than the following ϕ-phrase.

The motivation for this work lies in the following two points.

i. Phonological phrasing plays an important role in language comprehension. The information of ϕ-phrase boundaries is requisite in training data for developing a text-to-speech synthesis system with non-robotic voice quality. This work fulfills the requirement of ϕ-phrasing in Hindi text-to-speech synthesis system development.

ii. The role of spectral peaks in phonological phrasing as a predictor variable is investigated for both normal and fast tempo speech.

The rest of the paper is organized as follows. Section 2 describes the experimental details. Section 3 is the description of the algorithm for phonological phrasing in Hindi. Section 4 describes the significant acoustic cues which signal the phonological phrase boundary to the listeners. The conclusion is written in section 5.

2 Experimental Details

This section describes linguistic data collection and speech recording. It also describes the acoustic cues extracted for the analysis.

2.1 Linguistic Data

Fifty spoken sentences were selected for recording. The sentences were a combination of simple and complex declarative. The smallest sentence has four words, the largest sentence has fifteen words. The total count is 447 words in all 50 sentences. Ten speakers 5 males and 5 females were recorded, resulting into a total of 500 sentences. The speakers were either Delhite(born and brought up in Delhi) or one who has been studying in Delhi for the last 10 years. Each speaker is given few minutes to get familiar especially with the long sentences to mitigate hesitation while recording. If hesitation occurs for a sentence; speakers were advised to repeat for that sentence.

The sentences were recorded in two tempos—normal and fast. Both the tempos were used in neutral context only. The normal tempo for this study is the rate at which a speaker normally speaks. The recording was carried out in a noise proof sound recording studio. The speech was recorded at 44.1 kHz sampling rate and stored as 16 bits PCM data. The sentences for recording were selected from news websites covering news ranging from national to international, weather forecast, sports and entertainment. The sentences selected from these news websites were first corrected for Unicode rendering and then used for the recording.

2.2 Perceptual Experiment for ϕ-phrase boundary

A perception based experiment is performed to determine the ϕ-phrasing in Hindi. Ten persons participated in the experiment who are the native speakers of Hindi. Neither they have any formal background in linguistics nor they were taught about the phonological phrasing. The stimuli presented to the informants using the Praat's experiment MFC program. The response options were of four possible types of ϕ-phrases for each sentence. The reason for the limited number of possible response types are the following.

a. There can be many logical options depending upon the complexity of a sentence.

b. The best four plausible response choices are used for each experiment which in turn is decided by the expert.

The phrases were separated by square bracket. The participant were told that the square bracket denotes the short pause; click on the response which suitably shows the short pause in the stimuli. The participants were also asked to choose the confidence measure ranging from 1(for poor)—5(good). "Replay" button can be used for playing the same speech files again and again upto 10 times and "OOPS" button is for listening to the previous sound file. A test experiment having seven files is run first, and participants are asked to choose the suitable option. It is ensured that every participant understood the experiment clearly. At the end of the test experiment, they are asked two questions: 1—"Are you ok with the experiment?" and 2—"Do you have any question to ask?". The actual set of fifty sentences for both tempos are mixed randomly and run to each participant separately. The participants were advised to take a break of 15 minutes after continuously listening for 1 hour. The process completed in two days. The average time taken by informants is 11 hours and 42 minutes in two days. For clarity, see the Figure 1.

All utterances are annotated by all 10 annotators and the average pairwise kappa values are calculated for inter-informant agreement. The kappa values for inter-informant agreement for normal and fast tempo speech lie in the range of 0.7—0.9 and 0.6—0.7 respectively. The response option getting highest agreement is picked up for the analysis in both tempos. It is found that 2 sentences have different phrasing patterns for normal and fast tempos. Therefore, 2×10 (because the same sentence was recorded by all 10 speakers) are dropped and not analyzed in this study. The remaining 480 sentences show same phonological phrasing. The phonological phrasing rules based on the phrasing patterns selected by participants are presented in section 3.

2.3 Acoustic cues Extracted at ϕ-phrase Boundaries

Nine acoustic cues are extracted from the pre-boundary and the postboundary syllable of each ϕ-phrase, for clarity see the Figure 2 & 3.

These acoustic cues include the variants of temporal and spectral cues. These are the minimum pitch at the start of a syllable (InF0Min), max pitch (F0Max), minimum pitch in the end of a syllable (FiF0Min), mean intensity(AvgInt), minimum intensity (MinInt), maximum intensity (MaxInt), three spectral peaks at first, second and third formants (SpecInt1, SpecInt2 and SpecInt3). The acoustic cues pitch, intensity and duration are the most accepted and investigated predictor variables at phrase boundaries (Oller, 1973)(Streeter, 1978). Duration is not included as an acoustic cue in this experiment. Because, there are ample studies which unanimously accepted it as a relevant cue for the prosodic phrasing and prominence (Klatt, 1975)(Oller, 1973) (Lehiste and Lass, 1976) (Mac-Donald, 1976) (Roy, 2014). Therefore, less established acoustic cues are included in this study. The objective is to investigate the relevance of new

acoustic cues in phonological phrasing rather than reaffirming the importance of an already established acoustic cue. In this investigation spectral peaks are included as predictors because it signal perceptual stress(Sluijter et al., 1997) in an utterance. All nine cues are extracted using Praat software for speech signal analysis (Boersma and Weenink, 2013). The analysis of the importance of these cues in ϕ-phrasing is discussed in section 4.

3 Rules for ϕ-phrasing in Hindi

Hindi is a relatively free word order language. It follows SOV (subject followed by an object and then followed by a verb) structure. Based on the data collected from the performance and perception based experiment presented in section 2.2, the rules for ϕ are illustrated with examples. An intonation based analysis by (Patil et al., 2008) suggests that each content word in Hindi could be a prosodic phrase. The present analysis partially disagree to (Patil et al., 2008) as explained below (Parse tree is shown in Figure 4—7). See the following examples (the ϕ-phrases shown below for each sentence is the same chosen by the participants during the perception experiment).

a. raːm aːm kʰaːtaː hæː / Ram eats a mango/

[raːm]ϕ [aːm]ϕ [kʰaːtaː hæː]ϕ (normal & fast tempo)

b. siːtaː eːk gaːjikaː hæː. /Sita is a singer/
[sitaː]ϕ [eːk gaːjikaː hæː]ϕ (normal & fast tempo)

c. raːm neː siːtaː koː kitaːb diː /Ram gave a book to Sita/
[raːm -neː]ϕ [siːtaː koː]ϕ [kitaːb diː]ϕ (normal & fast tempo)
d. billi məmmi keː piːtʃheː bɦaːgiː / Cat ran behind the mother/
[billiː]ϕ [mə mmi keː]ϕ [piːtʃʰeː bɦaːgiː] ϕ
In the above example (a), which is of type [NP NP V] for which informants choose the phrasing pattern [NP]ϕ [NP]ϕ [V]ϕ. The example (b) which is of the same pattern as of (a). However the phrasing rules of (a) if applied on (b), the phrases breaks into the length of 1+2+1. Such phrasing patterns violate the principle of increasing units and thus restructuring applies. And finally it becomes [NP]ϕ [NP V]ϕ; with phrase

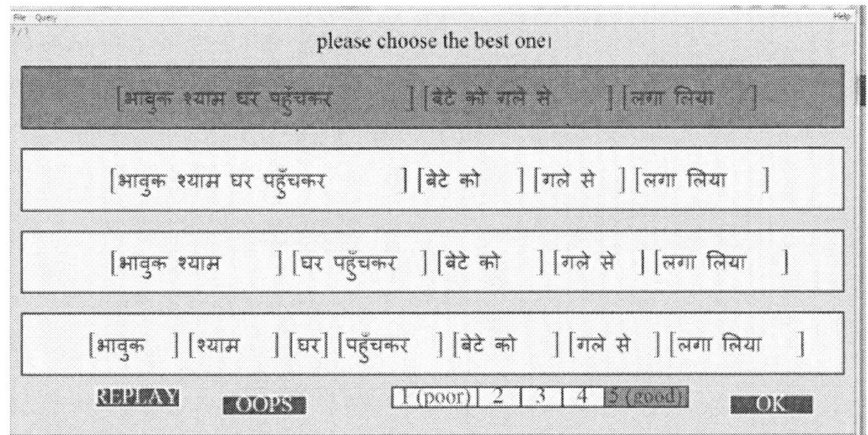

Figure 1: Praat's MFC experiment having four choices for the sentence "भावुक श्याम घर पहुँचकर बेटे को गले से लगा लिया", where square brackets denote short pauses or phonological phrase boundaries.

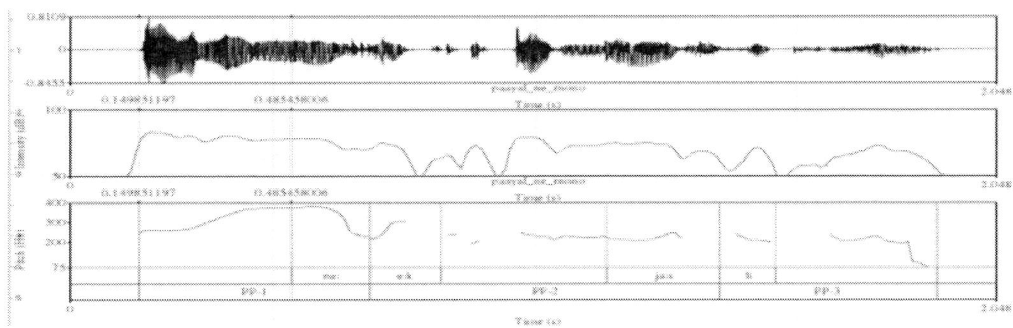

Figure 2: Preboundary and Postboundary syllables in the sentence, pa:jəl ne: e:k upənja:s likha: hei spoken in normal tempo. PP-1, PP-2 and PP-3 are three phonological phrase for which boundary is marked.

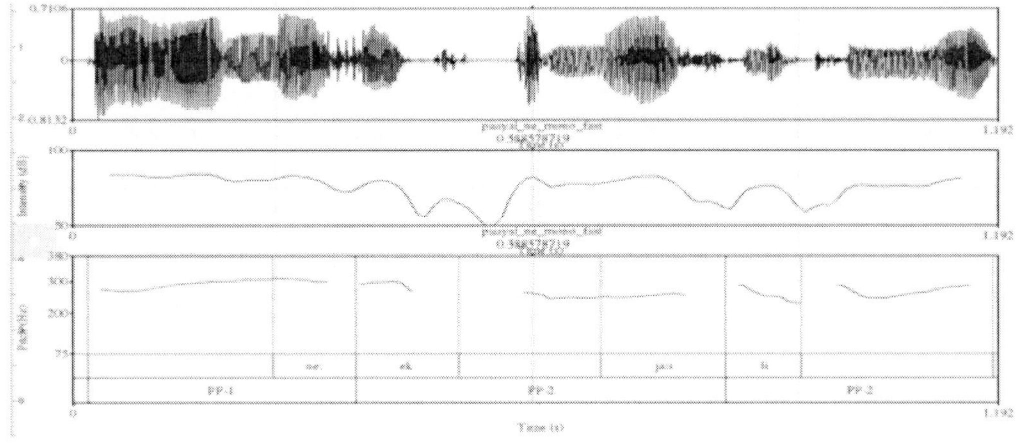

Figure 3: Preboundary and Postboundary syllables in the sentence, pa:jəl ne: e:k upənja:s likha: hei spoken in fast tempo. PP-1, PP-2 and PP-3 are three phonological phrase for which boundary is marked.

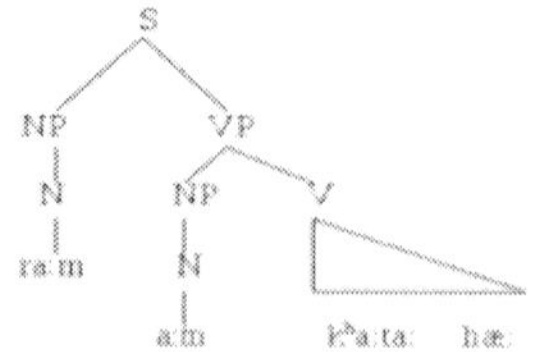

Figure 4: parse tree example1

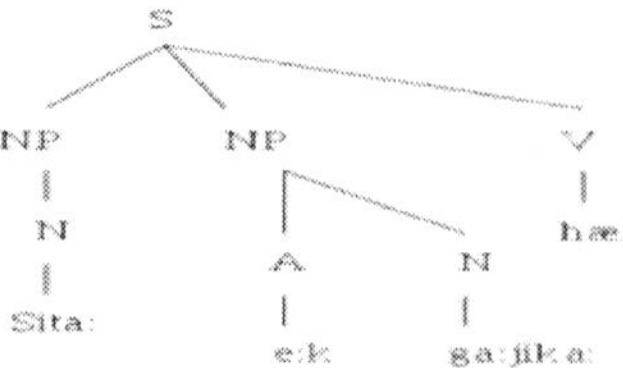

Figure 5: parse tree example2

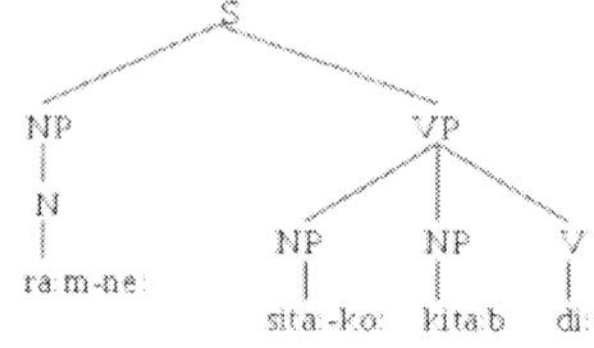

Figure 6: parse tree example3

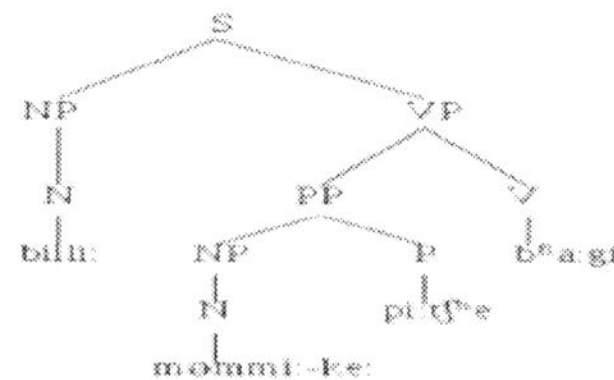

Figure 7: parse tree example4

length in increasing pattern i.e., 1+3. Example (b) also states that copula restructures itself with preceding ϕ-phrase. The example (c) is same as of the example (b), but differs on the category of verb at ultimate position. In this case it is a main verb and restructure itself with the preceding ϕ-phrase. The most important one is the fourth example (d), where the phrasing should be either [NP]ϕ [PP]ϕ [V]ϕ or [NP]ϕ [NP]ϕ [P]ϕ [V]ϕ but informants chose the phrasing pattern [NP]ϕ [NP]ϕ [P V]ϕ. It concludes that the restructuring takes place because both of the phrasing patterns i.e 1+3+1 and 1+2+1+1 violates principle of increasing units. Another important point need to

be highlighted here is that in the ϕ-phrase [P V]ϕ, the postposition (P) modifies the verb. Therefore P is no longer a postposition rather an adverb. Thus the word pi:tʃʰe: /behind/ in example (d), is a content word which along with another content word constitutes a ϕ-phrase. There are many such examples in Hindi where a single content word does not form a ϕ-phrase by itself rather restructure with some other content word. This implies that the process of ϕ-restructuring is of central significance in Hindi, and the claim that each content word could be a ϕ-phrase seems feeble.

Algorithm: ϕ-phrasing

i. Parse the input sentence.

ii. Apply end based rule(Selkirk, 1986).

iii. If phrase are not in increasing units, restructure it using principle of increasing units (Ghini, 1993)

4 Significance of Acoustic cues in ϕ-phrasing

The acoustic cues described in section 2.3 are analyzed. One way ANOVA modeling is applied at α=0.01. The ϕ-phrases are categorized into three types like initial ϕ-phrase (PhInit), medial ϕ-phrase (PhMed) and final ϕ-phrase (PhFin). The acoustic cues become factors and three phrases work as the level for ANOVA modeling.

The Table 1 and Table 2 describe the result of ANOVA Modeling for both normal and fast tempos speech respectively. The result indicates that the different type of acoustic cues are responsible for the ϕ-phrase break in normal and fast tempos, even though their ϕ-phrases have same boundaries for a sentence.

For normal tempo F0Max is the most significant parameter and other two significant acoustic cues are MaxInt and SpecInt1. The average difference of 10.1 Hz—22.4 Hz (approx) is found for F0Max at the ϕ-phrase boundaries. The comparison of MaxInt at consecutive ϕ-phrase boundaries shows that there is an average difference of 3dB—13.4 dB (approx) between the syllables at preceding and succeeding ϕ-phrase at boundaries. The noticed range of difference is significant, which provides listeners a cue for break. The significance of spectral peak at first formant (i.e., SpecInt1) states that intensity at higher frequency too is an important factor in determining ϕ-phrase boundary. SpecInt1 shows a significant difference at the boundary and difference lies in the range of 3.8 dB to 22.6dB (approx). Such pattern infers that each of these acoustic cues show declination between two consecutive ϕ-phrase boundaries as can be seen in Figure 2. The effect of declination in these acoustic cues are perceived as a short break or ϕ-phrase boundary to the listeners.

For Fast tempo F0Max is the most significant parameter and the other significant parameter is FiF0Min. MaxInt and SpecInt1 are not the significant parameters in fast tempo speech. F0Max shows significant change at phrase boundaries as in normal tempo, however it is not declination always. In other words, the next ϕ-phrase may have higher F0Max then the preceding one. The average difference in F0Max at consecutive ϕ-phrase boundaries lies in the range of 5.8 Hz to 16.9 Hz. FiF0Min in fast tempo shows pitch reset phenomena as can be seen in Figure 3. Each ϕ-phrase will have different level of pitch range from the beginning. The average difference for FiF0Min at consecutive ϕ-phrase boundaries are in the range of 8.6Hz—17.9Hz.

These results can be analyzed from different perspective. One perspective is that both normal and fast tempos show significant change in F0Max at ϕ-phrase boundaries. In other words, phrase break is signaled by the declining value in F0Max in normal tempo speech, but both rise and decline in F0Max are the factor signalling for ϕ-phrase boundaries in fast tempo speech. Also in normal tempo speech at phrasal boundaries speakers max intensity and spectral peak at first formant show declination but in fast tempo this effect is not found. Hence in normal tempo, speakers form a negative slope for these intensities between two adjacent boundaries. But in fast tempo speakers keep their intensity value almost constant between the adjacent boundaries.

5   Conclusion

The phonological phrasing in Hindi for a given sentence is same irrespective of the rate of speech. That is, both tempos yield same phonological phrasing. The phonological phrase restructuring rule in normal tempo follows the the principle of increasing units by (Ghini, 1993). The acoustic cues signaling phonological phrase boundary vary for both tempos. The acoustic parameters F0Max, MaxInt and SpecInt1 are the significant contrib-

utors for phonological phrasing in normal tempo speech, but for fast tempo F0Max and FiF0Min are the significant contributors for the phonological phrasing.

cues	F-Value	Pr>(F)	Significance
F0Max	11.584	1.93e-05	0.001
MaxInt	5.673	0.00412	0.01
SpecInt1	4.866	0.00882	0.01

Table 1: Anova Modeling for Significant Acoustic Cues in Normal Tempo Speech

cues	F-Value	Pr>(F)	Significance
F0Max	8.115	0.000491	0.001
FiF0Min	8.3	00.000417	0.001

Table 2: Anova Modeling for Significant Acoustic Cues in Fast Tempo Speech

References

Paul Boersma and David Weenink. 2013. Praat software. *Amsterdam: University of Amsterdam.*

Mirco Ghini. 1993. Phi-formation in italian: a new proposal. *Toronto Working Papers in Linguistics,* 12(2).

Bruce Hayes and Aditi Lahiri. 1991. Bengali intonational phonology. *Natural Language & Linguistic Theory,* 9(1):47–96.

Dennis H Klatt. 1975. Vowel lengthening is syntactically determined in a connected discourse. *Journal of phonetics,* 3(3):129–140.

Ilse Lehiste and Norman J Lass. 1976. Suprasegmental features of speech. *Contemporary issues in experimental phonetics,* 225:239.

Nina H MacDonald. 1976. Duration as a syntactic boundary cue in ambiguous sentences. In *Acoustics, Speech, and Signal Processing, IEEE International Conference on ICASSP'76.,* volume 1, pages 569–572. IEEE.

Marina Nespor and Irene Vogel. 1986. *Prosodic phonology,* volume 28. Walter de Gruyter.

John J Ohala. 1978. Production of tone. *Tone: A linguistic survey,* pages 5–39.

D Kimbrough Oller. 1973. The effect of position in utterance on speech segment duration in english. *The journal of the Acoustical Society of America,* 54(5):1235–1247.

Umesh Patil, Gerrit Kentner, Anja Gollrad, Frank Kügler, Caroline Féry, and Shravan Vasishth. 2008. Focus, word order and intonation in hindi. *Journal of South Asian Linguistics*, 1(1).

Somnath Roy. 2014. Prominence detection in hindi: A mathematical perspective. In *Computational Science and Computational Intelligence (CSCI), 2014 International Conference on*, volume 2, pages 119–124. IEEE.

Elisabeth O Selkirk. 1986. *Phonology and syntax: the relationship between sound and structure*. MIT press.

Agaath MC Sluijter, Vincent J Van Heuven, and Jos JA Pacilly. 1997. Spectral balance as a cue in the perception of linguistic stress. *The Journal of the Acoustical Society of America*, 101(1):503–513.

Lynn A Streeter. 1978. Acoustic determinants of phrase boundary perception. *The Journal of the Acoustical Society of America*, 64(6):1582–1592.

Hubert Truckenbrodt. 1995. *Phonological phrases— their relation to syntax, focus, and prominance*. Ph.D. thesis, Massachusetts Institute of Technology.

Author Index